An Introduction to Object-Oriented Programming and **Smalltalk**

Lewis J. Pinson

Richard S. Wiener

University of Colorado at Colorado Springs

ADDISON-WESLEY PUBLISHING COMPANY

Reading, Massachusetts • Menlo Park, California • New York
Don Mills, Ontario • Wokingham, England • Amsterdam • Bonn
Sydney • Singapore • Tokyo • Madrid • San Juan

Sponsoring Editor: James T. DeWolf
Production Supervisor: Bette J. Aaronson
Production: Michael Bass & Associates
Manufacturing Supervisor: Hugh Crawford
Text Design: R. Kharibian & Associates
Cover Design: Marshall Henrichs

Library of Congress Cataloging-in-Publication Data

Pinson, Lewis J.
An introduction to object-oriented programming and Smalltalk / by
Lewis J. Pinson and Richard S. Wiener.
    p.   cm.
  Bibliography: p.
  Includes index.
  ISBN 020119127
  1. Object-oriented programming (Computer science) 2. Smalltalk
(Computer program language) I. Wiener, Richard, 1941–
II. Title.
QA76.6.P56 1988
005.13'3—dc19   88-466
                                      CIP

The programs and applications presented in this book have been included for their instructional value. They have been tested with care but are not guaranteed for any particular purpose. The publisher does not offer any warranties or representations, nor does it accept any liabilities with respect to the programs or applications.

ABCDEFGHIJ-DO-898

Preface

Introduction and Objectives for the Book

Object-oriented problem solving and object-oriented programming represent a way of thinking and a methodology for computer programming that are quite different from the usual approach supported by structured programming languages. Object-oriented languages provide powerful features supporting concepts that make computer problem solving a more "natural" activity. They take advantage of the availability of increased hardware capability at reduced cost.

Object-oriented problem solving has its roots in simulation theory, and modern object-oriented languages trace their concepts back to Simula. Of the modern object-oriented languages, the one that is most true to the object-oriented philosophy is Smalltalk, developed at Xerox Palo Alto Research Center in the 1970s. The current commercial release of Smalltalk-80™* Version 2 is continually being revised. Other object-oriented environments are provided as shells over an existing language such as C or Lisp.

To be considered object-oriented, a language must support the concepts of abstraction, encapsulation, inheritance, and polymorphism. Beyond support for these four features, the details of the existing object-oriented languages are quite different. This book uses the Smalltalk language as a vehicle for illustrating the concepts of object-oriented programming and object-oriented problem solving.

The primary objective for this book is to present the principles of object-oriented problem solving through discussion of concepts, through summary descriptions of the Smalltalk image, and through presentation of examples that illustrate the concepts. A second objective is to provide an easy-to-use primer for object-oriented programming in Smalltalk. Many of the key features of the Smalltalk language are presented at an introductory level. No attempt is made to present the complete Smalltalk language. Rather, methods for understanding the Smalltalk system are given and applied to a subset of the language features. For

*Smalltalk-80™ is a trademark of ParcPlace Systems, Palo Alto, California.

a full description of the functionality of Smalltalk the reader is referred to *Smalltalk-80: The Language and Its Implementation* by Goldberg and Robson (Addison-Wesley 1983). A complete list of references can be found following the appendices.

This book is for the professional computer scientist/programmer/engineer who wishes to understand object-oriented programming methodology. As a secondary and necessary goal, many of the key features of the Smalltalk language are presented on an introductory level. No attempt is made to present the complete Smalltalk language. Rather, methods for understanding the Smalltalk system are given and applied to a subset of the language features.

This book is also intended to serve as a textbook at the advanced undergraduate or early graduate level. Exercises are given at the end of each chapter to test the knowledge acquired in the chapter.

General Organization of the Book

This book can be divided into two parts. The first eight chapters are intended to serve as an introduction to and an illustration of the concepts of object-oriented problem solving and Smalltalk. Examples are chosen that illustrate the power of the concepts of inheritance, abstraction, encapsulation, generics, polymorphism and data hiding. An introduction to Smalltalk is presented as a tutorial roadmap to the Smalltalk system image. It concentrates on selected classes and methods that provide functionality similar to constructs in other programming languages.

The book begins with an introductory chapter that gives a broad overview and definition for object-oriented problem solving. Basic concepts are discussed, and incremental problem solving is defined and illustrated by example. Comparisons are given that contrast object-oriented and structured programming methods.

Subsequent chapters develop general concepts supported by concise examples for specific classes in the Smalltalk system image. The beginning chapters discuss the fundamental features of Smalltalk that make it an object-oriented language, provide an introduction to using the Smalltalk environment, define essential syntactic features of Smalltalk, and illustrate concepts of object-oriented problem solving using classes such as **Magnitude, Stream,** and **Collection** that are familiar to programmers using procedural languages.

The second part of the book comprises Chapters 9 through 11. Less familiar classes that are peculiar to Smalltalk are discussed here. Each chapter begins with a discussion about the class and its functionality in general terms. A protocol summary is given for many of the Smalltalk classes. New classes are added to support specific problem solutions. Then examples are presented that use selected messages available to objects of that class. The objective is to provide just enough detail to show flexibility without overloading the user with too many new messages.

These last three chapters focus on expanded problem solving using object-oriented methodologies. Concepts and examples in this second part use more advanced classes and methods from the Smalltalk system image and add new functionality to the Smalltalk image. The emphasis is on incremental problem solving—incremental problem solving and object-oriented methodologies, as applied to larger problems, are illustrated by examples.

Intended Audience for the Book

This book is intended primarily for professional programmers and students wishing to learn object-oriented programming and to get a "user-friendly" start with Smalltalk. It is suitable for use in short courses, advanced undergraduate and introductory graduate level courses in engineering or computer science, and for self-learning.

Acknowledgments

The authors wish to thank a number of people who have contributed in various ways to the writing of this book. First we thank Mark Dalton, Jim DeWolf, and John Thompson of Addison-Wesley for their support on this project. We also express our thanks to the production staff at Addison-Wesley. Our copy editor Ellen Silge has significantly reduced the number of errors in a book where choice of typeface is critical to understanding. We would also like to acknowledge the efforts of several helpful reviewers. They include: Andrew Bernat, University of Texas, El Paso; Tim Budd, Oregon State University; Ralph E. Johnson, University of Illinois, Urbana-Champaign; Jeff McKenna, Tektronix; Eliot B. Moss, University of Massachusetts; Jean B. Rogers, Stanford University.

Through the efforts of Jim DeWolf and John Thompson, a state-of-the-art Tektronix 4406 workstation was obtained for developing the new Smalltalk code described in the book. We thank Tektronix, in particular Michael Taylor and Larry Stanley for their support and help. Thanks to Alan Kay and all the people at Xerox PARC who have been involved in the Smalltalk project. A special note of thanks is extended to Adele Goldberg.

Although we take full responsibility for the content of the book, our reviewers made many helpful suggestions that we incorporated into the manuscript. And finally, we thank our friends who have supported the strange working habits that we developed during the completion of the project. In particular, we thank Ellen, Leah, Gerry, Sharon, Don, Kathy, and Gene.

L.J.P.
R.S.W.

Table of Contents

Appendix 3   Descriptive Protocol Summaries for Selected Classes   458

List of Figures

List of Listings

List of Examples

What Is Object-Oriented Programming?

Object-oriented programming is defined in its purest sense as programming implemented by sending messages to objects. With this definiti n, problem solution that uses object-oriented programming principles consists of identifying the objects, messages, and object-message sequences to effect a solution. Object-oriented programming is further clarified by a discussion of the properties of objects. Computer languages are object-oriented if they support the four specific object properties called *abstraction, encapsulation, inheritance,* and *polymorphism.*

The goal of this chapter is to provide a thorough understanding of the principles of the object-oriented paradigm for computer problem solving. It presents concepts that are purely object-oriented without reference to specific computer languages.

The first section gives alternative definitions for object-oriented problem solving. The bulk of the chapter deals with the properties of objects and how these properties relate to problem solving. A number of examples are given throughout to illustrate each concept. A brief summary of several object-oriented computer languages is given in Section 1.6.

1.1   Definition of Object-Oriented Problem Solving

Object-oriented problem solving is a way of thinking. It is consistent with the way in which humans think about solving problems. It consists of identifying objects and what is to be done with those objects as specific steps in a problem solution. This is the object-oriented approach. There are no restrictions on the availability of data structures or instruction sets for use in the problem solution. Thus there is no need to force the steps in a solution to fit around a limited set of constructs supported by a computer language. An object-oriented language must support the flexibility of adding new objects and messages.

We define object-oriented problem solving as the solution of problems by developing steps that consist of *sending messages to objects.* The result of sending a message to an object is also an object. The following examples illustrate object-oriented problem solving. Each example is relatively simple and has solutions using other paradigms. The solutions presented here seek to represent the object-oriented paradigm. The initials OOP indicate object-oriented problem solving and object-oriented programming and are used throughout the book in both text and example titles.

The steps of an object-oriented approach are: (1) stating the problem, (2) identifying the objects in a solution, (3) identifying messages to which those objects should respond, and (4) establishing a sequence of messages to the objects that provide a solution to the stated problem. These four steps are identified in the following examples of solutions to simple problems.

OOP Example 1A

Problem statement—Examine each character in a text file and report the number of vowels.

Object identification—From the problem statement the following objects are identified:

textFile—the file that contains an unspecified number of characters.

aCharacter—any character in the text file.

count—an object that has value equal to the number of vowels.

booleanExpression—an object that evaluates to true or false. This object is not explicit in the problem statement. It is required for conditional testing. The term **booleanExpression** is used here to represent any sequence of actions that evaluates to true or false. A variety of different kinds of object-message sequences may satisfy this requirement.

Message identification—These objects must respond to the following messages as part of a problem solution.

openForRead—a message sent to object **textFile** that establishes the text file for *read only* status and positions the file pointer to the beginning of the file.

next—a message to object **textFile** that returns the next character in the file and advances the file pointer by one.

atEnd—a message to object **textFile** that returns a boolean true if the end of file has been reached; else false.

isVowel—a message to object **aCharacter** that returns a boolean true if the character is a vowel; else false.

increment—a message sent to object **count** that increments the value of count by one.

whileFalse:—a message sent to object **booleanExpression** that executes a block of expressions (blocks are delimited by square brackets, e.g., [expression(s)]) until the Boolean expression becomes true. The value of the Boolean expression is tested prior to each execution of the block of expressions. The Boolean expression may also be a block of expressions.

ifTrue—a message sent to object **booleanExpression** that executes a block of expressions one time only if the Boolean expression is true; else do nothing.

initialize—a message to object **count** that initializes the value of count to zero.

print—a message to object **count** that displays the value of count.

Object-message sequences—Using the above defined objects and messages, a solution to the problem is given by the following object-message sequence. Periods separate the individual expressions. Precedence is left to right unless altered by parentheses. The convention used here is to list the object first and its message or messages after the object name. The object to which a message is sent is referred to as the *receiver* object.

```
count initialize.
textFile openForRead.
[textFile atEnd] whileFalse:
    [ textFile next isVowel if True [ count increment ] ].
count print.
```

Concatenation of messages as in **textFile next isVowel if True** is possible because the result of a message being sent to an object is also an object. In this example the object-message pair **textFile next** produces an object **aCharacter** (implicit in this example), which is then sent the message **isVowel**. The result of that message is a **booleanExpression** object that is then sent the message **if True**. Only if the Boolean expression is true does the value of count get incremented. This sequence of messages is repeated until **textFile atEnd** evaluates to true. Finally the value of **count** is printed by the object-message pair **count print**.

There are many cases in which a message to an object requires that additional data be provided in the form of parameters. The parameters are objects also. The next example illustrates how the object-oriented approach is modified to accept parameters as part of a message. The ability of the object-message approach to include parameters as part of a message is essential to solving many problems, including the simple addition of two numbers.

OOP Example 1B

Problem statement—Compute the sum of two numbers and print the result. (This is an example that requires a message with a parameter.)

Object identification—The following objects are identified as part of the solution.

number1—the first number (object) forming the sum.

number2—the second number (object) forming the sum.

sum—an object that is the result of the addition of the two numbers.

Message identification—The following messages are required.

+ **aNumber**—a message sent to the receiver object number with parameter aNumber. The result of this message is an object **sum** representing the sum of the receiver object and **aNumber**.

print—a message that displays the value of the receiver object to which the message is sent.

Object-message sequences—The following object-message sequence solves the problem.

(number1 + number2) print

In words, the object **number1** is sent the message + with the object **number2** as a parameter. The result is an object (the sum of **number1** and **number2**), which is sent the message **print**. Parentheses are included to avoid any ambiguity as to which message is activated first. Note that the three objects, **number1**, **number2**, and **sum**, are all numbers. That is, they are distinct objects with many common features. The significant differences in these three objects are their numerical values.

One of the most important features of object-oriented problem solving is the ease with which capability can be added incrementally to an existing solution. If a particular kind of problem has been solved using the OOP approach, a similar but different problem can usually be solved by making incremental changes in the object-message protocol that already exists. In many cases the only requirement is the addition of new messages. In other cases there is a need to add new kinds of objects and new messages to which those objects respond.

OOP Example 1C

This example illustrates an incremental enhancement of OOP Example 1A and also illustrates the use of messages with multiple parameters.

Problem statement—Examine every character in a text file, replace every occurrence of a vowel with the string of characters 'Vowel', save the modified file, and report the number of vowels.

Object identification—The following new objects are required for solving this problem. Objects identified in OOP Example 1A are also a part of the solution. The following objects are added to the existing solution for Example 1A.

vowelString—an object consisting of the string of characters 'Vowel'.

Message identification—The following new messages are added in addition to those in OOP Example 1A for providing an incremental solution to this example.

openForReadWrite—a message sent to object **textFile** that opens the file for reading or writing and positions the file pointer at the beginning of the file.

replace: aCharacter **with:** vowelString—a message sent to object **textFile** that replaces object **aCharacter** with object **vowelString**. This is an example of a message that has two parameters. The two keyword components of the message, **replace:** and **with:**, are distinguished from objects by the colon terminator. This syntactic feature varies with different object-oriented languages. Its inclusion in this simple example is not essential; however, it does help the reader distinguish between the message and its parameters.

Object-message sequences—The following object-message sequence is a possible solution to the problem. Comparison of this solution with OOP Example 1A shows much similarity. This is a simple example of incremental problem solving. The application of incremental problem solving to larger, more advanced problems is the topic of Chapter 11. In addition, many of the examples developed throughout the text are incremental solutions.

```
count initialize.
textFile openForReadWrite.
[textFile atEnd] whileFalse:
    [ (aCharacter ← textFile next) isVowel if True [
            textFile replace: aCharacter with: vowelString.
            count increment ] ].
count print.
```

This example uses object **aCharacter** explicitly because it appears in the later message sequence **replace: with:** as a parameter. In this respect it is different from OOP Example 1A. The left arrow symbol, ←, is used to denote assignment. The exact symbol for assignment is typically language dependent. The details of the implementation of **replace: with:** are also language dependent. The important feature to understand here is the concept of what each message implies as an action for the object to which it is sent.

The above discussion and examples serve to illustrate the concept of object-oriented problem solving as identifying objects, messages, and object-message sequences to achieve a problem solution. This discussion is now expanded to include the *essential* properties of an OOP language and another definition of required features for an object-oriented approach to problem solving.

In the chapter he contributed to Krasner's book on Smalltalk, Dan Ingalls describes three properties of the object-oriented style of programming as

- data stored as objects with automatic deallocation
- processing effected by sending messages to objects
- object behavior described in classes

He further states, "In spite of opinions to the contrary, we consider these to be the hallmarks of the 'object-oriented' style of computing." We agree with these statements. Storing data as objects with automatic deallocation is an implementation detail of the object-oriented approach. Sending messages to objects has been demonstrated in the above examples as a methodology for problem solving. The concept of a class and its relationship to objects are discussed in Section 1.2. Classes form a central theme to the remainder of this book and to the understanding of OOP languages.

An additional hallmark of object-oriented problem solving is that it fully supports incremental solutions to problems. In the language of software engineering, the OOP paradigm supports the development of easily maintained, reusable software components. Of course, other languages and problem-solving methods provide support for incremental solutions and for reusability of software—the OOP paradigm just does it better. It is better from the standpoint of the ease with which existing software components can be modified and/or incorporated into new problem solutions. Fallout effects from modifications to software components are minimized by the way in which the object-oriented paradigm encapsulates the data and functional abstractions. Section 1.2 provides more detail on encapsulation for the OOP paradigm.

An object-oriented language has been defined as one that supports the four object properties: abstraction, encapsulation, inheritance, and polymorphism. Since object-oriented problem solving is achieved by using object-oriented languages, there is a tendency to reverse-engineer the definition of object-oriented problem solving to be "the use of these four properties." However, it is possible to solve problems with a number of OOP languages (that support these four properties) that do not require adherence to the above stated hallmarks of an OOP approach. This leads to discussions of the relative 'OOPness' or purity of object-oriented languages.

It is not our intent to add fuel to any disagreements about what constitutes a true object-oriented language. Rather we wish to show the advantages of using an object-oriented approach to problem solving. Adherence to the object-oriented paradigm is enforced by some languages and is dependent on programmer discipline in other languages.

Our definition for object-oriented programming is expanded from that given earlier. It includes adherence to the three hallmarks given by Ingalls. It supports incremental problem solving and the development of software components. Finally, it supports the four definitive properties: abstraction, encapsulation, inheritance, and polymorphism as defined and illustrated by examples in Sections 1.2 and 1.3.

1.2   Classes and Objects as Instances of Classes— Abstraction and Encapsulation

In the most general sense, an *abstraction* is a concise representation for a more complicated idea or object. Details of the implementation of an abstraction are not essential to an understanding of its purpose and functionality. Thus using and understanding an abstraction enables higher-level human functioning than is possible if one has always to dig into the details. Abstraction is supported by several procedural languages; its support by object-oriented languages is essential since *objects are encapsulations of abstractions.*

Definition of new abstractions in an object-oriented problem solution requires definition of new objects. For each new object one specifies sets of properties, features, and messages to which the object can respond. A problem solution can contain many objects. Some of those objects will have similar properties. This leads to the concept of grouping similar objects into classes. Common properties of objects within a class are defined in the class. Each object is then an instance of a class, and its behavior is defined by a set of properties that are consistent for all objects of that class. The use of classes to define properties for objects reduces the redundancy that occurs if properties are defined for each individual object.

The addition of new abstractions consists of first defining new classes and then creating objects as instances of the new classes. For a particular problem solution, a class definition is required for each kind of object. One or more instances of each class may be used in the problem solution.

Classes are also objects and must have their properties defined in a class description. The details for describing the properties of objects that are classes are handled differently by the various object-oriented languages.

A *class description protocol* is the complete definition of all properties, features, and messages that are descriptive of any object that is an instance of that class. Ways for establishing new instances of the class (new objects) must be included in the class description protocol. The class structure is a natural way to define various kinds of objects. Biological classes are an analog with which most people are familiar.

Encapsulation is the process by which individual software components are defined. A good method of encapsulation has the following desirable features:

- A clear boundary defining the scope of all its internal software
- A well-defined interface that describes how the software component interacts with other software
- A protected internal implementation that gives the details of the functionality provided by the software component

The concept of encapsulation is related to class descriptions; however, it provides an additional refinement on how the various components of a problem solution are grouped. The unit of encapsulation in an object-oriented approach to problem solving is the object. An object will have properties described by its class. Some of these properties are shared with other objects of the same class. Some of these properties will be private to each individual object. This distinctness of private features for an object is the refinement mentioned above. Encapsulation as objects is more specific than saying that a class represents encapsulation. With this definition for encapsulation, each instance of a class is a separate encapsulation or component in a problem solution.

An object (encapsulation) has the following features as given in the class description protocol:

- *Private Data*—other objects that are descriptive parameters of any instance of the given class. All objects that are instances of the class will have these parameters, but they will typically have different values. An object can only access its own private data.

- *Shared Data*—other objects that are descriptive parameters of any instance of the given class. These parameters have the same values for all objects that are instances of the class. All instances of the class have access to shared data.

- *Global Shared Data*—In some cases data (objects) can be shared by instances of several classes. Global shared data have the same values for all objects that share them.

- *Messages*—a set of messages to which the object responds. All objects that are instances of a given class will respond to the same set of messages.

With the object as the unit of encapsulation, the scope of all messages, identifiers, shared data, and private data is limited to the individual object. Concern about duplication of identifiers and messages is then restricted to the protocol description of an individual object. As will be shown later, an object's protocol is that given in its class plus protocol inherited from its superclasses. This significantly reduces the problem of controlling fallout effects during maintenance of a software system. The object represents a complete software component. It responds to its own protocol of messages and can send messages to other objects.

The objects and messages used in the three examples presented in Section 1.1 can be grouped into categories (classes). Four classes are identified from those examples. Encapsulation then consists of defining the *class description protocol* for each class and creating objects as instances of a given class. The concepts of abstraction and encapsulation are illustrated by the following examples. The convention that class names begin with uppercase letters is used.

Abstraction/Encapsulation Example 1A

This example first identifies the four classes developed from the earlier examples. It then develops the class description protocol for each class.

Identification of Classes of Objects

TextFile—A kind of object that represents a file on an external storage medium. The file contains text (ASCII characters). The private data of an instance of **TextFile** consists of an indexable collection of characters of unspecified size. Objects of this class were used in OOP Example 1A and OOP Example 1C.

Character—A kind of object that represents one of the ASCII characters.

Objects that are instances of class **Character** can have one of 256 predefined values (those values represented by the ASCII standard plus extended set of characters). This class will be able to access the shared data that is a list of allowed ASCII characters. Objects of this class were used implicitly in OOP Example 1A and explicitly in OOP Example 1C.

Boolean—A kind of object whose only allowed values are true or false. Objects of class **Boolean** can be created directly, or they may be created indirectly as the resulting object produced by other object-message sequences. For example, the expression num1 < num2 sends the message < to object num1 with object num2 as a parameter and produces a Boolean object as the result. OOP Example 1A and OOP Example 1C used objects of class **Boolean** that were created indirectly as the result of a Boolean expression involving objects of other classes.

Number—Objects of class **Number** are numbers. Protocol for objects of this class must include all the standard operations for numbers, given as messages. OOP Examples 1A, 1B, and 1C used objects of class **Number.**

Protocol for the Classes

Descriptions of the protocol for these four classes is given below. In each case the private data, shared data, global shared data, and messages for the class are described.

■ **TextFile** Class Description

Private data—Although there are many possibilities for defining the kinds of private data that an instance of **TextFile** may have, the following serve to illustrate the concept of what private data is and how it relates to the object it represents.

fileMode—an object whose value is a code (either integer or character) that identifies the mode of an instance of **TextFile.** Codes are required for the normal modes (read only, write only, read/write) and possibly others. Every object that is an instance of **TextFile** will have a value for fileMode that determines its own mode.

filePosition—an object representing the indexable position into a text file. This private data parameter will most likely be an integer. Its value is changed by messages that move the file pointer as part of their definition.

Shared data—The following object is given as an example of the kind of data that can be shared among all instances of class **TextFile.**

Buffer—an object that represents a fixed-size storage area in fast memory for transferring data to or from a text file. There is no reason for this parameter to be different for each instance of **TextFile;** therefore, it is shared by all instances of **TextFile.**

BufferSize—an object, probably an integer, that is the size in bytes of Buffer. This object is shared by all instances of **TextFile.**

Global shared data—There are no requirements for an object of class **TextFile** to access any specific global data.

Messages—The following list of messages is extracted from the examples in Section 1.1. Clearly, there are additional messages that are of interest to objects of class **TextFile.**

openForRead—an initialization message that establishes the instance as a read only text file. Set the value of **fileMode** to reflect 'read only'. Used in OOP Example 1A.

openForReadWrite—an initialization message that establishes the instance as a read/write text file. Set the value of **fileMode** to reflect 'read/write'. Used in OOP Example 1C.

atEnd—a testing message that returns true if the file pointer is at the end of the text file; else false. Test the value of private data object **filePosition** to determine correct response. Used in OOP Example 1A and OOP Example 1C.

next—an accessing message sent to an object of class **TextFile** that returns the character pointed to by the current **filePosition** and advances the **filePosition** to the next character. Used in OOP Example 1A and OOP Example 1C.

replace: aCharacter **with:** vowelString—an accessing message that replaces a character with a string of characters in the instance of **TextFile.** Used in OOP Example 1C.

■ **Character** Class Description

Private data—Characters are inherently identified by a code. Each instance of class **Character** will have a unique code value associated with it. This value is the only private data required of instances of class **Character.**

value—an object (typically an integer with value between 0 and 255) that represents the ASCII code for an instance of class **Character.** The message next in class **TextFile** returns an object that is an instance of class **Character.**

Shared data—All instances of class **Character** share a tabular mapping of characters to ASCII codes. This character mapping is also required by classes that display text on a screen. For that reason it is listed as global shared data.

Global shared data—A mapping of characters to ASCII codes.

CharacterTable—an object that is a table of character/code pairs, representing the 256 ASCII characters and their equivalent codes.

Messages—The following message is derived from examples in Section 1.1 and does not represent a complete list of messages desired for objects of class **Character.**

isVowel—a message that tests if the character object is a vowel and returns true; else false. Used in OOP Example 1A and OOP Example 1C.

■ **Boolean** Class Description

Private data—The only private data of interest to any Boolean object is its value. That value must be **true** or **false**.

    value—an object that is either the object **true** or the object **false**. Remember that all private or shared data must be objects and must have values that are objects.

Shared data—None required.

Global shared data—None required.

Messages—Examples in Section 1.1 created Boolean objects as the result of messages to other kinds of objects. These indirectly created Boolean objects were then sent the following messages. Remember that the object (parameter) **aBlock** was defined as a group of expressions delimited by square brackets, [ ]. These messages were used in OOP Example 1A and OOP Example 1C.

    whileFalse: **aBlock**—an iteration message that evaluates all expressions in **aBlock** until the receiver Boolean object evaluates to **true**.

    ifTrue: **aBlock**—a conditional message that evaluates the expressions in **aBlock** one time, if and only if the receiver Boolean object evaluates to **true**.

■ **Number** Class Description

Private data—Numbers may need private data to represent their internal states, depending on the kind of number that is represented. For example, complex numbers can be represented by two values: a real value and an imaginary value. Floating point numbers and integers are typically represented by a single value. This disparity in the way that the internal state of a number is represented leads to the consideration of different classes to represent different kinds of numbers. This topic is discussed in more detail in Section 1.3. For now consider a single class, called **Number,** that represents numbers with a single value.

    value—an object that is the actual value of an instance of class **Number.**

Shared data—Specific number classes discussed in later chapters have shared data across instances of those classes. For the examples given in Section 1.1, there is no need for shared data for the numbers used.

Global shared data—None needed in the examples.

Messages—The following messages include those in the examples of Section 1.1 plus some that are necessary for other applications.

    + **aNumber**—an operator message, with one parameter, that produces an object of the same class, **Number,** that is the sum of the receiver **Number** object and the parameter **aNumber**.

    − **aNumber**—an operator message, with one parameter, that produces an object of the same class, **Number,** that is the difference of the receiver **Number** object minus the parameter aNumber.

* aNumber—an operator message, with one parameter, that produces an object of the same class, **Number,** that is the product of the receiver **Number** object and the parameter aNumber.

/ aNumber—an operator message, with one parameter, that produces an object of the same class, **Number,** that is the quotient of the receiver **Number** object divided by the parameter aNumber.

increment—an operator message that increments the value of the receiver **Number** object by one.

initialize—an initialization message that establishes an initial value of zero for the receiver **Number** object. Initialization of numbers can be done this way or by assignment of a literal value to the receiver **Number** object. Most languages support literal numbers.

print—an output message that displays the value of a number in a specified way.

A second example further illustrates the concepts of abstraction and encapsulation. Categories (classes) of objects and their protocol for representing binary tree data structures are defined. At the highest level, two objects are identified as being essential to representing binary trees. The first of these is the binary tree itself; binary tree objects will be represented as instances of a class called **Tree.** Since binary trees consist of nodes, a second kind of object is represented by instances of a class called **TreeNode.**

For these two new classes one can define private data, shared data, and messages that are the protocol for describing the binary tree abstraction. Ways for adding protocol to describe specific kinds of binary trees will be discussed in Section 1.3.

Abstraction/Encapsulation Example 1B

Identification of Classes of Objects

Tree—Instances of class **Tree** are binary search trees and have the following properties. A binary search tree consists of tree nodes, with one special node referred to as the root node. All access to the tree object is through its root node. Nodes in a binary tree are ordered relative to some key object, with lesser key values being in the left subtree and larger key values being in the right subtree for any node. Insertion and deletion of nodes in a binary search tree must produce an object that is a binary search tree.

TreeNode—Instances of class **TreeNode** are the objects that form a binary search tree. Each tree node must contain one object as private data that is the key for determining order of a search tree. A node can contain additional information other than the key. A binary tree node must contain two objects that point to left and right subtrees for the node.

Protocol for classes **Tree** and **TreeNode** that represents only the properties of a general binary search tree is defined below. Additional protocol, illustrating incremental problem solving, is added in Section 1.3 and in later chapters for specific kinds of binary trees.

Protocol for the Classes

■ **Tree** Class Description

Private data—The root of a binary search tree is an essential private data object that is used to access any instance of class **Tree.** Two other examples of private data for the search tree are included that are not essential but that add clarification to instances of **Tree.**

root—an essential object that identifies the top node in a binary tree. All access to the binary tree is through this object. The root is an instance of **TreeNode.**

maxLevel—an object, probably an instance of class **Number,** that is the greatest level in a binary tree. The root node is considered to be at level 1, its offspring at level 2, and so on.

avgLevel—an object, probably an instance of class **Number,** that is the average of the levels of all nodes in a binary tree.

Shared data—There are no requirements for an object of class **Tree** to have shared data.

Global shared data—There are no requirements for an object of class **Tree** to access any specific global data.

Messages—The following messages represent a partial set of messages for an object that is an instance of the general class called **Tree.**

new—an instance creation message that creates a new instance of class **Tree.** It sets the values of private data **root** to nil, **avgLevel** to 0.0, and **maxLevel** to 0.

root—an accessing message that returns the object that is the root node of an instance of class **Tree.**

insert: aNode—parameter aNode is an instance of class **TreeNode** that is to be inserted into the receiver binary tree. Insertion must maintain rules of order for all nodes.

delete: aNode—parameter aNode is an instance of class **TreeNode** that is to be deleted from the receiver binary tree if it is in the binary tree. Deletion must maintain rules of order for all nodes. The object returned by this message is an instance of **Tree** if the object aNode was found and successfully removed.

isPresent: aKey—a testing message that returns a **Boolean** object with value true if the parameter object **aKey** is in the receiver binary tree.

empty—a testing message that returns a **Boolean** object with value true if the receiver binary tree is empty (root = nil).

inorderDisplay—an enumeration message that displays the contents of every node in the receiver binary tree in ascending order of their keys.

postorderDisplay—an enumeration message that displays the contents of every node in the receiver binary tree in postorder of their keys.

■ **TreeNode** Class Description

Private data—The key of a tree node is an essential private data object that is used to determine the order of any instance of class **TreeNode.** Two other examples of essential private data for the tree node are the left and right offspring for the node.

key—an essential object whose value is the basis for determining order of tree nodes in a binary tree.

leftNode—an object, also an instance of class **TreeNode,** that is the left offspring of the receiver tree node.

rightNode—an object, also an instance of class **TreeNode,** that is the right offspring of the receiver tree node.

Shared data—There are no requirements for an object of class **TreeNode** to have shared data.

Global shared data—There are no requirements for an object of class **TreeNode** to access any specific global data.

Messages—The following messages represent a partial set of messages for an object that is an instance of the general class called **TreeNode.**

new: aKey—an instance creation message that creates a new instance of class **TreeNode.** It sets the values of private data leftNode and rightNode to nil. The key value is special for each kind of node generated. Examples of how this specialization is accomplished are given in the next section and in later chapters.

key—an accessing message that returns the object that is the value of the key of an instance of class **TreeNode.**

key: anObject—The parameter **anObject** is established as the key in the receiver tree node. Included here only for describing protocol common to all subclasses. The implementation of this message is the responsibility of each subclass.

successor—Returns an object that is an instance of **TreeNode** satisfying the condition that it is the inorder successor of the receiver tree node. Both nodes are part of the same binary tree.

isEmpty—a testing message that returns a **Boolean** object with value true if the receiver tree node has a value of nil.

isLeaf—a testing message that returns a **Boolean** object with value **true** if the receiver tree node has two empty offspring (**leftNode** = **rightNode** = **nil**).

inorderDo: aBlock—a recursive enumeration message that executes the expressions in **aBlock** for every node in a binary tree. The order is ascending, based on the key value in each node.

postorderDo: aBlock—a recursive enumeration message that executes the expressions in **aBlock** for every node in a binary tree. The order is postorder, based on the key value in each node.

The two examples just given serve to illustrate the concepts of abstraction and encapsulation. Abstraction is represented by a class protocol description that defines the properties of any object that is an instance of that class. Objects are then the encapsulation of all private data, shared data, global shared data, and messages of specific instances of a class. The major differences among instances of a class are the values for private data.

The examples given so far are distinct in that objects within one class have little if anything in common with objects in a different class. Among all the objects that may be part of a problem solution, many will be related, yet not enough that they represent instances of the same class. In the next section our concepts of abstraction and encapsulation are refined to provide for a class hierarchy, with some classes existing as subclasses of others. This leads to a discussion of the other two object properties: inheritance and polymorphism.

1.3 Subclasses—Inheritance and Polymorphism

The limited examples presented in the previous two sections demonstrate that the object-oriented approach to problem solving uses objects as a method of encapsulation and defines objects to be instances of classes. The classes provide, through a protocol description, the properties of those instances. The protocol description includes private data, shared data, global shared data, and messages.

In this section the concept of a class hierarchy is introduced, where some classes are subordinate to others; i.e., subclasses. Subclasses are considered to be special cases of the class under which they are grouped in the hierarchy. The lower levels in a class hierarchy represent an increased specialization; higher levels in a class hierarchy represent more generalization.

The concepts of inheritance and polymorphism as properties for objects are a result of the arrangement of different kinds of objects in a hierarchy of classes. These two object properties are defined below. Their significance is discussed and illustrated through application examples.

Figure 1.1
Inheritance and
Class Hierarchy

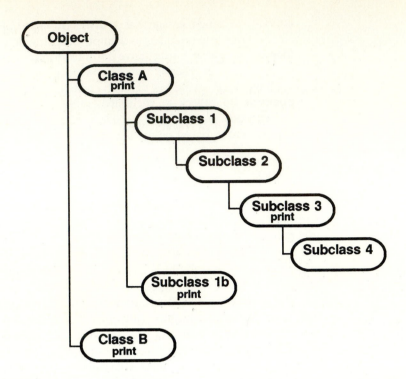

1.3.1   Inheritance

Given a hierarchy of classes such that **SubClass1** is a subclass of **ClassA,** objects that are instances of **SubClass1** can be described as more specialized instances of **ClassA.** It is then possible to state that instances of **SubClass1** have at least the same properties as instances of **ClassA.** Because of their more specialized nature, instances of **SubClass1** may have new properties that are not descriptive of the more general instances of **ClassA.** Instances of **SubClass1** inherit the properties of **ClassA.** These inherited properties can include private data, shared data, and messages. **ClassA** is called a superclass of **SubClass1.** Inheritance is the property of objects, which are instances of a specific class, whereby they inherit properties from their superclasses.

Subclasses can be nested to several levels. A class at the lowest level in a class hierarchy inherits properties from all its superclasses. In Figure 1.1, **Sub-Class4** inherits properties from **SubClass3, SubClass2, SubClass1,** and **ClassA. ClassB** is at the same hierarchical level as **ClassA.** They are essentially independent classes. **SubClass1b** is at the same hierarchical level as **SubClass1.** They both inherit properties from **ClassA,** but not from **ClassB.** Further, **SubClass2** does not inherit properties from **SubClass1b.**

Because of inheritance, the scope of an object that is an instance of **Sub-Class4** includes the scope of all its superclasses. An instance of **SubClass4** has access to all private data, shared data, and messages of all its superclasses. The reverse statement is not true. For example, **ClassA** does not have access to the private data, shared data, or messages that are specific to any of its subclasses.

The concept of multiple inheritance is also a part of the object-oriented paradigm. Multiple inheritance means that a class inherits properties from two or more classes that are not related as superclass or subclass of each other. Most object-oriented languages provide limited support for multiple inheritance.

1.3.2   Polymorphism

Polymorphism allows us to send the same message to different objects and have each object respond in a way appropriate to the kind of object it is. For example, one may wish to print the value of a variety of different kinds of objects. Polymorphism allows us to send the same message, print, to all these objects and achieve the desired result. Each object knows how to respond to the message print.

The ability to use the same message for a similar operation on different kinds of objects is consistent with the way that human beings think about solving problems. It is not natural to use different terminology for printing integers, floating point numbers, characters, strings of characters, or data records. Polymorphism is a key feature in the object-oriented paradigm for problem solving.

Polymorphism also supports the process of passing different kinds of objects as parameters of messages sent to other objects. For example, the message insert: aNode given as part of the protocol for class **Tree** in Abstraction/Encapsulation Example 1B works properly for instances of aNode that represent different classes.

Polymorphic redefinition of a message can be used in subclasses as well as across classes at equal hierarchical levels, as indicated in Figure 1.1. Polymorphic redefinition of operator symbols, called operator overloading in structured languages, is just another case of message polymorphism in an object-oriented language. Recall that operators are interpreted as messages also.

With reference to Figure 1.1, a message print is defined in **ClassA, ClassB, SubClass1b,** and **SubClass3.** Objects that are instances of each class will respond to the message print in accordance with its definition for that class. These four definitions for message print are examples of polymorphism. Objects that are instances of the other classes in Figure 1.1 also respond to the message print because of inheritance. Instances of **SubClass1** and **SubClass2** inherit the print message from **ClassA.** Instances of **SubClass4** inherit the print message from **SubClass3.**

Examples of inheritance and polymorphism are given as enhancements to the binary tree example given in Abstraction/Encapsulation Example 1B. The first example defines a new class called **ExpressionTree** that is a specialization of the **Tree** class. Expression trees contain nodes that are special cases of class **Tree-Node.** The other examples define several subclasses of **TreeNode** to represent the nodes of an expression tree. For each new class a class description protocol is given that identifies inherited properties, new properties, and polymorphic (redefined) properties.

An expression tree is a binary tree whose nodes and structure are determined by a special set of rules using tokens in an algebraic expression as the keys. The tokens are grouped into two categories: operators and operands. Operators are the special character symbols representing the allowed algebraic operations. Operands may be identifiers (variables whose value can be assigned later) or literal numbers. The general rules for building an expression tree are: (1) Generate a binary tree of operators only, using precedence rules to determine order, and (2) add operands to the operator tree as leaf nodes, based on their order of occurrence in the algebraic expression.

The rules for insertion of nodes into an expression tree are unique, and deletion of nodes from an expression tree is never required. Other operations on expression trees are compatible with the operations on a general binary search tree. Logically, **ExpressionTree** should be a subclass of **Tree.** Polymorphic redefinition of the **insert** message is required, and **delete** should be blocked. Further, the expression tree class needs additional private data as well as new protocol for certain operations.

Inheritance/Polymorphism Example 1A

ExpressionTree Class Description

Private data—Expression trees are built from strings of characters that represent an algebraic expression. Part of the private data of an instance of **ExpressionTree** is that string of characters.

> **exprString**—(new protocol) a string of characters representing an algebraic expression. The string should have no blanks, to minimize storage requirements.

> **operands**—(new protocol) a collection of operand/value pairs that serves as a lookup table. Values for operands are used during the numerical evaluation of an expression.

> **root, maxLevel, avgLevel**—(inherited protocol) from class **Tree.** Private data, maxLevel, and avgLevel have little significance in evaluating algebraic expressions. Although they are inherited by class **Expression-Tree,** there is no requirement that they be used.

Shared data—There is no requirement for shared data.

Global shared data—There is no requirement for global shared data.

Messages—Messages for class **ExpressionTree** can be grouped into four categories: (1) inherited and used, (2) new protocol not given in class **Tree,** (3) inherited and polymorphically redefined (including those messages that serve no purpose for expression trees, but would cause an error if used), and (4) inherited but not used (with no error created by their use). The following messages include examples in each category. They are not intended to be a complete list of messages that may be of value to objects of class **ExpressionTree.**

new, root, empty, postorderDisplay—(inherited and used as is).

insert: aNode—(polymorphically redefined) Insert parameter **aNode** into the expression tree using precedence rules for algebraic expressions. Insertion is restricted to operator nodes and operand nodes.

delete: aNode—(polymorphically redefined) Create an error message since nodes are not to be removed from expression trees.

isPresent: aKey—(inherited but not used) No error is created by checking the presence of a particular key. Evaluation of algebraic expressions simply does not require this message. It can be blocked by polymorphic redefinition or left as is.

inorderDisplay—(inherited but not used) The inorder traversal of an expression tree gives the algebraic expression in order but without parentheses, so precedence relations are lost. An alternative is to redefine this message to reinsert parentheses prior to display of the inorder expression.

getExpression—(new protocol) Prompt the user to enter an algebraic expression. The result is assigned to private data, **exprString.**

buildTree—(new protocol) Build an expression tree from the algebraic expression stored in instance variable, **exprString.**

evaluate—(new protocol) Establish values for all operands and compute the numerical value for the algebraic expression represented by the expression tree.

The next example on inheritance and polymorphism shows details of adding class **OperatorNode** as a subclass of **TreeNode.** An instance of **OperatorNode** contains a key value that is one of the allowed operator symbols in an algebraic expression. These include **+, −, *,** and **/** as a minimum.

Inheritance/Polymorphism Example 1B

OperatorNode Class Description

Private data—The precedence of operators used by class **ExpressionTree** to build an instance of an expression tree is dependent on the particular operator and upon the presence of parentheses to alter normal precedence rules. Each operator node has private data that keeps track of the number of parentheses for determining relative precedence.

info—(new protocol) an integer object that has value given by the difference in number of left parentheses and right parentheses encountered in an algebraic expression prior to the occurrence of the current operator instance.

leftNode, rightNode, key—(inherited from **TreeNode**).

Shared data—There is no requirement for shared data.

Global shared data—There is no requirement for global shared data.

Messages—Messages for class **OperatorNode** can also be grouped into four categories: (1) inherited and used, (2) new protocol not given in class **TreeNode,** (3) inherited and polymorphically redefined (including those messages that serve no purpose for operator nodes but would cause an error if used), and (4) inherited but not used (with no error created by their use). The following messages include examples in each category. They are not intended to be a complete list of messages that may be of value to objects of class **OperatorNode.**

new: aKey—(polymorphic redefinition) Installs an instance of an operator as the key value in a new instance of **OperatorNode.** It also uses the inherited message **new: withInfo:** from superclass **TreeNode** to establish nil values for leftNode and rightNode and to set the value of info to 0.

key, isEmpty, isLeaf, postorderDo: aBlock—(inherited and used) from **Tree-Node** and used as is.

key: anObject—(polymorphic redefinition) Parameter anObject is established as the key in the receiver operator node.

successor—(polymorphic redefinition) inherited but not used. Redefine, giving an error message. The inorder successor of a node in an expression tree has no application.

inorderDo: aBlock—(inherited but not used) An inorder traversal of nodes in an expression tree has no significant meaning. However, the operation causes no error and there may be other uses for it.

evaluate—(new protocol) a recursive message that combines the leftNode evaluate result with the rightNode evaluate result, using rules based on the key value operator in the current **OperatorNode.** The object produced by sending the message evaluate to an instance of **OperatorNode** is a numerical value.

A second kind of tree node containing operands as keys is needed for the expression tree example. The next example adds class **OperandNode** as a subclass of **TreeNode.** Instances of **OperandNode** have keys that are either variable identifiers or numeric literals.

Inheritance/Polymorphism Example 1C

OperandNode Class Description

Private data—Objects of class **OperandNode** inherit private data from the superclass **TreeNode.**
leftNode, rightNode, key—(inherited from **TreeNode**).

Shared data—There is no requirement for shared data.

Global shared data—There is no requirement for global shared data.

Messages—Messages for class **OperandNode** can also be grouped into four categories: (1) inherited and used, (2) new protocol not given in class **TreeNode,** (3) inherited and polymorphically redefined (including those messages that serve no purpose for operator nodes but would cause an error if used), and (4) inherited but not used (with no error created by their use). The following messages include examples in each category. They are not intended to be a complete list of messages that may be of value to objects of class **OperandNode.** The patterns of inheritance and polymorphic redefinition for class **OperandNode** are similar to those of class **OperatorNode.** They are different in some cases.

new: aKey—(polymorphic redefinition) Installs an instance of an operand as the key value in a new instance of **OperandNode.** It also uses the inherited message new: from superclass **TreeNode** to establish nil values for leftNode and rightNode.

key, isEmpty, postorderDo: aBlock—(inherited and used) from **TreeNode** and used as is.

isLeaf—(polymorphic redefinition) An operand node is always a leaf node.

key: anObject—(polymorphic redefinition) Parameter **anObject** is established as the key in the receiver operand node.

successor—(polymorphic redefinition) inherited but not used. Redefine, giving an error message. The inorder successor of a node in an expression tree has no application.

inorderDo: aBlock—(inherited but not used) An inorder traversal of nodes in an expression tree has no significant meaning. However, the operation causes no error and may have other applications.

evaluate—(new protocol) a message that returns the value of an operand node. The object produced by sending the message **evaluate** to an instance of **OperandNode** is a numerical value that is either the key or an associated value for a variable operand key.

The decision to make both **OperatorNode** and **OperandNode** subclasses of **TreeNode** at the same hierarchical level is not the only solution to the expression tree problem. It could be argued that **OperandNode** should be a subclass of **OperatorNode.** In fact the only significant differences in objects of class **OperandNode** from those of class **OperatorNode** are the value of the key, the fact that operand nodes are always leaf nodes, and the details of what is meant by evaluate.

In terms of choices for subclasses or subclass protocol, there is more than one solution for any given problem. Thus, object-oriented problem solving (like other paradigms) requires creativity and intelligence in establishing the "best" solution to a problem. As a general rule, the best solution using the OOP para-

Figure 1.2
Graphical
Summary of
Expression Tree
Classes

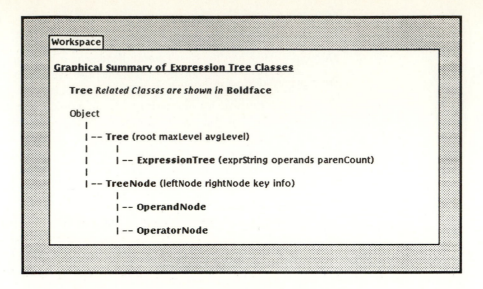

The examples illustrating inheritance and polymorphism indicate that

digm is one that is most true to that paradigm. For specific application problems, issues of efficient utilization of computer resources may be the criteria for what is best.

The examples illustrating inheritance and polymorphism indicate that object-oriented problem solutions involve the addition of subclasses to an overall class hierarchy. Figure 1.2 shows one graphical method for summarizing the status of the classes that have been added in these examples. For connectivity in Figure 1.2 a class called **Object** is introduced, which is the superclass of all objects. Private data are listed in parentheses after each class name. Private data names begin with a lowercase letter.

1.4   Comparison and Contrast of Object-Oriented Problem Solving with Structured Problem Solving

There are relatively few references on the object-oriented paradigm and its relationship to other problem-solving paradigms. Aside from definitions for object-oriented problem-solving methodology, examples and experience are required for us to understand what OOP is all about. Smalltalk, as the language most true to the object-oriented paradigm, is a good starting point. Definitions and examples are given by Goldberg and Robson in their 1983 work on Smalltalk and in Goldberg's 1984 book (see list of references). Kaehler and Patterson present an excellent discussion with comparative examples of object-oriented versus structured solutions to a problem. Further discussions of the object-oriented paradigm are given in Cox's book published in 1986.

For many years programmers have learned the methods of structured programming to solve problems on computers. Languages that support structured programming are typified by a small set of available instructions. These instructions were developed to solve specific kinds of problems in an efficient manner. Their application to problems other than their original intent is often cumbersome, if possible at all.

A structured problem solution using procedural languages consists of molding the steps in the solution to fit the set of available instructions and data structures provided by the language. Since we are familiar with structured languages, we may conclude that the solution is natural. Closer inspection will often reveal that the solution is not only awkward, but conceptually difficult to follow. This conclusion is more easily reached for some problem solutions than others.

In understanding what object-oriented problem solving really is, comparison with other familiar problem-solving methodologies is a useful technique. Most of the modern computer languages widely used for problem solving are procedural languages. In this section comparisons are made between problem solutions using the object-oriented approach and those using the structured approach. Comparisons are made in terms of the following features:

1. Method for accomplishing actions with data
2. Abstraction and encapsulation
3. Inheritance and polymorphism
4. Extensibility and relative status of new protocol
5. Iteration versus true object-oriented solutions to a simple problem
6. Accessing objects by nested indices versus sending messages to objects
7. Refinement of class hierarchy versus equivalent status of all software components
8. Passing objects as parameters and passing records as parameters

Each of these comparison features is discussed below, with examples that illustrate the differences between solutions that are object-oriented and solutions that are structured.

1.4.1 Method for accomplishing actions with data

A first comparison of the object-oriented paradigm and the structured paradigm for computer problem solving looks at the way in which actions on data are accomplished. In the OOP approach messages (actions) are sent to objects (data). The object responds to the message in a predetermined way. In a structured approach parameters (data) are sent to procedures (actions). The procedures operate on the data in a predetermined way. A closer examination of the details of these two approaches reveals that the receiver object in an OOP approach must be included as another parameter in the structured approach. For example, the OOP message that was a part of OOP Example 1C in Section 1.1, given by

textFile replace: aCharacter with: vowelString

can be implemented in the structured paradigm by the procedure call

replace (textFile, aCharacter, vowelString).

The OOP approach is in many ways more readable than the structured approach. Further explanation is required for the procedure call that explains which parameters are input, which are output, and which are input/output. This explanation, if it is included, must be in the form of comments attached to the parameters.

Keywords in the message of an OOP approach give information about what is to be done with parameters. The keywords **replace: with:** in the example just given provide information about how the parameters **aCharacter** and **vowelString** are to be used. In the structured approach, this information must be added as comments. Typically, the addition of such comments is not done in a consistent fashion, if at all.

1.4.2   Abstraction and encapsulation

Discussions on abstraction often center around two major categories: data abstractions and functional abstractions. In an object-oriented language, data abstractions are represented by selected classes of objects, and functional abstractions are represented by messages. Not all classes can be considered to be data abstractions. Rather they are abstractions for certain physical objects, ideas, processes, or concepts. Classes can be defined to represent any abstraction. This is a more general capability than provided by data abstraction alone. The central focus is on classes of objects and how they can be used to represent the other abstractions.

In a procedural language, data abstractions are typically represented by some combination of predefined data types provided by the specific language. Functional abstractions are represented as procedures operating on the data abstractions. The central focus is on data types and how they can be used to represent various data abstractions as well as more general abstractions.

Aside from differences in implementation details, the major difference between an object-oriented language and a procedural language for representing abstractions is one of focus. Data types are the central focus for procedural languages, and classes are the central focus for object-oriented languages.

The method of encapsulation for OOP versus procedural languages is significantly different. In an object-oriented approach to problem solving the unit of encapsulation is the object. It consists of the complete protocol as given in its class description and the private data of the particular instance of that class. A class description is for one kind of object only. Multiple objects that are instances of the same class are separate units of encapsulation.

Figure 1.3
Abstraction and
Encapsulation for
the Object-
Oriented and
Structured
Paradigms

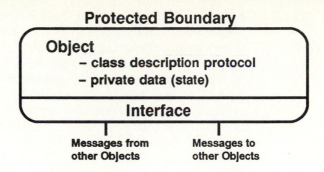

a) Object-Oriented Encapsulation

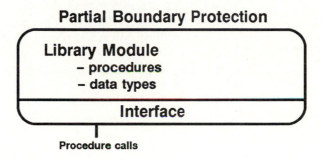

b) Structured Encapsulation

In a procedural language, encapsulation is usually in the form of library software components. Such components may contain more than one data abstraction, as well as the associated functional abstractions. Depending upon the particular language, the interface definition may or may not be separate from the implementation. Further, in some procedural languages the internal implementation details are not protected.

A summary comparison of abstraction and encapsulation for object-oriented versus structured paradigms is given in Figure 1.3.

1.4.3 Inheritance and polymorphism

By definition all object-oriented languages support inheritance and polymorphism; procedural languages in general do not. Limited polymorphism is provided in procedural languages in the form of operator overloading by Ada. Because of the lack of support for inheritance, software components and the data abstractions they represent are of equal hierarchical level in non–object-oriented languages. This is a severe restriction in understanding the relationships among various components of a problem solution. Lack of support for polymorphism causes a number of complicating factors in the choice of names for procedures. Similar operations in different component libraries must be distinct, either through choice of identifier or by qualification upon use.

Support for inheritance and polymorphism leads to a more natural solution to problems. The ability to show dependency relationships through subclassing and the reduction of redundancy are beneficial. Examples in Section 1.3 illustrate the concepts of inheritance and polymorphism.

1.4.4   Extensibility and relative status of new protocol

Extensibility is a property of computer languages that allows the user to define new constructs. Most modern languages are extensible; however, there are significant differences in the methodology supported by individual languages for adding new constructs. In most languages, the new constructs have status that is secondary to those constructs provided by the language. This typically means that the new constructs suffer significant degradation in efficiency.

In a truly object-oriented language all objects have equal status. This includes objects that are user-generated and objects that are part of the system kernel. This consistency of status is achieved at the expense of overall efficiency for existing OOP languages. The tradeoff is consistency versus local optimization.

1.4.5   Iteration versus true object-oriented solutions to a simple problem

Kaehler and Patterson give one indication of non–object-oriented programming as "too many loops." Even object-oriented languages provide constructs for looping. The use of an OOP language does not guarantee that an object-oriented solution has been accomplished. In fact, it is possible to translate solutions in structured languages into equivalent solutions in OOP languages.

Two partial solutions to a single problem are given below that contrast the object-oriented approach with a structured approach. The example examines the problem of defining an array with specified size and initializing the array elements to zero. This is a very short example that seeks to illustrate the principle without adding too much detail or introducing too much language-related syntax. In both cases, the solution uses object-message sequences.

Object vs. Structured Example 1A

Structured Partial Solution (using object-message sequences)

```
myArray ← Array new: size.
1 to: size do: [ :index | myArray at: index put: 0.0 ].
```

Parameter **index** is a block parameter that takes on the values **1** to **size** for the iteration message **to: do:**.

Object-Oriented Partial Solution

myArray ← Array new: size withAll: 0.0

_____

The two solutions in Object vs. Structured Example 1A accomplish the same result. The more object-oriented approach decomposes the problem differently. It places more emphasis on objects and messages that are simple. Higher-level abstractions are used with details kept as simple as possible within any message implementation. Iteration details are in the implementation for the message **new: withAll:**.

1.4.6   Accessing objects by nested indices versus sending messages to objects

Another feature of object-oriented problem solving discussed by Kaehler and Patterson is given as "limited use of nested indexing structures." The following example illustrates the simple operation of incrementing the count in a histogram of the relative occurrences of alphabetic characters. The object **string** is an array of characters of length **size**. Object **histogram** represents the relative occurrences of the letters *a* through *z* in **string**. The partial solutions presented are the expressions that increment a specific histogram value.

Object vs. Structured Example 1B

Structured Partial Solution (using object-message sequences)

```
1 to: string size do: [ :index |
    charCode ← (string at: index) asciiValue—$a acsiiValue).
    histogram at: charCode put: ((histogram at: charCode) + 1)]
```

Object-Oriented Partial Solution

```
string do: [ :aCharacter | histogram add: aCharacter ]
```

Note that the class of object **histogram** may differ in the two solutions. Some of the details for updating a specific histogram value have been delegated to the message **add:** in the object-oriented approach. The second implementation is more readable.

_____

1.4.7 Refinement of class hierarchy versus equivalent status of all software components

Because an object-oriented approach to problem solving supports inheritance and polymorphism, it also supports the development of a hierarchy of classes. This has the advantage that many problem solutions consist of adding incremental capability to an existing class hierarchy through subclasses.

In a structured approach to problem solving, in which inheritance and polymorphism are not supported, new software components all have equal status. They cannot draw on existing capability without redundant storage of copies of selected procedures. Further, the interdependence of various software components is not clear without a hierarchical structure. Procedural languages use variations on modular design charts to show relative interdependence of the software components.

The expression tree example given in Section 1.3 includes the addition of subclasses with inherited protocol. A solution in a procedural language must define separate and complete library software components for each of the subclasses. Much of the functional abstraction protocol would have to be repeated.

1.4.8 Passing objects as parameters in an OOP approach and passing records as parameters in a structured approach

Both object-message sequences and procedure calls have the ability to pass structured parameters in or out. In a procedural language this is accomplished with the data type *record*. In an object-oriented language, parameters are objects. Each object has its own private data as well as shared data. Passing an object as a parameter makes available (through appropriate messages) the private and shared data for that object.

The significant difference is one of encapsulation. A record parameter in a procedural language can be accessed in any way by the receiving procedure. An object parameter sent to another object can be accessed by that object only in ways provided by the protocol of the object parameter. The chance for errors from misuse are essentially eliminated by the object-oriented encapsulation.

1.5   A Summary of the Characteristics and Features of an Object-Oriented Approach to Problem Solving

The central feature of an object-oriented approach to problem solving is the concept of an object. Objects are the unit of encapsulation and consist of the private data, shared data, and messages as given in the class description protocol for that object. Objects are instances of a class. Abstractions are represented as

TABLE 1.1   Summary of Object-Oriented Programming

1. Programming consists of sending messages to objects.

2. The result of sending a message to an object is an object.

3. Problem solving consists of: (a) identifying the objects in a problem statement, (b) identifying the messages associated with each object, and (c) developing a sequence of messages to objects that solves the problem.

4. OOP languages must support encapsulation, abstraction, inheritance, and polymorphism.

5. The unit of encapsulation is the object, which includes private data, shared data, and message descriptions.

6. Abstraction is supported by a hierarchy of classes representing different kinds of objects. A class description protocol defines the properties of each abstraction. New abstractions are added by adding new subclasses.

7. Subclasses inherit the properties of their superclasses, including private data, shared data, and messages.

8. Inherited messages can be polymorphically redefined by subclasses.

9. Polymorphic definition of the same message in different classes is supported.

10. Data are stored as objects with automatic deallocation.

11. Full support for incremental problem solving is provided.

12. System objects and user-defined objects have equal status.

13. Extensibility is supported fully.

14. The use of iterative structures and multilevel indexing is minimized and localized to implementation details of simple messages.

kinds of objects through a hierarchy of classes. Object-oriented programs consist of object-message sequences, and messages are sent to objects.

The earlier sections of this chapter have defined the object-oriented paradigm, described its features, and illustrated object-oriented programming by examples. Table 1.1 summarizes the features of object-oriented programming and the object-oriented paradigm for solving problems.

1.6   Object-Oriented Languages

There are several languages that support object-oriented problem solving. Of these, Smalltalk is the most consistent with definitions and properties of the object-oriented paradigm as described in earlier sections of this chapter.

Smalltalk evolved from ideas of Alan Kay and a simulation language called

Simula.* It has been under development at Xerox, Palo Alto Research Center since the early 1970s. Three versions of Smalltalk have existed. The first commercial version, Smalltalk-80, Version 2.0, was released in 1983. The definition for the Smalltalk language is given in the Goldberg and Goldberg and Robson references already mentioned. A third book describing the MVC triad and how to develop graphics-based applications will be published by Addison-Wesley in 1988. Two recent books, *A Taste of Smalltalk,* by Kaehler and Patterson and Budd's *A Little Smalltalk* (see list of references), provide introductory material on the language. A series of conferences on object-oriented systems, languages, and applications (OOPSLA) was started in 1986. These are the major sources of information on Smalltalk.

Smalltalk is more than a language. It is an extensive program development environment whose standard image includes over two hundred classes and several thousand methods. Although the language is small in terms of reserved words and symbols, the entire system is large. It takes time to learn Smalltalk. Although it is not the only widely used object-oriented language (see the following paragraphs for an overview of others), the Smalltalk language and system continue to serve as an inspiration and model for object-oriented problem solving.

C++ was developed by AT&T Bell Laboratories in the early 1980s. It is based on the C language and is a superset of C. It adds polymorphism and inheritance to support object-oriented programming, while maintaining the speed and efficiency of C. Early versions of C++ include a translator for converting C++ code to C before compilation and linking with other C libraries. For more information on this important object-oriented language, the reader is referred to the companion of this book, *An Introduction to Object-Oriented Programming and C++,* by Wiener and Pinson, and to Stroustrup's *The C++ Programming Language.*

Another important and major object-oriented language based on the C language is Objective-C, developed by Productivity Products International, Inc., Sandy Hook, Connecticut, in 1978. It is described in Cox's book, along with other languages. A programmer can freely mix the structured features of C with the new object-oriented features of Objective-C. Objective-C is closer in structure to Smalltalk than is C++. The software-IC, which is the centerpiece of Objective-C, is the unit of encapsulation and reusability. All the major properties of object-oriented programming—abstraction, encapsulation, inheritance, and polymorphism—are supported by Objective-C.

Other object-oriented languages include: Object Pascal developed by Apple Computer; Neon (based on Forth) by Krygia Systems; ExperCommonLisp (based on Lisp) by ExperTelligence; Objective Logo (based on Logo) by Coral Software; CommonObjects (based on Lisp) by Hewlett Packard; Flavors (based on Lisp)

[ni:ən]

---

*Alan Kay was instrumental in the development of the object-oriented approach used in Smalltalk. Smalltalk was developed at Xerox Palo Alto Research Laboratories. It is continually being improved and marketed by Xerox ParcPlace Systems, 2400 Geng Road, Palo Alto, CA 94303.

X췰믁

[flo mingmun]taitə]

invented at MIT and developed by Symbolics, Inc.; Eiffel developed by Interactive Software Engineering; and Flamingo developed at Carnegie Mellon University. There are other object-oriented languages currently existing and under development. This list is not intended to be complete.

Exercises

1.1 In your own words, develop a concise definition for object-oriented problem solving.

1.2 Give two reasons why there is an advantage to the idea that a message sent to an object results in an object. Do these reasons apply to all object-message expressions? If not, does the requirement that an object-message produce an object cause any undesirable fallout effects?

1.3 Consider the following problem: A rollbook is to be developed and maintained for keeping class records. It must allow the entry of student names and grades, modification of existing grades, removal of student names (and grades), computation of grades based on user-specified weighting schemes, and printout of grades in alphabetical or rank order. Define the objects, messages, and object-message sequences that provide an interactive solution to this problem. (An interactive solution is one whereby the user has complete control over all options in the solution.)

1.4 It is required to establish a program that simulates normal transactions in a bank. Normal transactions include customer arrivals based on some statistical law, service by tellers of customers based on some statistical law, and computation of significant statistics. Define the objects and messages that are part of this simulation program. Include as much detail as you think is necessary for a reasonable simulation.

1.5 Based on capabilities of state-of-the-art printers (laser, dot-matrix, or daisy-wheel), define objects and messages that are significant for controlling computer output to those printers. Consider the output of both text and graphic images. Generate your objects and messages in generic terms that are understandable without specific knowledge of any printer protocol.

1.6 For the class **TextFile** described in Section 1.2, define at least six other messages to which objects that are instances of this class should respond.

1.7 For class **Tree,** defined in Section 1.3, consider the special binary tree that obeys AVL rules. Define a new subclass of **Tree** for AVL trees. Identify any new private data objects, new messages, inherited messages that still apply, and polymorphically redefined messages for AVL trees.

1.8 List and discuss the four most significant comparison features that you feel provide an advantage to object-oriented problem solving over structured problem solving. Justify your answers.

1.9 Why is polymorphism an important feature for a programming language to support?

1.10 List and discuss any problems you envision with a hierarchical class structure for representing kinds of objects. Do not restrict your thinking to computer problem solutions.

1.11 Exercise 1.4 requests definition for objects and messages that are part of a bank simulation program. Compare the required objects and messages for a simulation program that uses a single waiting line versus one that has separate waiting lines for each teller. Discuss the ramifications of establishing a class hierarchy that (a) makes the multi-line simulation a subclass of the single-line simulation or (b) makes the single-line simulation a subclass of the multi-line simulation.

1.12 Many procedural languages provide constructs that are well suited to the solution of numerical problems. Consider the following numerical problem. A two-dimensional array of numbers is to be processed using a window averaging scheme. That is, each value in the array is to be replaced with the average of itself and its eight closest neighbors (the process is a 3×3 averaging window centered about each value). Special cases include all values around the border of the matrix (those that do not have eight neighboring values). Develop solutions in one procedural language of your choice and in the object-oriented paradigm. For the object-oriented solution define all objects, messages, and the object-message sequence representing a solution. Compare the two solution approaches in terms of readability, efficiency, and ease of understanding.

CHAPTER

2

Object-Oriented Programming in Smalltalk

This chapter presents a detailed overview of the underlying features of the Smalltalk language, with emphasis on how those features support the object-oriented paradigm. It describes the five key components (object, class, instance, message, method) of Smalltalk. The Smalltalk user interface is described in Chapter 3. For additional details of the Smalltalk language the reader is referred to Goldberg and Robson's *Smalltalk 80: The Language and Its Implementation* (Addison-Wesley, 1983).

Smalltalk is an interpretive language that uses an intermediate compiler. Smalltalk source code is compiled into byte codes and made a part of the Smalltalk *virtual image* (hereafter referred to as the image). During program execution, the Smalltalk interpreter translates byte codes into appropriate actions. Smalltalk source code for all functionality in the language is available for viewing or modification by the user. The only exception is a group of low-level operations known as primitives, which are usually implemented in assembly language.

Smalltalk is *not* small! The size, completeness, and variety of functionality provided in the Smalltalk system image is at the same time one of its strong features and one of its drawbacks. Smalltalk is not just another language, but a complete environment. Further, the Version 2 Smalltalk image has already within it the capability for solving many standard problems in computer applications. In a typical Smalltalk implementation the image occupies about 1.3 megabytes and the source code occupies about 1.5 megabytes. Both of these grow in size as new capabilities are added to the system. Smalltalk is not small.

How does one know what's in the Smalltalk image, and how does one find it? Although there are several tools for exploring the Smalltalk image, there is no easy way. Gaining familiarity with Smalltalk takes time, but it is time well spent. One of the major goals of this book is to make the process of learning Smalltalk a faster, easier, and more logical process than has been possible in the past. In the long run there is no substitute for *knowing what's in the image*. It is the purpose of this book to reduce the time required for obtaining that knowledge.

Of all the object-oriented languages, Smalltalk is most true to the object-oriented paradigm. It supports all the features and properties for object-oriented problem solving described in Chapter 1. As an interpretive language it provides rapid testing of incremental changes to the image. Many problems are solved by using (and/or modifying) existing classes and methods in the system image.

Because it is interpretive, Smalltalk programs execute more slowly than those written in competing object-oriented languages that are compiled. Compilers for Smalltalk programs that produce machine code are currently under development. Their success will eliminate the speed disadvantage for Smalltalk production software systems.

Sections 2.1 through 2.5 of this chapter illustrate the object-oriented paradigm in Smalltalk. Section 2.6 gives the protocol that is used to define different kinds of classes. Section 2.7 provides a general overview of the classes that are part of the Version 2 Smalltalk image.

The reader not familiar with Smalltalk syntax is encouraged to review Appendix 1 and use it as a supplement to syntax details given in this chapter.

2.1   Objects and Messages—Sending Messages to Objects

All programming in Smalltalk is accomplished by sending messages to objects. The result of sending a message to an object is another object. An initial approach to problem solving is to use existing kinds of objects and messages in the Smalltalk image. An object-message sequence is developed that accomplishes the desired goals for the problem solution. The following examples are given in standard Smalltalk syntax.

Objects are *instances* of a particular *class*. The *messages* to which an object can respond are defined in the protocol for its class. *Methods* give the implementation details for messages and are a part of the class description protocol for a given class. These are the fundamental relationships among the five key components (*object, instance, class, message, method*) of the Smalltalk system. It has been said that understanding these five key components and their relationships is understanding Smalltalk. However, doing anything useful with Smalltalk requires knowledge of the Smalltalk image as well.

For the following examples, concentrate on the meanings of the objects and messages. For now accept our word that they are legitimately defined somewhere in the Smalltalk image. In Chapter 3, the reader will learn to use the tools that allow verification of the existence of all the messages used in these examples.

2.1.1   Three kinds of messages

There are three kinds of messages in Smalltalk: unary, binary, and keyword. Unary messages require no parameters. Binary messages are identified by special symbols and have exactly one parameter. Keyword messages are identified by a colon-terminated message selector followed by a parameter. Keyword messages may include any number of message selector–parameter pairs. Remember that the result of sending any message to an object is another object.

Each of the three kinds of messages is illustrated in the following examples, which use actual Smalltalk syntax. Comments are enclosed in double quotes.

Unary Message

A unary message is a single message selector with no parameters sent to a single object. For example:

9 factorial   "Answer the factorial of 9."

theta sin   "Answer the sin of theta."

Date today   "Answer a new instance of class **Date**."

Smalltalk inspect   "Inspect details of the Smalltalk system dictionary."

'hello' outputToPrinter   "Send the string 'hello' to the printer."

Binary Message

A binary message is a single message selector (usually a special symbol) with one parameter sent to a single object. The parameter is also an object. For example:

x + y   "Answer the sum of the receiver x and the parameter y. The symbol + represents a binary message."

a // b   "Answer the integral part of object a divided by parameter b."

23 @ 50   "Answer a two-dimensional point with x-coordinate = object 23 and y-coordinate = parameter 50."

c ~= d   "Answer true if object c is not equal to parameter d; else answer false. The message ~= is sent to object c with parameter d."

Keyword Message

A keyword message is a message to a single object with any number of message selector-parameter pairs. Message selectors are typically colon-terminated identifiers. For example:

Array new: 10

"Answer a new instance of class Array with ten elements. The message new: is sent to object Array with parameter 10."

'myFile.txt' printFile: 5

"Send file named myfile.txt to the printer with 5-space left margin indentation. Note that message printFile: is sent to a string that is the name of a file. String literals in Smalltalk are delimited by single quotes."

aDate day: dayInteger year: yearInteger

"Set the private data for object aDate to day = dayInteger and year = yearInteger. Private data is discussed in more detail in Section 2.3."

aMagnitude between: min and: max
> "Answer true if object aMagnitude is between parameter min and parameter max; else answer false. The message selector for this example is the combination between: and: with parameters min and max. Message selector - parameter pairs are distributed in Smalltalk for enhanced readability."

aString replaceFrom: start to: stop with: replacement startingAt: repStart
> "In the receiver object, aString, replace elements from start to stop with elements in replacement, starting at repStart. Answer the modified receiver, aString."

2.1.2   Precedence

Precedence in Smalltalk is left to right unless altered by the presence of parentheses or by message priorities. The precedence of the three kinds of messages is (from highest to lowest) unary, binary, and keyword. The following examples illustrate how precedence can be used to develop expressions with several messages. If in doubt, use parentheses to force the desired precedence.

Adherence to left-to-right precedence in Smalltalk produces a result for arithmetic expressions that is unexpected. Most languages support higher precedence for selected operators. Programmers are accustomed to interpreting arithmetic expressions where these operator-specific precedence rules apply. Recognition of this difference for arithmetic expressions in Smalltalk requires some retraining of thought processes. For example the expression 3 + 4 / 4 is interpreted in the following way in "Smalltalkese." The object **3** is sent the message + with parameter object **4**. The result is an object, **7**. Object **7** is sent the message / with parameter **4**. The final result is the object **7/4**.

Binary–Binary

3 + 4 / 4.

The result is **7/4**, not **4**. Note that both messages are binary and thus have equal precedence. Therefore, left-to-right precedence prevails.

Unary–Binary

1.5 + 2.1 sin.

The result is **1.5** + **sin(2.1)**. The unary message **sin** has precedence and is sent to the object **2.1** first. The resulting object, **sin(2.1)**, is the parameter for the binary message + sent to object **1.5**.

Unary–Unary

3.2 truncated factorial.

The result is **3!** or **6**. The object **3.2** is sent the message **truncated**, resulting in an object, **3**. Object **3** is sent the message **factorial**, resulting in the object **6**.

Unary–Keyword

Complex real: $A asciiValue imaginary: $B asciiValue asFloat.

The result is the complex number (65 + j66.0). The unary messages are sent first, in the following order. Character literal object $A is sent the message asciiValue, resulting in an integer object, 65. Character literal object $B is sent the message asciiValue, resulting in an integer object, 66. Integer object 66 is sent the message asFloat, resulting in a floating point object, 66.0. The class object **Complex** is sent the message real: imaginary:, with parameters 65 and 66.0, which creates a new complex number object, (65 +j66.0).

Binary–Keyword

'This string' displayAt: 100 @ 200.

The binary message @ is first sent to the integer object 100 with integer parameter 200, resulting in a point object with coordinates x = 100 and y = 200. The string literal object, 'This string', is sent the message displayAt:, with a parameter defined by the point object, x = 100 and y = 200. The result is the display of 'This string', beginning at coordinate point 100@200 on the screen.

Multiple Unary–Binary–Keyword

$A asciiValue = 65 ifTrue: ['Yes' displayAt: $A asciiValue − 64 ∗ 20 @ 200].

The character literal object $A is sent the unary message asciiValue, resulting in an integer object, 65. The object 65, which results from the first message, is sent the binary message = with parameter 65, resulting in the Boolean object **true** (since the asciiValue of $A is equal to 65). The Boolean object **true** is sent the keyword message ifTrue:, with the result that statements in the **block**, delimited by square brackets, are to be evaluated one time. The statement(s) in the block on the screen display the string 'Yes' at coordinates x = 20 (computed from 65 − 64 ∗ 20) and y = 200.

Forced Precedence

The above examples are valid Smalltalk expressions that take full advantage of the precedence rules. In no case were parentheses required. There are cases, however, in which precedence must be forced with the use of parentheses. The following examples illustrate cases where precedence must be forced to achieve the desired result. Comments are delimited by double quotation marks.

3 + (4 / 4)   "Result is 4"

(1.5 + 1.2) sin   "Result is sin (2.7)"

Complex real: $A asciiValue imaginary: 0 asFloat   "Result is a complex number, (65 + j0.0)"

TABLE 2.1   **Precedence Rules for Smalltalk**

General	Precedence is left to right
Messages	Unary (highest), Binary, Keyword(lowest)
Forced	Use enclosing parentheses
Assignment	Lowest precedence except for Return
Return	Lowest precedence

(Complex real: $A asciiValue imaginary: 0) asFloat   "Result is a floating point number, 65.0"

3 + j4 = Complex real: 3 imaginary: 4   "Result is an error."

For the last expression, object **3** is sent the message + with parameter j4 (an imaginary literal, not supported by the Smalltalk image unless added as a new class of objects—see Chapter 6), resulting in a complex number object, **3 + j4.** The object **3 + j4** is sent the binary message = with parameter object **Complex,** producing an error. Message = expects a parameter with a real and imaginary value, but object **Complex** has no real or imaginary value. The solution is simple. Force the keyword message **real: imaginary:** to be sent to object **Complex** *before* the comparison message = is sent to **3 + j4.** The correct message is given by

3 + j4 = (Complex real: 3 imaginary: 4)   "The result is Boolean object true."

Precedence rules for Smalltalk are summarized in Table 2.1. General precedence, messages, and forced precedence have been illustrated in the preceding examples. See Appendix 1 for definitions of *assignment* and *return.*

2.2   Abstraction—Objects and Methods

Objects in Smalltalk are encapsulations of *abstractions.* Abstractions include both data and functional abstractions. Data abstractions take the form of private and shared data, as discussed in Chapter 1. These data define the properties of the object. Functional abstractions take the form of methods that give the details of how an object is to respond to messages. There is a method for each message to which an object can respond.

All objects are instances of a specific class. Each class has a name and represents a specific kind of object. Objects are created by sending instance creation messages to the class name. All the data and functional abstractions for an object are defined in its *class description protocol.* This includes messages for instance creation (creating new objects of that class), private data, shared data, and methods.

The most general kind of object must include all possible kinds of objects. This most general kind of object is represented by a class called **Object. Object** is the superclass of all other classes in the Smalltalk system. Its class description protocol includes messages and corresponding methods, private and shared data, and instance creation methods that are common to any kind of object. Subclasses may polymorphically redefine any of the methods that are part of class **Object,** as required. Subclasses may also add new private or shared data.

In developing a software system such as Smalltalk, much effort must be devoted to defining the kinds of objects it is to support and the functional abstractions that must be available for each kind of object. The capability to modify and improve the existing Smalltalk image with relative ease is by far the most important feature to include. The latest Smalltalk virtual image represents the effort of many people over a period of many years. It provides a wide range of capabilities for problem solving and includes classes of objects that support the user in modifying and learning about the Smalltalk image.

The Smalltalk image consists of over two hundred classes representing as many abstractions. These classes are organized according to categories and according to a dependency hierarchy. Section 2.7 gives an overview of the organization of the Smalltalk image.

Some of the classes in the image are *abstract* classes. Abstract classes are identified by the following properties:

- No objects are instances of an abstract class. They will always be instances of a subclass of the abstract class.

- Methods contained in abstract classes represent protocol common to all its subclasses. Subclasses can polymorphically redefine methods and add new data.

- Abstract classes provide a logical hierarchical organization by serving as an umbrella for related subclasses of equal stature.

In the remainder of this section examples are given that illustrate the concept of *kind of object* and method details for selected messages sent to those objects. They show how abstraction is implemented in Smalltalk. The examples include messages whose actions are similar to operations, such as control and iteration, performed with other languages. The method implementation details are taken from the Smalltalk image. Most of the Smalltalk program segments are executable. Exceptions include those program segments that attempt to read an external file (the file must exist). Methods are not directly executable.

There are only two **Boolean** objects allowed in the Smalltalk system. Object true is the only instance of class **True.** Object false is the only instance of class **False.** Attempts to define new instances of either class **True** or class **False** produce an error message. Note that true and false are reserved words in Smalltalk representing objects that are instances of class **True** and **False** respectively. They cannot be redefined. The result of a Boolean expression (comparison or testing) is either the object true or the object false. Messages to which objects true and false respond form one basis for control in Smalltalk.

In the Smalltalk image, classes **True** and **False** are subclasses of **Boolean.** **Boolean** has no instances and serves to define protocol (messages) that are common to both **True** and **False. Boolean** is called an abstract class since it has no instances. The image includes other abstract classes that are discussed later in the book.

The protocol description for classes **True** and **False** lists several messages and their methods (functional abstractions) that can be used for control. Several of these are first illustrated by example. Then their implementation details (methods) are given.

Object/Method Example 2A—Boolean Objects and Control Messages

I. Unary conditional testing and control—Evaluate a block of expressions if a conditional Boolean expression is true; else do nothing.

'string1' < 'string2' if True: [↑ 'string1'].

The literal string object '**string1**' is sent the message < with the parameter literal string '**string2**'. The result is the object **true**. The object **true** is sent the message if True:, which evaluates the **block** (delimited by square brackets), returning the string literal '**string1**' (the up arrow denotes "return the value of"). If the result of the message < had been **false**, nothing would have happened. This is illustrated by the following method details for the message if True:, as implemented in class **True** and in class **False.** The term 'controlling' is a category name, within which method if True: is grouped, in the class description protocol for classes **True** and **False.**

True methodsFor: 'controlling'
if True: alternativeBlock
    "Answer the value of alternativeBlock since the receiver is true."
    ↑ alternativeBlock value

False methodsFor: 'controlling'
if True: alternativeBlock
    "Answer the false alternative, nil, since the receiver is false."
    ↑ nil

The message **value**, sent to **alternativeBlock**, evaluates the expressions in **alternativeBlock** one time. The identifier **nil** is a reserved word in Smalltalk. It represents an object with no value.

II. Binary conditional testing and control—If a Boolean expression evaluates to **true**, execute a block of expressions. If the Boolean expression is **false**, execute a different block of expressions.

'string1' < 'string2'
       if True: [↑ 'string1']
       ifFalse: [↑ 'string2']

If the literal string 'string1' is less than the literal string 'string2', then return 'string1'; else, return 'string2'. The message if True: ifFalse: could be sent to either object **true** or object **false**, depending on the result of the Boolean expression. Details of the method for message if True: ifFalse: are given below for classes **True** and **False.**

True methodsFor: 'controlling'
if True: trueAlternativeBlock **ifFalse:** falseAlternativeBlock
 "Answer the value of trueAlternativeBlock."
 ↑ trueAlternativeBlock value

False methodsFor: 'controlling'
if True: trueAlternativeBlock **ifFalse:** falseAlternativeBlock
 "Answer the value of falseAlternativeBlock."
 ↑ falseAlternativeBlock value

 III. Boolean logic and multiconditional testing for control—Smalltalk provides a rich variety of messages for performing complex Boolean logic. It does not provide messages designed specifically for multiconditional testing and control, such as that provided by the CASE statement in many languages. It is possible, however, to design and implement in Smalltalk a message that replicates the functionality of a CASE statement. The following example illustrates one way to test if the value of a number falls within one of several ranges.

```
num1 > 0 & ( num1 < 50 )
        ifTrue: [
                num1 < 25
                        ifTrue: [ ↑ 'Number between 0 and 24.']
                        ifFalse:[ ↑ 'Number between 25 and 50.']]
        ifFalse:[ ↑ 'Number is out of range.']
```

The binary message & is defined in both classes **True** and **False** as given below.

True methodsFor: 'logical operations'
& alternativeObject
 "Logical conjunction - Answer alternativeObject since receiver is true."
 ↑ alternativeObject
False methodsFor: 'logical operations'
& alternativeObject
 "Logical conjunction - Answer false since the receiver is false."
 ↑ self

 As we note in Appendix 1, **self** is a reserved word in Smalltalk. It is a pseudovariable (an object used in methods) that always refers to the receiver of the message that invoked the method. In the above example, **self** refers to an instance of class **False.** Further, since the only allowed instance of class **False** is the object false, ↑ **self** is equivalent to returning false.

 Iteration in Smalltalk is supported by messages sent to objects of classes **Number, BlockContext,** and the **Collection** classes. Objects of class **Block-**

Context are identifiable by the fact that they are delimited by square brackets. Some of the previous examples have used blocks. There are many subclasses under class **Collection** that will be discussed in more detail in Chapter 7. One of the most familiar **Collection** subclasses is class **Array.** It has the same functionality as arrays do in other languages.

Object/Method Example 2B—Collection, Number, and BlockContext Objects and Iteration Messages

I. An equivalent for *loop in Smalltalk*—A simple iterative loop with a specified number of iterations is accomplished in Smalltalk using messages from class **Number.** Consider the following example.

```
| anArray |
anArray ← Array new: 10.
1 to: 10 do: [ :i | anArray at: i put: 0.0 ].
1 to: 10 by: 2 do: [ :i | anArray at: i put: 3.0 ]
```

This example is a little more complete than previous examples and illustrates additional features of the Smalltalk language. The identifier **anArray**, delimited by the vertical bars, is a *temporary variable* (an object of unspecified class whose scope is limited to the block of code in which it is declared). The second line assigns (the left arrow means assignment in Smalltalk) **anArray** to be an object of class **Array** with space for 10 elements. Elements in the array can be any kind of object. The third line illustrates the message to: do: from class **Number.** It executes the block 10 times. The :i followed by a vertical bar signifies a block parameter. It takes on consecutive values from 1 to 10 in the example. The fourth line, using the message to: by: do: from class **Number,** is an iterative loop wherein the block parameter is incremented by 2 each time. It sets the odd indexed values in **anArray** equal to 3.0.

Methods in class **Number** supporting the messages to: do: and to: by: do: are given below.

Number methodsFor: 'intervals'
```
to: stop do: aBlock
    "Create an interval from the receiver up to the argument stop, incrementing by 1. For each
        element of the interval, evaluate aBlock."
    | nextValue |
    nextValue ← self.
    [ nextValue <= stop ]
        whileTrue: [
                aBlock value: nextValue.
                nextValue ← nextValue + 1 ]
to: stop by: step do: aBlock
    "Create an interval from the receiver up to the argument stop, incrementing by step. For
        each element of the interval, evaluate aBlock."
    | nextValue |
    nextValue ← self.
```

```
step < 0
    ifTrue: [[ stop <= nextValue ]
            whileTrue: [
                    aBlock value: nextValue.
                    nextValue ← nextValue + step ]]
    ifFalse:[[ stop >= nextValue ]
            whileTrue: [
                    aBlock value: nextValue.
                    nextValue ← nextValue + step ]]
```

Messages **ifTrue:** and **ifFalse:** were defined in Example 2AII. Message **while-True:** is described below. The message **value:** with parameter **nextValue**, sent to object **aBlock**, is defined in class **BlockContext.** It is valid only if **aBlock** has exactly one block parameter.

II. An equivalent while *loop in Smalltalk*—Messages available to objects of class **BlockContext** provide functionality equivalent to that of the while loop in other languages. The following example reads characters from *'myFile.txt'*, strips all blank spaces, and writes the result to *'yourFile.txt'*.

```
| textFile aCharacter outFile |
textFile ← FileStream oldFileNamed: 'myFile.txt'.
outFile ← FileStream newFileNamed: 'yourFile.txt'.
[ textFile atEnd ] whileFalse: [
        aCharacter ← textFile next.
        [ aCharacter = Character space ]
                whileTrue: [ aCharacter ← textFile next ].
        outFile nextPut: aCharacter ].
outFile close
```

The general format for the loop message **whileTrue:** is given by [testBlock] **whileTrue:** [executeBlock]. First, **testBlock** is evaluated. If it is **true**, then **executeBlock** is executed. This process is repeated until **testBlock** evaluates to **false**. Similar logic is followed by the loop message **whileFalse:**.

Details of the methods in class **BlockContext,** supporting messages **whileTrue:** and **whileFalse:**, are given below.

```
BlockContext methodsFor: 'controlling'
whileTrue: aBlock
    "Evaluate the argument aBlock as long as the receiver is true."
    ↑ self value
        ifTrue: [
                aBlock value.
                self whileTrue: aBlock]
whileFalse: aBlock
    "Evaluate the argument aBlock as long as the receiver is false."
    ↑ self value
        ifFalse: [
                aBlock value.
                self whileFalse: aBlock]
```

Please note that the implementations of these two messages are recursive.

III. Other iterative loops in Smalltalk—Messages available for objects in the

Collection classes provide a variety of iteration schemes. The following example illustrates five iteration messages sent to a string object (strings are collections of characters). For each of the five messages, the block is evaluated once for each element in the receiver, aString.

```
| aString count |
count ← 0.
aString ← 'Object-Oriented'. "String objects can be created by literal assignments."
aString do: [ :aChar | aChar isUppercase
    ifTrue: [ count ← count + 1 ] ].
aString collect: [ :aChar | aChar asUppercase ].
aString select: [ :aChar | aChar isUppercase ].
aString reject: [ :aChar | aChar isUppercase ].
aString detect: [ :aChar | aChar isUppercase ]
```

The parameter for each of the five messages is a block with a single block argument. Results for each of the five messages are given by the following.

do: aBlock—Answer the value of count (2), the number of uppercase characters in aString.

collect: aBlock—Answer a new collection with one element that is the result of evaluating the block, for each element in the receiver. The above result is a string, 'OBJECT-ORIENTED'.

select: aBlock—Answer a new collection containing the elements in aString for which the block evaluates to true. The above result is a string containing only the uppercase letters, 'OO'.

reject: aBlock—Answer a new collection containing only the elements for which the block evaluates to false. The above result is the string 'bject-riented'.

detect: aBlock—Answer the first element in the receiver for which the block evaluates to true. The above result is the character $O.

Details of the methods supporting the above messages are given in the Smalltalk image, under the **Collection** classes. They can be viewed using the Smalltalk System Browser, as described in Chapter 3. The method details are not reproduced here.

A variety of objects have the property called *magnitude*. Foremost among objects that have magnitude are numbers. Other objects with magnitude include time, dates, and characters. A consistent set of functional abstractions used with all magnitude objects is that of comparison. In the Smalltalk image, class **Magnitude** has the subclasses **Time, Date, Number,** and **Character,** among others.

Class **Magnitude** is called an abstract class. It has no instances and provides method protocol common to all its subclasses. Selected methods for comparison are listed below as additional examples of functional abstraction in Smalltalk. Each subclass of **Magnitude** will add its own specific functional and data abstractions. Chapter 6 provides a more complete discussion of the **Magnitude** classes.

Object/Method Example 2C—Objects with Magnitude and Messages for Comparison

Magnitude methodsFor: 'comparing'

< aMagnitude
  "Compare the receiver with the argument and answer true if the receiver is less than the
      argument. Otherwise answer false."
    ↑ self subclassResponsibility

= aMagnitude
  "Compare the receiver with the argument and answer true if the receiver is equal to the
      argument. Otherwise answer false."
    ↑ self subclassResponsibility

> aMagnitude
  "Compare the receiver with the argument and answer true if the receiver is greater than the
      argument. Otherwise answer false."
    ↑ aMagnitude < self

>= aMagnitude
  "Compare the receiver with the argument and answer true if the receiver is greater than or
      equal to the argument. Otherwise answer false."
    ↑ (self < aMagnitude) not

<= aMagnitude
  "Compare the receiver with the argument and answer true if the receiver is less than or
      equal to the argument. Otherwise answer false."
    ↑ (self > aMagnitude) not

max: aMagnitude
  "Answer the receiver or the argument, whichever has greater magnitude."
  self > aMagnitude
      ifTrue: [↑ self]
      ifFalse: [↑ aMagnitude]

min: aMagnitude
  "Answer the receiver or the argument, whichever has lesser magnitude."
  self < aMagnitude
      ifTrue: [↑ self]
      ifFalse: [↑ aMagnitude]

between: min **and:** max
  "Answer whether the receiver is less than or equal to the argument max and greater than
      or equal to the argument min."
    ↑ self >= min and: [self <= max]

The purpose in showing so many comparison methods for magnitudes is to demonstrate how the methods within a category often are built on one or two key methods. This layering of abstractions makes maintenance easier by focusing on the key methods when changes are made. In the above examples, lessthan (<) and equality (=) are the key methods upon which several of the others depend. Note also that the methods for lessthan and equality are not implemented here. Their implementation will be different for each subclass and will be given in the protocol for the subclass. The message subclassResponsibility is implemented as a method in class **Object.** It is therefore available to all objects in the Smalltalk system. This message produces the error message 'My subclass should have overridden one of my messages.'. It is sent unless the subclass does override the message.

This section has shown by example how Smalltalk implements abstractions. The abstractions, both data and functional, are encapsulated in the objects. The next section provides additional information about the data abstractions associated with an object. It discusses the differences in messages sent to objects (instances of a class) and messages sent to class names.

2.3   Encapsulation—Grouping Methods for Objects into Classes

Encapsulation as objects in Smalltalk is based on the class description protocols for individual classes. The protocol for a specific class defines the properties of its instances (objects). Properties of objects include descriptive parameters (other objects) and details of how the object responds to messages. This section describes the fundamental elements of a class description protocol, with selected examples. Section 2.6 gives a more formal definition of the class description protocol, using a complete example in Smalltalk syntax.

The fundamental elements of a class description protocol are given below. Not every class will have all these elements. The existence of private data or shared data depends on the nature of the objects represented by the class. The number and type of methods depend strongly on the complexity and richness of functional abstractions to which objects of the class must respond.

- *Definition*—a concise statement that identifies the location of the class in the image hierarchy. It also lists identifiers for private, shared, and pool data objects that are part of the class.

- *Private data*—descriptive parameters (also objects) whose values are private to individual instances of the class. Private data are represented by *instance variables,* which can be accessed only by instance methods. Details of how the private data objects are accessed are also subject to the protocol of each object's class.

- *Shared data*—descriptive parameters (also objects) whose values are shared by all instances of the class. Shared data are represented by *class variables,* which can be accessed by both instance methods and class methods. Here also, access is governed by the protocol of each object's class.

- *Pool data*—descriptive parameters (also objects) whose values are shared across multiple classes. Access to pool data must be specifically expressed in the class description protocol. Pool data are represented by *pool dictionaries,* which can be accessed by both instance methods and class methods. However, since pool data are typically instances of another class, their access is restricted to the use of messages provided by that class. The Version 2 Smalltalk image has only one pool dictionary, named **Text-Constants.** It is shared by approximately 13 classes.

- *Instance methods*—implementation details for messages to which instances of the class can respond. The messages these methods represent can be sent only to instances of the class. They are called *instance methods.*

- *Class methods*—implementation details for messages to which the class can respond. The messages these methods represent can be sent only to the class name. They are called *class methods.* Class methods typically are used to initialize class variables, to create instances of the class, or to provide general inquiries without instance creation.

The following example describes class **Date.** It has private data in the form of two instance variables, shared data in the form of five class variables, and no pool dictionaries. It has a rich variety of both class methods and instance methods. Only a summary of the methods is presented. This method of summarizing the protocol for a class is used throughout the book and in Appendix 3. It serves to provide a quick overview of the properties, complexity, and kinds of messages to which instances of a class respond. Examples that use the protocol of class **Date** are presented in Chapter 6.

Class Example 2A—Class Date Description Summary

Definition—The hierarchy for class **Date** is **Object—Magnitude—Date.** It has two instance variables, **day** and **year.** It has five class variables, DaysInMonth, First-DayOfMonth, MonthNames, SecondsInDay, and WeekDayNames. It has no pool dictionaries. It has 14 class methods in three categories and 27 instance methods in seven categories. Objects of class **Date** represent dates.

Private data—Class **Date** has two instance variables.

   day—an instance of **Integer** representing the day of a year (values range from 1 to 366).

   year—an instance of **Integer** representing the year (values range from beginning of Roman calendar).

Shared data—Class **Date** has five class variables.

   DaysInMonth—an instance of **Array,** containing 12 integers that are the number of days in the 12 months.

   FirstDayOfMonth—an instance of **Array,** containing 12 integers that are the accumulative day in the year for each of the first days of the 12 months. (For example, the sixth element in the array is the integer 152. The first day of June is the 152nd day of the year.)

   MonthNames—an instance of **Array,** containing symbols for the 12 month names (e.g., #January, etc.) Symbols in Smalltalk are preceded by the # sign.

SecondsInDay—an instance of **Integer,** with value $24 * 60 * 60 = 86,400$—the number of seconds in a day.

WeekDayNames—an instance of **Array,** containing symbols for the seven names of the weekdays (e.g., **#Monday,** etc.).

Instance methods—There are 27 instance methods in seven categories. The categories and corresponding number of methods are:

comparing—four methods including methods for testing equality and lessthan.

accessing—six methods including **day** and **year,** which return values of the instance variables **day** and **year** respectively. It is common practice in Smalltalk to assign identical message names and private data variable names for methods that access the private data.

arithmetic—Three methods for adding or subtracting days from a date.

inquiries—Six methods for inquiring about particular days, months, and years of an instance of **Date.**

converting—One method, **asSeconds,** that answers the number of seconds from January 1, 1901 to the date of the receiver. Time of day is assumed the same for both dates.

printing—Four methods for printing the date in a specified format. Method **printOn:** is implemented in all classes. It defines the format for printing the object on the display screen.

private—Three methods that support access to instance variables for instance creation. For example, class methods for instance creation call the private method **day: year:** to establish values for the instance variables **day** and **year.** Recall that class methods cannot access private data. Private methods are accessible externally; however, they are intended for use only by other methods within the class description.

Class methods—There are 14 class methods in three categories. The categories and corresponding number of methods are:

class initialization—one method, **initialize,** that sets values for the five class variables.

instance creation—five methods including **today,** which creates an instance with the current day and year.

general inquiries—eight methods including **dateAndTimeNow,** which returns the current date and time.

The above example is a summary description of the class called **Date.** It describes in general terms all the data and functional abstractions that are part of the class. Complete protocol descriptions including all method details can be examined using the Smalltalk System Browser, described in Chapter 3. Hardcopy printout of complete class description protocols can be obtained using messages and methods described in class **PrinterStream,** which is discussed in detail in Chapter 5. Menu options that are part of the System Browser make it possible to obtain hardcopy printout. In Chapter 3 the reader will learn to obtain hardcopy for methods, categories of methods, classes, categories of classes, and even the entire Smalltalk source code, as well as any text file.

2.4   Inheritance—The Class Hierarchy and Subclasses

One of the requirements for an object-oriented language is that it must support inheritance. Inheritance has no meaning unless classes are arranged in a hierarchy in which some classes are subordinate to others. Subclasses inherit from their superclasses. Superclasses do not inherit from their subclasses, and subclasses in a different hierarchical subtree generally do not inherit from each other. Things inherited by a subclass include private data, shared data, instance methods, and class methods. A subclass inherits from all its ancestors, from its immediate parent class all the way to class **Object.**

If a subclass has no protocol (including data and methods) that is different from its superclass, then one must question the need for its existence. Therefore subclasses do include new data and/or methods that were not a part of the protocol of their parent classes. Also, a subclass may need to redefine methods inherited from a superclass. Redefinition of inherited methods is called method overriding. It is a form of polymorphism. A more detailed discussion of polymorphism is given in Section 2.5.

The purpose of this section is to define the rules for inheritance in Smalltalk and to present an example in summary form that illustrates inheritance. The example is taken from the Smalltalk image for a specific inheritance subtree.

The rules for inheritance in Smalltalk, stated informally above, are specifically:

1. A subclass inherits only from its hierarchical chain of superclasses as given by its class description protocol. It inherits from its immediate superclass and all its superclasses up to class **Object.**

2. All classes are subclasses of class **Object,** except of course class **Object,** which has no superclass.

3. Superclasses do not inherit from subclasses.

4. Some implementations of Smalltalk support multiple inheritance. This means that a class may be declared to be a subclass of more than one hierarchical chain. It then inherits from each hierarchical chain. More details of multiple inheritance are given in Section 2.6.

5. A subclass inherits private data, shared data, instance methods, and class methods from its superclasses.

6. Rules for access to private and shared data for inherited protocol are the same as for the class description protocol.

7. A subclass may add new protocol for private data, shared data, instance methods, or class methods in addition to inherited protocol.

8. A subclass may redefine inherited instance or class methods to have new meanings. Redefined methods may serve to block response by instances of the subclass to messages that are legitimate for the superclasses.

The concept of inheritance is presented in two examples below. Since class **Object** is the superclass of all classes, its protocol is inherited by all classes. Inheritance Example 2A gives a summary of the protocol of class **Object.** Inheritance Example 2B describes inheritance properties of class **Character.** A summary is given of its inherited, new, and redefined protocol.

Inheritance Example 2A—Protocol Summary of Class **Object,** the Superclass of All Classes

Definition—The hierarchy for class **Object** is **Object.** It has no instance variables, two class variables, DependentsFields and ErrorRecursion, and no pool dictionaries. It has 11 class methods in 4 categories and 87 instance methods in 17 categories. **Object** is the superclass of all classes. It provides default behavior for all objects, such as class access, copying, and printing.

Shared data—Class **Object** has two class variables.

DependentsFields—an instance of **IdentityDictionary,** containing for every object in the system an **OrderedCollection** of dependents. Dependents are objects that should be notified if there is a change in the receiver object.

ErrorRecursion—an instance of **True** or **False.** The value of ErrorRecursion is initialized to **false.** It is set to **true** when certain error conditions exist.

Instance methods—There are 87 instance methods in 17 categories. The categories and corresponding number of methods are:

initialize-release—One method, **release,** establishes protocol for breaking dependents. It removes references to objects that may refer to the receiver.

accessing—eight methods, including **at:, at: put:,** and **size,** for accessing indexable objects. The method **yourself** answers the receiver.

testing—Three methods, **isInteger, isNil,** and **notNil,** answer **true** or **false** for any object.

comparing—six methods including methods for testing equality and identity.

copying—five methods for making different kinds of copies of an object. Differences relate to whether data are shared or copied.

dependents access—three methods for adding, viewing, or removing the dependents of the receiver object.

updating—eight methods for notifying all dependents of changes in the receiver object.

printing—eight methods for printing objects on the screen or storing objects on a file.

class membership—four methods for determining the class, testing class membership, or testing response to a message for the receiver object.

message handling—five methods that implement messages with zero, one, two, three, or more arguments.

error handling—ten methods, including **subclassResponsibility** and **halt,** that provide standard error handling protocol for all objects.

user interface—two methods for inspecting objects in the Smalltalk system.

system primitives—four methods for low-level operations.

system simulation—five methods that are templates for primitive calls.

private—thirteen methods intended for use only by other methods within the **Object** class description.

Class methods—There are 11 class methods in four categories. The categories and corresponding number of methods are:

class initialization—one method, **initialize,** that sets values for the two class variables.

instance creation—three methods for creating an instance from either a stream (streams are discussed in Chapter 8) or a file.

documentation—Two methods, **whatIsAPrimitive** and **howToModifyPrimitives,** contain only text and are for infomational purposes only.

private—five methods, including methods for initializing the class variables.

The summary description above does not include all the information one needs to use class **Object.** However, it is a good starting point. The reader is encouraged to become more familiar with this class since its protocol affects all objects in the system. Additional detail for this class can be obtained by using the System Browser or by printing the class description protocol for class **Object.**

The following example lists protocol for class **Character.** It separates the available protocol for instances of **Character** into three categories: (1) new protocol, (2) inherited protocol from class **Magnitude,** and (3) inherited protocol from class **Object.**

Inheritance Example 2B—Class Character Protocol Summary

Definition—The hierarchy for class **Character** is **Object—Magnitude—Character.** It has one instance variable, value. It has one class variable, Character-Table. It has no pool dictionaries. It has 13 class methods in five categories and 28 instance methods in six categories. Class **Character** represents the ASCII characters by storing the extended code (0–255) for each character.

Instances of class **Character** are unique (i.e., all instances $A are identical). Character literals in Smalltalk are preceded by a $ sign.

Private data—Class **Character** has one instance variable.

value—the ASCII code for an instance of class **Character.**

Shared data—Class **Character** has one class variable.

CharacterTable—an instance of **Array,** whose elements are the character instances (256 unique characters). The ASCII code for each character is its index position in CharacterTable minus 1.

Instance methods—There are 28 instance methods in six categories. The categories and corresponding number of methods are:

comparing—five methods including methods for testing equality and lessthan/greaterthan.

accessing—two methods, **asciiValue** and **digitValue,** for accessing the value of a character and for parsing numbers of base 2–36, respectively.

testing—eight methods for testing the kind of character that the receiver is.

copying—three methods for making different kinds of copies of a character.

printing—five methods for printing characters on the screen or storing characters on a file.

converting—five methods for converting characters to another kind of character or another kind of object.

Class Methods—There are 13 class methods in five categories. The categories and corresponding number of methods are:

class initialization—one method, **initialize,** that sets values for the Character-Table. In the Tektronix implementation, the details of this method are not shown, to prevent possible redefinition with catastrophic consequences.

instance creation—three methods for creating an instance. Method **new,** which is inherited from **Object,** is redefined to give an error message. No new instances of **Character** are allowed; only the unique 256 ASCII characters defined in CharacterTable are allowed.

accessing untypable characters—Seven methods for accessing nonprintable characters such as the escape key and formfeed are included. Additional methods may be desirable in this category and can be easily added.

constants—One method, **characterTable,** answers the contents of the class variable CharacterTable.

private—One method, **readDefinitionFrom: map:,** is used in creating new objects (redefined from class **Object**).

Protocol inherited from **Magnitude**—Class **Magnitude** is the immediate superclass of **Character. Character** inherits the following protocol from **Magnitude.**

Private data—none. Class **Magnitude** has no instance variables.

Shared data—none. Class **Magnitude** has no class variables.

Pool data—none. Class **Magnitude** has no pool dictionaries.

Instance methods—Class **Magnitude** has 10 instance methods in one category, 'comparison'. Of these, three were implemented as **subclassResponsibility** by **Magnitude**. Details for the three are given in **Character**. Two of the inherited methods are polymorphically redefined in **Character**. The remaining five methods are inherited and unchanged.

Class methods—none. Class **Magnitude** has no class methods.

Protocol inherited from **Object**—Class **Object** is the superclass of **Magnitude**. **Character** inherits the following protocol from **Object**.

Private data—none. Class **Object** has no instance variables.

Shared data—two. Class **Object** has the class variables DependentsFields and ErrorRecursion.

Pool data—none. Class **Object** has no pool dictionaries.

Instance methods—Class **Object** has 87 instance methods in 17 categories. Of these, three are polymorphically redefined in **Character**. Of the remaining 84 methods, all are inherited and unchanged. However, many of the inherited methods have no meaning for objects of **Character**. For example, the 'accessing' method **at: put:** is intended for use with collections, streams, and potentially with other kinds of objects. An attempt to use it with characters produces an error message.

Class methods—Class **Object** has 11 class methods in four categories. Of these, 3 are polymorphically redefined. The remaining 8 are inherited as they exist. Their application to characters may be limited.

The above examples indicate that inherited protocol may or may not be useful in all subclasses of a particular class. This disparity increases near the top of the image hierarchy because of increasing generalization.

2.5 Polymorphism—Sending the Same Message to Different Objects

The scope of a message selector in Smalltalk is restricted to the class description protocol for each class and its subclasses (through inheritance) in the image. Thus identical message selectors may exist in many classes. When messages are sent to objects, the meaning of a message is determined by the protocol description of the object's class. The ability of different objects to respond appropriately to the same message selector is *polymorphism*.

Polymorphism enhances the readability of software by allowing the same message selector, indicating a particular action, to be sent to different kinds of

objects. For example the message printOn: can be sent to any object in the Smalltalk system. The only requirement is that the details for printOn: be included
somewhere in the hierarchy path of the object's class. Conceptually, printOn: implies a particular action to be taken. The concept is identical for any object; only
the implementation details may be different.

The following example illustrates polymorphism by presenting various implementations for the message printOn: as it is given in several class descriptions.
The message has one parameter, an object of class **Stream.** In every case, the
message printOn: aStream, when sent to an object, appends a representation of
the object to aStream. Details vary widely for different classes.

Polymorphism Example 2A—Message printOn: aStream

Definition—"Answer a representation of the receiver appended to aStream. The
representation is a sequence of characters identifying the receiver."

Method for class **Object**—Default is to append the class name of the object; e.g.,
'a Fraction', 'a Complex', 'a Character', 'an Array'.

```
printOn: aStream
| title |
title ← self class name.
aStream nextPutAll: ((title at: 1) isVowel
                ifTrue: [ 'an ' ]
                ifFalse:[ 'a '])
        ,title
```

Method for class **Fraction**—Fractions are represented as rational numbers enclosed in parentheses; e.g., (3/4). Note that a polymorphic version of printOn;
is sent to numerator, an instance of **Number,** as part of this implementation.

```
printOn: aStream
        aStream nextPut: $(.
        numerator printOn: aStream.
        aStream nextPut: $/.
        denominator printOn: aStream.
        aStream nextPut: $)
```

Method for class **Complex**—Added as a new class in Chapter 6, complex numbers are printed in rectangular form and enclosed in parentheses; e.g., (3.0
+j4).

```
printOn: aStream
aStream nextPut: $(.
real printOn: aStream.
(imaginary >= 0)
        ifTrue: [aStream nextPutAll: ' +j'.
                imaginary printOn: aStream]
        ifFalse:[aStream nextPutAll: ' −j'.
                imaginary abs printOn: aStream].
aStream nextPut: $)
```

Method for class **Character**—Characters are printed as literals, the actual character preceded by a $ sign.

```
printOn: aStream
        aStream nextPut: $$.
        aStream nextPut: self
```

Method for class **Array**—**Array** is a subclass of **Collection.** The maximum number of characters printable to represent a collection is arbitrarily set to 5000 by the message maxPrint, defined in class **Collection.** Elements of an array are separated by blank spaces, and the entire array is enclosed in parentheses; e.g., (10 20 30 40 50).

```
printOn: aStream
        | tooMany |
        tooMany ← aStream position + self maxPrint.
        aStream nextPut: $(.
self do: [ :element |
                aStream position > tooMany
                        ifTrue: [aStream nextPutAll: '. .etc. . .)'. ↑ self].
                element printOn: aStream.
                aStream space].
        aStream nextPut: $)
```

There are many other examples of **printOn:** in the Smalltalk image. Almost every class has its own polymorphic definition for this important method.

2.6   Class Protocol—Classes, Metaclasses, Objects, Instances, and Messages

This section introduces the concept of *metaclass* as the class of a class (classes are objects and must therefore have a class). It shows how the components (instance variables, class variables, instance methods, class methods, and pool dictionaries) that are part of a class description protocol are formally defined. Simple classes are chosen for illustrating the complete class description protocol. Different types of subclasses are defined (*variableSubclass, subclass, variableWordSubclass, variableByteSubclass, nonVariableSubclass*) and illustrated by example.

2.6.1   Classes and metaclasses

In previous sections of this chapter, the reader has seen examples that send messages to objects that are instances of a class. In some cases messages were sent to the class name. All the class methods described in the examples above are details of messages sent to a class name. If this activity is to be consistent with the object-oriented paradigm, then classes must also be objects. As objects, classes must have a class and have properties defined by the protocol description in that class. It should be clear that this argument is circular and results in an infinite recursion of class levels.

To unravel the circular argument, the concept of a *metaclass* as the class of a class is introduced. Metaclasses are unique and have properties different from other classes. Every time a new class is defined, its metaclass is automatically defined. Having different metaclasses for each class removes the restriction that all classes have the same protocol. The following properties of metaclasses help clarify their function.

- There is exactly one metaclass for each class in the Smalltalk image.

- A metaclass has only one instance, the class for which it is the metaclass.

- Protocol for a class object is contained in its metaclass. Class variables and class methods are part of the metaclass protocol description for a class. For convenience, the class description and metaclass description are combined. Both can be viewed and modified from the System Browser.

- A metaclass is not an instance of another metaclass. Instead, all metaclasses are instances of a single class called **Metaclass. Metaclass** is a part of the image hierarchy.

- Since **Metaclass** is a class (not a metaclass), it also has a metaclass. The metaclass of **Metaclass** is also an instance of **Metaclass.**

- A class named **Class** is an abstract superclass of all the metaclasses. It serves the same function for metaclasses as **Object** does for classes. Yes, **Class** also has a metaclass that is an instance of **Metaclass.**

- Metaclasses have a hierarchy that matches the hierarchy for classes except for the highest levels. Remember that **Object** is the superclass of all other classes, including metaclasses.

- Rules for inheritance and polymorphism apply to metaclasses in the same way they apply to classes.

If this all sounds confusing, it is. Understanding the concept of classes and metaclasses requires multiple exposure and experience in working with the Smalltalk image. Imagine how confusing the above discussion would be without the aid of different type fonts and case sensitivity. Sometimes a graphic description is helpful. Figure 2.1a is a hierarchical diagram for the **Number** subclass. Figure 2.1b is a hierarchical diagram for the metaclass of the **Number** subclass.

Classes **Behavior** and **ClassDescription** are abstract superclasses of **Class** and also of **Metaclass.** With this example it should be possible to trace the hierarchy of any class or any metaclass in the virtual image. The reader is also referred to the discussion on metaclasses in Goldberg and Robson, with special

Figure 2.1a
Hierarchy for
Subclass **Number**

Object

    Magnitude

        Number

Figure 2.1b
Hierarchy for
Metaclass of
Subclass **Number**

Object

    Behavior

        ClassDescription

            Class

                Object metaclass

                    Magnitude metaclass

                        Number metaclass

attention to the graphic depiction of classes and metaclasses on pages 82–83. One of the menu options available in the System Browser displays either the class or metaclass hierarchy for any class in the system.

2.6.2   A formal class description protocol example

In addition to the elements already described as being part of the class description protocol, each class is assigned a category. Additionally, comments can be added that describe the role of the class. As an example, the complete protocol description for class **True** is given in Listing 2.1. It is a relatively small class and has already been discussed in previous examples. The purpose here is to show a precise protocol description.

The class and metaclass hierarchies for class **True** are shown in Figure 2.2. A complete list of all the protocol available to class **True** includes protocol inherited from its superclasses. Listing 2.1 includes only the protocol defined in class **True;** it does not include inherited protocol.

The order of information in the class description protocol is:

1. *Description*—Class description including superclass, kind of subclass, class name, list of instance variables, list of class variables, list of pool dictionaries, and category.

Listing 2.1
Protocol
Description for
Class **True**

```
Boolean subclass: #True
    instanceVariableNames: ''
    classVariableNames: ''
    poolDictionaries: ''
    category: 'Kernel-Objects'
```

True comment: 'I describe the behavior of my sole instance, true'

True methodsFor: 'logical operations'

& alternativeObject
"Evaluating conjunction -- answer alternativeObject since receiver is true."
↑alternativeObject

not
"Negation--answer false since the receiver is true."
↑false

| aBoolean
"Evaluating disjunction (OR) -- answer true since the receiver is true."
↑self

True methodsFor: 'controlling'

and: alternativeBlock
"Nonevaluating conjunction -- answer the value of alternativeBlock since the receiver is
    true."
↑alternativeBlock value

ifFalse: alternativeBlock
"Since the condition is true, the value is the true alternative, which is nil. Execution does
    not actually reach here because the expression is compiled in-line."
↑nil

ifFalse: falseAlternativeBlock ifTrue: trueAlternativeBlock
"Answer the value of trueAlternativeBlock. Execution does not actually reach here
    because the expression is compiled in-line."
↑trueAlternativeBlock value

ifTrue: alternativeBlock
"Answer the value of alternativeBlock. Execution does not actually reach here because
    the expression is compiled in-line."
↑alternativeBlock value

ifTrue: trueAlternativeBlock ifFalse: falseAlternativeBlock
"Answer with the value of trueAlternativeBlock. Execution does not actually reach here
    because the expression is compiled in-line."
↑trueAlternativeBlock value

or: alternativeBlock
    "Nonevaluating disjunction -- answer true since the receiver is true."
    ↑self

True methodsFor: 'printing'

printOn: aStream
    aStream nextPutAll: 'true'

True class
    instanceVariableNames: ''

True class comment: ''

True class methodsFor: 'private'

readDefinitionFrom: aStream **map:** anOrderedCollection
    "Reads a definition of an object from aStream. It is essential that the object be created
        and appended to anOrderedCollection BEFORE any recursive calls (e.g., to
        readStructureFrom:map:) are made. The syntax should correspond to that which is
        written out by storeDefinitionOn:auxTable:"
    ↑self readFixedDefinitionFrom: aStream map: anOrderedCollection value: true

Figure 2.2a
Hierarchy for
Subclass **True**

    Object

        Boolean

           True

Figure 2.2b
Hierarchy for
Metaclass of
Subclass **True**

    Object

        Behavior

           ClassDescription

                Class

                    Object metaclass

                        Boolean metaclass

                            True metaclass

2. *Class Protocol*—Comment relating to instances of the class. List of instance method details by category.

3. *Metaclass Protocol*—Comment relating to the class. List of class method details by category.

For class **True** described in Listing 2.1, the kind of subclass is simply **subclass:**. Please note that the class description is in the form of a message sent to **Boolean.** The message consists of the message selectors, subclass: instanceVariableNames: classVariableNames: poolDictionaries: category:, with appropriate parameters. This message sequence is invoked to create the subclass definition. It is an instance method in class **Class.**

There are actually six different kinds of subclasses, identified by an appropriate kind of class identifier in the subclass creation message. The six are listed below.

- **subclass:**—This is the standard initialization message for creating a new class as a subclass. The majority of classes are this kind of subclass.

- **variableSubclass:**—This is the standard initialization message for creating a new subclass with indexable pointer variables. The number of private data elements is indexable and in many cases variable in size. An example of a variableSubclass is class **Array.** Each element of an array is represented by an indexable pointer. For most implementations of Smalltalk, pointers are 32-bit quantities.

- **variableByteSubclass:**—This is the standard initialization message for creating a new subclass with indexable, byte-sized, nonpointer variables. An example of a variableByteSubclass is class **String.**

- **variableWordSubclass:**—This is the standard initialization message for creating a new subclass with indexable, word-sized, nonpointer variables. An example of a variableWordSubclass is class **WordArray.** Words are typically 16-bit quantities.

- **nonVariableSubclass:**—This is the standard initialization message for creating a new subclass of an existing variable subclass that does not have indexable variables. An example of a nonVariableSubclass is class **MethodDictionary.**

- **subclass: otherSupers:**—This is the standard initialization message for creating a new subclass with more than one superclass. The resulting class exhibits multiple inheritance. There are no examples of multiple inheritance in the Smalltalk image.

Listing 2.2 gives details of the complete subclass creation methods described above. They are all listed as 'subclass creation' instance methods in class **Class.**

Listing 2.2
Protocol
Description for
subclasscreation
Methods in Class
Class

Class methodsFor: 'subclass creation'

nonVariableSubclass: t instanceVariableNames: f
    classVariableNames: d **poolDictionaries:** s **category:** cat
    "This is the standard initialization message for creating a new class as a subclass of an
        existing class (the receiver) in which the subclass does not have indexable pointer
        variables but self is variable."
    self isBits
        ifTrue:
            [↑self error:
                'cannot make a pointer subclass of a class with non-pointer fields'].
    ↑self class name: t
        inEnvironment: Smalltalk
        subclassOf: self
        instanceVariableNames: f
        variable: false
        words: true
        pointers: true
        classVariableNames: d
        poolDictionaries: s
        category: cat
        comment: nil
        changed: false

subclass: t instanceVariableNames: f
    classVariableNames: d **poolDictionaries:** s **category:** cat
    "This is the standard initialization message for creating a new class as a subclass of an
        existing class (the receiver)."
    self isVariable
        ifTrue:
            [self isPointers
                ifTrue: [↑self
                        variableSubclass: t
                        instanceVariableNames: f
                        classVariableNames: d
                        poolDictionaries: s
                        category: cat].
            self isBytes
                ifTrue: [↑self
                        variableByteSubclass: t
                        instanceVariableNames: f
                        classVariableNames: d
                        poolDictionaries: s
                        category: cat].
            ↑self
                variableWordSubclass: t
                instanceVariableNames: f
                classVariableNames: d
                poolDictionaries: s
                category: cat].

Listing 2.2
(continued)

```
↑self class
    name: t
    inEnvironment: Smalltalk
    subclassOf: self
    instanceVariableNames: f
    variable: false
    words: true
    pointers: true
    classVariableNames: d
    poolDictionaries: s
    category: cat
    comment: nil
    changed: false

subclass: t otherSupers: others
    instanceVariableNames: f classVariableNames: d category: cat
    "This is the standard initialization message for creating a new class as a subclass of an
        existing class (the receiver)."
    self isVariable
        ifTrue:
            [self isPointers
                ifTrue: [↑self
                                variableSubclass: t
                                instanceVariableNames: f
                                classVariableNames: d
                                poolDictionaries: ''
                                category: cat].
            self isBytes
                ifTrue: [↑self
                                variableByteSubclass: t
                                instanceVariableNames: f
                                classVariableNames: d
                                poolDictionaries: ''
                                category: cat].
            ↑self
                variableWordSubclass: t
                instanceVariableNames: f
                classVariableNames: d
                poolDictionaries: ''
                category: cat].
    ↑self class
        name: t
        inEnvironment: Smalltalk
        subclassOf: self and: others
        instanceVariableNames: f
        variable: false
        words: true
        pointers: true
        classVariableNames: d
        poolDictionaries: ''
        category: cat
        comment: nil
        changed: false
```

variableByteSubclass: t **instanceVariableNames:** f
  classVariableNames: d **poolDictionaries:** s **category:** cat
  "This is the standard initialization message for creating a new class as a subclass of an
     existing class (the receiver) in which the subclass is to have indexable byte-sized
     nonpointer variables."
  self instSize > 0
    ifTrue: [↑self error: 'cannot make a byte subclass of a class with named fields'].
  (self isVariable and: [self isWords])
    ifTrue: [↑self error: 'cannot make a byte subclass of a class with word fields'].
  (self isVariable and: [self isPointers])
    ifTrue: [↑self error:
           'cannot make a byte subclass of a class with pointer fields'].
  ↑self class name: t
    inEnvironment: Smalltalk
    subclassOf: self
    instanceVariableNames: f
    variable: true
    words: false
    pointers: false
    classVariableNames: d
    poolDictionaries: s
    category: cat
    comment: nil
    changed: false

variableSubclass: t **instanceVariableNames:** f
  classVariableNames: d **poolDictionaries:** s **category:** cat
  "This is the standard initialization message for creating a new class as a subclass of an
     existing class (the receiver) in which the subclass is to have indexable pointer
     variables."
  self isBits
    ifTrue:
      [↑self error:
          'cannot make a pointer subclass of a class with non-pointer fields'].
  ↑self class name: t
    inEnvironment: Smalltalk
    subclassOf: self
    instanceVariableNames: f
    variable: true
    words: true
    pointers: true
    classVariableNames: d
    poolDictionaries: s
    category: cat
    comment: nil
    changed: false

variableWordSubclass: t **instanceVariableNames:** f
  classVariableNames: d **poolDictionaries:** s **category:** cat
  "This is the standard initialization message for creating a new class as a subclass of an
     existing class (the receiver) in which the subclass is to have indexable word-sized
     nonpointer variables."

Listing 2.2
(continued)

```
self instSize > 0
    ifTrue: [↑self error:
                'cannot make a word subclass of a class with named fields'].
self isBytes
    ifTrue: [↑self error: 'cannot make a word subclass of a class with byte fields'].
(self isVariable and: [self isPointers])
    ifTrue: [↑self error:
                'cannot make a word subclass of a class with pointer fields'].
↑self class name: t
    inEnvironment: Smalltalk
    subclassOf: self
    instanceVariableNames: f
    variable: true
    words: true
    pointers: false
    classVariableNames: d
    poolDictionaries: s
    category: cat
    comment: nil
    changed: false
```

2.7   The Smalltalk Image—An Initial Hierarchy of Classes

This section is designed to help the reader organize his or her thoughts with respect to what is already available in the Smalltalk image. It starts at a level of categorization higher than the class categories used by the System Browser. The discussion is of a summary nature; the intent is to provide a global view of what is in the standard Smalltalk image and what it can accomplish. Information about the big picture is helpful when one dives into Smalltalk and gets quickly lost in all the detail.

Classes in the Smalltalk image can be grouped into several categories, as in the System Browser. The following summary discussion provides a more global grouping of classes. Its aim is to provide a general overview of some of the major functionality provided by the Smalltalk image.

- *Magnitude classes*—These classes define objects that can be compared, measured, ordered, and counted. They include numbers, dates, times, characters, and associations (key/value pairs). Objects in these categories are the easiest to understand and the most frequently used.

- *Stream classes*—These classes are used for accessing external devices (such as printers), files, and internal objects as sequences of characters or other objects. Instances of the stream classes provide a combination of sequential and random accessing and maintain a record of the current position.

- *Collection classes*—The collection classes are the data structures in Smalltalk. Collections are groups of related objects. There is a rich variety of collection subclasses representing various data structures. Collection subclasses differ in their properties related to size, ordering, duplication of elements, and accessibility by keys.

- *Windows*—Windows are described by a model, a view, and a controller. A model-view-controller triad exists for any window opened in the Smalltalk system. There are numerous classes supporting specific standard views and controllers. Models may be instances of many different classes. Since Smalltalk is a window-oriented environment, understanding the MVC triad is essential to the development of consistent application software.

- *Graphics*—Smalltalk provides rich support for graphics based on a bit-mapped display. There are many classes that deal with graphics objects and the mechanism by which they are displayed.

- *Kernel classes*—Kernel classes provide the protocol for many of the fundamental and essential operations of the Smalltalk system. These include classes for creation of new subclasses, organization of the class hierarchy, protocol common to all classes, support for processes, and support for methods and messages.

- *System classes*—System classes provide support for maintaining changes to the Smalltalk image, for compiling new methods, for status checking and benchmarking, and for creating clean versions of the image.

- *Interface classes*—Interface classes provide a wide variety of capabilities for accessing the operating system, for inspecting parts of the Smalltalk system, and for supporting standard windows such as the System Browser.

These eight global categories of the Smalltalk classes combine and in many cases overlap the categories of classes listed in the System Browser. They present a more high-level and general view of the Smalltalk system capabilities.

Smalltalk has within it the tools for describing itself at any level of detail. Some of these tools are already a part of the image. Other tools can be easily developed after the user gains a certain level of familiarity with the existing classes and methods. The System Browser provides tools for examining every detail of the Smalltalk source code. It allows the user to view definitions, abbreviated lists of protocol for any class, comments, and details of any method, and it even provides explanations for almost any token within a method. Other tools provided by the browser are described in Chapter 3.

It is sometimes easier to understand complex relationships from printed hardcopy of pertinent information than it is to scan through graphical data in a window on a display screen. All the tools for investigating the image in the System Browser can be redirected to provide hardcopy output. This capability is not part of the standard Smalltalk image, but can be added with relative ease (see Chapter 5).

Information about the Smalltalk image can be very simple, such as a hierarchical summary (with indentation to show hierarchical level) of every class in the system. This information may be of use to the seasoned Smalltalk user, but it provides limited information to the newcomer. Information can also be as complex as a complete protocol description of every class in the system. The very size of this information boggles the mind of all users.

There are several levels of complexity between the two extremes mentioned above for presenting information about the Smalltalk image. One approach that has been used in previous sections of this chapter is to summarize the protocol for a given class. While this approach is useful, it is a huge project to undertake for all classes unless Smalltalk can be modified to accomplish the task automatically.

Appendix 2 represents an intermediate level of complexity in summarizing the class descriptions. The listing in Appendix 2 was produced automatically by adding incremental capability to existing classes in Smalltalk. It is a hierarchical listing of all classes that includes the instance variables. The next level of sophistication would add lists of method categories and the number of methods in each category.

This chapter has presented both summary information and selected details about Smalltalk. It is a large system that requires time for its understanding. In Chapter 3, the reader is introduced to the Smalltalk environment and the tools it provides. Additional discussion and examples of Smalltalk syntax are also presented in Chapter 3.

Exercises

2.1 How is programming accomplished in Smalltalk?

2.2 Explain in your own words the significance of the existence of binary messages for supporting normal arithmetic operations.

2.3 Evaluate the mathematical expression $2 * (4 + 3 / 2) + 3 * 4$, using (a) Smalltalk precedence rules and (b) precedence rules for Pascal.

2.4 Modify the expression in Exercise 2.3 so that it gives the same value for both Smalltalk and Pascal precedence rules.

2.5 **Fraction** is a subclass of **Number**. Based on examples given in the chapter for iteration using the messages to: do: and to: by: do: and your understanding of inheritance by subclasses, is the following expression valid?

```
| sum |
sum ← 1/2.
1/2 to: 15/2 by: 1/4 do: [ :value | sum ← sum + value ]
```

If the expression is valid, give your reasoning. What action with respect to the messages defined in **Fraction** can ensure that this expression will not be valid?

2.6 In Object/Method Example 2C, eight comparison methods are defined for class **Magnitude.** If a new subclass of **Magnitude** is to be added, what methods must be defined in that new subclass for its instances to be able to respond to all eight of the comparison messages? What conclusions can you draw about the relative importance of methods? How does this affect future maintenance of the Smalltalk system?

2.7 Class **Object** is the superclass of all classes in Smalltalk. It has no instance variables. Give reasons why this is desirable.

2.8 In the hierarchy chain shown in Figure 2.1b for the metaclasses of **Number,** why is **Metaclass** not a part of the figure?

2.9 Develop a complete protocol summary for class **Object** including all the methods that are part of the class description. Identify key methods, those that are implemented as subclassResponsibility or that are sent by other methods in class **Object.**

Using the Smalltalk Environment and Language

This chapter presents an overview of the Smalltalk environment and how to use it. Examples show how to use the major system windows in Smalltalk and how to generate, execute, and save Smalltalk programs. More details of the Smalltalk syntax are presented and more example Smalltalk programs are given.

3.1 The Smalltalk Environment

The first-time user of Smalltalk needs some relatively simple instructions and examples on how to find what is in the image, how to generate and save Smalltalk source code, and how to execute Smalltalk programs. This section of this chapter seeks to provide an easy set of steps for achieving those functions. Brief mention is made of some of the more advanced features of the Smalltalk environment that are discussed in more detail later in the book.

Windows were described briefly in Chapter 2 as one of the major categories of classes in the Smalltalk image. There are a number of *standard system windows* that provide the tools for user interaction with the Smalltalk system. The user interacts with these windows through positioning of a mouse-driven cursor, through clicking or pressing buttons on the mouse, and through keyboard input.

The Version 2 Smalltalk system requires a three-button mouse. The function of each button in many cases depends upon the window within which the cursor is positioned; however, the following general rules apply. The left button (or red button) is typically used for selection of windows or text or objects on the screen. The middle button (or yellow button) is typically used to display a window-sensitive menu of options for user action. The right button (or blue button) is typically used to display a menu of options that is standard for all system windows. Although few if any mice have colored buttons, the convention of referring to buttons by color is unfortunately used throughout the Smalltalk image, so both color and position references are included in this chapter.

The user interface is one of the most friendly and easily learned features of Smalltalk. With limited instruction, most readers will soon be able to explore the Smalltalk system on their own. Additional details of user interface are given in Goldberg's work.

There are five standard system windows that are most often used for exploring the Smalltalk system and for interacting with external storage media. They are the *System Browser, System Workspace, File List, Workspace,* and *System Transcript* windows. These windows are accessible from a system menu, which is obtained by first moving the cursor to a background area of the display (one with no underlying window) and then pressing the yellow (middle) mouse button. Clicking means a quick depression and release of the button; whereas pressing means continuous depression of a button. Multiple copies of these windows, except for the System Workspace and System Transcript, can be opened at the same time.

The details for invoking the Smalltalk system vary for different computers and implementations. On the Tektronix 4406, Smalltalk is initially invoked by typing 'smalltalk' and pressing the 'return' key. After the system is loaded, the user is presented an initial screen with several of the standard system windows open. Figure 3.1 shows one possible initial screen that contains exactly one of each of the five standard system windows listed above. Options on invoking Smalltalk provide a way to select different images that have been saved from previous sessions.

Using the blue-button list of menu options (activated by first moving the cursor within a window and then pressing the right button), any system window can be moved, reframed, collapsed to a small rectangle containing only the name, or closed. Thus it is possible to change the display of windows on the screen with almost unlimited flexibility. Using Projects, described in Section 3.1.7, it is possible to maintain several screen display configurations for easy access.

The visual display of each window is referred to as a *view*. Recall from Chapter 2 that all windows have an associated model-view-controller triad. Some windows will have subdivided parts, referred to as *subviews*. For example, the System Browser window has seven subviews (see Figure 3.1), identifiable as separate rectangular regions within the view. Each of the five standard system views listed above is described further in the following subsections. The functionality of each window is described and illustrated with examples.

3.1.1 The System Browser window—finding what's in the Smalltalk image

Probably the most important window in the entire Smalltalk system, the System Browser is a window on all the source code that is part of the Smalltalk image. It is the window with which a Smalltalk user spends most of his or her time. The standard system view for the System Browser is shown in Figure 3.2, with se-

Figure 3.1 Initial Screen Display of the Standard Smalltalk Image

System Transcript

System Workspace

The Smalltalk–80tm System Version T2.2.0c

Copyright (c) 1983 Xerox Corp.
All rights reserved.
Copyright (c) 1984, 1985, 1986 Tektronix, Inc.
All rights reserved.

Create File System

"Make the Smalltalk home directory an absolute path"
Disk + FileDirectory directoryNamed: '/public'.

File List

/smalltalk/fileIn

System Browser

Numeric–Magnitud
Numeric–Numbers
Collections–Abstra
Collections–Unord
Collections–Sequer

class

Workspace

An Introduction to
Object–Oriented
Programming and
Smalltalk

by: Lewis Pinson
and Richard Wiener

Initial Screen Display
of the Standard
Smalltalk Image
Showing Various
Window Options

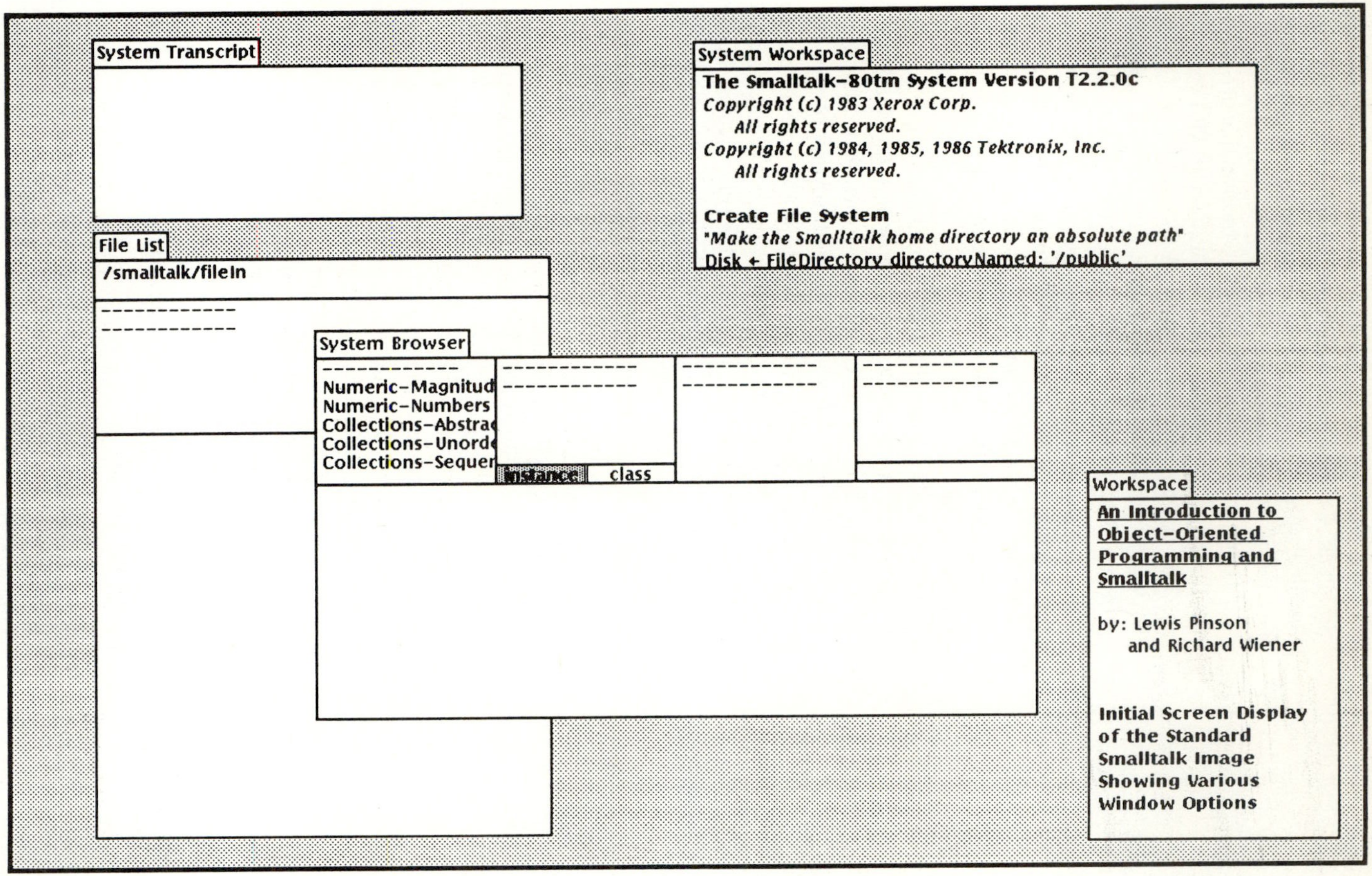

Figure 3.2
The Smalltalk
System Browser
Window

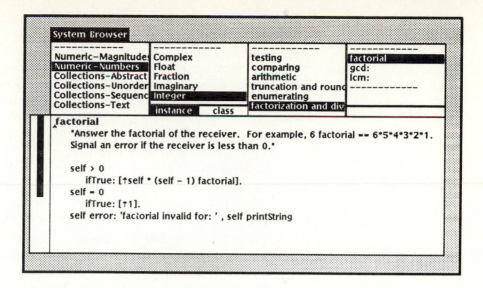

lected examples of objects to be displayed in each subview. The subviews and their purpose are described below.

- *Class Category Subview*—The upper left rectangular region of the System Browser shown in Figure 3.2. This subview contains a list of categories for classes in the Smalltalk image. The category *Numeric-Numbers* has been selected, as indicated by its being displayed in reverse video. With the cursor positioned in this subview, a scroll bar appears to the left of the subview. This scroll bar indicates there are more categories than can fit within the window. Other categories can be moved into the window by appropriate scrolling action (using the left mouse button).

- *Class Name Subview*—Immediately to the right of the class category subview in Figure 3.2. This subview lists the names of all classes that are in the selected class category, *Numeric-Numbers*. This category has 10 classes in it, of which 5 are visible in the class name subview in Figure 3.2. Others are viewed by scrolling. The class named **Integer** has been selected.

- *Instance Subview*—Part of the class name subview, containing the single word **instance**. When selected, as shown in the figure, the two subviews to the right of the class name subview will contain information relating to instance methods (class protocol).

- *Class Subview*—Part of the class name subview, containing the single word **class**. When selected, the two subviews to the right of the class name subview will contain information relating to class methods (metaclass protocol). The class subview and instance subview are mutually exclusive; only one may be selected at any given time.

■ *Message Category Subview*—Immediately to the right of the class name subview in Figure 3.2. This subview lists categories of messages for the selected class. The categories represent either instance methods or class methods, depending on whether the class subview or the instance subview has been selected. In Figure 3.2 the instance message category *factorization and divisibility* has been selected. It is one of 12 categories for **Integer** instance methods. Other categories can be viewed by scrolling.

■ *Message Selector Subview*—The far right rectangular region in Figure 3.2. This subview contains a list of message selectors for the chosen class and message category. They are instance message selectors or class message selectors depending on the selection of either the instance subview or class subview. In the figure, the three message selectors invoke instance methods in the category *factorization and divisibility* of class **Integer.**

■ *Text Subview*—The large bottom rectangular region in Figure 3.2. This subview contains textual information that depends on the selections (or lack of selections), and menu options of the other subviews. For the state of selected items shown in Figure 3.2, this subview contains source code for the method that represents the message selector **factorial.**

Except for the instance subview and the class subview, all the subviews in the System Browser have pop-up menus that can be viewed by pressing the yellow (middle) mouse button. The following hierarchy and rules apply when attempting to view pop-up menus in the various subviews.

■ *Text Subview Menu*—The menu for this subview is the standard pop-up menu for a text view. It is available anytime the System Browser window is displayed by moving the cursor into the text subview and pressing the middle button on the mouse. Options in this menu include the usual text related menu items such as cut, copy, paste, accept (save), and others.

■ *Class Category Subview Menu*—This menu is viewed by moving the cursor into the class category subview and pressing the middle button on the mouse. One menu is available if no category has been selected. A different menu is available if a category has been selected. Some of the more important options in these menus are adding, renaming, or removing categories, finding a class, and filing out. The importance of filing out is discussed in Chapter 4. It is an important step in sharing, backing up, and maintaining multiple Smalltalk images.

■ *Class Name Subview Menu*—This subview has one pop-up menu that is activated by selecting both a class category and a class name, then moving the cursor into the class name subview, and pressing the middle button on the mouse. Nothing happens unless both a category and a class have been selected (reverse videoed). Important menu options for classes include checking external references to the class, its instance variables, and class variables, examining the definition, comment, hierarchy, or protocol summaries for the class, and filing out.

- *Message Category Subview Menu*—This subview has two menus, neither of which is activated unless both a class category and class name have been selected. One menu is available when no message category has been selected. The other menu is available when a message category has been selected. In either case the menu can be viewed by moving the cursor into the message category subview and pressing the middle button on the mouse. Important options for message selector categories include adding, renaming, or removing categories and filing out.

- *Message Selector Subview Menu*—This menu is available only if selections have been made for a class category, a class name, a message selector category, and a message selector. It is activated in a manner similar to that used for activating the other menus. Menu options in this subview include the ability to remove a message, test the senders, implementors, or messages that are part of the selected message, and filing out.

There are a wide variety of menu options on each of these pop-up menus. They provide the capability to explore every facet of the Smalltalk image and to modify the Smalltalk image. The reader is encouraged to experiment with the menu options and to use the Goldberg reference.

It is possible to remove existing options from a menu or to add new options. Discussed in Section 3.1.6 are examples that add capability for easily obtaining hardcopy printout of selected source code, from the System Browser.

Contents of the text subview change depending on the state of selected items from other subviews in the browser and on menu options. As selections are made from the other subviews, there are default text displays in the text subview. With no selection made for the class category subview, all other subviews are empty, as in Figure 3.3. Selection of a class category results in the

Figure 3.3
Smalltalk System
Browser Window—
Initial View

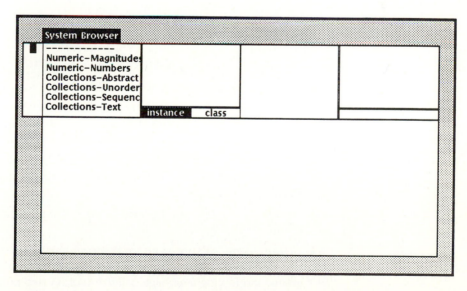

default display of a class description template. This is useful for defining new subclasses.

Selection of a class name causes the text subview to display the class description for the selected class. A menu option in the class name subview, *definition,* causes the same display. Selection of a message selector category causes a message template to be displayed in the text subview. This is useful for generating new messages. And finally, as shown in Figure 3.2, selection of a particular message selector causes the display of its method details.

3.1.2   The System Workspace window—key information about the system and maintenance

The System Workspace is a standard system window with a single text subview. Its contents can be edited as with any other text window. Only one System Workspace window can be open at any given time. The purpose of this window is to maintain a list of executable Smalltalk expressions that serve as general utilities. They are grouped in categories. The following list is a summary of the capabilities typically found in the System Workspace.

- *Create File System*—This category contains expressions for establishing the home directory, printing catalog files, naming the Smalltalk sources and changes files, creating a clean Smalltalk system, and turning off all accessability to the disk.

- *Files*—This category includes expressions for file input/output. Expressions for filing in (installing in the Smalltalk image) a file, saving changes to a file, and editing an external file can be executed.

- *Changes*—Modify or examine the internal record of changes to the Smalltalk image.

- *Inquiry*—Ask the system dictionary for information about the Smalltalk environment. Some of these expressions are also invoked by menu options in the System Browser.

- *Dependents*—Expressions for examining and releasing dependents.

- *Globals*—A list of existing global variables and expressions for inspecting or examining their contents. There is one global variable called **Smalltalk** that is an instance of class **SystemDictionary.** This global variable is very important for examining the Smalltalk environment.

- *Fonts and Text Styles*—Expressions for examining and changing default text styles and fonts.

- *Display*—Expressions for changing size, color, background, and other features of the display.

- *Measurements*—Expressions for determining the size of the Smalltalk system, determining free disk space, timing the execution of Smalltalk programs, and forcing a garbage collection of unused pointers.

■ *Change Management and Crash Recovery*—Smalltalk has tools for recovering from a system crash. It takes real effort to cause a crash that cannot be recovered. However, it's still a good idea to have backups.

Execution of Smalltalk code consists of selecting the text to be executed and then choosing the middle-button menu items *do it* or *print it*. *Print it* always displays the result of the execution (the value of some object) on the screen immediately following the selected code. If the expressions being executed provide their own display messages or cause an action to happen that does not require display, then *do it* is the preferred execution option.

Several examples of the expressions in the System Workspace are shown in Figures 3.4 through 3.7 after having been executed using *print it* or *do it*. Figure 3.4 shows the result of evaluating the expression

Disk := FileDirectory directoryNamed: '/public'

It sets the value of global variable **Disk** to the directory /public.

Figure 3.5 shows the result of evaluating the expression

Smalltalk inspect

The user is prompted to define a rectangular window that becomes an inspector window on class **SystemDictionary.** The Global variable **Smalltalk** is the single instance of class **SystemDictionary.** The left subview of the inspector window contains a list of all global variables that are part of the **SystemDictionary.** By selecting one of these global variables, the user can obtain information about the variable in the right subview. As indicated by the size of the scroll bar, there are many more global variables in **Smalltalk** than those shown in the window.

Figure 3.6 shows how the display can be easily modified using expressions

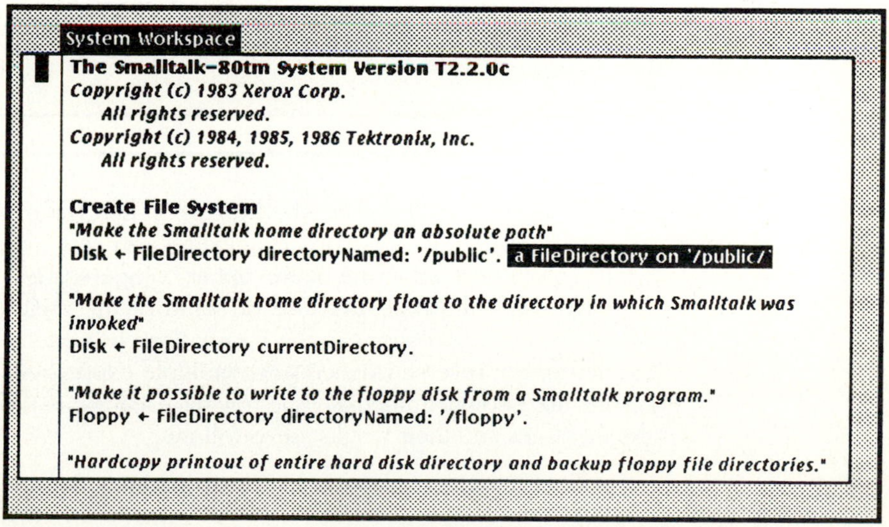

Figure 3.4
Executable
Smalltalk Utilities
in the System
Workspace

```
System Workspace

The Smalltalk–80tm System Version T2.2.0c
Copyright (c) 1983 Xerox Corp.
    All rights reserved.
Copyright (c) 1984, 1985, 1986 Tektronix, Inc.
    All rights reserved.

Create File System
"Make the Smalltalk home directory an absolute path"
Disk ← FileDirectory directoryNamed: '/public'.    a FileDirectory on '/public/'

"Make the Smalltalk home directory float to the directory in which Smalltalk was
invoked"
Disk ← FileDirectory currentDirectory.

"Make it possible to write to the floppy disk from a Smalltalk program."
Floppy ← FileDirectory directoryNamed: '/floppy'.

"Hardcopy printout of entire hard disk directory and backup floppy file directories."
```

Figure 3.5
Inspecting the
Smalltalk System

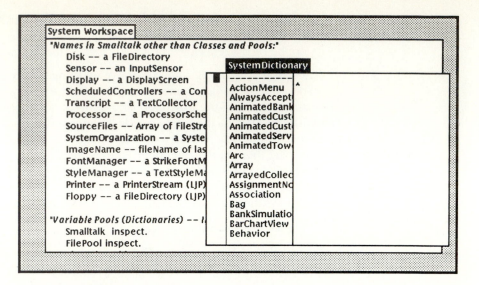

Figure 3.6
Setting Display
Options from the
System Workspace

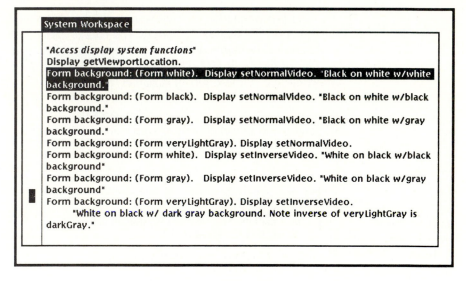

kept in the System Workspace. The expression in reverse video in Figure 3.6 was executed with *do it*. This particular expression sets the background color to white, as can be seen in the figure. Other colors (shades of gray) are possible.

Figure 3.7 illustrates the use of some of the measurement expressions. There are five expressions in the figure. Each was executed with *print it*. The results are not reverse videoed since multiple expressions were evaluated. The results are shown immediately following each expression. Interpretations of the messages and their results are as follows.

■ Smalltalk core—answers an array containing the number of objects in the system and the number of words they occupy. When this message was

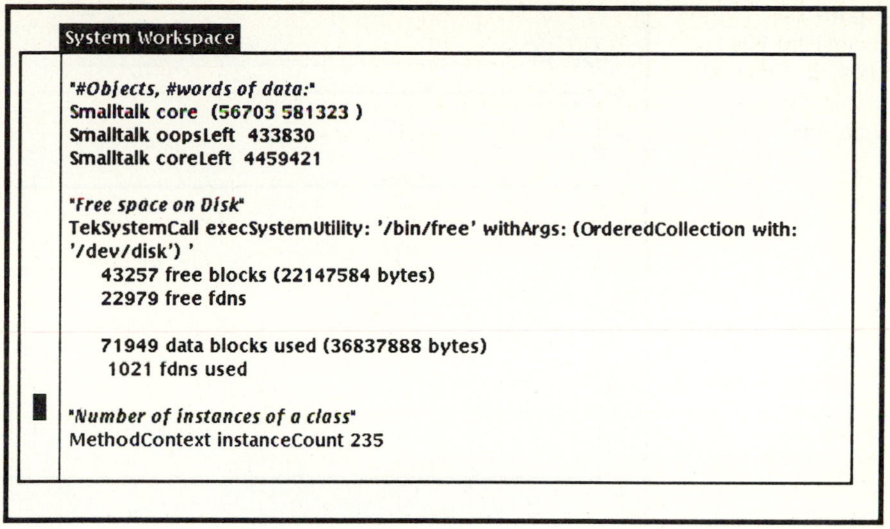

Figure 3.7
System
Measurements
from the System
Workspace

```
┌─────────────────────────────────────────────────────────────┐
│ ┌──────────────────┐                                         │
│ │ System Workspace │                                         │
│ ├──────────────────┴──────────────────────────────────────┐ │
│ │                                                          │ │
│ │ "#Objects, #words of data:"                              │ │
│ │ Smalltalk core  (56703 581323 )                          │ │
│ │ Smalltalk oopsLeft  433830                               │ │
│ │ Smalltalk coreLeft  4459421                              │ │
│ │                                                          │ │
│ │ "Free space on Disk"                                     │ │
│ │ TekSystemCall execSystemUtility: '/bin/free' withArgs: (OrderedCollection with: │ │
│ │ '/dev/disk') '                                           │ │
│ │    43257 free blocks (22147584 bytes)                    │ │
│ │    22979 free fdns                                       │ │
│ │                                                          │ │
│ │    71949 data blocks used (36837888 bytes)               │ │
│ │     1021 fdns used                                       │ │
│ │                                                          │ │
│ │ "Number of instances of a class"                         │ │
│ │ MethodContext instanceCount 235                          │ │
│ │                                                          │ │
│ └──────────────────────────────────────────────────────────┘ │
└─────────────────────────────────────────────────────────────┘
```

executed there were 56,703 objects in the system and they occupied 581,323 words (or 1,162,646 bytes).

- Smalltalk oopsLeft—answers the number of remaining object pointers that can be allocated before the object table is full (*oops* are object pointers). The figure indicates that 433,830 object pointers can still be allocated.

- Smalltalk coreLeft—answers the number of unallocated words in the object space. The figure indicates 4,459,421 words are unallocated.

- TekSystemCall execSystemUtility: '/bin/free' withArgs: (OrderedCollection with: '/dev/disk')—executes the operating system function *free*. The result is that 43,257 blocks (or 22,147,584 bytes) are free with capability for generating 22,979 file descriptor nodes. There are 71,949 blocks used (or 36,837,888 bytes) that are described by 1021 file descriptor nodes.

- MethodContext instanceCount—answers the number of instances of **MethodContext.** The result is 235.

There are numerous other utility expressions in the System Workspace. The user may modify, delete, or add expressions as desired.

3.1.3   The File List window—saving text as files on disk

File List windows can be opened by choosing the appropriate option on the system pop-up menu. Any number of File List windows can be open at one time. They provide access to files on an external storage medium. These files can be accessed, modified, saved, and filed in. (Filing in is the counterpart to filing out that was previously discussed above for source code in the Smalltalk image.)

Figure 3.8
Examining File
Lists, on External
Media, from
Smalltalk

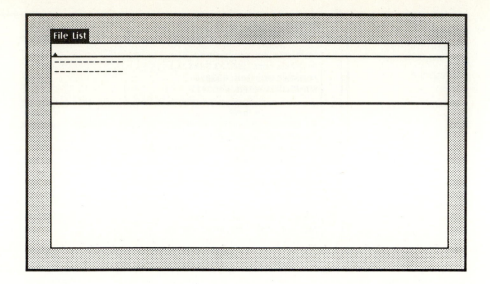

Not all examples of Smalltalk code become part of the Smalltalk image. Yet it may be desirable to save those code segments. Files are the logical way to save textual information. The File List window is the mechanism for doing this in Smalltalk. Figure 3.8 shows an initial view of a File List window.

The view for a File List window consists of three subviews. The wide, thin rectangular region at the top of the File List window in Figure 3.8 is called the file pattern subview. The user types a pattern in this subview that may include directory paths, existing single file names, wild card characters that return multiple files, or a new file name. This subview has a yellow-button pop-up menu that includes the option *accept*.

When the user *accepts* the file pattern in the file pattern subview, a list of files matching that pattern is displayed in the file list subview immediately below it. When a file in the list is selected, information about its size and date and time stamp is displayed in the bottom text subview. If the selected item in the list is a directory, the word *-Directory-* appears in the text subview.

After a file name has been selected, a pop-up menu can be accessed from the file list subview. Among the options provided by this menu are the ability to remove or rename the file, obtain the contents of the file (displayed in the text subview), and file it in. If a directory has been selected, the menu options include removing or renaming, listing contents, and spawning a new File List window on the directory.

Menu options in the text subview, activated by selecting a file name from the file name subview, include the usual cut, copy, paste, and editing options. This menu also provides options for filing in and saving (put) the text file.

Figure 3.9 shows the result of *accepting* all files in a directory called */smalltalk/fileIn*. The asterisk is a wild card character that returns all files in the direc-

Figure 3.9
Using the File
List Window

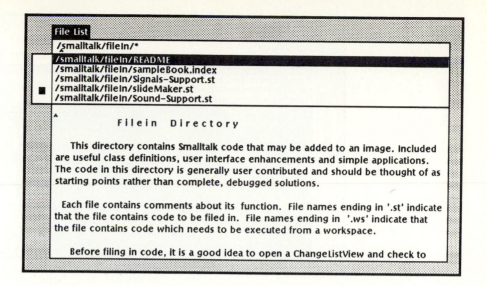

tory. The file named *README* has been selected and the first part of its contents are displayed in the bottom subview. It is possible to copy, cut, and paste text among text subviews of any open window. Pasting text selections into the File List window is a good way to generate and save information on disk.

3.1.4 The Workspace window—flexible but temporary

The concept of a scratchpad window is introduced in the form of the Workspace window. It is a window for generating temporary text that may be informative or executable Smalltalk code. The Workspace window is not unique in this feature. Any of the previously discussed windows can also be used as scratchpad workspaces. Transfer of text between text views is demonstrated in examples below.

The Workspace window consists of a single text view and has the standard yellow-button pop-up menu for manipulating text. Menu options include cut, copy, paste, and so forth. Like all other system views, it has a blue- (right) button menu with options for framing, collapsing, moving, closing, and other operations.

Figure 3.10 shows how text from a File List view is copied into a Workspace and executed. Figure 3.10a shows a File List with the file named *sieve.st* selected. The middle-button menu from the File List allows the selected text to be copied into a buffer. Next the Workspace window is selected and the middle-button menu option for *paste* is selected. The text for *sieve.st* is pasted into the Workspace window as shown in Figure 3.10b. The entire code for the sieve is obtainable from the Figure 3.10a and b.

The code in Figure 3.11 has been selected and executed with *do it* since the code includes expressions for displaying the result. The result of the exe-

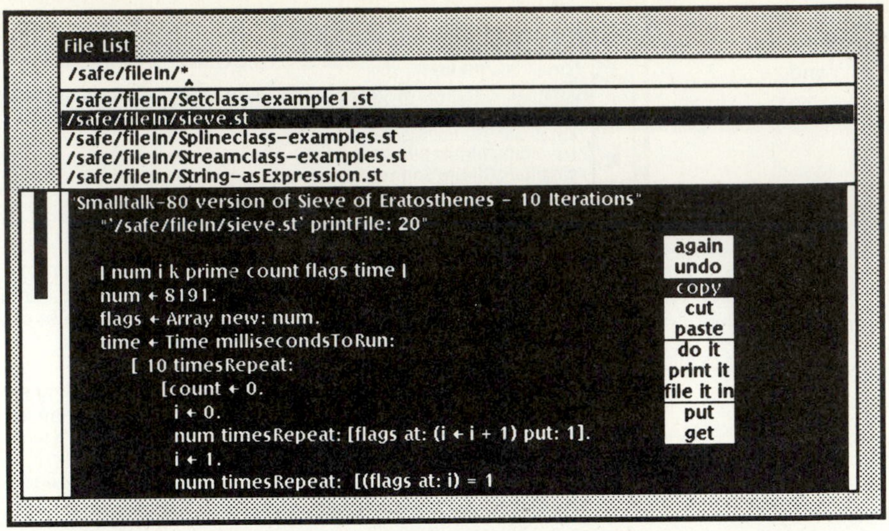

Figure 3.10a
Copying Text from
File List to
Workspace

```
File List
/safe/fileIn/*
/safe/fileIn/Setclass-example1.st
/safe/fileIn/sieve.st
/safe/fileIn/Splineclass-examples.st
/safe/fileIn/Streamclass-examples.st
/safe/fileIn/String-asExpression.st
'Smalltalk-80 version of Sieve of Eratosthenes - 10 Iterations'
  "'/safe/fileIn/sieve.st' printFile: 20"

| num i k prime count flags time |       again
num ← 8191.                              undo
flags ← Array new: num.                  copy
time ← Time millisecondsToRun:           cut
  [ 10 timesRepeat:                      paste
    [count ← 0.                          do it
     i ← 0.                              print it
     num timesRepeat: [flags at: (i + i + 1) put: 1].  file it in
     i ← 1.                              put
     num timesRepeat:  [(flags at: i) = 1   get
```

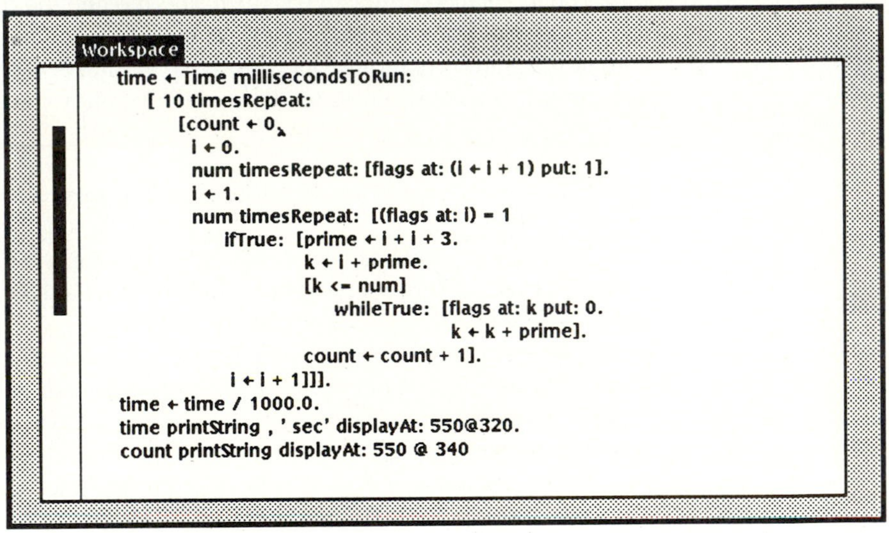

Figure 3.10b
Copying Text from
File List to
Workspace

```
Workspace
      time ← Time millisecondsToRun:
        [ 10 timesRepeat:
          [count ← 0.
           i ← 0.
           num timesRepeat: [flags at: (i + i + 1) put: 1].
           i ← 1.
           num timesRepeat:  [(flags at: i) = 1
             ifTrue:  [prime ← i + i + 3.
                       k ← i + prime.
                       [k <= num]
                         whileTrue:  [flags at: k put: 0.
                                      k ← k + prime].
                       count ← count + 1].
             i ← i + 1]]].
      time ← time / 1000.0.
      time printString , ' sec' displayAt: 550@320.
      count printString displayAt: 550 @ 340
```

cution is shown on the screen in reverse video. For ten iterations of the sieve, 26.116 seconds were required.

The only significant advantage to a Workspace window over other windows with text subviews is that it provides a larger area for displaying text, since it has only the one view. For systems with small screens this may be desirable.

Text generated in the Workspace window can be saved to disk with the

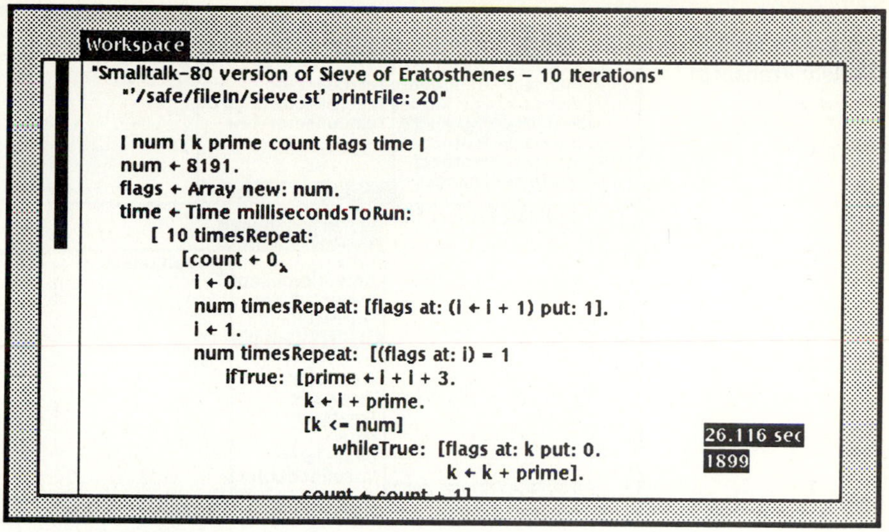

Figure 3.11
Executing
Smalltalk Code in
the Workspace

```
Workspace
"Smalltalk–80 version of Sieve of Eratosthenes – 10 Iterations"
"'/safe/fileIn/sieve.st' printFile: 20"

| num i k prime count flags time |
num ← 8191.
flags ← Array new: num.
time ← Time millisecondsToRun:
    [ 10 timesRepeat:
        [count ← 0.
        i ← 0.
        num timesRepeat: [flags at: (i ← i + 1) put: 1].
        i ← 1.
        num timesRepeat: [(flags at: i) = 1
            ifTrue: [prime ← i + i + 3.
                    k ← i + prime.
                    [k <= num]
                        whileTrue: [flags at: k put: 0.
                                    k ← k + prime].
                    count ← count + 1]
```

26.116 sec
1899

middle-button menu option *file out*. This capability is not part of the standard Version 2 image. It was supplied as a user-generated feature with the Tektronix system. This menu option prompts for a file name and defaults to *Workspace.ws*. During the development of new methods for addition to the Smalltalk image, the Workspace window is useful for maintaining a list of test expressions that can be saved to disk for later review or debugging.

3.1.5   The System Transcript window—display of textual messages from execution of Smalltalk code

The System Transcript window is used for displaying a variety of information. Textual output from a program can be displayed in this window. The Smalltalk system uses the System Transcript to display status and messages related to specific actions taken by the system, such as snapshots or filing out. For example, the transcript window in Figure 3.1 contains a message about the last snapshot taken. A snapshot means that the image was saved either when exiting Smalltalk or in response to the *save* option on the system pop-up menu.

The System Transcript window has a single text subview; therefore, its contents can be edited as with other text views. In many of the figures in this chapter, the System Transcript has been used as a text display for the results of executing examples.

Program output is directed to the System Transcript window by sending messages to the global variable **Transcript.** Figure 3.12 shows an inspector on **Smalltalk,** the single instance of **SystemDictionary.** It identifies **Transcript** as

Figure 3.12
Identifying the
System Transcript

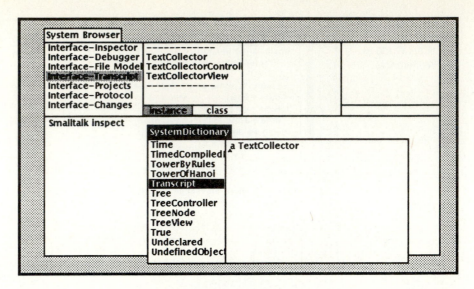

aTextCollector. Shown also in the figure is where to find protocol for class **Text-Collector** in the System Browser. Note there are three classes listed under the category *Interface-Transcript*. These classes correspond to the model, view, and controller for the System Transcript window. For a list of messages to which **Transcript** responds, the reader is encouraged to explore the protocol for class **TextCollector** and its superclasses, **StringHolder** and **Object.**

Figure 3.13 illustrates the use of the transcript for displaying output from a program. It also illustrates the common practice of providing examples of the use of a specific class's protocol as class methods in the class protocol description. The System Browser at the bottom of Figure 3.13 shows the details of a class method called **example** in class **TextCollector.** This example was executed with the resulting display shown in the System Transcript. As shown in the figure, the method includes a comment, "TextCollector example," that can be selected and executed. It then sends the message **example** to the object **TextCollector.** This avoids the necessity of having to select the entire source code of the method. This practice is common also. The expressions in the example method illustrate the process of sending multiple messages to the same object by separating the messages with semicolons.

Methods within the protocol description of a class are generally not executable as stand-alone Smalltalk code. The example methods are. It is constructive and helpful to other users if example methods are included by the developer of new class protocol. This technique is used in larger example software systems throughout this book. It maintains the software system within the Smalltalk image, without the necessity for external, separate files of Smalltalk code. This is one of the most important concepts for maintaining Smalltalk code.

Figure 3.13
Executing Code
with Display in the
System Transcript
Window

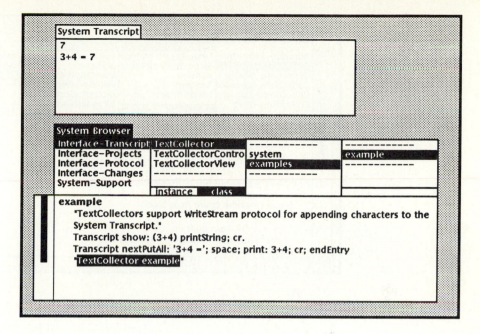

3.1.6 The System Browser window revisited—changing the Smalltalk image

In this section several examples are used to illustrate how the Smalltalk image can be modified. Existing methods within a class can be changed, or new methods can be added. Examples of both techniques are given. The System Browser provides all the tools necessary for modifying the Smalltalk image.

New Method Example 3A—Adding **sieve** to Class **Integer**

In Section 3.1.4, the sieve was introduced as an executable Smalltalk program that was saved on disk. Execution of the program required that it be found in a disk file, displayed in a text subview, selected, and executed with *do it* from the middle-button menu. The number of iterations was set at 10. This is a lot of steps to perform every time the sieve is to be run. The process is greatly simplified by adding a method for running the sieve to the Smalltalk image.

A logical first choice for location of the sieve method is in class **Integer.** It has the added flexibility that the receiver integer object can be used to denote number of iterations. Then the object-message pair **10 sieve** causes the iteration to be performed 10 times.

Figure 3.14
Adding a New
Method to the
Smalltalk Image

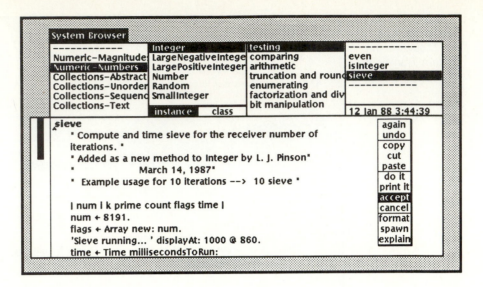

Figure 3.14 shows the System Browser with class **Integer** selected. There is an existing category of instance methods called *testing* that is also selected. Under this category there are already two methods, **even** and **isInteger**. This is a logical place for **sieve**. Note that the text subview shows a template for the components of any method. This is a simple reminder of the expected format. It can be deleted as the details for the new method are added.

The user next adds details in the text subview for the intended new method. After completion, select *accept* from the text subview middle-button menu. The method statements are compiled. If compilation is successful, the new method selector will appear in the message selector subview. If there are errors, the user is notified with appropriate error messages. Figure 3.15 shows the result of successfully adding the details for method **sieve**. Only a partial listing of the sieve method is shown in Figure 3.15. For complete details of the method, see Listing 3.1. There are minor differences in the sieve method and the sieve program discussed in Section 3.1.4.

New Method Examples 3B and 3C—Adding Instance Methods outputToPrinter and printFile: to Class String

The Smalltalk standard image does not provide a class or methods for sending text or graphics to the printer. These are essential tools that can be added with relative ease. Since most printers deal with strings of characters, it seems logical that a message **outputToPrinter** added to class **String** is the fundamental message upon which to build new protocol for printer output. Printers and other devices

Figure 3.15
A Successfully
Compiled New
Method

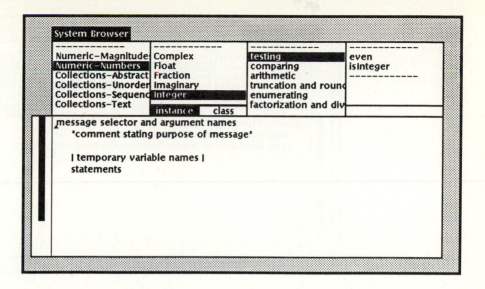

Listing 3.1
Method sieve
Added to Class
Integer

Integer methodsFor: 'testing'

sieve
```
    " Compute and time sieve for the receiver number of iterations. "
    " Added as a new method to Integer by L. J. Pinson"
    "            March 14, 1987"
    " Example usage for 10 iterations -->  10 sieve "
    | num i k prime count flags time |
    num ← 8191.
    flags ← Array new: num.
    'Sieve running... ' displayAt: 1000 @ 860.
    time ← Time millisecondsToRun: [
        self timesRepeat: [
            count ← 0.
        i ← 0.
        num timesRepeat: [flags at: (i ← i + 1) put: 1].
        i ← 1.
        num timesRepeat: [(flags at: i) = 1 ifTrue: [
                prime ← i + i + 3.
                k ← i + prime.
                [k < = num] whileTrue: [
                    flags at: k put: 0.
                    k ← k + prime].
                count ← count + 1].
                i ← i + 1]]].
    time ← time / 1000.0.
    'Sieve in Smalltalk-80: ' , self printString , ' iterations'
        displayAt: 1000 @ 900.
    time printString , ' sec' displayAt: 1000 @ 920.
    count printString displayAt: 1000 @ 940
```

Figure 3.16
Adding Instance
Method
outputToPrinter to
Class **String**

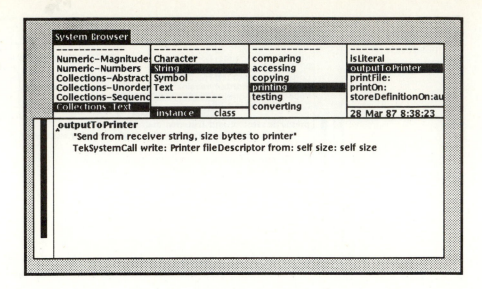

are typically treated as files by most software operating systems. The details of
outputToPrinter must access that file system.

Figure 3.16 shows the result of having added and successfully accepted
code for the message outputToPrinter. It has been added to class **String** under the
existing category *printing*. **TekSystemCall** is a class that provides access to the
underlying operating system. The message write: from: size:, sent to class name
TekSystemCall, writes a specified number of bytes from a specified source to a
specified "file." A literal interpretation of the message and its parameters is:
"Write the number of bytes in the receiver string to the file identified by the
fileDescriptor of **Printer.**" **Printer** is a global parameter, added to the system dictionary, that identifies the printer. Details of **Printer** and its protocol are given in
Chapter 5.

The message outputToPrinter can be sent to objects that are instances of
String. This provides the capability for sending text to the printer and for sending control codes (as strings of escape sequences). From this fundamental abstraction, it is possible to build other useful tools as methods for printer output.
The next example builds on outputToPrinter to provide an easy way for printing
the contents of disk files. Since disk files are usually accessed by a file name (an
instance of **String**), the method printFile: is included as a *printing* method in
class **String** also. Details are given in Figure 3.17 and in Listing 3.2.

In Listing 3.2, there are several new messages to **Printer** that are described in
detail in Chapter 5. Many of these messages eventually emit the message output-
ToPrinter to a string of characters (as text or control codes). Most of the complexity of this method stems from the desire to capture special characters and codes
for formatting. All the listings included in this book were generated by sending
the message printFile: to an appropriate file name string.

Figure 3.17
Adding Instance
Method printFile:
to Class **String**

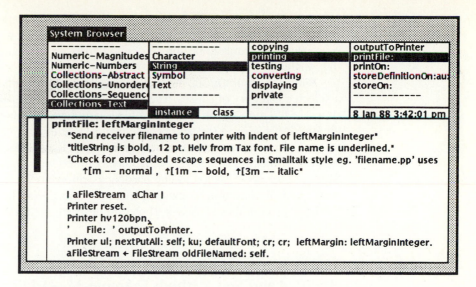

Listing 3.2
Method printFile:
Added to Class
String

String methodsFor: 'printing'

printFile: leftMarginInteger
 "Send receiver filename to printer with indent of leftMarginInteger"
 "titleString is bold, 12 pt. Helv from Tax font. File name is underlined."
 "Check for embedded escape sequences in Smalltalk style eg. 'filename.pp' uses
  ^[m -- normal , ^[1m -- bold, ^[3m -- italic"

 | aFileStream aChar |
 Printer reset.
 Printer hv120bpn.
 '   File: ' outputToPrinter.
 Printer ul; nextPutAll: self; ku; defaultFont; cr; cr; leftMargin: leftMarginInteger.
 aFileStream ← FileStream oldFileNamed: self.
 [aFileStream atEnd] whileFalse: [
  aChar ← aFileStream next.
  (aChar asciiValue = 27)
   ifTrue: [aChar ← aFileStream next. aChar ← aFileStream next.
    aChar = $m ifTrue: [Printer kb; ki].
    aChar = $1 ifTrue: [Printer ki; bo. aChar ← aFileStream next].
    aChar = $3 ifTrue: [Printer kb; it. aChar ← aFileStream next]]
   ifFalse: [Printer nextPut: aChar]].
 Printer ff

   The System Browser provides an on-screen method for inspecting and viewing the details of any part of the Smalltalk image. In many cases it is useful and desirable to be able to view several different parts of the image at the same time. One approach that works is to open more than one browser. As many as four browsers can be displayed on a large (19″) screen and still show adequate detail.

Additional browsers can be opened, but the problem becomes one of increased overlap of the windows or reduced size of the text subview. For this and other reasons it is desirable to be able to obtain hardcopy printout of selected parts of the Smalltalk source code.

Within the four top subviews of the browser, there are options for filing out a selected category of classes, a selected class, a selected category of messages, or a selected message. In each case a file is generated in "chunk format." Files in chunk format serve a special purpose that is described in more detail in Chapter 4. There is also a menu option (*print out*) for producing a file with embedded formatting codes. This capability, coupled with printFile: added to class **String,** forms the basis for adding hardcopy options to the browser menus. The result is a modification to existing methods and the addition of several new methods in a number of classes. These are described in the following examples.

Modified and New Methods Example 3A—Adding Hardcopy Menu Options to Browser Subviews

Details are given for the modified and new methods required to add the option *to printer* to the middle-button pop-up menu of the class category subview of the System Browser window. Similar modifications are added to the other three selector subviews. The modifications can be summarized as follows.

1. Modify the appropriate menu method for each of the four subviews. These are listed as instance methods in class **Browser.** For the four subviews of interest the menu methods are called categoryMenu, classMenu, protocol-Menu, and selectorMenu.

2. Add a new method corresponding to the new menu item, *to printer,* for each subview in class **Browser.** The new methods are called toPrinterCategory, toPrinterClass, toPrinterProtocol, and toPrinterMessage, respectively. These methods are patterned after existing methods for generating the formatted file output described above.

3. Add new methods in existing classes that deal directly with the category, class, protocol, and message outputs to printer. These methods are patterned after existing similar methods in those classes for generating the formatted file output. The methods added are toPrinterCategory in class **System-Organizer,** printerOut in class **Class,** toPrinterCategory in class **ClassDescription,** and toPrinterMessage in class **ClassDescription.**

Details of the modified and new methods for the class category subview of the browser are given in Listing 3.3. Details of the methods for the remaining three subviews may be developed as an exercise for the reader.

Listing 3.3
Modified and New
Methods for
Hardcopy Options
in System Browser

Browser methodsFor: 'category list'

categoryMenu
    "Browser flushMenus"
    category = = nil ifTrue: [↑ActionMenu
        labels:
                'add category\update\edit all\find class\save entry\restore entry' withCRs
        lines: #(1 3)
        selectors: #(addCategory updateCategories editCategories findClass
                saveEntry restoreEntry)].
    CategoryMenu = = nil ifTrue: [CategoryMenu ← ActionMenu
        labels: 'file out\file out *.pp\to printer\spawn\add category
                \rename\remove\update\edit all\find class\save entry
                \restore entry' withCRs
        lines: #(4 7 9)
        selectors: #(fileOutCategory printOutCategory toPrinterCategory
                spawnCategory addCategory renameCategory removeCategory
                updateCategories editCategories findClass saveEntry restoreEntry)].
    ↑ CategoryMenu

Browser methodsFor: 'category functions'

toPrinterCategory
    "Send category to printer"
    organization toPrinterCategory: category

SystemOrganizer methodsFor: 'fileIn-Out'

toPrinterCategory: category
    "Send description of classes in this category to printer. Use temporary file."

    | aFileStream |
    aFileStream ← Disk file: (category , '.prn') asFileName.
    aFileStream emphasis: 3.   "italic"
    Smalltalk timeStamp: aFileStream.
    aFileStream cr; cr.
    self printOutCategory: category on: aFileStream.
    aFileStream close.
    (category, '.prn') asFileName printFile: 20.
    aFileStream remove.

3.1.7   Customizing the Smalltalk environment—Projects

This section specifically deals with Projects, collapsed or framed windows, multiple windows, multiple file lists, the use of multiple browsers for examining the Smalltalk image, screen attributes, and other options for customizing the working environment.

Figure 3.18 Customizing the Main System Display

System Transcript

Snapshot at: (2
November 1987 5:52:12
pm)

Workspace

**An Introduction to Object-Oriented
Programming and Smalltalk**
by: *Lewis Pinson and Richard Wiener*
Slide Number: ^

System Workspace | **File List**

BigWorkspace | OS-Commands | BigBrowser

System Browser

BigExecute | BigFileList | BigSystemWorkspace

Numeric–Magnitu
Numeric–Number
Collections–Abstra

instance | class

Customizing the main system display

Active Windows: *System Browser, System Transcript, Workspace*
Collapsed Windows: *System Workspace, File List*
Collapsed Project Windows: *BigWorkspace, OS-Commands, BigBrowser*
BigExecute, BigFileList, BigSystemWorkspace

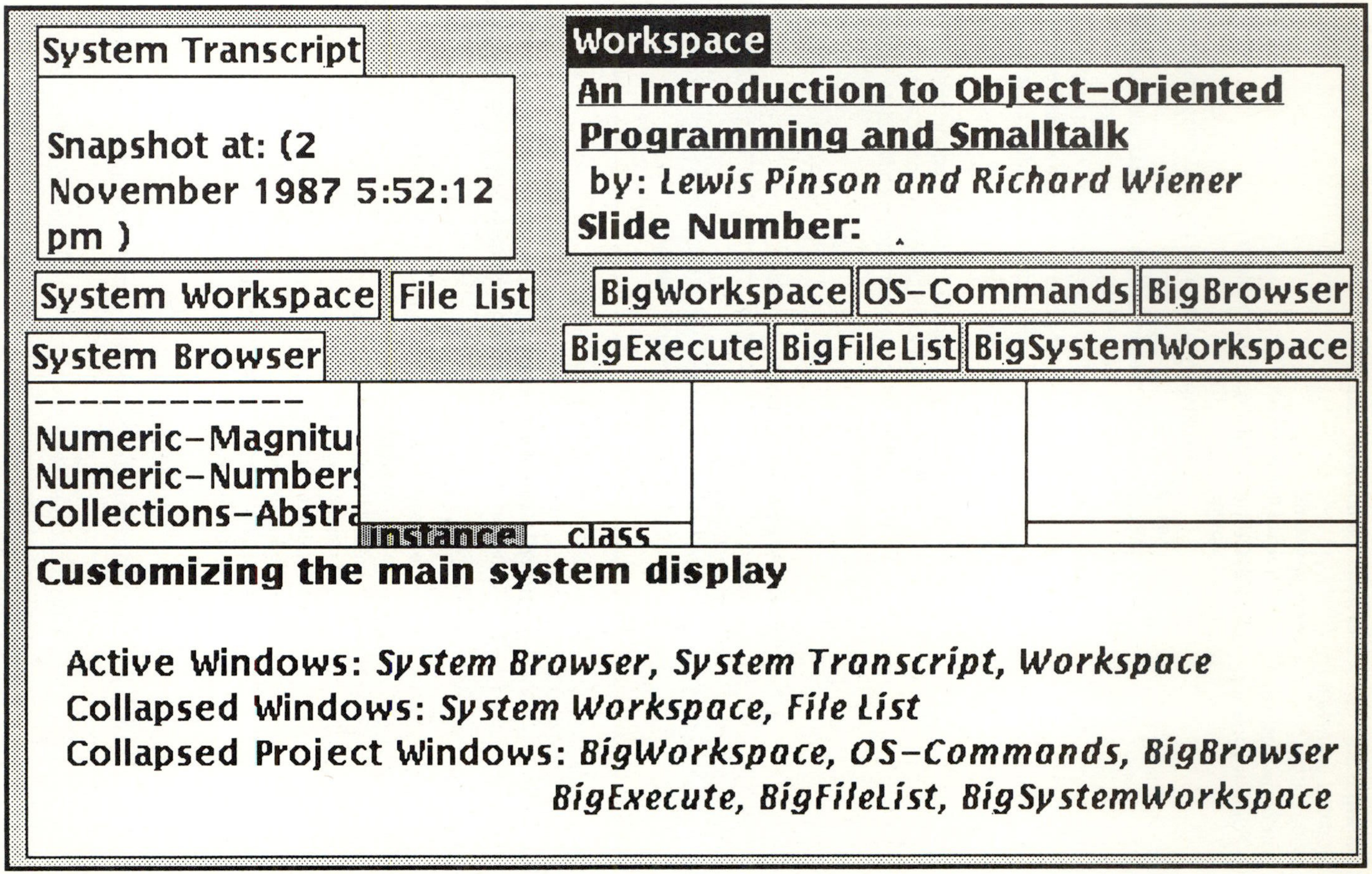

Some of the utility messages for customizing the Smalltalk display were shown in Section 3.1.2 as part of the protocol saved in the System Workspace window. **Display** is a global variable that is an instance of class **DisplayScreen.** It represents the current video display. There are many messages defined in class **DisplayScreen** and its superclasses for modifying the display. For example, the outer black border of the figures is generated by the message expression: **Display borderWidth: 4.** Options are available on background pattern and reverse or normal video. Background patterns are saved when the Smalltalk system is exited. Reverse video and border width as options are not saved.

Each system window on the Smalltalk screen has a blue- (right) button pop-up menu that allows the window to be reframed, moved, collapsed to a small rectangle containing only its title, or closed. Closed windows do not appear on the screen at all. In addition to the five system windows described already (System Browser, System Workspace, File List, Workspace, and System Transcript), there is also a system window called *Project*. Projects provide the capability of maintaining different screens that support several software development activities without continually redefining windows.

With all these options it is possible to customize several screens as projects that can be entered from the main screen display. Each project can be arranged to best support a particular kind of activity. Most of the figures shown in this chapter are projects with displays designed to show the features of a specific window. New projects can be defined by selecting the *project* option of the main system menu.

Figure 3.18 shows a main system screen with several windows. Three active windows, System Transcript, Workspace, and System Browser, are shown with eight collapsed windows. Six of the collapsed windows (*BigExecute, BigSystemWorkspace, BigFileList, BigBrowser, BigWorkspace,* and *OS-Commands*) are projects. They can be invoked by selecting and framing the collapsed window, then choosing the *enter* option from the Project window middle-button menu. Two of the collapsed windows (File List and System Workspace) are regular windows that can be made active by selecting and framing.

Figure 3.18 was generated with a special version of the Smalltalk image called *slideMaker.** New protocol for converting to the slideMaker image was included in the */smalltalk/fileIn* directory examined in Section 3.1.3 using the File List window. The slideMaker version essentially magnifies all the views and text for easier readability. This of course restricts the amount of information that can be displayed on the screen. For comparison, Figure 3.19 shows the normal screen font sizes, with a number of active windows and collapsed Project windows. The arrangement of any screen is preserved when a snapshot of the image is taken (by choosing the *save* option in the main system menu).

The goal of this discussion on the Smalltalk environment has been to intro-

*For information about slideMaker contact Tektronix, Technical Support Services, P.O. Box 1000, Beaverton, OR 97070.

Figure 3.19 Initial Smalltalk Screen

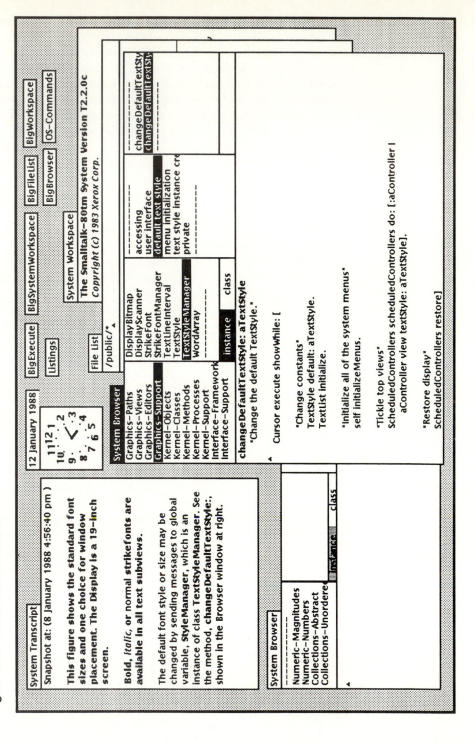

duce the reader to the major system windows that allow access to the underlying software and hardware. The System Browser, in particular, is the most useful tool in the Smalltalk system. It provides the capability for examining the image, modifying the image, and for entering and executing Smalltalk program code. Section 3.2 presents more discussion of Smalltalk syntax and gives additional examples of Smalltalk program code.

3.1.8   Inspectors and debuggers

Inspectors

An *inspector* is a window that allows inspection of the variables of an object. It is invoked by sending the message inspect to a receiver object. The user is then prompted to define a window on the screen. The window has a number of subviews that show details of the variables of the object being inspected.

The message inspect is part of the protocol of class **Object** and is therefore available to all subclasses. The message inspect can be sent to objects that are class names, variable names, private data, shared data, or global data. It can be sent to any object that is part of the Smalltalk system dictionary. As shown earlier in this chapter, it can also be sent to the single instance of **SystemDictionary,** which is **Smalltalk.** When sent to private data of a class, inspect is restricted to be a part of the instance methods of that class. This is consistent with the restriction that only instance methods have access to the private data of a class. The inspect message can be sent to global variables from any window in the Smalltalk system.

The inspect message is polymorphically redefined in classes **Dictionary** and **View** to provide special kinds of inspectors on the contents of a dictionary and a model-view-controller triad. (The MVC triad inspector is demonstrated in Chapter 9.) A dictionary inspector is illustrated below.

Figure 3.20 lists some of the global variables in the Smalltalk system. Any one of these globals can be inspected.

Inspector Example 3A—Inspecting Global Variables

Figure 3.21 shows an inspector opened on global variable **Disk.** It was implemented by executing the expression Disk inspect, shown in the Workspace window with menu option *do it*. As indicated in the inspector window, **Disk** is an instance of class **FileDirectory.**

The left subview of the inspector window in Figure 3.21 shows a list of the instance variables of **FileDirectory** and the pseudovariable self. Since self has been selected, the right subview shows what self is. Global variable **Disk** is a **FileDirectory** on '/public/'. Values for the instance variables of **Disk** can be examined by selecting the appropriate variable name in the left subview of the inspector window.

Figure 3.20
Globals in
Smalltalk

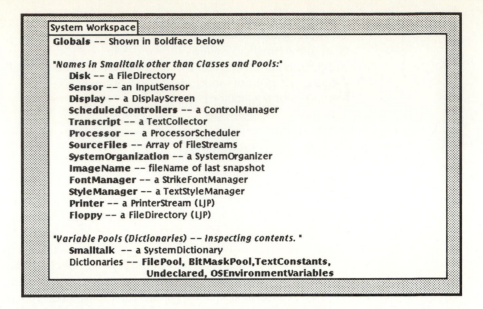

Figure 3.21
Inspecting Global
Variable Disk

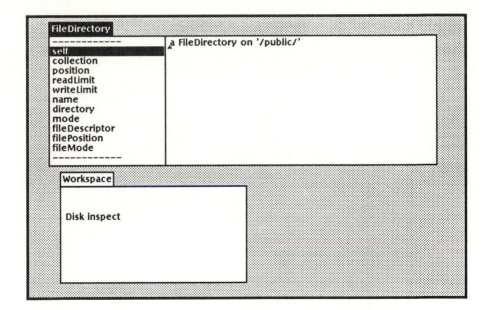

The right subview of the inspector window is a textview. It has the set of editing menu options (using the mouse middle button) that is standard for a textview. The left subview has a mouse middle-button menu option, *inspect,* that allows the user to open an inspector on any selected instance variable in the list.

Figure 3.22
Inspecting Class
Date

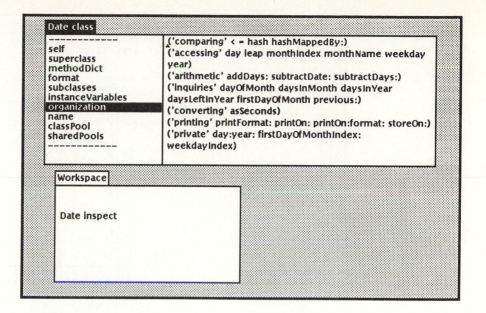

Inspector Example 3B—Inspecting a Class

A class (for example class **Date**) can be inspected as shown in Figure 3.22 by executing the expression in the Workspace window. A number of features for a class can be inspected, as indicated by the list in the left subview. In the figure the *organization* is being examined. The *organization* shows message categories and messages in each category for the class. The inspector for a class has the same menu options as described above for a global variable.

Inspector Example 3C—Inspecting a Dictionary

An example of the inspector for instances of **Dictionary** is given in Figure 3.23. Global variable **BitMaskPool** is an instance of **Dictionary.** Dictionaries are associations (key/value pairs). The dictionary inspector lists keys in the left subview with the corresponding value of a selected key in the right subview.

In the figure, key Bitoff in **BitMaskPool** is selected with its value shown in the right subview. The *inspect* menu option has also been selected for Bitoff. The middle inspector window shows Bitoff to be an instance of **Array.** Arrays have indexable instance variables. The third element in Bitoff has been selected, and its value of −5 is shown in the right subview of the inspector on Bitoff.

Figure 3.23
Inspecting a
Dictionary

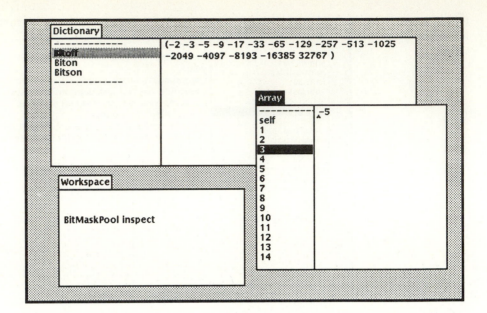

The dictionary inspector has additional options in its left subview menu. These additional options are (in addition to *inspect*) *references, add field,* and *remove.* The *add field* and *remove* options allow the user to add or delete keys in the dictionary. The *references* option opens a browser on all messages that reference the selected key. If no references are found, the message *Nobody* is displayed in the System Transcript window.

Debuggers

Debuggers are special windows that allow the user to examine source code that fails to execute. The Debugger window provides options on inspecting the details of any object, for modifying source code, and for continuing execution of the program.

The debugger can be invoked whenever a Smalltalk program encounters a condition that causes a halt. This occurs whenever run-time errors are encountered. It can also be intentionally invoked by inserting the message **self halt** into any part of the program code.

Debugger Example 3A

Figure 3.24 illustrates the second, intentional method for invoking the debugger. The method isLiteral in class **Array** has been modified by replacing ↑ **true** with the expression **self halt** into the block parameter for **detect: ifNone:**. Whenever

Figure 3.24
Program halt—
Invoking the
Debugger

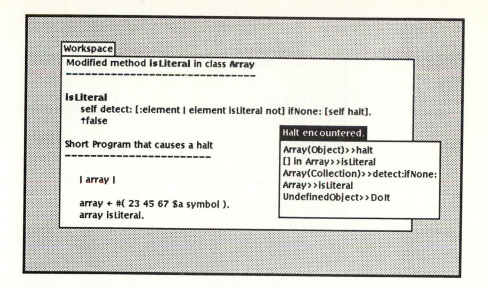

this message (isLiteral) is sent to a literal array, the halt will occur. Simple code for causing this condition is shown in the figure. The notifier window includes the two menu options *proceed* and *debug* as part of the middle-button menu. The user may elect to proceed, ignoring the error, or invoke the debugger.

Debugger Example 3B

Proceeding with Debugger Example 3A, Figure 3.25 shows the Debugger window opened by selecting the *debug* menu option in the notifier window. The top subview of the Debugger window contains a reverse-order abbreviated list of message sends prior to encountering the halt. The middle textview shows details of the message send that is selected in the top subview. The bottom of the window contains two inspectors on objects in the selected message. The left inspector is on the object receiving the selected message. The right inspector is on the temporary variables and parameters of the message. The title bar of the Debugger window shows the error that caused program interruption (halt encountered in this example).

Code in the textview can be edited to make changes. Menu options in the top subview include *restart, proceed,* and *step* for continuing execution. Also included are the options *implementors, senders,* and *messages* for examining details of any part of a message. One option, *full stack,* provides a complete list of the message sequences currently on the execution stack.

Figure 3.25
Program halt—The
Debugger Window

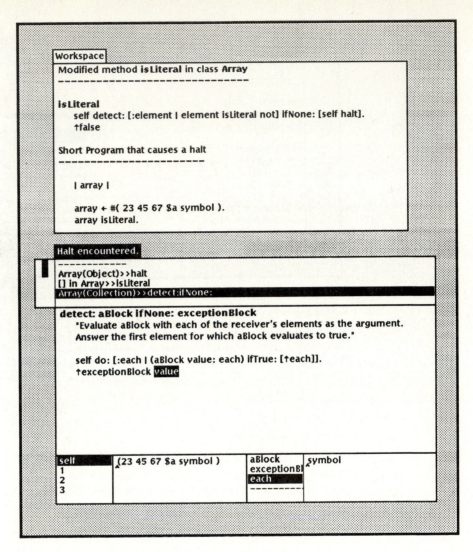

Workspace

Modified method **isLiteral** in class **Array**
----

isLiteral
    self detect: [:element | element isLiteral not] ifNone: [self halt].
    ↑false

Short Program that causes a halt

    | array |

    array ← #(23 45 67 $a symbol).
    array isLiteral.

Halt encountered.

Array(Object)>>halt
[] in Array>>isLiteral
Array(Collection)>>detect:ifNone:

detect: aBlock ifNone: exceptionBlock
    "Evaluate aBlock with each of the receiver's elements as the argument.
    Answer the first element for which aBlock evaluates to true."

    self do: [:each | (aBlock value: each) ifTrue: [↑each]].
    ↑exceptionBlock value

self	(23 45 67 $a symbol)	aBlock	symbol
1		exceptionBl	
2		each	
3		----------	

3.2   Writing Smalltalk Programs

This section gives an overview of selected features of Smalltalk syntax, reserved words, expressions, and selected methods. At the end of this chapter the reader should feel at home generating, saving, and executing a limited variety of Smalltalk "programs." The syntax discussion seeks to clarify concepts related to syntax. Appendix 1 gives a list of syntax rules without clarification.

3.2.1   Literals

There are five standard literals supported in Smalltalk. They are characters, numbers, strings, symbols, and arrays. Each of these is supported by a class of which it is an instance. Properties of each of the five standard literals are given below.

- *characters*—Instances of class **Character.** They are identified by a preceding $ sign (e.g., $A $c $9 $$). Characters have protocol defined in the hierarchy chain **Object—Magnitude—Character.**

- *numbers*—**Number** literals are supported in all the standard number subclasses. They can be instances of classes **Float, Fraction,** or **Integer** (and its subclasses). Numbers must begin with either a numeral (0..9) or a minus sign. Some implementations support numbers beginning with a decimal point. Because Smalltalk provides user access to the compiler, it is possible to add literal support for new classes of numbers. This is examined in Chapter 6 for imaginary and complex numbers. Protocol for numbers is supported by the hierarchy chain **Object—Magnitude—Appropriate Number Subclass.**

- *strings*—Strings are sequences of characters enclosed in single quotes (e.g., 'This is a string.' and 'What''s a string?'), with embedded single quotes doubled. Strings can be concatenated using the comma (,) message selector. Strings are instances of class **String.** Protocol for strings is supported by the hierarchy chain **Object—Collection—SequenceableCollection—ArrayedCollection—String.**

- *symbols*—Symbols are special identifiers with a preceding # sign. They are created as unique strings of characters and are instances of class **Symbol. Symbol** is a subclass of **String,** so symbols inherit all the protocol of strings.

- *arrays*—Arrays are collections of integer-indexable objects. Objects in an array need not be instances of the same class. **Array** literals are enclosed in parentheses and preceded by the # sign. Arrays can be nested. Symbols and arrays when included as elements in an array do not use the preceding # sign; e.g., #($a 10 aSymbol (4 $b 'string')). The protocol of arrays is given by the hierarchy chain **Object—Collection—Sequenceable-Collection—ArrayedCollection—Array.**

In addition to the instance creation methods for establishing objects as new instances of a class, instances can be created by assigning literal values to identifiers. For example, the assignment

aTempVariable ← 22.3

establishes aTempVariable as an instance of class **Float** with a value of 22.3, independently of its previous status or class membership.

3.2.2   Pseudovariables and reserved words

Smalltalk has five reserved words: nil, true, false, self, and super. Definition and examples of their use are given in this section. Three of the reserved words, nil, true, and false, are unique instances (objects) of classes within the Smalltalk image. They always have the same meaning. The other two, self and super, are objects that have meaning dependent on the context within which they are used. All five of these words are global in nature; they can be referenced by any method at any level.

self

The reserved word **self** is used as a pseudovariable in methods and always refers to the receiver of the message that the method represents. As an object, **self** is also sent messages. The pseudovariable **self** always refers to the original object of a message, even when used in a superclass method. The protocol for the messages is found in the class of the receiver that **self** represents. Consider the following example message sent to an instance of class **Float.** It answers the result of converting 60.0 degrees to radians.

60.0 degreesToRadians

Details of the method for **degreesToRadians** are

degreesToRadians
        ↑ **self** * RadiansPerDegree

In this example, **self** refers to the receiver object, **60.0**. It returns the product of **60.0** and the class variable RadiansPerDegree. The binary message * sent to **self** is found in the protocol for class **Float,** the class of the object to which **self** refers (**60.0**).

super

The reserved word **super** is used as a pseudovariable in methods and, like **self**, always refers to the receiver of the message that the method represents. However, it is different from **self** in that the protocol for messages sent to **super** is found by looking first in the immediate superclass of the receiver that **super** represents. Messages to **super** are used when both the superclass and the class of the receiver have methods with the same message selector, and the desired action is represented by the superclass method. Sending the message to **super** instead of to **self** causes the system to skip the class protocol of the receiver and start looking for the message in the superclass chain of the receiver.

Consider the following example message sent to an instance of class **File-Stream.** It makes a copy of the object **aFileStream** with a different file descriptor. This requires that the file first be closed.

aFileStream copy

Details of the invoked messages are given below.

FileStream methodsFor: 'copying'
copy

"Answer a copy of the file with a different file descriptor."
self close.
↑ super copy

Object methodsFor: 'copying'
copy

"Answer another instance just like the receiver."
↑ self shallowCopy

shallowCopy

"Answer a copy of the receiver that shares the receiver's instance variables."
"Details can be viewed using the System Browser."

The method copy in **FileStream** sends the superclass message copy from **FileStream**'s superclass to the object aFileStream. In the class hierarchy for **FileStream (Object—Stream—PositionableStream—WriteStream—ReadWrite-Stream—ExternalStream—FileStream),** the first occurrence of copy is sought beginning from **ExternalStream** and working up the hierarchy. The first occurrence is in class **Object.** In class **Object,** copy sends the message shallowCopy to self. In this case, self still refers to aFileStream. The system starts looking for shallowCopy in the protocol for **FileStream.** The first occurrence up the hierarchy tree from **FileStream** is found in class **Object.**

Other examples of super appear in various parts of the book.

nil

The reserved word nil is a constant-valued pseudovariable that is the only instance of class **UndefinedObject.** It is used to represent the value of objects that have not been initialized and for results that are meaningless. Thus even uninitialized objects have an object as their value. The protocol for nil is given in the class description for **UndefinedObject.** It has 2 class methods in one category and 10 instance methods in five categories. Some of the methods block attempts to create new instances of **UndefinedObject** or to copy nil. Useful methods include testing and printing.

true

The reserved word true is the only instance of class **True.** It represents the Boolean value for logical truth. Protocol for true is defined in its class, **True,** and its superclass, **Boolean.**

false

The reserved word false is the only instance of class **False.** It represents the Boolean value for logical nontruth. Protocol for false is defined in its class, **False,** and its superclass, **Boolean.**

3.2.3   Returning values from methods

The special symbol ↑ (up arrow) is used to denote values to be returned from a method. This symbol has been used in several of the previous examples. In this section, the return symbol is examined in more detail to illustrate its properties.

Return Example 3A

In the simplest case, a single return symbol is used to return the object that results from evaluating an expression. In the method respondsTo: aSymbol (shown below) from class **Object,** the expression self class canUnderstand: aSymbol is evaluated to produce a **Boolean** object. The **Boolean** object (either true or false) is returned.

Object methodsFor: 'class membership'
   respondsTo: aSymbol
      "Answer a Boolean as to whether the method dictionary of the receiver's class
      contains aSymbol as a message selector."
      ↑ self class canUnderstand: aSymbol

Return Example 3B

A second kind of return statement is illustrated by a two-way Boolean test, as shown in the following example method from class **Object.** The returned result is either true or the result of the expression self class inheritsFrom: aClass.

Object methodsFor: 'class membership'
   isKindOf: aClass
      "Answer a Boolean as to whether the class aClass is a superclass or class of the
      receiver."
      self class == aClass
               ifTrue: [↑ true]
               ifFalse:[↑ self class inheritsFrom: aClass]

A similar example is given by the following method from class **Integer.** It returns either a **0** or a **1**. Note the difference in the return statements for the two examples. Either implementation style can be used for either method.

Integer methodsFor: 'bit manipulation'
   bitAt: i
      "Answer the bit at the ith position."
      ↑ (self bitAnd: (1 bitShift: i - 1)) = 0
               ifTrue: [0]
               ifFalse:[1]

Return Example 3C

A more complicated return example is given by the following **Integer** method for computing factorial. The method either returns a value of 1, returns the result of a recursive call to itself, or returns nothing. If the first test, **self** > **0**, is true, then all the other statements are skipped because of the return in that expression block. The first valid return statement is the only one in effect for any method.

Integer methodsFor: 'factorization and divisibility'
> **factorial**
>> "Answer the factorial of the receiver. Signal an error if the receiver is less than zero."
>> self > 0
>>> ifTrue: [↑ self ∗ (self - 1) factorial].
>> self = 0
>>> ifTrue: [↑ 1].
>> self error: 'factorial invalid for: ', self printString

3.2.4   Block expressions—deferred execution

This section defines the class **BlockContext** and shows how it represents deferred execution. Some of the messages to which blocks respond include automatic evaluation of the block. This section also points out the use of blocks by other classes such as **True** and **False** that automatically execute the block.

The hierarchy for class **BlockContext** is **Object— InstructionStream—ContextPart—BlockContext.** It has three instance variables: nargs, startpc, and home and no class variables. It has no class methods but has 27 instance methods in nine categories. In addition, **BlockContext** has inherited protocol from its three superclasses.

The three instance variables in **BlockContext** have the following functions. Instance variable nargs is an instance of **Integer** representing the number of block arguments. Instance variable startpc is an instance of **Integer** that points to the beginning of a block of code. It is essentially an initial program counter for the block. And instance variable home is an instance of **MethodContext** whose **CompiledMethod** contains the block represented by an instance of **BlockContext.**

Expressions in blocks, delimited by square brackets, represent code for deferred execution. The code is executed only when the appropriate value (there are several value messages dependent on the number of block arguments) message is sent to the block. Blocks can be assigned to variable names, as in the following example.

Block Example 3A—Deferred Execution Using Blocks

| aBlock |
aBlock ← [Transcript show: 'This is deferred execution code.'].
aBlock value "Execute the block with no arguments, aBlock."

The string, 'This is deferred execution code' is displayed in the Transcript window only when the second expression, aBlock value, is executed. Blocks can be defined anywhere within a code segment and executed anywhere after the definition within the code segment.

Block Example 3B—Messages That Include Automatic Execution of Blocks

The receiver and/or parameters of the message can be blocks.

I. An instance of **BlockContext** is the receiver and a parameter.

[a boolean block] whileTrue: [a block to execute]

This is a message sent to an instance of **BlockContext** with a single parameter that is also an instance of **BlockContext.** Details of the meaning of this message sequence are given in the method description for whileTrue:, listed below. It evaluates [a boolean block] one time. If it evaluates to false nothing else happens. If it evaluates to true, then [a block to execute] is evaluated. This cycle is repeated until [a boolean block] evaluates to false.

BlockContext methodsFor: 'controlling'
   whileTrue: aBlock
          "Evaluate the argument aBlock as long as the value of the receiver is true. Ordinarily
               compiled in-line for increased efficiency."
     ↑ self value
         ifTrue:
               [aBlock value.
               self whileTrue: aBlock]

II. An instance of **BlockContext** is a parameter in a message to a receiver of another class. The method has two parameters, both of which are blocks. The parameter **aBlock** is a block with one parameter, and parameter **exceptionBlock** has no parameters.

Collection methodsFor: 'enumerating'
   detect: aBlock **ifNone:** exceptionBlock
          "Evaluate aBlock with each element of the receiver as the argument. Answer the first
          element for which aBlock evaluates to true. Evaluate exceptionBlock if none
          of the receiver elements produces a true result for aBlock."
          self do: [:each | (aBlock value: each) ifTrue: [↑ each]].
           ↑ exceptionBlock value

3.2.5   Variables

There are six kinds of variables in the Smalltalk system. Many of these have been discussed or illustrated already in previous examples. In this section they are formally listed and defined. The six kinds of variables are *instance, class, global, pool, temporary,* and *pseudo.* Instance variables are private to a class description. Class, pool, and global variables are shared data objects. Temporary variables are private to a method or program segment. Pseudovariables cannot be redefined (they are unique). The two kinds of pseudovariables are reserved words and parameters within a message selector.

- *instance variables*—Private data defined in the class description protocol of a given class. They can be accessed only by instance methods of the defining class and its subclasses.

- *class variables*—Shared data defined within the class protocol description (for the metaclass) of a given class. They can be accessed only by the class and instance methods of the defining class and its subclasses.

- *global variables*—Global variables are accessible to any part of the Smalltalk system. The global variable **Smalltalk** is an instance of class **System-Dictionary.** It is a dictionary of all global variables, including itself. Global variables can be added or deleted from **Smalltalk.** Every class name is a global variable. In addition to the class names there are several other global variables, which are shown in Figure 3.20. Some are pool dictionaries and some are not. Inspectors can be opened on any global variable by executing the expression **GlobalVarName inspect.**

- *pool variables*—Shared data, defined as global variables, representing instances of a particular class that are accessible by specified classes as pool dictionaries. The designation as a pool dictionary is only significant semantically. As a global variable, a pool dictionary is accessible by the entire Smalltalk system. For example, the pool dictionary **TextConstants** is specified for access by 13 specific classes. However, the expression **Text-Constants at: #Underlined** can be executed from any Smalltalk text subview. The result is 4.

- *temporary variables*—Data that is private to either a method or to a Smalltalk program segment. The scope of the temporary variable is limited to the code segment in which it is defined, with the vertical bar delimiters. Temporary variables belong to class **UndefinedObject** until they are assigned values. They then take on the class of the values assigned to them. A temporary variable may be an instance of many different classes within the same program segment. For example, temp below is first an integer and then a string.

```
| temp |
temp ← 25.
temp ← 'Temp is now a string.'
```

- *pseudovariables*—The five reserved words in Smalltalk (**self, super, nil, true,** and **false**) were described earlier as pseudovariables whose values cannot be reassigned. The parameter objects within a method description behave as pseudovariables, also. Within the method their values cannot be reassigned.

This chapter has presented information about the Smalltalk system windows and how they support investigating the capability of Smalltalk. Examples clarified parts of the Smalltalk language. In Chapter 4, more detail is presented on exactly how new protocol is added to the Smalltalk image. Specific examples are presented that show how to maintain a consistent Smalltalk image for members of a software development team.

Exercises

3.1 Using the System Browser window, examine the protocol for class **System-Dictionary.** Investigate information about the system by sending selected messages to the global variable **Smalltalk.** These message expressions can be typed in any system text window, selected, and executed with *print it.*

3.2 Using protocol in class **SystemDictionary,** open a browser on all implementors of the message printOn:.

3.3 Open an inspector window on **Smalltalk** and verify the number of classes in the system. In addition list all other keys in **Smalltalk,** identify their classes, and give their functions. What kind of inspector is opened on **Smalltalk?**

3.4 Practice using the File List window by copying a method from some class in the System Browser into the textview of the File List window and saving it under a selected file name. Verify that the file contains the correct information.

3.5 Using the browser, develop a list of messages to which the global variable **Transcript** responds. Messages to **Transcript** are used for displaying program results in the System Transcript window. **Transcript** is an instance of **TextCollector.**

3.6 Using the code for outputToPrinter in Figure 3.16 as a basis, develop an equivalent method for the system upon which you have access to Smalltalk. This is a new method to be added to class **String.**

3.7 Implement a version of printFile: in Listing 3.2 for the system upon which you have access to Smalltalk. Make it a **String** method.

3.8 Add hardcopy capability to the browser subviews of your system. Use the examples given in this chapter as a guide.

3.9 Use the browser to explore messages for the global variable **Display.** Experiment with the use of these messages for controlling the display "color," for bordering, and other display operations. **Display** is an instance of **DisplayScreen.**

3.10 Design three project screens that can be accessed from the main display screen of your Smalltalk system. Give them appropriate names and save them as collapsed windows on the main display. One project should be designed to provide maximum display size for browsing. A second project should be designed for interacting with file lists. The third project should contain an active inspector on **Smalltalk.**

3.11 Design a project that includes expressions representing all the demonstrations or examples in a single window. The user should be able to open this project, select an expression, and evaluate any example or demonstration in the system. Since many examples use the Transcript Window to display results, this project should include that window.

3.12 Using protocol in class **SystemDictionary,** find how many times the return message (↑) is used in your Smalltalk system. Select any 10 of these occurrences and explain in words what is being returned.

3.13 Explain the methods for evaluating an instance of **BlockContext.** Depending on your implementation of Smalltalk, there may be five or fewer methods that are used to evaluate blocks with zero or more parameters. Develop an example that uses each method.

3.14 Using protocol in **SystemDictionary,** find how many occurrences of the pseudovariables **self** and **super** are in your Smalltalk system. Find any four occurrences of **super** and explain in words what the method that uses it does.

3.15 Practice using the *browser* menu option for filing out selected portions of Smalltalk code (methods, categories of methods, classes, categories of classes). Test the *file in* option in the File List window by first deleting the filed-out code from the Smalltalk image and then filing it back in. Keep notes on any difficulties encountered.

4

Adding New Classes to Smalltalk and Maintaining the Smalltalk Image

This chapter describes the techniques for adding new subclasses to Smalltalk and gives some guidelines and hints for maintaining the Smalltalk system. In particular it gives methods for keeping a clean image and for incorporating new classes from members of a software team. It discusses the rationale for where to add a new subclass in the image hierarchy and presents through example the concepts of how to make the added protocol more consistent with the object-oriented paradigm. A consistent example with subclasses is used throughout the chapter to illustrate the reasoning behind choices, the use of inheritance, and the use of polymorphism. The new classes added to the image are those that support the binary tree and expression tree objects discussed in Chapter 1. Additional discussion of the classes, their private data, and methods is given in this chapter. Complete protocol listings for the new classes are given.

4.1 Adding New Subclasses—Protocol Description

One of the first steps in an object-oriented solution to a problem is definition of the objects. Once the objects are defined, the next step is to develop a complete description of each object that is part of the solution. This description includes the characteristics of the objects and the actions to which each object must respond. The more important characteristics of an object can be defined in terms of other objects. These become the private or shared data for this kind of object. The actions become method details with appropriate message selectors to indicate the expected response.

The Smalltalk image offers a rich variety of existing classes to represent objects. Some problem solutions can be achieved using objects that fit within these existing classes. Many problem solutions will require the addition of new classes to represent objects that are not found within the existing class structure. These are the more interesting problems since the software developer has more latitude in defining the characteristics of the new objects.

Given that one or more new classes is to be added to the Smalltalk image for a particular problem solution, there are several questions and concerns that arise. First, where are the new classes to be attached to the existing hierarchy? This question is best answered by example and development of logical reasoning for where to attach new classes. Familiarity with what is already in the image is of great help also. Several new classes are added to the Smalltalk image throughout this book. In each case, beginning with this chapter, the reasoning for where to add the classes is presented.

A second concern that eventually arises after many new classes have been added to the Smalltalk image is how to manage the increasing complexity. This had to be one of the major concerns of the developers of Smalltalk. Why is the image so large, and are all those classes really necessary? Obviously, as the user adds new classes the questions become even more important.

Smalltalk is large, even with a pared down set of "essential" classes. With computers that have powerful processors, a large amount of cheap memory, high-capacity hard disks, and virtual memory support, Smalltalk can grow to be very large. The real concern is with development of an image (even a large one) that is logical, well-structured, and consistent. The task is similar to the development of a filing system when the objects to be filed are received one at a time in random order. No advance knowledge is provided for the kinds of objects that are likely to be added. New classes added to the Smalltalk image may fit best at one point in the hierarchy when they are first added. They may need to be moved as other related classes are added. The Smalltalk image is a continually evolving entity.

Fortunately, Smalltalk has classes and methods that make changes in its structure more manageable. Redefinition of any part of a class (its superclass, private data, shared data, or methods) automatically invokes this change management support when the new class description is "accepted." Examples and additional methods for maintaining the Smalltalk image are given in Section 4.2.

The following subsections discuss techniques and rationale for adding new classes to the Smalltalk image. The new classes are relatively simple, yet varied enough to illustrate many of the concerns and tradeoffs. The new classes provide support for binary tree operations and the generation and evaluation of algebraic expression trees.

4.1.1   Where in the hierarchy do I add a new class?

The first step in finding a place to attach new classes to the class hierarchy is definition of the objects in a solution and definition of their classes. Any object that is part of the solution may fit within an existing class or may require definition of a new class. After this is completed, the logic is presented for choosing where in the existing image hierarchy to add the new classes. The choice is not unique, so logical arguments are presented with examples to give experience with making an initial choice. This section also examines the process of choosing a category for a new class and the concepts of grouping classes in categories.

Many of the objects related to binary trees and expression trees were discussed in Chapter 1. The objects supporting binary tree operations include the following.

- *Binary Tree*—an object representing the binary tree. No existing class in the Smalltalk image provides the necessary properties or protocol for binary trees. A new class is to be defined to represent binary trees.

- *Tree Nodes*—objects that are the nodes of a binary tree. These nodes must contain private data for defining left and right offspring, as well as a key value. Binary trees have an order specified by the key values in the nodes. Class **Node** in the Smalltalk image appears at first glance to be a potential class for these objects. However, class **Node** has only one pointer to another node. Binary tree nodes require two. It is possible to add a subclass of **Node** that adds a second node pointer; however, the terminology used for the node pointer in **Node** is misleading. The pointer **next** is not consistent with a node that has **left** and **right** pointers. For this reason, a new class is defined to represent the nodes of a binary tree.

- *Expression Trees*—These objects are a special case of the binary tree objects. Their major differences are that the nodes contain only operators or operands and that rules for insertion are different. A new class is defined to represent expression trees. It is best defined as a subclass of the binary tree class.

- *Operator Nodes*—These are required nodes for supporting expression trees. Each node contains a valid operator (for algebraic operations) and an information field that determines relative precedence (required as part of the new insertion rules). These objects are special cases of the tree node objects. A new class is defined as a subclass of the tree node objects.

- *Operand Nodes*—These are required to support expression trees. Each operand node contains an identifier that is an operand in an algebraic expression. These objects are also special cases of tree node objects. A new class is defined and added as a subclass of the tree node objects.

- *Queue of Operands*—The algorithm that generates an expression tree puts operands on a queue before adding them to the tree. Queues are represented by an existing class, **OrderedCollection,** in the Smalltalk image. No new class is required.

- *Operators*—Operators are single characters that represent specific arithmetic operations. Class **Character** already exists in the Smalltalk image.

- *ValidOperators*—This object is a set of characters defining the characters that are valid operators. Class **Set** in the existing image represents this object.

- *Other Kinds of Nodes*—A binary tree can contain nodes with keys that are any kind of object. A subclass of the tree node class is defined for each new key object. This is required since creation of a binary tree depends on relative magnitudes of the keys. Comparison rules may differ for various keys. In addition, details of displaying the node contents may differ for various keys.

- *Information in a Node*—In addition to its key value, nodes often store a variety of other information. These information objects may be of any class, including those in the Smalltalk image.

- *Algebraic Expression Objects*—Typically these objects are instances of **String.** However, strings have added requirements to qualify as expressions. One method for adding these objects is to modify existing **String** protocol to ensure compliance with the new restrictions. An alternative approach is to add a new subclass to **String** to represent the expression objects.

- *Other Minor Objects*—Other objects of less significance are required to support the binary tree and expression tree objects. In most cases these are best included as private data of the major objects.

Based on the arguments and discussion above, several new classes are added to the Smalltalk image to support binary trees and expression trees. The hierarchy of these related classes is shown in Figure 4.1. The figure also identifies private data (instance variables) for each class by enclosing them in parentheses. These data objects are discussed in more detail in Section 4.1.2.

Figure 4.1
Hierarchy of the
Tree and
TreeNode Classes

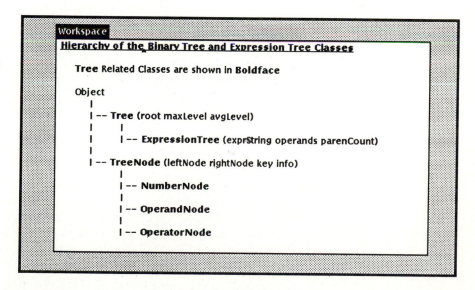

4.1.2   Defining private data and shared data

From the objects defined in Section 4.1.1, descriptions are developed that identify unique or common characteristics of instances of the new classes to represent these objects. These descriptions are used to define private, shared, or pool data for each class.

Characteristics of the defined objects for **Tree, TreeNode, ExpressionTree, NumberNode, OperatorNode,** and **OperandNode** are given below.

- *The root of a binary tree*—Every binary tree has a root node that is the topmost node in the tree. Access to the tree always begins at the root node. This object is an instance of **TreeNode** or one of its subclasses. It is different for each instance of **Tree** or its subclasses and is defined as instance variable **root** in class **Tree.**

- *The maximum level in a binary tree*—The root node is at level one. Its two offspring are at level two, and so on. It is often of interest to know the maximum level of any node in a tree. This value can change as nodes are inserted or deleted. It is a simple integer and is defined as an instance variable, **maxLevel**, in class **Tree.**

- *The average level in a binary tree*—A measure of the efficiency of a binary tree structure in terms of retrieving information in a node is given by the average level of all its nodes. This is an instance of **Float** and is defined as an instance variable, **avgLevel**, of **Tree.**

- *The key of a node*—Nodes in a binary tree are ordered by their key values. Every node in a binary tree has a **key** which is defined as an instance variable of **TreeNode.** Responsibility for assigning key values and displaying key values or other data is assigned to the subclasses of **TreeNode.**

- *The offspring of a binary tree node*—A node in a binary tree has two offspring that are other tree nodes or **nil**. Each instance of **TreeNode** or its subclasses must maintain a separate reference to its own offspring. Two instance variables, **leftNode** and **rightNode**, are defined for class **TreeNode** to represent these objects.

- *The information content of a tree node*—A node may contain information in addition to its key. An instance variable, **info**, is defined for class **TreeNode** to represent this object. Responsibility for installing or displaying the value for **info** is given to the subclasses of **TreeNode.**

- *The expression represented by an expression tree*—A binary expression tree is built from an algebraic expression that contains no blanks or other separators. Further, the expression must be valid in terms of rules for algebra. An instance variable, **exprString**, is a string of characters representing the valid expression. It is an instance variable in class **ExpressionTree.** New methods are added to ensure it is a valid expression.

- *The operands in an expression*—The rules for building an expression tree require that all operands first be pushed onto the end of a queue. After a tree of operators has been constructed, the operands are removed from the queue and added as leaf nodes to the tree. Intermediate storage of the operands in a queue is accomplished with an instance variable, operands, in class **ExpressionTree.** It is an instance of **OrderedCollection** (an existing Smalltalk class for supporting queues).

- *The precedence flag for building operator trees*—The rules for building a tree of operators from an expression require that relative precedence be measured for each operator. In Smalltalk, this requires only that a comparison be made of the relative number of nested parentheses for each operator. The instance variable parenCount in class **ExpressionTree** has a value that is the number of nested left parentheses at any given stage in the tree building. Its current value is installed as the info field in each **OperatorNode** when the operator node is added to the expression tree.

- *Valid operators in an operator node*—The characters that represent valid arithmetic operators are a small set of the 256 characters. A set that contains only the valid operator characters is useful for testing an 'operator' prior to inserting it in an operator node. The class variable ValidOperators is defined in class **OperatorNode.** It is a class variable because its contents are identical for all instances of **OperatorNode.** It is shared by all instances.

- *Values of nonnumber operands*—The identifier operands must be assigned numerical values prior to evaluation of the algebraic expression. A class variable, OperandValues, is defined in class **ExpressionTree.** It is an instance of **Dictionary.** Key/value pairs that are the identifier string and its numerical value are stored in the dictionary. Messages for evaluation prompt the user to input a value for each unique identifier in the dictionary.

4.1.3   Initialization and creation of instances

Class variables need to be initialized before any instances are created for the class. This is typically accomplished by a class method called initialize. It is generally placed in a message category called *class initialization*. Messages in this category for all classes provide information necessary to the successful use of the class. Once a class has been initialized, it need not be done again during the current Smalltalk session. If the image is saved on exiting Smalltalk, the class should not require initialization again when re-entering Smalltalk.

Messages that are used to create instances of a class are grouped in class method category *instance creation*. If no methods exist for a class, then instances are created using instance creation protocol of its superclasses. Recall that the superclass structure of metaclasses (representing class methods) ends with the class **Behavior.** Instance creation methods new and new: are defined in **Behavior** and inherited by all metaclasses.

Creation of a new instance of any class can be augmented to include the initialization of its private data (instance variables). The usual technique is to include one or more instance initialization messages as part of the instance creation message. These must be instance messages sent to the new object after it is created. Class methods do not have access to instance variables. For example, in class **Tree** the creation message **new** has the details given below. It both establishes a new instance of **Tree** and initializes instance variables.

Tree methodsFor: 'instance creation'
new
    "Answer a new instance with initialized instance variables"
    ↑ super new root: nil; maxLevel: 0; avgLevel: 0.0

The method first creates an instance of **Tree** with the message **super new**. The use of the pseudovariable **super** causes the message **new** to be sought in the superclass of **Tree** and not in **Tree** itself. Otherwise there would be an infinity of recursive calls to **new**. The message **new** is found in the superclass of **Tree** called **Behavior.** It returns an object that is a new instance of class **Tree.** This new **Tree** object is then sent the three instance messages **root:**, **maxLevel:**, and **avgLevel:** to establish values for the three instance variables. Instance variables can be accessed only by the instance methods of a class and its subclasses.

Instance methods of a class cannot access the private data of its subclasses. For example, instance methods in class **Tree** cannot access the instance variables **exprString, operands,** and **parenCount** in its subclass **ExpressionTree.** This makes sense after one thinks about it for a while. For example, a class has no knowledge about the existence or number of subclasses that may be defined under it.

4.1.4   Class methods and instance methods

The choice of categories for methods seems to be almost unlimited; however, maintaining consistency within the categories in the Smalltalk image has advantages. When looking for a polymorphic redefinition of a method in a subclass, the first and most likely place to look is in the same category in the subclass. If this rule is not fo!lowed, one must search all methods in the subclass. For classes like **View** that have over a hundred methods, the advantage of category consistency becomes more important.

Class methods are used for three main purposes: (1) initialization of the class, (2) instance creation, and (3) answering general inquiries. General inquiries include the return of useful information without the creation by the user of a new instance of the class. Class **Time** has several class messages under the category of *general inquiries*. For example, finding the current time does not require the user to create a new instance of **Time.** It is obtained by sending the class message **now** to the class name object, **Time.**

Instance methods provide access to the private data of an instance of the class plus many other operations specific to an instance of the class. There are numerous categories of instance messages in the Smalltalk system. A useful exercise is to outline the classes and their categories of messages. This provides insight into what is there. This limited protocol summary is used to describe many of the existing Smalltalk classes throughout this book. A summary is given of the binary tree classes in the next section.

4.1.5   Protocol summary of the binary tree classes

Protocol Summary for Class **Tree**

Definition—The hierarchy for class **Tree** is **Object—Tree.** Class **Tree** has three instance variables, root, maxLevel, and avgLevel. It has no class variables or pool dictionaries. It has 1 class method (excluding examples) in one category and 20 instance methods in six categories.

Private data—Class **Tree** has three instance variables.

root—an instance of **TreeNode** or its subclasses that is the root node in the tree.

maxLevel—an instance of **Integer** that is the level of the deepest node in the tree (root has level = 1).

avgLevel—an instance of **Number** that is the average level of all nodes in the tree.

Instance methods—Class **Tree** has 20 instance methods in six categories. A summary of the categories and methods follows.

accessing—four methods (**averagePathLength, maxPathLength, root, search:**) that access private data of the tree or search for a node with a specified key value. All four are new protocol.

deleting—six methods (**delete:, deleteLeft:, deleteRight:, deleteRoot, predecessorOf:, removeTree**) that are part of the process of deleting a node or all nodes from the tree. All six are new protocol.

inserting—one method (**insert:**) for inserting a node with a specified key into the tree. This method is new protocol.

testing—two methods (**empty, isPresent:**) for testing if a tree is empty and if it contains a specified key. Both are new protocol.

printing and display—four methods (**inorderDisplay, inorderPrint, postorderDisplay, postorderPrint**) that provide the capability to display on the screen or print on the printer all node contents. The order may be inorder or postorder. All four methods are new protocol.

private—three methods (**avgLevel:, maxLevel:, root:**) that set values for the private data of instances of class **Tree.** All three are new protocol.

Class methods—Class **Tree** has one class method in one category, which are summarized below.

instance creation—one method (**new**) that is used to create instances of the binary tree classes. It is inherited from **Behavior** and polymorphically redefined.

Protocol Summary for Class **TreeNode**

Definition—The hierarchy for class **Tree** is **Object—TreeNode.** Class **TreeNode** has four instance variables, leftNode, rightNode, key, and info. It has no class variables or pool dictionaries. It has 2 class methods in one category and 17 instance methods in five categories.

Private data—Class **TreeNode** has four instance variables.

   leftNode—an instance of **TreeNode** or its subclasses. It is the left offspring of the current node. This instance variable is initialized to nil.

   rightNode—an instance of **TreeNode** or its subclasses. It is the right off-spring of the current node. This instance variable is initialized to nil.

   key—an **Object** that has a distinct order (integers, characters, strings, and so forth). It is the key value in a node that determines its location in a binary tree.

   info—an **Object** that is additional information in a node. Subclasses have responsibility for defining values of this instance variable.

Instance methods—Class **TreeNode** has 17 instance methods in five categories. A summary is given below of the categories and methods.

   accessing—six methods (**info, key, left, right, predecessor, successor**) for accessing private data of a node and for finding its inorder predecessor or inorder successor. All six are new protocol.

   testing—three methods (**isEmpty, isLeaf, isParentOf:**) for testing the status of a node. All three are new protocol.

   enumerating—two methods (**inorderDo:, postorderDo:**) that support the inorder and postorder traversal of a binary tree. Both are new protocol.

   printing—two methods (**display, toPrinter**) that are the responsibility of the subclasses of **TreeNode.** They define how a node displays and prints its key value and information.

   private—four methods (**left:, right:, key:, info:**) for establishing the values of instance variables. Method **key:** is the responsibility of the subclasses of **TreeNode.** All four are new protocol.

Class methods—Class **TreeNode** has two class methods in one category as summarized below.

   instance creation—two methods (**new:, new: withInfo:**) that are used to create instances of the tree node classes. Method **new:** is inherited from **Behavior** and redefined. It creates an instance with a specified key value. The other method is new protocol and creates an instance with specified key value and information.

Protocol Summary for Class **NumberNode**

Instances of this class inherit protocol from the superclass **TreeNode.** In addition, the methods in **TreeNode** that are implemented as subclassResponsibility are given details in this class.

Definition—The hierarchy for class **NumberNode** is **Object—TreeNode—NumberNode.** Class **NumberNode** has no instance variables, class variables, or pool dictionaries. It has no class methods. It has three instance methods in two categories.

Instance methods—Class **NumberNode** has three instance methods in two categories. A summary is given below of the categories and methods.

> *printing and display*—two methods (**display, toPrinter**) that are implemented for nodes with number keys. These are inherited from **TreeNode** and defined. In **TreeNode,** they are implemented as subclassResponsibility.

> *private*—one method (**key:**) that sets the key value to a number. This method is inherited and redefined.

Class methods—Class **NumberNode** has no class methods.

Protocol Summary for Class **ExpressionTree**

This class represents a kind of binary tree that is used to evaluate algebraic expressions. In addition to protocol inherited from its superclass **Tree,** additional new protocol is necessary.

Definition—The hierarchy for class **ExpressionTree** is **Object—Tree—ExpressionTree.** Class **ExpressionTree** has three instance variables, exprString, operands, and parenCount. It has one class variable, OperandValues. It has no pool dictionaries. It has 2 class methods (excluding examples) in two categories and 14 instance methods in five categories.

Private data—Class **ExpressionTree** has three instance variables.

> **exprString**—an instance of **String** that has been processed to remove all separator characters and checked for matching parentheses.

> **operands**—an instance of **OrderedCollection** that is a queue of operands.

> **parenCount**—an instance of **Integer** that is a global count of the number of left parentheses encountered minus the number of right parentheses encountered in an expression string.

Shared data—Class **ExpressionTree** has one class variable.

> **OperandValues**—an instance of **Dictionary** that stores operand strings and their values. An entry is made for each unique operand string. This shared data is used as a lookup table.

Instance methods—Class **ExpressionTree** has 14 instance methods in five categories. A summary is given below of the categories and methods.

accessing—three methods (**decParenCount, exprString, incParenCount**) for accessing private data of expression trees. All three are new protocol.

deleting—one method (**delete:**) that is inherited from **Tree** and redefined to block its use. Deletion from expression trees is not allowed.

inserting—five methods (**insert:, insertOperator: inTree:, precedenceOf-TreeNodeIsGreater:, addToQueue:, addOperandsToTree**) for inserting objects in an expression into an expression tree. Method **insert:** is inherited from **Tree** and redefined. The other four methods are new protocol.

evaluation—one method (**evaluate**) that prompts the user to enter values for all nonnumerical operands and then evaluates the expression.

private—four methods (**buildTree, exprString:, getExpression, initialize**) that initialize the expression tree, prompt the user to enter an expression, and then build the expression tree. Once an expression tree is built, the expression can be evaluated for any set of operand values. All four are new protocol.

Class methods—Class **ExpressionTree** has two class methods in two categories. A summary is given below of the categories and the methods.

inquiries—one method (**operandValueAt:**) that returns the value of a specified operand string in class variable, OperandValues. It is new protocol.

instance creation—one method (**new**) that is inherited from **Tree** and redefined to provide initialization of the instance variables of **ExpressionTree.**

Protocol Summary for Class **OperatorNode**

Instances of **OperatorNode** have keys that are characters recognized as algebraic operators. This class inherits most of its necessary protocol from its superclass, **TreeNode.** It adds protocol for checking if a key is a valid operator and for evaluation.

Definition—The hierarchy for class **OperatorNode** is **Object—TreeNode—OperatorNode.** Class **OperatorNode** has no instance variables or pool dictionaries. It has one class variable, ValidOperators. It has two class methods in two categories and five instance methods in four categories.

Shared data—Class **OperatorNode** has one class variable.

ValidOperators—an instance of **Set** that maintains a set of characters that are valid algebraic operators. New operators may be added if the protocol for handling their indicated operation is also added to instance methods.

Instance methods—Class **OperatorNode** has five instance methods in four categories. A summary is given below of the categories and methods.

evaluation—one method (**evaluate**) that combines the value of the node's left and right subtrees using the operation indicated by the key operator character. This is new protocol and is implemented recursively.

private—one method (**key:**) that is inherited and defined. It checks if a key is a valid operator and then installs it as the key value.

printing and display—two methods (**display, toPrinter**) that are inherited from **TreeNode** as subclassResponsibility.

enumerating—one method (**inorderAdd:**) that is new protocol for supporting the addition of operands to an expression tree.

Class methods—Class **OperatorNode** has two class methods in two categories, as summarized below.

class initialization—one method (**initialize**) that creates the set Valid-Operators.

general inquiries—one method (**validOperators**) that answers the class variable ValidOperators. This message is sent by protocol of class **ExpressionTree**.

Protocol Summary for Class **OperandNode**

Instances of this class support expression trees. They contain key values that are either numerical values or identifier strings.

Definition—Hierarchy for class **OperandNode** is **Object—TreeNode—Operand-Node.** Class **OperandNode** has no instance variables, class variables, or pool dictionaries. It has no class methods. It has five instance methods in four categories. These are summarized below.

evaluation—one method (**evaluate**) that returns the numerical value of an operand. This is new protocol for this class hierarchy.

private—one method (**key:**) that is inherited from **TreeNode** as subclassResponsibility.

printing and display—two methods (**display, toPrinter**) that are inherited from **TreeNode** as subclassResponsibility.

testing—One method (**isLeaf**) is inherited from **TreeNode** and redefined to always be true. Operand nodes are always leaf nodes in a binary expression tree.

Class methods—Class **OperandNode** has no class methods.

The next section gives a complete protocol listing for the five classes that are summarized in this section. Although this may seem redundant, the purpose is to demonstrate in this chapter, with one example, all the methods used in the book for characterizing, describing, and using classes.

4.1.6   Protocol description and examples for the new classes

This section presents complete protocol listings for the tree classes and gives an example of the use of the new classes. Listing 4.1 gives details for the class **Tree.** It is the superclass of all binary tree objects, and its protocol provides methods for most generic binary tree operations.

Listing 4.1
Protocol
Description for
Class **Tree**

Object subclass: #Tree
    instanceVariableNames: 'root maxLevel avgLevel '
    classVariableNames: ''
    poolDictionaries: ''
    category: 'Trees-Ordered'

Tree comment: 'Ordinary binary search tree operations. Subclasses may add rebalance (AVL etc) methods. Subclasses would override methods for insert and delete.'

Tree methodsFor: 'deleting'

delete: aKey
    "Delete based on the key value in aNode subclass. Error if key doesn't match root key
        class."
    | parent |
    parent ← self search: aKey.
    parent isNil ifTrue: [↑self deleteRoot].
    (parent isParentOf: aKey)
        ifFalse:[Transcript cr; tab; show: 'Node with key ',
            aKey printString, ' is not in tree. No action taken.']
        ifTrue: [(parent left isNil not and: [parent left key = aKey])
           ifTrue: [self deleteLeft: parent]
           ifFalse:[self deleteRight: parent]]

deleteLeft: aNode
    "Delete left offspring of aNode."
    | nodeToDelete |
    nodeToDelete ← aNode left.
    nodeToDelete left isNil ifTrue: [↑aNode left: nodeToDelete right].
    nodeToDelete right isNil ifTrue: [↑Node left: nodeToDelete left].
    ↑aNode left: (self predecessorOf: nodeToDelete)

deleteRight: aNode
    "Delete right offspring of aNode."
    | nodeToDelete |
    nodeToDelete ← aNode right.
    nodeToDelete left isNil ifTrue: [↑aNode right: nodeToDelete right].
    nodeToDelete right isNil ifTrue: [↑Node right: nodeToDelete left].
    ↑aNode right: (self predecessorOf: nodeToDelete)

deleteRoot
    "Delete root node and answer a new tree."
    root left isNil ifTrue: [↑self root: root right].

    root right isNil ifTrue: [↑self root: root left].
    ↑self root: (self predecessorOf: root)

predecessorOf: aNode
    "Replace aNode with its inorder predecessor. "
    | predecessor |
    predecessor ← aNode predecessor.
    predecessor = aNode left ifFalse: [
       aNode left right: predecessor left.
       predecessor left: aNode left].
    predecessor right: aNode right.
    ↑predecessor

removeTree
    "Remove entire tree based on root."
    root postorderDo: [:aNode | aNode ← nil]

Tree methodsFor: 'printing and display'

computeBoundingBox
    "Answer the minimum rectangle for displaying the tree."
    ↑Rectangle origin: 0@0 extent: root setNodeDisplayParams

inorderDisplay
    "In order display in Transcript of tree contents"
    self empty
       ifTrue: [Transcript cr; show: 'Attempted to display empty binary tree.']
       ifFalse:[Transcript cr; cr; show: 'In-order Listing of Key Fields of a Binary Tree'.
          root inorderDo: [:aNode | aNode display]]

inorderPrint
    "In order printer listing of tree contents"
    Printer reset; ul; hv120bpn; tab: 5.
       'In-order Listing of Key Fields of a Binary Tree' outputToPrinter.
       Printer ku; defaultFont; cr; cr; tab: 10.
    root inorderDo: [:aNode | aNode toPrinter].
    Printer ff

postorderDisplay
    "Post order display of tree contents"
    self empty
       ifTrue: [Transcript cr; show: 'Attempted to display empty binary tree.']
       ifFalse:[Transcript cr; cr; show: 'Post-order Listing of Key Fields of a Binary Tree'.
          root postorderDo: [:aNode | aNode display]]

postorderPrint
    "Post order printer listing of tree contents"
    Printer reset; ul; hv120bpn; tab: 5.
       'Post-order Listing of Key Fields of a Binary Tree' outputToPrinter.
       Printer ku; defaultFont; cr; cr; tab: 10.
    root postorderDo: [:aNode | aNode toPrinter].
    Printer ff

Listing 4.1
(continued)

Tree methodsFor: 'accessing'

averagePathLength
    "Answer the average path length of the receiver Tree"
       " Not currently supported by insert and delete"
    ↑avgLevel

maxPathLength
    "Answer the maximum path length of the receiver Tree"
       " Not currently supported by insert and delete"
    ↑maxLevel

root
    "Return root node"
    ↑root

search: aKey
    "Answer parent of node containing the value, aKey, if present. Return nil if aKey is in root
        node. Else answer node that will be parent of a new node to insert, containing the
        value, aKey. This method supports both insertion and deletion."
    | aNode |
    self empty ifTrue: [↑self error: 'Tree is empty.'].
    aNode ← self root.
    (aKey isKindOf: aNode key class) ifFalse: [↑self error: 'Key is wrong class'].
    aNode key = aKey ifTrue: [↑nil]. "aNode is root node."
    [aNode isLeaf or: [aNode isParentOf: aKey]]
        whileFalse: [
            aKey < aNode key
            ifTrue: [aNode left isNil ifTrue: [↑aNode].
               aNode ← aNode left]
            ifFalse:[aNode right isNil ifTrue: [↑aNode].
               aNode ← aNode right]].
    ↑aNode

Tree methodsFor: 'inserting'

insert: aNode
    "insert based on the key value in aNode subclass. Error if key doesn't match root key."
    | parent |
    self empty ifTrue: [↑self root: aNode].
    parent ← self search: aNode key.
    (parent isNil or: [parent isParentOf: aNode key])
        ifTrue: [↑ Transcript cr; tab; show: 'Node with key ',
            aNode key printString, ' is already in tree. No action taken.'].
    aNode key < parent key
        ifTrue: [parent left: aNode]
        ifFalse:[parent right: aNode].
    ↑self

Tree methodsFor: 'testing'

empty
    ↑ root isNil

isPresent: aKey
    "Return true if key field of aNode is found. Error if key doesn't match root key."
    | node |
    self empty ifTrue: [↑Transcript cr; show: 'Tree is empty.'].
    node ← self root.
    (aKey isKindOf: root key class)
        ifFalse: [↑self error: 'Key is wrong class'].
    [aKey = node key or: [node isNil]]
        whileFalse: [
            aKey < node key
                ifTrue: [node ← node left]
                ifFalse:[node ← node right]].
        ↑node isNil not

Tree methodsFor: 'private'

avgLevel: aFloat
    avgLevel ← aFloat

maxLevel: anInteger
    maxLevel ← anInteger

root: aNode
    ↑root ← aNode

Tree class
    instanceVariableNames: ''

Tree class comment: ''

Tree class methodsFor: 'instance creation'

new
    "Answer a new instance with initialized instance variables."
    ↑super new root: nil; maxLevel: 0; avgLevel: 0.0

Tree class methodsFor: 'examples'

example1
    "Generate a binary tree with 15 random integer keys. Display keys inorder in Transcript.
        Delete even values and redisplay. Test inorder and postorder display."

    " Tree example1 "

Listing 4.1
(continued)

```
| tree rand |
Transcript clear; refresh;
      show: 'Insertion of random integers (0..9) into a binary tree.'.
tree ← Tree new.
rand ← Random new.
1 to: 15 do: [ :i | tree insert: (NumberNode new: (rand next * 10) truncated) ].
tree inorderDisplay.
tree postorderDisplay.
Transcript cr; cr;
      show: 'Delete even integers from the binary tree.'.
0 to: 9 do: [ :i |  i even ifTrue: [tree delete: i ]].
tree inorderDisplay.
tree postorderDisplay.
↑tree
```

example2
```
"Generate a binary tree with 10 integer keys. Display keys inorder and
      postorder in Transcript. Delete odd integers and redisplay."

" Tree example2 "

| tree |
Transcript clear; refresh;
      show: 'Insertion of integers (1..10) into a binary tree.'.
tree ← Tree new.
21 to: 30 do: [ :value | tree insert: (NumberNode new: value ) ].
tree inorderDisplay.
tree postorderDisplay.
Transcript cr; cr;
      show: 'Delete odd integers from the binary tree.'.
21 to: 30 do: [ :i | i odd ifTrue: [tree delete: i]].
tree inorderDisplay.
tree postorderDisplay.
↑tree
```

example2a
```
"Generate a binary tree with 10 integer keys. Display keys inorder and
      postorder in Transcript. Delete odd integers and redisplay."

 " Tree example2a "

| tree |
Transcript clear; refresh;
      show: 'Insertion of integers (1..10) into a binary tree.'.
tree ← Tree new.
tree insert: (NumberNode new: 50 ) .
tree insert: (NumberNode new: 45).
tree insert: (NumberNode new: 95).
tree insert: (NumberNode new: 75).
tree insert: (NumberNode new: 12000).
↑tree
```

example3
"Generate a binary tree with 10 integer keys. Display keys inorder and
    postorder in Transcript. Delete odd integers and redisplay."

" Tree example3 "

```
| tree |
Transcript clear; refresh;
    show: 'Insertion of integers (21..30) into a binary tree.'.
tree ← Tree new.
tree insert: (NumberNode new: 25);
    insert: (NumberNode new: 23);
    insert: (NumberNode new: 27);
    insert: (NumberNode new: 30);
    insert: (NumberNode new: 21);
    insert: (NumberNode new: 26);
    insert: (NumberNode new: 29);
    insert: (NumberNode new: 28);
    insert: (NumberNode new: 24);
    insert: (NumberNode new: 22).
tree inorderDisplay.
tree postorderDisplay.
Transcript cr; cr;
    show: 'Delete odd integers from the binary tree.'.
21 to: 30 do: [ :i | i odd ifTrue: [tree delete: i]].
tree inorderDisplay.
tree postorderDisplay
```

Listing 4.2 gives details for the class **TreeNode.** It represents generic properties and methods for all binary tree nodes. The major responsibility of its subclasses is to define details for display, printing, and assigning key values in
the node.

Listing 4.2
Protocol
Description for
Class **TreeNode**

Object subclass: #TreeNode
    instanceVariableNames: 'leftNode rightNode key info displaySize nodeImage '
    classVariableNames: 'Delta '
    poolDictionaries: ''
    category: 'Trees-Ordered'

TreeNode comment: '   This class represents an abstract, generic binary tree node with a
    'key' field and an 'info' field. The key field and info field assignments are subclass
    responsibility. Trees are built with instances of subclasses of TreeNode.

        displaySize -- aPoint, whose x & y values specify the minimum rectangle in pixels
            required to display the node and its subtrees.
        nodeImage -- aRectangle, that is large enough to display node contents. This
            instance variable is set by the subclasses of TreeNode.
        Delta -- aPoint specifying spacing between nodes for display.'

Listing 4.2
(continued)

TreeNode methodsFor: 'enumerating'

inorderDo: aBlock
    leftNode isNil ifFalse: [leftNode inorderDo: aBlock].
    aBlock value: self.
    rightNode isNil ifFalse: [rightNode inorderDo: aBlock]

postorderDo: aBlock
    leftNode isNil ifFalse: [leftNode postorderDo: aBlock].
    rightNode isNil ifFalse: [rightNode postorderDo: aBlock].
    aBlock value: self

TreeNode methodsFor: 'testing'

isEmpty
    ↑ self isNil

isLeaf
    ↑ (leftNode isNil) & (rightNode isNil)

isParentOf: aKey
    "First check if offspring are not nil. Answer true if either left or right offspring of the
       receiver contain aKey."
    ↑ ((self left isNil not) and: [self left key = aKey])
       or: [(self right isNil not) and: [self right key = aKey]]

TreeNode methodsFor: 'accessing'

displaySize
    "Answer the minimum size to display the node and its subtrees."
    ↑displaySize

info
    "Return the info field of the receiver treenode."
    ↑info

key
    "Return the key field of the receiver treenode."
    ↑key

left
    ↑leftNode

nodeImage
    "Answer the rectangle that is the node display image."
    ↑nodeImage

predecessor
>"Find in order predecessor of receiver node"
>| aNode |
>self left isNil
>>ifTrue: [self error: 'Left offspring is empty.']
>>ifFalse: [aNode ← self left.
>>>[aNode right isNil] whileFalse: [
>>>>aNode ← aNode right].
>>>↑aNode]

right
>↑rightNode

successor
>"Find in order successor of receiver node"
>| aNode |
>self right isNil
>>ifTrue: [self error: 'Right offspring is empty.']
>>ifFalse: [aNode ← self right.
>>>[aNode left isNil] whileFalse: [
>>>>aNode ← aNode left].
>>>↑aNode]

TreeNode methodsFor: 'private'

displaySize: aPoint
>"Set the extent of the display size for a node and its subtrees."
>displaySize ← aPoint

info: anObject
>info ← anObject

key: anObject
>"Assign anObject as key."
>↑self subclassResponsibility

left: aNode
>leftNode ← aNode

right: aNode
>rightNode ← aNode

setNodeImage
>"Set the rectangular image for the node, subclass responsibility."
>↑self subclassResponsibility

TreeNode methodsFor: 'printing and display'

display
>↑self subclassResponsibility

Listing 4.2
(continued)

```
setNodeDisplayParams
    "Answer the extent of the minimum display rectangle for the root."
    ↑self setNodeDisplayParams: self

setNodeDisplayParams: aNode
    "Set the nodeImage and answer the extent of the minimum display rectangle."
    | lSize rSize |
    aNode isNil ifTrue: [↑0@0].
    aNode setNodeImage.
    aNode isLeaf ifTrue: [aNode displaySize: aNode nodeImage extent].
    lSize ← self setNodeDisplayParams: aNode left.
    rSize ← self setNodeDisplayParams: aNode right.
    aNode displaySize: lSize x + rSize x + (Delta x max: aNode nodeImage extent x)
                @ (aNode nodeImage extent y + (lSize y max: rSize y)).
    ↑aNode displaySize

showImageAt: aPoint as: direction
    "Display the nodeImage at aPoint.
     Direction is left or right from parent node."
    | dx dy location line |
    line ← Line new form: (Form dotOfSize: 2).
    dx ← nodeImage extent x // 2 max: Delta x // 2.
    dy ← nodeImage extent y // 2 max: Delta y // 2.
    direction = #left
        ifTrue: [location ← aPoint + (0-dx@dy).
            self right isNil ifFalse: [
                location ← location - (self right displaySize x @ 0)]].
    direction = #right
        ifTrue: [location ← aPoint + (dx@dy).
            self left isNil ifFalse: [
                location ← location + (self left displaySize x @ 0)]].
    direction = #center ifTrue: [location ← aPoint + (dx@0).
            self left isNil ifFalse: [
                location ← location + (self left displaySize x @ 0)]].
    direction = #center ifFalse: [ line beginPoint: aPoint.
        line endPoint: location.
        line displayOn: Display].
    nodeImage displayOn: Display at: location.
    leftNode isNil ifFalse: [
        self left showImageAt: location + (0-dx@dy) as: #left].
    rightNode isNil ifFalse: [
        self right showImageAt: location + (dx@dy) as: #right].

toPrinter
    ↑self subclassResponsibility
```

TreeNode class
    instanceVariableNames: "

TreeNode class comment: "

TreeNode class methodsFor: 'instance creation'

new: aKey
    "Create a new node with nil left and right subnodes. Key is subclass responsibility."
    ↑self basicNew left: nil; right: nil; key: aKey

new: aKey withInfo: anObject
    "Answer an instance of me with aKey as the key and anObject as info."
    ↑ (self new: aKey) info: anObject

TreeNode class methodsFor: 'accessing'

setDelta: aPoint
    "Set the spacing between node images for display."
    Delta ← aPoint

Listing 4.3 gives details for class **NumberNode,** which is a subclass of **Tree-Node.** It adds new protocol for generation of binary trees whose nodes have key values that are numbers. An example is given later that builds a binary tree using nodes of this class.

Listing 4.3
Protocol
Description
for Class
NumberNode

TreeNode subclass: #NumberNode
    instanceVariableNames: "
    classVariableNames: "
    poolDictionaries: "
    category: 'Trees-Ordered'

NumberNode comment: This class represents binary treenodes with numbers as keys.
    Each node may contain additional information also.

NumberNode methodsFor: 'printing and display'

display
    "Screen display of binary tree."
    Transcript crtab;
        show: ('Number key = ', key printString).

Listing 4.3
(continued)

```
toPrinter
    "printer output of nodes of binary tree."
    Printer it; tab: 10.
    ('Number key = ', key printString) outputToPrinter.
    Printer cr
```

NumberNode methodsFor: 'private'

```
key: aNumber
    key ← aNumber
```

Listing 4.4 gives protocol for the class **ExpressionTree,** which is a subclass of **Tree.** Its instances are used to evaluate algebraic expressions using binary expression trees. Major differences in **ExpressionTree** from its superclass include methods for inserting nodes into a tree. In addition, deletion is not allowed from expression trees.

Listing 4.4
Protocol
Description
for Class
ExpressionTree

```
Tree subclass: #ExpressionTree
    instanceVariableNames: 'exprString operands parenCount '
    classVariableNames: 'OperandValues '
    poolDictionaries: ''
    category: 'Trees-Ordered'
```

ExpressionTree comment: New private data are:

> exprString -- an instance of string with all separators removed.
> operands -- an instance of OrderedCollection that is a queue of operands.
> parenCount -- an Integer that is the number of unanswered left parentheses on enumerating the characters in exprString. Increment by one when a left paren encountered. Decrement by one when a right paren encountered.
> OperandValues -- an instance of Dictionary that maps operand keys to operand values. Defined as a class variable to provide easy access by each operand node.

ExpressionTree methodsFor: 'private'

```
buildTree
    "Build an expression tree using exprString."
    | stream char |
    stream ← ReadStream on: exprString.
    stream position: 0.
    [ stream atEnd ] whileFalse: [
        char ← stream peek.
        (OperatorNode validOperators includes: char) ifTrue: [
            self insert: (OperatorNode new: stream next withInfo: parenCount )].
        (char isLetter or: [ char isDigit ]) ifTrue: [
            self addToQueue: stream ].
```

```
        char isOpenParen ifTrue: [parenCount ← parenCount + 1. stream next].
        char isClosingParen ifTrue: [parenCount ← parenCount - 1. stream next]].
    self addOperandsToTree
```

exprString: aString
```
    "Set exprString = aString."
    exprString ← aString
```

getExpression
```
    "Prompt the user to enter an expression. Check its validity."
    | expression |
    FillInTheBlank
        request: 'Enter an algebraic expression and press return.'
        displayAt: Display computeBoundingBox center - (344@100)
        centered: true
        action: [ :answer | expression ← answer]
        initialAnswer: ''.
    Transcript cr; cr; show: 'The string you entered is'; crtab; show: expression.
    expression ← expression asExpression.
    Transcript cr; cr; show: 'The equivalent expression is '; c tab; show: expression.
    expression isValidExpression
        ifTrue: [Transcript cr; cr; show: 'The expression is valid'.
            self exprString: expression]
        ifFalse:[ Transcript cr; cr; show: 'The expression is not valid'.
            self getExpression]
```

initialize
```
    operands ← OrderedCollection new.
    parenCount ← 0.
    OperandValues ← Dictionary new
```

ExpressionTree methodsFor: 'accessing'

decParenCount
```
    parenCount > = 1
        ifTrue: [parenCount ← parenCount - 1]
        ifFalse:[↑self error: 'Unmatching right parenthesis in expression.']
```

exprString
```
    ↑exprString
```

incParenCount
```
    parenCount ← parenCount + 1
```

ExpressionTree methodsFor: 'deleting'

delete: anObject
```
    ↑self error: 'Deletion from expression trees not allowed.'
```

Listing 4.4
(continued)

ExpressionTree methodsFor: 'inserting'

addOperandsToTree
    "Take operands from queue and add as leaf nodes to tree."
    | operandList |
    operandList ← operands deepCopy.   "Don't corrupt the original."
    self empty
        ifTrue: [↑self error: 'Expression tree is empty']
        ifFalse: [root inorderAdd: [:aNode |
           aNode left isNil ifTrue: [
               aNode left: (OperandNode new: operandList removeFirst)].
           aNode right isNil ifTrue: [
               aNode right: (OperandNode new: operandList removeFirst)]]].

addToQueue: stream
    "Find the operand, all chars up to next operator or right paren, and add to operands
queue."
    | opStream |
    opStream ← WriteStream on: (String new: 16).
    [stream atEnd or: [(OperatorNode validOperators includes: stream peek)
        or: [stream peek isClosingParen]]]
           whileFalse: [opStream nextPut: stream next].
    operands add: opStream contents.
    ↑stream

insert: aNode
    "Insert aNode as an operator.
        Special rules apply to precedence for operator nodes."
    aNode class = OperatorNode
        ifTrue: [↑self insertOperator: aNode inTree: self root].
    ↑self error: 'Expression trees contain only operators and operands'

insertOperator: aNode inTree: aTreeNode
    "Insert the operator node, aNode, in subtree at aTreeNode."
    self empty ifTrue: [↑self root: aNode].
    (self precedenceOfTreeNodeIsGreater: aTreeNode)
        ifTrue: ["replace aTreeNode with aNode, make aTreeNode left offspring of aNode"
           aTreeNode = root
               ifTrue: [aNode left: aTreeNode. self root: aNode]
               ifFalse: [aNode left: aTreeNode].
           ↑aNode]
        ifFalse: ["add aNode as right offspring of aTreeNode or go down right subtree."
           aTreeNode right isNil
               ifTrue: [aTreeNode right: aNode]
               ifFalse: [aTreeNode right:
                    (self insertOperator: aNode inTree: aTreeNode right)].
           ↑aTreeNode]

precedenceOfTreeNodeIsGreater: aNode
    "Answer true if precedence of operator in aNode is higher
        than newOperator, else false."

↑aNode info > = parenCount
"Only operators in parens have higher precedence.
   Else, precedence is left to right."

ExpressionTree methodsFor: 'evaluation'

evaluate
   "Evaluate the expression with user input values for independent variables.
    First Prompts user for a single value for each non-number operand."
   operands do: [:operand | OperandValues at: operand
      ifAbsent: [OperandValues add: (Association key: operand
         value: (operand firstIsDigit
            ifTrue: [operand asNumber]
            ifFalse:[(FillInTheBlank
               request: 'Enter numerical value for ',operand) asNumber]))]].
   Transcript cr; show: 'The value is --> ', root evaluate printString

ExpressionTree class
   instanceVariableNames: ''

ExpressionTree class comment: ''

ExpressionTree class methodsFor: 'examples'

example1
   "Prompt user for an algebraic expression, build tree and evaluate."
   "Prompts user for values of independent variables."
   self title.
   self new getExpression; buildTree; evaluate

   " ExpressionTree example1 "

title
   Transcript clear; refresh; show:
      'Algebraic Expression Evaluator - LJ Pinson August 1987'; cr; cr.

ExpressionTree class methodsFor: 'instance creation'

new
   "Answer an expression tree with initialized instance variables."
   ↑super new initialize

ExpressionTree class methodsFor: 'inquiries'

operandValueAt: aKey
   "Answer value in OperandValues dictionary at aKey"
   ↑OperandValues at: aKey

Listing 4.5 shows details of the **TreeNode** subclass **OperatorNode.** Its key values are valid arithmetic operator characters. New protocol for evaluation is required to support the evaluation of algebraic expression trees.

Listing 4.6 shows details of the **TreeNode** subclass **OperandNode.** Operand nodes contain either string identifiers or numbers. New protocol for evaluation is required.

Listing 4.5
Protocol
Description
for Class
OperatorNode

TreeNode subclass: #OperatorNode
    instanceVariableNames: ''
    classVariableNames: 'ValidOperators '
    poolDictionaries: ''
    category: 'Trees-Ordered'

OperatorNode comment: 'Private and shared data are:

    info (parenCount) -- an instance of Integer that establishes relative precedence rules.
        Its value is the number of nested left parens entered.
    ValidOperators -- an instance of Set whose elements are the valid operator
        characters'

OperatorNode methodsFor: 'evaluation'

evaluate
    "Recursively evaluate the expression in an OperatorNode."
    key = $+ ifTrue: [↑self left evaluate + self right evaluate].
    key = $- ifTrue: [↑self left evaluate - self right evaluate].
    key = $* ifTrue: [↑self left evaluate * self right evaluate].
    key = $/ ifTrue: [↑self left evaluate / self right evaluate].
    key = $↑ ifTrue: [↑self left evaluate raisedTo: self right evaluate]

OperatorNode methodsFor: 'private'

key: anOperator
    "Set key to be anOperator."
    (ValidOperators includes: anOperator)
        ifTrue: [key ← anOperator]
        ifFalse:[↑self error: 'Invalid operator in expression']

OperatorNode methodsFor: 'printing and display'

display
    "Screen display of binary tree."
    Transcript crtab;
        show: ('Operator key = ', key printString).

toPrinter
    "Send the key character to the printer"
    (String with: key) outputToPrinter

OperatorNode methodsFor: 'enumerating'

inorderAdd: aBlock
    leftNode isNil ifFalse: [leftNode inorderAdd: aBlock].
    aBlock value: self.
    (rightNode isNil not and: [ValidOperators includes: rightNode key])
        ifTrue: [rightNode inorderAdd: aBlock]

OperatorNode class
    instanceVariableNames: ''

OperatorNode class comment: ''

OperatorNode class methodsFor: 'class initialization'

initialize
    "Create the set of valid operator characters."
    ValidOperators ← Set new.
    ValidOperators
        add: $+;
        add: $-;
        add: $*;
        add: $/;
        add: $↑   "Raise to power"

    " OperatorNode initialize"

OperatorNode class methodsFor: 'general inquiries'

validOperators
    ↑ValidOperators

Listing 4.6
Protocol
Description
for Class
OperandNode

TreeNode subclass: #OperandNode
    instanceVariableNames: ''
    classVariableNames: ''
    poolDictionaries: ''
    category: 'Trees-Ordered'

OperandNode comment: ''

OperandNode methodsFor: 'evaluation'

evaluate
    "Answer the value of the operand node."
    ↑ExpressionTree operandValueAt: key

Listing 4.6
(continued)

OperandNode methodsFor: 'private'

```
key: anOperand
    (anOperand class = String)
        ifTrue: [ key ← anOperand ]
        ifFalse:[ ↑self error: 'Illegal operand in expression']
```

OperandNode methodsFor: 'testing'

```
isLeaf
    ↑true
```

OperandNode methodsFor: 'printing and display'

```
display
    "Screen display of binary tree."
    Transcript crtab;
        show: ('Operand key = ', key printString).

toPrinter
    "Send the key character to the printer"
    (String with: key) outputToPrinter
```

Listing 4.7
Tree example1
Details

Tree class methodsFor: 'examples'

```
example1
    "Generate a binary tree with 15 random integer keys. Display keys inorder in Transcript.
        Delete even values and redisplay. Test inorder and postorder display."

    " Tree example1 "

    | tree rand |
    Transcript clear; refresh;
        show: 'Insertion of random integers (0..9) into a binary tree.'.
    tree ← Tree new.
    rand ← Random new.
    1 to: 15 do: [ :i | tree insert: (NumberNode new: (rand next * 10) truncated) ].
    tree inorderDisplay.
    tree postorderDisplay.
    Transcript cr; cr;
        show: 'Delete even integers from the binary tree.'.
    0 to: 9 do: [ :i |  i even ifTrue: [tree delete: i ]].
    tree inorderDisplay.
    tree postorderDisplay.
    ↑tree
```

Binary Tree Example 4A

This example shows the generation of a binary tree containing integer keys. Its nodes are instances of **NumberNode.** Insertion, deletion, inorder display, and postorder display are demonstrated. The details of the **Tree** class method **example1** are given in Listing 4.7. The example attempts to add 15 integers between 0 and 9 to a binary tree. Duplicates are not allowed.

Results of the example are shown in Figure 4.2. The example illustrates how attempts to insert an existing number in the tree are handled. Also, attempts to

Figure 4.2
Tree example1—
A Binary Tree with
Random Integers

```
System Transcript
Insertion of random integers (0..9) into a binary tree.
    Node with key 5 is already in tree. No action taken.
    Node with key 2 is already in tree. No action taken.
    Node with key 5 is already in tree. No action taken.
    Node with key 2 is already in tree. No action taken.
    Node with key 1 is already in tree. No action taken.
    Node with key 0 is already in tree. No action taken.
    Node with key 1 is already in tree. No action taken.
    Node with key 5 is already in tree. No action taken.


In-order Listing of Key Fields of a Binary Tree
    Number key = 0
    Number key = 1
    Number key = 2
    Number key = 5
    Number key = 6
    Number key = 7
    Number key = 8

Post-order Listing of Key Fields of a Binary Tree
    Number key = 1
    Number key = 2
    Number key = 6
    Number key = 5
    Number key = 0
    Number key = 7
    Number key = 8

Delete even integers from the binary tree.
    Node with key 4 is not in tree. No action taken.

In-order Listing of Key Fields of a Binary Tree
    Number key = 1
    Number key = 5
    Number key = 7

Post-order Listing of Key Fields of a Binary Tree
    Number key = 1
    Number key = 5
    Number key = 7
```

Listing 4.8
ExpressionTree
example1 Details

ExpressionTree class methodsFor: 'examples'

example1
    "Prompt user for an algebraic expression, build tree and evaluate."
      "Prompts user for values of independent variables."

    self title.
    self new getExpression; buildTree; evaluate

    " ExpressionTree example1 "

Figure 4.3
ExpressionTree
example1—
Evaluating
Algebraic
Expressions

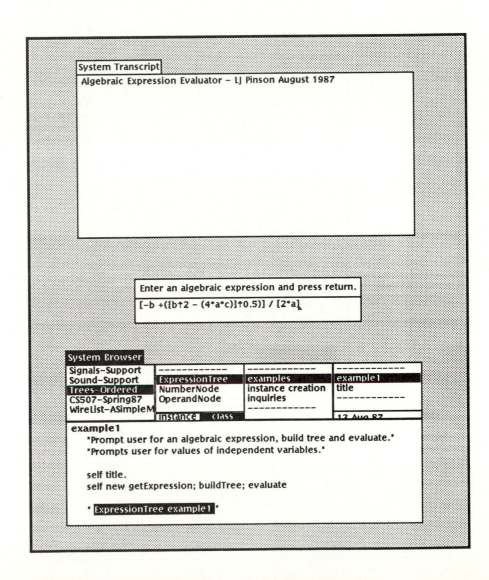

delete a number not in the tree simply result in a message displayed in the Transcript window.

Binary ExpressionTree Example 4A

This example illustrates the generation and evaluation of binary expression trees. Details of the **ExpressionTree** class method example1 are given in Listing 4.8. The user is prompted to enter an algebraic expression, as indicated in Figure 4.3. The expression may contain the three kinds of parentheses shown in the figure. If the expression contains identifiers, the user is prompted for values for each unique identifier, as shown in Figure 4.4. The final result is indicated in

**Figure 4.4
ExpressionTree**
example1—Prompt
for Identifier Values

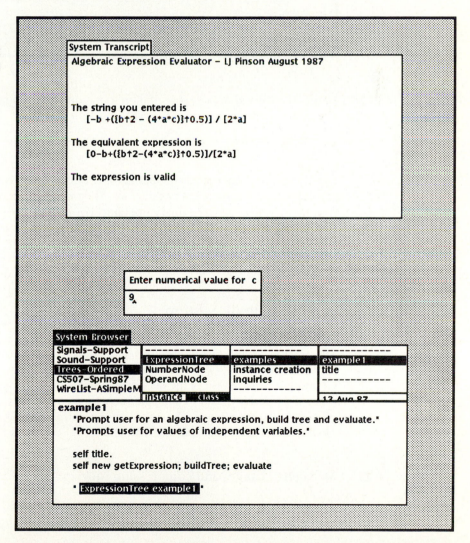

**Figure 4.5
ExpressionTree**
example1—Result

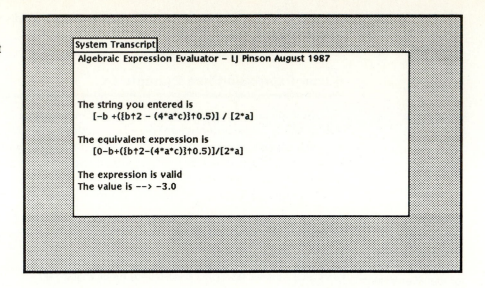

Figure 4.5. The expression is a solution to the quadratic equation a*x ↑ 2 + b*x + c = 0, with a = 1, b = 6, and c = 9.

The expression tree class supports only binary operators; it currently does not support unary operators or functions. The only exception is that it does support the negative sign as a unary operator. For example, −(3 + 4) is correctly interpreted as −7. It is left as an exercise for the reader to include protocol for handling functions such as sin and cos.

4.2   Maintaining the Smalltalk System

This section defines techniques for maintaining a clean image and gives details for the management of a system that is being developed by a software team. In addition to a discussion of the supporting Smalltalk classes for change management, a rational set of steps and rules is presented for the maintenance of complicated software systems. The rules are not complicated, but they may not be obvious to the first-time user of Smalltalk.

4.2.1   Managing changes and compressing sources

The process of maintaining a clean Smalltalk system consists of several possible operations. The first of these compresses the changes file to include only those actions affecting the working Smalltalk image. The second and more complete "cleanup" operation consists of compressing the changes file and the source file into a new source file, a new image, and an empty changes file. This section outlines these steps and provides cautions for protection against lost or corrupted files.

Compressing the Changes File

The message condenseChanges in class **SystemDictionary** is sent to the global variable **Smalltalk** to condense the changes file. The exact protocol is

Smalltalk condenseChanges.

It creates a compacted changes file that contains only the source code that has been changed since the last creation of a new sources file. All references to *do it*s are removed. All multiple changes to a single method or class are replaced with the latest change. A significant reduction in the size of the changes file is achieved. The sources file and image are not affected.

As an example of the relative gain in storage efficiency, the development of new classes in this chapter and in Chapter 11 produced a changes file of size 476,473 bytes. After execution of the above expression to condense the changes, the new changes file contains only 65,240 bytes.

Condensing the changes file is easy to execute and takes little time. The result is a changes file that reflects only the important changes to the current sources file. It is recommended as a periodic maintenance technique.

Compressing the Sources File

Occasionally it is desirable to incorporate all valid changes into the sources file and start fresh with an empty changes file. This operation is also accomplished with protocol in class **SystemDictionary.** The following expression can be evaluated with *do it* from any window. It creates a new sources file with updated source information and an empty changes file. Both can be attached to the current image file.

Smalltalk newSourceFile: newVersionName without: setOfClasses

The expression generates two files, **newVersionName.sources** and **newVersionName.changes**. All classes in **setOfClasses** are excluded from the new source file. Generally, for updating one's own system, no classes are to be excluded. This is accomplished by defining **setOfClasses** as an empty array; e.g.,

Smalltalk newSourceFile: myFile without: (Array new)

This expression takes several minutes to execute because it rewrites every class in the system to the new sources file while incorporating all changes. The parameter **myFile** must be a different file name than used by the current version, or else problems occur.

After the compression is completed, the current image file can be bound to the new sources and changes files by saving ("taking a snapshot"). Changing the image file name to be '*myFile.im*' is recommended when taking the snapshot to give a consistent naming pattern to all the system files.

At this point there will be two complete and different sets of system files, the old files and the ones with name '*myfile*'. The user can change these file names at any time; however, there is one additional requirement if Smalltalk is to function properly. A global variable, **SourceFiles,** in the system dictionary is an array containing two file names. The file name at position 1 in the array is the name (including path) of the sources file. The second array position contains the name (including path) of the changes file. This global variable is set to contain '*path/myFile.sources*' and '*path/myFile.changes*' for the new system files generated by the newSourceFile: without: message.

If a user assigns new file names (e.g., newName) to the sources and changes files, then the user must enter Smalltalk and set the values in **SourceFiles** to match the new names. This is easily accomplished by the following expressions.

```
SourceFiles ← Array new.
SourceFiles at: 1 put: (FileStream oldFileNamed: 'path/newName.sources').
SourceFiles at: 2 put: (FileStream oldFileNamed: 'path/newName.changes').
```

The final step is to save the change by taking a snapshot (using the main system menu option *save* or by quitting and saving).

4.2.2   Managing changes for a team approach to Smalltalk software development

This section presents an approach for making maintenance of the composite image of a software team manageable. Responsibilities are given for the maintenance executive and for each team member. Detailed procedures for the use of file out, file in, source compression, backup of changes, and system integration are given.

The most important feature of any software development effort is the design of new classes and their relative place in the existing image hierarchy. If this task is completed correctly, then maintenance becomes easy. Each team member may add new subclasses to the classes for which he or she has responsibility. However, the addition of classes that attach to other parts of the hierarchy must be coordinated with the team.

Because of the encapsulation provided by Smalltalk, there is little chance for conflict from independent actions by team members. The major area of potential conflict is the addition of new global variables to the system dictionary **Smalltalk.** New globals must be coordinated with the team members.

As each team member adds new protocol to his or her working system, each will have unique and noncompatible image and changes files. There are several easy steps required to regain compatibility and for merging all the efforts of the team into one working software system. First, it is recommended that one team member be assigned the responsibility of producing that merged software system. No other team member is part of this activity.

The team now has two categories of members, which are given different names for easy reference. They are:

- *Maintenance executive*—Has responsibility for acquiring modified source code from all team members and producing a merged, consistent Smalltalk system. The Smalltalk system consists of updated sources, changes, and image files. These updated files are returned to the team members on a periodic basis so all team members have updated system files.

- *Team members*—Different from the maintenance executive in that they never produce a set of new system files. The only updating that team members do is to condense their own changes files.

The maintenance process consists of the following steps and responsibilities.

Responsibilities of Team Members

- Develop new protocol in the form of new classes and methods. This protocol is restricted to assigned responsibilities for each team member.

- Periodically condense the changes file using the expression **Smalltalk condenseChanges**.

- Create a chunk format file for each new class as it is completed (debugged and "working"). This is done by using the *file out* menu option from the browser.

- On a regular schedule, deliver to the maintenance executive a copy of all file outs. These are source code for classes and methods added since the last system update.

- Use the updated system files returned by the maintenance executive for additional software development.

Responsibilities of the Maintenance Executive

- On a periodic basis collect all chunk format source code files generated by each team member.

- Add the new source code to the existing system by selecting the *file in* option from a File List window.

- Create a set of new system files by using the expression **Smalltalk newSourceFile: fileName without: (Array new)**. This creates the new system sources, changes, and image files.

- Deliver the updated system files to each team member.

Variations on this set of steps may reduce the time required to keep updates; however, this is the safe way to maintain a complex software system. In addition to these steps, all team members must keep backup copies (in a different file directory) of their own work. The maintenance executive must keep multiple copies of the current system files and never attempt to create a new set of system files without this multiple backup.

It is recommended that each team member update his or her own backup copies at the end of each session or sooner. Lost code is difficult to reproduce and requires time. As each new method is accepted, the team member is encouraged to file it out. Testing of new protocol has been known to cause error loops that can only be stopped by exiting Smalltalk in an unceremonious way. All new source code not filed out or saved with a snapshot of the image is then lost. Don't let this happen.

As a final note on maintenance, there are even techniques for partially recovering from disaster. These techniques are described by Goldberg. The best approach is not to let disasters occur.

Exercises

4.1 In Section 4.1.1 the algebraic expression object is discussed as being a string with special properties. It is suggested that these objects can be implemented as special cases of class **String** by adding limited new protocol to the class. It is also suggested that a subclass of **String** can be defined to represent this new object. Examine the tradeoffs for choosing one method versus the other. Criteria such as amount of new protocol needed versus the conceptual separation of expression strings from other kinds of strings form the basis for this comparison.

4.2 The chosen hierarchy for the binary tree classes has three node subclasses, **OperatorNode, OperandNode,** and **NumberNode,** all at the same hierarchical level. Each of the three kinds of node has a different key value (operator, operand, or number). Given that the keys in each could be represented by a string of characters, give reasons why three separate classes offer advantages over a single class with strings for keys.

4.3 Explain in your own words why the pseudovariable **super** is an essential part of the message **new** defined in Section 4.1.3.

4.4 Add the new classes and supporting protocol for the binary tree classes to your Smalltalk system and test their functionality. Add a new method isValidExpression to class **String** that simply determines if there are matching parentheses in the expression string.

4.5 Based on the protocol summaries and complete protocol descriptions for the binary tree classes, summarize each class in terms of its new, inherited, and redefined protocol.

4.6 Discuss ways to handle the inclusion of unary operators in a binary expression tree algorithm.

4.7 Based on the results of Exercise 4.6, select at least three unary operators (e.g., sin, cos, tan) for inclusion in the binary expression tree classes. Implement and test the new capability.

4.8 Practice using the **SystemDictionary** protocol for compressing changes and sources.

4.9 Repeat Exercise 4.4 using a team approach in which different team members are responsible for the details of adding each class. Does this approach cause any problems when two different team members are adding a class and its subclass? If so, how can these problems be handled?

5

Fundamental Input/Output Operations in Smalltalk

This chapter presents a discussion of the objects, classes, and methods for performing "standard" input/output operations such as prompted keyboard input, screen output, printer output, mouse input, graphics output to screen or printer, and file I/O. Existing classes for keyboard input, mouse input, and screen text output are discussed and illustrated with examples. A new class called **Printer-Stream** is introduced for sending text output to a printer. Initial concepts for presenting graphical images to the screen or printer are given. New methods in classes **Form** and **DisplayScreen** are described that support graphics output to a printer. (A more detailed discussion of the graphics classes is given in Chapter 9.)

5.1 Prompted User Input from the Keyboard

There are several classes in the Smalltalk image that support prompting and accepting keyboard input from the user. This section gives a summary of the protocol for those classes and gives several examples of the more commonly used methods. Two classes, **BinaryChoice** and **FillInTheBlank,** provide fundamental support for prompting and accepting input from the user. Since each of these classes involves the display of a *prompt* window on the display screen, each is supported by a model-view-controller triad.

The classes supporting the MVC triad for user input are contained in the class category *Interface - PromptAndConfirm* in the System Browser. There are seven classes in that category since there are two controller classes for **FillInThe-Blank.** Figure 5.1 shows the classes in that category.

To use the prompt and confirm capabilities of Smalltalk requires sending messages to the model class names. That is, class messages in the protocol for **BinaryChoice** and **FillInTheBlank** are the ones to use. In this section only the model and its use are examined. To look only at the model requires examining the protocol of the classes **BinaryChoice** and **FillInTheBlank.** It does not require a detailed examination of the view and controller classes.

Figure 5.1 shows an example of the use of the **BinaryChoice** prompter. The upper right browser shows details of a class method called **example** that is part of the protocol for **BinaryChoice.** The comment in that method, "BinaryChoice example", was selected and executed with *do it.* The resulting binary choice view, shown in the System Transcript window, was displayed at a point selected by positioning the cursor and clicking the left mouse button (a result of the expression **displayAt: Sensor waitButton**). Although it is not shown in the figure, the cursor changes to a *ThumbsUp* shape when in the *yes* subview of the binary choice view and a *ThumbsDown* shape when in the *no* subview.

The user must respond to the binary choice prompter before any other action can be taken. Movement of the cursor outside the binary choice view causes the view to blink, indicating a response is required.

The example method in class **BinaryChoice** sends a single message with five selector-parameter pairs to itself (class name **BinaryChoice**). The lower left browser window in Figure 5.1 shows details for the method representing that message. Understanding of the details requires examination of other messages called by the method. Understanding of its functionality requires only that one read the explanatory comment. The message selector subview of the lower left browser (hidden in the figure) lists five messages for creating instances of **BinaryChoice.** Differences among the five messages relate to where the prompt window is to be displayed and options on true or false alternatives. Each of the remaining four instance creation messages send the message pattern **message: displayAt: centered: ifTrue: ifFalse:** (shown in Figure 5.1), with appropriate parameters. Details are given in Section 5.1.2 below.

Figure 5.2 shows an example of the use of a **FillInTheBlank** prompter. The expression in comments in the upper right browser, "FillInTheBlank example1", was selected and executed with *do it.* The cursor was moved to the System Transcript window and the left mouse button was clicked. This caused display of the prompter window shown in the figure with the **initialAnswer**, L. J. Pinson, reverse videoed as shown. This name can be accepted using the middle-button menu in the prompter window. Or the default name can be changed by simply typing in a new name. The name must be accepted by using the *accept* menu option, or nothing happens.

Unlike the **BinaryChoice** window, which required a response, the **FillInThe-Blank** window does not require a user response. It remains on the screen with no action taken if the cursor is clicked outside the prompter view. At any time the user can activate the prompter window and respond with the expected result. Or the user can close the prompter window with no action taken.

The message **example1** sends a single message with five selector-parameter pairs to its class name, **FillInTheBlank.** This is one of six instance creation messages for this class. Details for the message sent by **example1** are given in the text subview of that browser. Again, the comment in the method explains what is accomplished (not how it is accomplished).

Two other examples are listed in the *examples* protocol category for class **FillInTheBlank.** The **example2** message is similar to **example1**, except that it uses a different controller, one that adds the feature that the text in the prompter

Figure 5.1 Example of the Use of **BinaryChoice** Prompter

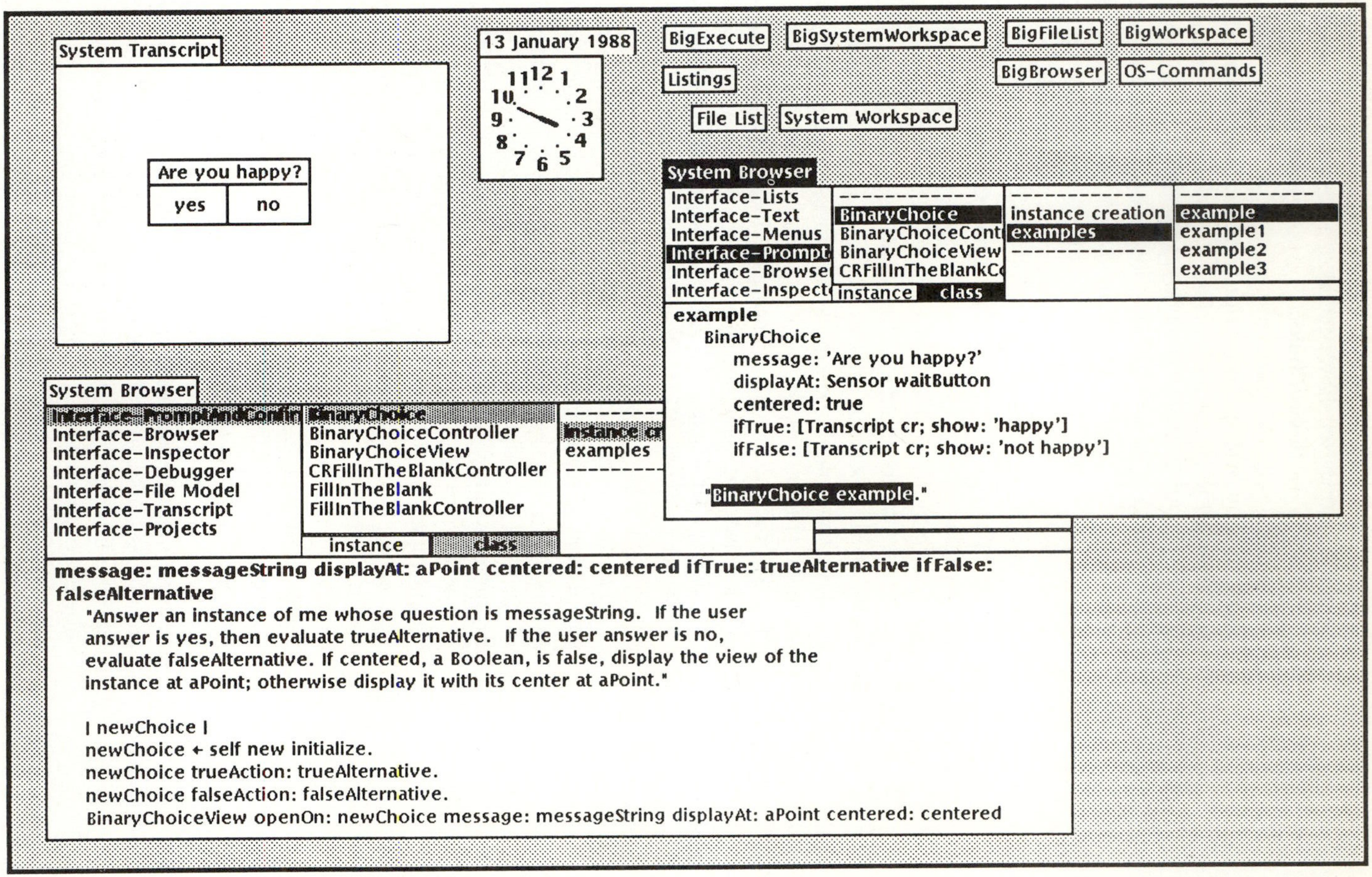

System Transcript

13 January 1988

Are you happy?

| yes | no |

BigExecute | BigSystemWorkspace | BigFileList | BigWorkspace

Listings | BigBrowser | OS-Commands

File List | System Workspace

System Browser

Interface-Lists
Interface-Text
Interface-Menus
Interface-Prompt
Interface-Browse
Interface-Inspect

BinaryChoice
BinaryChoiceCont
BinaryChoiceView
CRFillInTheBlankC

instance creation
examples

example
example1
example2
example3

instance   class

example
    BinaryChoice
        message: 'Are you happy?'
        displayAt: Sensor waitButton
        centered: true
        ifTrue: [Transcript cr; show: 'happy']
        ifFalse: [Transcript cr; show: 'not happy']

"BinaryChoice example."

System Browser

Interface-PromptAndConfirm
Interface-Browser
Interface-Inspector
Interface-Debugger
Interface-File Model
Interface-Transcript
Interface-Projects

BinaryChoice
BinaryChoiceController
BinaryChoiceView
CRFillInTheBlankController
FillInTheBlank
FillInTheBlankController

instance creation
examples

instance   class

message: messageString displayAt: aPoint centered: centered ifTrue: trueAlternative ifFalse:
falseAlternative

"Answer an instance of me whose question is messageString. If the user
answer is yes, then evaluate trueAlternative. If the user answer is no,
evaluate falseAlternative. If centered, a Boolean, is false, display the view of the
instance at aPoint; otherwise display it with its center at aPoint."

| newChoice |
newChoice ← self new initialize.
newChoice trueAction: trueAlternative.
newChoice falseAction: falseAlternative.
BinaryChoiceView openOn: newChoice message: messageString displayAt: aPoint centered: centered

Figure 5.2 Example of the Use of **FillInTheBlank** Prompter

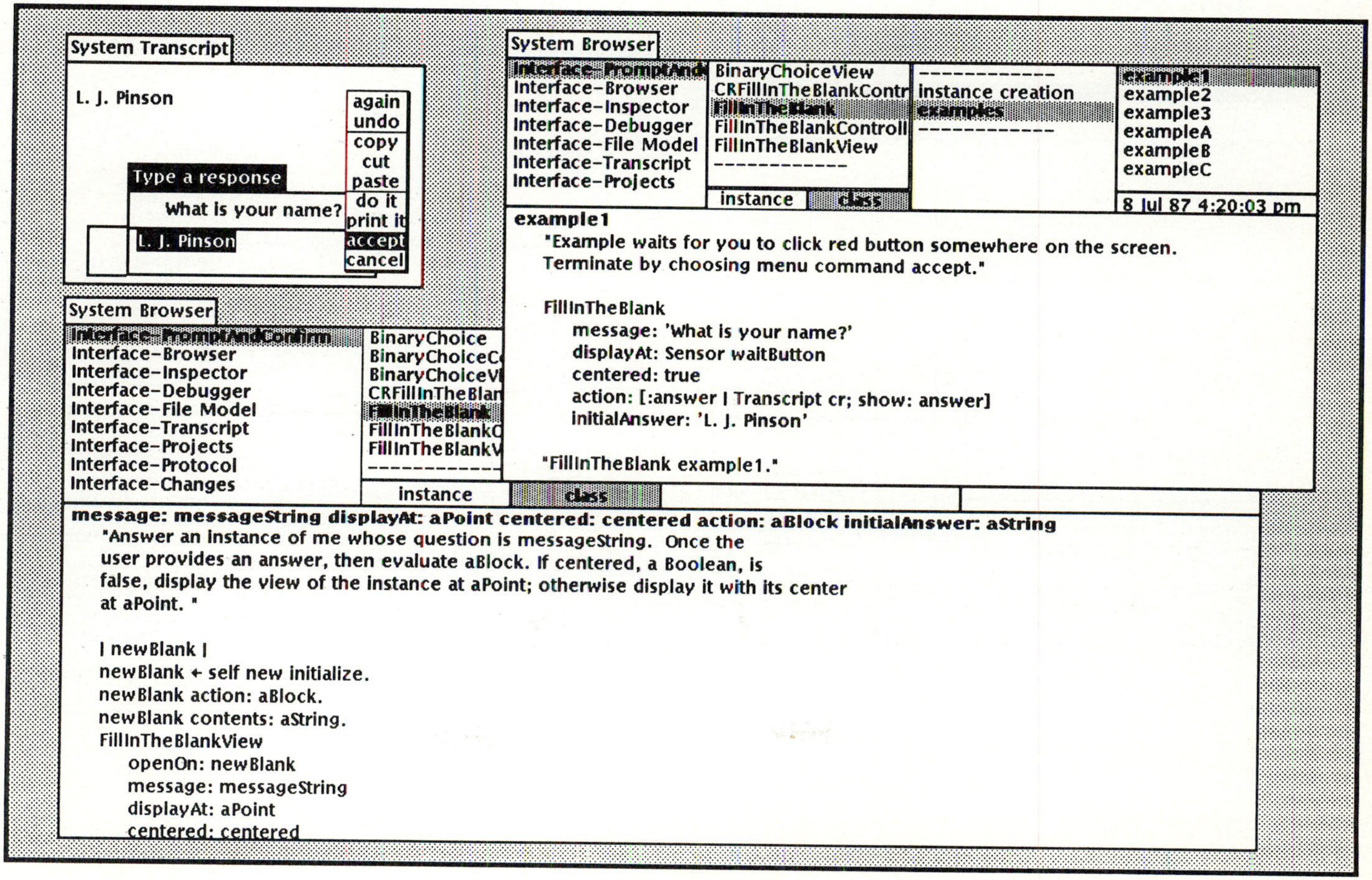

System Transcript

L. J. Pinson

Type a response

what is your name?

L. J. Pinson

again
undo
copy
cut
paste
do it
print it
accept
cancel

System Browser

Interface-Prompt/And/Confirm
Interface-Browser
Interface-Inspector
Interface-Debugger
Interface-File Model
Interface-Transcript
Interface-Projects
Interface-Protocol
Interface-Changes

BinaryChoice
BinaryChoiceC
BinaryChoiceV
CRFillInTheBlan
FillInTheBlank
FillInTheBlankC
FillInTheBlankV

instance   class

message: messageString displayAt: aPoint centered: centered action: aBlock initialAnswer: aString

"Answer an Instance of me whose question Is messageString. Once the
user provides an answer, then evaluate aBlock. If centered, a Boolean, is
false, display the view of the instance at aPoint; otherwise display it with Its center
at aPoint."

l newBlank l
newBlank ← self new initialize.
newBlank action: aBlock.
newBlank contents: aString.
FillInTheBlankView
    openOn: newBlank
    message: messageString
    displayAt: aPoint
    centered: centered

System Browser

Interface-Prompt/And
Interface-Browser
Interface-Inspector
Interface-Debugger
Interface-File Model
Interface-Transcript
Interface-Projects

BinaryChoiceView
CRFillInTheBlankContr
FillInTheBlank
FillInTheBlankControll
FillInTheBlankView

instance creation
examples

example1
example2
example3
exampleA
exampleB
exampleC

instance   class

8 Jul 87 4:20:03 pm

example1

"Example waits for you to click red button somewhere on the screen.
Terminate by choosing menu command accept."

FillInTheBlank
    message: 'what is your name?'
    displayAt: Sensor waitButton
    centered: true
    action: [:answer | Transcript cr; show: answer]
    initialAnswer: 'L. J. Pinson'

"FillInTheBlank example1."

class

149

Figure 5.3 FillInTheBlank Prompter Using Class **Text**

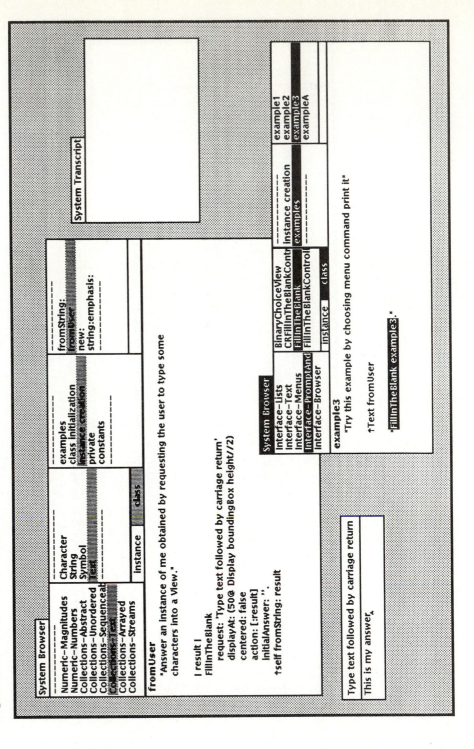

window can be accepted by entering a carriage return from the keyboard. The controller used by **example1** required that the middle-button menu option *accept* be selected.

The **example3** message is different in that it uses protocol in a different class, **Text,** for creating an instance of **FillInTheBlank.** Figure 5.3 shows the result of executing **example3.** Note that it sends the message fromUser to the class name **Text.** Details of the message fromUser, shown in the upper left browser in Figure 5.3, indicate that it calls one of the instance creation messages available in class **FillInTheBlank.**

Note that the message in fromUser sent to **FillInTheBlank** begins with the selector request:. This means that the prompter window requires a response before any other action can be taken by the user. The message sent by **example1** began with the selector message:. Recall that it could be responded to or ignored.

Finally, if **example3** was executed with *print it,* as suggested in its comment, the result is **Text** for 'This is my answer.' It would appear immediately to the right of the expression **FillInTheBlank example3,** in the lower right browser in Figure 5.3.

5.1.1 Protocol summary for classes **BinaryChoice** and **FillInTheBlank**

Brief summaries are given here of the protocol provided in classes **BinaryChoice** and **FillInTheBlank.** More complete protocol summaries are given in Appendix 3.

Protocol Summary for Class **BinaryChoice**

Class **BinaryChoice** is used when there is a need to prompt the user with a message to which the answer is yes or no. Options within this class provide alternatives for executing a block of expressions dependent on which response the user makes. It also provides a message for simply returning true or false, with no other actions taken.

The hierarchy for class **BinaryChoice** is **Object—BinaryChoice.** It has three instance variables, trueAction, falseAction, and actionTaken. It has no class variables or pool dictionaries. It has six class methods in two categories and seven instance methods in three categories. **BinaryChoice** also inherits protocol from its superclasses (both classes and metaclasses).

The three instance variables have the following descriptions. Instance variable **trueAction** is an instance of **BlockContext,** representing a sequence of expressions to execute if the positive choice is made. Instance variable **falseAction** is an instance of **BlockContext,** representing the sequence of expressions to execute if a negative choice is made. And instance variable **actionTaken** is an instance of **Boolean** that is true or false depending on which action has been taken.

Protocol Summary for Class **FillInTheBlank**

Class **FillInTheBlank** provides options not only for prompting the user with instructions, but also for accepting a response in the form of a string entered by the user in the prompter window. Appropriate conversions must be applied to the response string for information that is to be interpreted as other kinds of objects; e.g., numbers.

The hierarchy for class **FillInTheBlank** is **Object—StringHolder—FillInThe-Blank.** It has two instance variables, actionBlock and actionTaken. It has no class variables or pool dictionaries. It has nine class methods in two categories and five instance methods in three categories.

FillInTheBlank has two instance variables with the following descriptions. Instance variable **actionBlock** is an instance of **BlockContext,** representing a sequence of expressions to execute with the user response as a parameter. Instance variable **actionTaken** is an instance of **Boolean** that is true or false depending on whether the action block has been executed at least once.

5.1.2   More examples of prompted user response

In this section examples are given for most of the instance creation methods in classes **BinaryChoice** and **FillInTheBlank.**

BinaryChoice Example 5A

This is the most generic of the examples for **BinaryChoice.** It sends the instance creation message **message: displayAt: centered: ifTrue: ifFalse:** to its own class name. This message provides the most flexibility in terms of how to display the prompter window and what responses can be handled.

```
BinaryChoice methodsFor: 'examples'
    example1
        BinaryChoice
            message: 'Most generic instance creation.'
            displayAt: 1050@700
            centered: true
            ifTrue: [Transcript show: 'You selected yes']
            ifFalse:[Transcript show: 'You selected no']
        "BinaryChoice example1"
```

The preceding example displays a binary choice prompter window with the message 'Most generic instance creation'. The window is centered about point

1050@700 on the screen. If the user selects *yes* the string, 'You selected yes' is displayed in the System Transcript. If the user selects *no* the string 'You selected no' is displayed in the System Transcript.

The following example uses a different prompt message and does not center the prompter view about point 1050@700. Rather it displays the prompter view with its upper left origin at the specified point. This example sends the message **message: displayAt: ifTrue: ifFalse:** to **BinaryChoice.** An examination of the details of this message reveals that it sends the same message as **example1** above, with the parameter for the message selector **centered:** set to **false.**

BinaryChoice Example 5B

BinaryChoice methodsFor: 'examples'
   example2
       BinaryChoice
             message: 'Example 1 without Prompter centered.'
             displayAt: 1050@700
             ifTrue: [Transcript show: 'You selected yes']
             ifFalse:[Transcript show: 'You selected no']
       "BinaryChoice example2"

A third example uses another of the instance creation messages, **message: displayAt: ifTrue:**. It displays the prompter view without centering and takes no action for a *no* response. This message also calls the message in **example1**, with parameters **false** for **centered:** and **[nil]** for **ifFalse:**.

BinaryChoice Example 5C

BinaryChoice *methodsFor:* 'examples'
   example3
       BinaryChoice
             message: 'Nothing happens for No.'
             displayAt: 1050@700
             ifTrue: [Transcript show: 'You selected yes']
       "BinaryChoice example3"

The following example is similar to **example3**, except that nothing happens for a *yes* response. In this case the message from **example1** is sent with the parameter **[nil]** for the message selector **ifTrue:**.

BinaryChoice Example 5D

BinaryChoice methodsFor: 'examples'
   example4
      BinaryChoice
            message: 'Nothing happens for Yes.'
            displayAt: 1050@700
            ifFalse: [Transcript show: 'You selected no']
      "BinaryChoice example4"

A fifth example illustrates the simplest of all the **BinaryChoice** messages, with the fewest options. It returns either a true or false depending on whether the user response is *yes* or *no,* respectively. The prompter window is centered about the current location of the cursor. Addition of the return symbol (up arrow) in this example allows the user to obtain the result (true or false) by executing this example with *print it.*

BinaryChoice Example 5E

BinaryChoice methodsFor: 'examples'
   example5
      ↑ BinaryChoice
            message: 'Are you learning Smalltalk.'
      "BinaryChoice example5"

Details of the method for **message:** are given below. Note that the only parameter in the method that is not predetermined is **messageString**.

BinaryChoice methodsFor: 'instance creation'
   message: messageString
      "Answer an instance of me whose question is messageString. If the user answers yes, return true. If the user answers no, return false. Center the prompter window about the current cursor location."
      self
            message: messageString
            displayAt: Sensor cursorPoint
            centered: true
            ifTrue: [↑ true]
            ifFalse:[↑ false]

One of the fundamental instance creation messages in **FillInTheBlank** is the message **request: displayAt; centered: action: initialAnswer: useCRController:.** It provides the most flexibility for prompting the user for a required response. Three other instance creation messages form a four-level hierarchy with this message.

The messages become simpler with fewer options. The following four examples illustrate increasingly simpler messages with less flexibility.

FillInTheBlank Example 5A

FillInTheBlank methodsFor: 'examples'
  exampleA
      "Example waits for user to click red button somewhere on screen. Terminate by
      choosing menu command accept. Return user response as a number."
      | aNumber |
      ↑ aNumber ← FillInTheBlank
              request: 'Enter number of iterations.'
              displayAt: Sensor waitButton
              centered: true
              action: [:answer | ↑ answer asNumber]
              initialAnswer: '10'
              useCRController: false
      " FillInTheBlank exampleA"

The **action:** part of the preceding message above causes the block following it to be sent the message **value:**, with the user response as a parameter. Specifically, **aNumber** is assigned the user response interpreted as a number.

The next example loses the flexibility of whether to use the **CRController** or not. It defaults to **true**, meaning that the user can accept a response by either the command menu *accept* or by entering a carriage return (*cr*).

FillInTheBlank Example 5B

FillInTheBlank methodsFor: 'examples'
  exampleB
      "Example waits for user to click red button somewhere on screen. Terminate by
      choosing menu command accept or by a cr. Return user response as a number."
      | aNumber |
      ↑ aNumber ← FillInTheBlank
              request: 'Enter number of iterations.'
              displayAt: Sensor waitButton
              centered: true
              action: [:answer | ↑ answer asNumber]
              initialAnswer: '10'
      " FillInTheBlank exampleB"

The third example allows the user to specify only a message and initial response. It defaults to displaying the prompter centered about the current cursor position and to accepting with a carriage return. Note that no action is specified for the user response. The action described in details of this method is to simply return the user response, which will be a string. The example returns a number by sending the message **asNumber** to the string returned by the message to **FillInTheBlank.**

FillInTheBlank Example 5C

FillInTheBlank methodsFor: 'examples'
    exampleC
        "Example centers prompter about current cursor position. Terminate by choosing menu command accept or by a cr. Return user response as a number."
        | aNumber |
        ↑ aNumber ← (FillInTheBlank
                request: 'Enter number of iterations.'
                initialAnswer: '10') asNumber
       " FillInTheBlank exampleC"

A fourth example is the simplest of the request messages. It is similar to **FillInTheBlank** Example 5C except that a default value is no longer specified.

FillInTheBlank Example 5D

FillInTheBlank methodsFor: 'examples'
    exampleD
        "Example centers prompter about current cursor position. Terminate by choosing menu command accept or by a cr. Return user response as a number."
        | aNumber |
        ↑ aNumber ← (FillInTheBlank
                request: 'Enter number of iterations.') asNumber
       " FillInTheBlank exampleD"

An illustration of the instance creation message **message: displayAt: centered: action: initialAnswer:** was given as **example1** in Figure 5.2. The examples given should be sufficient for enabling the reader to construct custom prompter windows.

5.2   Sending Text to the Screen

This section describes the methods available for output to the System Transcript window as well as other classes and methods for displaying text results on the screen. Methods in class **Form** and its related classes are introduced that control the entire display screen.

Smalltalk provides rich support for text, with stylized variation. However, for simple display, there is no need to study all the protocol of classes supporting text manipulation. The beginning Smalltalk user initially has need only for an ability to display textual output on the screen.

Simple screen output is accomplished rather painlessly with messages sent to objects of either class **String** or class **TextCollector** (**Transcript** is a global variable that is an instance of **TextCollector**). Most program operation results that need to be displayed on the screen can be easily converted to strings with existing methods in the Smalltalk image. These strings are then displayed on the screen, using the message displayAt: from class **String.** They can also be displayed in the System Transcript window by sending various messages to **Transcript.**

It is possible to specify an "output" window using messages defined in class **Rectangle** (as well as class **View** and its subclasses). Then text can be displayed in the output window. Although not essential, this approach is certainly aesthetically pleasing. Using views requires an understanding of the MVC triad, and no examples of that approach are given in this chapter.

The following examples illustrate sending text to the display screen without reference to a window and sending text to two kinds of windows. Sending text to the System Transcript window is easy because protocol already exists to support it. Sending text to a rectangular window defined as an instance of class **Rectangle** requires the user to specify coordinates that fall inside the window.

5.2.1   Displaying strings anywhere on the screen

Class **String** provides two messages that support the display of text at any location on the screen. They are displayAt: and displayOn: at:. Details of the methods for these two messages are given below.

String methodsFor: 'displaying'
    displayAt: aPoint
        "Show representation of the receiver as DisplayText at location aPoint on
            the screen."
        self asDisplayText displayAt: aPoint
    displayOn: aDisplayMedium **at:** aPoint
        "Show representation of the receiver as DisplayText at location aPoint on
            aDisplayMedium."
        self asDisplayText displayOn: aDisplayMedium at: aPoint

The first message always refers to the display screen. The second refers to a specified display medium (an instance of class **DisplayMedium** or its subclasses) that may or may not be the display screen. The parameter aPoint is always relative to the coordinate origin of aDisplayMedium. Note that both methods convert the string represented by **self** to an instance of class **DisplayText** using the message asDisplayText. The resulting display text is then sent an appropriate message from the protocol of **DisplayText.**

The display location, aPoint, can be specified in a number of ways. One way is to specify a literal value for an instance of class **Point,** such as 100@200. A second way to specify a value for **aPoint** is to use the mouse. Whenever the mouse is moved to a position and the left button clicked, the result is a point. The following two examples illustrate the use of these methods for sending text to the screen.

Strings, as literals or instances of the class, **String,** may be sent the message displayAt: or displayOn: at: for sending the receiver to the display screen. Two examples are added as class methods under the category '*display and print examples*' in class **String,** illustrating the use of these two messages.

String Example 5A

String class methodsFor: 'display and print examples'
> **example**
> > "Displaying strings on the screen at the cursor location."
> > "To see the string displayed at the cursor point, execute this expression and select a point by pressing a mouse button."
> > 'This is text to be displayed at a mouse-selected point.'
> > > displayOn: Display at: Sensor waitButton
> > " String example"
> **example1**
> > "Displaying strings at a specified point on the screen."
> > "To see the string displayed at the specified point, execute the expression."
> > 'Display text at a specified point.' displayAt: 0@0
> > " String example1 "

The first example above shows how the cursor can be used with the mouse buttons to determine where the string is to be displayed. In the example the string is displayed on **Display,** thus it could have been implemented with the message displayAt: just as easily. The second example illustrates a message that always refers to **Display** and that allows the user to specify a point. In **example1,** the string will be displayed with its upper left boundary at location 0@0.

5.2.2   Displaying text in the Transcript window

Protocol for the Transcript window is given in class **TextCollector,** and messages to the Transcript window are sent to the global variable **Transcript** (**Transcript** is an instance of **TextCollector**). An example of the use of the Transcript window for program output was given in Chapter 3. This section begins with a summary of the protocol for **TextCollector** and then gives examples of its use for displaying program text output.

Protocol Summary for Class **TextCollector**

Class **TextCollector** provides options for displaying text or objects as streams in the System Transcript window. It provides the most convenient protocol for displaying the result of programs.

Definition—The hierarchy for class **TextCollector** is **Object—StringHolder—TextCollector.** It has one instance variable, entryStream. It has no class variables or pool dictionaries. Aside from examples as class methods, it has 1 class method in one category. It has 20 instance methods in seven categories.

Private data—Class **TextCollector** has one instance variable.
   entryStream—an instance of **WriteStream,** representing a stream of characters to be displayed in the System Transcript window. This makes it possible to build and display a text message with the help of the protocol in the stream classes also. This is particularly important for displaying representations of noncharacter objects.

Instance methods—There are 20 instance methods in seven categories. They provide a minimal set of protocol for displaying text in the Transcript window. The categories and corresponding number of methods are:
   initialize-release—One method, **initialize,** sets the value for the instance variable entryStream by creating a new instance of a **WriteStream.** It also initializes inherited instance variables from its superclass, **StringHolder.**
   accessing—four methods for adding characters or collections of characters to the entryStream. One method, **show:,** also includes protocol for actually displaying the resultant entryStream.
   clearing—two methods, **clear** and **refresh,** that initialize the Transcript window to contain no characters and bring the window to the front on the screen, respectively.
   entry control—four methods for controlling the contents of entryStream. Included are messages for creating, adding to, accessing, or displaying the contents of entryStream.
   character writing—five methods for appending carriage return, space, or tabs to entryStream.
   printing—two methods for handling objects that are not character strings. These methods send messages that convert the object to a string of characters and then append the character representation to entryStream.
   private—two methods that set size limits and default contents for entryStream.

Class methods—There is one method in one category. However, a number of example methods are also added in the category *examples* to illustrate the use of **TextCollector** protocol.
   system—one method, **newTranscript:,** used by the Smalltalk system to create an instance of **TextCollector,** called **Transcript,** as a global variable.

The following examples have been added as class methods in **TextCollector** to illustrate the use of messages for displaying results in the Transcript window.

Transcript Example 5A

Figure 5.4 illustrates the messages that deal with characters or strings of characters directly. It shows the result of evaluating the message **example1**.

Transcript Example 5B

Figure 5.5 shows examples of how noncharacter objects are displayed in the Transcript window using the message print: with a noncharacter object as a parameter. It shows the result of evaluating the message **example2**. This use of print is illustrated with the number and literal array examples. A second way of displaying noncharacter objects is to convert an object to a string using the message printString. It can then be displayed using character-specific messages, as illustrated with the display of the default size limit, which is an integer object.

Figure 5.4
Example for
Display of
Characters and
Strings in
Transcript Window

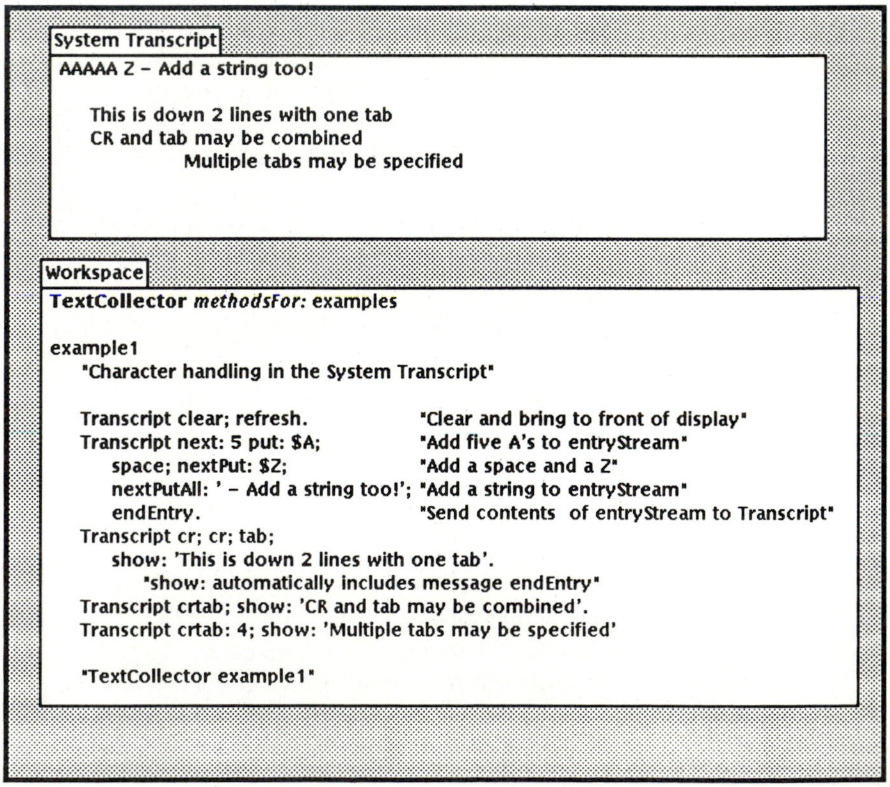

```
┌─────────────────────────────────────────────────────┐
│  System Transcript                                    │
│  AAAAA Z – Add a string too!                          │
│                                                        │
│     This is down 2 lines with one tab                 │
│     CR and tab may be combined                        │
│                 Multiple tabs may be specified         │
│                                                        │
└─────────────────────────────────────────────────────┘

┌─────────────────────────────────────────────────────┐
│  Workspace                                            │
│  TextCollector methodsFor: examples                   │
│                                                        │
│  example1                                             │
│      "Character handling in the System Transcript"    │
│                                                        │
│      Transcript clear; refresh.          "Clear and bring to front of display" │
│      Transcript next: 5 put: $A;         "Add five A's to entryStream"          │
│         space; nextPut: $Z;              "Add a space and a Z"                   │
│         nextPutAll: ' – Add a string too!'; "Add a string to entryStream"       │
│         endEntry.                        "Send contents  of entryStream to Transcript" │
│      Transcript cr; cr; tab;                          │
│         show: 'This is down 2 lines with one tab'.    │
│            "show: automatically includes message endEntry" │
│      Transcript crtab; show: 'CR and tab may be combined'. │
│      Transcript crtab: 4; show: 'Multiple tabs may be specified' │
│                                                        │
│      "TextCollector example1"                         │
└─────────────────────────────────────────────────────┘
```

Figure 5.5
Example for
Display of
Noncharacter
Objects in
Transcript Window

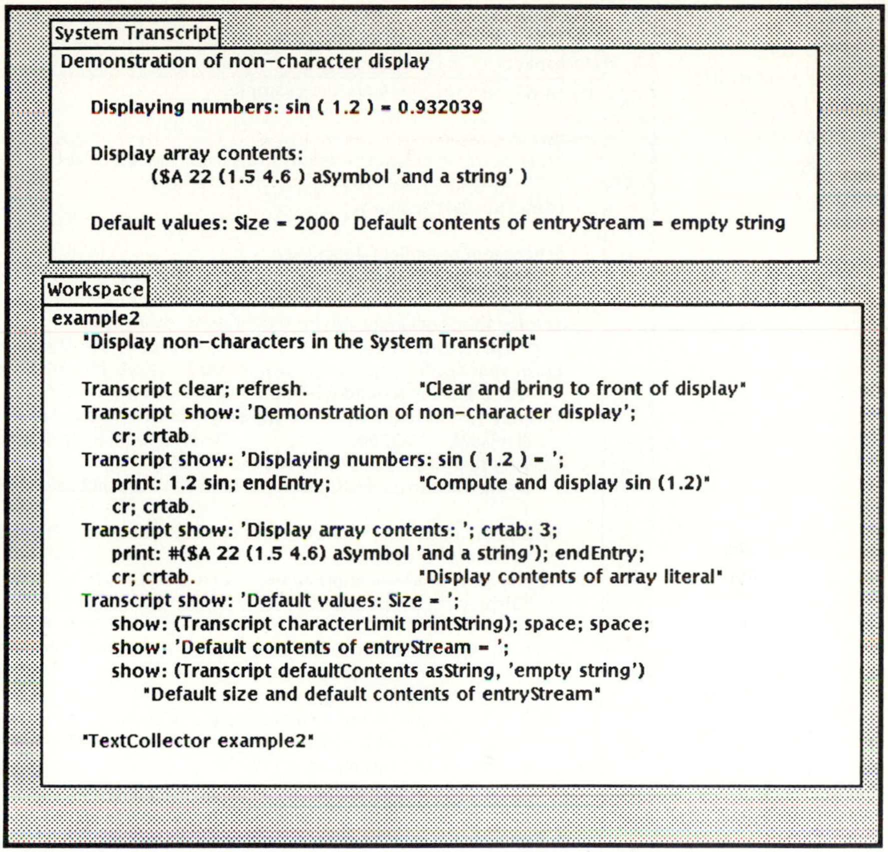

```
┌─────────────────────────────────────────────────────────────┐
│  System Transcript                                            │
│  ┌─────────────────────────────────────────────────────────┐ │
│  │ Demonstration of non-character display                  │ │
│  │                                                         │ │
│  │    Displaying numbers: sin ( 1.2 ) = 0.932039           │ │
│  │                                                         │ │
│  │    Display array contents:                              │ │
│  │         ($A 22 (1.5 4.6 ) aSymbol 'and a string' )      │ │
│  │                                                         │ │
│  │    Default values: Size = 2000  Default contents of     │ │
│  │                     entryStream = empty string          │ │
│  └─────────────────────────────────────────────────────────┘ │
│  Workspace                                                    │
│  ┌─────────────────────────────────────────────────────────┐ │
│  │ example2                                                │ │
│  │   "Display non-characters in the System Transcript"     │ │
│  │                                                         │ │
│  │   Transcript clear; refresh.       "Clear and bring to  │ │
│  │                                     front of display"   │ │
│  │   Transcript  show: 'Demonstration of non-character     │ │
│  │       display';                                         │ │
│  │       cr; crtab.                                        │ │
│  │   Transcript show: 'Displaying numbers: sin ( 1.2 ) = ';│ │
│  │       print: 1.2 sin; endEntry;    "Compute and display │ │
│  │                                     sin (1.2)"          │ │
│  │       cr; crtab.                                        │ │
│  │   Transcript show: 'Display array contents: '; crtab: 3;│ │
│  │       print: #($A 22 (1.5 4.6) aSymbol 'and a string'); │ │
│  │       endEntry;                                         │ │
│  │       cr; crtab.                   "Display contents of  │ │
│  │                                    array literal"       │ │
│  │   Transcript show: 'Default values: Size = ';           │ │
│  │       show: (Transcript characterLimit printString);    │ │
│  │       space; space;                                     │ │
│  │       show: 'Default contents of entryStream = ';       │ │
│  │       show: (Transcript defaultContents asString,       │ │
│  │       'empty string')                                   │ │
│  │          "Default size and default contents of          │ │
│  │          entryStream"                                   │ │
│  │                                                         │ │
│  │   "TextCollector example2"                              │ │
│  └─────────────────────────────────────────────────────────┘ │
└─────────────────────────────────────────────────────────────┘
```

5.2.3   Displaying text in user-defined windows

This section illustrates some of the capability provided for defining windows and displaying text within those windows. It involves messages sent to a number of classes that deal with the display screen. Keep in mind that the examples given are only a small subset of the possible ways to creatively send display text to the screen. The classes that are important to the development of an understanding of these examples are the following:

- **ControlManager**—The global variable **ScheduledControllers** is an instance of this class. It keeps track of all active windows on the display screen, among other things. Messages sent to **ScheduledControllers** are essential to the display of text within user-specified windows and to subsequent restoration of the original screen view.

- **DisplayScreen** *and Its Superclasses*—The global variable **Display** is an instance of class **DisplayScreen.** It represents the physical display screen. Code for displaying anything on the screen eventually must send messages to **Display.**

Figure 5.6
Example for
Sending Text to the
Display Screen
with User-Defined
Windows

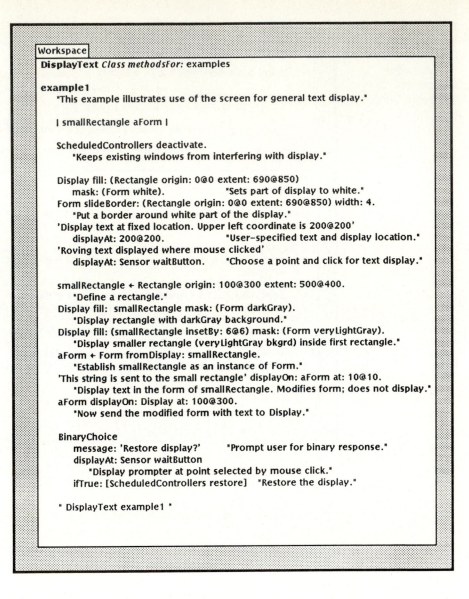

```
Workspace

DisplayText Class methodsFor: examples

example1
    "This example illustrates use of the screen for general text display."

    | smallRectangle aForm |

    ScheduledControllers deactivate.
        "Keeps existing windows from interfering with display."

    Display fill: (Rectangle origin: 0@0 extent: 690@850)
        mask: (Form white).          "Sets part of display to white."
    Form slideBorder: (Rectangle origin: 0@0 extent: 690@850) width: 4.
        "Put a border around white part of the display."
    'Display text at fixed location. Upper left coordinate is 200@200'
        displayAt: 200@200.          "User-specified text and display location."
    'Roving text displayed where mouse clicked'
        displayAt: Sensor waitButton.     "Choose a point and click for text display."

    smallRectangle ← Rectangle origin: 100@300 extent: 500@400.
        "Define a rectangle."
    Display fill:  smallRectangle mask: (Form darkGray).
        "Display rectangle with darkGray background."
    Display fill: (smallRectangle insetBy: 6@6) mask: (Form veryLightGray).
        "Display smaller rectangle (veryLightGray bkgrd) inside first rectangle."
    aForm ← Form fromDisplay: smallRectangle.
        "Establish smallRectangle as an instance of Form."
    'This string is sent to the small rectangle' displayOn: aForm at: 10@10.
        "Display text in the form of smallRectangle. Modifies form; does not display."
    aForm displayOn: Display at: 100@300.
        "Now send the modified form with text to Display."

    BinaryChoice
        message: 'Restore display?'       "Prompt user for binary response."
        displayAt: Sensor waitButton
            "Display prompter at point selected by mouse click."
        ifTrue: [ScheduledControllers restore]    "Restore the display."

    " DisplayText example1 "
```

- **Form**—a superclass of **DisplayScreen** that has protocol for defining rect-angular display areas (using protocol from class **Rectangle**) with specified bordering and background characteristics.

- **Rectangle**—Contains protocol for defining a rectangle.

- **DisplayText**—This is the class that represents textual objects to be dis-played on the screen. The examples given below are implemented as class methods in **DisplayText.**

Figure 5.6 shows details of the method for example1 in class **DisplayText.** It illustrates methods for performing the following operations.

Figure 5.7
Result of
DisplayText
example1

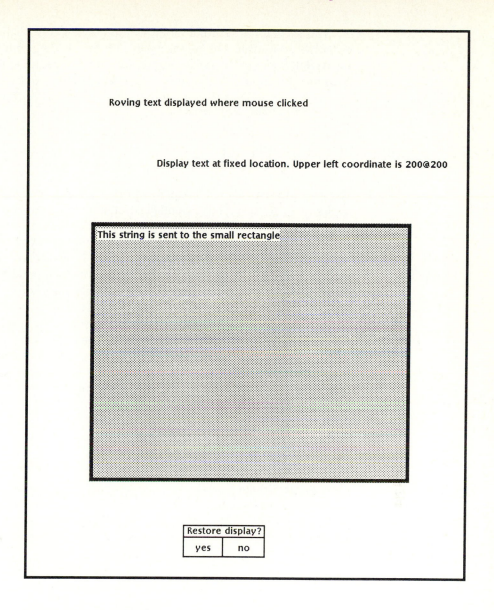

1. Clearing the display
2. Displaying text on the cleared screen (1) at a specified point, and (2) at a point selected by the mouse
3. Specifying a rectangular window
4. Displaying text in the rectangular window at coordinates relative to the upper left corner
5. Restoring the display (from a binary choice prompter)

Figure 5.7 shows the result of evaluating **DisplayText** example1.

This section has shown a variety of ways to send text to the display screen. By far the easiest way is to use the protocol for interacting with the global object **Transcript.** Some of the details required in the last example for defining windows are also applicable to graphics applications as discussed in Chapter 9.

5.3   Sending Text to the Printer

The ability to send textual output to a printer is fundamental to most computer applications. However, this capability is not part of the standard Smalltalk image. Since most operating systems treat printers as files with special names, it is relatively easy to add printer capability to Smalltalk by building on the existing file handling classes. Class **PrinterStream** is added as a subclass of **WriteStream.** It inherits existing protocol from **WriteStream** and its superclasses. Additionally, **PrinterStream** defines new protocol for controlling the mode and fonts of the printer.

In this section, a complete summary is given of the protocol for **PrinterStream.** In addition, several methods are described in detail, and examples are given of the use of **PrinterStream.** A single instance of **PrinterStream** is installed in **Smalltalk** as the global variable **Printer.** This decision plus the choice of selected class variables indicates a system with only one printer. Modifications to support multiple printers could be easily made.

Protocol Summary for Class **PrinterStream**

Class **PrinterStream** provides protocol for sending text and control codes to a printer. It depends on the fundamental method outputToPrinter, defined earlier as new protocol for class **String.** The purpose of most methods in class **PrinterStream** is to build streams of characters that can be sent to a printer (by outputToPrinter) for both control and display of text.

Definition—The hierarchy for class **PrinterStream** is **Object—Stream—PositionableStream—WriteStream—PrinterStream.** It has two instance variables, fileDescriptor and currentFont. It has six class variables, DefaultFont, DefaultMode, DeviceID, El, Esc, and PrinterType. It has no pool dictionaries. It has 67 class methods in four categories and 75 instance methods in six categories.

Private data—Class **PrinterStream** has two instance variables.

    fileDescriptor—an instance of **SmallInteger,** representing a code assigned by the operating system to the **FileStream** representing the printer. This instance variable is assigned a value by a message sent to class **TekSystemCall** (or the appropriate class representing the operating system).

    currentFont—an instance of **String** that is the appropriate control sequence for the current printer font. Its value is updated every time the font is changed.

Shared data—Class **PrinterStream** has six class variables.

DefaultFont—an instance of **String** that is the control sequence for the default font.

DefaultMode—an instance of **String** that may consist of several control codes for establishing default printer options.

DeviceID—an instance of **String** that is the device identification required by the resident operating system for the printer. (In the uniflex operating system on the Tektronix 4406, the device id is */dev/printer.*)

El—a character representing the lower case of the letter *L*. This is defined only as a convenience for easy distinction between lowercase el and the numeral one.

Esc—the escape character (ASCII code 27) represented as an instance of **Character.** Many printers use escape sequences for control codes.

PrinterType—an instance of **String** that simply identifies the type of printer; e.g., *'HP Laserjet II'.*

Instance methods—There are 75 instance methods in seven categories. Many of these methods deal with sending control codes to the printer for changing fonts or other features. The large number of methods is a result of the rich set of features available on the HP Laserjet II printer. The categories and corresponding number of methods are:

initialize—one method, **reset,** that must always be the first message sent to an instance of class **PrinterStream.** It resets the printer and establishes default values. More importantly, it attaches a valid file descriptor to the printer device string. All references to the printer must be through this file descriptor.

accessing—six methods for adding characters or collections of characters to the **PrinterStream** or accessing values of the two instance variables.

printer mode—seven methods for setting portrait, landscape, or graphics mode. Also included are methods for controlling the graphics mode.

printer control—seventeen methods for controlling printer parameters such as left margin, underline, bold, italic, cursor location, and graphic resolution in dots per inch.

fonts—thirty-nine methods for setting fonts. These include a number of downloadable fonts.

private—five methods used by other methods for opening and closing the printer (remember it acts like a file) and for setting fonts or mode parameters.

Class methods—There are 67 methods in four categories. Most of these methods simply establish a string of control characters for setting fonts and setting printer parameters. They are given in class methods to localize the effects of a specific printer on the overall functionality provided by **PrinterStream.** The class can be adapted to other printers by redefining the code sequences given in these class methods.

initialize—two methods—**new,** which establishes values for the class variables and returns an instance of **PrinterStream,** and **initialize,** which establishes global variable **Printer** as an instance of **PrinterStream.**

general escape codes—twenty-eight methods that return escape code sequences for controlling parameters of the printer.

times roman softfont—eighteen methods that return escape code sequences for setting each of 18 variations of the Times Roman downloadable soft font.

helvetica softfont—eighteen methods that return escape code sequences for setting each of 18 variations of the Helvetica downloadable soft font.

As a part of the initial installation of **PrinterStream,** one must install the global variable **Printer** in the Smalltalk system dictionary as an instance of **PrinterStream.** Thereafter, using the printer requires sending the message **reset** to the object **Printer.** This invokes several other message expressions that get the printer ready to receive text.

PrinterStream Example 5A—Initializing the Printer

The message sequence given in Listing 5.1 is invoked by the user sending the following messages:

```
PrinterStream initialize.
Printer reset.
```

PrinterStream Example 5B—Sending Characters and Strings to the Printer

With the message outputToPrinter already installed in class **String,** it should be a simple process to send strings to the printer. The message nextPutAll:, with aString as the single parameter, does send aString to the printer.

The details of the method for this message are complicated by the fact that Smalltalk source code uses some special symbols that are not part of the standard lower ASCII set of characters. The left arrow is used for assignment, and the up arrow is used to denote a return. In order to display these symbols correctly when printing Smalltalk source code, it is necessary to trap them and change to a font that supports their display. (Note: Not all printers support such font descriptions.) Listing 5.2 shows the details of methods for sending a character or a string to the printer.

Listing 5.1
Initializing the
Printer for Text
Output from
Smalltalk—
Message
Sequence

PrinterStream class methodsFor: 'initialize'

initialize
    Printer ← PrinterStream new

    "PrinterStream initialize"

new
    DeviceID ← '/dev/printer'.
    PrinterType ← 'HPLaserjet II'.
    Esc ← String with: (27 asCharacter).
    El ← String with: (108 asCharacter).
    DefaultMode ← self crlf, self sop, self lineWrap, self portrait.
    DefaultFont ← self hv100rpn.
    ↑self basicNew

PrinterStream methodsFor: ' initialize'

reset
    "Must be first message to Printer - use only once."
    self open.
    (Esc, 'E') outputToPrinter.
    self normal

PrinterStream methodsFor: 'private'

open
    "Open the printer device if not already open-- get a valid fileDescriptor."
    (TekSystemCall validFileDescriptor: fileDescriptor) ifFalse:
        [fileDescriptor ← TekSystemCall openForWrite: DeviceID]

normal
    self setPrinter: DefaultMode.
    self defaultFont

In Listing 5.2, the method for **nextPut:** shows how special symbols are trapped. If the symbol is a left arrow, then **aString** is a concatenated escape sequence that first changes fonts and displays the left arrow (**assignString** does this) and then resets the font to its previous state (**currentFont** does this). A similar sequence of operations using **returnString** prints the up arrow. If the character is not a left arrow or an up arrow, then it is simply sent to the printer as a one-character string.

In the method for **nextPutAll:**, the input string **aString** is first scanned for occurrences of the left arrow and up arrow. At each occurrence, a sequence of control characters is inserted into the string to change fonts, display the symbol, and return to the current font.

An example illustrating the use of various messages in class **PrinterStream** is

Listing 5.2
Trapping Special
Symbols and
Changing Fonts
to Print Them

PrinterStream methodsFor: 'accessing'

nextPut: aChar
  "Output aChar to the printer. Special since DefaultFont does not include left arrow or up
     arrow."
  | aString |
  (aChar = $←) ifTrue: [aString ← (PrinterStream assignString, currentFont)].
  (aChar = $↑) ifTrue: [aString ← (PrinterStream returnString, currentFont)].
  (aChar = $←) | (aChar = $↑)
     ifFalse: [aString ← String with: $.
        aString at: 1 put: aChar].
  aString outputToPrinter.

nextPutAll: aString
  "Output aString to the printer. Special since DefaultFont does not include left arrow or up
     arrow. "
  | outString |
  outString ← String new.
  aString do: [:aChar |
     (aChar = $←) ifTrue: [
        outString ← outString, PrinterStream assignString, currentFont].
     (aChar = $↑) ifTrue: [outString ← outString, PrinterStream returnString, currentFont].
     (aChar = $←) | (aChar = $↑)
        ifFalse: [outString ← outString, (String with: aChar)]].
  outString outputToPrinter

Listing 5.3
Example Method
for Illustrating
PrinterStream
Protocol

PrinterStream class methodsFor: 'examples'

example
  "Illustrate the protocol for sending text to a printer."

  Printer reset.
  Printer tab: 10;
     nextPutAll: 'Listing 5.4 Result of Evaluating the PrinterStream Example Method'.
  Printer hv140bpn.
  Printer cr; tab: 5;
     nextPutAll: '--'.
  Printer cr; cr; tab: 15.
  Printer tab: 5; nextPutAll: 'This title is 14 point Helvetica bold face.'.
  Printer cr; cr; defaultFont; tab: 15.
     'This is default font (10 point Helvetica) with a tab of 15.' outputToPrinter.
  Printer bo; cr; cr; tab: 15.
     'This is default font size in bold face with tab of 15.' outputToPrinter.
  Printer kb; it; cr; cr; tab: 15;
     nextPutAll: 'This is default font size in italics with tab of 15.'.
  Printer cr; cr; cr; cr; hv060rpn; tab: 20; ul;
     nextPutAll:
        'This is 6 point Helvetica regular font, underlined and tabbed 20 little spaces.'.
  Printer ku; hv140bpn; cr; cr; tab: 5;
     nextPutAll: '--'.
  Printer ff

  " PrinterStream example "

This title is 14 point Helvetica bold face.

This is default font (10 point Helvetica) with a tab of 15.

This is default font size in bold face with tab of 15.

This is default font size in italics with tab of 15.

<u>This is 6 point Helvetica regular font, underlined and tabbed 20 little spaces.</u>

----

included as a class method in that class. Details of the method **example** are given in Listing 5.3, and the result of executing that example is included as Listing 5.4. The example exercises a subset of the available protocol.

The key messages and methods for adding printer capability to the Smalltalk image have been given in this section. Other methods for various font and printer control functions can be developed from these; this is left as an exercise for the reader.

5.4   Reading and Writing Text Files

Class **FileStream,** its subclass **FileDirectory,** and its superclasses support standard file input/output operations in Smalltalk. In this section a summary is given of the protocol for **FileStream.** Examples of reading from and writing to files are given, along with other file operations such as creating, opening, and closing files.

Protocol Summary for Class **FileStream**

Class **FileStream,** in conjunction with class **FileDirectory,** provides protocol for file manipulation. A more complete protocol summary for **FileStream** is given in Appendix 3.

The hierarchy for class **FileStream** is **Object—Stream—Positionable-Stream—WriteStream—ReadWriteStream—ExternalStream—FileStream.** It has six instance variables, name, directory, mode, fileDescriptor, filePosition, and file-Mode. It has three class variables, BufferSize, OpenFileStreams, and SystemCall. It has no pool dictionaries. It has 12 class methods in 3 categories and 67 instance methods in 16 categories. In addition, **FileStream** inherits protocol from all its superclasses.

Class **FileStream** has six instance variables with the following functions. Instance variable **name** is an instance of **String** identifying the file within a directory. Instance variable **directory** is an instance of **FileDirectory** containing the file. If the directory is unknown, this instance variable has a value of nil. Instance variable **mode** is an instance of **Symbol,** representing the mode of the file (e.g., #ReadOnly, #WriteOnly, #ReadWrite).

Instance variable **fileDescriptor** is an instance of **SmallInteger,** representing a code assigned by the operating system to the **FileStream.** This instance variable is assigned a value by a message sent to class **TekSystemCall** (or the appropriate class representing the operating system). Instance variable **filePosition** is an instance of **Integer,** representing the position within a file. Instance variable **fileMode** is an instance of **Symbol** indicating the current permission for the file-Descriptor of the file.

The three class variables in **FileStream** are: (1) **BufferSize**—an instance of **Integer** that is the size in bytes of the file buffer (default value is 1024), (2) **Open-FileStreams**— an instance of **OrderedCollection** (each time a new file is opened, it is added to this collection), and (3) **SystemCall**—set equal to the class name **TekSystemCall.**

FileStream Example 5A

This example deals with creating a text file, writing to a text file, and reading from a text file. It uses protocol from both **FileStream** and **FileDirectory** to illustrate the flexibility that is part of the Smalltalk image. The example is shown in Figure 5.8, along with the results of its execution in the Transcript window.

This example defines two instances of **FileStream** on the same file name, 'writeFile.txt'. This makes it possible to maintain two independent pointers into the file and to either access or modify its contents with messages to both text-File1 and textFile2.

Two instance creation messages are illustrated. The first, in class **FileStream,** creates a new file and attaches the file descriptor for textFile1 to that file name. If the file name already exists on the external medium, a notifier is displayed prompting the user for permission to redefine. The second instance creation method, from class **FileDirectory,** opens the file stream textFile2 on either an existing or new file with the name, 'writeFile.txt'.

The remainder of the example illustrates some of the protocol available to instances of class **FileStream.** It demonstrates that the independent pointers into textFile1 and textFile2 can be manipulated to achieve a variety of results.

Near the end of this example, the message **remove** is sent to textFile1. The effect of this message is to disassociate the file descriptor in textFile1 from the

Figure 5.8
Operations on Text
Files Using
Protocol in Class
FileStream

System Transcript

Name for textFile1: writeFile.txt

Name for textFile2: writeFile.txt

This is a string that is added to the file.

Changes a string that is added to the file.

 Add some to end.

Changes a STRING that is added to the file. Add some to end.

textFile1 is text file? true

textFile2 has lost its file.

Workspace

FileStream *methodsFor:* examples

example1

```
| textFile1  textFile2 |

textFile1 ← FileStream newFileNamed: 'writeFile.txt'.      "New write only file."
textFile2 ← FileDirectory currentDirectory file: 'writeFile.txt'.
    "Now we have a readWrite filestream on this file."
Transcript clear; refresh;
    show: 'Name for textFile1: ',textFile1 name.      "Both textFile1 & textFile2"
Transcript cr; cr;                                   "are attached to"
    show: 'Name for textFile2: ',textFile2 name.      "the same file name."

textFile1 nextPutAll: 'This is a string that is added to the file.'.
                                                "Can write using textFile1."
Transcript cr; cr;
    show: (textFile2 next: (textFile1 size)).  "and read using textFile2."
textFile1 reset;  nextPutAll: 'Change'.        "Move pointer to start and overwrite."
Transcript cr; cr;
    show: (textFile1 reset; next: (textFile1 size)).  "Effect of the overwrite."
textFile1 nextPutAll: ' Add some to end.'.        "Since pointer is at end."
Transcript cr; cr;
    show: (textFile2  next: 18).              "textFile2 pointer still at end of first part."
textFile2 position: 10; nextPutAll: 'STRING'. " Overwrite contents of position 10."
Transcript cr; cr;
    show: (textFile1 reset; next: (textFile2 size)).  "textFile1 reflects change."

Transcript cr; cr;
    show: ('textFile1 is text file? ',textFile1 isText printString).  "Type of textFile1"
textFile1 remove.                                "Remove 'writeFile.txt'."
textFile2 exists ifFalse: [
    Transcript cr; cr; show: 'textFile2 has lost its file.']. "Verfiy textFile2 is affected."

" FileStream example1 "
```

Figure 5.9 Operation on Integer Files Using Protocol in Classes **FileStream** and **ExternalStream**

Workspace

FileStream *methodsFor:* examples

example2

"Protocol for writing and reading is in class ExternalStream."

| integerFile |

Transcript clear; refresh.
integerFile ← Disk file: 'testFile.int'.
integerFile binary.
−5 to: 128000 by:30000 do: [:value | integerFile nextNumber: 4 put: value].
integerFile reset.
−5 to: 128000 by:30000 do: [:value | value + integerFile nextNumber: 4.
        Transcript cr; print: value; endEntry].

integerFile reset. Transcript cr.
100 to: 64000 by: 10000 do: [:value | integerFile nextWordPut: value].
integerFile reset.
100 to: 64000 by: 10000 do: [:value | value + integerFile nextWord.
        Transcript cr; print: value; endEntry].

integerFile reset. Transcript cr.
−2 to: 2 do: [:value | integerFile nextWordPut: value].
integerFile reset.
−2 to: 2 do: [:value | Transcript cr; print: (integerFile nextWord); endEntry].

integerFile reset. Transcript cr.
−2 to: 2 do: [:value | integerFile nextWordPut: value].
integerFile reset.
−2 to: 2 do: [:value | Transcript cr; print: (integerFile nextSignedInteger); endEntry].

" FileStream example2 "

System Transcript

5
29995
59995
89995
119995

100
10100
20100
30100
40100
50100
60100

65534   "Should be −2"
65535   "Should be −1"
0
1
2

−65538   "Should be −2"
−65537   "Should be −1"
0
1
2

file name 'writeFile.txt'. In addition it removes 'writeFile.txt' from the external medium. Although **textFile2** still has an active file descriptor, the file name to which it was associated has been removed. Thus, in effect, **textFile2** has also been removed.

The example in Figure 5.8 shows how Smalltalk code can be made more compact by cascading messages and by concatenating strings. The message expression **show:**('textFile1 is text file? ', textFile1 isText printString) concatenates the string literal with the result of **textFile1 isText printString**. The message **isText** returns a Boolean **true**, which must be converted to a string using **printString**. It can then be concatenated with the string literal as the parameter of **show:**.

FileStream Example 5B

This example shows how integers can be written to a binary file and read from the file. Protocol in class **ExternalStream** provides the messages for reading and writing for binary files in which the objects are interpreted as integers.

Figure 5.9 shows the details of method **example2a** in class **FileStream.** Results of execution of the example are shown in the Transcript window in that figure.

The object **integerFile** is established as an instance of **FileStream** by using the message **file:**, sent to **Disk. Disk** is a global variable that is an instance of **File-Directory.** The instance **integerFile** is converted to a binary file by sending it the message **binary**. All subsequent messages sent to **integerFile** assume the file represents an array of bytes instead of an array of characters.

The example has four parts that write different data sets into **integerFile** and then read and display the contents in the Transcript window. The results of the four parts are separated by an extra carriage return in the Transcript window display.

Part 1 demonstrates the use of messages for saving objects that have a specified number of bytes for their representation. In the example, four bytes are used to represent integer values ranging up to 128,000. As can be seen from the result of this part, it does not handle negative integers. The protocol description for these messages states that they are for positive integers only. The single negative value, −5, is simply treated as a positive value of 5.

Part 2 demonstrates the use of "word-size" messages (words are assumed to be two bytes). It provides a way to write and read two-byte integers. As can be seen by the results of Part 2, integers may range up to 65535 (or 60100 in the example). This implies that all 16 bits are interpreted as positive values only.

Part 3 verifies the conclusion about positive values only for the "word-size" messages. As is evident from the results for Part 3, this is inconsistent with the way that actual integer values are represented in the Smalltalk system. Clearly, the first two results obtained in Part 3 are two's complement representations for

Figure 5.10 Numbers and Binary Files Using Protocol in Classes **FileStream** and **ExternalStream**

```
workspace

FileStream methodsFor: examples

example3
    "Writing numbers to a binary file and reading numbers from a binary file."

    | writeStream number readStream |

    Transcript clear; refresh; show: 'Numbers and Binary Files';cr; cr.
    Transcript show: 'Integer numbers from a binary file'; cr.

    writeStream ← Disk file: 'strings.txt'.                    "Write integers to binary file"
    writeStream binary.
    12 to: 20 do: [:value | writeStream nextStringPut: value printString].
    writeStream close.

    readStream ← Disk file: 'strings.txt'.          "Read integers from binary file"
    readStream binary.
    12 to: 20 do: [ :number | number ← (readStream nextString) asNumber.
        Transcript cr; print: number; endEntry].

    Transcript cr; cr; show: 'Real numbers from a binary file'; cr.

    writeStream reset.                              "Write floats to binary file"
    12 to: 20 do: [:value | writeStream nextStringPut: value sin printString].
    writeStream close.

    readStream reset.                               "Read floats from binary file"
    12 to: 20 do: [ :number | number ← (readStream nextString) asNumber.
        Transcript cr; print: number; endEntry].

    " FileStream example3 "
```

```
System Transcript

Numbers and Binary Files

Integer numbers from a binary file

12
13
14
15
16
17
18
19
20

Real numbers from a binary file

-0.536573
0.420167
0.990607
0.650288
-0.287903
-0.961397
-0.750987
0.149877
0.912945
```

−2 and −1, respectively. Yet the message **nextWord** interpreted them as positive large integers.

An even stranger result is obtained for Part 4, using the message **nextSigned-Integer** to read the "word-size" quantities from the file. These inconsistencies in the way that integers are handled by the system and by the file messages make the use of this protocol risky. It is not clear that the problem is one of concept or of implementation.

The authors recommend the methods described in the next two examples for handling integer objects as well as other noncharacter objects for file input/output.

FileStream Example 5C

This is a better method for writing and reading numbers to and from a binary file. It handles both integers and floating point numbers. This example is shown in Figure 5.10 as the class method **example3**.

Results of executing the example are shown in the Transcript window in that figure. The messages **nextStringPut:** and **nextString** are the write and read messages, respectively. Both are part of the protocol of class **ExternalStream.** These two methods accept and return strings from and to the user. The strings are, however, stored on the file in binary form. Conversion of the returned string to a number is accomplished by the message **asNumber**, which is part of the protocol of class **String.**

A useful exercise is to add new protocol to class **FileStream,** in the form of new messages for handling file input/output of numbers. This would make the user interaction with files considerably simpler, if done properly.

The next example illustrates how noncharacter objects can be written to a file and read from a file. The approach is to store on the file a character representation that can be read in and used to reconstruct the object with all its private data. This approach is supported by the fact that most classes in the system have a message, **printOn:**, that stores a string representation for the object on a stream. Objects that have a complicated structure store a string representation that, when executed, reconstructs the object.

FileStream Example 5D

Figure 5.11 shows an example method for storing complex objects on an external file and for reconstructing the object from the file. Objects are stored on a

Figure 5.11
Text Files for
Object Storage and
Reconstruction

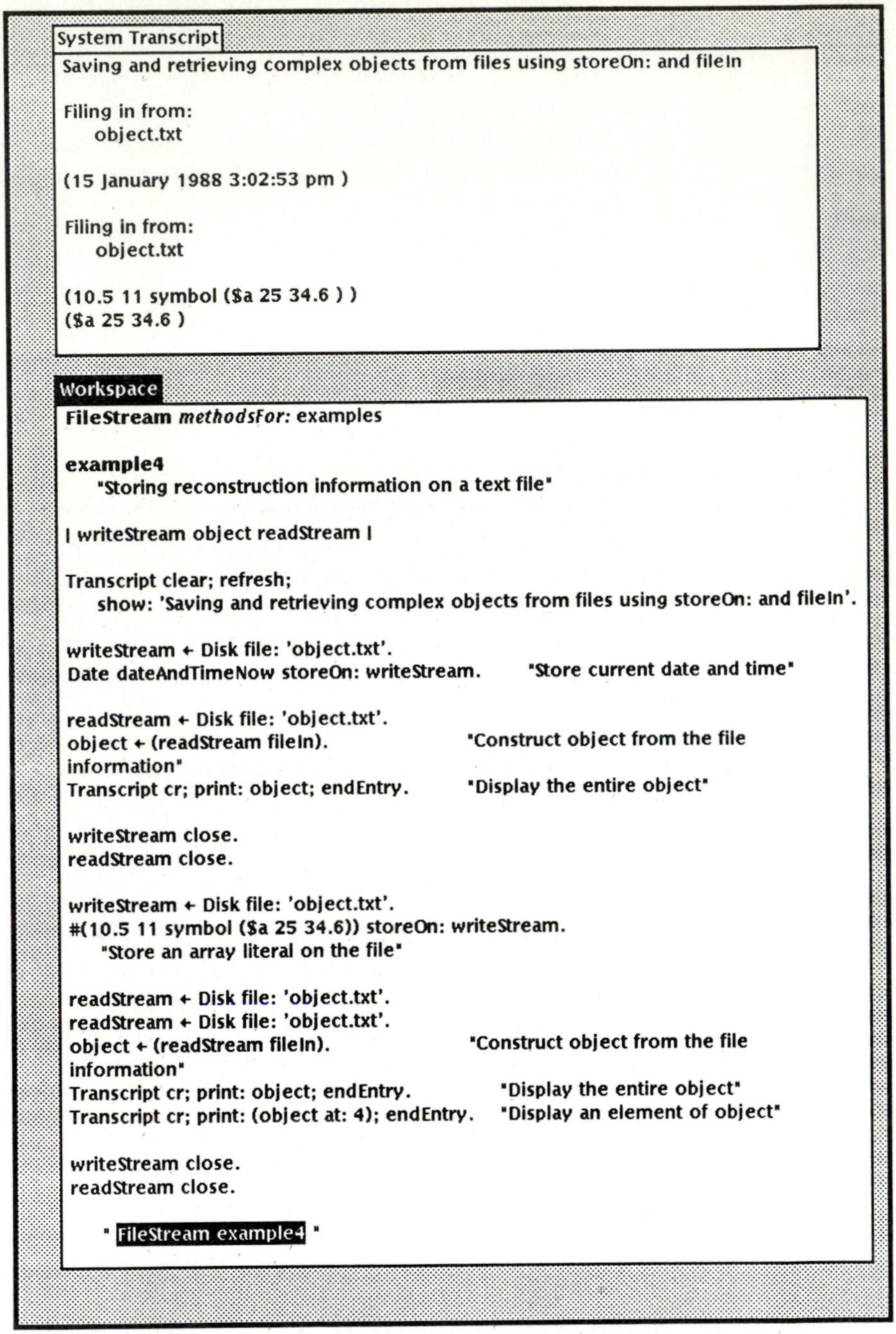

System Transcript

Saving and retrieving complex objects from files using storeOn: and fileIn

Filing in from:
    object.txt

(15 January 1988 3:02:53 pm)

Filing in from:
    object.txt

(10.5 11 symbol ($a 25 34.6)))
($a 25 34.6)

Workspace

```
FileStream methodsFor: examples

example4
    "Storing reconstruction information on a text file"

| writeStream object readStream |

Transcript clear; refresh;
    show: 'Saving and retrieving complex objects from files using storeOn: and fileIn'.

writeStream ← Disk file: 'object.txt'.
Date dateAndTimeNow storeOn: writeStream.        "Store current date and time"

readStream ← Disk file: 'object.txt'.
object ← (readStream fileIn).              "Construct object from the file
information"
Transcript cr; print: object; endEntry.      "Display the entire object"

writeStream close.
readStream close.

writeStream ← Disk file: 'object.txt'.
#(10.5 11 symbol ($a 25 34.6)) storeOn: writeStream.
    "Store an array literal on the file"

readStream ← Disk file: 'object.txt'.
readStream ← Disk file: 'object.txt'.
object ← (readStream fileIn).                "Construct object from the file
information"
Transcript cr; print: object; endEntry.        "Display the entire object"
Transcript cr; print: (object at: 4); endEntry.  "Display an element of object"

writeStream close.
readStream close.

    " FileStream example4 "
```

file using the message **storeOn:**. Most objects in complex classes support this protocol. The stored object with all its data intact can be reconstructed by sending the message **fileIn** to the file and assigning the result to a variable. This is illustrated in Figure 5.11 for an instance of class **Date** and for a literal array.

Results of executing **example4** are shown in the Transcript window. Access into indexable objects such as arrays is possible from the reconstructed object. The reconstructed object has all the features of the original object that was stored on the file. More details of the stream classes are given in Chapter 8.

5.5 Sensors—Mouse Inputs

This section presents a brief description of the classes and methods that support user inputs from the mouse (either cursor positioning or button pressing). It also discusses in general terms the concept of other sensors. The discussion is kept simple and is not intended to be complete. Included are the class **InputSensor** and the global variable **Sensor,** which is an instance of **InputSensor.** A summary of the protocol of class **InputSensor** is presented, followed by an example of its use.

Protocol Summary for Class **InputSensor**

Class **InputSensor** provides protocol for interfacing with user input devices. Support is provided for the mouse, the keyboard, and the cursor. Another class, **InputState,** represents the state of input devices by maintaining a number of instance and class variables. An instance of **InputState** is used in class **InputSensor** as a class variable. Only the protocol of **InputSensor** is briefly described here; a more complete protocol summary for **InputSensor** is given in Appendix 3.

The hierarchy for class **InputSensor** is **Object—InputSensor.** It has one instance variable, keyboardMap. It has three class variables, CurrentCursor, CurrentInputState, and DefaultKeyboardMap. It has no pool dictionaries. It has 5 class methods in three categories and 30 instance methods in four categories.

Private data for class **InputSensor** includes only one instance variable. Instance variable **keyboardMap** is an instance of **String** containing 5 * 256 characters. These characters represent the keyboard map for five different states of the *shift, control,* and *caps lock* keys. The keyboard can be remapped by the user.

Class **InputSensor** has three class variables: (1) **CurrentCursor,** an instance of **Cursor** that is a 16-by-16 pixel pattern representing the cursor, (2) **CurrentInputState,** an instance of **InputState,** representing the attached hardware, and (3) **DefaultKeyboardMap,** the default mapping of the keyboard. The private data variable, **keyboardMap,** is initialized to be equal to this default.

Figure 5.12
Interacting with the
Mouse Using Class
InputSensor and
Its Global Instance,
Sensor

System Transcript

Test 1: left button response (press to continue).
Press red (left) button to continue
Press red (left) button to continue

Test 2: any button response (press to continue).

Test 3: yellow button to show mouse coordinates, blue button to quit.
Mouse coordinates: 11@14
Mouse coordinates: 1298@946

Test 4: Mouse coordinates and cursor coordinates. Move cursor and click any button
Cursor coordinates: 419@385   Mouse coordinates: 419@385

Test 5: Move cursor about to display. Press any button to quit.

Workspace

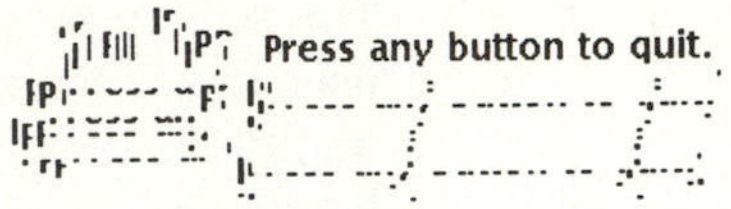

InputSensor *methodsFor:* examples

example1
    "Interaction with the mouse"   Press any button to quit.

"Test 1"   Transcript clear; refresh;
                show: 'Test 1: left button response (press to continue).'.
                [Sensor waitButton; redButtonPressed] whileFalse: [
                    Transcript cr; show: 'Press red (left) button to continue'].

"Test 2"   Transcript cr; cr;
                show: 'Test 2: any button response (press to continue).'.
                [Sensor waitButton; anyButtonPressed] whileFalse: [
                    Transcript cr; show: 'Press any button to continue'].

"Test 3"   Transcript cr; cr;
                show: 'Test 3: yellow button (mouse coords), blue button to quit.'.
                [Sensor waitButton; blueButtonPressed] whileFalse: [
                    Sensor yellowButtonPressed ifTrue: [
                        Transcript cr; show: 'Mouse coordinates: ',
                        Sensor mousePoint printString]].

"Test 4"   Transcript cr; cr;
                show: 'Test 4: Mouse & cursor coords. Move cursor, click any button'.
                Transcript cr; show: 'Cursor coordinates: ',
                    Sensor waitClickButton printString,'
                    Mouse coordinates: ',
                    Sensor mousePoint printString.

"Test 5"   Transcript cr; cr;
                show: 'Test 5: Move cursor about to display. Press any button to quit.'.
                [Sensor noButtonPressed] whileTrue: [
                    'Press any button to quit.' displayAt: Sensor mousePoint].

        " InputSensor example1 "

InputSensor **Example 5A**

This example illustrates the use of protocol in **InputSensor** for interacting with the mouse. Figure 5.12 shows details of the class method **example1** in class **Input-Sensor.** As with other examples in this chapter, the results are shown in the Transcript window. There are five tests that demonstrate most of the protocol in the category *mouse* of this class. The five tests are summarized below.

- *Test 1*—The message "Press red (left) button to continue" is displayed in the Transcript window every time a button other than the left button is pressed. Once the left button is pressed, the example proceeds to Test 2.

- *Test 2*—This test simply waits for any button to be pressed before proceeding to Test 3.

- *Test 3*—During this test, the user can move the cursor to different locations on the screen. At any location, a press of the yellow (middle) button causes the cursor coordinates to be displayed in the Transcript window. Pressing the blue (right) button terminates this test.

- *Test 4*—This test shows that coordinates for the mouse and coordinates for the cursor are identical.

- *Test 5*—This test continually displays the string "Press any button to quit" at the current cursor location. As the cursor is moved with the mouse, it displays without erasing. That is why the display in Figure 5.12 looks the way it does. Pressing any button causes this test to terminate.

Low-level interaction with the keyboard can be accomplished with protocol in the *keyboard* category of class **InputSensor.** Examples of this kind of interaction are not included in this book. The protocol described in Section 5.1 for prompters provides easy keyboard interaction by the user during program execution.

5.6   Graphical Output to the Printer

This section describes a limited number of methods and classes for displaying graphical images on the screen and for dumping those images to a printer. New methods in class **PrinterStream,** class **Form,** and class **DisplayScreen** that support printer bitmap dumps are described and illustrated with examples.

Details of the techniques for printing of graphic images are strongly dependent on the particular printer being used. For that reason it is advantageous to implement a limited number of key methods that handle all the printer-specific protocol. Other methods can build on top of these key methods, which minimizes maintenance when changing to a different printer. This limited number of key methods is the approach used in the following new protocol.

The printer used for this example is the Hewlett-Packard Laserjet Series II (for more information on this printer see the printer manual). Details may vary for other printers; however, the printing of a bit-mapped image consists of the following five steps:

1. *Position the cursor.* This command establishes the location of the printhead on a page.

2. *Specify the raster graphics resolution.* This command specifies the resolution in dots per inch for the printer display.

3. *Specify the left raster graphics margin.* This command allows the user to specify either the current cursor position or zero as the left margin on the page.

4. *Transfer the data to the printer.* Each row of dots is transferred as a string of bytes. The number of dots in the row is 8 * the number of bytes in the row. Each bit is translated into a pixel. The pixel is black or white depending on the value of the bit. Gray images can be displayed only by varying the spatial density of black and white pixels.

5. *End the raster graphic image transfer.* This command tells the printer that the graphic image is complete. It causes the printer to print the image and exit graphics mode.

In support of graphics operations, several new methods are added to class **PrinterStream.** Most of these implement the specific command strings for performing the above five steps. The following new methods are added to **PrinterStream.**

- **resetCursor**—Set the cursor position to zero.

- **setCursor:** aPoint—Set the cursor position to **aPoint.**

- **setRes:** resolution—Set the value of the parameter **resolution** in dots per inch (for the Laserjet II, resolution may be 75, 100, 150, or 300 dpi).

- **startGraphicsReset**—Initiate graphics mode with the left margin set to zero.

- **startGraphics**—Initiate graphics mode with the left margin set to the x-coordinate of the current cursor location.

- **rasterTransfer**—This is the initial escape sequence for initiating a raster transfer. It requires that the number of bytes, the character *W,* and the row of bytes (raster data) follow this initial sequence as a single command sent to the printer. Construction of the complete command is accomplished by the message **outputToPrinterVert: offset:,** implemented in class **Form.** Forms are the objects whose bitmaps are typically sent to the printer.

- **endGraphics**—Send the end graphics command to the printer.

Listing 5.5
Key Method for
Sending **Form**
Bitmaps to the
Printer

Form methodsFor: 'printing'

outputToPrinterVert: resolution **offset:** aPoint
    "Output the form to the printer in portrait mode at resolution dpi starting at offset 'aPoint'.
       Example use --
         (Form dotOfSize: 200) outputToPrinterVert: 150 offset: 200@300 "

    | widthInWords widthInBytes rasterRow wordAsInt index |
    Printer reset; setCursor: aPoint; setRes: resolution; startGraphics.
    widthInWords ← width + 15 // 16.
    widthInBytes ← 2 * widthInWords.
    rasterRow ← String new: widthInBytes.
    1 to: height do: [:rowIndex |
       index ← 0.
       1 to: widthInWords do: [: colIndex |
          wordAsInt ← (bits at: ((rowIndex - 1) * widthInWords + colIndex)) asInteger.
          rasterRow at: (index ← index + 1) put: ((wordAsInt bitShift: -8) asCharacter).
          rasterRow at: (index ← index + 1) put: ((wordAsInt bitAnd: 255) asCharacter)].
       (PrinterStream rasterTransfer, widthInBytes printString, 'W', rasterRow)
         outputToPrinter].
    Printer endGraphics; ff

With this new protocol in class **PrinterStream** it is possible to develop a single key method in class **Form** for sending graphic images to the printer. That key method, given in Listing 5.5, is sent to an instance of class **Form,** whose bitmap will be printed as a graphic image on the printer. The default mode for the printer is portrait mode. The user of this message specifies both the resolution in dots per inch and the offset for printing the image on a page. The offset is given in pixels from the upper left corner on the page.

For printing a graphic image in landscape mode, a new message, output-ToPrinterHor: offset:, is added to class **Form.** It uses the existing protocol message rotate: in class **Form** to rotate the image by 90 degrees. This rotated image is then sent the message outputToPrinterVert: offset:. With this approach, the interpretation of offset is always the same.

Class **DisplayScreen,** a subclass of **Form,** represents forms that are the entire display screen. Four new methods are added to class **DisplayScreen** for printing graphic images of the display screen. The four messages are described below. All are sent to the global object **Display,** which is the only instance of **Display-Screen.**

- **outputToPrinterHor**—Print a graphic image of the full display screen in landscape mode. Resolution and offset are given default values for centering the image on the page. This method rotates the screen image and sends the message outputToPrinterVert: offset: in its superclass, **Form.**

- **outputToPrinterHor: resolution**—Print a graphic image of the full display screen in landscape mode with specified resolution. For resolutions of 150 or 300 dpi, the image is automatically centered on the page. A resolution of 100 or 75 dpi cannot display the entire image on a single page (it is not recommended). This method also rotates the screen image and sends the message outputToPrinterVert: offset: in its superclass, **Form.**

- **outputToPrinterVert**—Print a graphic image of the display in portrait mode at a resolution of 150 dpi. This produces an image that will almost but not quite fit on the page. At this resolution, the maximum number of pixels that can be printed across the width of a page is 1200. The Tektronix display screen has 1376 pixels horizontally.

- **outputToPrinterVert:** resolution—Print a graphic image of the display in portrait mode with the specified resolution in dots per inch. The Laserjet II automatically expands graphic images transferred at less than 300 dpi to 300 dpi during printing. This produces a magnification in both the x and y directions of 2 for 150 dpi, 3 for 100 dpi, and 4 for 75 dpi.

Listing 5.6 gives the details of the four new methods added to class **Display-Screen.**

Listing 5.6
Four Methods for
Graphic Printing of
the Display Screen

DisplayScreen methodsFor: 'printing'

outputToPrinterHor
```
    "Print display screen in Landscape mode, default resolution of 150 dpi"
    | screenForm extent |
    extent ←
        (FillInTheBlank
            request: 'Enter x dimension in pixels'
            initialAnswer: '1376') asNumber @
        (FillInTheBlank
            request: 'Enter y dimension in pixels'
            initialAnswer: '1024') asNumber.
    screenForm ← (Form fromDisplay: (0@0 extent: extent)) rotateBy: 1.
    screenForm outputToPrinterVert: 150 offset: 150@130
```

outputToPrinterHor: resolution
```
    "Print display screen in Landscape mode, 'resolution' dpi"
    | screenForm aPoint |
    resolution = 300
        ifTrue: [ aPoint ← 680@900 "centered"]
        ifFalse: [ aPoint ← 0@0 "start at lower left"].
    screenForm ← (Form fromDisplay: (0@0 extent: 1376@1024)) rotateBy: 1.
    screenForm outputToPrinterVert: resolution offset: aPoint
```

outputToPrinterVert
```
    "Print display screen in Portrait mode, default resolution of 150 dpi"
    self outputToPrinterVert: 150
```

outputToPrinterVert: resolution
```
    "Print display screen in Portrait mode with resolution dpi"
    | screenForm |
    screenForm ← (Form fromDisplay: (0@0 extent: 1376@1024)).
    screenForm outputToPrinterVert: resolution offset: 0@0.
```

Figure 5.13
DisplayScreen
Example Methods for Printing Graphic Images

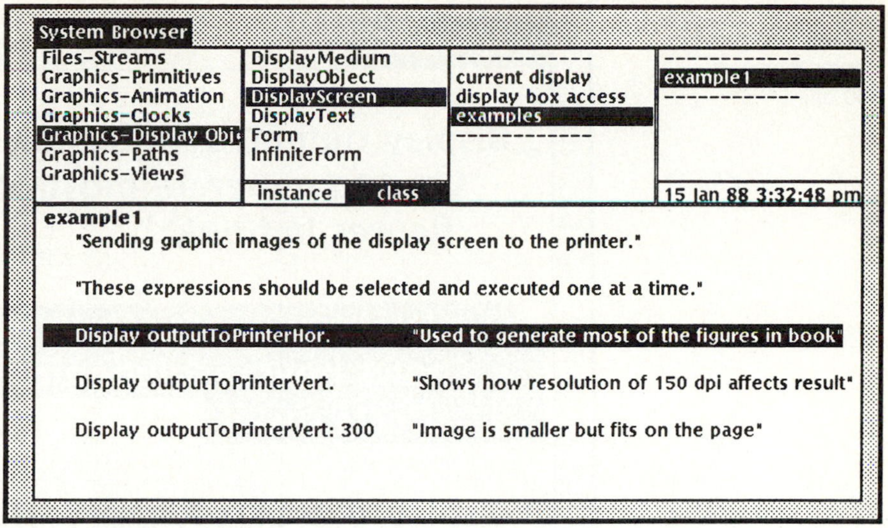

DisplayScreen Example 5A

This example is added as a class method, **example1**, to class **DisplayScreen.** It illustrates the use of protocol for printing graphic images of the display screen.

Figure 5.13 shows the result of evaluating the first expression in the example. This is the expression used to generate most of the figures in this book.

Figure 5.14 shows the result of evaluating the second expression. It produces a portrait orientation printout at the default of 150 dpi resolution. This results in part of the display screen image being clipped on the printed page.

Figure 5.15 shows another example of the portrait orientation at a resolution of 300 dpi. It produces a smaller image that does fit on the page.

Form Example 5A

This example illustrates the techniques for printing graphical images other than the display screen. Instances of class **Form** can be of just about any size. These graphical objects can be printed using the methods **outputToPrinterVert: offset:** and **outputToPrinterHor: offset:**, defined in class **Form.** A class method called **examplePrints** that illustrates their use has been added to **Form.**

Figure 5.16 shows details of the method for **examplePrints**. There are two parts to the example. Part 1 generates a small (350v-by-345h pixels) graphics image in the center of the screen. It then creates an instance of **Form,** whose bitmap is taken from the screen image. This image is printed in portrait mode with a resolution of 75 dpi. This means that the pixels are all exploded by a factor of four in the resultant printout. Figure 5.17 shows the result of this first part.

Figure 5.14
Portrait Orientation
Printer Image at
150 dpi

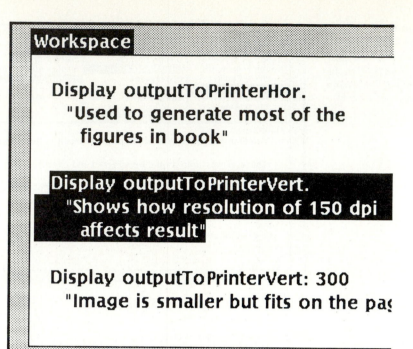

Figure 5.15
Portrait Orientation
Printer Image at
300 dpi

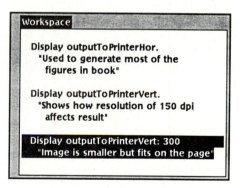

Part 2 generates a large (690v-by-690h pixels) graphics image and uses the same process to print the image at 150-dpi resolution. Figure 5.18 shows the resultant printout. The difference in scaling for the two parts is seen by comparing the background pattern and text in the two figures. On the display screen, the background and text are the same size.

The sequence of steps used in both parts is the following.

1. Generate a mandala pattern by sending the message **mandala: diameter:** to a new instance of class **Pen.** Details of this method cause the display screen to be cleared first.

Figure 5.16
Printing Graphic
Images—
Examples for
Sending Instances
of Class **Form** to
the Printer

```
Workspace
Form methodsFor: examples

examplePrints
    "Printing graphic images of forms. The first part prints a small form at 75 dpi.
        The second part prints a large form at 300 dpi."
    | rectangle  form |

    "Part 1 – Small forms printed at low resolution produce a large printed image."

    Pen new mandala: 10 diameter: 250.
        "Generate a 250 pixel diameter mandala on white background"
    rectangle ← (Rectangle origin: 0@0 extent: 344@350) center: 688@512.
        "Define a rectangular region around the mandala"
    Display fill: rectangle rule: Form under mask: Form veryLightGray.
        "Paint the gray rectangle under the mandala"
    '350v x 345h Image at 75 dpi' displayAt: 520@650.
        "Add a text description inside the rectangle"
    form ← (Form fromDisplay: rectangle). form borderWidth: 4.
        "Create an instance of Form from the display area. Add border."
    form displayOn: Display at: 516@337.
        "Send the form with border to the display"
    form outputToPrinterHor: 75 offset: 0@0.
        "Print the form in landscape mode at 75 dpi"

    "Part 2 – Large forms must be printed at higher resolution, producing a smaller
                printed image, if they are to fit on the page."

    Pen new mandala: 20 diameter: 600.
        "Generate a large mandala using most of the screen"
    rectangle ← (Rectangle origin: 0@0 extent: 690@690) center: 688@512.
        "Define a rectangle about the mandala"
    Display fill: rectangle rule: Form under mask: Form veryLightGray.
        "Paint the gray rectangle under the mandala"
    '690v x 690h Image at 150 dpi' displayAt: 360@835.
        "Add a text description inside the rectangle"
    form ← (Form fromDisplay: rectangle). form borderWidth: 4.
        "Create an instance of Form from the display area. Add border."
    form displayOn: Display at: 343@167.
        "Send the form with border to the display"
    form outputToPrinterHor: 150 offset: 0@0.
        "Print the form in landscape mode at 150 dpi"

    ScheduledControllers restore.
        "Restore the screen"

    " Form examplePrints "
```

Figure 5.17
350v × 345h
Image at 75 dpi

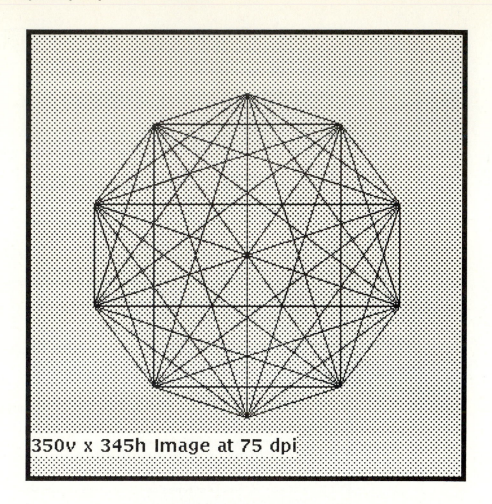

350v x 345h Image at 75 dpi

2. Next a rectangle is defined of a specified size and centered. This sets the origin and corner to the appropriate point values. It does not display the rectangle.

3. Fill in the defined rectangular region with a **veryLightGray** pattern, using the rule that the pattern is displayed under the existing pattern (the mandala). There are several other display rules to choose from in class **Form.**

4. Add text in the form of a string to the calculated display location for proper positioning.

5. Define a new instance of **Form** whose bitmap is taken from the specified rectangular region on the display screen.

6. Add a four-pixel black border to the new form.

7. Redisplay the form on the display screen. Until this is done, the border added in Step 6 does not appear.

Figure 5.18
690v × 690h
Image at 150 dpi

690v x 690h Image at 150 dpi

8. Send the form to the printer with specified resolution and offset.

9. As a final step the screen display is restored to clear the mandala image and restore the active windows. This is accomplished by the expression **ScheduledControllers restore**.

This chapter has presented summaries of the classes that are essential to performing standard operations such as keyboard input, mouse input, text output to the screen, limited graphics display to the screen, text output to a printer, and graphics output to a printer. Use of the class protocol has been demonstrated by examples that in most cases are added as class methods within the class protocol. The tools presented in this chapter should make user interaction with the Smalltalk system more friendly.

Exercises

5.1 Of the five methods for creating instances of **BinaryChoice,** four of them send the fifth with appropriate parameters. Comment on the significance of the fifth message in terms of maintenance of the Smalltalk system.

5.2 Develop an example program that prompts the user to enter a string of characters and then displays the string of characters on the display screen beginning in the upper left corner. Repeat this process until the user enters a specified termination character. Each successive string is to be displayed below the previous string. Use the default character size, font, and style.

5.3 Modify Exercise 5.2 to use a variety of character styles (e.g., italics, boldface, underlined). One suggestion is to change the style for each new string in a cyclic fashion.

5.4 Repeat Exercise 5.2 for an increasing font size from minimum to maximum. Be careful of line spacings.

5.5 Repeat Exercise 5.2, but display the text in the Transcript window.

5.6 Repeat Exercise 5.2, but display the text in a user-specified window. See the example in Figure 5.6 for hints.

5.7 Based on the protocol summary of class **PrinterStream** and details of key methods given in this chapter, develop a working **PrinterStream** class on your Smalltalk system that supports the output of text to your available printer. Test the functionality of this new class.

5.8 Implement a short Smalltalk program that reads an existing text file, computes a histogram of the occurrences of the alphabetic characters (a through z without case sensitivity), and prints the histogram values on the printer as key/value pairs.

5.9 Add incremental capability to the solution in Exercise 5.8. This incremental capability is to write the histogram key/value pairs to a file, which involves writing mixtures of characters and integers.

5.10 Develop an example in class **InputSensor** that does the following: Clicking the mouse left button reverse videos the display, clicking the mouse center button clears the display, and clicking the mouse right button restores the display and terminates the program.

5.11 Add the graphics protocol described in Section 5.6 to your Smalltalk system. Test the protocol by sending the screen graphic image to the printer.

5.12 Using your Smalltalk system and platform, develop the required protocol to connect the pressing of a specified function key with an automatic graphics screen dump to the printer.

6

Object-Oriented Programming Using Magnitude Classes

This chapter describes class **Magnitude** and its subclasses. Three of the primary subclasses of **Magnitude** (**Number, Date,** and **Time**), represent objects that are familiar to most readers. The purpose of this chapter is to provide more familiarity with Smalltalk classes and object-oriented programming methods. By choosing examples from classes that represent familiar objects, more time can be focused on understanding the object-oriented methodology and less time on explaining the objects.

Two new classes, **Complex** and **Imaginary,** are added that support complex and imaginary numbers. Examples are given that illustrate the concept of generality of numbers. Support for literals is provided for the **Imaginary** and **Complex** number classes. This feature of Smalltalk that allows the user to add support for new literals is unique. New methods are added to existing classes to support the two new classes.

6.1   Class Hierarchy of the Magnitude Classes

This section presents a hierarchy summary of the magnitude classes and describes in general terms what a "magnitude" class is. Listing 6.1 gives a hierarchy list of the **Magnitude** classes. Instance variables in each class are shown in parentheses in the listing. A summary has been given of class **Character** in a previous chapter. This chapter concentrates on the **Time, Date,** and **Number** subclasses with particular emphasis on the new **Number** subclasses **Complex** and **Imaginary.** An example of the use of **Association** is given in Chapter 7 in conjunction with collections.

Protocol Summary for Class **Magnitude**

Magnitude is an abstract class. It defines protocol that is common to its subclasses. No objects are instances of class **Magnitude.** They will be instances of one of its subclasses and will have access to protocol defined in **Magnitude** in

Listing 6.1
Hierarchy for
the **Magnitude**
Classes, Instance
Variables in
Parentheses

Object ()

    Magnitude ()
        Character ('value')
        Date ('day' 'year')
        LookupKey ('key')
            Association ('value')
        MessageTally ('class' 'method' 'tally' 'receivers')
        Number ()
            Complex ('real' 'imaginary' 'modulus' 'angle')
            Float ()
            Fraction ('numerator' 'denominator')
            Imaginary ('magnitude')
            Integer ()
                LargeNegativeInteger ()
                LargePositiveInteger ()
                SmallInteger ()
      Time ('hours' 'minutes' 'seconds')
        SimTime ()

addition to the protocol of their own specific class. Instances of **Magnitude** are objects that have a linear measure.

Definition—The hierarchy for class **Magnitude** is **Object—Magnitude.** It has no instance variables, class variables, or pool dictionaries. It has no class methods. It has 10 instance methods in one category. The details of most of the instance methods have already been given in Chapter 2.

Instance methods—Class **Magnitude** has 10 instance methods in one category, called *comparing.* The 10 message selectors are $<$, $<=$, $=$, $>$, $>=$, **between: and:, hash:, hashMappedBy:, min:,** and **max:.** Details of most of the methods are given in Chapter 2. They are not repeated here.

Class methods—Class **Magnitude** has no class methods. As an abstract class **Magnitude** should have no instances.

6.2   Class **Time** and Class **Date**

Two of the major subclasses of **Magnitude** are **Time** and **Date.** A protocol summary for class **Date** was given in Chapter 2. In this section an abbreviated protocol summary is given for class **Time.** A more complete protocol summary is given in Appendix 3. Examples are given that illustrate protocol of both classes **Time** and **Date.**

These two classes provide a good example of why and when class methods are preferable to instance methods as vehicles for providing useful functionality. Certain standard inquiries about times and dates are provided as class methods. Results are obtained by sending appropriate messages to the class names **Time** and **Date.** There is no need to create an instance of the class. An example is given in this section that uses only class methods.

Protocol Summary for Class **Time**

Instances of class **Time** represent times.

The hierarchy for class **Time** is **Object—Magnitude—Time.** Class **Time** has three instance variables, hours, minutes, and seconds. It has no class variables or pool dictionaries. It has 14 class methods in three categories and 14 instance methods in six categories.

Class **Time** has three instance variables. Instance variable **hours** is an instance of **Integer,** representing the number of hours in the instance of time. Instance variable **minutes** is an instance of **Integer,** representing the number of minutes in the instance of time. Instance variable **seconds** is an instance of **Integer,** representing the number of seconds in the instance of time.

Time and Date Example 6A

This example shows the use of general inquiries that return information about specific times and dates. All messages are sent to the class names.

Figure 6.1 shows the details of a class method, example1, in class **Magnitude** that illustrates these messages sent to class names **Time** and **Date.** Results are shown in the Transcript window in the figure.

There are two interesting points to be made about the code here. First, the expression **Time** abbreviatedDateAndTimeNow returns a string. It is the only expression in this example that does not have to be sent the message printString, before inclusion as part of the string parameter for the **Transcript** message show:. Second, the expression for determining if a specified year is a leap year, DateleapYear: 1960, returns an integer that is 1 for a leap year and 0 for a non-leap year. As the expression is constructed, it concatenates the string, 'not ', depending on the Boolean result, ((DateleapYear: 1960) = 1). The return symbol (up arrow) in the block for ifFalse: is redundant. Its use is optional.

Time and Date Example 6B

This example illustrates the use of the timing message millisecondsToRun: for timing the execution of a block of code. Figure 6.2 shows details for class method example2 in class **Magnitude.**

Figure 6.1
An Example
Showing the Use
of General
Inquiries Sent to
Class Names **Time**
and **Date**

System Transcript

dateAndTimeNow sent to Date or Time gives: (15 January 1988 8:01:00 pm)
    An abbreviated version from Time gives: 15 Jan 88 8:01:00 pm

Total seconds from Jan 1, 1901 (corrected for time zone and DST) is: 2746728060

Returning numbers about dates
Index for day of week, Wednesday is: 3
Index for month in year, August is: 8
Number of days in year 1942 was: 365
Number of days in February, 1960 was: 29
1961 was not a leap year

Returning names of days or months.
The name of the day with index of 5 is: Friday
The name of the month with index of 6 is: June

Workspace

Magnitude *methodsFor:* examples

example1
    "This example illustrates general inquiry messages sent to Time and Date"

"Time and Date Examples"
    Transcript clear; refresh.
    Transcript show: 'dateAndTimeNow sent to Date or Time gives: ',
        Time dateAndTimeNow printString.
    Transcript cr; tab; show: 'An abbreviated version from Time gives: ',
        Time abbreviatedDateAndTimeNow.
    Transcript cr; cr; show:
        'Total seconds from Jan 1, 1901 (corrected for time zone and DST) is: ',
        Time totalSeconds printString.

"Numbers for Dates"
    Transcript cr; cr; show: 'Returning numbers about dates'; cr.
    Transcript show: 'Index for day of week, Wednesday is: ',
        (Date dayOfWeek: #Wednesday) printString; cr.
    Transcript show: 'Index for month in year, August is: ',
        (Date indexOfMonth: #August) printString; cr.
    Transcript show: 'Number of days in year 1942 was: ',
        (Date daysInYear: 1942) printString; cr.
    Transcript show: 'Number of days in February, 1960 was: ',
        (Date daysInMonth: #February forYear: 1960) printString; cr.
    Transcript
        show: ('1961 was ',(((Date leapYear: 1961) = 1) ifFalse: ['not ']), 'a leap year').

"Names for Dates"
    Transcript cr; cr; show: 'Returning names of days or months.'; cr.
    Transcript show: 'The name of the day with index of 5 is: ',
        (Date nameOfDay: 5) printString; cr.
    Transcript show: 'The name of the month with index of 6 is: ',
        (Date nameOfMonth: 6) printString; cr.

    " Magnitude example1 "

Figure 6.2
An Example
Showing the Use
of Messages in
Time for Timing
Block Execution

System Transcript

Example showing how execution time for blocks is evaluated.
(15 January 1988 8:19:47 pm) Millisecond clock value: 29578573

Execution time for do nothing looping: 646   milliseconds

Execution time for assignment looping: 711   milliseconds

Execution time for real arithmetic looping: 5283   milliseconds

Execution time for function calc. looping: 1756   milliseconds

Running millisecond clock value: 3479   milliseconds

                                                    29591043

Workspace

Magnitude *methodsFor:* examples

example2
    "This example illustrates messages sent to Time for timing the execution of blocks."
    | value |

"Time and Date & milliseconds"
    Transcript clear; refresh;
        show: 'Example showing how execution time for blocks is evaluated.'; cr.
    Transcript show: Time dateAndTimeNow printString, ' Millisecond clock value: ',
        Time millisecondClockValue printString; cr; cr.

"Time various loops of 10000"
    Transcript show: 'Execution time for do nothing looping: ',
        (Time millisecondsToRun: [1 to: 10000 do: [:i |]]) printString,
            ' milliseconds'; cr; cr.   "do nothing"
    Transcript show: 'Execution time for assignment looping: ',
        (Time millisecondsToRun: [1 to: 10000 do: [:i | value + i]]) printString,
            ' milliseconds'; cr; cr.   "integer assignment"
    Transcript show: 'Execution time for real arithmetic looping: ',
        (Time millisecondsToRun: [1 to: 10000 do: [:i | i * 5.2]]) printString,
            ' milliseconds'; cr; cr.   "real multiplication"
    Transcript show: 'Execution time for function calc. looping: ',
        (Time millisecondsToRun: [1 to: 10000 do: [:i | i tan]]) printString,
            ' milliseconds'; cr; cr.   "compute tan"

"100 displays of millisecond clock"
    Transcript cr; show: 'Running millisecond clock value: ',
        (Time millisecondsToRun: [1 to: 100 do: [:i |
            Time millisecondClockValue printString displayAt: 500@300]])
            printString, ' milliseconds'.

    " Magnitude example2 "

Two messages are sent to class name **Time.** The first message, millisecond-ClockValue, returns the number of milliseconds that have elapsed since the millisecond clock was last reset or rolled over. Accuracy of this clock is limited to 32 bits.

The second message, millisecondsToRun: aBlock, returns the time in milliseconds to execute the expression in **aBlock.** The method details for this message send the message millisecondClockValue prior to and after completion of the message **aBlock value.** The difference is returned as the execution time in milliseconds.

The results of executing **example2** are shown in the Transcript window in Figure 6.2. The results show execution times for 10,000 loops that (a) do nothing, (b) assign integers, (c) multiply two reals, and (d) compute the tangent.

A final part of this example shows the time required to access the millisecond clock, convert the result to a string, and display the result on the screen 100 times. The result shows an average of 34.79 (3479/100) milliseconds to perform these three steps one time.

6.3   **Number** as an Abstract Class— Inheritance and Polymorphism

This section gives a protocol summary for the abstract class **Number.** In addition it gives a summary of the new, inherited, and polymorphically redefined methods of three **Number** subclasses. They are **Integer, Float,** and **Fraction.**

Protocol Summary for Class **Number**

Class **Number** is an abstract superclass of all the number classes. As such it provides protocol common to all number classes and has no instances. It inherits protocol from classes **Magnitude** and **Object.**

Definition—The hierarchy for class **Number** is **Object—Magnitude—Number.** It has no instance variables, class variables, or pool dictionaries. Excluding examples, it has 1 class method in one category. It has 55 instance methods in eight categories. Some of these methods are added to support new classes, **Complex** and **Imaginary,** described later in this chapter. They are not part of the standard Smalltalk image.

Instance methods—Class **Number** has 55 instance methods in eight categories. The categories and number of methods are given below.

arithmetic—eleven methods (***, +, −, /, //, abs, negated, quo:, reciprocal, rem:, **) representing basic arithmetic operations. Four of these (***, +, −, /**) are implemented as subclassResponsibility.

mathematical functions—fourteen methods (**arcCos, arcSin, arcTan, cos,**

exp, floorLog:, ln, log:, raisedTo:, raisedToInteger:, sin, sqrt, squared, tan) that represent the most common mathematical functions, including transcendental functions and logarithms. Eleven of these methods first convert the number to an instance of **Float** and send the same message to the **Float** instance. These 11 mathematical functions are implemented as primitives using floating point numbers as arguments. Protocol for these functions is included here so the messages can be sent to other number classes with no error (e.g., **2 exp** is a valid expression and is interpreted as **2.0 exp**).

testing—six methods (**even, negative, odd, positive, sign, strictlyPositive**) that test the sign, oddness, and evenness of numbers.

truncation and round off—six methods (**ceiling, floor, rounded, roundTo:, truncated, truncateTo:**) for truncation and round off.

coercing—three methods (**coerce:, generality, retry: coercing:**), two of which (coerce:, generality) are subclassResponsibility. The third is the method for the message retry: coercing:, which supports the concept of generality of numbers.

converting—eight methods (**@, asComplex, asImaginary, asInteger, asPoint, degreesToRadians, pi, radiansToDegrees**) for converting to points, radians, degrees, integers, or multiples of pi.

intervals—four methods (**to:, to: by:, to: by: do:, to: do:**) for iteration. These methods have been illustrated in previous examples.

printing—three methods (**printStructureOn:, storeOn:, storeStructureOn: auxTable:**) for printing and storing numbers on a stream.

Class methods—Class **Number** has one class method in one category, as described below.

instance creation—one class method (**readFrom:**) that creates a new instance of **Number** as described on a stream.

Subclasses of **Number** inherit, redefine, and define new protocol for objects that are instances of the respective class. In the discussion below, a summary is given of the inherited, redefined, and new protocol for three major subclasses of **Number—Integer, Float,** and **Fraction.** The purpose of these descriptive summaries is to illustrate the properties of inheritance and polymorphism in Smalltalk. It also emphasizes how subclasses can define new protocol in the form of new private or shared data and in the form of new instance or class methods. Since class **Number** has no private, shared, or pool data, none of its subclasses will inherit any data from it. Protocol inherited from class **Number** consists of only the 55 instance methods and 1 class method defined in it.

New, Inherited, and Redefined Protocol in Class **Integer**

Class **Integer** has no private, shared, or pool data. It has 3 class methods in 1 category and 66 instance methods in 12 categories. The methods are either new or redefined protocol. In addition some methods are inherited from **Number** and used by class **Integer.** The following is a summary of the new, inherited, and redefined protocol in class **Integer.**

New protocol—New protocol in class **Integer** consists of 2 new class methods and 40 new instance methods. A list by category is given below.
Class Methods
instance creation—two methods (**new: neg:, readFrom: radix:**).
Instance Methods
testing—one method (**sieve**).
converting—three methods (**asCharacter, asFloat, asFraction**).
printing—three methods (**printOn: base:, printStringRadix:, storeString-Radix:**).
enumerating—one method (**timesRepeat:**).
factorization and divisibility—three methods (**factorial, gcd:, lcm:**).
bit manipulation—thirteen methods (**allMask:, anyMask:, bitAnd:, bitAt:, bitInvert, bitOr:, bitShift:, bitXor:, fillBySignExtendFrom:, highBit, noMask:, putBit: at:, showBits**).
system primitives—two methods (**lastDigit, lastDigitGet:**).
private—fourteen methods (**anyBitTo:, copyTo:, denominator, digitAdd:, digitCompare:, digitDiv: neg:, digitLogic: op: length:, digitLshift: bytes: lookfirst:, digitMultiply: neg:, digitRshift: bytes: lookfirst:, digitSub-tract:, growby:, growto:, numerator**).

Inherited protocol—Forty-four instance methods are inherited by **Integer** from **Number.** A summary list of the methods and their categories is given below.
Instance Methods
arithmetic—four methods (**abs, negated, reciprocal, rem:**).
testing—five methods (**negative, odd, positive, sign, strictlyPositive**).
converting—seven methods (**@, asComplex, asImaginary, asPoint, de-greesToRadians, pi, radiansToDegrees**).
coercing—one method (**retry: coercing:**).
mathematical functions—fourteen methods (**arcCos, arcSin, arcTan, cos, exp, floorLog:, ln, log:, raisedTo:, raisedToInteger:, sin, sqrt, squared, tan**).
truncation and round off—six methods (**ceiling, floor, rounded, roundTo:, truncated, truncateTo:**).
intervals—four methods (**to:, to: by:, to: by: do:, to: do:**).
printing—three methods (**storeOn:, printStructureOn:, storeStructureOn: auxTable:**).

Class **Integer** also inherits protocol from **Object** and **Magnitude.** Details of that inherited protocol are not given here. **Integer** does redefine 11 instance methods inherited from these superclasses, and those 11 methods are listed below.

Redefined protocol—A total of 16 methods are polymorphically redefined in class **Integer** to override their implementations in class **Number.** Of these 16, 1 is a class method and 15 are instance methods. Six of the methods were implemented as subclassResponsibility in **Number.** They should always be redefined in the subclass. Four of the methods are not really redefined; they are just relisted. Following is a summary list of the 16 redefined methods and their categories. In addition, 11 other instance methods are inherited from classes **Magnitude** or **Object** and redefined in **Integer.**

Class Methods

instance creation—one method (**readFrom:**).

Instance Methods

arithmetic—seven methods (*****, **+**, **−**, **/**, **//**, **quo:**, ****), of which four (*****, **+**, **−**, **/**) were implemented as subclassResponsibility in **Number.**

testing—One method (**even**) is inherited from **Number** and redefined. One method (**isInteger**) is inherited from **Object** and redefined.

converting—One method (**asInteger**) is inherited from **Number** and redefined.

coercing—two methods (**generality, coerce:**), both of which were implemented as subclassResponsibility in **Number.**

comparing—seven methods (**<, <=, =, >, >=, hash, hashMappedBy:**), of which three (**<, =, hash**) are implemented as subclassResponsibility, inherited from **Magnitude** and polymorphically redefined. One method (**~=**) is inherited from **Object** and polymorphically redefined.

printing—Two methods (**isLiteral, printOn:**) are inherited from **Object** and redefined in **Integer.**

truncation and round off—Four methods (**ceiling, floor, rounded, truncated**) are relisted but not redefined. They are thus inherited and used as defined in **Number.**

New, Inherited, and Redefined Protocol in Class **Float**

Class **Float** has no private or pool data. It has 15 class variables, most of which represent special numbers such as infinity or coefficients required in mathematical function evaluations. **Float** has 8 class methods in 3 categories and 50 instance methods in 10 categories. The methods are either new or redefined protocol. In addition some methods are inherited from **Number** or its superclasses, **Magnitude** and **Object,** and used by class **Float.** The following is a summary of the new, inherited, and redefined protocol in class **Float.**

New protocol—New protocol in class **Float** consists of 15 new class variables, 5 new class methods, and 16 new instance methods. A list by category is given below.

Class Variables

Class **Float** has 15 new class variables (**ExpPCoefficients, ExpQCoefficients, Fourthpi, Halfpi, Ln2, LnCoefficients, NegativeInfinity, NotANumber, Pi, PositiveInfinity, RadiansPerDegree, SinCoefficients, Sqrt2, TanCoefficients, Twopi**).

Class Methods
instance creation—one method (**notANumber:**).
constants—four methods (**negativeInfinity, notANumber, pi, positiveInfinity**).
Instance Methods
arithmetic—one method (**mod:**).
mathematical functions—one method (**log**).
testing—five methods (**infinity, isNAN, isNegativeInfinity, isNormal, isPositiveInfinity**).
converting—two methods (**asFloat, asFraction**).
truncation and round off—two methods (**fractionPart, integerPart**).
private—five methods (**absPrintOn: digits:, exponent, mantissa:, printOn: digits:, timesTwoPower**).

Inherited protocol—Thirty-two instance methods are inherited by **Float** from **Number.** A summary list of the methods and their categories is given below.
Instance Methods
arithmetic—six methods (**//, abs, quo:, reciprocal, rem:, **).
mathematical functions—three methods (**log:, raisedTo:, raisedToInteger:**)
testing—six methods (**even, negative, odd, positive, sign, strictlyPositive**).
converting—six methods (**@, asComplex, asImaginary, asInteger, asPoint, pi**).
coercing—one method (**retry: coercing:**).
truncation and round off—four methods (**ceiling, floor, roundTo:, truncateTo:**).
intervals—four methods (**to:, to: by:, to: by: do:, to: do:**).
printing—two methods (**storeOn:, storeStructureOn: auxTable:**).

Class **Float** also inherits protocol from **Object** and **Magnitude.** Details of that inherited protocol are not given here. **Float** does redefine 12 instance methods and 1 class method inherited from these superclasses, plus 1 class method inherited from **Behavior.** Those methods are listed under redefined protocol.

Redefined protocol—A total of 23 methods are polymorphically redefined in class **Float** to override their implementations in class **Number.** Of these, 1 is a class method and 22 are instance methods. Six of the methods were implemented as subclassResponsibility in **Number.** They should always be redefined in the subclass. Given below is a summary list of the redefined methods and their categories. In addition, 12 other instance methods and 1 class method are inherited from classes **Magnitude** or **Object** and redefined in **Float.** One class method is inherited from **Behavior** and redefined.
Class Methods
instance creation—One method (**readFrom:**) is inherited from **Number** and redefined. One method (**new**) is inherited from **Behavior** and redefined.
class initialization—One method (**initialize**) is inherited from **Object** and redefined.

Instance Methods

arithmetic—Five methods (***, +, −, /, negated**), of which four (***, +, −, /**) were implemented as subclassResponsibility in **Number,** are inherited and redefined.

converting—Two methods (**degreesToradians, radiansToDegrees**) are inherited from **Number** and redefined.

comparing—Seven methods (**<, <=, =, >, >=, hash, hashMappedBy:**), of which three (**<, =, hash**) are implemented as subclassResponsibility, are inherited from **Magnitude** and polymorphically redefined. One method (**~=**) is inherited from **Object** and polymorphically redefined.

coercing—Two methods (**generality, coerce:**), both of which were implemented as subclassResponsibility in **Number,** are inherited and redefined.

printing—Two methods (**isLiteral, printOn:**) are inherited from **Object** and redefined. One method (**printStructureOn:**) is inherited from **Number** and redefined.

copying—Two methods (**deepCopy, shallowCopy**) are inherited from **Object** and redefined.

mathematical functions—Ten methods (**arcCos, arcSin, arcTan, cos, exp, floorLog:, ln, sin, sqrt, tan**) are inherited from **Number** and redefined.

truncation and round off—Two methods (**rounded, truncated**) are inherited from **Number** and redefined.

New, Inherited, and Redefined Protocol in Class **Fraction**

Class **Fraction** has no shared or pool data. It has two instance variables representing the numerator and denominator of its instances. It has 1 class method in one category and 20 instance methods in seven categories. The methods are either new or redefined protocol. In addition some methods are inherited from **Number** and its superclasses, **Magnitude** and **Object,** and used by class **Fraction**. The following is a summary of the new, inherited, and redefined protocol in class **Fraction**.

New protocol—New protocol in class **Fraction** consists of two new instance variables, one new class method and six new instance methods. A list by category is given below.

Private Data

Class **Fraction** has two new instance variables (**numerator, denominator**).

Class Methods

instance creation—one method (**numerator: denominator:**).

Instance Methods

converting—two methods (**asFloat, asFraction**).

private—four methods (**denominator, numerator, reduced, setNumerator: denominator:**).

Inherited protocol—Forty-six instance methods are inherited by **Fraction** from **Number.** A summary list of the methods and their categories follows.

Instance Methods

arithmetic—five methods (//, **abs, quo:, rem:, **).

testing—six methods (**even, negative, odd, positive, sign, strictlyPositive**).

converting—eight methods (**@, asComplex, asImaginary, asInteger, asPoint, degreesToRadians, pi, radiansToDegrees**).

coercing—one method (**retry: coercing:**).

mathematical functions—fourteen methods (**arcCos, arcSin, arcTan, cos, exp, floorLog:, ln, log:, raisedTo:, raisedToInteger:, sin, sqrt, squared, tan**).

truncation and round off—five methods (**ceiling, floor, rounded, roundTo:, truncateTo:**).

intervals—four methods (**to:, to: by:, to: by: do:, to: do:**).

printing—three methods (**storeOn:, printStructureOn:, storeStructureOn: auxTable:**).

Class **Fraction** also inherits protocol from **Object** and **Magnitude**. Details of that inherited protocol are not given here. **Fraction** does redefine five instance methods inherited from these superclasses. Those five methods are listed below.

Redefined protocol—A total of 14 methods are polymorphically redefined in class **Fraction** to override their inherited implementations. Of these, 9 are instance methods inherited from **Number** and redefined. Four instance methods from **Magnitude** and 1 instance method from **Object** are inherited and redefined. Four of the methods were implemented as subclassResponsibility in **Number** and 3 were subclassResponsibility in **Magnitude.** They should always be redefined in the subclass. Given below is a summary list of the 14 redefined methods and their categories.

Instance Methods

arithmetic—six methods (***, +, −, /, negated, reciprocal**), of which four (***, +, −, /**) were implemented as subclassResponsibility in **Number,** are inherited and redefined.

comparing—four methods (**<, =, hash, hashMappedBy:**), of which three (**<, =, hash**) are implemented as subclassResponsibility, are inherited from **Magnitude** and polymorphically redefined.

coercing—two methods (**generality, coerce:**), both of which were implemented as subclassResponsibility in **Number.**

printing—One method (**printOn:**) is inherited from **Object** and redefined.

truncation and round off—One method (**truncated**) is inherited from **Number** and redefined.

In tracing the details of a segment of Smalltalk code, it is sometimes necessary to find details of all the messages and objects in the code. This includes looking up method details for the messages and understanding the private data objects and shared data objects. Even a relatively simple block of code can lead one on a merry chase through the Smalltalk image. This chase is complicated by inheritance. Knowing the class of an object does not always lead directly to the details of a message sent to that object. It may be part of the protocol in a superclass.

Sometimes it becomes necessary to switch among several hierarchy paths at different levels to find all the details of a block of code. There are tools in the System Browser that make this possible, if not easy. Having multiple browser windows open also helps. *In the long run there is no substitute for familiarity with the Smalltalk image.* That is why so much effort in this book is devoted to summarizing numerous classes.

One can also think of additional tools for helping track the path through the image for a particular block of code. Generation of an execution history of all object-message pairs that can be viewed would be helpful. It may even be of manageable size for relatively simple software systems.

6.4   Generality of Numbers Versus Strong Type Checking

The concept of strong type checking is used in many modern computer languages. A strongly typed language does not allow the mixing of different types of numbers (e.g., reals and integers) in an expression. Some languages are weakly typed and allow restricted mixing of types, such as reals and integers, that are forced to give a result compatible with both (in this case a real). The product of an integer and a real must be a real. Smalltalk takes the concept of mixed types a step further. It uses the concept of *generality of numbers.* This removes from the user the burden of checking number types in an expression.

The concept of the generality of numbers is stated in the following way: *When numbers of two different types appear in an expression, the system coerces the numbers to both be of the type that is the most general of the two. Then the operation can be performed with the numbers now being of the same type.* This concept requires that each type (class) of number be assigned a "generality index."

For most of the number classes, the generality index is easily determined. For the three classes **Float, Integer,** and **Fraction,** the following relationships hold.

1.   Floating point numbers are the most general. The other two classes of numbers can be thought of as special cases of instances of class **Float.**

2.   Fractions are numbers represented as rational numbers. Rational numbers can always be expressed as the ratio of two integers. Not all floating point numbers have a rational number representation, but all rational numbers can be represented by floating point numbers. This is within the constraints of accuracy limitations. Therefore, instances of **Fraction** are a subset of **Float.**

3. Integers are a special case of rational numbers whose ratio produces a new integer value from the indicated division. Or, an integer can be considered to be a rational number whose denominator is 1. As such, instances of class **Integer** are a subset of **Fraction.**

From these relationships a generality hierarchy from highest to lowest is **Float—Fraction—Integer.** From this hierarchy one can assign ascending numbers to represent the generality index for each class. This is done in the Smalltalk system. Generality indices for these three classes are, from highest to lowest, 80−60−40.

Application of the concept of generality to a binary operation such as num1 * num2 produces the following result: If num1 and num2 are not instances of the same class, then the one with the lower generality index is coerced to be an instance of the class with the higher generality index. The multiply operation can then be performed.

The advantage of the concept of generality of numbers over strong type checking is that the user can define what specific mix of classes of numbers can be combined and how. This allows the programmer to use numbers in a way that is closer to the way that people normally use them.

The key method for handling generality of numbers is implemented in class **Number.** It is called retry: coercing:. The purpose of this method is to retry a particular binary operation on numbers that are of different classes, coercing the one with the lower generality index to be an instance of the class of the one with the higher generality index. For example,

1/5 * 4 / 0.8

gives the result 1.0. The first number, 1/5, is actually an integer division of 1 by 5. Protocol in class **Integer** recognizes the result is not a valid integer and returns an instance of **Fraction** (protocol in class **Integer** uses the message // to indicate true integer division). This fraction is sent the multiply message with the integer 4 as a parameter. Since the fraction has a higher generality index, the multiply operation first converts 4 to a fraction with value 4/1. It then multiplies 1/5 by 4/1 and gets the result 4/5. This object is next sent the divide message with 0.8 as the parameter. Since **Float** has a higher generality index than **Fraction,** the fraction 4/5 is converted to a real value of 0.8. The division then produces an instance of **Float,** which is the result 1.0.

Methods for arithmetic within a **Number** subclass first check to see if the receiver and parameter are of the same class. If not, the message retry: coercing: is sent to the receiver with the errant parameter to be coerced. The method for retry: coercing: handles cases in which either the receiver or parameter have higher generality index.

Listing 6.2 shows the details of the method retry: coercing: in class **Number,** provided in the standard Smalltalk image. This method is later modified to handle the new classes **Imaginary** and **Complex.** The message perform: aSymbol with: anObject used in Listing 6.2 is a message implemented (using a primitive) in class **Object.** This message is interpreted to mean, "Send the receiver the mes-

Listing 6.2
Details of Standard
Method retry:
coercing: in Class
Number

Number methodsFor: 'coercing'

retry: aSymbol coercing: aNumber
"Arithmetic represented by the symbol, aSymbol, could not be performed with the
    receiver and the argument, aNumber, because of the differences in representation.
    Coerce either the   receiver or the argument, depending on which has higher
    generality, and try again. If the symbol is the equals sign, answer false if the
    argument is not a Number. If the generalities are the same, create an error
    message."

(aSymbol = = #= and: [(aNumber isKindOf: Number) = = false])
    ifTrue: [↑false].
self generality < aNumber generality
    ifTrue: [↑ (aNumber coerce: self) perform: aSymbol with: aNumber].
self generality > aNumber generality
    ifTrue: [↑self perform: aSymbol with: (self coerce: aNumber)].
self error: 'coercion attempt failed'

Listing 6.3
Example of How
retry: coercing:
Is Called

Float methodsFor: 'arithmetic'

+ aNumber
    "Add the receiver to the argument and return the result as a Float. Fail if the
    argument is not a Float. Essential. See Object documentation
    whatIsAPrimitive. "

    <primitive: 41>
    ↑self retry: #+ coercing: aNumber

sage represented by **aSymbol** with a single parameter given by **anObject**." For
example, the statement

20.0 perform: #+ with: (20.0 coerce: 3/4)

first coerces the fraction 3/4 to be a floating 0.75 and then performs the addition
of 20.0 and 0.75. The message is equivalent to

20.0 + (20.0 coerce: 3/4).

Listing 6.3 shows details of the message for addition in class **Float.** Imple-
mentation details of the message are contained in primitive method number 41.
If the primitive method fails, as will be true if **aNumber** is not also an instance of
Float, the expression retry: #+ coercing: aNumber is sent to the receiver object.
The parameter of the selector, retry:, is a symbol representing the indicated bi-
nary operation (+ in this example).

In the next two sections, imaginary and complex numbers are added to the
Smalltalk image as new **Number** subclasses. If these new kinds of numbers are to
be consistent with the generality of numbers concept, they must be assigned
generality indices that produce correct results in mixed operations.

For some cases, simple coercion does not work. For example, if the product of a real number and an imaginary number is indicated, it makes no sense to try to coerce either number to be of the same class as the other. This will produce an incorrect result. There are several special cases that have to be handled when adding imaginary and complex numbers to the image.

Instances of class **Imaginary** are given a generality index higher than that of floating point numbers. This has the advantage that the special cases can be handled in the protocol for class **Imaginary.** The protocol for the lower generality classes should require little if any changes.

Instances of class **Complex** are given the highest generality. It is easy to argue that all the other kinds of numbers are special cases of complex numbers. Thus in the modified Smalltalk image the number classes have generality from highest to lowest given by **Complex—Imaginary—Float—Fraction—Integer.**

6.5   Class **Imaginary**—A New **Number** Subclass with Support for Literals

In this section the class **Imaginary** is added as a subclass of **Number** to represent pure imaginary numbers. The concept of adding new literals to the Smalltalk image is discussed and explained as it is implemented for class **Imaginary.** Imaginary numbers are displayed and identified by a preceding j character. Thus a literal imaginary number is entered by simply typing j, followed by a number (e.g., j3, j3.4, j3/4).

To handle imaginary numbers as literals, modifications must be made both to existing methods in the **Number** classes and to the system compiler classes. Fortunately, Smalltalk provides the flexibility for modifying its compiler classes. This section presents a discussion of the required modification to existing classes and a summary of the protocol for class **Imaginary.** Imaginary numbers have a generality index higher than floating point numbers. A floating point number may be considered to be a special case of the imaginary number (e.g., its magnitude). In Section 6.6, complex numbers are introduced as new protocol to the Smalltalk image. Complex numbers have the highest generality index.

Protocol Summary for Class **Imaginary**

Class **Imaginary** represents imaginary numbers. Instances of this class are represented as numbers preceded by the symbol j.

The hierarchy for class **Imaginary** is **Object—Magnitude—Number—Imaginary.** It has one instance variable, **magnitude.** It has no class variables or pool dictionaries. It has 1 class method in one category and 15 instance methods in seven categories.

Class **Imaginary** has one instance variable, **magnitude,** that is a number representing the magnitude of the imaginary number.

Complete protocol for class **Imaginary**

Listing 6.4 gives the complete protocol description for class **Imaginary.** It is included as an example of how new capability can be added to the Smalltalk image. The class category, definition, and all protocol details were added to the image using the System Browser as described in Chapters 3 and 4.

6.5.1 Required modifications to existing **Number** classes necessitated by adding classes **Imaginary** and **Complex**

To provide consistency with the concept of the generality of numbers, the addition of classes **Complex** and **Imaginary** necessitates several modifications to the existing number classes. These modifications are minimized by taking full advantage of the generality concept. Support for mixing instances of classes **Imaginary** and **Complex** with instances of the other classes in ordinary arithmetic operations and for comparisons must be provided.

A summary of the specific support for generality and the protocol changes in other **Number** classes is given below. Features that are known not to be supported are also listed.

1. Generality support is provided for the four major arithmetic operations ($+$, $-$, $*$, $/$) and for the six major comparison operations ($<$, $<=$, $=$, $>$, $>=$, $\sim=$).

2. **Integer** arithmetic operations such as **/, \\,** and **quo:** are not supported but could be included by making minor additional modifications.

3. Some of the inherited protocol from **Number** is supported, and some is not. For example, testing methods **negative, positive, sign,** and **strictlyPositive** are supported, but **even** and **odd** are not since they send the integer message \\.

4. Inherited mathematical functions are not supported. Their implementations first attempt to coerce a number to be an instance of **Float.** Coercing imaginary or complex numbers to be floating point numbers is like coercing apples to be oranges. Some mathematical functions used in engineering applications do have meaning for complex and imaginary numbers. A good exercise is to add support for these.

5. The three numeral classes (**Float, Integer, Fraction**) can be coerced to be complex and cause no inconsistency. They are essentially assigned to be the real part of a complex number that has zero imaginary part. Instances of

Listing 6.4
Complete Protocol
Listing for New
Class **Imaginary**

Number subclass: #Imaginary
    instanceVariableNames: 'magnitude '
    classVariableNames: ''
    poolDictionaries: ''
    category: 'Numeric-Numbers'

Imaginary comment: 'New Number subclass : added April 20, 1987 by Lewis J. Pinson.
    Imaginary numbers are identified by a number preceded by the character, j. No spaces
    are allowed between j and the number. A lone j is treated as j1. Literals are supported.
    Class Imaginary has one instance variable,magnitude, that is the value, including sign, of
    the imaginary number. Addition of this class required mods to existing Number
    subclasses, the Number methods: retry:coercing: and readFrom:. The Scanner class was
    modified to support literals.'

Imaginary methodsFor: 'printing'

printOn: aStream
    "Append the receiver to aStream"
    self magnitude > = 0
        ifTrue: [aStream nextPutAll: ' +j']
        ifFalse: [aStream nextPutAll: ' -j'].
    magnitude abs printOn: aStream

Imaginary methodsFor: 'coercing'

coerce: aNumber
    self error: 'should not coerce a number to be imaginary'

generality
    ↑100

Imaginary methodsFor: 'converting'

asComplex
    ↑Complex real: 0 imaginary: self magnitude

asImaginary
    ↑self

Imaginary methodsFor: 'arithmetic'

* aNumber
    (aNumber isMemberOf: Imaginary)
        ifTrue: [↑(self magnitude * aNumber magnitude) negated]
        ifFalse: [(aNumber isMemberOf: Complex)
            ifTrue: [↑self retry: #* coercing: aNumber]
            ifFalse:[↑Imaginary new: (self magnitude * aNumber)]]

```
+ aNumber
    (aNumber isMemberOf: Imaginary)
        ifTrue: [ ↑Imaginary new: (self magnitude + aNumber magnitude) ]
        ifFalse: [ ↑self retry: #+ coercing: aNumber]

- aNumber
    (aNumber isMemberOf: Imaginary)
        ifTrue: [ ↑Imaginary new: (self magnitude - aNumber magnitude) ]
        ifFalse: [ ↑self retry: #- coercing: aNumber]

/ aNumber
    (aNumber isMemberOf: Imaginary)
        ifTrue: [ ↑(self magnitude / aNumber magnitude)  ]
        ifFalse: [ (aNumber isMemberOf: Complex)
            ifTrue: [ ↑self retry: #/ coercing: aNumber]
            ifFalse:[ ↑Imaginary new: (self magnitude / aNumber)]]
```

Imaginary methodsFor: 'accessing'

magnitude
```
    ↑magnitude
```

Imaginary methodsFor: 'comparing'

```
< aNumber
    (aNumber isMemberOf: Imaginary)
        ifTrue: [  ↑magnitude < aNumber magnitude]
        ifFalse:[ ↑self retry: #< coercing: aNumber]

= aNumber
    (aNumber isMemberOf: Imaginary)
        ifTrue: [  ↑magnitude = aNumber magnitude]
        ifFalse:[ ↑self retry: #= coercing: aNumber]
```

hash
```
    "Hash is reimplemented because = is implemented"
    ↑self magnitude asFloat hash
```

hashMappedBy: map
```
    "My hash is independent of my oop"
    ↑self hash
```

Imaginary methodsFor: 'private'

setMagnitude: aNumber
```
    (aNumber isKindOf: Complex)
        ifTrue: [ self error: 'invalid assignment of imaginary number']
        ifFalse:[ magnitude ← aNumber]
```

Listing 6.4
(continued)

Imaginary class
    instanceVariableNames: ''

Imaginary class comment: ''

Imaginary class methodsFor: 'instance creation'

new: aNumber
    ↑self new setMagnitude: aNumber

these three classes can also be coerced to be imaginary (as the magnitude). This coercion produces an inconsistent result; however, it is useful in some applications. Both coercions are provided for these three classes. The details of the methods for two new messages (**asImaginary, asComplex**) are given below. The methods are identical for **Float, Integer,** and **Fraction.** Therefore they are included as instance methods in superclass **Number** under the category *converting.*

Number methodsFor: 'converting'
asComplex
        "Answer a new complex number with real = self and imaginary = 0."
        ↑ Complex real: self imaginary: 0.0
asImaginary
        "Answer a new imaginary number with magnitude = self."
        ↑ Imaginary new: self

6. A new method, **mod:**, is added to class **Float.** It supports modulo arithmetic for floating point numbers. This support is required for computing the polar form angle of a complex number. Its details are:

Float methodsFor: 'arithmetic'
mod: aFloat
        "Answer the receiver modulo aFloat truncated toward zero."
        ↑ self—((self/aFloat) truncated * aFloat)

7. Method **sqrt**, in class **Float** is modified to return an imaginary number for the square root of a negative numeral. The modified method for **sqrt** is shown below.

Float methodsFor: 'mathematical functions'
sqrt
        | guess |
        <primitive 150>
        self <= 0.0 ifTrue: [self = 0.0
                ifTrue: [↑ 0.0]
                ifFalse:[↑ Imaginary new: self abs sqrt]].
        guess s self timesTwoPower: 0 - (self exponent // 2).
        5 timesRepeat: [guess ← self - (guess*guess) / (guess * 2.0) + guess].
        ↑ guess.

8. The **Number** method retry: coercing: is modified to handle all the special cases caused by mixing imaginary numbers with other kinds of numbers. Details of this modified method are given in Listing 6.5. The rules implemented by the added code in this method are the following:

- Complex numbers can be mixed with the three numeral types and with imaginary numbers by using the concept of generality. No modifications are necessary to handle complex numbers.

- An addition or subtraction that mixes a numeral with an imaginary number returns an imaginary number if the numeral is zero. If the numeral is not zero, a complex number is returned. For example, $0 - j3$ returns $-j3$, and $2 + j4$ returns $(2 + j4)$.

- A multiplication or division that mixes a numeral with an imaginary number returns an imaginary number whose magnitude is the product or

Listing 6.5
Modified Listing of
Number Method
retry: coercing:

Number methodsFor: 'coercing'

retry: aSymbol **coercing:** aNumber
  "Arithmetic represented by the symbol, aSymbol could not be performed with the
    receiver and the argument, aNumber, because of the differences in representation.
    Coerce either the receiver or the argument, depending on which has higher
    generality, and try again. If the symbol is the equals sign, answer false if the
    argument is not a Number. If the generalities are the same, create an error message.
    If the receiver or the argument have a preceding 'j' return a Complex literal."

  (aSymbol = = # = and: [(aNumber isKindOf: Number) = = false]) ifTrue: [↑false].

  ((self isMemberOf: Imaginary) or: [aNumber isMemberOf: Imaginary]) ifTrue: [
    (aSymbol = = # + or: [aSymbol = = #-]) ifTrue: [
      self = = 0
          ifTrue: [↑self asImaginary perform: aSymbol with: aNumber]
          ifFalse:[↑self asComplex perform: aSymbol with: (aNumber asComplex)]].
    (aSymbol = = #* or: [aSymbol = = #/]) ifTrue: [
      ((self isMemberOf: Complex) not and: [(aNumber isMemberOf: Complex) not])
        ifTrue:[↑Imaginary new: (
            self generality > aNumber generality
              ifTrue: [self magnitude perform: aSymbol with: aNumber]
              ifFalse:[self perform: aSymbol with:
                ((aSymbol = = #/
                    ifTrue: [-1]
                    ifFalse:[1]) * (aNumber magnitude))])]].
    (aSymbol = = # = or: [aSymbol = = # <]) ifTrue: [↑false]].

  self generality < aNumber generality
    ifTrue: [↑ (aNumber coerce: self) perform: aSymbol with: aNumber].
  self generality > aNumber generality
    ifTrue: [↑self perform: aSymbol with: (self coerce: aNumber)].
  self error: 'coercion attempt failed'

quotient of the numeral and the magnitude of the imaginary number. Logic based on generality is used to determine which (**self** or **aNumber**) is the imaginary number (imaginary has higher generality than numerals). For division, when the divisor is the imaginary number, the resulting imaginary number will be negated. For example, 2.0 * j3 returns j6.0, j4 / 2 returns j2, and 3.0 / j2 returns −j1.5.

6.5.2   Adding support for **Imaginary** literals—the compiler classes

Class **Scanner,** a subclass of **Object,** provides protocol for scanning expressions and returning tokens. Method **scanToken** is an instance method in that class with major responsibility for tokenizing an expression. To provide support for imaginary literals as numerals preceded by the character j, a minor modification is made to **scanToken**. An additional modification is made to the instance creation method **readFrom:** in class **Number.**

Listing 6.6 shows the details of the modified method **scanToken**. It simply traps a j that precedes a digit and signals the scanner to expect a number. This results in sending the message **xDigit**, whose purpose is to acquire the number token and return it. Listing 6.7 shows the details for the method **xDigit**. The significant message in this method is the class method **readFrom:**, sent to **Number.**

Listing 6.6
Modified Version of
Scanner Method
scanToken—
Imaginary Literals

Scanner methodsFor: 'expression types'

scanToken
```
    [(tokenType ← typeTable at: hereChar asciiValue) = = #xDelimiter]
        whileTrue: [self step].  "Skip delimiters fast, there almost always is one."
    mark ← source position - 1.
    (hereChar = $j and: [(typeTable at: aheadChar asciiValue) = = #xDigit])
        ifTrue: [tokenType ← #xDigit].
    (tokenType at: 1) = $x "x as first letter"
        ifTrue: [self perform: tokenType "means perform to compute token & type"]
        ifFalse:[token ← self step asSymbol "else just unique the first char"].
    ↑token
```

Listing 6.7
Details of **Scanner**
Method xDigit

Scanner methodsFor: 'multi-character scans'

xDigit
```
    "form a number"

    tokenType ← #number.
    (aheadChar = EndChar and: [source atEnd
            and: [source skip: -1. source next ~ = EndChar]])
        ifTrue: [source skip: -1 "Read off the end last time"]
        ifFalse: [source skip: -2].
    token ← Number readFrom: source.
    self step; step
```

Listing 6.8
Modified **Number**
Class Method
readFrom:

Number class methodsFor: 'instance creation'

```
readFrom: aStream
    "Answer an instance of me as described on the stream, aStream"

    | value radix fraction fracpos sign imaginary |
    radix ← 10.
    sign ← (aStream peekFor: $-) ifTrue: [-1] ifFalse: [1].
    imaginary ← (aStream peekFor: $j).
    value ← Integer readFrom: aStream.
    (aStream peekFor: $r)
        ifTrue:
            ["<radix>r<integer>"
            (radix ← value) < 2 ifTrue: [^self error: 'Invalid Radix'].
            value ← Integer readFrom: aStream radix: radix].
    (aStream peekFor: $.)
        ifTrue:
            ["<integer>.<fraction>"
            (aStream atEnd not and: [aStream peek digitValue between: 0 and: radix - 1])
                ifTrue:
                    [fracpos ← aStream position.
                    fraction ← Integer readFrom: aStream radix: radix.
                    radix ← radix asFloat.
                    fraction ←
                        fraction asFloat / (radix raisedTo: aStream position - fracpos).
                    value ← value asFloat + (value < 0
                                    ifTrue: [fraction negated]
                                    ifFalse: [fraction])]
                ifFalse:
                    ["oops - just <integer>."
                    aStream skip: -1.        "un-gobble the period"
                    imaginary
                        ifTrue: [↑ (value * sign) asImaginary]
                        ifFalse:[↑value * sign]
                                "Number readFrom: (ReadStream on: '3r-22.2')"]].
    (aStream peekFor: $e)
        ifTrue:
            ["<integer>e<exponent>"
            imaginary
                ifTrue: [↑ (value * sign * (radix raisedTo: (Integer readFrom: aStream)))
                        asImaginary]
                ifFalse:[↑value * sign * (radix raisedTo: (Integer readFrom: aStream))]].
    imaginary
        ifTrue: [↑ (value * sign) asImaginary]
        ifFalse:[↑value * sign]
```

The purpose of readFrom: is to read the number token from the source stream (which contains the expression being scanned).

Listing 6.8 shows the modified **Number** class method readFrom:. The message peekFor: (defined in the protocol of class **PositionableStream**) used in the method peeks into the receiver stream for occurrence of a specified character. If

Figure 6.3 An Example Showing the Use of Instances and Literals of Class **Imaginary**

System Transcript

Test 1: Literal support for imaginary numbers (Very large imaginary numbers).
+j30614062   +j30614166   +j30614288   +j30614398   +j30614507

Test 2: Operations on imaginary literals.
-j4 + j6 = +j2; -j4 * j6 = -24; -j4 / j6 = (-2/3); -j4 * j3 .2 = 12.8

Test 3: Operations on imaginary variables.
Imag1 + imag2 = +j2; imag1 * imag2 = 24; imag1 / imag2 = (-2/3); float product = 12.8

Test 4: Mixed operations with imaginary numbers.
Imag1 + (3/4) = ((3/4) - j4.0); imag1 * 5 = -j20; -4 / imag2 = +j(2/3); imag1 / 6 = -j(2/3); float product = -j12.8

Workspace

Number *methodsfor:* examples
"Number example1"

example1
  "Adding literal support for imaginary numbers and mixing imaginary and numerals."
  | imag1 imag2 |
"Test 1"
  Transcript clear; refresh; show: 'Test 1: Literal support for imaginary numbers (Very large imaginary numbers).'; cr.
  5 timesRepeat: [Transcript show: (Imaginary new: (Time millisecondClockValue)) printString, '   '].
"Test 2"
  Transcript cr; cr; show: 'Test 2: Operations on imaginary literals.'; cr.
  Transcript show: '-j4 + j6 = ', (-j4+j6) printString, '; -j4 * j6 = ', (-j4*j6) printString,
    '; -j4 / j6 = ', (-j4/j6) printString, '; -j4 * j3.2 = ', (-j4*j3.2) printString.
"Test 3"
  Transcript cr; cr; show: 'Test 3: Operations on imaginary variables.'; cr.
  imag1 + Imaginary new: -4. imag2 + Imaginary new: 6.
  Transcript show: 'Imag1 + imag2 = ', (imag1+imag2) printString, '; imag1 * Imag2 = ', (imag1*imag2) printString,
    '; imag1 / imag2 = ',(imag1/imag2) printString, '; float product = ', (imag1* (imag2 + Imaginary new: 3.2)) printString.
"Test 4"
  Transcript cr; cr; show: 'Test 4: Mixed operations with imaginary numbers.'; cr.
  imag1 + Imaginary new: -4. imag2 + Imaginary new: 6.
  Transcript show: 'Imag1 + (3/4) = ', (Imag1+(3/4)) printString, '; imag1 * 5 = ', (imag1*5) printString,
    '; -4 / Imag2 = ',(-4/imag2) printString, '; imag1 / 6 = ',(imag1/6) printString, ';' float product = ', (imag1* 3.2) printString.

the character is there, it is skipped and a value of true is returned. If the character is not there, nothing happens except that a value of false is returned. The temporary variable imaginary is set to true if a j is part of the number. If a j is found then the method returns the number as an instance of **Imaginary.** The method as modified correctly returns imaginary exponents as well as base numbers. However, no other protocol is available for using numbers with imaginary exponents. This additional support could be added since numbers with imaginary exponents are another representation for complex numbers.

Imaginary Example 6A

This example illustrates the support for literals and for mixed operations with other **Number** classes for instances of class **Imaginary.** It is added as a class method called example1 in **Number.** Figure 6.3 shows the method and the result of its execution. Test 1 in the figure creates five new instances of class **Imaginary** by sending the instance creation message new:, to class name **Imaginary** with the value of the millisecond clock as its magnitude. Test 2 demonstrates the use of imaginary literals and the four standard arithmetic operations. Test 3 demonstrates arithmetic operations using variables as instances of **Imaginary.** And, finally, Test 4 shows mixed arithmetic operations using imaginary numbers and instances of the three numeral classes, **Float, Fraction,** and **Integer.**

6.6   Class **Complex**—A New Subclass of **Number**

In this section the class **Complex** is defined and added to the Smalltalk image. Criteria for testing equality, coercing, generality, and operations with other numbers are presented in descriptive form and supported by examples. The default method (rectangular form) for "printing" complex numbers is presented.

Class **Complex** is the most general of all the **Number** classes. Complex numbers represented in rectangular form have literal support because they are combinations of instances from the other **Number** classes (including **Imaginary**), all of which have support for literals.

Protocol Summary for Class **Complex**

Class **Complex** represents complex numbers. Instances of this class are represented in both rectangular form as a real and imaginary part or in complex form as a magnitude and an angle.

The hierarchy for class **Complex** is **Object—Magnitude—Number—Complex.** It has four instance variables, real, imaginary, modulus, and angle. It has no class variables or pool dictionaries. It has 2 class methods in one category and 21 instance methods in seven categories.

Class **Complex** has four instance variables. They are: (1) **real,** a number representing the real part of the complex number in rectangular form; (2) **imaginary,** a number representing the imaginary part of a complex number in rectangular form; (3) **modulus,** a number representing the modulus of a complex number in polar form; and (4) **angle,** a number representing the angle of a complex number in polar form.

Complete protocol for class **Complex**

Listing 6.9 gives the complete protocol for class **Complex.** It is given as an example of how new protocol can be added to the Smalltalk image.

Listing 6.9
Complete Protocol
Listing of New
Number Subclass
Complex

Number subclass: #Complex
    instanceVariableNames: 'real imaginary modulus angle '
    classVariableNames: ''
    poolDictionaries: ''
    category: 'Numeric-Numbers'

Complex comment: 'New subclass of Number: Added March 1987 by Lewis J. Pinson.
    This class provides standard operations on complex numbers. New instances are
    created by specifying either the real and imaginary parts or the modulus and phase
    angle. Both rectangular and polar forms are stored as instance variables for either
    method of instance creation. Literals are supported in class Imaginary."

Modification: April 20, 1987 by Lewis J. Pinson
    Support for literals added along with support for a new Number subclass, Imaginary.'

Complex methodsFor: 'accessing'

angle
    "Return real part of complex number."
    ↑angle

imaginary
    "Return imaginary part of complex number."
    ↑imaginary

modulus
    "Return real part of complex number."
    ↑modulus

real
    "Return real part of complex number."
    ↑real

Complex methodsFor: 'private'

setModulus: aNumber1 **setAngle:** aNumber2
    "Establish both forms of a complex number."
    " a + jb   and   r , theta"
    | r th |
    modulus ← (r ← aNumber1).
    angle ← (th ← aNumber2).
    real ← r * (th degreesToRadians cos).
    imaginary ← r * (th degreesToRadians sin).

setReal: aNumber1 **setImaginary:** aNumber2
    "Establish both forms of a complex number."
    " a + jb   and   r , theta"
    | a b |
    real ← (a ← aNumber1).
    imaginary ← (b ← aNumber2).
    modulus ← ((a*a) + (b*b)) sqrt.
    (a = 0)
          ifTrue: [angle ← (b sign) * 90]
          ifFalse: [angle ← (b/a) arcTan radiansToDegrees.
              (a < 0) ifTrue: [angle ← angle + 180]]

Complex methodsFor: 'arithmetic'

* aNumber
    "Answer the product of receiver and aNumber"
    | a b |
    (aNumber isMemberOf: Complex)
        ifTrue:[a ← self modulus * aNumber modulus.
           b ← (self angle + aNumber angle) mod: 360.
           ↑(Complex modulus: a angle: b)]
        ifFalse:[↑self retry: #* coercing: aNumber]

+ aNumber
    "Answer the sum of receiver and aNumber"
    | a b |
    (aNumber isMemberOf: Complex)
        ifTrue:[a ← self real + aNumber real.
           b ← self imaginary + aNumber imaginary.
           ↑(Complex real: a imaginary: b)]
        ifFalse:[↑self retry: #+ coercing: aNumber]

- aNumber
    "Answer the difference of receiver and aNumber"
    | a b |
    (aNumber isMemberOf: Complex)
        ifTrue:[a ← self real ← aNumber real.
           b ← self imaginary - aNumber imaginary.
           ↑(Complex real: a imaginary: b)]
        ifFalse:[↑self retry:#- coercing: aNumber]

Listing 6.9
(continued)

```
/ aNumber
    "Answer the quotient of receiver by aNumber"
    | a b |
    (aNumber isMemberOf: Complex)
        ifTrue:[ a ← self modulus / aNumber modulus.
            b ← (self angle - aNumber angle) mod: 360.
                ↑(Complex modulus: a angle: b)]
        ifFalse:[↑self retry: #/ coercing: aNumber]
```

Complex methodsFor: 'coercing'

coerce: aNumber
```
    ↑aNumber asComplex
```

generality
```
    ↑120
```

Complex methodsFor: 'printing'

printOn: aStream
```
    "Print in rectangular form on aStream."
    aStream nextPut: $(.
    real printOn: aStream.
    (imaginary > = 0)
        ifTrue:[ aStream nextPutAll: ' + j'.
            imaginary printOn: aStream]
        ifFalse:[ aStream nextPutAll: ' - j'.
            imaginary abs printOn: aStream].
    aStream nextPut: $).
```

printPolar
```
    "Returns  the complex number in polar form on aStream as a string."
    | outString modString angString aStream |
    modString ← ( self modulus printString).
    angString ← ( self angle printString).
    outString ← '(', modString, ' < ', angString, ')'.
    ↑(aStream ← WriteStream with: outString) contents
```

printPolar: aStream
```
    "Returns  the complex number in polar form on aStream."
    aStream nextPut: $(.
    modulus printOn: aStream.
    aStream nextPutAll: ' angle '.
    angle printOn: aStream.
    aStream nextPut: $)
```

Complex methodsFor: 'comparing'

```
< aNumber
    (aNumber isMemberOf: Complex)
        ifTrue: [↑modulus < aNumber modulus]
        ifFalse:[ (aNumber isMemberOf: Imaginary)
            ifTrue: [↑imaginary < aNumber magnitude and: [real = 0]]
            ifFalse: [↑false]]
```

```
= aNumber
    (aNumber isMemberOf: Complex)
        ifTrue: [↑real = aNumber real and: [imaginary = aNumber imaginary]]
        ifFalse:[ (aNumber isMemberOf: Imaginary)
            ifTrue: [↑imaginary = aNumber magnitude and: [real = 0]]
            ifFalse: [↑false]]
```

hash
    "Hash is reimplemented because = is implemented"
    ↑self modulus asFloat hash

hashMappedBy: map
    "My hash is independent of my oop"
    ↑self hash

Complex methodsFor: 'converting'

asComplex
    ↑self

asImaginary

    self real = 0.0
        ifTrue: [↑Imaginary new: self imaginary]
        ifFalse:[↑'Can''t convert to imaginary']

Complex class
    instanceVariableNames: ''

    Complex class comment: '"New instances are created with class methods real:imaginary:
        and modulus:angle:."'

Complex class methodsFor: 'instance creation'

modulus: modulusNumber **angle:** angleNumber
    "Create a new complex number"
    ↑self new setModulus: modulusNumber setAngle: angleNumber

real: realNumber **imaginary:** imaginaryNumber
    "Create a new complex number"
    ↑self new setReal: realNumber setImaginary: imaginaryNumber

Figure 6.4 An Example Showing the Use of Instances and Literals of Class **Complex**

System Transcript

Test 1: Operations on complex literals.
(2 – j4) + (–3 – j6) = (0 – j10.0); (2 – j4) * (–3 – j6) = (–36.0 – j18.0); (2 – j4) / (–3 – j6) = (0.399999 + j0.533334); (2 – j4) * (1/3 + j3 .2) = (13.4667 + j5.06667)

Test 2: Operations on complex variables.   cx1 = (2.0 + j4)   cx2 = ((3/4) + j(1/3))
cx1 + cx2 = (2.75 + j(13/3)); cx1 * cx2 = (0.166666 + j3.66667); cx1 / cx2 = (4.20619 + j3.46392)

Test 3: Mixed operations with complex numbers.
cx1 + (3/4) = (2.75 + j4.0); cx1 * 5 = (10.0 + j20.0); –4 / cx2 = (–4.4536 + j1.97939); cx1 / 6 = (0.333333 + j0.666667)

Test 4: yellow button to show mouse coordinates as x + jy, blue button to quit.
Mouse coordinates: (257 + j772)

Workspace

```
Number methodsFor: examples
    "Number example2 "

example2
"Adding literal support for imaginary numbers and mixing imaginary and numerals."
| cx1 cx2 |  cx1 ← Complex real: 2.0 imaginary: 4. cx2 ← Complex real: 3/4 imaginary: 1/3.
"Test 1"
Transcript clear; refresh; show: 'Test 1: Operations on complex literals.'; cr.
Transcript show: '(2 – j4) + (–3 – j6) = ', ((2–j4)+(-2–j6)) printString, '; (2– j4) * (–3 – j6) = ', ((2–j4)*(-j3–j6)) printString,
        '; (2 – j4) / (–3 – j6) = ',((2–j4)/(-3–j6)) printString, ';  (2 – j4) * (1/3 +  j3 .2) = ', ((2–j4)*(1/3+j3.2)) printString.
"Test 2"
Transcript cr; cr; show: 'Test 2: Operations on complex variables.',  '   cx1 = ', cx1 printString, '   cx2 = ', cx2 printString; cr.
Transcript show: 'cx1 + cx2 = ',(cx1+cx2) printString, '; cx1 * cx2 = ', (cx1*cx2) printString, '; cx1 / cx2 = ',(cx1/cx2) printString.
"Test 3"
Transcript cr; cr; show: 'Test 3: Mixed operations with complex numbers.'; cr.
Transcript show: 'cx1 + (3/4) = ', (cx1+(3/4)) printString, ';  cx1 * 5 = ', (cx1*5) printString,
        '; –4 / cx2 = ',(-4/cx2) printString, '; cx1 / 6 = ',(cx1/6) printString.
"Test 4"
Transcript cr; cr; show: 'Test 4: yellow button to show mouse coordinates as x + jy, blue button to quit.'.
[Sensor waitButton; blueButtonPressed] whileFalse: [
    Sensor yellowButtonPressed ifTrue: [
        Transcript cr; show: 'Mouse coordinates:  ',(Complex real: Sensor mousePoint x imaginary: Sensor mousePoint y) printString]].
```

Complex **Example 6A**

This example illustrates the various operations defined for instances of class **Complex.** It shows how literals are supported and how the concept of generality of numbers is supported for complex numbers mixed with instances of the other number classes. It is implemented as a class method called **example2** in **Number.** Details of the method and the result of its evaluation are shown in Figure 6.4.

Test 1 shows the results of the four standard arithmetic operations on complex number literals. Test 2 shows the four arithmetic operations using complex variables. Test 3 shows the result of mixed arithmetic operations between complex numbers and instances of classes **Float, Fraction,** and **Integer.** And, finally, Test 4 demonstrates the creation of complex numbers from mouse-selected coordinate points on the screen. The coordinates are created as complex numbers in the form $x + jy$, where (x,y) are the screen coordinates.

Complex **Example 6B**

This example illustrates the accessing of private data and the conversion protocol in classes **Imaginary** and **Complex.** Figure 6.5 shows details of the method **example3** added to class **Number.** Results of evaluating the method are given in the Transcript window in the figure.

Test 1 demonstrates how the private data of instances of **Complex** and **Imaginary** can be accessed. Test 2 shows the allowed conversion of all the **Number** classes to either complex or imaginary. Test 3 shows how complex numbers can be displayed in both rectangular and polar forms. The symbol $<$ is used to indicate angle for the polar display.

This chapter has illustrated object-oriented programming with familiar objects that are instances of the **Magnitude** classes. The flexibility of the Smalltalk system is illustrated through definition of two new major **Number** subclasses, **Imaginary** and **Complex.** Finally, access to Smalltalk compiler classes is illustrated by adding support for **Imaginary** literals.

Figure 6.5 Accessing Private Data and Converting **Complex** and **Imaginary**

Test 1: Accessing private data.   cx1 = (2.0 + j4)   cx2 = ((3/4) + j(1/3))
cx1 private data: real = 2.0; imaginary = 4; modulus = 4.47214; angle = 63.435   degrees
cx2 private data: real = (3/4); imaginary = (1/3); modulus = 0.820738;   angle = 23.9625   degrees
imag1 magnitude = 25.6

Test 2: Converting to/from Complex and Imaginary
2 as Complex = (2 + j0.0); 23.9 as Complex = (23.9 + j0.0);   3/4 as Complex = ((3/4) + j0.0);   j5 as Complex = (0 + j5)
2 as Imaginary = +j2; 23.9 as Imaginary = +j23.9;   3/4 as Imaginary = +j(3/4);   0 + j4 as Imaginary = +j4
3 + j4 as Imaginary = Can't convert to imaginary

Test 3: Options for displaying complex numbers.
cx1 in rectangular form = (2.0 + j4);   cx1 in polar form = (4.47214 < 63.435)
cx2 in rectangular form = ((3/4) + j(1/3));   cx2 in polar form = (0.820738 < 23.9625)

example3

"Accessing the private data and converting complex and imaginary numbers"   "Number example3"
| cx1 cx2 imag1 |
cx1 ← Complex real: 2.0 imaginary: 4.   cx2 ← Complex real: 3/4 imaginary: 1/3.   imag1 ← Imaginary new: 25.6.
Transcript clear; refresh; show: Test 1: Accessing private data.   cx1 = ', cx1 printString,   cx2 = ', cx2 printString;cr.   "Test 1 "
Transcript show: 'cx1 private data: real = ', cx1 real printString, ';   imaginary = ',cx1 imaginary printString,
    ';   modulus = ', cx1 modulus printString, ';   angle = ', cx1 angle printString, '   degrees'; cr;
    show: 'cx2 private data: real = ', cx2 real printString, ';   imaginary = ',cx2 imaginary printString,
    ';   modulus = ', cx2 modulus printString, ';   angle = ', cx2 angle printString, '   degrees';
cr; show: 'imag1 magnitude = ',imag1 magnitude printString.
Transcript cr; cr; show: 'Test 2: Converting to/from Complex and Imaginary.'; cr.   "Test 2 "
Transcript show: '2 as Complex = ', 2 asComplex printString, ';   23.9 as Complex = ', 23.9 asComplex printString,
    ';   3/4 as Complex = ', (3/4) asComplex printString, ';   j5 as Complex = ', j5 asComplex printString; cr;
    show: '2 as Imaginary = ', 2 asImaginary printString, ';   23.9 as Imaginary = ', 23.9 asImaginary printString,
    ';   3/4 as Imaginary = ', (3/4) asImaginary printString, ';   0 + j4 as Imaginary = ', (0+j4) asImaginary printString;
    cr; show: '3 + j4 as Imaginary = ', (3+j4) asImaginary.
Transcript cr; cr; show: 'Test 3: Options for displaying complex numbers.'; cr.   "Test 3 "
Transcript show: 'cx1 in rectangular form = ', cx1 printString, ';   cx1 in polar form = ', cx1 printPolar; cr;
    show: 'cx2 in rectangular form = ', cx2 printString, ';   cx2 in polar form = ', cx2 printPolar.

Exercises

6.1 Develop an example program that utilizes all the protocol in classes **Time** and **Date.**

6.2 In class **Number,** the methods for the four basic arithmetic operations (***, +, −,** /) are implemented as subclassResponsibility. Why then are they included in the **Number** class at all?

6.3 Give reasons why the mathematical functions are implemented in class **Number** when most of them require floating point numbers as arguments.

6.4 Give reasons why the 15 class variables defined as new protocol in class **Float** are not and should not be defined in class **Number.**

6.5 We normally think of subclasses as inheriting protocol from their superclasses and superclasses as not having access to the methods of their subclasses. In terms of the definitions for mathematical functions in classes **Number** and **Float,** it appears that the superclass **Number** does indeed have access to the methods of its subclass **Float.** Review the method definitions and discuss this apparent inconsistency with the rules of inherited protocol.

6.6 In the method retry: coercing: in class **Number,** exceptions were included for the case in which either number in an arithmetic operation was of class **Imaginary.** Explain why this must be true, and discuss the desirability of coercing other number types to be imaginary.

6.7 Make modifications to the classes **Imaginary** and **Complex** to provide support for the arithmetic operations //, \\, and quo:. Also add support for **even** and **odd.** Discuss what evenness and oddness mean for both imaginary and complex numbers.

6.8 Discuss methodologies for expanding the interpretation of the mathematical functions to include arguments that are imaginary or complex. Describe at least one approach to modifying the Smalltalk number classes to provide consistency for computing mathematical functions with arguments that are of any number class. Identify those mathematical functions for which imaginary or complex arguments should not be allowed.

6.9 Develop a list of new protocol to add to classes **Imaginary** and **Complex.** Implement and test the new protocol.

7

Object-Oriented Programming Using Collection Classes

This chapter describes the class **Collection** and all its subclasses. The collection classes represent data structures in Smalltalk and are representative of objects with which most readers can identify. The purpose of the chapter is to provide an overview of what the collection classes are and how they are used. Numerous small examples are presented to illustrate the use of "collections".

A Word about Examples: In previous chapters, examples have been presented as class methods with results, in many cases, displayed in the Transcript window. Details of the examples are shown in a browser window and the complete screen display is given as a figure. As the length of the examples increases it becomes desirable to show details of an example as a separate listing. The results in most cases are still displayed in the Transcript window and presented as a figure. This new approach is used in this chapter whenever a method is too large to fit on the display screen with the results. The figures are custom sized to present only the details of the example execution.

7.1   Class Hierarchy of the Collection Classes

This section presents the hierarchy of the collection classes and describes how the various subclasses are different. It includes an abbreviated summary of selected material. Conversion among various collection subclasses is discussed with its limitations. Protocol summaries are given for many of the collection classes.

A collection is a group of objects. Objects in the collection are the *elements* of the collection. Relationships among the objects can be structured or nonstructured. The wide variety of collection subclasses available in the Smalltalk image indicates the richness of kinds of collections. There are even kinds of collections that are not included in the Smalltalk image. Virtually any data structure can be thought of as being a kind of collection.

Listing 7.1 is a hierarchical diagram of the collection classes from the Tektronix Version 2.2.0c Smalltalk image. Various hierarchy levels are shown by in-

Listing 7.1
Hierarchy Diagram
for the Collection
Classes

Object ()

Collection ()
    Bag ('contents')
    MappedCollection ('domain' 'map')
    SequenceableCollection ()
        ArrayedCollection ()
            Array ()
                LiteralArray ()
            ByteArray ()
                BytecodeArray ()
            RunArray ('runs' 'values')
            String ()
                Symbol ()
            Text ('string' 'runs')
            WordArray ()
                DisplayBitmap ()
        Interval ('start' 'stop' 'step')
            TextLineInterval ('internalSpaces' 'paddingWidth')
        LinkedList ('firstLink' 'lastLink')
            Semaphore ('excessSignals')
        OrderedCollection ('firstIndex' 'lastIndex')
            Signal ()
            SortedCollection ('sortBlock')
            WireList ()
    Set ('tally')
        Dictionary ()
            Histogram ()
            IdentityDictionary ('valueArray')
                MethodDictionary ('keyArray')
            LiteralDictionary ()
            StrikeFontManager ()
            SystemDictionary ()
            TextStyleManager ()
        IdentitySet ()

dentation. Instance variables for each class are shown in parentheses. Class **Collection** has four major subclasses, **Bag, MappedCollection, Sequenceable-Collection,** and **Set.** Each major subclass and its subclasses is discussed in the remaining sections of this chapter. More emphasis is placed on some selected classes than others.

Collections can be categorized in a number of ways based on their properties. This approach is used in defining the original collection classes in the Smalltalk image. These properties include the following.

- *Order of the elements*—The elements of a collection can be ordered or unordered. This feature breaks collections into two major subcategories. Of the four major subclasses of **Collection,** two (**Bag, Set**) are unordered and two (**SequenceableCollection, MappedCollection**) are ordered.

- *Basis for determining order*—This feature applies only to the subclasses **SequenceableCollection** and **MappedCollection,** which have ordered elements. It does not apply to subclasses (**Bag, Set**) without ordered elements. There are two ways in which the order of a collection is determined. It can may be determined externally by an index or a key value. A second way that order can be determined is internally by a comparison rule for sorting (as with instances of **SortedCollection**) or by a rule for generating elements in the collection (as with instances of **Interval**).

- *Accessible by a key*—The elements in a collection can be accessible by an external key such as an integer index or another object. Integer indices are typically used as external keys for collections that have order (such as the subclasses of **ArrayedCollection**); however, all collections that have order do not have external keys (for example, classes **LinkedList** and **OrderedCollection**). Unordered collections can be accessible by external keys (such as classes **Dictionary** and **IdentityDictionary**). Keys for unordered collections can be any object.

- *Duplicate elements allowed*—By definition a **Set** does not allow duplicate elements and its elements have no order or accessibility by keys. Interestingly enough, the elements of two of its subclasses (**Dictionary, IdentityDictionary**) have unordered elements that are accessible by keys. The elements of a **Bag** have no order, are not accessible by keys, and can be duplicated. Duplicate elements are allowed in all the ordered collections.

- *Class of elements allowed*—Various collection subclasses have different rules about the class membership of its elements. They range from homogeneous collections of a specified class (**ByteArray, String, Text, Interval, LinkedList**) to mixes of any object (**SortedCollection, Array, RunArray, OrderedCollection**) for the ordered collections. The unordered collections accept any object as an element.

Collection is an abstract superclass of all the collection classes. It does not have instances; rather, its subclasses will have instances that inherit protocol defined in **Collection. Collection** defines protocol that is common to all collections. In some cases a subclass will redefine an inherited method or block its use.

Of the numerous methods defined in class **Collection,** three are of primary significance. These three are add:, remove: ifAbsent:, and do:. They are implemented as subclassResponsibility, and most of the other methods depend on the implementation of the three. One can think in terms of a hierarchy of methods with these three at the top for the collection classes.

Protocol Summary for Class **Collection**

Definition—The hierarchy for class **Collection** is **Object—Collection.** Class **Collection** has no instance variables or pool dictionaries. It has three class variables, DefaultMaximumSize, MaxObjectSize, and MaxStringSize. It has 6 class methods in three categories and 31 instance methods in eight categories.

Shared data—Class **Collection** has three class variables.

DefaultMaximumSize—an instance of **Integer,** initialized to have value (2 raised to power 30) −1. This is the largest size that a collection can have.

MaxObjectSize—an instance of **Integer** defining the maximum size for an object, initialized to have value (2 raised to power 24) −1. This is the largest size that an element of the collection can have.

MaxStringSize—an instance of **Integer** defining the maximum size for a string, initialized to have value (2 raised to power 24) −1.

Instance methods—Class **Collection** has 31 instance methods in eight categories. A summary of the categories and methods follows.

accessing—one method (**size**) that returns the number of elements in the receiver collection.

testing—three methods (**isEmpty, includes:, occurrencesOf:**) that test emptiness of a collection, presence of an element, and number of occurrences of an element in a collection.

removing—three methods (**remove:, removeAll:, remove: ifAbsent:**) for removing an element, a collection of elements, or removal with an alternative if the element is absent. Instances of **SequenceableCollection** cannot respond to the message **remove: ifAbsent:**. This key method will be blocked in that class definition.

adding—two methods (**add:, addAll:**) for adding one or a collection of elements to the receiver. The method **add:** is one of the key methods in this class.

enumerating—seven methods (**collect:, detect:, detect: ifNone:, do:, inject: into:, reject:, select:**) for enumerating the elements of a collection and performing a specified set of actions with each element as the parameter. Method **do:** is the key method.

printing—two methods (**printOn:, storeOn:**) for printing or storing collections on a stream.

converting—five methods (**asBag, asOrderedCollection, asSet, asSorted-Collection, asSortedCollection:**) for converting one kind of collection to another kind of collection. Only those conversions listed are allowed.

private—eight methods (**emptyCheck, errorEmptyCollection, errorNoMatch, errorNotFound, errorNotKeyed, growSize, maxPrint, maxSize**) that are used by other methods in the protocol for class **Collection.**

Class methods—Class **Collection** has six class methods in three categories, as summarized below.

class initialization—one method (**initialize**) that sets values for the three class variables.

instance creation—four methods (**with:, with: with:, with: with: with:, with: with: with: with:**) that are used to create instances of the collection subclasses.

constants—one method (**maxSize**) that answers the value of the class variable DefaultMaximumSize.

Examples of collections are given in the subclass discussions below, since no instances of **Collection** can be created. The key message in the protocol for **Collection** that prevents any instances of itself to be created is **add:**. All four instance creation messages send the message **add:**, and it is implemented as **subclassResponsibility**. Thus the expression, Collection with: anObject produces an error message instead of creating a new collection.

7.2   Class **Bag** and Class **Set**

Classes **Bag** and **Set** and their subclasses represent collections of objects that are unordered. In this section, properties of these two classes and the **Dictionary** subclasses of **Set** are given, along with examples of their use. Abbreviated protocol summaries are given here. More complete protocol summaries can be found in Appendix 3.

7.2.1   Bags—the most general kind of collection

A bag is unordered, it allows duplicates, and its elements are not accessible by a key (either internal or external). Bags can be converted to other kinds of collections with keys if there is a need to access individual elements. Further, the enumeration protocol defined in superclass **Collection** provides a way to access and modify the elements in the bag. It is important to note that multiple occurrences of objects in a bag are not stored separately. They are stored one time with a tally for the number of occurrences. This is accomplished by using an instance of class **Dictionary** to store the contents of the bag.

The protocol summary for class **Bag** is given below, followed by an example of its use.

Protocol Summary for Class **Bag**

The hierarchy for class **Bag** is **Object—Collection—Bag.** Class **Bag** has one instance variable, contents. It has no class variables or pool dictionaries. It has 1 class method in one category and 12 instance methods in six categories.

Private data for class **Bag** includes one instance variable. Instance variable **contents** is an instance of **Dictionary** that contains the contents (the objects) of the bag. An object is stored once, and a tally is kept of the occurrences of each unique object.

Bag Example 7A

This example is added as class method example1 to **Bag.** It demonstrates the protocol defined within the class and some of the inherited protocol from classes **Behavior** and **Collection.** Details of the example are given in Listing 7.2 and the results as shown in the Transcript window are shown in Figure 7.1.

Three different methods are demonstrated for creating instances of **Bag.** The bag called mixedBag has a variety of different kinds of objects in it. After the bags are created, their contents are displayed, using the printString message to first convert the stored representation of a bag to a string.

Next the protocols for adding, removing, and conditional removing are illustrated. The message remove: ifAbsent: seeks to find the character $x in bag mixedBag. If it fails (and it does) the block is executed and the string, 'error', is added to mixedBag. This is a convenient way to track errors.

Two of the methods for accessing (sortedCounts, sortedElements) are demonstrated. The first gives a list of the contents of the bag sorted according to the one with the highest number of counts. This method works for any of the bags in the example. The second message, which sorts based on the elements, should only be sent to bags that contain homogeneous elements. Sending the message sortedElements to mixedBag will produce an error. This error occurs when the method attempts to determine the order of two dissimilar objects (e.g., numbers and strings).

Finally, it is demonstrated how instances of **Bag** can use protocol from its superclass. The message reject:, sent to mixedBag removes all objects in the bag that are of class **String.** The contents of the resultant mixedBag are displayed in Figure 7.1.

7.2.2 Sets—collections with unique membership

Sets are unordered, allow no duplicates, and are not accessible by a key or index. They are compatible with the definition of sets as defined in mathematical theory. Much of the protocol of class **Set** implements standard operations performed on sets, such as adding, removing, and testing for membership of an element.

Protocol Summary for Class **Set**

The hierarchy for class **Set** is **Object—Collection—Set.** Class **Set** has one instance variable, tally. It has no class variables or pool dictionaries. It has 4 class methods in three categories and 22 instance methods in eight categories.

The private data of class **Set** consists of one instance variable. Instance variable **tally** is an instance of **Integer** that is the number of elements in a set.

Of the 22 instance methods and 4 class methods defined in **Set,** 11 instance

Listing 7.2
Details of **Bag**
example1

Bag class methodsFor: 'examples'

example1
"This example shows most of the protocol defined in class Bag, plus some inherited
protocol from Collection."

```
| bagOfOneKind mixedBag junkBag |
Transcript clear; refresh; show: 'Results of evaluating example1 in class Bag';
    cr; cr; show: 'Contents of three new bags:'; cr.

junkBag ← Bag new.

    "Create an empty bag."
bagOfOneKind ← Bag with: $A with: $L with: $$ with: $L.
    "Create a bag with four characters."
mixedBag ← Bag new. mixedBag add: $A; add: 'string' withOccurrences: 3.
    "Create an empty bag, then add a character and 3 identical strings."

"Display contents of the bags"
Transcript tab; show: 'junkBag --> ', junkBag printString.
Transcript crtab; show: 'bagOfOneKind --> ', bagOfOneKind printString.
Transcript crtab; show: 'mixedBag --> ', mixedBag printString; cr.

bagOfOneKind remove: $L.
Transcript cr; show: 'Remove one object only, $L:'; crtab;
    show: 'bagOfOneKind --> ', bagOfOneKind printString; cr.
mixedBag remove: $x ifAbsent: [ mixedBag add: 'error'].
Transcript cr; show: 'Add ''error'' if try to remove an absent object ($x):'; crtab;
    show: 'mixedBag --> ',
    mixedBag printString; cr.

mixedBag
    add: #symbol withOccurrences: 5;
    add: 10.6 withOccurrences: 2;
    add: j7 withOccurrences: 4.
Transcript cr; show: 'There are two ways to get a summary of the contents of a bag: ';
    cr; show: 'sorted on counts or elements (only if elements can be sorted).'; crtab.
Transcript show: 'Sorted by decreasing count (mixedBag)'; crtab; tab;
    show: mixedBag sortedCounts printString; crtab;
    show: 'Sorted by element (bagOfOneKind)' ;crtab; tab;
    show: bagOfOneKind sortedElements printString; crtab.
Transcript show: 'mixedBag now has a total of ',
    mixedBag size printString, ' elements.'; tab;
    show: 'It does ', ((
    mixedBag includes: 'error') ifFalse: ['not ']), 'include the element ''error''.';
    crtab; show: 'It includes ',(
    mixedBag occurrencesOf: #symbol) printString, ' copies of #symbol.';cr; cr.

Transcript show: 'One example of enumeration, rejects all strings in mixedBag.'; crtab;
    show: 'The new mixedBag contains '; crtab; tab;
    show: (mixedBag reject: [ :i | i class = = String] ) printString.

" Bag   example1  "
```

Figure 7.1
Class Method
example1 in Class
Bag—Protocol
for Bags

```
┌─────────────────────────────────────────────────────────────────┐
│ System Transcript                                                 │
│ Results of evaluating example1 in class Bag                       │
│                                                                   │
│ Contents of three new bags:                                       │
│     junkBag --> Bag ()                                            │
│     bagOfOneKind --> Bag ($A $$ $L $L )                           │
│     mixedBag --> Bag ($A 'string' 'string' 'string' )            │
│                                                                   │
│ Remove one object only, $L:                                       │
│     bagOfOneKind --> Bag ($A $$ $L )                              │
│                                                                   │
│ Add 'error' if try to remove an absent object ($x):               │
│     mixedBag --> Bag ($A 'string' 'string' 'string' 'error' )    │
│                                                                   │
│ There are two ways to get a summary of the contents of a bag:     │
│ sorted on counts or elements (only if elements can be sorted).    │
│     Sorted by decreasing count (mixedBag)                         │
│         SortedCollection (5->symbol 4-> +j7 3->'string' 2->10.6 1->$A 1->'error' ) │
│     Sorted by element (bagOfOneKind)                              │
│         SortedCollection ($$->1 $A->1 $L->1 )                     │
│     mixedBag now has a total of 16 elements. It does include the element 'error'. │
│     It includes 5 copies of #symbol.                              │
│                                                                   │
│ One example of enumeration, rejects all strings in mixedBag.      │
│     The new mixedBag contains                                     │
│         Bag ($A symbol symbol symbol symbol symbol +j7 +j7 +j7 +j7 10.6 10.6 ) │
└─────────────────────────────────────────────────────────────────┘
```

methods and all 4 class methods are polymorphic redefinitions of inherited methods. Aside from the 9 private methods, only 2 new methods are defined in class **Set**. The key instance methods in class **Set** are add:, remove: ifAbsent:, and do:. The methods **new** and **new:** are redefined to include initialization of the instance variable tally.

Set Example 7A

This example illustrates the use of protocol in class **Set.** The details of a method called **example1** added to class **Set** are shown in Listing 7.3. Results of executing the example are shown in Figure 7.2.

Three sets are created using different instance creation messages. A display of the size of each set indicates that they all have a size of zero. This is true because the message **size** returns the number of elements that exist in a set, not the space that was allocated upon instance creation.

The next block of code adds the 10 upper- and lowercase vowels to **set3** and displays its contents. A mixed collection of element types is added to **set1**, to indicate the generic nature of set elements. The contents of **set1** are displayed for verification.

Listing 7.3
Details of **Set**
example1

Set class methodsFor: 'examples'

example1
"This example illustrates the use of protocol in class Set."

```
| set1 set2 set3 char |
Transcript clear; refresh;
     show: 'Example that uses protocol of class Set.'; cr; cr.

set1 ← Set new.                    "Defaults to 16 element size."
set2 ← Set new: 0.                 "Creates an instance of size 1."
set3 ← Set new: 10.                "A set of vowels, uc and lc."

"Show the sizes of the three sets. Note: they are all empty at this point."
Transcript tab;
     show: 'Initial:    set1 size is: ', set1 size printString; tab;
     show: 'set2 size is: ', set2 size printString; tab;
     show: 'set3 size is: ', set3 size printString; cr.

"Add all vowels to set3."
$a asciiValue to: $z asciiValue do: [ :num |
     num asCharacter isVowel ifTrue: [
          set3 add: num asCharacter.
          set3 add: num asCharacter asUppercase ]].
Transcript crtab; show: 'set3 now contains: ', set3 printString;cr.

Transcript crtab; show: 'Create a set of mixed elements (set1).'; crtab.
set1 add: #(2 4.5 ($a symbol) 'string').
set1 add: 2; add: 4.5; add: $a; add: #symbol; add: 'string'.
Transcript show: 'set1 now contains: ', set1 printString; cr.

set2 ← set1.                 "Size of set2 is adjusted to accomodate by calling grow."
Transcript crtab;
     show: 'set2 assigned equal set1 contains: '; crtab; tab;
     show: set2 printString; crtab.
Transcript tab;
     show: 'set1 size is: ', set1 size printString,
     '    set2 size is: ', set2 size printString.

Transcript cr; crtab;
     show: 'Test membership of keyboard entry in the vowel set, set3.';crtab.
Transcript show: 'Press any keyboard key (return to quit).'; crtab: 2;
     show: 'Character from keyboard: '.
[(char ← Sensor keyboard) asciiValue = 13] whileFalse: [
     Transcript
          nextPut: char;
          show: ' is'.
     (set3 includes: char) ifFalse: [ Transcript show: ' not'].
     Transcript show: ' a vowel.';crtab; tab;
          show: 'Character from keyboard: '].
Transcript show: 'return'; cr.
```

" Set example1 "

Figure 7.2
Class Method
example1 in Class
Set—Protocol
for Sets

```
System Transcript
Example that uses protocol of class Set.

    Initial:    set1 size is:  0    set2 size is:  0    set3 size is:  0

set3 now contains:  Set ($e $A $i $U $E $o $I $a $u $O )

Create a set of mixed elements (set1).
set1 now contains:  Set (4.5 $a 2 symbol 'string' (2 4.5 ($a symbol ) 'string' ) )

set2 assigned equal set1 contains:
    Set (4.5 $a 2 symbol 'string' (2 4.5 ($a symbol ) 'string' ) )
    set1 size is:  6     set2 size is:  6

Test membership of keyboard entry in the vowel set, set3.
Press any keyboard key (return to quit).
    Character from keyboard:  a  is a vowel.
    Character from keyboard:  e  is a vowel.
    Character from keyboard:  i  is a vowel.
    Character from keyboard:  o  is a vowel.
    Character from keyboard:  u  is a vowel.
    Character from keyboard:  A  is a vowel.
    Character from keyboard:  E  is a vowel.
    Character from keyboard:  I  is a vowel.
    Character from keyboard:  O  is a vowel.
    Character from keyboard:  U  is a vowel.
    Character from keyboard:  b  is not a vowel.
    Character from keyboard:  B  is not a vowel.
    Character from keyboard:  z  is not a vowel.
    Character from keyboard:  Z  is not a vowel.
    Character from keyboard:  g  is not a vowel.
    Character from keyboard:  G  is not a vowel.
    Character from keyboard:  return
```

The next part of this example assigns **set2** to be equal to **set1**. Recall that **set2** was defined to contain zero elements (the instance creation method defaults to one element). One might think a problem occurs if attempting to assign a set (**set1**) that contains six elements to a set (**set2**) that is defined to contain one element. However, set sizes are adjusted automatically whenever assignments or additions are made. Figure 7.2 verifies that **set2** contains the same elements as **set1** and that both have a new size of 6.

The last part of **example1** demonstrates the testing of set membership. It accepts single keystrokes from the keyboard and answers if the key is a vowel or not. This example illustrates for the first time keyboard methods in class **Input-Sensor** as well. The expression **Sensor keyboard** returns the next character from the keyboard buffer.

7.2.3   Dictionaries—**Smalltalk** and the **SystemDictionary** class

Dictionary is a subclass of **Set.** Dictionaries are unique sets that have as their elements instances of the class **Association.** The hierarchy for class **Association** is **Object—Magnitude—LookupKey—Association. LookupKey** has one instance variable, key. **Association** has one instance variable, value. An association consists of two parts, a key and a value (the instance variables of itself and its superclass, **LookupKey**). These key/value pairs are the elements stored in dictionaries. The concept is not unusual, since dictionaries are typically thought of as storing one-to-one relationships among words and definitions (i.e., key and value).

Dictionary has several subclasses, the most interesting of which is **System-Dictionary. SystemDictionary** has only one instance, **Smalltalk,** that is the dictionary for all global variables in the system. These include the class names. Protocol for **SystemDictionary** includes messages for making inquiries and for maintaining the Smalltalk system.

In this section protocol summaries are given for **Dictionary** and **System-Dictionary.** (A more complete protocol summary for class **Dictionary** is given in Appendix 3.) Then several examples are given of the use of both.

Protocol Summary for Class **Dictionary**

The hierarchy for class **Dictionary** is **Object—Collection—Set—Dictionary.** Class **Dictionary** has no instance variables, class variables, or pool dictionaries. It has no new class methods. It has 38 instance methods in 12 categories.

Of the 10 methods for accessing, 2 (**at:, at: put:**) were blocked in class **Set.** They are defined to be valid in class **Dictionary.** Methods **add:** and **do:** are also redefined.

Two methods (**remove:, remove: ifAbsent:**), inherited respectively from **Collection** and **Set,** are redefined to block their use by instances of **Dictionary.** Removal of an element from a dictionary consists of removing an association. This must be done by accessing the key in the association. New protocol for correct removal of elements in a dictionary is added in the category *dictionary removing.*

Four methods (**removeAssociation:, removeAssociation: ifAbsent:, remove-Key:, removeKey: ifAbsent:**) that provide protocol for removing elements from a dictionary based on finding their key value or a specified association are added under the category *dictionary removing.*

Class **SystemDictionary** with its single instance, **Smalltalk,** is one of the most important classes in the Smalltalk system. Certain messages sent to **Smalltalk** provide detailed information about the entire system, and other messages provide the capability for maintaining the Smalltalk image. It is one of the larger classes in terms of number of methods provided. A detailed protocol summary is given below for this important class.

Protocol Summary for Class **SystemDictionary**

Definition—The hierarchy for class **SystemDictionary** is **Object—Collection—Dictionary—SystemDictionary.** Class **SystemDictionary** has no instance variables or pool dictionaries. It has nine class variables, CachedClass-Names, Frills, LowSpaceProcess, LowSpaceSemaphore, OopsLeftLimit, Save-Space, SpecialSelectors, SystemChanges, and WordsLeftLimit. It has 2 class methods in 2 categories and 82 instance methods in 16 categories.

Shared data—Class **SystemDictionary** has nine class variables.

CachedClassNames—an instance of **SortedCollection** that contains the names of all the classes in Smalltalk.

Frills—an instance of **Boolean.** When set to false, Smalltalk eliminates some of the special features to improve performance on slow machines. For example, the default timing interval is changed from 16 to 60 ticks, the standard system view repainting process does not repaint previously occluded parts of a view, and the explainer gives less detail. (The explainer is invoked as a menu item in a text subview as part of the Tektronix Version 2.2.0c image.)

LowSpaceProcess—an unscheduled instance of **Process** that is invoked whenever the amount of space (in number of object pointers [oops] remaining) or the amount of memory (from core measurements) becomes low.

LowSpaceSemaphore—an instance of **Semaphore** that serves as a flag to notify the system whenever a low-space or low-memory condition occurs. The method for setting this flag is implemented as a primitive, <primitive 116>.

OopsLeftLimit—an instance of **Integer** representing a threshold number of remaining object pointers (oops). If the actual number of available oops falls below this number, the LowSpaceProcess is invoked.

SaveSpace—an instance of **Boolean** that determines if the system is in a spacesaving mode or not. Protocol in **SystemDictionary** allows the user to specify whether spacesaving mode is in effect. This variable should be set to true on machines with limited memory. One effect is that forms for windows are not saved. This causes repainting of the windows to be slower.

SpecialSelectors—an instance of **Array** containing the 32 special message selectors that can be sent directly by issuing a bytecode. See Goldberg and Robson, page 545, for a list.

SystemChanges—an instance of **ChangeSet**, a class that maintains and tracks changes made to the system in several categories. **ChangeSet** has five instance variables representing the changes in system status.

WordsLeftLimit—an instance of **Integer** representing a threshold number of remaining words of core memory. If the actual number of available memory words falls below this number, the LowSpaceProcess is invoked.

Instance methods—Class **SystemDictionary** has 82 instance methods in 16 categories. A summary is given below of the categories and methods.

initialize-release—one method (**install**) that installs the system. It initializes class variables within **SystemDictionary,** and it initializes several classes, the display, the input sensor, and the cursor.

accessing—two methods (**at: put:, valueAtNewKey: put: atIndex: declareFrom:**). The first is inherited from **Dictionary** and redefined to check for and fix up undeclared objects. The second is new protocol that should be used instead of atKey: put: inherited from **Dictionary.** It also checks and fixes up any undeclared references.

enumerating—three new methods (**allBehaviorsDo:, allClassesDo:, pointersTo: do:**) that evaluate a user-specified block for all behaviors, classes, or pointers in the Smalltalk system, respectively.

browsing—six methods (**browseAllCallsOn:, browseAllCallsOn: and:, browseAllImplementorsOf:, browseAllSelect:, browseChangedMessages, showMenuThenBrowse:**) for opening browsers on selected parts of the Smalltalk system. Many of these methods are used by the browser classes under menu control.

retrieving—seven methods (**allCallsOn:, allCallsOn: and:, allClassesImplementing, allImplementedMessages, allImplementorsOf:, allSelect:, collectPointersTo:**) that are used by the browsing methods to actually retrieve the indicated parts of Smalltalk for browsing.

class names—three methods (**classNames, flushClassNameCache, newClassNames**) for managing the contents of the class variable CachedClassNames.

compiling—three methods (**recompileAllFrom:, recompileCallsOn:, recompileMethodsForWhich:**) that provide selective hierarchical recompilation of classes from a specified class name, methods that call a specified literal, or any method for which a user-specified block evaluates to true.

change management—seven methods (**changes, logChange:, newChanges:, noChanges, recover:, removeClassNamed:, renameClass: as:**) for initializing, accessing, removing, or adding to the change set represented by the class variable SystemChanges.

memory space—sixteen methods (**core, coreLeft, coreLeftLimit, coreLeftLimit:, frills, frills:, garbageCollect, garbageCollect:, oopsLeft, oopsLeftLimit, oopsLeftLimit:, resetLowSpaceSignal, resetSpaceLimits, saveSpace, saveSpace:, signal: atOopsLeft: wordsLeft:**) for accessing the amount of memory or object pointers remaining, for setting frills, spacesaver option, oops left, memory left, and for garbage collection.

special selectors—four methods (**hasSpecialSelector: ifTrueSetByte:, specialNargsAt:, specialSelectorAt:, specialSelectorSize**) for accessing various features of the class variable SpecialSelectors.

system compression—five methods (**condenseChanges, appendChangesToSourceFileWithout:, forgetDoIts, newSourceFile: without:, renameSystemFiles:**) for compressing system changes and sources files.

    printing—three methods (**isUniqueValue, printOn:, storeDefinitionOn: auxTable:**), of which the first (isUniqueValue) is inherited from **Object** and redefined. The other two (printOn:, storeDefinitionOn: auxTable:) are inherited from **Dictionary** and redefined.

    private—eight methods (**exitToDebugger, lowSpaceNotificationLoop, postSnapshot, quitPrimitive, releaseExternalViews, snapshotPrimitive, snapshotPrimitive:, specialSelectors**) that are used by other methods in the protocol for class **SystemDictionary.**

    system backup-out—eight methods (**copyChangesTo:, getImageName, quit, saveAs: thenQuit:, shutdown, snapshot, snapshotAs: onReload-Do:, snapshotAs: thenQuit:**) that support quitting, saving, filing out of sources file, and snapshots.

    time-versions—five methods (**copyright, timeStamp:, version, version-Name, versionNumber**) for accessing the version, copyright, and time stamp for Smalltalk.

    copying—one method (**structureCopyWithDict:**) inherited from **Set** and redefined.

Class methods—Class **SystemDictionary** has two class methods in two categories, as summarized below.

    class initialization—one method (**initialize**) that sets the current project to have no changes.

    private—one method (**readDefinitionFrom: map:**) that adds **Smalltalk** to a stream.

Dictionary Example 7A

This example shows the use of protocol from class **Dictionary.** It demonstrates how a dictionary can be used to generate a histogram of the occurrence of characters in a text file. This example is implemented as a class method, **example1**, in class **Dictionary.** The details of the example are given in Listing 7.4, and the resulting histogram display is shown in Figure 7.3.

Listing 7.4
Details of
Dictionary
example1

Dictionary class methodsFor: 'examples'

example1
  "This example illustrates the use of a dictionary for computing histograms. It illustrates associations, file I/O, and simple graphics also. Special attention is suggested to the message, storeOn: ."

  | sourceFile key histogram outputFile dispRect x y ymax dx |
  ScheduledControllers deactivate.
    "Keep system windows from interfering with the display."

Listing 7.4
(continued)

```
"Open file for read only and build histogram as a Dictionary of Associations."
sourceFile ← FileStream oldFileNamed: '/safe/fileIn/project1.st'.
histogram ← Dictionary new: 27.
[sourceFile atEnd] whileFalse:[
    (key ← sourceFile next) isLetter
        ifTrue: [ histogram at: (key ← key asLowercase) put:
                        ((histogram at: key ifAbsent: [histogram at: key put: 0]) + 1) ]
        ifFalse: [ histogram at: $( put:
                        ((histogram at: $( ifAbsent: [histogram at: $( put: 0]) + 1) ]].


"Store the histogram  on the outputFile in a way that allows reconstruction."
outputFile ← FileStream newFileNamed:  '/safe/fileIn/project1.hst'.
histogram storeOn: outputFile.
outputFile close.


"Open the histogram file for read only and plot histogram on the screen."
outputFile ← FileStream oldFileNamed: '/safe/fileIn/project1.hst'.
histogram ← outputFile fileIn.
    "Rebuild the histogram as a Dictionary from outputFile."
x ←  dx ← 20.
ymax ← 500.
Display veryLightGray.
dispRect ← Rectangle origin: 0@0 corner: (51*dx)@ymax.
Display fill: dispRect rule: Form over mask: Form black.
Display fill: (dispRect insetBy: 2@2) rule: Form over mask: Form white.
ymax ← ymax - 40.
histogram associationsDo: [:anAssociation |
    (String with: (anAssociation key)) displayAt: x@(ymax+20).
    ((y ← anAssociation value) < = (ymax - 20))
        ifTrue: [ dispRect ←  Rectangle
                origin:  (x @ (ymax - y ))
                corner: ((x + dx) @ ymax).
            y printString displayAt:  x@(ymax - y - 20)]
        ifFalse: [ dispRect ← Rectangle
                origin: ( x @ 30)
                corner: ((x + dx) @ ymax).
            ((String with: $*), (y printString)) displayAt: x @ 10].
    Display fill: dispRect rule: Form over mask: Form black.
    Display
        fill: (dispRect insetBy: 2@2)
        rule: Form over
        mask: Form veryLightGray.
    x ← x + (2*dx)].
outputFile remove.
'Histogram of characters in File: "/safe/fileIn/project1.st"' displayAt: 60@100.
BinaryChoice
    message: 'Restore Display?'
    displayAt: 1100 @ 700
    ifTrue: [ScheduledControllers restore].


" Dictionary example1 "
```

Figure 7.3 Class Method example1 in Class **Dictionary**—Protocol for Dictionaries

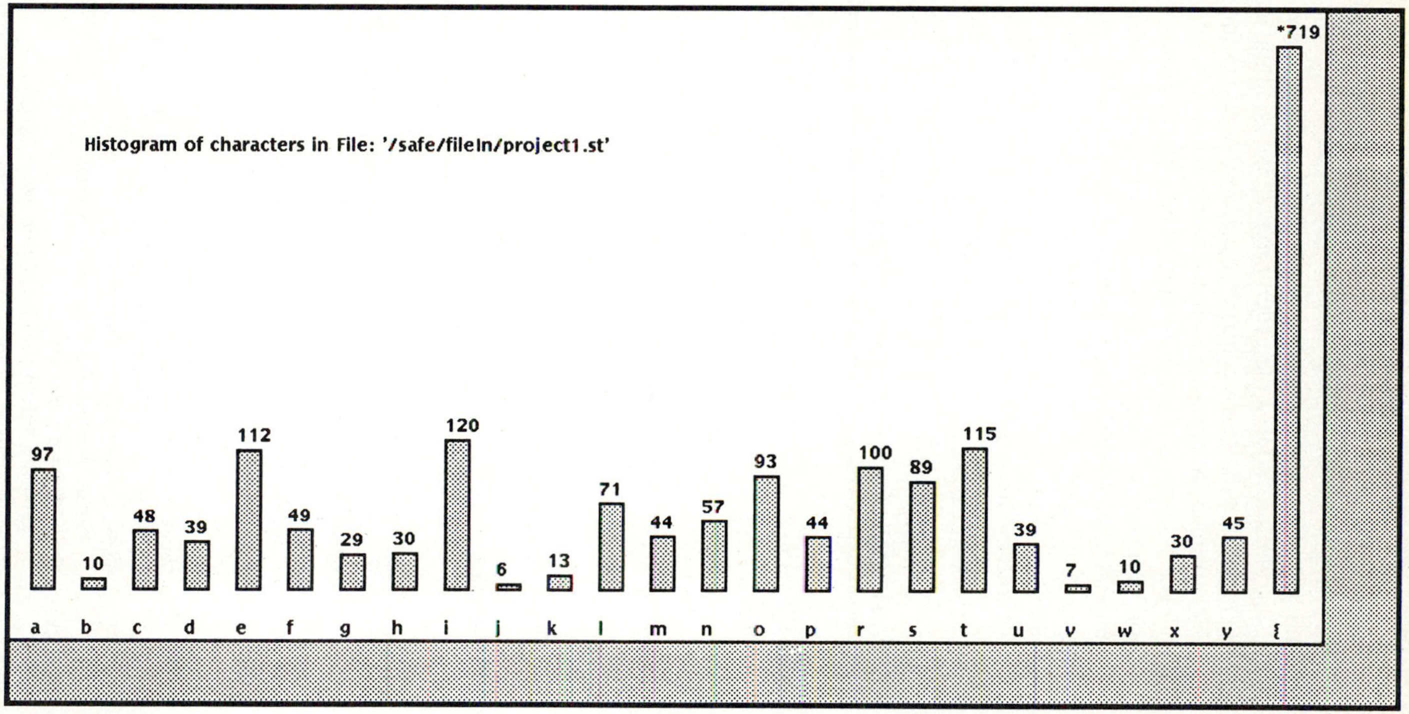

Histogram of characters in File: '/safe/fileIn/project1.st'

This example reads a file called *project1.st* in directory */safe/fileIn*. Any other directory can be used to store the file. It generates a histogram as a dictionary of associations. In each association, the key is the character of the alphabet, and the value is the number of occurrences in the text file. Once computed, the histogram is saved to a file called *project1.hst* using the storeOn: message. This message saves the receiver object in a form that allows for reconstruction of the object using a fileIn message sent to the file name.

The histogram is reconstructed as an object in fast memory by the expression histogram ← outputFile fileIn. The remainder of the example deals with generating and displaying a bar chart of the histogram. This example is not representative of good object-oriented programming. It does show all the steps in one place. A more object-oriented approach is to define a **Histogram** class and methods for automatically sizing the graphics display.

SystemDictionary (Smalltalk) Example 7A

This example illustrates how messages to **Smalltalk** can be used to access information about version, time stamps, memory remaining, and number of object-oriented pointers (oops) that can still be allocated. It shows how any category of information about classes, behaviors, or pointers in the system can be accessed.

Listing 7.5 shows details of the example. It is installed as a class method, example1, in **SystemDictionary**. Results are given in Figure 7.4.

Listing 7.5
Details of
SystemDictionary
example1

SystemDictionary class methodsFor: 'examples'

example1
    "This example shows how Smalltalk can be used to access system information."

    | count | count ← 0.

    Transcript clear; refresh; show: 'SystemDictionary example1 - System Information by
Sending Messages to Smalltalk.'; cr;cr;
        show: 'General system information for the current system.'; cr.

    Transcript tab; show: 'Number of objects and words occupied = ',
            Smalltalk core printString; crtab;
        show: 'Number of unallocated words in object space = ',
            Smalltalk coreLeft printString; crtab;
        show: 'Low threshold on core left = ',
            Smalltalk coreLeftLimit printString; crtab;
        show: 'Currently, frills are ',
            (Smalltalk frills ifFalse: ['not ']), 'in effect.'; crtab;
        show: 'Number of unallocated object pointers in object table = ',
            Smalltalk oopsLeft printString; crtab;

```
        show: 'Low threshold on oops left = ',
            Smalltalk oopsLeftLimit printString; crtab;
        show: 'Space saving option is ',
            (Smalltalk saveSpace ifFalse: ['not ']), 'in effect.'; crtab; show:
            'Although not done here, low threshold for core and oops can be set by user.';
            cr; cr.


    Transcript show:      'Garbage collection is invoked at any level from 0(newest objects) to
7(oldest objects).'; crtab;
        show: 'Smalltalk garbageCollect --> Evoke garbage collection at level 7.' ; crtab;
        show: 'Smalltalk garbageCollect: k --> Evoke garbage collection at level k.';cr; cr.
    Smalltalk garbageCollect.          "Do a level 7 garbage collection"
    Transcript tab;
        show: 'After garbage collection, objects and words = ',
            Smalltalk core printString.


    Smalltalk allClassesDo: [ :className | count ← count + 1].
    Transcript cr; cr;
        show: 'Enumeration messages provide easy way to go through all classes.'; crtab;
        show: 'Total number of classes in this version of Smalltalk = ',
            count printString; crtab;
        show: 'Total number of messages in this version of Smalltalk = ',
            Smalltalk allImplementedMessages size printString; cr.


    " SystemDictionary example1  "
```

Figure 7.4
Class Method
example1 in Class
SystemDictionary—
Accessing System
Information

```
System Transcript
SystemDictionary example1 – System Information by Sending Messages to Smalltalk.

General system information for the current system.
    Number of objects and words occupied = (61241 626777 )
    Number of unallocated words in object space = 4205291
    Low threshold on core left = 0
    Currently, frills are in effect.
    Number of unallocated object pointers in object table = 410314
    Low threshold on oops left = 0
    Space saving option is not in effect.
    Although not done here, low threshold for core and oops can be set by user.

Garbage collection is invoked at any level from 0(newest objects) to 7(oldest objects).
    Smalltalk garbageCollect  --> Evoke garbage collection at level 7.
    Smalltalk garbageCollect: k  --> Evoke garbage collection at level k.

    After garbage collection, objects and words = (59049 576516 )

Enumeration messages provide easy way to go through all classes.
    Total number of classes in this version of Smalltalk = 297
    Total number of messages in this version of Smalltalk = 3671
```

Figure 7.5 Class Method example2 in Class **SystemDictionary**—Accessing Protocol Information

---

System Transcript

SystemDictionary example2 – Protocol Information by sending Messages to Smalltalk.

Browsing the Smalltalk system.
Browse all implementors of a particular message selector -- at: put:
    Execute the expression: Smalltalk browseAllImplementorsOf: #at:put:
    Result is the browser window shown to the right.

The message that does the work is -- allImplementorsOf:
    It returns a SortedCollection of all the methods that implement -- at: put:
    Contents of that sorted collection are:
    SortedCollection ('Bag at:put:' 'CompiledMethod at:put:' 'ContextPart at:put:' 'Dictionary at:put:' 'DisplayBitmap at:put:'
'IdentityDictionary at:put:' 'Interval at:put:' 'LinkedList at:put:' 'MappedCollection at:put:' 'MethodContext at:put:' 'Object at:put:'
'OrderedCollection at:put:' 'Path at:put:' 'Set at:put:' 'SortedCollection at:put:' 'StrikeFontManager at:put:' 'String at:put:' 'Symbol at:put:'
'SystemDictionary at:put:' 'Text at:put:' 'TextStyleManager at:put:')

Workspace

example2
    "This example shows how Smalltalk can be used to access selected protocol."

Transcript clear; refresh;
    show: 'SystemDictionary example2 – Protocol Information by sending Messages to Smalltalk.'; cr;
    cr;cr; show: 'Browsing the Smalltalk system.'; cr.

Transcript tab; show: 'Browse all implementors of a particular message selector -- at: put:';
    cr; tab; show:' Execute the expression: Smalltalk browseAllImplementorsOf: #at:put:';
    cr; tab; show:'   Result is the browser window shown to the right.'; cr; cr.

Transcript tab; show: 'The message that does the work is -- allImplementorsOf:'; cr;
    tab; show:'   It returns a SortedCollection of all the methods that implement -- at: put:'; cr;
    tab; show:'   Contents of that sorted collection are: '; cr; tab; tab; show:
    (Smalltalk allImplementorsOf: #at:put:) printString.

    Smalltalk browseAllImplementorsOf: #at:put:.

    " SystemDictionary example2 "

Implementors of at:put:

Symbol at:put:
SystemDictionary at:put:
Text at:put:
TextStyleManager at:put:
----

at: aKey put: anObject
    "Override from Dictionary so that
    can check Undeclared and fix up
    references of undeclared
    variables."

    | index element |
    index ← self findKeyOrNil: aKey.
    element ← self basicAt: index.
    element == nil
    ifTrue:
        [self
            valueAtNewKey: aKey
            put: anObject

Information given by the messages to **Smalltalk** here provides a good summary of the system status. It is interesting to note that the current version (the one that existed when this example was executed) of the image contains 297 classes and 3671 message selectors. (Smalltalk is not small!) After performing a level 7 garbage collection, the number of objects and words occupied by the system fell from (61241 626777) to (59049 576516), as shown in Figure 7.4.

SystemDictionary (Smalltalk) Example 7B

This example shows messages to **Smalltalk** that return a collection of class names, browse calls, implementors, senders, and so forth, of selected Smalltalk protocol. Much of the protocol shown in this example is implemented as menu items in the System Browser. The purpose of the example is to show how the browser does it (i.e., where the protocol is for supporting those menu items).

Figure 7.5 shows details of two of the possible messages for accessing protocol information in **Smalltalk.** A new class method called example2 is shown in the text subview of the workspace.

When example2 is executed, it produces the output shown in the Transcript window and also produces the user-defined window in the upper-right portion of the figure. This window is a browser window on all implementors of the message selector at: put:. There are more classes implementing at: put: than can be shown in the space provided. Partial details of the implementation of at: put: in class **SystemDictionary** are shown in the text subview of the browser.

SystemDictionary (Smalltalk) Example 7C

This example demonstrates one message, classNames, that returns all the class names in the system as a **SortedCollection.** Figure 7.6 shows details of the example, listed as example3 in **SystemDictionary.** Results are shown in the Transcript window as a sorted collection of 297 class names.

SystemDictionary (Smalltalk) Example 7D

This example demonstrates more options on change management and compression of the changes or system. Chapter 3 gave one example of how to use some of the protocol for condensing sources and the changes file. This example gives a more detailed demonstration of those capabilities.

Figure 7.6
Class Method
example3 in Class
SystemDictionary—
Listing All the
Class Names

```
System Transcript
SystemDictionary example3 – Listing the classes.

    SortedCollection (ActionMenu AlwaysAcceptCodeController AnimatedBankSim
AnimatedCustomer AnimatedCustomerQueue AnimatedServer AnimatedTowerOfHanoi
Arc Array ArrayedCollection AssignmentNode Association Bag BankSimulation
BarChartView Behavior Benchmark BinaryChoice BinaryChoiceController
BinaryChoiceView BitBlt BitEditor BlockContext BlockNode Boolean BooleanView
BounceInBoxNode Browser BrowserTimeView BrowserView Button ByteArray
BytecodeArray CascadeNode Change ChangeController ChangeList
ChangeListController ChangeListView ChangeScanner ChangeSet Character
CharacterBlock CharacterBlockScanner CharacterScanner Checker Circle Class
ClassCategoryReader ClassChange ClassCommentChange ClassDefinitionChange
ClassDescription ClassOrganizer ClassOtherChange ClassRelatedChange
ClassReorganizationChange ClockController ClockView CodeController CodeView
Collection CompiledMethod Compiler Complex ComplexSignal CompositionScanner
ContextInspector ContextPart Controller ControlManager CRFillInTheBlankController
Cursor Curve Customer CustomerQueue Date Debugger Decompiler
DecompilerConstructor Delay Dictionary DictionaryInspector DisplayBitmap
DisplayMedium DisplayObject DisplayScanner DisplayScreen DisplayText
DisplayTextView DrunkenCockroach Encoder EvaluationNode Explainer ExpressionTree
ExternalStream False FileDirectory FileList FileModel FileStream FillInTheBlank
FillInTheBlankController FillInTheBlankView FinancialHistory FinancialHistoryController
FinancialHistoryView Float Form FormButtonCache FormEditor FormHolderView
FormMenuController FormMenuView FormView Fraction HanoiDisk HanoiDiskRules
HanoiProgs Histogram HistogramController HistogramView IconPopUpMenu
IdentityDictionary IdentitySet Imaginary IndicatorOnSwitchController InfiniteForm
InputSensor InputState Inspector InspectorView InstructionPrinter InstructionStream
Integer Interval KeyboardEvent LargeNegativeInteger LargePositiveInteger LeafNode
Line LinearFit Link LinkedList ListController ListView LiteralArray LiteralDictionary
LiteralNode LockedListController LockedSwitchController LookupKey Magnitude
MappedCollection Message MessageNode MessageTally Metaclass
MetaclassForMultipleInheritance MethodChange MethodContext
MethodDefinitionChange MethodDescription MethodDictionary MethodListBrowser
MethodNode MethodOtherChange MorseCode MouseMenuController MovieController
MovieView MovingNode MultiLineBankSimulation MusicFormatter NoController
NotifierController NotifierView Number NumberNode Object OneOnSwitch
OnlyWhenSelectedCodeController OnlyWhenSelectedCodeView OpaqueForm
OperandNode OperatorNode OrderedCollection OtherChange Paragraph
ParagraphEditor ParseNode Parser ParseStack Path Pen Pipe PipeReadStream PipeStream
PipeWriteStream Point PopUpMenu PositionableStream PositionNode PrinterStream
Process ProcessHandle ProcessorScheduler Project ProjectBrowser ProjectController
ProjectView ProtocolBrowser Quadrangle Random ReadStream ReadWriteStream
Rectangle RemoteString ReturnNode RunArray Scanner ScreenController
```

```
Workspace
example3
    "This example shows how to obtain a sorted list of class names."

    Transcript clear; refresh;
        show: 'SystemDictionary example3 – Listing the classes.'; cr; cr; tab;
        show: Smalltalk classNames printString.

   "  SystemDictionary example3  "
```

The following expressions and their results are given for managing the Smalltalk system.

Smalltalk appendChangesToSourceFileWithout: setOfClasses

"Add source in changes file to the source file. Changes files not affected. All references to class names in **setOfClasses** are omitted."

Smalltalk condenseChanges

"Create a new changes file that removes redundancies. Source file unaffected."

Smalltalk newSourceFile: filename without: setOfClasses

"Create a new source file containing all the changes. Create an empty new changes file. Rename the image file for consistency. Exclude all references in changes file to class names in **setOfClasses**."

Smalltalk renameSystemFiles: newVersion

"Rename the sources, changes, and image files."

Smalltalk changes

"Answer the current system change set."

Smalltalk noChanges

"Create an empty change set."

The preceding examples illustrate only a small portion of the available protocol for instances of **Dictionary** and specifically **SystemDictionary.** Development of a thorough understanding of messages to **Smalltalk** is recommended. These messages provide the mechanism for learning about any part of the Smalltalk image.

7.3   **SequenceableCollection** as an Abstract Class— Inheritance and Polymorphism

This section defines **SequenceableCollection** and shows how it is characterized as an abstract class. Properties of sequenceable collections are described and illustrated through examples for the subclasses of **SequenceableCollection.** There are four major subclasses under **SequenceableCollection.** These are **ArrayedCollection, Interval, LinkedList,** and **OrderedCollection.** Each of these major subclasses is described in subsections of this section. First, an abbreviated protocol summary for **SequenceableCollection** is presented. A more complete summary is given in Appendix 3.

SequenceableCollection is an abstract superclass of the collection classes that have a well-defined order associated with their elements. It does not have instances; rather, its subclasses will have instances that inherit protocol defined in **SequenceableCollection.**

Protocol Summary for Class **SequenceableCollection**

The hierarchy for class **SequenceableCollection** is **Object—Collection—SequenceableCollection.** Class **SequenceableCollection** has no instance variables, class variables, or pool dictionaries. It has no class methods. It has 35 instance methods in eight categories.

Ten new methods for accessing the elements of a **SequenceableCollection** are added. These methods take advantage of the fact that sequenceable collections have indexed elements.

One method (**remove: ifAbsent:**) is polymorphically redefined to block its usage by a **SequenceableCollection.**

One method (**grow**) for making the instance larger by a specified size called growSize is added. The size of a sequenceable collection is essentially doubled until doubling is not possible. Then it is incremented by an amount that brings its total size up to DefaultMaximumSize (as defined by the class variable in **Collection**).

The comma (,) operator is introduced under the category *copying*. It provides concatenation of sequenceable collections.

7.3.1   Class **ArrayedCollection**

This section gives a protocol summary for the class **ArrayedCollection** and application examples of its subclasses. A protocol summary is not given of the subclasses of **ArrayedCollection.** This is left as an exercise for the reader. Examples are designed to exercise a variety of messages for objects of each subclass.

ArrayedCollection is an abstract superclass of all the collection classes that have a fixed-range integer, external key. It does not have instances; rather, its subclasses will have instances that inherit protocol defined in **ArrayedCollection.** Since the methods for instance creation for most of the subclasses of **ArrayedCollection** are identical, the instance creation protocol is defined in **ArrayedCollection** instead of its subclasses. This discussion illustrates a long chain of abstract classes supporting the subclasses that actually represent objects that may be created. That is, the chain of classes given by **Object—Collection—SequenceableCollection—ArrayedCollection** is an abstract chain defining protocol for use by the subclasses of **ArrayedCollection.**

Protocol Summary for Class **ArrayedCollection**

The hierarchy for class **ArrayedCollection** is **Object—Collection—SequenceableCollection—ArrayedCollection.** Class **ArrayedCollection** has no instance variables, class variables, or pool dictionaries. It has seven class methods in two categories and five instance methods in four categories. Most of the protocol of its subclasses is inherited.

One key change is that method **add:,** as inherited from **Collection,** is redefined to block its use. All instances of subclasses of **ArrayedCollection** have a fixed number of elements. Therefore elements cannot be added.

An example illustrates the protocol for arrays of heterogeneous objects. The hierarchy for objects of class **Array** is **Object—Collection—SequenceableCollection—ArrayedCollection—Array.** Because of this long inheritance chain and the richness of protocol defined in its superclasses, **Array** objects respond to a large number of messages. In the following example, messages are used that are found in the protocol of all the superclasses of **Object.** Not all the available protocol is demonstrated in the example.

Array Example 7A

Listing 7.6 gives details for an example that illustrates some of the protocol for objects of class **Array.** It is implemented as a class method, example1, in class **Array.** Results of execution of the example are given in Figure 7.7. One of the most powerful and convenient message selectors in the Smalltalk system is the comma (,) for concatenating two objects. The objects must be instances of a subclass of **SequenceableCollection.** This includes arrays as well as strings and some other kinds of objects. This message selector is demonstrated for arrays in this example.

The following example illustrates the use of special arrays that contain byte-sized elements. The elements are stored as small integers with compacted storage; for example, two elements of a byte array are stored per 16-bit word.

ByteArray Example 7A

Listing 7.7 gives details for the method example1 in class **ByteArray.** The results are shown in Figure 7.8. A significant minor difference is illustrated for the

Listing 7.6
Details of **Array**
example1

Array class methodsFor: 'examples'

example1
    "This example illustrates protocol for arrays."

    | array1 array2 array3 |

    array1 ← Array new.   "Size defaults to zero."
    array2 ← Array new: 5.   "Contents default to nil."
    array3 ← Array new: 5 withAll: 0.0.   "Initialize contents to 0.0."

    Transcript clear; refresh; show: 'Array example1 -- Protocol for arrays.'; cr; crtab;
        show: 'Instance creation and initialization of arrays'; crtab;
          show: ' array1 size and contents: ', array1 size printString, ' --> ', array1 printString;
            crtab;
          show: ' array2 size and contents: ', array2 size printString, ' --> ', array2 printString;
            crtab;
          show: ' array3 size and contents: ', array3 size printString, ' --> ', array3 printString;
            cr; cr.

    Transcript tab; show: 'Accessing, adding and removing objects in an array.'; cr.
    array2 at: 2 put: 'string'; at: 1 put: $F; at: 5 put: 21; at: 3 put: #(3 $x).
    Transcript tab;
        show: ' New array2 contents --> ',array2 printString; crtab;
        show:
         ' array2 Index of element 21 is: ', (array2 indexOf: 21) printString, ' (0 if absent)';
           crtab;
        show: ' first element in array2 is: ', array2 first printString; tab; tab;
        show: 'last element in array2 is: ', array2 last printString; crtab;
        show: ' array2 contents after removing element 3 --> '.
    array2 at: 3 put: nil.   "This is the only way to remove an array object."
    Transcript show: array2 printString; cr; cr.

    array3 ← #(1 2 3 4 5).
    Transcript tab; show:
        'Enumerating across elements in an array (do:, select:, reject:, collect: reverse).';
        crtab; show: ' Literal array --> ', array3 printString; crtab;
        show: ' Squares --> '.
          array3 do: [:elem | Transcript show: ' ', (elem*elem) printString].
    Transcript crtab; show: ' Odd elements --> ',
        (array3 select: [:elem | elem odd]) printString.   "returns a new array of odds."
    Transcript cr; tab; show: ' Even elements --> ',
        (array3 reject: [:elem | elem odd]) printString.   "returns a new array of evens."
    array3 ← array3 collect: [:elem | elem*elem].   "Redefine array3 to be squares."
    Transcript crtab;
        show: ' Redefinded array3 to be squares --> ',   array3 printString; crtab.
    Transcript show: ' array2 reversed contains --> ', array2 reverse printString; cr; cr.

    Transcript tab; show: 'Concatenate (,) array2 & array3, assign to array1.'; cr; tab;
        show: ' New array1 contents --> '.
    array1 ← array2, array3.
    Transcript print: array1; endEntry.

    " Array example1 "

Figure 7.7
Class Method
example1 in Class
Array—Array
Protocol Usage

```
System Transcript
Array example1 -- Protocol for arrays.

    Instance creation and initialization of arrays
      array1 size and contents: 0 --> ()
      array2 size and contents: 5 --> (nil nil nil nil nil )
      array3 size and contents: 5 --> (0.0 0.0 0.0 0.0 0.0 )

    Accessing, adding and removing objects in an array.
      New array2 contents --> ($F 'string' (3 $x ) nil 21 )
      array2 index of element 21 is: 5  (0 if absent)
      first element in array2 is: $F     last element in array2 is: 21
      array2 contents after removing element 3 --> ($F 'string' nil nil 21 )

    Enumerating across elements in an array (do:, select:, reject:, collect: reverse).
      Literal array --> (1 2 3 4 5 )
      Squares -->   1  4  9  16 25
      Odd elements --> (1 3 5 )
      Even elements --> (2 4 )
      Redefinded array3 to be squares --> (1 4 9 16 25 )
      array2 reversed contains --> (21 nil nil 'string' $F )

    Concatenate (,) array2 & array3, assign to array1.
      New array1 contents --> ($F 'string' nil nil 21 1 4 9 16 25 )
```

Listing 7.7
Details of
ByteArray
example1

ByteArray class methodsFor: 'examples'

example1
　"Protocol for byte arrays."

　　| byteArray0 byteArray1 byteArray2 |

　　byteArray0 ← ByteArray new: 6.
　　byteArray1 ← ByteArray new: 10 withAll: 95.
　　byteArray2 ← ByteArray with: 66 with: 98 with: 109 with: 120.

　　Transcript clear; refresh;
　　　　show: 'ByteArray example1 -- Manipulating Arrays of Bytes.'; cr; crtab;
　　　　show: 'Instance creation options.'; crtab;
　　　　show: ' Uninitialized array (default element is 0) byteArray0 --> ',
　　　　　　byteArray0 printString; crtab;
　　　　show: ' Initialized array byteArray1 --> ', byteArray1 printString; crtab;
　　　　show: ' Initialized differently byteArray2 --> ', byteArray2 printString; cr.

　　Transcript crtab; show: 'Accessing 1, 2, or 4 bytes.'; crtab;
　　　　show: ' Byte 3 of byteArray2 is --> ', (byteArray2 at: 3) printString; crtab;
　　　　show: ' Word beginning at byte 2 of byteArray2 is --> ',
　　　　　　(byteArray2 wordAt: 2) printString; crtab;
　　　　show: ' Long word (4 bytes) beginning at byte 3 of byteArray1 is --> ',
　　　　　　(byteArray1 doubleWordAt: 3) printString; cr.

Listing 7.7
(continued)

```
Transcript crtab; show: 'Reassigning 1, 2, or 4 bytes.'; crtab.
    byteArray0 at: 1 put: 20. Transcript
        show: ' Set byte 1 in byteArray0 to 20 --> ', byteArray0 printString; crtab.
    byteArray0 doubleWordAt: 3 put: (byteArray1 doubleWordAt: 6). Transcript
        show: ' Set long word beginning at 3 in byteArray0 to be 1600085855 ';
        crtab; tab; show: '--> ', byteArray0 printString; crtab.
    byteArray1 wordAt: 3 put: (byteArray2 wordAt: 2). Transcript
        show: ' Set word beginning at 3 in byteArray1 to be 28024';
        crtab; tab; show: '--> ', byteArray1 printString; crtab.
    byteArray1 doubleWordAt: 2 put: (byteArray2 doubleWordAt: 1). Transcript
        show: ' Set long word beginning at 2 in byteArray1 to be 1600085855 ';
        crtab; tab; show: '--> ', byteArray1 printString; crtab.
    byteArray1 doubleWordAt: 3 put: (byteArray2 doubleWordAt: 1). Transcript
        show: ' Set long word beginning at 3 in byteArray1 to be 1600085855 ';
        crtab; tab; show: '--> ', byteArray1 printString; crtab.
    byteArray2 wordAt: 2 put: (0). Transcript
        show: ' Set word beginning at 2 in byteArray2 to be 0 ';
        crtab; tab; show: '--> ', byteArray2 printString; cr.

    " ByteArray example1  "
```

Figure 7.8
Class Method
example1 in Class
ByteArray—
ByteArray Protocol
Usage

```
┌─────────────────────────────────────────────────────────────────┐
│ System Transcript                                               │
│ ┌─────────────────────────────────────────────────────────────┐ │
│ │ ByteArray example1 -- Manipulating Arrays of Bytes.         │ │
│ │                                                             │ │
│ │    Instance creation options.                               │ │
│ │       Uninitialized array (default element is 0) byteArray0 --> ByteArray (0 0 0 0 0 0 ) │ │
│ │       Initialized array byteArray1 --> ByteArray (95 95 95 95 95 95 95 95 95 95 ) │ │
│ │       Initialized differently byteArray2 --> ByteArray (66 98 109 120 ) │ │
│ │                                                             │ │
│ │    Accessing 1, 2, or 4 bytes.                              │ │
│ │       Byte 3 of byteArray2 is --> 109                       │ │
│ │       Word beginning at byte 2 of byteArray2 is --> 28024   │ │
│ │       Long word (4 bytes) beginning at byte 3 of byteArray1 is --> 1600085855 │ │
│ │                                                             │ │
│ │    Reassigning 1, 2, or 4 bytes.                            │ │
│ │       Set byte 1 in byteArray0 to 20 --> ByteArray (20 0 0 0 0 0 ) │ │
│ │       Set long word beginning at 3 in byteArray0 to be 1600085855 │ │
│ │          --> ByteArray (20 0 95 95 95 95 )                  │ │
│ │       Set word beginning at 3 in byteArray1 to be 28024     │ │
│ │          --> ByteArray (95 95 95 95 109 120 95 95 95 95 )   │ │
│ │       Set long word beginning at 2 in byteArray1 to be 1600085855 │ │
│ │          --> ByteArray (95 66 98 109 120 120 95 95 95 95 )  │ │
│ │       Set long word beginning at 3 in byteArray1 to be 1600085855 │ │
│ │          --> ByteArray (95 66 66 98 109 120 95 95 95 95 )   │ │
│ │       Set word beginning at 2 in byteArray2 to be 0         │ │
│ │          --> ByteArray (66 98 0 0 )                         │ │
│ └─────────────────────────────────────────────────────────────┘ │
└─────────────────────────────────────────────────────────────────┘
```

methods that reassign either words (two bytes) or long words (four bytes) in a byte array. The messages wordAt: put: and doubleWordAt: put: assign either two bytes or four bytes to consecutive locations in the byte array. However, the index position into the byte array is in words for the two-byte assignment and in bytes for the four-byte assignment. This discrepancy in interpretation of the index is illustrated by the examples for setting words and long words in byteArray1.

The following example illustrates some of the protocol for manipulating strings. Strings are among the most important objects in the system. They form the basis for most of the interfaces between Smalltalk and the user. Class **String** inherits a rich variety of protocol from all its superclasses and defines new protocol as well. Smalltalk also supports string literals.

String Example 7A

Listing 7.8 gives details of example4 in class **String.** It illustrates general protocol usage for objects of class **String.** Results are given in Figure 7.9. Concatenation by the comma message selector is used in the show: message to **Transcript.** Full support is provided in Smalltalk for a very complete set of string messages.

Listing 7.8
Details of String
example4

String class methodsFor: 'display & print examples'

example4
   "This example illustrates general protocol for strings."

   | string1 string2 string3 |

   string1 ← 'fromString:'.
   string2 ← 'I am string2.'.
   string3 ← String perform: string1 asSymbol with: string2.
   string3 ← string3 copyReplaceAll: '.' with: ' (actually I am string3).'.

   Transcript clear; refresh;
       show: 'String example4 -- General String protocol Usage'; cr; crtab;
       show: 'Three initial string assignments'; crtab;
       show: ' string1 contents --> ', string1; crtab;
       show: ' string2 contents --> ', string2; crtab;
       show: ' string3 contents --> ', string3; cr; crtab.

   Transcript
       show: 'Comparing, accessing, and copying strings.'; crtab;
       show: ' string1 is ', (string1 < string2 ifFalse: ['not ']), 'less than string2'; crtab;
       show: ' string3 is ', (string3 < string2 ifFalse: ['not ']), 'less than string2'; crtab.

Listing 7.8
(continued)

```
Transcript
    show: ' Part of string3 does ',
        ((string2 copyUpTo: $2) = (string3 copyUpTo: $2) ifFalse: [ 'not ']),
        'match part of string2.'; crtab;
    show: ' "string" is ',
        (('*string*' match: string1) ifFalse: ['not ']), 'found in string1'; crtab;
    show: ' The contents of string3 up to and including $l are --> ',
        (string3 copyUpTo: $l), 'l'; cr; crtab.


Transcript
    show: 'Converting strings to objects of other clases.'; crtab;
    show: ' string1 as lower case is --> ', string1 asLowercase; crtab;
    show: ' string1 as upper case is --> ', string1 asUppercase; crtab;
    show: ' string1 as symbol is --> ';
        print: (string1 asSymbol); endEntry; show: ' is an instance of class ',
        string1 asSymbol class printString; crtab;
    show: ' "2345" as a number is --> ';
        print: ('2345' asNumber); endEntry; crtab;
    show: ' "12-15-87" as a date is --> ';
        print: ('12-15-87' asDate); endEntry; crtab;
    show: ' Embedded backslashes converted to cr"s -->',
        ('\      line 1\      line 2\      line 3 \' withCRs).


"String example4"
```

Figure 7.9
Class Method
example4 in Class
String—General
Protocol Usage

```
System Transcript

String example4 -- General String protocol Usage

    Three initial string assignments
      string1 contents --> fromString:
      string2 contents --> I am string2.
      string3 contents --> I am string2 (actually I am string3).

    Comparing, accessing, and copying strings.
      string1 is less than string2
      string3 is less than string2
      Part of string3 does match part of string2.
      'string' is found in string1
      The contents of string3 up to and including $l are --> I am string2 (actual

    Converting strings to objects of other clases.
      string1 as lower case is --> fromstring:
      string1 as upper case is --> FROMSTRING:
      string1 as symbol is --> fromString: is an instance of class Symbol
      '2345' as a number is --> 2345
      '12-15-87' as a date is --> 15 December 1987
      Embedded backslashes converted to cr's -->
        line 1
        line 2
        line 3
```

Figure 7.10
An Example
Method That Has
Too Many Literals

```
Workspace
example1
    "This example illustrates general protocol for texts."

    | text1 text2 text3 text4 string1 string2 string3 |

    text1 ← (string1 ← 'fromString:') asText.
    text2 ← (string2 ← 'I am text2 in boldface.') asText allBold.
    string3 ← String perform: text1 asString asSymbol with: text2 asString.
    text3 ← (string3 copyReplaceAll: '.' with: ' (actually I am text3 in italic).' )asText.
    text3 emphasizeFrom: 1 to: text3 size with: 3. "code for italic"
    text4 ← Text string: 'This is underlined text.' emphasis: 13.

    Transcript clear; refresh;
        show: 'Text example1 -- General Text Protocol Usage';
        cr; cr; tab; show: 'Three initial text assignments'; cr; tab;
        show: ' text1 contents --> ', text1 printString; cr; tab;
        show: ' text2 contents --> '; print: text2; endEntry; cr; tab;
        show: ' text3 contents --> ', text3 printString; cr; tab;
        show: ' text4 contents --> ', text4 printString; cr; cr.

    Transcript tab; print:
Notifier t string: 'Comparing, accessing, and copying strings.' emphasis: 1); endEntry;
    More than 64 literals referenced.  You must split or otherwise simplify this method

    Transcript crtab; show: ' Part of string3 does ',
        ((string2 copyUpTo: $2) = (string3 copyUpTo: $2) ifFalse: ['not ']),
        'match part of string2.'; crtab; show: ' "string" is ',
        (('*string*' match: string1) ifFalse: ['not ']), 'found in string1'; crtab;
        show: ' The contents of string3 up to and including $I are --> ',
        (string3 copyUpTo: $I), 'I'; cr; cr.

    Transcript tab; print:
        ((Text fromString: 'Converting strings to objects of other classes.' ) allBold);
        endEntry; crtab; show: ' string1 as lower case is --> ', string1 asLowercase;
        crtab; show: ' string1 as upper case is --> ', string1 asUppercase; crtab;
        show: ' string1 as symbol is --> '; print: (string1 asSymbol); endEntry;
            show: ' is an instance of class ', string1 asSymbol class printString; crtab;
        show: ' "2345" as a number is --> '; print: ('2345' asNumber); endEntry;
        crtab; show: ' "12-15-87" as a date is --> '; print: ('12-15-87' asDate);
            endEntry; cr; crtab;
        print: (Text string: ' Embedded backslashes converted to cr''s -->' emphasis: 2);
            endEntry; show: '\        line 1\        line 2\        line 3 \' withCRs.

    " Text example1 "
```

Texts are strings with style. That is, the characteristics of the characters may be given emphasis such as boldface, underline, or italic.

In developing the next example, many of the details included in the **String** Example 7A were kept. This led to an interesting result that identifies a limitation of methods. A method is limited to no more than 64 literals (this number is undoubtedly implementation-dependent). The first attempt is shown in Figure 7.10, with the error notifier shown over a workspace containing the errant example code. The error was obtained from the browser while attempting to *accept* the listed example. For purposes of displaying the entire method details, the code was moved from the browser window to a workspace window, as shown.

Text Example 7A

Listing 7.9 shows details of example1 in **Text.** It demonstrates several key features of instances of **Text.** First, as seen in Figure 7.11, display of instances of **Text** are not supported by the Transcript window. This means that the emphasis (bold, italic, underline) is lost in the Transcript display. Second, the only support for displaying text is provided in class **DisplayText.** Thus displaying an instance of **Text** with the proper emphasis shown requires that it first be converted to a display text and displayed with the message displayAt:. Other display messages in the protocol for **DisplayText** can also be used.

It is significant that the emphasis is added to the instances of **Text,** and it is retained in the conversion to instances of **DisplayText.** It is a bit tedious, but text handling never seems to be easy.

Listing 7.9
Details of **Text**
example1

Text class methodsFor: 'examples'

example1
　"This example illustrates general protocol for texts."

　| text1 text2 text3 text4 string1 string2 string3 |

　text1 ← (string1 ← 'fromString:') asText.
　text2 ← (string2 ← 'I am text2 in boldface.') asText allBold.
　text3 ← (string2 copyReplaceAll: '.' with: ' (actually I am text3 in italic).')asText.
　text3 emphasizeFrom: 1 to: text3 size with: 3.　　"code for italic"
　text4 ← Text string: 'This is underlined text.' emphasis: 13.

　Transcript clear; refresh;
　　　show: 'Text example1 -- General Text Protocol Usage';cr; crtab;
　　　show: 'Three initial text assignments'; crtab;
　　　show: ' text1 contents --> ', text1 printString; crtab;
　　　show: ' text2 contents --> '; print: text2; endEntry; crtab;
　　　show: ' text3 contents --> ', text3 printString; crtab;
　　　show: ' text4 contents --> ', text4 printString; cr; crtab.

　text1 asDisplayText displayAt: 100@500.
　text2 asDisplayText displayAt: 100@520.
　text3 asDisplayText displayAt: 100@540.
　text4 asDisplayText displayAt: 100@560.

```
Transcript print:
    ((Text fromString: 'Converting strings to objects of other classes.' ) allBold);
        endEntry; crtab;
    show: ' string1 as lower case is --> ', string1 asLowercase; crtab;
    show: ' string1 as upper case is --> ', string1 asUppercase; crtab;
    show: ' string1 as symbol is --> ';
        print: (string1 asSymbol); endEntry; show: ' is an instance of class ',
        string1 asSymbol class printString; crtab;
    show: ' "2345" as a number is --> ';
        print: ('2345' asNumber); endEntry; crtab;
    show: ' "12-15-87" as a date is --> ';
        print: ('12-15-87' asDate); endEntry; cr; crtab;
    print: (Text string: ' Embedded backslashes converted to cr''s -->' emphasis: 2);
        endEntry;
    show: '\      line 1\      line 2\      line 3 \' withCRs.


" Text example1 "
```

Figure 7.11
Text example1 for
Converting Strings
to Text and
Displaying Them

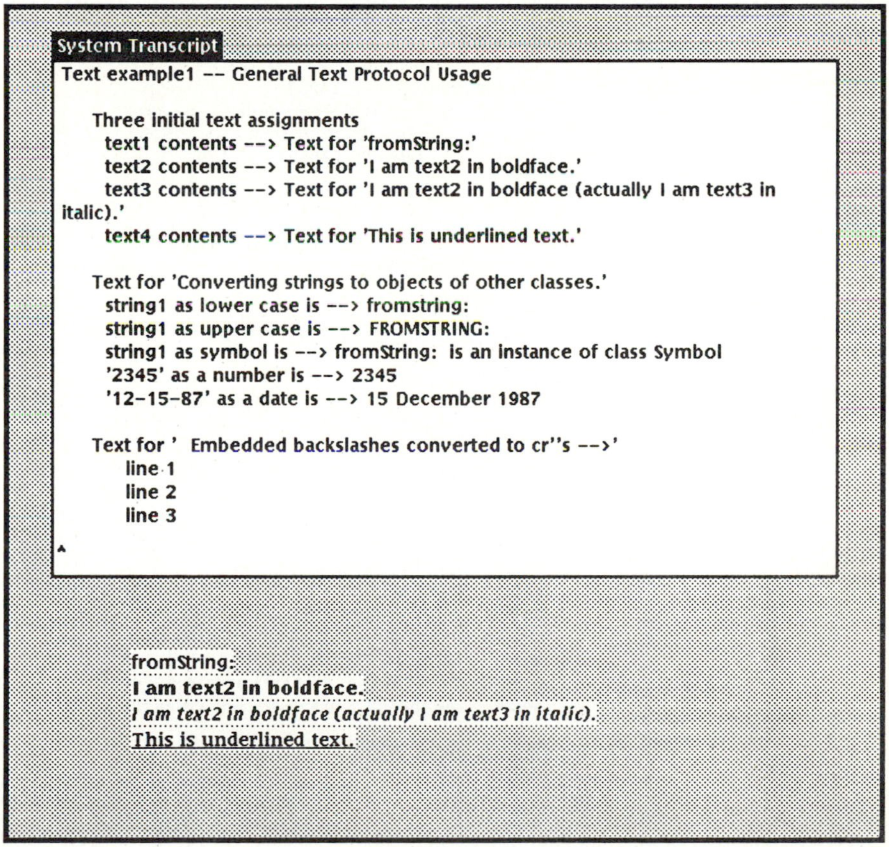

```
System Transcript
Text example1 -- General Text Protocol Usage

    Three initial text assignments
    text1 contents --> Text for 'fromString:'
    text2 contents --> Text for 'I am text2 in boldface.'
    text3 contents --> Text for 'I am text2 in boldface (actually I am text3 in
italic).'
    text4 contents --> Text for 'This is underlined text.'

    Text for 'Converting strings to objects of other classes.'
    string1 as lower case is --> fromstring:
    string1 as upper case is --> FROMSTRING:
    string1 as symbol is --> fromString:  is an instance of class Symbol
    '2345' as a number is --> 2345
    '12-15-87' as a date is --> 15 December 1987

    Text for '  Embedded backslashes converted to cr''s -->'
        line 1
        line 2
        line 3


        fromString:
        I am text2 in boldface.
        I am text2 in boldface (actually I am text3 in italic).
        This is underlined text.
```

Word arrays are most often used for storing the bitmaps of class **Form.** The next example shows how those bitmaps are stored. Emphasis is on the subclass of **WordArray** called **DisplayBitmap.**

WordArray Example 7A

Figure 7.12 shows details of example1 in class **DisplayBitmap.** The Transcript window shows results of some statistics that are available using protocol in **DisplayBitmap** and its superclass, **WordArray.** In addition to accessing statistical information about the bitmap, it is possible to access the contents of any word and to set the contents of any word.

The expression bits at: 12830 put: 16rFFFF sets all bits to one in the 12830th

**Figure 7.12
DisplayBitmap**
example1—
Accessing and
Setting Display Bits

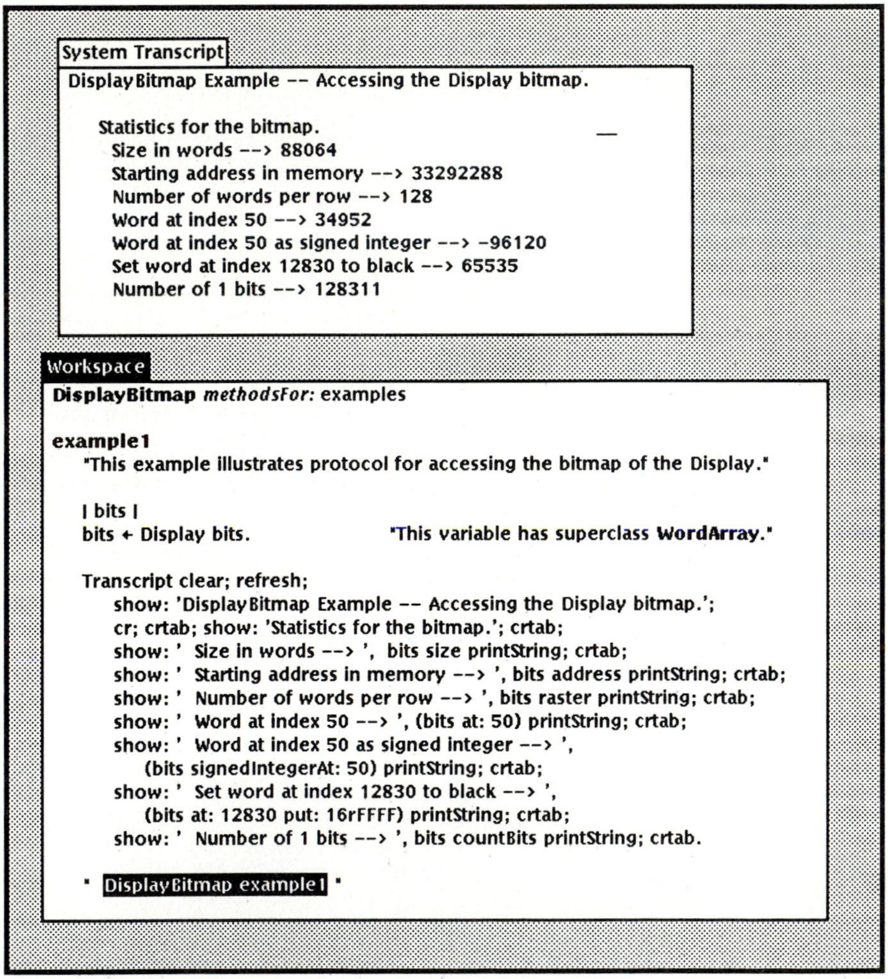

```
System Transcript
DisplayBitmap Example -- Accessing the Display bitmap.

    Statistics for the bitmap.                          —
        Size in words --> 88064
        Starting address in memory --> 33292288
        Number of words per row --> 128
        Word at index 50 --> 34952
        Word at index 50 as signed integer --> -96120
        Set word at index 12830 to black --> 65535
        Number of 1 bits --> 128311
```

```
Workspace
DisplayBitmap methodsFor: examples

example1
    "This example illustrates protocol for accessing the bitmap of the Display."

    | bits |
    bits ← Display bits.              "This variable has superclass WordArray."

    Transcript clear; refresh;
        show: 'DisplayBitmap Example -- Accessing the Display bitmap.';
        cr; crtab; show: 'Statistics for the bitmap.'; crtab;
        show: ' Size in words --> ',  bits size printString; crtab;
        show: ' Starting address in memory --> ', bits address printString; crtab;
        show: ' Number of words per row --> ', bits raster printString; crtab;
        show: ' Word at index 50 --> ', (bits at: 50) printString; crtab;
        show: ' Word at index 50 as signed integer --> ',
            (bits signedIntegerAt: 50) printString; crtab;
        show: ' Set word at index 12830 to black --> ',
            (bits at: 12830 put: 16rFFFF) printString; crtab;
        show: ' Number of 1 bits --> ', bits countBits printString; crtab.

  •  DisplayBitmap example1 •
```

word of bits. On the display this corresponds to the word at y = 12830 // 128, or pixel row 100. Its x-coordinate corresponds to x = 12830 \\ 128, or the 30th word across. The result is seen as the thin black line in the upper right part of the Transcript window. The length of the line is one word (or 16 pixels).

7.3.2　Class **Interval**

This section gives an application example of the **SequenceableCollection** subclass **Interval.** The example is designed to exercise a variety of messages for objects of this class. Development of a protocol summary for class **Interval** is left as an exercise for the reader.

Interval Example 7A

Class **Interval** has three instance variables **first, last,** and **step.** Instances of this class are fixed-size arithmetic progressions that go from **first** to **last** by **step.** A simple example, given in Figure 7.13, illustrates some of the protocol for intervals.

7.3.3　Class **LinkedList**

The implementation of **LinkedList** represents a simple linked list of instances of **Link.** It is a connected list of pointers only; the links contain only a pointer to the next link. To include other objects in the links as information fields requires that subclasses be added to **Link** that have the appropriate objects as private data. Links are added and removed at the front or end only to instances of **LinkedList.** This limitation is satisfactory for implementing stacks or queues but is inadequate for insertion into an ordered linked list. The solution to this problem is to add a subclass to **LinkedList** that includes new protocol for both insertion and deletion based on ordering rules.

Instances of class **SortedCollection** achieve the same functionality as an ordered linked list. Instances of **OrderedCollection** also provide protocol for maintaining stack or queue data structures.

7.3.4　Class **OrderedCollection**

This section gives an abbreviated protocol summary for the class **OrderedCollection** and application examples of its use. A more complete protocol summary is given in Appendix 3.

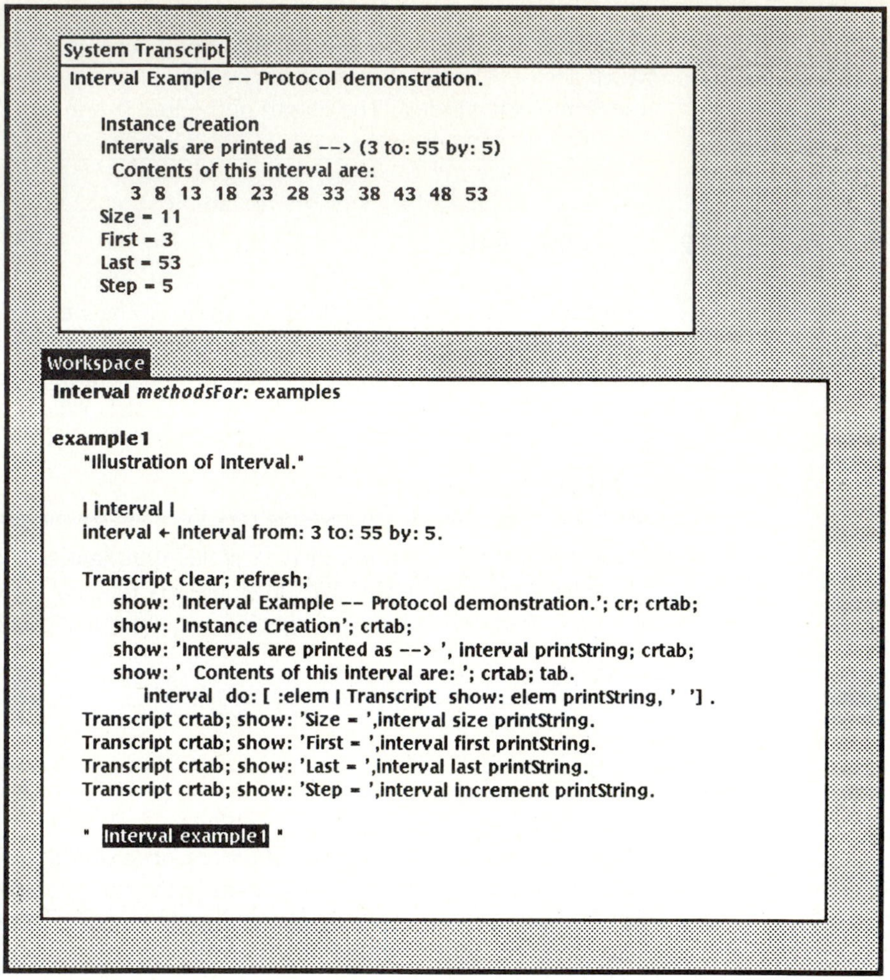

**Figure 7.13
Interval**
example1—
Accessing Intervals

```
┌─────────────────────────────────────────────────────┐
│ System Transcript                                    │
│ Interval Example -- Protocol demonstration.          │
│                                                      │
│   Instance Creation                                  │
│   Intervals are printed as --> (3 to: 55 by: 5)      │
│    Contents of this interval are:                    │
│       3  8  13  18  23  28  33  38  43  48  53       │
│   Size = 11                                          │
│   First = 3                                          │
│   Last = 53                                          │
│   Step = 5                                           │
└─────────────────────────────────────────────────────┘

┌─────────────────────────────────────────────────────┐
│ Workspace                                            │
│ Interval methodsFor: examples                        │
│                                                      │
│ example1                                             │
│   "Illustration of Interval."                        │
│                                                      │
│   | interval |                                       │
│   interval ← Interval from: 3 to: 55 by: 5.          │
│                                                      │
│   Transcript clear; refresh;                         │
│       show: 'Interval Example -- Protocol demonstration.'; cr; crtab; │
│       show: 'Instance Creation'; crtab;              │
│       show: 'Intervals are printed as --> ', interval printString; crtab; │
│       show: ' Contents of this interval are: '; crtab; tab. │
│          interval do: [ :elem | Transcript show: elem printString, ' '] . │
│   Transcript crtab; show: 'Size = ',interval size printString. │
│   Transcript crtab; show: 'First = ',interval first printString. │
│   Transcript crtab; show: 'Last = ',interval last printString. │
│   Transcript crtab; show: 'Step = ',interval increment printString. │
│                                                      │
│   " Interval example1 "                              │
└─────────────────────────────────────────────────────┘
```

Instances of **OrderedCollection** have order that is determined by the sequence in which objects are added or removed. They are accessible by keys that are external indices. Instances of this class are used to implement stacks, queues, deques, or ordered linked lists.

Protocol Summary for Class **OrderedCollection**

The hierarchy for class **OrderedCollection** is **Object—Collection—SequenceableCollection—OrderedCollection.** Class **OrderedCollection** has two instance variables, firstindex and lastindex. It has no class variables or pool dictionaries. It has 3 class methods in two categories and 40 instance methods in six categories. Private data in class **OrderedCollection** consists of two instance variables.

The instance variable **firstindex** is an instance of **Integer** representing the index position of the first element in the **OrderedCollection.** The instance variable **lastindex** is an instance of **Integer** representing the index of the last element in the **OrderedCollection.**

Key new methods for accessing, adding, and removing elements are added. These include the following messages: **after:, before:, first, last, removeFirst, removeLast, addAfter:, addBefore:, addFirst, addLast:.**

The following two examples illustrate how an ordered collection is used to represent the stack and queue data structures. In both cases the data structures are totally generic, meaning that mixed types of objects can be stored in a single instance of either. This feature of Smalltalk is difficult to duplicate in other languages.

Instances of **OrderedCollection** can be used to represent ordered linked lists as well. There is adequate protocol in the class description to support normal operations on all three data structures (stack, queue, and linked list).

OrderedCollection (Stack) Example 7A

This example uses an instance of **OrderedCollection** to represent a purely generic stack and its most standard operations. Operations include push, pop, stackTop, size, enumerating without clearing, and clearing.

Listing 7.10 shows details of class method example1 added to class **OrderedCollection** to demonstrate stack operations. The message new sent to **OrderedCollection** establishes an ordered collection with a default of 10 elements. Results of the example1 message evaluation are shown in Figure 7.14. The implementation is truly generic and dynamic in nature; it satisfies all the defined properties for a stack data structure. Even mixed classes of objects can be stored on the same stack with no difficulty. This feature is very difficult, if even possible, to implement in most languages.

OrderedCollection (Queue) Example 7B

This example illustrates how an instance of class **OrderedCollection** can represent a queue and its operations. A true generic representation is again used. The operations of adding, removing, determining size, enumerating without clearing, and clearing are demonstrated.

Listing 7.11 gives details for class method example2 in class **OrderedCollection.** Figure 7.15 shows the result of evaluating the expression OrderedCollection example2. Again, the full support for generics is demonstrated.

Listing 7.10
Details of
OrderedCollection
example1

OrderedCollection class methodsFor: 'examples'

example1
"This example shows how an OrderedCollection can represent a stack.
   It implements the stack operations:
      push, pop, isEmpty, stackTop, reverse, size, clearing."

```
| stack1 stack2 |
stack1 ← OrderedCollection new.                "Initialize to 10 elements, but still empty"
stack2 ← OrderedCollection with: 'bottom'.     "Initialize to contain one string"

Transcript clear; refresh;
    show: 'OrderedCollection example1 -- Implementing a Stack.'; cr; crtab;
    show: 'Instance Creation (two ways)'; crtab;
    show: ' stack1 contents --> ', stack1 printString; crtab;
    show: ' stack2 contents --> ', stack2 printString; cr; crtab.

Transcript
    show: 'Adding and removing operations (push and pop)'; crtab;
    show: ' Add 5 integers to stack1 --> '.
1 to: 5 do: [ :i | stack1 add: i*i. Transcript show: ' ', (i*i) printString ].
Transcript crtab;
    show: ' Add array to stack2 --> ',
        (stack2 add: #($s 2 symbol 'me')) printString; crtab;
    show: ' Add integer to stack2 --> ',
        (stack2 add: 125) printString; crtab;
    show: ' Add character to stack2 --> ',
        (stack2 add: $P) printString; crtab;
    show: ' Pop stack1 to get --> ',
        (stack1 removeLast) printString; crtab;
    show: ' Push contents of stack2 onto stack1 --> '; crtab; tab;
    show: (stack1 addAllLast: stack2) printString.

Transcript cr; crtab; show: 'Accessing the stack.'; crtab;
    show: ' New stackTop for stack1 is --> ', (stack1 last) printString; crtab;
    show: ' New stackTop for stack2 is --> ', (stack2 last) printString; crtab;
    show: ' stack1 size is --> ', stack1 size printString; crtab;
    show: ' stack2 size is --> ', stack2 size printString.

Transcript cr; crtab;
    show: 'Iterating across the generic elements, and clearing'; crtab;
    show: ' The contents of stack1 are:'.
    stack1 reverseDo: [ :each | Transcript crtab; tab; print: each; endEntry ].
Transcript crtab;
    show: ' Empty stack1 and verify contents --> ',
        (stack1 ← stack1 copyEmpty) printString.

" OrderedCollection example1 "
```

Figure 7.14
OrderedCollection
example1—Stack
Operations

```
┌─────────────────────────────────────────────────────────┐
│ System Transcript                                       │
│ ┌─────────────────────────────────────────────────────┐ │
│ │ OrderedCollection example1 -- Implementing a Stack.  │ │
│ │                                                      │ │
│ │    Instance Creation (two ways)                      │ │
│ │     stack1 contents --> OrderedCollection ()         │ │
│ │     stack2 contents --> OrderedCollection ('bottom' )│ │
│ │                                                      │ │
│ │    Adding and removing operations (push and pop)     │ │
│ │    Add 5 integers to stack1 -->  1  4  9  16  25     │ │
│ │    Add array to stack2 --> ($s 2 symbol 'me' )       │ │
│ │    Add integer to stack2 --> 125                     │ │
│ │    Add character to stack2 --> $P                    │ │
│ │    Pop stack1 to get --> 25                          │ │
│ │    Push contents of stack2 onto stack1               │ │
│ │      --> OrderedCollection ('bottom' ($s 2 symbol 'me' ) 125 $P ) │ │
│ │                                                      │ │
│ │    Accessing the stack.                              │ │
│ │     New stackTop for stack1 is --> $P                │ │
│ │     New stackTop for stack2 is --> $P                │ │
│ │     stack1 size is --> 8                             │ │
│ │     stack2 size is --> 4                             │ │
│ │                                                      │ │
│ │    Iterating across the generic elements, and clearing │ │
│ │     The contents of stack1 are:                      │ │
│ │       $P                                             │ │
│ │       125                                            │ │
│ │       ($s 2 symbol 'me' )                            │ │
│ │       'bottom'                                       │ │
│ │       16                                             │ │
│ │       9                                              │ │
│ │       4                                              │ │
│ │       1                                              │ │
│ │    Empty stack1 and verify contents --> OrderedCollection () │ │
│ │                                                      │ │
│ └─────────────────────────────────────────────────────┘ │
└─────────────────────────────────────────────────────────┘
```

Listing 7.11
Details of
OrderedCollection
example2

OrderedCollection class methodsFor: 'examples'

example2
   "This example shows how an OrderedCollection can represent a queue.
         It implements the queue operations:
              add, remove, isEmpty, size, and clearing."

```
| queue1 queue2 queue3 |
queue1 ← OrderedCollection new.          "Initialize to 10 elements, but still empty"
queue2 ← OrderedCollection with: 'June'.   "Initialize to contain one string"
```

Listing 7.11
(continued)

```
Transcript clear; refresh;
     show: 'OrderedCollection example2 -- Implementing a Queue.'; cr; crtab;
     show: 'Instance Creation (two ways)'; crtab;
     show: ' queue1 contents --> ', queue1 printString; crtab;
     show: ' queue2 contents --> ', queue2 printString; cr; crtab.

Transcript
     show: 'Adding and removing operations'; crtab;
     show: ' Add 5 names to queue1 --> ',
          ' ', (queue1 add: 'Donna'), ' ', (queue1 add: 'Leah'),
          ' ', (queue1 add: 'Vicki'), ' ', (queue1 add: 'Judy'),
          ' ', (queue1 add: 'Jan'); crtab.
Transcript
     show: ' Add array to queue2 --> ',
          (queue2 add: #($s 2 symbol 'me')) printString; crtab;
     show: ' Add integer to queue2 --> ', (queue2 add: 125) printString; crtab;
     show: ' Add character to queue2 --> ', (queue2 add: $P) printString;cr; tab;
     show: ' Add 2 names to queue2 --> ',' ',
          (queue2 add: 'Jackie'), ' ', (queue2 add: 'Julie'); crtab;
     show: ' Add two integers to queue2 --> '.
1 to: 2 do: [ :i | Transcript show: ' ', (queue2 add: i) printString].

Transcript cr; crtab;
     show: 'Contents of queue1 --> '; crtab; tab; show: queue1 printString; crtab;
     show: 'Contents of queue2 --> '; crtab; tab; show: queue2 printString.

Transcript cr; crtab;
     show: 'Add names from queue2 to queue1 --> '.
queue2 do: [ :nam | (nam isKindOf: String) ifTrue: [
     queue1 add: nam. Transcript show: ' ', nam] ] .
Transcript crtab;
     show: 'New contents of queue1 --> '; crtab; tab;
     show: queue1 printString.

Transcript cr; crtab; show: 'Accessing the queue.'; crtab;
     show: ' Last name in queue1 is --> ', (queue1 last) printString; crtab;
     show: ' First name in queue1 is --> ', (queue1 first) printString; crtab;
     show: ' Last object in queue2 is --> ', (queue2 last) printString; crtab;
     show: ' queue1 size is --> ', queue1 size printString; crtab;
     show: ' queue2 size is --> ', queue2 size printString.

Transcript cr; crtab;
     show: 'Iterating across the generic elements, and clearing.'; crtab;
     show: ' The in-order contents of queue2 are:'.
queue2 do: [ :each | Transcript crtab; tab; print: each; endEntry ].
Transcript crtab;
     show: ' Empty queue1 and verify contents --> ',
          (queue1 ← queue1 copyEmpty) printString.

" OrderedCollection example2 "
```

**Figure 7.15
OrderedCollection**
example2—Queue
Operations Using
Ordered
Collections

```
System Transcript
OrderedCollection example2 -- Implementing a Queue.

    Instance Creation (two ways)
    queue1 contents --> OrderedCollection ()
    queue2 contents --> OrderedCollection ('June' )

    Adding and removing operations
    Add 5 names to queue1 -->   Donna  Leah  Vicki  Judy  Jan
    Add array to queue2 --> ($s 2 symbol 'me' )
    Add integer to queue2 --> 125
    Add character to queue2 --> $P
    Add 2 names to queue2 -->   Jackie   Julie
    Add two integers to queue2 -->   1  2

Contents of queue1 -->
    OrderedCollection ('Donna' 'Leah' 'Vicki' 'Judy' 'Jan' )
Contents of queue2 -->
    OrderedCollection ('June' ($s 2 symbol 'me' ) 125 $P 'Jackie' 'Julie' 1 2 )

Add names from queue2 to queue1 -->   June Jackie Julie
New contents of queue1 -->
    OrderedCollection ('Donna' 'Leah' 'Vicki' 'Judy' 'Jan' 'June' 'Jackie' 'Julie' )

Accessing the queue.
    Last name in queue1 is --> 'Julie'
    First name in queue1 is --> 'Donna'
    Last object in queue2 is --> 2
    queue1 size is --> 8
    queue2 size is --> 8

Iterating across the generic elements, and clearing.
    The in-order contents of queue2 are:
        'June'
        ($s 2 symbol 'me' )
        125
        $P
        'Jackie'
        'Julie'
        1
        2
    Empty queue1 and verify contents --> OrderedCollection ()
```

7.4   Mapped Collections

A mapped collection is a collection whose elements are determined by a specified mapping from an existing collection with external keys such as a dictionary
or sequenceable collection. This class of objects is particularly useful for defining subsets of existing collections based on some mapping rule. The mapping

rule can be selected so that it changes the relational meaning between an element and its key. Examples are given that illustrate this redefinition of meaning. First, a protocol summary is given for the class **MappedCollection.**

A **MappedCollection** represents an access mechanism to an existing collection. Mapping can determine a reordering or partial listing of the collection. The key elements of an instance of **MappedCollection** are its domain and map. The domain has key/value pairs that map the elements from an existing collection into a mapped collection. The domain is the existing collection.

Protocol Summary for Class **MappedCollection**

The hierarchy for class **MappedCollection** is **Object—Collection—MappedCollection.** Class **MappedCollection** has two instance variables, map and domain. It has no class variables or pool dictionaries. It has 2 class methods in one category and 12 instance methods in six categories.

The private data of class **MappedCollection** consists of two instance variables. Instance variable **map** is an instance of **Dictionary** or a subclass of **SequenceableCollection** that gives a one-to-one correspondence between the keys of the mapped collection and keys in the existing collection. This mapping determines the value for any key in the mapped collection as the value of the mapped key in the existing collection. Instance variable **domain** is an instance of **Dictionary** or a subclass of **SequenceableCollection,** representing the existing collection from which the mapped collection is generated.

The next example shows how a mapped collection is created from an existing collection. It demonstrates some of the protocol available to instances of **MappedCollection.** The definition for **MappedCollection** indicates that the domain and the map may be instances of either class **Dictionary** or one of the **SequenceableCollection** classes. The only requirement is that they be accessible by external keys. The elements of dictionaries are accessible by keys that can be instances of any object. Typically they are symbols or strings. Keys for instances of **SequenceableCollection** are integers.

A typical application of a mapped collection can use dictionaries as the map and domain. To demonstrate that a map can associate integer keys, the example uses instances of **Array** for the map and for the domain.

MappedCollection **Example 7A**

Listing 7.12 gives details of class method example1 in class **MappedCollection.** It defines two arrays for the map and the domain of a mapped collection. The map provides a mapping of the odd-numbered elements of the domain in reverse

Listing 7.12
Details of
MappedCollection
example1

MappedCollection class methodsFor: 'examples'

example1
"A mapped collection using integer keys."

```
| map domain mapcol |
domain ← Array new: 10.
map ← Array new: 5.

domain at: 1 put: 'string'; at: 3 put: 'short'; at: 5 put: 'a';
    at: 7 put: 'is'; at: 9 put: 'This'.
domain at: 2 put: $z; at: 4 put: 25; at: 6 put: 'aString';
    at: 8 put: #symbol; at: 10 put: $a.
1 to: 5 do: [ :index |  map at: index put: 10 - (index * 2 - 1) ].
mapcol ← MappedCollection collection: domain map: map.

Transcript clear; refresh;
    show: 'Mapped Collection example1 -- Array map and domain'; cr; crtab;
    show: 'The map selects only the odd elements of the domain in reverse order.';crtab;
    show: ' domain contents --> ', domain printString; crtab;
    show: ' map contents --> ', map printString; crtab;
    show: ' mapped collection size = ', mapcol size printString; crtab: 2;
    show: 'definition --> ', mapcol printString; cr; crtab.

Transcript
    show: 'Domain elements can be changed via the map.';crtab;
    show: ' mapcol ', ' at: 3 put: ',
        (mapcol at: 3 put: 'some') printString, ' at: 4 put: ',
        (mapcol at: 4 put: 'new') printString; crtab;
    show: ' domain contents --> ', domain printString; crtab;
    show: ' mapcol contents --> ', mapcol contents printString; cr; crtab.

Transcript
    show: 'Select all the elements beginning with $s'; crtab: 2;
    show: (mapcol select: [ :each | (each at: 1) = $s] ) printString.

" MappedCollection example1 "
```

order into the mapped collection. The **select:** iteration message is demonstrated. Results are shown in Figure 7.16.

This chapter has presented protocol summaries for the collection classes and examples of their use. Collections are among the most often used classes in the Smalltalk image. They represent data structures. Chapter 8 introduces stream classes and discusses thieir relationship to the class **Collection.**

Figure 7.16
MappedCollection
example1—
Mapping Arrays

```
┌─────────────────────────────────────────────────────────────────────┐
│ System Transcript                                                     │
│ Mapped Collection example1 -- Array map and domain                    │
│                                                                       │
│     The map selects only the odd elements of the domain in reverse order. │
│       domain contents --> ('string' $z 'short' 25 'a' 'aString' 'is' symbol 'This' $a ) │
│       map contents --> (9 7 5 3 1 )                                   │
│       mapped collection size = 5                                      │
│         definition --> MappedCollection ('This' 'is' 'a' 'short' 'string' ) │
│                                                                       │
│     Domain elements can be changed via the map.                       │
│       mapcol   at: 3 put: 'some'  at: 4 put: 'new'                    │
│       domain contents --> ('string' $z 'new' 25 'some' 'aString' 'is' symbol 'This' $a ) │
│       mapcol contents --> ('This' 'is' 'some' 'new' 'string' )        │
│                                                                       │
│     Select all the elements beginning with $s                         │
│       ('some' 'string' )                                              │
│                                                                       │
└─────────────────────────────────────────────────────────────────────┘
```

Exercises

7.1 For class **Array** make a complete list of all its new, inherited, and redefined protocol. Comment on the significance of redefined protocol.

7.2 Based on discussions of various classes in the text, what criteria can you find for identifying the key messages in any class hierarchy?

7.3 Class **Array** has four abstract superclasses. Verify that all but one of the superclasses meet the constraint that no instances can be defined for them. Identify the specific reasons for each class. Comment on the fact that instances can be created for class **Object** but not for some of its subclasses.

7.4 Class **Bag** is not indexable; therefore messages such as at: put: and at: are blocked for instances of **Bag.** Yet the contents of **Bag** are represented by an instance of **Dictionary,** which is accessible by keys. Since you know this to be true, is it not possible to actually access the contents of **Bag** by keys? Why or why not? Is this desirable or not?

7.5 Define a new category of messages for class **Set** called *set operations*. Implement new protocol for performing the ordinary set operations of intersection, union, difference, and symmetric difference.

7.6 In Listing 7.4, the block of code that begins with histogram associationsDo: has the purpose of plotting the histogram on the display screen. Examine this expression carefully and develop an algorithm that explains the steps in the expression.

7.7 Using class **OrderedCollection,** implement an example that illustrates an ordinary linked list. Demonstrate operations for creating a linked list, inserting, deleting, and enumerating elements in a linked list.

7.8 Repeat Exercise 7.7 using class **LinkedList.** Comment on the two approaches from the viewpoint of consistency with the object-oriented paradigm and ease of maintenance.

7.9 Discuss the generic nature of stacks generated using class **OrderedCollection.** Compare with generic stack implementations in any other non–object-oriented language.

7.10 Repeat the example shown in Listing 7.4 using an instance of **Bag** to create the histogram values. Use conversion protocol in class **Collection** to order and display the contents of the **Bag.** Comment on the two approaches.

7.11 Message add: is blocked for use by class **ArrayedCollection.** Thus it is not possible to add elements to an instance of its subclass **Array.** Yet there is a way to increase the size of an array. Use the browser to search protocol of the superclasses of **Array** and find how this can be done. Verify with an example program.

CHAPTER
8

Streams and Their Relationship to Other Objects

This chapter describes the class **Stream** and its subclasses. The purpose is to provide a descriptive overview of the stream classes and their functionality. It further has the purpose of illustrating through examples how the stream classes can be used. Examples are chosen to illustrate the use of streams for interacting with the display screen, files, and the printer. The relationship of streams to collections is clarified and illustrated through examples.

8.1   Class Hierarchy of the Stream Classes

This section presents a summary of the class hierarchy for **Stream** and its subclasses with descriptive information about the functionality of each class. **Stream** is a subclass of **Object** and has several nested subclasses under it. Listing 8.1 shows the hierarchy chain for the stream classes, with indentation level corresponding to hierarchy level. Instance variables are shown in parentheses for each class. The hierarchy shown is the Tektronix version 2.2.0c image with modifications by the authors (e.g., **PrinterStream** is a new class added by the authors).

A stream provides the ability to maintain a *position* reference into a *collection* of objects. The collection of objects is most often an instance of one of the collection classes that have externally indexed elements. The position reference and the external indices provide easy access to the objects in both a sequential and random manner. The collection classes provide messages for storing and messages for enumerating across their elements. However, the storing and enumerating operations cannot be intermingled. Streams, on the other hand, provide the ability to intermingle the operations of storing and enumerating. This difference is illustrated in **Stream** Example 8A below.

An instance of **Stream** is said to "stream over a collection." It is possible to create several streams that stream over the same collection, thus providing several independent position references into that collection. This ability is also illustrated in the following example.

Listing 8.1
Hierarchy for the
Stream Classes

Object ()

Stream ()
    PositionableStream ('collection' 'position' 'readLimit')
        ReadStream ()
        WriteStream ('writeLimit')
            PrinterStream ('fileDescriptor' 'currentFont')
            ReadWriteStream ()
                ExternalStream ()
                    FileStream ('name' 'directory' 'mode' 'fileDescriptor' 'filePosition'
                            'fileMode')
                      FileDirectory ()
                  PipeStream ('fileDescriptor' 'mode')
                    PipeReadStream ('foundEnd')
                    PipeWriteStream ()
    Random ('seed')

Stream Example 8A

This example illustrates the difference in the properties of collections and streams. Specifically, it shows how the storing and enumerating operations can be mixed for streams. The concept of maintaining multiple position references into a collection by defining multiple streams on the same collection is also illustrated.

In this example, three streams are created, using either Method 2 or 3 below. Instances stream1 and stream3 are created to stream over the same collection, array. Instance stream2 is created to stream over a separate collection that is a subarray of array. See Listing 8.2 for details.

Since **Stream** is an abstract class, this **Stream** example uses instances of one of its subclasses, **ReadWriteStream.** First there are several options in the super-class chain of **ReadWriteStream** (**Object—Stream—PositionableStream—Write-Stream—ReadWriteStream**) for creating an instance of this class. The choices are listed below with their corresponding characteristics. Based on these characteristics (and they are different), a choice is made for how to create an instance of **ReadWriteStream.** Interestingly enough, class **ReadWriteStream** has no new protocol for instance creation.

8.1.1 Method choices for instance creation of a **ReadWriteStream** object—working up the hierarchy chain

1. **on:** aCollection **from:** firstindex **to:** lastIndex (in class **WriteStream**)—This method creates a stream on a portion of aCollection from firstIndex to last-Index. It creates an instance with readLimit = writeLimit = the smaller of last-Index or the length of aCollection. This method sets the position reference before the element at firstIndex (i.e., at the beginning of the specified sub-

Listing 8.2
Details of **Stream**
example1

Stream class methodsFor: **'examples'**

example1
"This example uses an instance of ReadWriteStream to illustrate differences between
    stream and collections. Specifically it shows how the position reference makes it
    possible and easier to enumerate over selected portions of the streamed collection
    and store new values simultaneously."

"The collection streamed over is an array."

```
| stream1  stream2  stream3  array |
array ← #( $B 1.25 23 symbol ('smallarray') ).
stream1 ← ReadWriteStream with: array.
stream2 ← ReadWriteStream with: array from: 3 to: 5.        "This is a different array."
stream3 ← ReadWriteStream with: array.

Transcript clear; refresh;
    show: 'Stream example1 -- Stream Properties vs Collection Properties.'; cr; crtab;
    show: 'Instance Creation for Streams on an Array.'; crtab;
    show: ' The array streamed over --> ', array printString; crtab;
    show: ' stream1 definition --> ', stream1 printString, ' over ',
        stream1 contents printString; crtab;
    show: ' stream2 definition --> ', stream2 printString, ' over ',
        stream2 contents printString; crtab;
    show: ' stream3 definition --> ', stream3 printString, ' over ',
        stream3 contents printString; cr; crtab.

Transcript
    show: 'The position references are initially at the end.'; crtab;
    show: ' stream1&3 position --> ', stream1 position printString,
                ' stream2 position --> ', stream2 position printString; cr; crtab.

Transcript
    show: 'Store a new value in stream1 and see effect on stream3.'; crtab;
    show: ' Store 6.5 at position5 in stream1. '; crtab;
    show: ' new stream3 contents --> '.
stream1 position: 4; nextPut: 6.5.
    Transcript
    print: stream3 contents; endEntry; crtab;
    show: ' Positions now:   stream1 --> ',
        stream1 position printString, '   stream3 --> ',
        stream3 position printString; cr; crtab.

Transcript
    show: 'Add the Array to end of stream2''s array.'; crtab;
    show: ' stream2 new contents --> '.
stream2 nextPutAll: array.
Transcript
    show: stream2 contents printString; crtab;
    show: '   stream2 position reference --> ',
        stream2 position printString; crtab;
    show: ' That''s possible but not easy using collection protocol.'.
```

```
Transcript cr; crtab;
    show: 'Enumerating store, replace elements 3-5 in stream2 with "insert"'; crtab;
    show: ' new stream2 contents --> '.
stream2 position: 2; next: 3 put: 'insert'.
Transcript show: stream2 contents printString; cr; crtab.


Transcript
    show: 'Redefine stream2 to include all its elements through first "insert".'; crtab;
    show: ' new stream2 contents --> '.
stream2 ← stream2 reset through: 'insert'.
Transcript print: stream2; endEntry.


Transcript cr; crtab;
    show: 'Enumerating and simultaneous store'; crtab.
(stream1 reset;  contents) do: [ :object |  stream1 nextPut: 'change' ].
Transcript show: ' stream1 new contents --> ', stream1 contents printString.


"  Stream example1  "
```

collection). Only the elements of aCollection between firstIndex and last-
Index, inclusive, are initially included in the stream. However, **WriteStream**
provides protocol for writing beyond the end of an instance, providing access beyond lastIndex. The reset message resets the position to zero, providing access to elements prior to firstIndex.

2. **with:** aCollection (in class **WriteStream**)—This method creates a new stream
on aCollection. It sets private data readLimit = writeLimit = the size of aCollection. It sets the position reference to the end of aCollection. This is the normal position for adding new objects to the collection over which one is
streaming. The collection size is actually increased by selected messages.
The user must be aware that the position reference is initially at the end of
aCollection.

3. **with:** aCollection **from:** firstIndex **to:** lastIndex (in class **WriteStream**)—This
method combines results of the first two. It creates a stream on aCollection
from firstIndex to lastIndex. It sets the initial conditions writeLimit = readLimit
= the number of elements in the subcollection from firstIndex to lastIndex
inclusive. It sets the position reference to the end of the subcollection. Messages sent to this instance have no effect on the original collection, aCollection. Rather, a separate subcollection, created as an extraction from
aCollection, is being streamed over. The new collection can be expanded in
size by selected protocol.

4. **on:** aCollection (in class **PositionableStream**)—Creates a stream instance
that streams over aCollection. The private data readLimit is set to the size of
aCollection. The position reference is set to the beginning of aCollection.
WriteStream private data (writeLimit), which is inherited by **ReadWrite-
Stream,** is not initialized because **PositionableStream** is higher in the hier-

archy. Because of this, writeLimit will have a value of nil. Although it is likely to cause no error, this is not the best message for creating an instance of **ReadWriteStream.**

5. **on:** aCollection **from:** firstIndex **to:** lastIndex (in class **PositionableStream**)— This method creates a stream in the same way as Message 4. The only difference is that it streams over a separate subcollection created from aCollection between indices firstIndex and lastIndex, inclusive. Other comments in Method 4. apply to this stream instance.

6. **basicNew:** size (in class **Behavior**)—This message attempts to create an instance of **ReadWriteStream** with size-indexable elements. This is inconsistent with the definition of a stream and produces a primitive failed error.

7. **basicNew** (in class **Behavior**)—This is the fundamental message for creating a new instance of any object in the system. It can be used to create a new instance of **ReadWriteStream.** It will not have any of its private data initialized; that is, the user must still specify the collection to stream over, the read limit, the write limit, and the position reference. Messages 1 through 5 above use this message and then proceed to initialize private data as described. This message by itself does not produce a usable instance of **ReadWriteStream.**

The contents of the arrays being streamed over for all three instances are displayed in the Transcript window (see Figure 8.1). It is interesting to note that the stream classes have no redefined versions of the messages printOn: and storeOn:. Thus the printString message sent to an instance of any stream class defaults to the version in class **Object.** This default implementation simply appends the class name preceded by *'a'* or *'an'* for grammatical accuracy. To display the contents of the collection over which the stream is streaming, one must use the message contents, followed by printString. Correct application of this principle is illustrated in Listing 8.2.

This example verifies that initially the position reference is at the end of the respective collections. The contents of the collection of a stream can be modified by protocol messages to the stream instance. Since stream1 and stream3 are defined over the same array, contents of the array can be modified by separate messages to either one. This is illustrated by sending a message to stream1 and observing the effect on stream3.

This example is one of the most general for showing the properties of streams since instances of **ReadWriteStream** have protocol for both reading and writing access. The last four parts of the example illustrate: (1) how the contents of one stream can be appended to the contents of another stream, (2) how to enumerate across a portion of the collection of a stream and store new objects, (3) how to redefine a stream so that its collection includes elements up through a specified object in the old collection, and (4) how to simultaneously enumerate across the stream contents and change the object at each location.

Figure 8.1
Stream
example1—
General Properties
of Streams

```
System Transcript
Stream example1 -- Stream Properties vs Collection Properties.

    Instance Creation for Streams on an Array.
    The array streamed over --> ($B 1.25 23 symbol ('smallarray' ) )
    stream1 definition --> a ReadWriteStream over ($B 1.25 23 symbol ('smallarray' ) )
    stream2 definition --> a ReadWriteStream over (23 symbol ('smallarray' ) )
    stream3 definition --> a ReadWriteStream over ($B 1.25 23 symbol ('smallarray' ) )

    The position references are initially at the end.
    stream1&3 position --> 5   stream2 position --> 3

    Store a new value in stream1 and see effect on stream3.
    Store 6.5 at position5 in stream1.
    new stream3 contents --> ($B 1.25 23 symbol 6.5 )
    Positions now:   stream1 --> 5   stream3 --> 5

    Add the Array to end of stream2's array.
    stream2 new contents --> (23 symbol ('smallarray' ) $B 1.25 23 symbol 6.5 )
       stream2 position reference --> 8
    That's possible but not easy using collection protocol.

    Enumerating store, replace elements 3-5 in stream2 with 'insert'
    new stream2 contents --> (23 symbol 'insert' 'insert' 'insert' 23 symbol 6.5 )

    Redefine stream2 to include all its elements through first 'insert'.
    new stream2 contents --> (23 symbol 'insert' )

    Enumerating and simultaneous store
    stream1 new contents --> ('change' 'change' 'change' 'change' 'change' )
```

Stream Example 8A has shown some of the protocol available to instances of the stream classes. Additional messages are described and used in examples for instances of other specific subclasses in the subsections below.

There are three ways to relate the position reference to a particular object in the collection. (1) The position reference can be set equal to an external integer index (as with the **PositionableStream** classes). (2) The position reference can be determined from a seed value that is used to generate new objects in the stream (as in class **Random**). (3) Finally, the position reference can be kept as private data that represents the last object accessed (none of the existing stream classes support this approach). This requires that the object have protocol for accessing the next object in the collection. For example, a new **Stream** subclass called **LinkedListStream** can be defined to stream over an instance of the collection class **LinkedList.**

In the standard image, there are two major subclasses of **Stream** (**Random, PositionableStream**). **Random** is a class representing random numbers. It uses the second method of maintaining a seed value for generating new objects to add to the stream. Protocol in this class provides the messages for generating sequences of random numbers. The default probability law for the random numbers is a uniform distribution between zero and one, exclusive of the end points.

Class **PositionableStream** is an abstract superclass of all the other stream subclasses. Instances of the subclasses of **PositionableStream** stream over a collection of objects that are elements of an indexable collection. The positionable stream has the ability to maintain and vary a **position** reference within that indexable collection.

8.1.2 Class **Stream** Protocol Summary

Stream is an abstract superclass of all the stream classes. It does not have instances; rather, its subclasses will have instances that inherit protocol defined in **Stream. Stream** defines protocol that is common to all streams. In some cases a subclass will redefine an inherited method or block its use.

Protocol Summary for Class **Stream**

The hierarchy for class **Stream** is **Object—Stream.** Class **Stream** has no instance variables, class variables, or pool dictionaries. It has 1 class method in one category and ten instance methods in three categories.

Eight accessing methods are provided that return or change the contents of a stream. These methods are all new protocol; some are redefined by subclasses. Three of the methods (**next, nextPut:, contents**) are key methods in the inheritance hierarchy, since they are implemented as subclassResponsibility in **Stream.** These three methods can be blocked at any subclass level and effectively block most of the other five *accessing* methods that appear to be inherited and usable.

One method (**atEnd**) that answers whether the **position** is at the end of the stream is also a key method and is implemented as subclassResponsibility.

One method (**do:**) is provided for enumerating across the elements of a stream. It evaluates the parameter block for all elements in the stream from the current position to the end of the stream. It is the responsibility of the user to establish the **position** in the stream.

The instance creation method (**new**) is inherited from class **Behavior** and redefined to block its use. New instances of the stream subclasses are created with the messages **on:** and **with:.**

Since class **Stream** is an abstract class, no examples are given of its use. Instances of the subclasses of **Stream** will be illustrated in examples in the following sections.

8.2   Generating Random Numbers as a Stream

This section defines the **Random** subclass of **Stream** and gives examples of its usage. Random numbers have application in many computer problem solutions that require statistical data or statistical analyses. One of the most commonly used probability laws is the continuous uniform law, which describes values that are uniformly distributed over a specified interval. For simplicity, that interval is normalized to be from zero to one by most random number generators. The actual interval can be easily translated and scaled from the normalized interval.

Several other probability laws are obtainable as functions of the uniform law. This adds to its utility and explains why most computer systems provide support for generating normalized, uniform random numbers. Smalltalk does the same in its **Random** class. Examples of its use for various probability laws are included in this and remaining chapters of the book. Chapter 21 in Goldberg and Robson gives a class hierarchy framework for developing support for a wide variety of both discrete and continuous probability laws.

Instances of **Random** are streams whose initial element value is determined from a clock-driven seed. Subsequent values are derived from the previous value using algorithms for producing the desired uniform distribution of numbers. The protocol for instances of **Random** is limited and requires polymorphic blocking of certain inherited protocol messages.

Protocol Summary for Class **Random**

The hierarchy for class **Random** is **Object—Stream—Random.** Class **Random** has one instance variable, **seed.** It has no class variables or pool dictionaries. It has one class method in one category and five instance methods in three categories.

Class **Random** has one instance variable, **seed,** an instance of **Integer** limited to 16-bit accuracy. This is required by the algorithm for generating the elements of a **Random** stream.

Method **atEnd** is inherited from **Stream** and redefined to always return false. A stream of random numbers has no end so long as the next message is sent. Thus the user generates exactly as many random numbers as desired, without prespecifying how many.

The instance creation method **new** that is inherited from class **Stream** is redefined. Recall that this message was blocked in class **Stream.** It is the preferred way to create an instance of **Random.**

A more complete protocol summary is given in Appendix 3.

Although class **Random** is a subclass of **Stream,** it is placed in the class category *Numeric-Numbers* because the objects that are elements of its instances are numbers. A random number generator logically fits in the category of numbers.

Random Example 8A

This example illustrates the protocol in class **Random** for generating uniformly distributed random numbers. Many continuous probability laws are specified completely by two of their first and second moments (e.g., mean and variance). The uniform probability law can be specified in this way or by its interval (a − b; a < b). The relationship among these two parameters (a,b) and the moments is given by the following equations, written as Smalltalk expressions. Think of them as Boolean expressions that evaluate to true.

```
mean = ( b + a ) / 2.
variance = ( b − a ) squared / 12.
a = mean − ( 3 * variance ) sqrt.
b = mean + ( 3 * variance ) sqrt.
```

The details of the example are given in Listing 8.3. It is implemented as class method uniform: a: b: in class **Random.** The example generates 10,000 random numbers that are uniformly distributed between 3.0 and 10.0. The actual number is obtained from the output of the 0.0 to 1.0 random number generator by scaling and then shifting, using the relationship randomNumber = rand next * (b − a) + a. For this example, only the bin numbers (not the actual random numbers) need to be generated.

In this example the histogram for the 10,000 random numbers is generated but not yet plotted. The expression histogram displayNormalizedAt: 50@50 includes a message whose details have not yet been added to class **Dictionary.** Details of the method called displayNormalizedAt: are given below.

```
Dictionary methodsFor: 'displaying'
displayNormalizedAt: aPoint
    "Display on the screen self value vs. self key normalized to maximum value."
    self associationsDo: [:assoc |
        (Form dotOfSize: 4)
            displayOn: Display
            at: (( 2 * assoc key + 50) @ (5 * assoc value + 50))]
```

Summary statistics for the random numbers (range, mean, standard deviation, and maximum histogram value) are displayed in the Transcript window. The maximum histogram value varies from run to run. For one example run, the maximum histogram value was 125. On the average there should be exactly 100 values in each of the 100 bins for 10,000 uniformly distributed random numbers.

This example also illustrates the use of the halt message to **Smalltalk.** It is used because the last expression contains a message to histogram that has not yet been implemented. This message, displayNormalizedAt: offset, is added to class **Dictionary** as a standard graphic normalized display of a histogram. The parameter offset defines the upper left corner point of the displayed histogram. The graphic display of this random number example is left as an exercise for the reader.

Listing 8.3
Details of **Random**
Method uniform:
a: b:

Random class methodsFor: 'examples'

uniform: anInteger **a:** aNum1 **b:** aNum2
"This example generates anInteger random numbers uniformly distributed over the
interval [a, b, a < b]. It generates and plots the histogram for the random numbers
on the screen display. The relationships
mean = (a + b) / 2 and,
sd = (b - a) / (12 sqrt)
give mean and standard deviation respectively.
Random numbers generated by:

random number = rand next * (aNum2 - aNum1) + aNum1."

```
| rand histogram mean sd bin binSize max |
max ← 0.
rand ← Random new.
histogram ← Dictionary new: 100.
1 to: 100 do: [ :i | histogram at: i put: 0].
binSize ← (aNum2 - aNum1) /100.0.
mean ← (aNum1 + aNum2) /2.0.
sd ← (aNum2 - aNum1) / 12 sqrt.
anInteger timesRepeat: [
    bin ← ((rand next * (aNum2 - aNum1)) / binSize) truncated + 1.
    histogram at: bin put: (histogram at: bin) + 1].
histogram associationsDo: [ :assoc | max ← max max: assoc value ].
Transcript clear; refresh;
    show: 'For ', anInteger printString, ' random numbers, max histogram value is ',
        max printString; crtab;
    show: 'a = ', aNum1 printString, '  b = ', aNum2 printString,
        ' mean = ', mean printString, '  sd = ', sd printString.
```

Smalltalk halt.

"The following method is to be implemented in class Dictionary later."
histogram displayNormalizedAt: 50@50.

" Random uniform: 10000 a: 3.0 b: 10.0 "

Random **Example 8B**

This example uses protocol in class **Random** to generate random numbers that
have a gaussian distribution with specifiable mean and standard deviation. An
approximation to a gaussian-distributed random number is achieved by adding
together a large number of values that have a uniform probability distribution
(this follows from the Law of Large Numbers described in references on probability theory). The approximation is relatively good for the addition of only 12
such numbers, producing a truncated gaussianlike distribution that ranges plus
or minus six standard deviations about the mean.

Listing 8.4
Details of **Random**
Method gaussian:
mean: sd:

Random class methodsFor: 'examples'

gaussian: anInteger **mean:** aNum1 **sd:** aNum2
   "Chapter 8 examples on random numbers, class Random. This example creates
       anInteger random numbers between mean-6*sd and mean+6*sd, with a pseudo-
       Gaussian distribution of mean aNum1 and standard deviation of aNum2. It computes
       and displays the histogram of those numbers."

```
| rand histogram bin binSize max rNum |
max ← 0.
rand ← Random new.
histogram ← Dictionary new: 100.
1 to: 100 do: [ :i | histogram at: i put: 0].
binSize ← (12 * aNum2) /100.0.
anInteger timesRepeat: [ rNum ← 0.0.
    12 timesRepeat: [ rNum ← rNum + rand next ].
    rNum ← (rNum - 6.0) * aNum2 + aNum1.
    bin ← ((rNum - aNum1 + (6.0 * aNum2)) / binSize) truncated + 1.
    histogram at: bin put: (histogram at: bin) + 1].
histogram associationsDo: [ :assoc | max ← max max: assoc value ].
Transcript clear; refresh;
    show: 'For ', anInteger printString, ' random numbers, max histogram value is ',
        max printString; crtab;
    show: 'range of values = ',(aNum1 - (6.0 * aNum2)) printString,
        ' to ', (aNum1 + (6.0 * aNum2)) printString,
        ' mean = ', aNum1 printString, '  sd = ', aNum2 printString.
```

Smalltalk **halt.**

   "The following method is to be implemented in class Dictionary later."
      histogram displayNormalizedAt: 50@50.

   "Random gaussian: 10000 mean: 3.0 sd: 2.0"

If 12 independent random numbers that have a uniform distribution from 0 to 1 (mean = 0.5, variance = 1/12) are added, their sum has a distribution with mean = 6 and variance = 1. The range of the sum of random numbers is from 0 to 12. Their probability density function is a 12-fold convolution of the uniform probability density function (its shape is very close to gaussian).

This example illustrates this technique for generating nearly gaussian random numbers with specifiable mean and standard deviation. It is a class method called **gaussian: mean: sd:**, in class **Random.** Details of this method are shown in Listing 8.4.

For the parameters chosen (mean = 3.0, standard deviation = 2.0, 10,000 numbers generated) in executing this example, the range of values is from −9.0 to +15.0 and the maximum histogram value is 486. This represents the integral over one bin width (((15 − (−9)) / 100 = 0.24, corresponding to plus or minus

0.06 standard deviations about the mean) of the resultant probability density function.

Random Example 8C

This example uses protocol in class **Random** to generate numbers representing exponentially distributed interarrival times. These are useful for discrete event simulations, where the arrivals have a Poisson distribution. This example shows how random numbers with an exponential probability distribution can be obtained from the random numbers uniformly distributed over the interval from zero to one.

The probability density function for an exponentially distributed random variable is given by $p(t) = (1/T) \exp(-t/T)$, where T is the mean value. If this equation is integrated from zero to some value, t, the result is a number between zero and one. This is a property of the cumulative distribution function for any probability law. The result of this integration is $r = 1 - \exp(-t/T)$, where r is a random value between zero and one. Rearranging this equation gives $\exp(-t/T) = 1 - r$. If r is distributed between zero and one, then so is the quantity $r' = 1 - r$. Solving for the time, t, gives: $t = -T * \ln(r')$.

With t as the interarrival time and T as the average interarrival time, the generation of random arrivals is given by the expression 0 − aNum * rand next ln, in Listing 8.5. The parameter aNum is the mean value and rand is the random number between zero and one. For 10,000 numbers generated with a mean of 1.0, the maximum histogram value is 506.

Listing 8.5
Details of
Random Method
exponential: mean:

Random class methodsFor: 'examples'

exponential: anInteger **mean:** aNum
   "This example creates anInteger random numbers representing an exponentially
      distributed time interval between events of a Poisson process. It computes and
      displays the histogram of the time intervals from values of zero to 5 times the mean,
      aNum."

```
| rand histogram bin binSize max |
max ← 0.
rand ← Random new.
histogram ← Dictionary new: 100.
1 to: 100 do: [ :i | histogram at: i put: 0].
binSize ← 5.0 * aNum /100.0.
anInteger timesRepeat: [
    bin ← ( 0 - aNum * rand next ln / binSize) truncated + 1.
    bin < = 100 ifTrue: [
        histogram at: bin put: (histogram at: bin) + 1] ].
```

Listing 8.5
(continued)

```
histogram associationsDo: [ :assoc | max ← max max: assoc value ].
Transcript clear; refresh;
    show: 'For ', anInteger printString, ' random numbers, max histogram value is ',
        max printString; crtab; show: 'Exponential distribution: ',
        ' mean = ', aNum printString.

Smalltalk halt.

"The following method is to be implemented in class Dictionary later."
    histogram displayNormalizedAt: 50@50.

"Random exponential: 10000  mean: 1.0 "
```

8.3   **PositionableStream** as an Abstract Class— Inheritance and Polymorphism

This section defines protocol in **PositionableStream** that is common to most of the stream subclasses. Since **PositionableStream** is an abstract class, it has no instances. Examples are presented in the appropriate section for each subclass under **PositionableStream**.

The description summaries for class **PositionableStream** and its subclasses identify which methods are inherited and unchanged, inherited and polymorphically redefined, and new. This approach illustrates how dependent the hierarchical class structure of Smalltalk is on inheritance and polymorphism—two key concepts of an object-oriented language.

A positionable stream is one that streams over an indexable collection. One of the instance variables defined in this class is an instance of the particular class of collection that the positionable stream is streaming over.

PositionableStream is an abstract superclass of many of the stream classes. It does not have instances; rather, its subclasses will have instances that inherit protocol defined in **PositionableStream. PositionableStream** defines protocol that is common to all its subclasses. In some cases a subclass will redefine an inherited method or block its use. A complete protocol summary is given for this important abstract stream class.

Protocol Summary for Class **PositionableStream**

Definition—The hierarchy for class **PositionableStream** is **Object—Stream— PositionableStream.** Class **PositionableStream** has three instance variables, collection, position, and readLimit. It has no class variables or pool dictionaries. It has 2 class methods in one category and 18 instance methods in five categories.

Private data—Class **PositionableStream** has three instance variables.

collection—an instance of one of the integer indexable collection classes. The instance of **PositionableStream** will stream over this collection.

position—an instance of **Integer** that is the integer position reference into the collection.

readLimit—an instance of **Integer** that is the size of the collection in number of elements.

Instance methods—Class **PositionableStream** has 18 instance methods in five categories. A summary is given below of the categories and methods.

accessing—Six methods (**contents, next:, peek, peekFor:, through:, upTo:**) that return selected elements, with and without moving the position reference, in the stream's collection. Two of the methods (**contents, next:**) are inherited from **Stream** and redefined. The other four are new protocol.

testing—Two methods (**atEnd, isEmpty**) that test whether the position reference is at the end of the collection and emptiness of the collection. The method (**atEnd**) is inherited from **Stream,** where it is implemented as subclassResponsibility. The method (**isEmpty**) is new protocol.

positioning—Six methods (**position, position:, reset, setToEnd, skip:, skipTo:**) for determining the current position reference and various ways of setting a new position reference. All these methods are new protocol.

fileIn-Out—Two methods (**nextChunk, skipSeparators**) that answer contents of the collection up to the next terminator character ($!) and move the position reference past any separators respectively (separators are the characters: **space, cr, tab, line feed, form feed**). Both these methods are new protocol. The terminator character ($!) has special meaning for filing in or filing out of blocks of Smalltalk code.

private—Two methods (**on:, positionError**) that are used to set initial values for the instance variables and to check for out of bounds position references respectively. Both these methods are new protocol. Subclasses that are writable streams must override the positionError message, since their size can grow.

Class methods—Class **PositionableStream** has two class methods in one category. A summary is given below of the categories and the methods.

instance creation—two methods (**on:, on: from: to:**) that are used to create instances of the positionable stream subclasses. The first message opens a stream on a collection. The second message opens a stream on a portion of a collection from a starting index to an ending index. Both these methods are new protocol.

The following subsections define protocol for subclasses of **PositionableStream** and give examples that use that protocol. The examples also use the protocol inherited from the superclasses **PositionableStream, Stream,** and **Object.**

The two major subclasses of **PositionableStream** are **ReadStream** and **WriteStream.** As their names imply, one is intended for read only status and the other is intended for write only status. There are occasions when it is desirable to be able to both read from a stream and to write to it. The class **ReadWrite-Stream** is a subclass of **WriteStream.** Many of the streams that interact with external devices are read-write streams (e.g., file streams).

Instances of class **ReadWriteStream** are interpreted as being write streams that have the capability to read as well. Some of the protocol in **WriteStream** that blocks reading must be polymorphically overridden in class **ReadWriteStream.**

8.3.1 Class **ReadStream**

This section gives a protocol summary for class **ReadStream.** It also defines properties of read streams and gives examples of the use of read only streams.

Class **ReadStream** redefines two accessing methods (next and nextPut:). The redefinition for next is done to invoke a primitive method and improve efficiency. The method nextPut: is redefined to block its use. All the other storing messages defined in superclasses of **ReadStream** are also blocked because they send the message nextPut:.

Instances of **ReadStream** can be created in several ways. These include two messages sent to **PositionableStream** and one new message sent to **ReadStream.** The options include creation of a read only stream on a specified collection, on the elements from firstIndex to lastIndex of the specified collection, or on a new collection created as a subcollection of a specified collection. These options were discussed in **Stream** Example 8A; their meaning is the same here. For read streams the position reference is initialized to be at the beginning of its collection (the normal position).

Read streams are useful whenever the contents of the collection being streamed over need to be accessed but protected from changes. **ReadStream** is a class whose instances are set for reading only. The protocol for writing to these instances is blocked. An abbreviated protocol summary for **ReadStream** is given below. A more complete summary is given in Appendix 3.

Protocol Summary for Class **ReadStream**

The hierarchy for class **ReadStream** is **Object—Stream—PositionableStream—ReadStream.** Class **ReadStream** has no instance variables, class variables, or pool dictionaries. It has one class method in one category and three instance methods in two categories.

> *accessing*—The accessing method **nextPut:** is inherited from **Stream** and blocked. Read streams cannot write.
> *instance creation*—Instances of **ReadStream** are created using the message **on: from: to:,** inherited from **PositionableStream** and redefined.

ReadStream **Example 8A**

This example shows protocol for instances of **ReadStream.** Results of the two instance creation methods for defining a stream on a portion of an existing collection are of particular interest. The methods used for positioning, enumerating, and accessing are inherited from the superclasses of **ReadStream.**

Details of the class method example1 in **ReadStream** are shown in Listing 8.6. Results of executing the example are shown in the Transcript window in Figure 8.2.

Listing 8.6
Details of
ReadStream
example1

ReadStream class methodsFor: 'examples'

example1
"This example illustrates how read streams provide protection for their collection."

```
| rStream1 rStream2 rStream3  array  string |

array ← #( $a $b symbol 'hi' (6 5) 12.5).
string ←
    'This is a Special string ( #Joe #Ernie #Rich #Gerry ) that I don''t want to corrupt.'.
rStream1 ← ReadStream on: array.
rStream2 ← ReadStream on: string.
rStream3 ← ReadStream on: string.
Transcript clear; refresh;
    show: 'ReadStream Example -- Streaming over Collections Without Corruption'; cr;
    crtab; show: 'Instance Creation'; crtab;
    show: '  rStream1 collection contents --> ',
        rStream1 contents printString; crtab;
    show:  '  rStream2 collection contents --> ';
        crtab; tab; show:  rStream2 contents printString; crtab;
    show:  '  rStream3 collection contents --> ';
        crtab; tab; show:  rStream3 contents printString; cr; tab;
    show: '  rStream1, rStream2, and rStream3  position reference at index --> ',
        rStream1 position printString; cr; crtab.

Transcript
    show: 'Simple accessing of elements.'; crtab;
    show: '  Position 4 in rStream1 is --> ', (rStream1 position: 3; next) printString,
            '  Position 28 in rStream2 is --> ', (rStream2 position: 27; next)
            printString; cr; crtab.

Transcript
    show: 'Skipping past a sentinel in the collection.'; crtab;
    show: '  Find all words after a # sign using rStream3 (still positioned at beginning.)';
        crtab; tab.
[ rStream3 atEnd ] whileFalse: [
        rStream3 skipTo: $#.
        Transcript show: (rStream3 through: $  ) printString ].
```

Listing 8.6
(continued)

```
Transcript crtab;
    show: ' Find all words after a # sign using rStream2 ( positioned at 1st #.)';
    crtab; tab.
[ rStream2 atEnd ] whileFalse: [
    rStream2 skipTo: $#.
    Transcript show: (rStream2 through: $  ) printString ].


Transcript cr; crtab;
    show: 'Redefine rStream1 and rStream2 on a subcollection of string.'; crtab.
rStream3 reset.
rStream1 ← ReadStream on: string from: 26 to: (rStream3 skipTo: $); position).
rStream2 ← PositionableStream on: string from: 26 to: rStream3 position.
Transcript
    show: 'New contents of the stream collections.'; crtab;
    show: '  rStream1 collection contents --> ';
        crtab; tab; show: rStream1 contents printString; crtab;
    show: '  rStream2 collection contents --> ', rStream2 contents printString; crtab;
    show: '  rStream3 collection contents --> ';
        crtab; tab; show: rStream3 contents printString; crtab;
    show: '  rStream1 position --> ', rStream1 position printString,
        '  rStream2 position --> ', rStream2 position printString,
        '  rStream3 position --> ', rStream3 position printString.


    " ReadStream example1  "
```

Figure 8.2
ReadStream
example1—
Properties of
Read Streams

```
┌─────────────────────────────────────────────────────────────────────────┐
│ System Transcript                                                         │
├───────────────────────────────────────────────────────────────────────── │
│ ReadStream Example -- Streaming over Collections Without Corruption        │
│                                                                           │
│   Instance Creation                                                       │
│     rStream1 collection contents --> ($a $b symbol 'hi' (6 5 ) 12.5 )     │
│     rStream2 collection contents -->                                      │
│       'This is a Special string ( #Joe #Ernie #Rich #Gerry ) that I don''t want to corrupt.' │
│     rStream3 collection contents -->                                      │
│       'This is a Special string ( #Joe #Ernie #Rich #Gerry ) that I don''t want to corrupt.' │
│     rStream1, rStream2, and rStream3  position reference at index --> 0    │
│                                                                           │
│   Simple accessing of elements.                                           │
│     Position 4 in rStream1 is --> 'hi'     Position 28 in rStream2 is --> $# │
│                                                                           │
│   Skipping past a sentinel in the collection.                             │
│     Find all words after a # sign using rStream3 (still positioned at beginning.) │
│       'Joe ''Ernie ''Rich ''Gerry '''                                     │
│     Find all words after a # sign using rStream2 ( positioned at 1st #.)   │
│       'Ernie ''Rich ''Gerry '''                                           │
│                                                                           │
│   Redefine rStream1 and rStream2 on a subcollection of string.            │
│   New contents of the stream collections.                                 │
│     rStream1 collection contents -->                                      │
│       'This is a Special string ( #Joe #Ernie #Rich #Gerry )'             │
│     rStream2 collection contents --> '( #Joe #Ernie #Rich #Gerry )'       │
│     rStream3 collection contents -->                                      │
│       'This is a Special string ( #Joe #Ernie #Rich #Gerry ) that I don''t want to corrupt.' │
│     rStream1 position --> 25   rStream2 position --> 0   rStream3 position --> 53 │
└─────────────────────────────────────────────────────────────────────────┘
```

In this example three instances of **ReadStream** are created using the message on:, inherited from **PositionableStream.** Contents of the collection streamed over and the position reference are printed, for all three, in the Transcript window. Positioning and accessing are demonstrated for rStream1 and rStream2.

The next part of the example shows how certain objects can be found using skipTo: to skip past a sentinel (in this case the character $#). This message is used in conjunction with the through: message to extract the names in the string. Care must be taken to know where the position reference is, since many messages produce results that start at the current position. This is demonstrated by performing the same extraction using the two read streams defined on string. Their position references are independent of each other.

Finally, the example illustrates how the two instance creation messages (on: from: to:—one in class **ReadStream** and one in its superclass **Positionable-Stream**) produce different results. Normally one would think the method in the subclass, which overrides its superclass version, is preferred. In this case, the subclass method produces a somewhat confusing result.

Instance rStream1 is defined to stream over the collection string from position **26** (the opening left parenthesis) through the position containing the closing right parenthesis. It is created by sending on: from: to: to class **ReadStream.** Details of this instance creation method are such that the following happens. No new subcollection is created. The readLimit is reassigned to be at the end of the specified subcollection (at the index of the right parenthesis). The position reference is set to the beginning of the subcollection (immediately before the left parenthesis).

Instance rStream2 is defined to stream over the same range of string. It is created by sending the on: from: to: message to superclass **PositionableStream.** The major difference in these two implementations of the same message is small but significant. In **PositionableStream,** a new collection is created from the specified range in string. The readLimit is set to the last element in the new collection. In this example, that is a smaller number than for rStream1. The position reference is set to the index position immediately before the first element (it is zero here).

Aside from the differences in values for readLimit and position, another difference is significant. The message contents returns all elements in the private data, collection, from its first element up to the readLimit. This explains the result for the new contents of rStream1.

8.3.2   Class **WriteStream**

Properties and examples of write only streams are given in this section. Instances of **WriteStream** are used throughout the Smalltalk system. In particular, three messages that are used extensively (printString, printOn:, and storeOn:) make use of write streams. Since the accessing message next is blocked in the protocol for **WriteStream,** many of the inherited methods from **Positionable-**

Stream for accessing are also blocked. The only method for returning objects in a write stream is provided by the message **contents**. It returns the **collection** over which the write stream is streaming.

Instances of **WriteStream** have write only status. The size of their collections can grow as needed to accommodate new elements written onto the stream.

Protocol Summary for Class **WriteStream**

The hierarchy for class **WriteStream** is **Object—Stream—PositionableStream—WriteStream.** Class **WriteStream** has one instance variable, writeLimit. It has no class variables or pool dictionaries. It has 3 class methods in one category and 21 instance methods in six categories.

Class **WriteStream** has one instance variable, **writeLimit,** an instance of **Integer** that is initialized to equal the number of elements in the collection over which an instance of **WriteStream** is streaming. Its value is increased whenever additional elements are written onto the collection.

The accessing method **next** is inherited from **PositionableStream**. Its definition in **WriteStream** is to block its use, since write streams cannot access using next.

Eight character-writing methods are added for appending special characters to the stream. Most of these are self-explanatory or easily understood from their method details. All are new protocol.

One method is added for filing out (**nextChunkPut:**) that appends its parameter string to the stream and adds terminators (**$!**) where appropriate. Chunks are the format used for creating files that can be filed in (i.e., added to a Smalltalk image). This method is new protocol.

Three methods are included that are used to create instances of **WriteStream.** A more complete protocol summary is given in Appendix 3.

WriteStream Example 8A

This example illustrates additional protocol for write streams. Much of the protocol is already demonstrated in **Stream** Example 8A, early in the chapter. The emphasis for this example is on how other objects in the Smalltalk system are stored on streams. Listing 8.7 gives details of the class method example1 in **WriteStream.** Results of executing the method are shown in Figure 8.3.

In the example, four different methods for displaying the value of a complex number in the Transcript window are shown. All send messages that invoke other messages similar to those given in the last method in the listing.

Listing 8.7
Details of
WriteStream
example1

WriteStream class methodsFor: 'examples'

example1
"How complex objects are represented on streams."

```
| wStream1 wStream2 wStream3 complex |
complex ← Complex real: 2 imaginary: -6.
wStream1 ← WriteStream with: String new.
wStream2 ← WriteStream with: 'This is the complex number ---> '.
wStream3 ← WriteStream with: String new.

Transcript clear; refresh;
    show: 'WriteStream Example - Storing Objects on Streams'; cr; crtab;
    show: 'Create an empty writestream collection and add object description.'; crtab;
    show: ' Description of a complex number --> ', complex printString; crtab;
    show: ' Same result, a different way ------> '.
complex printOn: wStream1.
Transcript show: wStream1 contents; crtab;
    show: ' Same result a third way ------> ',
        (wStream3 print: complex) contents; crtab;
    show: 'Now the detailed way (all the others use something similar to this). ';
        crtab: 2.
wStream2 nextPut: $(.
complex real printOn: wStream2.
( complex imaginary > = 0)
    ifTrue:[ wStream2 nextPutAll: ' + j'.
        complex imaginary printOn: wStream2]
    ifFalse:[ wStream2 nextPutAll: ' - j'.
        complex imaginary abs printOn: wStream2].
wStream2 nextPut: $).
Transcript show: wStream2 contents.

" WriteStream example1 "
```

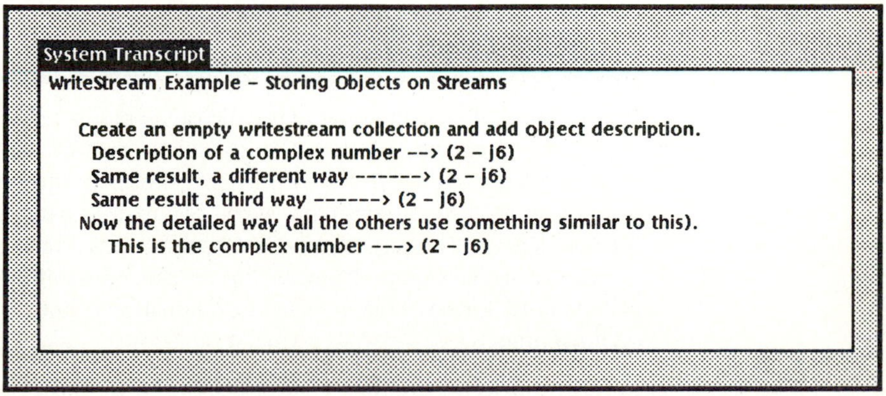

Figure 8.3
WriteStream
example1—
Properties of
Write Streams

System Transcript

WriteStream Example – Storing Objects on Streams

   Create an empty writestream collection and add object description.
     Description of a complex number --> (2 – j6)
     Same result, a different way ------> (2 – j6)
     Same result a third way ------> (2 – j6)
   Now the detailed way (all the others use something similar to this).
     This is the complex number ---> (2 – j6)

8.3.3   Class **ReadWriteStream**

Properties and examples of read/write streams are given in this section. Class **ReadWriteStream** is a subclass of **WriteStream.** No discussion of the rationale for the chosen hierarchy that places a **ReadWriteStream** as a subclass of **WriteStream** is given in the Smalltalk language reference by Goldberg and Robson. Logically, the hierarchy could have placed **ReadWriteStream** as a subclass of **PositionableStream.** Then **ReadStream** and **WriteStream** could have been equal hierarchy subclasses of **ReadWriteStream.** The existing protocol works.

Instances of **ReadWriteStream** can be thought of as write streams modified to permit reading as well. The following is an abbreviated summary of the protocol of **ReadWriteStream.** For more details see Appendix 3.

Protocol Summary for Class **ReadWriteStream**

The hierarchy for class **ReadWriteStream** is **Object—Stream—Positionable-Stream—WriteStream—ReadWriteStream.** Class **ReadWriteStream** has no instance variables, class variables, or pool dictionaries. It has no class methods. It has eight instance methods in three categories.

Two accessing methods (**contents, next**) are inherited from **WriteStream** and redefined. These two methods were blocked in **WriteStream** to disallow reading. They are redefined to be active for **ReadWriteStream.**

Five methods (**fileIn, fileOutChanges, fileOutChangesFor:, printOut-Changes, timeStamp**) are added that support filing in and filing out in chunk format of a specified file, all system changes, changes for a specified class, or the current time stamp. The message printOutChanges appends all changes to the receiver stream in a format that has standard emphasis added and no terminators ($!). It produces a more easily read copy of the changes. All five are new protocol.

ReadWriteStream Example 8A

This example illustrates some of the file out options included in protocol for this class. Listing 8.8 gives details for the class method example1 in **ReadWriteStream.** Figure 8.4 shows the resulting contents of the read/write stream. Only those changes for class **Float** that have been made since the last source compression are shown. The message fileOutChanges adds all the changes to the stream. There are usually quite a few of these. The figure illustrates the style that is called chunk format. Note the use of exclamation points to delimit separate compilation units.

Listing 8.8
Details of
ReadWriteStream
example1

ReadWriteStream class methodsFor: 'examples'

example1
    "Illustrate the file-out messages for ReadWriteStreams."

    | rwStream |
    rwStream ← ReadWriteStream with: String new.   "Create on empty string."

    Transcript clear; refresh;
        show: 'ReadWriteStream Example -- Filing out system changes on a stream.';
        cr; crtab;
        show: 'New ReadWriteStream on --> ', rwStream contents; cr; crtab.

    Transcript
        show: 'Append all changes made to class Float.'; cr.
    rwStream fileOutChangesFor: Float.
    Transcript cr; crtab;
        show: 'Contents of rwStream.'; cr; cr;
        show: rwStream contents.

    " ReadWriteStream example1 "

Figure 8.4
ReadWriteStream
example1—File
out Options with
Streams

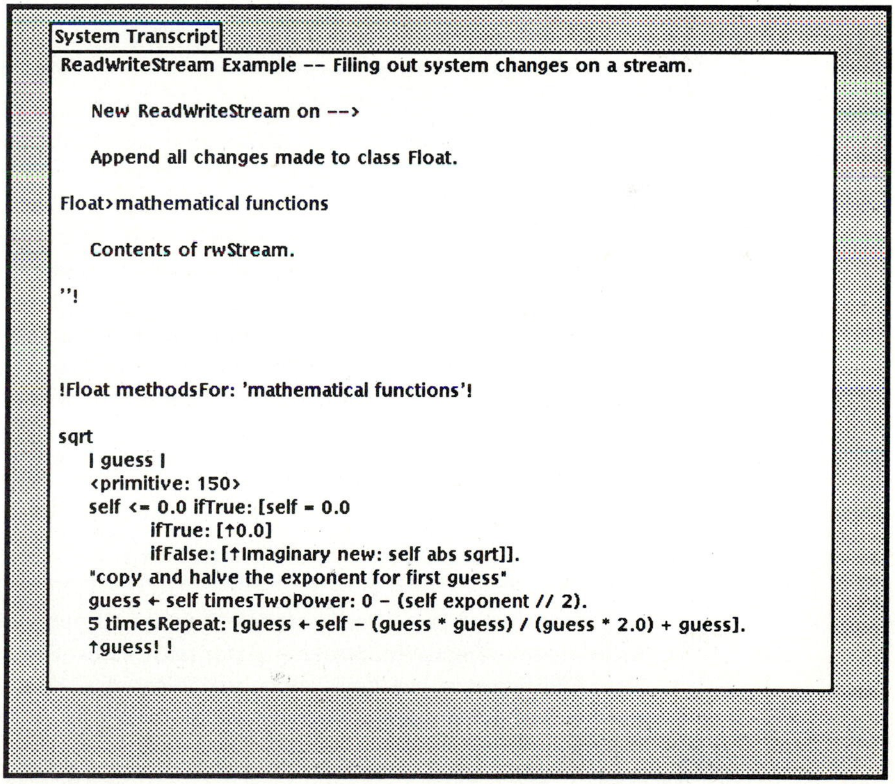

```
System Transcript
ReadWriteStream Example -- Filing out system changes on a stream.

    New ReadWriteStream on -->

    Append all changes made to class Float.

Float>mathematical functions

    Contents of rwStream.

''!


!Float methodsFor: 'mathematical functions'!

sqrt
    | guess |
    <primitive: 150>
    self <= 0.0 ifTrue: [self = 0.0
            ifTrue: [↑0.0]
            ifFalse: [↑Imaginary new: self abs sqrt]].
    "copy and halve the exponent for first guess"
    guess ← self timesTwoPower: 0 - (self exponent // 2).
    5 timesRepeat: [guess ← self - (guess * guess) / (guess * 2.0) + guess].
    ↑guess! !
```

8.3.4   Class **ExternalStream**

External streams represent external devices such as files and printers. These devices must typically be accessed in a special way such as by block transfer for files and character transfer for printers. Class **PrinterStream,** which represents printers, is not a subclass of **ExternalStream.** It fits more logically under **WriteStream** since printers are write only devices. Subclasses of **ExternalStream** have both read and write status. This is one example that shows how finding the "correct" place in the hierarchy for a new class is not always clear.

The Tektronix 2.2.0c version Smalltalk image has two major subclasses of **ExternalStream.** They are **FileStream** and **PipeStream.** Instances of **FileStream** provide protocol for interacting with files. Instances of **PipeStream** provide protocol for using UNIX pipes. Details of the **PipeStream** class and its use are not included in this book.

This section provides a discussion of the subclasses of **ExternalStream,** with emphasis on **FileStream** and **FileDirectory.** An abbreviated protocol summary is given for class **ExternalStream** and for **FileDirectory.** More detailed summaries are given in Appendix 3. (A summary for **FileStream** was given in Chapter 5.) An example that concentrates on the use of **FileDirectory** protocol is given after the class description summaries.

Protocol Summary for Class **ExternalStream**

The hierarchy for class **ExternalStream** is **Object—Stream—PositionableStream—WriteStream—ReadWriteStream—ExternalStream.** Class **ExternalStream** has no instance variables, class variables, or pool dictionaries. It has 1 class method in one category and 19 instance methods in five categories.

Seven new methods (**padTo:, padTo: put:, padToNextWord, padToNextWordPut:, skipWords:, wordPosition, wordPosition:**) for nonhomogeneous positioning of the stream position reference are provided.

Nine new methods (**nextBytes: into:, nextNumber:, nextNumber: put:, nextSignedInteger, nextString, nextStringPut:, nextWord, nextWordPut:, nextWords: into:**) for nonhomogeneous reading and writing of elements in the receiver stream are provided.

Protocol Summary for Class **FileDirectory**

The hierarchy for class **FileDirectory** is **Object—Stream—PositionableStream—WriteStream—ReadWriteStream—ExternalStream—FileStream—FileDirectory.** Class **FileDirectory** has no instance variables, class variables, or pool dictionaries. It has 5 class methods in one category and 30 instance methods in nine categories.

FileDirectory has methods for creating or deleting file directories. It also has methods for accessing, testing, adding, removing, and enumerating file names in a file directory.

ExternalStream (FileDirectory) Example 8A

Chapter 5 gives several examples of the use of protocol for manipulating individual files. This example illustrates protocol for managing directory information. It uses messages from **FileDirectory** and its superclasses, **FileStream** and **ExternalStream.**

This example, implemented as class method example1 in class **FileDirectory,** illustrates the various ways to create instances of a file directory. It also shows the kinds of operations possible for file directories. Details of the method are given in Listing 8.9. Results of executing the example are given in Figure 8.5.

Three separate file directories are created on existing directories of the authors' system. The first is on the current directory, '*/public*'. The third is on sub-

Listing 8.9
Details of
FileDirectory
example1

FileDirectory class methodsFor: 'examples'

example1
   "Protocol for file directories."

   | directory1 directory2 directory3 |
   directory1 ← FileDirectory currentDirectory.
   directory2 ← FileDirectory directoryNamed: '/safe'.
   directory3 ← FileDirectory directory: directory2 directoryName: 'pcat'.

   Transcript clear; refresh;
      show: 'FileDirectory Example -- Creating and Manipulating File Directories.'; cr;
      crtab; show: 'Instance Creation and Accessing of file directories.'; cr; crtab;
      show: ' directory1 definition --> ', directory1 completePathname,
         ' contains files only'.
   directory1 do: [:nam | Transcript crtab; tab; show: nam fullName].
   Transcript cr; crtab;
      show: ' directory3 definition --> ', directory3 completePathname,
         ' contains files only'.
   directory3 do: [:nam | Transcript crtab; tab; show: nam fullName].
   Transcript cr; crtab;
      show: ' directory2 definition --> ', directory2 completePathname,
         ' contains files and subdirectories'.
   directory2 do: [:nam | Transcript crtab; tab; show: nam fullName.
      Transcript tab; tab; show:
         (nam isDirectory ifTrue: [' is a directory '] ifFalse: [''])].

   " FileDirectory example1 "

Figure 8.5
FileDirectory
example1—
Creating and
Accessing File
Directories

```
System Transcript

FileDirectory Example -- Creating and Manipulating File Directories.

Instance Creation and Accessing of file directories.

  directory1 definition --> /public/  contains files only
    .login
    .shellbegin
    .shellhistory
    .backup.time
    stLJP2.sources
    stLJP2.changes
    stLJP2.im
    nostamp.im
    stFiles

  directory3 definition --> /safe/pcat/  contains files only
    /safe/pcat/numbers.st
    /safe/pcat/banksim.st
    /safe/pcat/trees.st
    /safe/pcat/histogram.st
    /safe/pcat/examples.st
    /safe/pcat/printer.st
    /safe/pcat/project1.st

  directory2 definition --> /safe/  contains files and subdirectories
    /safe/chapters          is a directory
    /safe/slide.changes
    /safe/stLJP2.changes
    /safe/stLJP2.im
    /safe/stLJP2.sources
    /safe/slide.im
    /safe/slide.sources
    /safe/newImage
    /safe/listings       is a directory
    /safe/pcat           is a directory
    /safe/fileIn         is a directory
```

directory, '*/safe/listings*', and the second is on the directory '*/safe*'. The first and third contain only files; whereas, the second (directory2) contains both files and subdirectories.

The example enumerates across the contents of each file directory and displays information about the files and/or subdirectories in each. The iteration message do: returns a **FileStream** on each name within the file directory. To test if that file stream is actually a directory requires sending the file stream message isDirectory.

Protocol in classes **FileDirectory** and **FileStream** provides the capability to create/rename/remove both directories and files. It also provides messages for accessing file lists in directories and contents of any file on the system.

Exercises

8.1. Develop an example program that illustrates all the instance creation methods available to class **FileDirectory.** Comment on the utility of each method.

8.2 Define protocol for a new class called **LinkedListStream** to stream over instances of class **LinkedList.** Implement the protocol and develop an example illustrating its use.

8.3 Discuss the rationale for realigning the stream classes so that both **ReadStream** and **WriteStream** are made subclasses of **ReadWriteStream.** What effect does this have on the placement of class **ExternalStream** and its subclasses?

8.4 Investigate the desirability of defining a new class called **Probability** whose subclasses represent various probability laws. Where should this new class structure be attached to the existing class hierarchy? Explain clearly how existing protocol in class **Random** is used by these new classes.

8.5 Implement method displayNormalizedAt: in class **Dictionary** and run the **Random** examples with the expression Smalltalk halt removed.

8.6 Develop a summary list of the new, inherited, and redefined protocol in the **Stream** classes. Comment on the significance of inheritance and polymorphism for these classes.

8.7 Since **PrinterStream** streams over an external device (the printer), why should it not be a subclass of **ExternalStream**? Give reasons for and against.

8.8 Based on an analysis of the protocol provided for classes **FileStream** and **FileDirectory,** give reasons for the existence of **FileDirectory** as a separate class and for its being a subclass of **FileStream.**

8.9 Explain as concisely and completely as possible the similarities and differences between streams and collections.

9

The Graphics Classes and the MVC Triad

This chapter describes the "graphics" classes in summary form. The graphics-related classes are grouped into categories and defined in general terms. These categories in the Smalltalk image are used to characterize the functionality of each graphics class. Examples are given that illustrate the use of selected graphics classes. The model-view-controller triad (MVC) concept is defined and discussed in terms of its functionality. A very simple example of the MVC triad is presented in this chapter, with a more detailed example given in Chapter 11.

Smalltalk is graphics! Probably more than any other existing language and environment, Smalltalk supports and even demands the use of graphics. The display of text on the screen is a graphics operation. The entire user interface is graphics-oriented to the extent that sending a simple string to a printer is more difficult than displaying it in a graphics window. (In fact, as was shown in Chapter 5, the Smalltalk image comes with no direct support for printers.)

Of the 297 classes found in the authors' version of Smalltalk (See **System-Dictionary** Example 7A in Chapter 7), over 90 of them are related to graphics. It is not possible to do justice to that many classes in one chapter of a book. Most of the classes that relate to the MVC triad are not described anywhere in public form, though Addison-Wesley is planning to publish such a book soon.

9.1   Hierarchy and Categories of the Graphics Classes

This section provides a hierarchy tree and a description of all the graphics-related classes. It discusses their categories in the Smalltalk image and seeks to provide a better understanding of what the graphic classes are and why they exist as they do. The concepts of storage, display object creation, transfer, and special purpose graphics are discussed.

There are six categories of classes in the Smalltalk image that have a graphics classification. These are: (1) *Display Objects,* (2) *Primitives,* (3) *Paths,* (4) *Support,* (5) *Editors,* and (6) *Views.* In addition, the controller classes grouped under the category *Interface-Framework,* along with other view classes in the same category, are important to the graphics concept. Early in this chapter, the emphasis is on the first four categories: *Display Objects, Primitives, Paths,* and *Support.* The classes in the *Editors* category are special applications and are not described here. *Views* and *Controllers* are part of the MVC triad and are described in Section 9.6.

Figure 9.1 shows the class hierarchy for the graphics-related classes. It is divided into four parts. In each part, the category of classes is numbered and shown in italics. The classes that are actually grouped under that category are shown in boldface under each category. Figure 9.1a shows the class hierarchy for the *Display Objects, Primitives,* and *Paths* categories. Figure 9.1b shows the class hierarchy for the *Support* and *Editors* categories. Figure 9.1c shows the full hierarchy of classes under the subclass **View.** Only five of the classes (shown in boldface) are grouped with the graphics categories. And finally, Figure 9.1d shows the full class hierarchy for the controller classes. Only four of these classes (shown in boldface) are grouped with the graphics categories.

The graphics concept can be described by three fundamental actions. They are the creation and transfer of display objects and the storage of display information.

9.1.1   Creation of display objects

Display objects are defined on a rectangular region that is characterized by its width, height, and display bitmap. The display bitmap is the primary storage object for a display object. The physical display screen is a special case of a display object. Display objects can be scaled, copied, displayed, translated, or transferred. As can be seen in Figure 9.1a, there are many existing classes of display objects in the Smalltalk image.

There are three major categories of display objects, represented by three of the major subclasses of **DisplayObject** (**DisplayMedium, DisplayText,** and **Path**). A display medium is an object that can be bordered and filled with various colors (patterns). A display text is an object that is a representation for text characters. A path is an object that represents a continuous path definable by some set of rules (or an equation). There are several classes in the Smalltalk image that support various kinds of display objects. In addition to the subclasses listed under **DisplayObject** in Figure 9.1a, the creation of display objects is strongly supported by the classes **Point, Rectangle,** and **Quadrangle.**

9.1.2   Storage of display information

A display bitmap is an object that stores bits. These bits map one-to-one to every pixel in a particular display object, based on a prescribed mapping method. The bit patterns are stored as 16-bit words in the Smalltalk system. The key parameters of a display object are its width, height, and display bitmap. The Smalltalk image has two classes (**WordArray** and **DisplayBitmap**) that support storage of bitmaps. They are subclasses of **Collection.** The class called **Bitmap** in the Goldberg and Robson reference has been renamed to **WordArray.**

Figure 9.1a
Graphics Classes
Hierarchy—Part 1

```
┌─────────────────────────────────────────────────────────────────┐
│ Workspace                                                        │
├──────────┬──────────────────────────────────────────────────────┤
```

Graphics Classes in the Smalltalk System by Categories (Classes in category in boldface)

Category 1: Display Objects

Object ()
   DisplayObject ()
      DisplayMedium ()
         Form ('bits' 'width' 'height' 'offset')
            Cursor ()
            DisplayScreen ()
         DisplayText ('text' 'textStyle' 'offset' 'form')
            Paragraph ('clippingRectangle' 'compositionRectangle' 'destinationForm'
                        'rule' 'mask' 'marginTabsLevel' 'firstIndent' 'restIndent'
                        'rightIndent' 'lines' 'lastLine' 'outputMedium')
            TextList ('list')
      InfiniteForm ('patternForm')
      OpaqueForm ('figure' 'shape')
      Path ('form' 'collectionOfPoints')
         Arc ('quadrant' 'radius' 'center')
            Circle ()
         Curve ()
         Line ()
         LinearFit ()
         Spline ('derivatives')

Category 2: Primitives

Object ()
   Rectangle ('origin' 'corner')
      CharacterBlock ('stringIndex' 'character')
      Quadrangle ('borderWidth' 'borderColor' 'insideColor')

   Point ('x' 'y')

   BitBlt ('destForm' 'sourceForm' 'halftoneForm' 'combinationRule' 'destX' 'destY'
      'width' 'height' 'sourceX' 'sourceY' 'clipX' 'clipY' 'clipWidth' 'clipHeight')
      Pen ('frame' 'location' 'direction' 'penDown')

Category 3: Paths

Object()
   DisplayObject ()
      Path ('form' 'collectionOfPoints')
         Arc ('quadrant' 'radius' 'center')
            Circle ()
         Curve ()
         Line ()
         LinearFit ()
         Spline ('derivatives')

Figure 9.1b
Graphics Classes
Hierarchy—Part 2

```
Workspace

Graphics Classes in the Smalltalk System by Categories (Classes in category in boldface)

Category 4: Support

Object ()
    BitBlt ('destForm' 'sourceForm' 'halftoneForm' 'combinationRule' 'destX' 'destY'
            'width' 'height' 'sourceX' 'sourceY' 'clipX' 'clipY' 'clipWidth' 'clipHeight' )
    CharacterScanner ('lastIndex' 'xTable' 'stopConditions' 'text' 'textStyle'
            'leftMargin' 'rightMargin' 'font' 'line' 'runStopIndex'
            'spaceCount' 'spaceWidth' 'outputMedium' )
        CharacterBlockScanner ('characterPoint' 'characterIndex' 'lastCharacter'
                'lastCharacterExtent' 'lastSpaceOrTabExtent' 'nextLeftMargin' )
        CompositionScanner ('spaceX' 'spaceIndex' )
        DisplayScanner ('lineY' 'runX' )
    Pen ('frame' 'location' 'direction' 'penDown' )

Object()
    Rectangle ('origin' 'corner' )
        CharacterBlock ('stringIndex' 'character' )

Object ()
    Collection ()
        SequenceableCollection ()
            ArrayedCollection ()
                WordArray()
                    DisplayBitmap ()
            Interval ('start' 'stop' 'step' )
                TextLineInterval ('internalSpaces' 'paddingWidth' )
        Set ('tally' )
            Dictionary ()
                StrikeFontManager ()
                TextStyleManager ()

Object ()
    StrikeFont ('xTable' 'glyphs' 'name' 'stopConditions' 'type' 'minAscii' 'maxAscii'
            'maxWidth' 'strikeLength' 'ascent' 'descent' 'xOffset' 'raster' 'subscript'
            'superscript' 'emphasis' 'ascentForStdAsciiChars' 'descentForStdAsciiChars' )
    TextStyle ('fontArray' 'lineGrid' 'baseline' 'alignment' 'firstIndent' 'restIndent'
            'rightIndent' 'tabsArray' 'marginTabsArray' 'outputMedium'
            'lineGridForLists' 'baselineForLists' 'lineGridForMenus' 'baselineForMenus' )

Category 5: Editors

Object ()
    View (Instance variables not shown to save space)
        FormMenuView ()
    FormButtonCache ('offset' 'form' 'value' 'initialState' )
    Controller ('model' 'view' 'sensor' )
        FormMenuController ()
        MouseMenuController  (Instance variables not shown to save space)
            BitEditor ('scale' 'squareForm' 'color' )
            FormEditor ('form' 'tool' 'grid' 'togglegrid' 'mode' 'previousTool' 'color'
                'unNormalizedColor' 'xgridOn' 'ygridOn' 'toolMenu' 'underToolMenu' )
```

Figure 9.1c
Graphics Classes
Hierarchy—Part 3

```
Workspace
Graphics Classes in the Smalltalk System by Categories (Classes in category in boldface)

Category 6: Views (Class View is in Category Interface-Framework)

Object ()
    View ('model' 'controller' 'superView' 'subViews' 'transformation' 'viewport'
            'window' 'displayTransformation' 'insetDisplayBox' 'borderWidth'
            'borderColor' 'insideColor' 'boundingBox' 'selectionSelected' )
        BinaryChoiceView ()
        BrowserTimeView ()
        DisplayTextView ('rule' 'mask' 'editParagraph' 'centered' 'textStyle')
        FormView ('rule' 'mask' )
            FormHolderView ('displayedForm' )
        ListView ('list' 'selection' 'topDelimiter' 'bottomDelimiter' 'lineSpacing'
                'isEmpty' 'textStyle' )
            ChangeListView ()
            SelectionInListView ('itemList' 'printItems' 'oneItem' 'partMsg'
                    'initialSelectionMsg' 'changeMsg' 'listMsg' 'menuMsg' )
        StandardSystemView ('labelFrame' 'labelText' 'isLabelComplemented'
                'savedSubViews' 'minimumSize' 'maximumSize' 'windowForm'
                'windowFormFlag' 'textStyle' )
            BrowserView ()
            ClockView ('cacheForm' 'cacheBox' 'myProject' 'date' )
            InspectorView ()
            NotifierView ('contents' )
        StringHolderView ('displayContents' 'textStyle' )
            FillInTheBlankView ()
            ProjectView ()
            TextCollectorView ()
            WorkspaceView ()
        SwitchView ('complemented' 'label' 'selector' 'keyCharacter' 'highlightForm'
                'arguments' 'textStyle' )
            BooleanView ()
        TextView ('partMsg' 'acceptMsg' 'menuMsg' 'textStyle' )
            CodeView ('initialSelection' )
                OnlyWhenSelectedCodeView ('selectionMsg' )
```

9.1.3   Transfer of display objects

Display objects are transferred by an operation called bit-block transfer (**BitBlt** for short). This operation could have been implemented as a set of instance methods in the display object classes, but because it is relatively complicated, it is implemented as a separate class called **BitBlt.** Even more importantly, implementation as a separate class provides a better encapsulation in support of the object-oriented method.

All text and images on the display screen are created by a bit-block transfer of the graphic image to the display. The fundamental method in class **BitBlt** is copyBits, which supports a wide range of options on how the copying is to be done. Among the specifiable parameters are the source display object, the desti-

Figure 9.1d
Graphics Classes
Hierarchy—Part 4

```
Workspace
Graphics Classes in the Smalltalk System by Categories (Classes in category in boldface)

Category 7: Controllers (Class Controller is in Category Interface-Framework)

Object ()
    Controller ('model' 'view' 'sensor' )
        BinaryChoiceController ()
        FormMenuController ()
        MouseMenuController ('redButtonMenu' 'redButtonMessages'
                'yellowButtonMenu' 'yellowButtonMessages' 'blueButtonMenu'
                'blueButtonMessages' )
            BitEditor ('scale' 'squareForm' 'color' )
            FormEditor ('form' 'tool' 'grid' 'togglegrid' 'mode' 'previousTool' 'color'
                    'unNormalizedColor' 'xgridOn' 'ygridOn' 'toolMenu' 'underToolMenu' )
        ScreenController ()
        ScrollController ('scrollBar' 'marker' 'savedArea' )
            ListController ()
                LockedListController ()
                    ChangeListController ()
                SelectionInListController ()
            ParagraphEditor ('paragraph' 'startBlock' 'stopBlock' 'beginTypeInBlock'
                    'emphasisHere' 'initialText' 'selectionShowing' 'currentFont'
                    'echoLocation' 'echoForm' )
                StringHolderController ('isLockingOn' )
                    ChangeController ()
                    FillInTheBlankController ()
                        CRFillInTheBlankController ()
                    ProjectController ()
                    TextCollectorController ()
                    WorkspaceController ()
                TextController ()
                    CodeController ()
                        AlwaysAcceptCodeController ()
                        OnlyWhenSelectedCodeController ()
        StandardSystemController ('status' )
            NotifierController ()
    NoController ()
    SwitchController ('selector' 'arguments' 'cursor' )
        IndicatorOnSwitchController ()
        LockedSwitchController ()
```

nation display object, and a combination rule for overwriting existing bitmap data. The user can also specify a rectangular region (the clipping rectangle) in the destination display object, outside which no effect is seen from the copy operation. **BitBlt** is a subclass of **Object.**

9.2 Classes **Point** and **Rectangle**— Geometry of Graphics Objects

This section defines the primitive graphic classes **Point, Rectangle,** and **Quadrangle** (a special subclass of **Rectangle**). It discusses their importance to graphics applications and provides several examples illustrating the flexibility and use of objects of these classes.

Instances of these classes define the basic geometric properties of display objects. They also define coordinates within a display object (or on the display screen) for transferring by bit-block transfer, and the clipping rectangle. They are categorized as *graphics primitives* (in the class category list) because they are fundamental to most of the other graphics classes.

Instances of **Point** are defined by the **Number** binary message @. A point is specified as xNumber @ yNumber, where xNumber and yNumber are the x,y-coordinates of the point. The coordinate origin is at the upper left corner on the display screen. For reasons of compatibility, this convention (and the use of integer values for the x,y-coordinates) should be maintained in the definition of other display objects as well. The x-coordinate increases to the right and the y-coordinate increases downward.

Points with negative x,y values are supported, and arithmetic operations on points can be done with appropriate messages. Scaling and translation operations make it easy to transform a point from one coordinate system to another.

In a rectangular x,y-coordinate system, a rectangle is defined by two of its diagonal corners. By convention, the upper left corner of a rectangle is referred to as the **origin**. The lower right corner of the rectangle is called its **corner**. Both **origin** and **corner** are instances of **Point.** A third parameter, called the **extent**, is defined as the point whose x,y values correspond to the width and height, respectively, of a rectangle. Thus rectangles are specified by **origin** and **corner** in absolute coordinates or **origin** and **extent** in relative coordinates.

It is possible to reverse the roles of the **origin** and **corner** by specifying a negative **extent**, such as the creation of a rectangle using the following expression in the protocol for points.

100 @ 100 extent: −50 @ −50

The result is a rectangle with **origin**, 100 @ 100, and **corner**, 50 @ 50. This rectangle does not represent a displayable object.

An abbreviated summary of the protocol for classes **Point** and **Rectangle** is given below. More complete protocol summaries are given in Appendix 3. The protocol summary for class **Quadrangle** is left as an exercise for the reader. An example is given at the end of this section that illustrates protocol from all three classes.

Protocol Summary for Class Point

The hierarchy for class **Point** is **Object—Point.** Class **Point** has two instance variables, **x** and **y**. It has no class variables or pool dictionaries. It has 1 class method in 1 category and 45 instance methods in 12 categories.

Class **Point** has two instance variables. The first is **x,** an instance of **Number** (preferably an integer) that is the x-coordinate of the point. The second instance variable is **y,** an instance of **Number** (preferably an integer) that is the y-coordinate of the point.

There are eight methods (**dist:, dotProduct:, grid:, normal, pointNearestLine: to:, transpose, truncatedGrid:, unitVector**), defined under category *point functions,* that are intended specifically for operating on instances of class **Point.** In each case the result of sending the message to a point is another point with characteristics determined by the particular message. All eight are new protocol.

Two methods (**coerce:, generality**) define the special coercing of a two-dimensional object and set its generality at 90. Since arithmetic operations are defined for points, and their private data consists of numbers, they are implemented to support the concept of generality of numbers described in Chapter 6. Although it has not been added, protocol to coerce a point to a complex number (with the x-coordinate as the real part and the y-coordinate as the imaginary part) could be useful for certain problem applications. New protocol can be added to class **Complex** for converting complex numbers to points. This would be useful for the display of complex numbers on a two-dimensional graph.

Two methods (**scaleBy:, translateBy:**) are provided for scaling and translating a point. The parameter in each case is also an instance of **Point.** This allows independent scaling or translation for the x- and y-directions.

Protocol Summary for Class **Rectangle**

The hierarchy for class **Rectangle** is **Object—Rectangle.** Class **Rectangle** has two instance variables, origin and corner. It has no class variables or pool dictionaries. It has 8 class methods in one category and 57 instance methods in eight categories.

Class **Rectangle** has two instance variables: **origin,** an instance of **Point** that is the upper left corner of the rectangle; and **corner,** an instance of **Point** that is the lower right corner of the rectangle.

There are 33 accessing methods (**area, bottom, bottom:, bottomCenter, bottomLeft, bottomRight, bottomRight:, center, center:, corner, corner:, extent, extent:, height, height:, left, left:, leftCenter, origin, origin:, origin: corner:, origin: extent:, right, right:, rightCenter:, top, top:, topCenter, topLeft, topLeft:, topRight, width, width:**) that return specific points or features of a rectangle or allow those features to be set to new values. As is common in Smalltalk protocol, messages without a colon terminator return information, and messages that use the same identifier with a colon terminator set new values for specified parameters. The intent of many of the 33 messages is apparent from the selector name. All these messages represent new protocol.

Eight rectangle *function methods* (**amountToTranslateWithin:, areasDiffering:, areasOutside:, expandBy:, insetBy:, insetOriginBy: cornerBy:, intersect:, merge:**) are provided that are specific to rectangles. In most cases the result is also a rectangle. These methods are new protocol.

Eight methods (**fromUser, fromUser:, fromUserAspectRatio, left: right: top: bottom:, origin: corner:, origin: extent:, originFromUser:, originFromUser: grid:**) are provided that are used to create instances of **Rectangle.**

The following example illustrates some of the protocol of classes **Point** and **Rectangle.** Emphasis is on the creation of rectangles, on arithmetic operations for both points and rectangles, and on transformations.

Point and Rectangle Example 9A

Listing 9.1 gives details for this example, installed as class method **example1** in class **Rectangle.** The results of executing this example method are shown in Figure 9.2.

This example creates five rectangles using three methods for specifying the private data by program expressions and two methods that let the user specify

Listing 9.1
Details of
Rectangle
example1

Rectangle class methodsFor: 'examples'

example1
    " Shows how rectangles may be created, transformed, and displayed on sceeen."

    | rect1 rect2 rect3 rect4 rect5 |

    Transcript clear; refresh;
        show: 'Rectangle/Point Example - Creation, Transforming, and Displaying.';
        cr; crtab;
        show: 'Create rectangles and display border, using various instance creation
methods.';
        cr; cr; cr; cr; cr; cr; cr; crtab;
        show: 'Please keep user-generated rectangles above this text, else they will be
overwritten.'.

    rect1 ← Rectangle origin: 100@120 extent: 100@75.
    rect1 showRect: rect1 origin.
    'rect1' displayAt: 130@150.
    rect2 ← Rectangle origin: 220@120 corner: 250@180.
    rect2 showRect: rect2 origin.
    'rect2' displayAt: 220@182.

    rect3 ← Rectangle left: 270 right: 400 top: 120 bottom: 220.
        rect3 showRect: rect3 origin.
        (Rectangle origin: rect3 leftCenter corner: rect3 corner)
            showRect: rect3 leftCenter.
        (Rectangle origin: rect3 topCenter corner: rect3 rightCenter + (0 @ 2))
            showRect: rect3 topCenter.
        (Rectangle origin: rect3 center corner: rect3 corner)
            showRect: rect3 center.
        'rect3' displayAt: rect3 center + (2@2).

    rect4 ← Rectangle originFromUser: 100@ 80.
    rect4 showRect: rect4 origin. 'rect4' displayAt: rect4 center.
    rect5 ← Rectangle fromUser.
    rect5 showRect: rect5 origin. 'rect5' displayAt: rect5 center.

```
Transcript cr; crtab;
    show: 'Transformations on rectangles and points.'; cr; crtab;
    show: 'rect1 translated by 300@150 gives ------> '; crtab;
    show: ' Shown in true coordinates on screen.'.
Transcript cr; cr; cr; cr; crtab;
    show: 'rect2 scaled by 8@0.8 gives -----------> '; crtab;
    show: ' True coordinates are:'; crtab; tab;
    show: 'origin: 2200@96 corner: 2500@144.'.
Transcript cr; cr; cr; crtab;
    show: 'rect3 origin scaled by 1.5@4.0 gives ----> '; crtab;
    show: ' Shown in true coordinates on screen.'.


rect1 ← rect1 translateBy: 300@150.
rect1 showRect: rect1 origin. 'new rect1' displayAt: rect1 center - (35@7).
rect2 ← rect2 scaleBy: 8@0.8.
rect2 showRect: 400@400. 'new rect2' displayAt: 500@420.
rect3 ← Rectangle origin: (rect3 origin scaleBy: 1.5@4.0) extent: rect3 extent.
rect3 showRect: rect3 origin. 'new rect3' displayAt: rect3 center - (35@7).


" Rectangle example1 "
```

Figure 9.2
Rectangle
example1—
Creating,
Displaying, and
Transforming
Points and
Rectangles

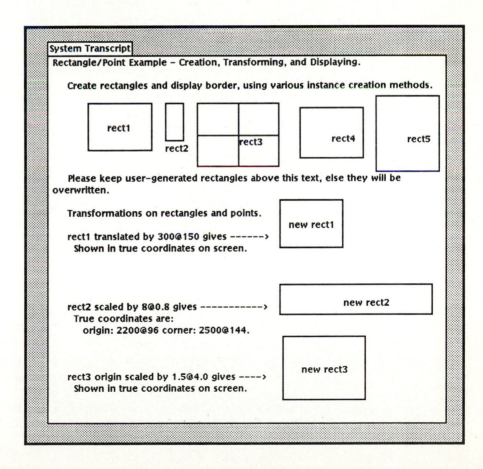

the private data by moving the cursor on the screen and clicking the mouse left button. Once the rectangles are created, they are displayed on the screen by filling them with a **veryLightGray** color, adding a 2-pixel wide border, and displaying.

All the rectangles are shown on the screen at their true coordinates, except for the scaled version of **rect2**. Being shown at their true coordinates means that a rectangle is displayed on the screen at coordinates matching its origin and corner. For example, **rect1** has an **origin** of 100@120 and a **corner** of 200@195. It is displayed on the screen with its **origin** at 100@120 and its **corner** at 200@195.

To support the repeated display of instances of **Rectangle** on the display screen, a new instance method called **showRect:** is added to the protocol for class **Rectangle.** Its details are given below. Several things are significant about this new method. First, the display of rectangles with noninteger private data causes an error. This is easily avoided by first rounding the **extent** of the rectangle to obtain an integer size. Next, an instance of **Form** is created that is the same size as the rectangle. The fill: rule: mask: message fills a specified rectangular region of a form with the color specified by the mask parameter based on the rule specified by the rule parameter. The result of this message is that the entire form contains the color **veryLightGray**. This form can now be displayed on the screen at any specified location. It is next bordered with a 2-pixel black border and displayed with its upper left corner at **aPoint**.

Rectangle methodsFor: 'example support'
showRect: aPoint
   "Display a 2-pixel border defining the receiver on the Display with its origin at aPoint."
   (Form extent: self rounded extent)
              fill: (0@0 extent: self rounded extent)
              rule: Form over
              mask: Form veryLightGray;
      borderWidth: 2;
      displayOn: Display at: aPoint

This example illustrates scaling of rectangles (**rect2**), the scaling of points (the **origin** of **rect3**), and the translation of rectangles (**rect1**). The display of text strings is done in several different ways. The labeling of **rect3**, **rect4**, and **rect5** illustrates the effect of displaying text at the center point of a rectangle. This center point becomes the upper-left origin of the displayed text string.

Point and Rectangle Example 9B

This example concentrates on protocol for point and rectangle functions. Details of class method **example2** in class **Rectangle** are given in Listing 9.2. Results of executing the example are given in Figure 9.3. Several rectangle functions and several point functions are demonstrated in the example.

All rectangles in this example are displayed in a surrounding box to give a constant reference among the various rectangle locations. All rectangles are dis-

Listing 9.2
Details of
Rectangle
example2

Rectangle class methodsFor: 'examples'

example2
   " Shows examples of rectangle functions and point functions."

   | rect1 rect2 pt1 pt2 box |

   rect1 ← Rectangle origin: 0@0 extent: 100@45.
   rect2 ← Rectangle origin: 50@25 extent: 110@50.
   box ← rect1 merge: rect2.
   pt1 ← 1@10.
   pt2 ← box corner.

   Transcript clear; refresh;
      show: 'Rectangle/Point Example - Rectangle Functions and Point Functions.';
        cr; crtab;
      show: 'Creation and merging of rectangles (shown relative to 0@0).'; crtab;
      show: ' rect1 (origin: 0@0 extent: 100@75) -----> '; cr; cr; cr; cr; crtab;
      show: ' rect2 (origin: 50@25 extent: 110@50) ---> '; cr; cr; cr; cr; crtab;
      show: ' result of merging rect1 and rect2 -------> '; cr; cr; cr; cr; crtab;
      show: ' result of intersecting rect1 and rect2 ----> '; crtab;
      show: ' Dark rectangle in middle is intersection.'; cr; cr; cr; crtab;
      show: ' areas differing between rect1 & rect2 ---> '; crtab;
      show: ' Rectangles in either one but not both.'; cr; cr; cr; crtab;
      show: ' rect1 with uniform inset --------------> '; cr; cr; cr; cr; crtab;
      show: ' rect2, different inset, origin and corner --> '; cr; cr; cr; cr; crtab;
      show: 'Point Functions for pt1 = ', pt1 printString, ' and pt2 = ', pt2 printString;
        cr;crtab;
      show: ' Distance between pt1 and pt2 is --------> ', (pt1 dist: pt2) printString; crtab;
      show: ' pt1 transposed is given by ------------> ', pt1 transpose printString; crtab;
      show: ' The pt on a normal to pt2 is given by ---> ', pt2 normal printString; crtab;
      show: ' pt2 as a unit vector is given by --------> ', pt2 unitVector printString; crtab;
      show: ' The dot product of pt1 and pt2 is -------> ', (pt1 dotProduct: pt2) printString.

   rect1 showRect: 450@105 in: box.
   rect2 showRect: 450@195 in: box.
   (rect1 merge: rect2) showRect: 450@285 in: box.
   rect1 showRect: 450@375 in: box.
   rect2 showRect: 450@375 in: box.
   (rect1 intersect: rect2) showRect: 450@375 in: box color: Form gray.
   (rect1 areasDiffering: rect2) do: [:eachRect |
      eachRect showRect: 450@465 in: box].
   rect1 showRect: 450@555 in: box color: Form white.
   (rect1 insetBy: 6@6) showRect: 450@555 in: rect1.
   rect2 showRect: 450@645 in: box color: Form white.
   (rect2 insetOriginBy: 6@6 cornerBy: 10@10)
      showRect: 450@645 + rect2 origin - box origin in: rect2.

   " Rectangle example2 "

Figure 9.3
Rectangle
example2—
Rectangle and
Point Functions

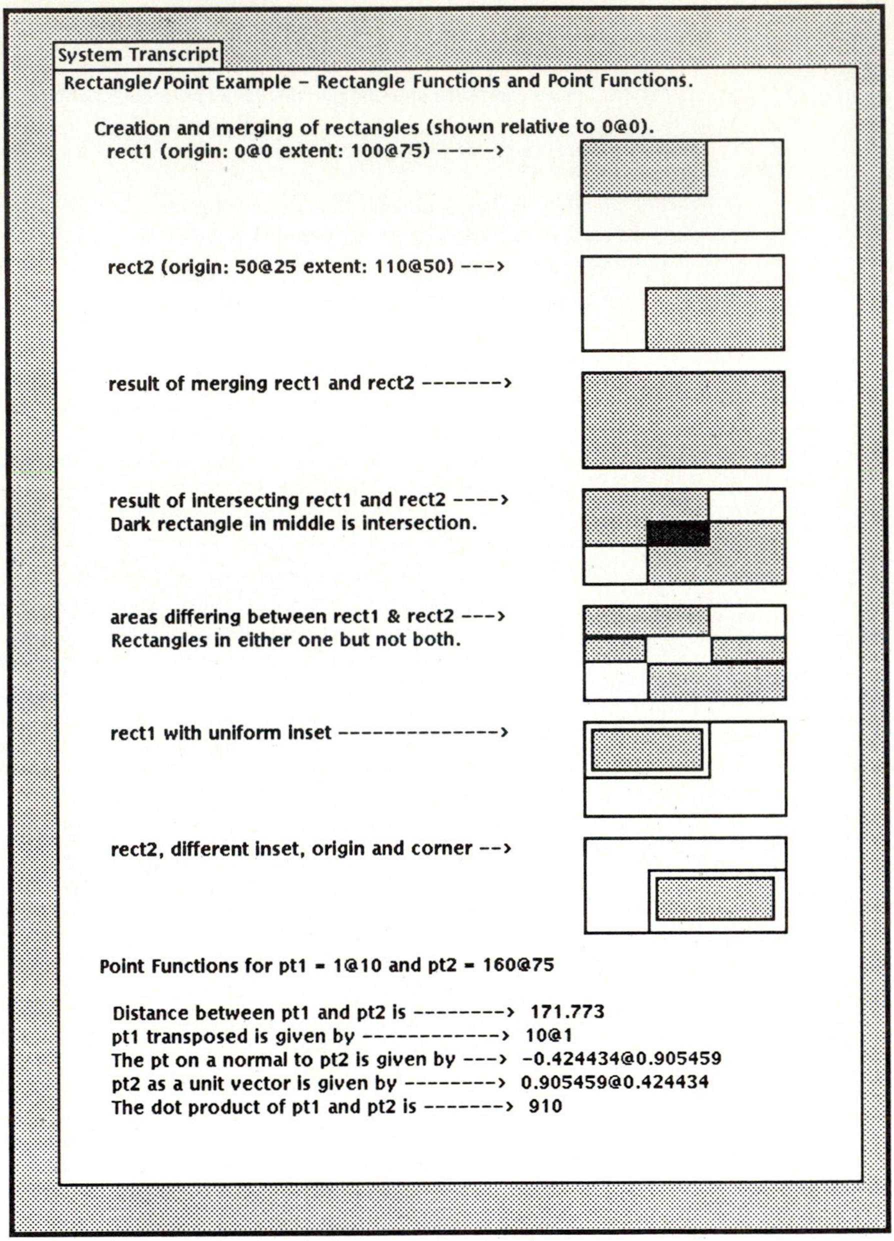

System Transcript

Rectangle/Point Example – Rectangle Functions and Point Functions.

Creation and merging of rectangles (shown relative to 0@0).
rect1 (origin: 0@0 extent: 100@75) ----->

rect2 (origin: 50@25 extent: 110@50) --->

result of merging rect1 and rect2 ------->

result of intersecting rect1 and rect2 ---->
Dark rectangle in middle is intersection.

areas differing between rect1 & rect2 --->
Rectangles in either one but not both.

rect1 with uniform inset -------------->

rect2, different inset, origin and corner -->

Point Functions for pt1 = 1@10 and pt2 = 160@75

Distance between pt1 and pt2 is -------> 171.773
pt1 transposed is given by -----------> 10@1
The pt on a normal to pt2 is given by ---> -0.424434@0.905459
pt2 as a unit vector is given by -------> 0.905459@0.424434
The dot product of pt1 and pt2 is ------> 910

played after the transcript messages have been sent. This is because a simple carriage return sent to Transcript clears the line from the current cursor position in the Transcript window to the right edge of the window. Display positions of the rectangles were chosen by trial and error to appear at the appropriate locations in the Transcript window. Although not elegant, this method works.

It can be seen from Figure 9.3 that the symmetric difference method, areas-Differing:, gives preference to the x-direction.

Rectangle and Quadrangle Example 9A

This example shows how rectangles and quadrangles can be created and displayed. Details of the class method example1 in class **Quadrangle** are given in Listing 9.3. Figure 9.4 shows the results of executing this example.

Listing 9.3
Details of
Quadrangle
example1

Quadrangle class methodsFor: 'examples'

example1
    "Examples of rectangles and quadrangles."

    | rect1 quad1 quad2 quad3 |

    rect1 ← Rectangle origin: 0@0 extent: 100@50.

    quad1 ← Quadrangle region: rect1
                borderWidth: 4
                borderColor: Form black
                insideColor: Form veryLightGray.
    quad2 ← Quadrangle region: rect1
                borderWidth:6
                borderColor: Form veryLightGray
                insideColor: Form black.
    quad3 ← Quadrangle region: rect1
                borderWidth:8
                borderColor: Form black
                insideColor: Form white.

    Transcript clear; refresh;
        show: 'Rectangle and Quadrangle Functions.';cr; crtab;
        show: 'Creation and merging of quadrangles. (shown relative to 0@0).';
          cr; cr; crtab;
        show: ' quad1 (borderwidth = 4 pixels) ---------> '; cr; cr; cr; cr; crtab;
        show: ' quad2 (borderwidth = 8 pixels, vlg) -----> '; cr; cr; cr; cr; crtab;
        show: ' quad3 (borderwidth = 8 pixels, black) ----> '; cr; cr; cr; cr; crtab;
        show: ' quad2 (new borderwidth & color) -------> '; cr; cr; cr; cr; crtab;
        show: ' quad2 (new inside color) -------------> '.

    quad1 displayOn: Display at: 450@105.
    quad2 displayOn: Display at: 450@195.
    quad3 displayOn: Display at: 450@285.
    (quad2 borderWidth: 5; borderColor: Form gray) displayOn: Display at: 450@375.
    (quad2 insideColor: Form veryLightGray) displayOn: Display at: 450@465.

    " Quadrangle example1 "

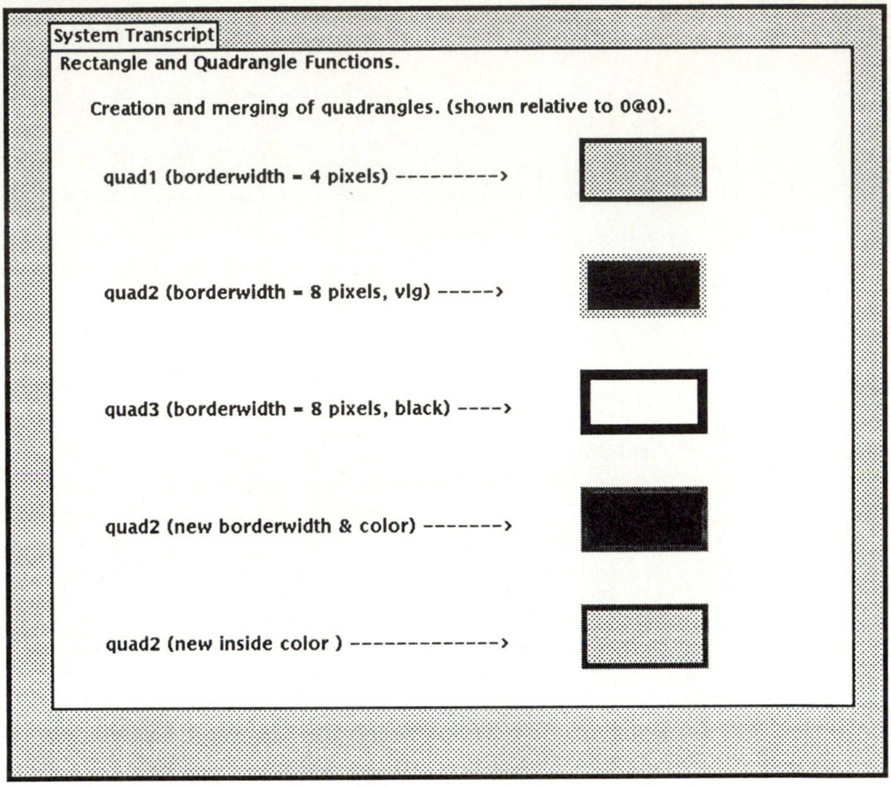

**Figure 9.4
Quadrangle**
example1—
Rectangle and
Quadrangle
Functions

```
System Transcript
Rectangle and Quadrangle Functions.

  Creation and merging of quadrangles. (shown relative to 0@0).


    quad1 (borderwidth = 4 pixels) --------->


    quad2 (borderwidth = 8 pixels, vlg) ----->


    quad3 (borderwidth = 8 pixels, black) ---->


    quad2 (new borderwidth & color) ------->


    quad2 (new inside color ) ------------->
```

Class **Quadrangle** is a subclass of **Rectangle.** It represents rectangular objects that have borders of a specified width and color, plus a specified inside color. Instances of **Quadrangle** have three new instance variables, borderWidth, borderColor, and insideColor, which define the quadrangle's features. Instances of **Quadrangle** make excellent bars for a bar chart.

9.3   Classes **WordArray** and **DisplayBitmap**—
Storage of Graphics Objects

The storage of graphic images is accomplished with objects in classes **WordArray** and **DisplayBitmap.** A protocol summary is given for class **DisplayBitmap,** and its properties are discussed. An example illustrates how the pixel data are stored in a display bitmap and how the bitmap can be accessed. Some of the protocol for this class was used in Chapter 7 in the discussion of the collection class **WordArray.**

Protocol Summary for Class DisplayBitmap

The hierarchy for class **DisplayBitmap** is **Object—Collection—Sequenceable-Collection—ArrayedCollection— WordArray—DisplayBitmap.** Class **Display-Bitmap** has no named instance variables, class variables, or pool dictionaries. As a variableWordSubclass, its private data consist of indexable words (16-bit quantities). It has three class methods in two categories and nine instance methods in two categories.

DisplayBitmap Example 9A

This example shows details of the structure of the private data of an instance of **DisplayBitmap.** Additionally, it illustrates accessing protocol for reading or setting display memory locations.

Instances of **DisplayBitmap** have instance variables that are of variable length and that consist of 16-bit words. The first five 16-bit words contain statistical information about the display bitmap, including a starting memory address for the actual bitmap.

Listing 9.4 shows details of class method example2 in class **DisplayBitmap.** Results of executing the example are shown in Figure 9.5.

Listing 9.4
Details of
DisplayBitmap
example2

DisplayBitmap class methodsFor: 'examples'

example2
"This example illustrates the structure of a display bitmap."

```
| bits |
bits ← Display bits.              "This variable has superclass WordArray."

Transcript clear; refresh;
    show: 'DisplayBitmap Example -- Structure of the Display bitmap.'; cr; crtab;
    show: 'Statistical words in the bitmap (indexable private data).'; crtab;
    show: ' Words 1 & 2: Size of bitmap in words --> ',
        bits size printString; crtab;
    show: ' Words 3 & 4: Starting address in memory --> ',
        bits address printString; crtab;
    show: ' Word 5: Number of words per row --> ',
        bits raster printString; cr; crtab;
    show: 'Display Words in the bitmap (indexable from starting address).'; crtab;
    show: ' Word at index 50 --> ',
        (bits at: 50) printString; crtab;
    show: ' Set word at index 12840 to black --> ',
        (bits at: 12840 put: 16rFFFF) printString; crtab;
    show: ' Verify word at 12840 --> ',
        (bits at: 12840) printString; crtab.

" DisplayBitmap example2 "
```

**Figure 9.5
DisplayBitmap**
example2—
Structure of
Bitmaps

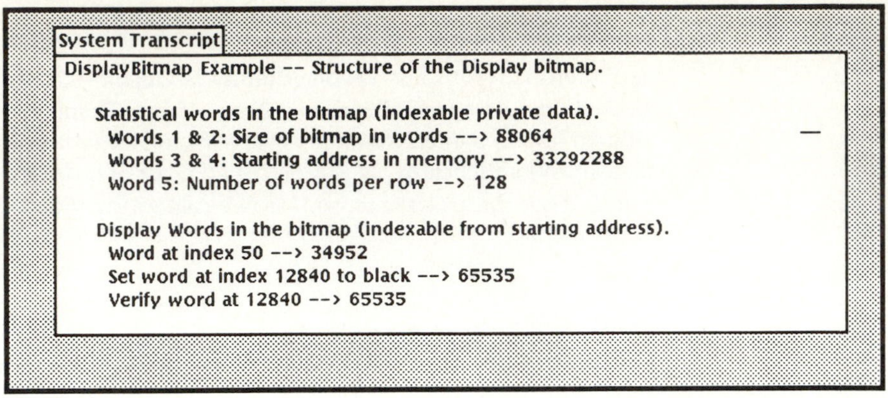

```
┌─────────────────────────────────────────────────────────────┐
│ ┌──────────────────┐                                         │
│ │System Transcript │                                         │
│ ├──────────────────┘                                         │
│  Display Bitmap Example -- Structure of the Display bitmap.   │
│                                                          ─    │
│  Statistical words in the bitmap (indexable private data).    │
│    Words 1 & 2: Size of bitmap in words --> 88064             │
│    Words 3 & 4: Starting address in memory --> 33292288       │
│    Word 5: Number of words per row --> 128                    │
│                                                               │
│  Display Words in the bitmap (indexable from starting address).│
│    Word at index 50 --> 34952                                 │
│    Set word at index 12840 to black --> 65535                 │
│    Verify word at 12840 --> 65535                             │
│                                                               │
└─────────────────────────────────────────────────────────────┘
```

The first five words in a display bitmap contain statistical data. As indicated in Figure 9.5, the first two words contain a 32-bit quantity that gives the size of the bitmap in words (88,064 words * 16 bits = 1376 * 1024 bits for the standard display size). The third and fourth words in the display bitmap contain a 32-bit quantity that is the starting memory address of the actual display bits.

The fifth 16-bit word gives the memory raster size in words per row (128). There are 128 memory words from the beginning of one row to the beginning of the next row. This information is essential for accessing specific pixels on the display. A little arithmetic shows that the rows are not stored contiguously (1376 pixels per row gives 1376/16 = 86 words per row of actual display information).

9.4   Classes **BitBlt** and **Pen**—Transfer of Graphics Objects

Class **BitBlt** is "the" class for transferring graphic images and its protocol is both summarized and described in detail in this section. Class **Pen** is a subclass of **BitBlt** with a modified protocol (summarized here) to make line drawing easier. Examples of the use of both classes are given.

Protocol Summary for Class BitBlt

The hierarchy for class **BitBlt** is **Object—BitBlt**. Class **BitBlt** has 14 instance variables, destForm, sourceForm, halftoneForm, combinationRule, destX, destY, width, height, sourceX, sourceY, clipX, clipY, clipWidth, clipHeight. It has no class variables or pool dictionaries. It has 3 class methods in two categories and 27 instance methods in four categories.

Private data—Class **BitBlt** has 14 instance variables. Examples given at the end of this section illustrate the definition of these instance variables and how different options on their values affect the transfer of images. The instance variables and their functions are defined as follows.

destForm—an instance of **Form** that is the destination object for the copy operation of a bit-block transfer.

sourceForm—an instance of **Form** that is the source object from which the copy operation is performed.

halftoneForm—a 16-by-16 pixel instance of **Form** that is repeatedly combined with each subarea of the source form prior to the copy operation. The bits actually copied into the destination form are the result of ANDing the halftone form and the source form.

combinationRule—an instance of **Integer** between 0 and 15 that is the code for one of the 16 possible combination rules for black-and-white pixels. Definitions for the combination rules are given in Goldberg and Robson on page 361. **BitBlt** Example 9A shows the graphic result of the 16 combination rules.

destX—an instance of **Integer** that is the x-coordinate of the origin of a rectangle in the destination form into which the copy operation is to be performed.

destY—an instance of **Integer** that is the y-coordinate of the origin of a rectangle in the destination form into which the copy operation is to be performed.

width—an instance of **Integer** that is the x-direction extent of the rectangle in the destination form into which the copy operation is to be performed. It is also the x-direction extent of the rectangle in the source form from which the copying is to be performed.

height—an instance of **Integer** that is the y-direction extent of the rectangle in the destination form into which the copy operation is to be performed. It is also the y-direction extent of the rectangle in the source form from which the copying is to be performed.

sourceX—an instance of **Integer** that is the x-coordinate of the origin of the rectangle in the source form from which the copying is to be performed.

sourceY—an instance of **Integer** that is the y-coordinate of the origin of the rectangle in the source form from which the copying is to be performed.

clipX—an instance of **Integer** that is the x-coordinate of the origin of the clipping rectangle in the destination form.

clipY—an instance of **Integer** that is the y-coordinate of the origin of the clipping rectangle in the destination form.

clipWidth—an instance of **Integer** that is the x-direction extent of the clipping rectangle in the destination form.

clipHeight—an instance of **Integer** that is the y-direction extent of the clipping rectangle in the destination form.

There are 20 accessing methods (**clipHeight:, clipRect, clipRect:, clipWidth:, clipX, clipY, combinationRule:, destForm:, destOrigin:, destRect:, destX:, destY:, height:, mask:, sourceForm:, sourceOrigin:, sourceRect:, sourceX:, sourceY:, width:**) that set values for the instance variables of **BitBlt.** One method (**clipRect**) returns the parameters defining the clipping rectangle. All these methods are new protocol.

The most important method (**copyBits**) performs the actual bit-block transfer. It requires that an instance of **BitBlt** first be established and that the appropriate parameters be established using other protocol in this class.

Protocol Summary for Class Pen

The hierarchy for class **Pen** is **Object—BitBlt—Pen.** Class **Pen** has four instance variables, frame, location, direction, and penDown. It has no class variables or pool dictionaries. It has 1 class method in one category and 25 instance methods in five categories.

Private data for class **Pen** consists of four instance variables. Instance variable **frame** is an instance of **Rectangle** that defines the rectangular region within which the pen can draw. Instance variable **location** is an instance of **Point** that is the current location of the pen. Instance variable **direction** is an instance of **Integer** that defines the direction in which the pen is pointing. Direction is measured in degrees clockwise from the positive x-direction (i.e., right is 0, up is 270). And instance variable **penDown** is an instance of **Boolean** that defines whether the pen is down (true) or not. A pen cannot draw unless it is down.

Category *geometric designs* has six methods (**dragon:, filberts: side:, hilbert: side:, hilberts:, mandala: diameter:, spiral: angle:**) that demonstrate the drawing of geometric patterns with instances of class **Pen.**

BitBlt Example 9A

This example illustrates the 16 combination rules for combining the source form with the destination form during a copy operation. It is added to class **BitBit** as the class method **example1**. The details of this method are given in Listing 9.5. The result of executing the example is shown in Figure 9.6.

Listing 9.5
Details of **BitBlt**
example1

BitBlt class methodsFor: 'examples'

example1
    "This tests BitBlt by displaying the result of all sixteen combination rules that BitBlt is
        capable of using."

    | ruleArray |
    ruleArray ← BitBlt setRuleArray.
    Display white.
    'The sixteen combination rules (no halftone mask used).' asText allBold asDisplayText
        displayOn: Display at: 20@15.
    ' Source' asText allBold asDisplayText
        displayOn: Display at: 280 @ 45.
    ' Destination' asText allBold asDisplayText
        displayOn: Display at: 380 @ 45.

```
' Result' asText allBold asDisplayText
    displayOn: Display at: 530 @ 45.
1 to: 16 do: [:index |
    BitBlt
        displayAt: 300 @ (25 + (45*index))
        spacing: 100 @ 0
        rule: index - 1
        mask: nil.
    ('Rule ', (index - 1) printString, ' gives ----------> ') asText allBold asDisplayText
        displayOn: Display at: 50 @ (30 + (45*index)).
    (ruleArray at: index) asDisplayText
        displayOn: Display at: 55 @ (50 + (45*index))]

"BitBlt example1."
```

Figure 9.6
BitBlt example1—
The 16
Combination Rules

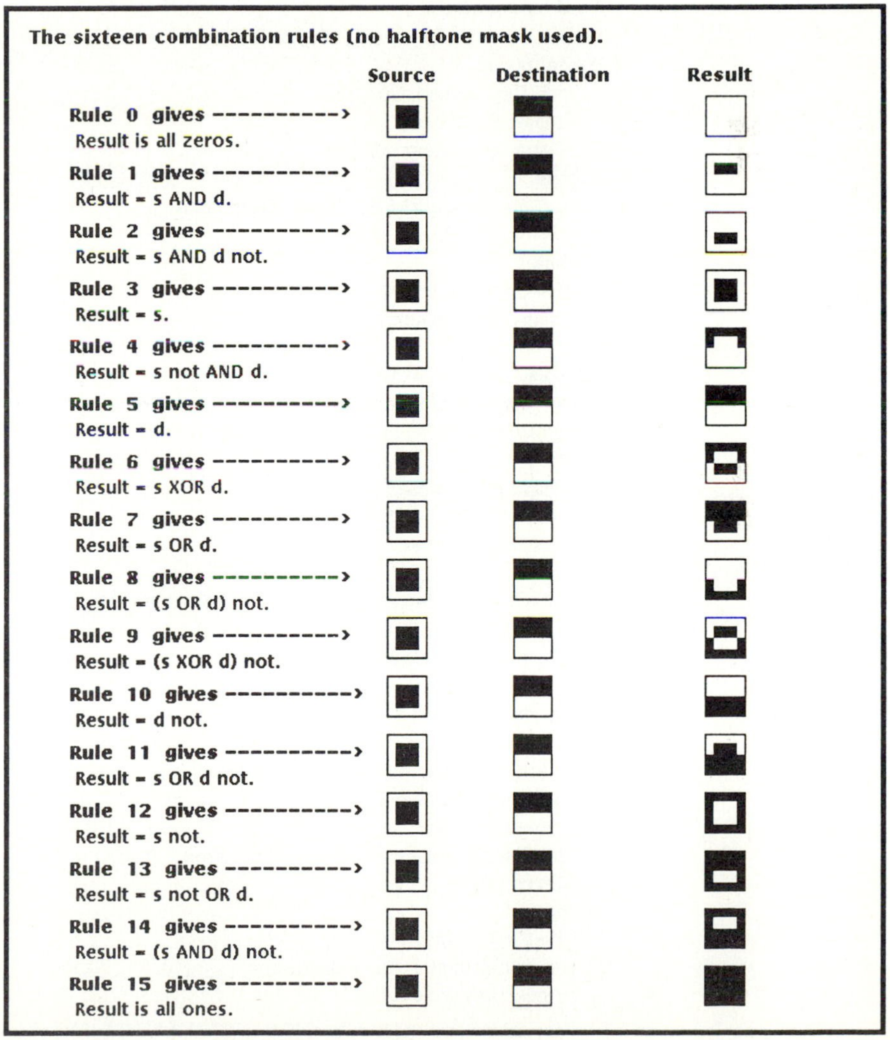

The sixteen combination rules (no halftone mask used).

	Source	Destination	Result
Rule 0 gives ----------> Result is all zeros.			
Rule 1 gives ----------> Result = s AND d.			
Rule 2 gives ----------> Result = s AND d not.			
Rule 3 gives ----------> Result = s.			
Rule 4 gives ----------> Result = s not AND d.			
Rule 5 gives ----------> Result = d.			
Rule 6 gives ----------> Result = s XOR d.			
Rule 7 gives ----------> Result = s OR d.			
Rule 8 gives ----------> Result = (s OR d) not.			
Rule 9 gives ----------> Result = (s XOR d) not.			
Rule 10 gives ----------> Result = d not.			
Rule 11 gives ----------> Result = s OR d not.			
Rule 12 gives ----------> Result = s not.			
Rule 13 gives ----------> Result = s not OR d.			
Rule 14 gives ----------> Result = (s AND d) not.			
Rule 15 gives ----------> Result is all ones.			

To support this example, two new methods are added as private class methods in **BitBlt.** The first, displayAt: spacing: rule: mask:, generates and displays the source and destination forms at a specified location on the screen and with a specified horizontal spacing. It then performs the actual bit-block transfer and shows the resulting form. It provides options for the rule and halftone mask. Details of displayAt: spacing: rule: mask: are given in Listing 9.6.

Listing 9.6
Details of **BitBlt**
Method displayAt:
spacing: rule:
mask:

BitBlt class methodsFor: 'private'

displayAt: originPoint **spacing:** deltaPoint **rule:** rule **mask:** mask
"This builds a source and destination form and copies the source to the destination using
the specified rule and mask. It is called from the method named example1."

```
| s d border aBitBlt |
border ← Form new extent: 32@32.
border black;
    fill: (1@1 extent: 30@30)
    mask: Form white.
s ← Form new extent: 32@32.
s white.
s fill: (7@7 corner: 25@25) mask: Form black.
d ← Form new extent: 32@32.
d white;
    fill: (0@0 corner: 32@16)
    mask: Form black.

s displayOn: Display at: originPoint.
border displayOn: Display at: originPoint rule: Form under.
d displayOn: Display at: originPoint + deltaPoint.
border
    displayOn: Display
    at: originPoint + deltaPoint
    rule: Form under.

d displayOn: Display at: originPoint + (2.5 * deltaPoint).
aBitBlt ← BitBlt
    destForm: Display
    sourceForm: s
    halftoneForm: mask
    combinationRule: rule
    destOrigin: originPoint + (2.5 * deltaPoint)
    sourceOrigin: 0 @ 0
    extent: s extent
    clipRect: Display computeBoundingBox.
aBitBlt copyBits.
border
    displayOn: Display
    at: originPoint + (2.5 * deltaPoint)
    rule: Form under.
```

Listing 9.7
Details of
BitBlt Method
setRuleArray

BitBlt class methodsFor: 'private'

setRuleArray
"Establish an array of string definitions for the 16 rules."

```
|array|
array ← Array new: 16.
array at: 1 put: 'Result is all zeros.'.
array at: 2 put: 'Result = s AND d.'.
array at: 3 put: 'Result = s AND d not.'.
array at: 4 put: 'Result = s.'.
array at: 5 put: 'Result = s not AND d.'.
array at: 6 put: 'Result = d.'.
array at: 7 put: 'Result = s XOR d.'.
array at: 8 put: 'Result = s OR d.'.
array at: 9 put: 'Result = (s OR d) not.'.
array at: 10 put: 'Result = (s XOR d) not.'.
array at: 11 put: 'Result = d not.'.
array at: 12 put: 'Result = s OR d not.'.
array at: 13 put: 'Result = s not.'.
array at: 14 put: 'Result = s not OR d.'.
array at: 15 put: 'Result = (s AND d) not.'.
array at: 16 put: 'Result is all ones.'.
↑array
```

This example uses a nil halftone mask, which means that the source and destination forms are combined without a mask and based only on the combination rule. A nil mask is equivalent to a black mask.

The second method added, **setRuleArray**, has the singular purpose of generating an array of 16 descriptive strings that define the 16 combination rules. Details of **setRuleArray** are given in Listing 9.7.

BitBlt Example 9B

This example shows the meaning of all the private data objects in class **BitBlt**. In particular, it illustrates the definition and meaning of the clipping rectangle. It is added as the class method **example2** in class **BitBlt**. Details of the example are given in Listing 9.8. Results are given in Figures 9.7 and 9.8.

The clipping rectangle in each case is defined with coordinates given by the actual location on the display screen to which the copy is to take place. Its size is defined as the size of the source rectangle with increasing inset border. In Figure 9.7, the source is a gray-filled rectangle. The destination form is a rectangular area of the same size as the source, filled with partial text. Since the source in this figure is uniformly gray, the result tells nothing about how the source is clipped, only that it is clipped.

Figure 9.8 shows a source form with text in it and a destination form showing as in Figure 9.7. In this figure, the clipping rectangle goes from full size at the
top to zero at the bottom. The source and destination rectangles are 100-by-56
pixels each, so a clipping rectangle reduced by a border of 28 pixels has zero
height. This gives the destination form at the lower right figure. This figure
shows that the clipping rectangle also serves as a masking window for the source
content. Any content in the source outside the clipping rectangle is not copied,
and the underlying destination form is unchanged.

Listing 9.8
Details of **BitBlt**
example2

BitBlt class methodsFor: 'examples'

example2
    "This tests BitBlt by showing the effect of the clipping rectangle on copying."

    | s d rect aBitBlt |

    rect ← 0@0 extent: 100@56.
    s ← Form fromDisplay: (rect translateBy: 40@750).
    s borderWidth: 1.
    d ← Form fromDisplay: (rect translateBy: 1100@175).
    d borderWidth: 1.
    Display white.
    'The Effect of Clipping Rectangle on copyBits.' asText allBold asDisplayText
        displayOn: Display at: 60@15.
    ' Source' asText allBold asDisplayText
        displayOn: Display at: 400 @ 65.
    ' Clipped Result' asText allBold asDisplayText
        displayOn: Display at: 550 @ 65.
    1 to: 8 do: [:index |
        aBitBlt ← BitBlt
            destForm: Display
            sourceForm: s
            halftoneForm: nil
            combinationRule: Form over
            destOrigin: 550 @ (50 + (80 * index))
            sourceOrigin: 0 @ 0
            extent: s extent
            clipRect: ((rect insetBy: 4*(index-1))
                translateBy: 550 @ (50+ (80 * index))).
        d displayOn: Display at: 550 @ (50 + (80 * index)).
        aBitBlt copyBits.
        s displayOn: Display at: 400 @ (50 + (80 * index)).
        ('Clipping rectangle smaller by ', (4*(index-1)) printString, ' pixel border')
            asDisplayText displayOn: Display at: 40@(55+ (80*index))]

    "BitBlt example2."

Figure 9.7
BitBit example2—
Effect of Clipping
Rectangle on
copyBits—Part 1

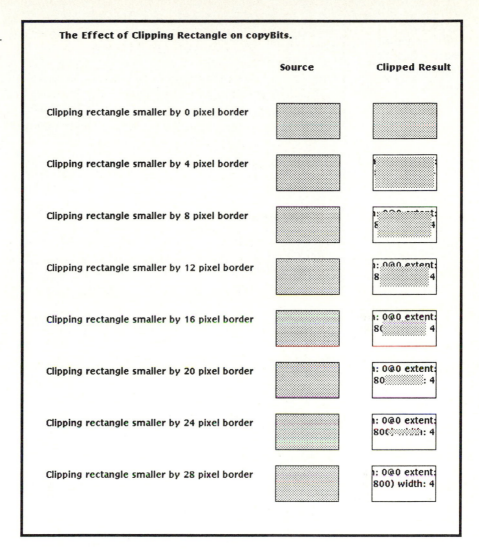

Pen Example 9A

This example illustrates some of the protocol in class **Pen.** It shows how pens can be used to plot graphical information. The example is listed in Listing 9.9 as class method **example2** in class **Pen.** In addition to this example, there are several geometric design methods as described in the protocol summary. Figure 9.9 shows the resulting plot of the sinc function (sin (pi $*$ x) / (pi $*$ x)).

Figure 9.8
BitBit example2—
Effect of Clipping
Rectangle on
copyBits—Part 2

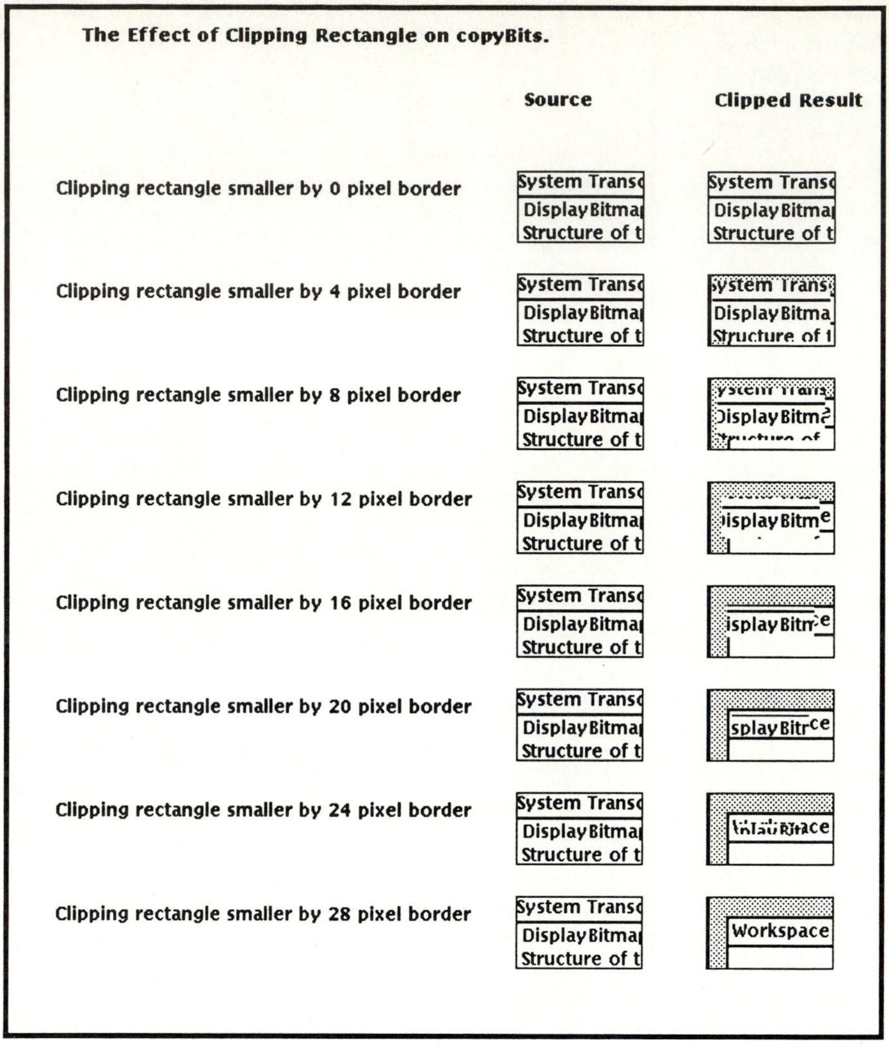

The Effect of Clipping Rectangle on copyBits.

	Source	Clipped Result
Clipping rectangle smaller by 0 pixel border	System Transc / Display Bitma / Structure of t	System Transc / Display Bitma / Structure of t
Clipping rectangle smaller by 4 pixel border	System Transc / Display Bitma / Structure of t	ystem Trans / Display Bitma / Structure of t
Clipping rectangle smaller by 8 pixel border	System Transc / Display Bitma / Structure of t	ystem Trans / Display Bitma / tructure of
Clipping rectangle smaller by 12 pixel border	System Transc / Display Bitma / Structure of t	isplay Bitm e
Clipping rectangle smaller by 16 pixel border	System Transc / Display Bitma / Structure of t	isplay Bitn ce
Clipping rectangle smaller by 20 pixel border	System Transc / Display Bitma / Structure of t	splay Bitr ce
Clipping rectangle smaller by 24 pixel border	System Transc / Display Bitma / Structure of t	nterface
Clipping rectangle smaller by 28 pixel border	System Transc / Display Bitma / Structure of t	Workspace

9.5 Classes That Support Definition of Display Objects

This section defines the classes that support generation of different kinds of display objects. Three major categories of display objects—*Images, Text,* and *Paths*—are described and illustrated by examples in the appropriate subsections below.

Display objects are defined on a rectangular region. There is protocol to support the modification of pixels within this rectangular region to produce any

Listing 9.9
Details of **Pen**
example2

Pen class methodsFor: 'examples'

example2
    " This example uses a pen to plot a sin x / x curve. "

    | pen axis rect sinc |

    pen ← Pen new sourceForm: (Form dotOfSize: 2).
    rect ← Rectangle origin: 50@50 extent: 600@220.
    (Form extent: rect extent)
        borderWidth: 2;
        displayOn: Display
        at: rect origin.
    pen frame: rect.
    axis ← rect bottomCenter - (0@90).
    pen
        place: rect origin x @ axis y;   "Draw axes"
        turn: 90;
        go: rect extent x;
        place: rect bottomCenter;
        north;
        go: rect extent y.
    pen
        sourceForm: (Form dotOfSize: 4);
        place: axis - (0@100).
    1 to: 300 do: [:x |
        sinc ← (x / 100.0 * Float pi) sin / (x/100.0 * Float pi).
        pen goto: axis - (x @ (100*sinc))].
    pen place: axis - (0@100).
    1 to: 300 do: [:x |
        sinc ← (x / 100.0 * Float pi) sin / (x/100.0 * Float pi).
        pen goto: axis + (x @ (0-100*sinc))]

    " Pen example2 "

Figure 9.9
Pen example2—
Plotting Curves
with Pens

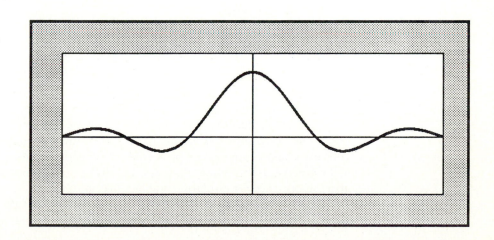

desired bitmap for the display object. The pixels of the bitmap can be set using direct memory access, using information from an array, using a bit editor, or using input from an external scanning device.

Class **DisplayObject** is an abstract superclass of all the display object classes. It does not have instances; rather, its subclasses will have instances that inherit protocol defined in **DisplayObject.** There are five major subclasses under **DisplayObject—DisplayMedium, DisplayText, InfiniteForm, OpaqueForm,** and **Path. DisplayObject** defines protocol that is common to all display objects. In some cases a subclass will redefine an inherited method or block its use. An abbreviated protocol summary for **DisplayObject** is given below. A more detailed summary is given in Appendix 3.

Protocol Summary for Class **DisplayObject**

The hierarchy for class **DisplayObject** is **Object—DisplayObject.** Class **DisplayObject** has no instance variables, class variables, or pool dictionaries. It has no class methods. It has 27 instance methods in six categories.

Of the 10 *displaying-generic* methods for displaying objects, the key method is displayOn: at: clippingBox: rule: mask:. It is called by the remaining 9 methods, and it is implemented as subclassResponsibility. All 10 are new protocol in this class.

Five *displaying-Display* methods (**backgroundAt:, display, displayAt:, follow: while:, moveTo: restoring:**) provide ways to display a display object on the display screen (represented by global variable **Display**). The background already on the display screen is preserved if desired.

9.5.1   Displaying images—classes **DisplayMedium, Form, Cursor,** and **DisplayScreen**

These classes support images that can be colored and bordered. Descriptions and examples are given for objects of these classes.

Class **DisplayMedium** is an abstract superclass of classes in this category. Instances of **Form** are private data in other classes of display objects. A clear understanding of the protocol in class **Form** is essential to understanding graphic display in Smalltalk. **Cursor** and **DisplayScreen** are subclasses of **Form** that represent the cursor and the display screen, respectively. In most cases, access to the cursor and its supporting protocol is of secondary interest and can be studied when the user has time. Access to the display screen is essential and of primary importance for displaying graphic objects.

Examples given at the end of this section emphasize forms and the display screen. There is one example that shows all the standard system cursor shapes and that defines a new cursor shape. A detailed summary of the protocol of class **DisplayMedium** is given below.

Protocol Summary for Class **DisplayMedium**

Definition—The hierarchy for class **DisplayMedium** is **Object—DisplayObject— DisplayMedium.** Class **DisplayMedium** has no instance variables, class variables, or pool dictionaries. It has no class methods. It has 24 instance methods in three categories.

Class **DisplayMedium** has 24 instance methods in three categories, which are summarized below.

coloring—eighteen methods (**black, black:, darkGray, darkGray:, fill:, fill: mask:, fill: rule: mask:, gray, gray:, lightGray, lightGray:, reverse, reverse:, reverse: mask:, veryLightGray, veryLightGray:, white, white:**) that set the entire display medium or a specified rectangular region (using the colon-terminated selectors) of the receiver to a specified shade of gray, based on various combination rules. All are new protocol. The key method (**fill: rule: mask:**) is implemented as **subclass-Responsibility**. All the other 17 methods depend on this key method for their implementation. This again illustrates the principles of encapsulation, inheritance, and polymorphism as implemented by Smalltalk. Seventeen higher-level abstractions are built on one lower-level abstraction. Maintenance requires only that the lower-level abstraction be changed.

bordering—four methods (**border: width:, border: width: mask:, border: widthRectangle: mask:, border: widthRectangle: mask: clippingBox:**), all of which are new protocol, for adding borders to an instance of subclasses of **DisplayMedium** All four depend on the implementation of the method fill: rule: mask:, as defined in the *coloring* category above. These four methods also depend on the lower-level abstraction, and their maintenance requires only changing that one method.

displaying—two methods (**copyBits: from: at: clippingBox: rule: mask:, drawLine: from: to: clippingBox: rule: mask:**) for performing the actual display using bit-block transfer. Both are subclassResponsibility and are new protocol.

Class methods—Class **DisplayMedium** has no class methods.

Instances of class **Form** are display objects that can be colored, bordered, displayed, copied, and transformed (translated, scaled) using protocol inherited from superclasses **DisplayMedium** and **DisplayObject** In addition to the inherited protocol implemented as subclassResponsibility in its superclasses, **Form** provides implementation for a variety of new methods as well.

Forms are rectangular in shape. Patterns can be shown within this rectangular shape by setting the appropriate combination of bits within the form. Instances of **Form** are private data for several other classes. **Form** is one of the key classes supporting graphics in Smalltalk. An abbreviated summary of the protocol for class **Form** is given below. More details are given in Appendix 3.

Protocol Summary for Class Form

The hierarchy for class **Form** is: **Object—DisplayObject—DisplayMedium—Form.** Class **Form** has four instance variables, bits, width, height, and offset. It has no pool dictionaries. It has one class variable, OneBitForm. It has 26 class methods in 4 categories and 49 instance methods in 15 categories.

Class **Form** has four instance variables: **bits,** an instance of **WordArray** that is the bitmap for the form; **width,** an instance of **Integer** that is the width in pixels of the rectangular form; **height,** an instance of **Integer** that is the height in pixels of the rectangular form; and **offset,** an instance of **Point** that gives the offset for displaying the form. If a form is to be displayed at aPoint, the offset is first added to aPoint and then displayed. This provides an easy mechanism for displaying the form centered about a point.

Shared data in class **Form** consists of one class variable, **OneBitForm,** that is an instance of **Form.** It is one-by-one bit in size and its bitmap contains only zeros.

Two methods (**follow: while:, moveTo: restoring:**) for displaying forms smoothly on the display screen are inherited from **DisplayObject** and redefined.

Two methods (**borderWidth:, borderWidth: mask:**) are provided for painting a black border of specified pixel width around a form. The second method allows specification of a mask color other than black. Both methods are new protocol.

One method (**fill: rule: mask:**) is inherited from **DisplayMedium** (where it was subclassResponsibility) and redefined. This is the key method for coloring the rectangular region of a form.

Eleven methods are provided for manipulating the size or orientation of a form's bitmap and other image characteristics. All are new protocol.

One method (**writeOn:**) is new protocol that saves the form on a specified file in a format that allows reconstruction of the form.

Ten methods (**dotOfSize:, extent:, extent: fromArray: offset:, extent: fromCompactArray: offset:, fromDisplay:, fromUser, fromUser:, readFormFile:, readFrom:, stringScanLineOfWidth:**) are provided for creating new instances of **Form.** Instances can be created by user specification from a rectangle on the display screen, by reading a form file, from an array, or as a circular dot. All methods are new protocol except for readFrom:, which is inherited from **Object** and redefined.

Six methods that give names to six of the combination rule codes used by **BitBlt** are provided in this class. Eight methods for returning or setting the background mask and for answering the form that represents various "colors" are also provided.

Instances of class **Cursor** are 16-by-16 forms whose bit patterns represent the various cursor shapes used by the Smalltalk system. There are 13 standard cursor shapes that are the class variables of **Cursor.** The user can easily define new cursor shapes if desired. The following is an abbreviated summary of the protocol of class **Cursor.** More details are given in Appendix 3.

Protocol Summary for Class Cursor

The hierarchy for class **Cursor** is **Object—DisplayObject—DisplayMedium— Form—Cursor.** Class **Cursor** has no instance variables or pool dictionaries. It has 14 class variables, BlankCursor, CornerCursor, CrossHairCursor, CurrentCursor, DownCursor, MarkerCursor, NormalCursor, OriginCursor, ReadCursor, Square-Cursor, UpCursor, WaitCursor, WriteCursor, and XeqCursor. It has 19 class methods in four categories and 8 instance methods in three categories.

Shared data in class **Cursor** consists of 14 class variables, which are described below. Each represents a specific system cursor shape in Smalltalk, except that CurrentCursor is the current cursor shape. **Cursor** Example 9A illustrates these cursor shapes and how the user can define a new cursor shape.

BlankCursor—an instance of **Cursor** that has a blank bitmap.

CornerCursor—an instance of **Cursor** that has the shape of a lower right corner of a rectangle.

CrossHairCursor—an instance of **Cursor** that has the shape of a crosshair.

CurrentCursor—an instance of **Cursor** that is the current cursor shape. It is typically one of the other cursor shapes defined as class variables in **Cursor.**

DownCursor—an instance of **Cursor** that has the shape of a downward-pointing half-arrow.

MarkerCursor—an instance of **Cursor** that has the shape of a boldface right-pointing arrow.

NormalCursor—an instance of **Cursor** that is a northwest-pointing arrow. This is the normal cursor shape.

OriginCursor—an instance of **Cursor** that has the shape of the upper left corner of a rectangle.

ReadCursor—an instance of **Cursor** that has the shape of a pair of glasses.

SquareCursor—an instance of **Cursor** that has the shape of a small square.

UpCursor—an instance of **Cursor** that has the shape of an upward-pointing half-arrow.

WaitCursor—an instance of **Cursor** that has the shape of an hourglass.

WriteCursor—an instance of **Cursor** that has the shape of a pencil.

XeqCursor—an instance of **Cursor** that has the shape of the normal cursor with a star positioned in its upper right corner.

Class **DisplayScreen** has one instance, the global variable **Display.** It is a subclass of **Form** that provides protocol for interacting directly with the display screen. A short summary of **DisplayScreen** is given below. A more detailed summary of its protocol is given in Appendix 3.

Protocol Summary for Class DisplayScreen

The hierarchy for class **DisplayScreen** is **Object—DisplayObject—Display-Medium—Form—DisplayScreen.** Class **DisplayScreen** has no instance variables, class variables, or pool dictionaries. It has 4 class methods in two categories and 30 instance methods in six categories.

Cursor Example 9A

This example shows the shape of all 13 standard system cursors and illustrates how the user can define a new cursor shape. The details of the class method example1 in class **Cursor** are given in Listing 9.10. The results are shown in Figure 9.10.

Note that defining the array for the cursor in binary numbers provides a visual clue to the cursor shape. The array could have been given as an equivalent set of 16 numbers in any other base.

The noticeable shift in the display of several of the cursors is due to the fact that the magnifyBy: message does not preserve the specified offset for displaying the cursor.

Form and DisplayScreen Example 9A

This example illustrates how forms may be created, how text information may be added to a form, and how forms may be displayed on the screen. In addition, the source code for bordering and printing a portion of the display screen is included. This is the method used to generate most of the figures in the book.

Details of the example are given in Listing 9.11 as the class method example1 in class **Form.** Results of executing the example are given in Figure 9.11.

Listing 9.10
Details of **Cursor**
example1

Cursor class methodsFor: 'examples'

example1
"This example shows the thirteen standard cursors plus one user defined cursor in both normal size and expanded size (by factor of 2)."

```
| myCursor cursors index |
index ← 1.
Display white.
cursors ← self standardCursors.
'The Thirteen Standard Cursor Shapes Plus One User-Defined Cursor' asText allBold
    asDisplayText displayOn: Display at: 20@15.
' CursorName' asText allBold asDisplayText
    displayOn: Display at: 40 @ 45.
' Cursor ' asText allBold asDisplayText
    displayOn: Display at: 380 @ 45.
' Cursor (2:1)' asText allBold asDisplayText
    displayOn: Display at: 480 @ 45.
cursors associationsDo: [ :cursor |
        (cursor key, ' has shape --------> ') asText allBold asDisplayText
            displayOn: Display at: 50 @ (30 + (50*index)).
        cursor value displayOn: Display at: 400 @ (35 + (50*index)).
        (cursor value magnifyBy: 2@2)
            displayOn: Display at: 500 @ (35 + (50*index)).
        index ← index + 1].
myCursor ← Cursor
    extent: 16@16
    fromArray: #(
        2r0000000000000000
        2r0000000110000000
        2r0000111001110000
        2r0011100000011100
        2r1110000000000111
        2r1100000000000011
        2r1100111001110011
        2r1100000000000011
        2r1101000000001011
        2r1100111111110011
        2r0110000110000110
        2r0011100000011100
        2r0000111001110000
        2r0000000110000000
        2r0000000000000000
        2r0000000000000000 )
    offset: 0@0.
('myCursor  has shape --------> ') asText allBold asDisplayText
    displayOn: Display at: 50 @ (30 + (50*14)).
myCursor displayOn: Display at: 400 @ (35 + (50*14)).
(myCursor magnifyBy: 2@2)
    displayOn: Display at: 500 @ (35 + (50*14))

" Cursor example1 "
```

**Figure 9.10
Cursor**
example1—
Standard and
User-Defined
Cursors

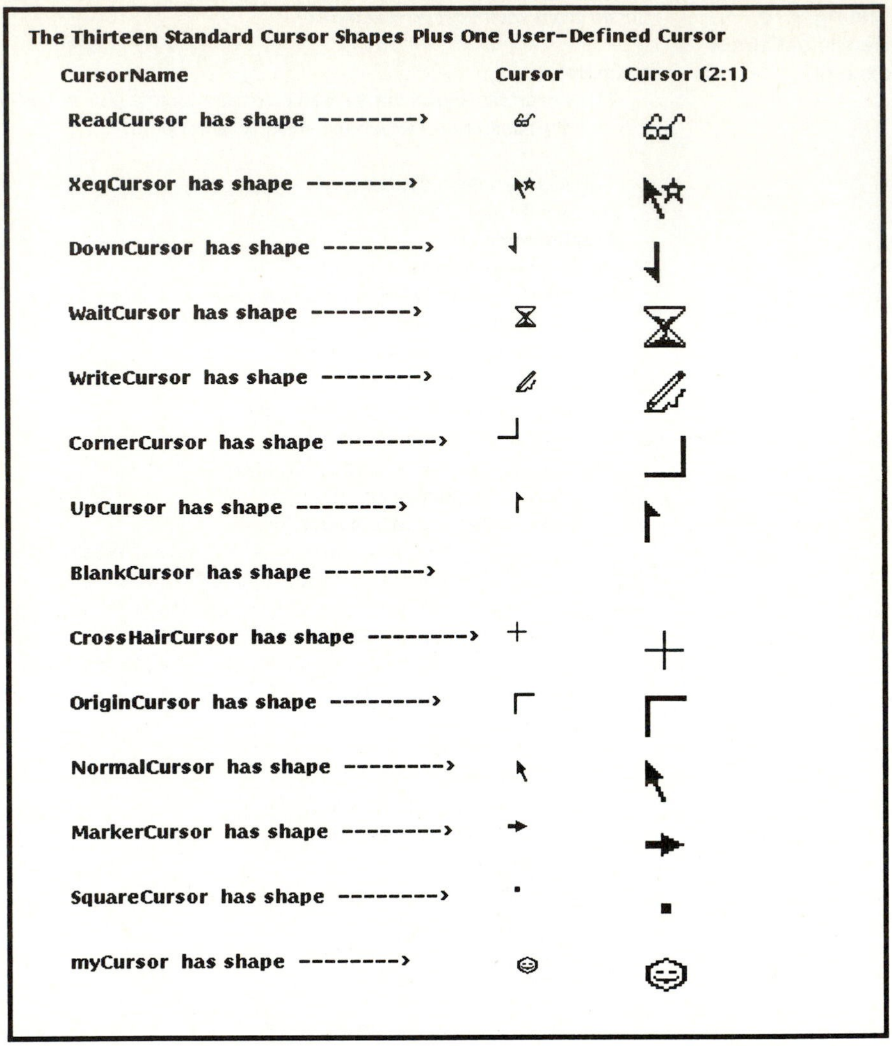

The Thirteen Standard Cursor Shapes Plus One User-Defined Cursor

CursorName	Cursor	Cursor (2:1)
ReadCursor has shape -------->		
XeqCursor has shape -------->		
DownCursor has shape -------->		
WaitCursor has shape -------->		
WriteCursor has shape -------->		
CornerCursor has shape -------->		
UpCursor has shape -------->		
BlankCursor has shape -------->		
CrossHairCursor has shape -------->		
OriginCursor has shape -------->		
NormalCursor has shape -------->		
MarkerCursor has shape -------->		
SquareCursor has shape -------->		
myCursor has shape -------->		

Listing 9.11
Details of **Form**
example1

Form class methodsFor: 'examples'

example1
    "This example illustrates the creation and display of forms."

    | rect form1 form2 form3 |

    rect ← Rectangle origin: 50@50 extent: 590@590.
    form1 ← (Form extent: rect extent) white.

```
'This large white rectangle is form1'
    displayOn: form1 at:  20@20.
(form1 borderWidth: 4)
    displayOn: Display
    at: rect origin
    rule: Form over.

form2 ← Form dotOfSize: 100.
'This is form2'
    displayOn: form2
    at: 20@ form2 height  // 2 - 7.

'Define a rectangular region to be form3'
    displayOn: Display
    at: (rect origin translateBy: 20@40).
form3 ← Form fromUser.
'Select location, click blueButton to display form2 (inverse dot, size 100)'
    displayOn: Display
    at: (rect origin translateBy: 20@60).

[ Sensor blueButtonPressed ] whileFalse: [].
form2 reverse
    displayOn: Display
    at: Sensor cursorPoint rule: Form over.

'This is form3'
    displayOn: form3
    at: 20@20.
'Select location and click redButton for displaying form3 with border.'
    displayOn: Display
    at: (rect origin translateBy: 20@80).
[ Sensor redButtonPressed ] whileFalse: [].
(form3 borderWidth: 1)
    displayOn: Display
    at: Sensor cursorPoint rule: Form over.

'Click yellow button to place border around the display and print.'
    displayOn: Display
    at: (rect origin translateBy: 20@100).
[ Sensor yellowButtonPressed ] whileFalse: [].
Form
    slideBorder: (rect ← 0@0 corner: rect corner + (50@50))
    width: 6.    "Border"
(Form fromDisplay: rect)
    outputToPrinterHor: 150
    offset: 150@130.        "Print"

" Form example1  "
```

Figure 9.11
Form and
DisplayScreen
example1—Form
Creation, Display,
and Printing

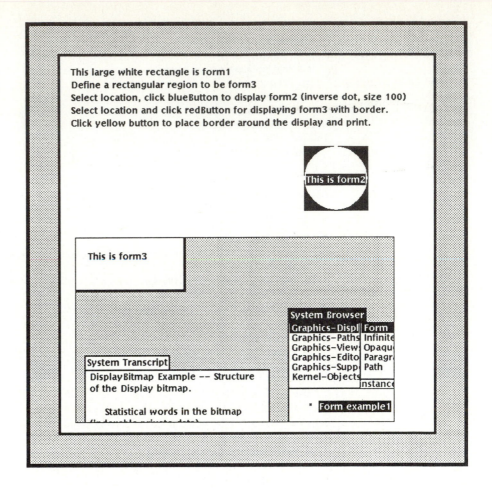

Form Example 9A

This example illustrates the image manipulation protocol that provides rotation and scaling of forms. It shows how forms can be rotated, magnified, reduced, reflected, displayed and printed. Details of the class method **example2** in class **Form** are given in Listing 9.12. Results of the example are given in Figure 9.12.

9.5.2   Classes for displaying text

The classes **DisplayText, Paragraph,** and **TextList** support text display objects. Instances of these classes provide the protocol for displaying text on the screen with emphasis if desired. The display text can be displayed anywhere on the

Listing 9.12
Details of **Form**
example2

Form class methodsFor: 'examples'

example2
    "This example illustrates the manipulation of forms."

    | rect form1 form2 form3 |
    rect ← Rectangle origin: 25@25 extent: 640@750.
    form1 ← (Form extent: rect extent) white.
    'This large white rectangle is form1'
        displayOn: form1 at: 20@20.
    (form1 borderWidth: 4)
        displayOn: Display
        at: rect origin
        rule: Form over.

    'Define a rectangular region to be form3 (size is fixed).'
        displayOn: Display
        at: (rect origin translateBy: 20@40).
    form3 ← Form fromDisplay: (Rectangle originFromUser: 150@100).
    'This is form3 as selected by the user ------> '
        displayOn: Display
        at: (rect origin translateBy: 20@80).
    (form3 borderWidth: 1)
        displayOn: Display
        at: (rect origin translateBy: 370@80)
        rule: Form over.

    'This is form3 rotated by 90 & 270 degrees --> '
        displayOn: Display
        at: (rect origin translateBy: 20@200).
    ((form3 rotateBy: 1) borderWidth: 1)
        displayOn: Display
        at: (rect origin translateBy: 370@200)
        rule: Form over.
    ((form3 rotateBy: 3) borderWidth: 1)
        displayOn: Display
        at: (rect origin translateBy: 500@200)
        rule: Form over.

    'This is form3 reflected vertically about itself -> '
        displayOn: Display
        at: (rect origin translateBy: 20@370).
    ((form3 reflect: 0@1) borderWidth: 1)
        displayOn: Display
        at: (rect origin translateBy: 370@370)
        rule: Form over.
    'This is form3 reflected horizontally -------> '
        displayOn: Display
        at: (rect origin translateBy: 20@490).
    ((form3 reflect: 1@0) borderWidth: 1)
        displayOn: Display
        at: (rect origin translateBy: 370@490)
        rule: Form over.

Listing 9.12
(continued)

```
'This is form3 magnified by 2@1'
    displayOn: Display
    at: (rect origin translateBy: 20@530).
((form3 magnifyBy: 2@1) borderWidth: 1)
    displayOn: Display
    at: (rect origin translateBy: 20@570)
    rule: Form over.

'This is form3 reduced by 1@2'
    displayOn: Display
    at: (rect origin translateBy: 370@610).
((form3 shrinkBy: 1@2) borderWidth: 1)
    displayOn: Display
    at: (rect origin translateBy: 370@650)
    rule: Form over.

'Click yellow button to place border around the display and print.'
    displayOn: Display
    at: (rect origin translateBy: 20@710).

[ Sensor yellowButtonPressed ] whileFalse: [].
Form
    slideBorder: (rect ← 0@0 corner: 690@800)
    width: 6.          "Add Border"
(Form fromDisplay: rect)
    outputToPrinterHor: 150
    offset: 150@130.    "Print"

" Form example2 "
```

screen, or it can be restricted to a specified window. A protocol summary is given for class **DisplayText.**

The display of text in varying fonts with varying emphasis is a complicated process supported by several classes within the Smalltalk image. Simple emphasis requirements such as bold, italic, and underlined are illustrated in other examples for instances of class **Text.** Since control of fonts is a special application area that has little direct impact on object-oriented programming, it is not included in this book.

Protocol Summary for Class **DisplayText**

The hierarchy for class **DisplayText** is **Object—DisplayObject—DisplayText.** Class **DisplayText** has four instance variables, text, textStyle, offset, and form. It has one pool dictionary, **TextConstants.** It has no class variables. It has 3 class methods in one category and 17 instance methods in five categories.

Class **DisplayText** has four instance variables: **text,** an instance of **Text** that is

Figure 9.12
Form and
DisplayScreen
example2—Form
Manipulation and
Display

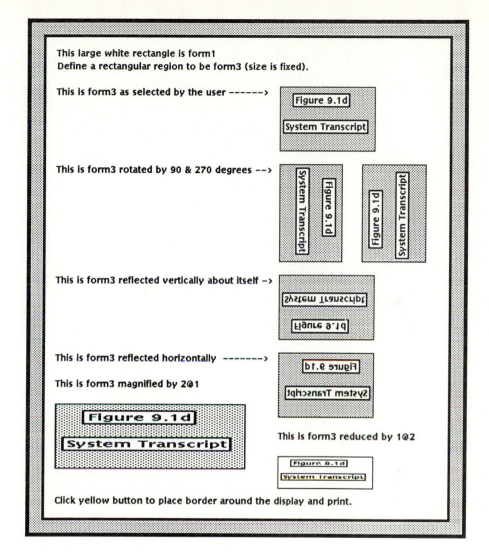

This large white rectangle is form1
Define a rectangular region to be form3 (size is fixed).

This is form3 as selected by the user ------>

Figure 9.1d

System Transcript

This is form3 rotated by 90 & 270 degrees -->

This is form3 reflected vertically about itself ->

This is form3 reflected horizontally ------->

This is form3 magnified by 2@1

Figure 9.1d

System Transcript

This is form3 reduced by 1@2

Click yellow button to place border around the display and print.

the text string to be displayed; **textStyle,** an instance of **TextStyle** that defines all the pertinent features for the font that is the display text; **offset,** an instance of **Point** that defines an offset from a display point for the actual display of the text; and **form,** an instance of **Form** used to cache the display text. It is set to nil in most cases. A value is assigned to this instance variable by sending the message form to the class name **DisplayText.**

Class **DisplayText** has one pool dictionary called **TextConstants** that is an instance of **Dictionary.** It defines defaults for keyboard control sequences, character features, and emphasis.

9.5.3   Classes for displaying lines

The classes **Path, Arc, Curve, Line, LinearFit,** and **Spline** support display objects that represent specific geometric shapes or methods for connecting points. Descriptions and examples are given for objects of these classes. A path is defined by a collection of points. Display protocol copies a specified form to the screen at each point of the path. The form can be any instance of **Form,** providing the mechanism for a wide variety of display effects. The subclasses of **Path** define some of the more commonly used graphics paths.

Path is an abstract superclass of its subclasses that represent specific kinds of paths. Paths are typically defined by an equation. As an abstract class, **Path** has no instances. It defines protocol shared by instances of its subclasses. An abbreviated description of the protocol for **Path** is given below. A more detailed description is in Appendix 3.

Protocol Summary for Class Path

The hierarchy for class **Path** is **Object—DisplayObject—Path.** Class **Path** has two instance variables, form and collectionOfPoints. It has no class variables or pool dictionaries. It has 2 class methods in one category and 27 instance methods in nine categories.

There are two instance variables in class **Path.** The first is **form,** an instance of **Form** that is the display object to be displayed at each point in the path. This instance variable defaults to a 1-pixel black dot unless defined differently by a creation method. The second instance variable is **collectionOfPoints,** an instance of **OrderedCollection** that contains points representing the path. As an ordered collection, points in the path have the order of their insertion. Addition of a new point always occurs at the end of the collection. However, accessing protocol provides the mechanism for changing any point in the collection.

Protocol for adding, removing, and enumerating the points in the collection of a **Path** are provided.

Path (Arcs and Circles) Example 9A

This example illustrates the use of arcs and circles as paths for displaying objects. Details of the example are given in Listing 9.13 as the class method **example1** in class **Circle.** The form used for displaying the center of the circle is a dot of size 5. The form used for drawing the circle is **edgeForm,** a 3-by-3 black square. Results are shown in Figure 9.13.

Note that the message size when sent to circle gives zero for the number of points in the instance variable collectionOfPoints. This is because the protocol for **Circle** does not actually generate a circle. It only displays a circle using the pri-

Listing 9.13
Details of **Circle**
example1

Circle class methodsFor: 'examples'

example1
    "This example shows circles and arcs."

    | circle edgeForm centerForm rect form1 arc |

    rect ← Rectangle origin: 50@200 extent: 500@500.
    form1 ← (Form extent: rect extent) white.
    (form1 borderWidth: 4)
        displayOn: Display
        at: rect origin
        rule: Form over.

    Transcript clear; refresh;
        show: 'Path (Arc & Circle) Example - Arcs and Circles.'; cr; crtab;
        show: 'Find space below for a 150 radius circle.'; crtab.

    centerForm ← Form dotOfSize: 5.
    edgeForm ← Form extent: 3@3.
    edgeForm black.
    circle ← Circle new.
    circle
        form: edgeForm;
        radius: 150;
        center: Sensor waitButton.

    centerForm
        displayOn: Display
        at: circle center.
    circle
        displayOn: Display.

    Transcript
        show: ' The circle contains ', circle size printString, ' points.'; crtab;
        show: ' It''s center is at point --> ', circle center printString; cr; crtab.

    arc ← Arc new.
    arc
        form: edgeForm;
        center: rect corner;
        radius: 120;
        quadrant: 2.
    arc displayOn: Display.
    Transcript
        show: 'The semicircle (Arc) has radius ', arc radius printString,
            ' and center at ', arc center printString.

    "Circle example1."

Figure 9.13
Circle example1—
Circles and Arcs

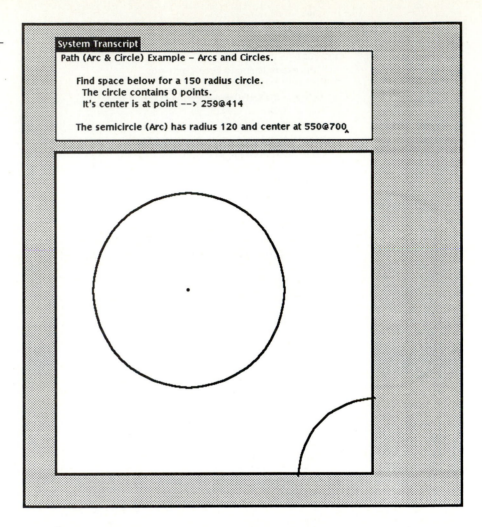

vate data center and radius, from its superclass **Arc.** All the essential details are contained in the instance methods displayOn: at: clippingBox: rule: mask: and displayOn: transformation: clippingBox: rule: mask:.

Path (LinearFit) Example 9B

This example illustrates the use of lines and objects of class **LinearFit** as paths for displaying objects. The example developed for class **Pen** is repeated here. It displays a sin x / x curve using only 13 points and a linear fit algorithm. The **Pen** example used 601 points. Details of the **LinearFit** class method example1 are given in Listing 9.14. The result is shown in Figure 9.14.

Listing 9.14
Details of
LinearFit
example1

LinearFit class methodsFor: 'examples'

example1
"This example shows a linear fit to a set of points."

```
| aLinearFit pathForm axis rect sinc pen |

aLinearFit ← LinearFit new.
pathForm ← Form new extent: 4@4 offset: -2@-2.
pathForm  black.
aLinearFit form: pathForm.
pen ← Pen new sourceForm: (Form dotOfSize: 2).
rect ← Rectangle origin: 50@50 extent: 605@220.
(Form extent: rect extent)
    borderWidth: 2;
    displayOn: Display at: rect origin.

axis ← rect bottomCenter - (0@90).
pen                                  "Draw axes"
    place: rect origin x @ axis y;
    turn: 90;
    go: rect extent x;
    place: rect bottomCenter;
    north;
    go: rect extent y.

-6  to: 6 do: [ :x | x = 0
    ifTrue: [ aLinearFit add: axis - (0 @ 100) ]
    ifFalse: [sinc ←  (x / 2 * Float pi) sin / (x / 2 * Float pi).
        aLinearFit add:  axis + ((x * 50) @ (0-100*sinc)) ] ].
aLinearFit displayOn: Display.
'Path Example Using Linear Fit'
    displayOn: Display
    at: rect origin  + (20@10).
'Linear Fit to 13 Points of sin x / x '
    displayOn: Display
    at: rect origin  + (20@30)
```

"LinearFit example1."

Figure 9.14
LinearFit
example1—Linear
Fit to Sets of Points

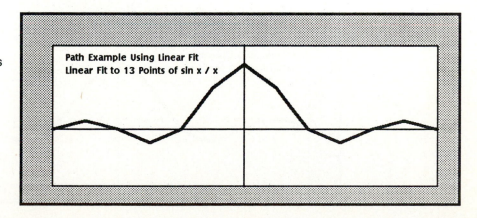

Path Example Using Linear Fit
Linear Fit to 13 Points of sin x / x

Listing 9.15
Details of **Spline**
example1

Spline class methodsFor: 'examples'

example1
   "This example shows a spline fit to a set of points."

```
| aSpline pathForm axis rect sinc pen |
aSpline ← Spline new.
pathForm ← Form new extent: 4@4 offset: -2@-2.
pathForm  black.
aSpline form: pathForm.
pen ← Pen new sourceForm: (Form dotOfSize: 2).
rect ← Rectangle origin: 50@50 extent: 605@220.
(Form extent: rect extent)
    borderWidth: 2;
    displayOn: Display
    at: rect origin.

axis  ← rect bottomCenter - (0@90).
pen place: rect origin x @ axis y;          "Draw axes"
    turn: 90;
    go: rect extent x;
    place: rect bottomCenter;
    north;
    go: rect extent y.

-6  to: 6 do: [ :x | x = 0
    ifTrue: [ aSpline add: axis - (0 @ 100) ]
    ifFalse: [sinc ← (x / 2 * Float pi) sin / (x / 2 * Float pi).
        aSpline add:  axis + ((x * 50) @ (0-100*sinc)) ] ].
aSpline computeCurve.
aSpline displayOn: Display.
'Path Example Using Spline Fit'
    displayOn: Display
    at: rect origin + (20@10).
'Spline Fit to 13 Points of sin x / x '
    displayOn: Display
    at: rect origin + (20@30)

"Spline example1."
```

**Figure 9.15
Spline**
example1—Spline
Fit to Sets of Points

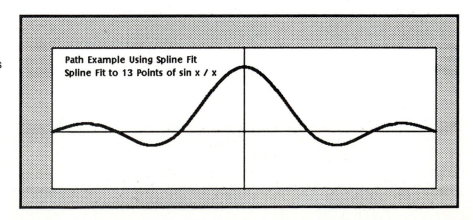

Path (Spline) Example 9C

This example illustrates the use of instances of subclass **Spline** to represent paths. It repeats **Path** Example 9B except that a spline function is used to connect the 13 points of sin x / x. Details are given in Listing 9.15 for the **Spline** class method **example1**. Results are shown in Figure 9.15.

Notice in Listing 9.15 that the spline curve must first be computed from its sample points before displaying. This is accomplished by the expression aSpline computeCurve. The advantage of the spline fit is that it provides a smoother curve with a few data points.

Path (Special Forms) Example 9D

This example illustrates the use of special forms displayed along various paths. The primary difference in this example and other **Path** examples is the use of a more complex form as the image replicated at each point in collectionOfPoints. Listing 9.16 shows details of the class method example1 in **Path.** Results are shown in Figure 9.16.

The method example1 generates a new instance of **Form** from a file called 'man4.form' in directory '/smalltalk/demo/forms/'. As can be seen from the result in

Listing 9.16
Details of **Path**
example1

Path class methodsFor: 'examples'

example1
    "Send an image of toothpaste man along a discrete path."

```
| form path |
form ← Form  readFrom: '/smalltalk/demo/forms/man4.form'.
path ← Path new.
path form: form.
1 to: 10 do: [ :i |  path add: (45*i) @ (500 - (200 * i ln))].
Display white.

path
    displayOn: Display
    at: 0@0
    clippingBox: Display computeBoundingBox
    rule: 7
    mask: Form black.

path form: (Form dotOfSize: 7).
path displayOn: Display at: 0@0 rule: Form over.
'Actual path is dotted curve.'
    displayOn: Display at: 50@50

" Path example1 "
```

Figure 9.16
Path example1—
Drawing with
Complex Forms

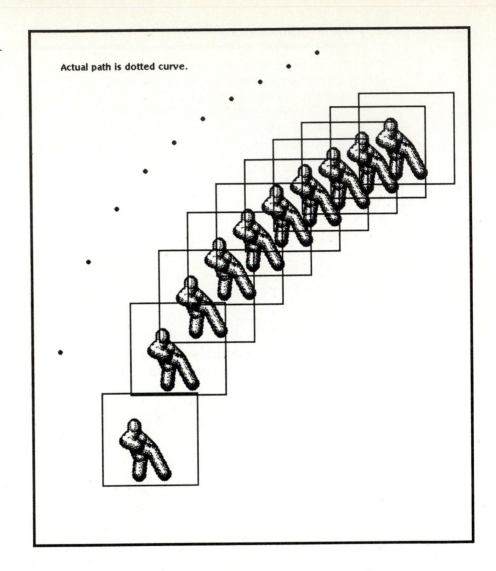

Figure 9.16, the form has an offset of approximately 75@75 from the path point. This is a feature of the form as it is stored in file 'man4.form'. The display of the complex form is done using an OR rule (code 7).

9.6   The Model-View-Controller Triad

Any window on the Smalltalk screen has three essential components associated with it, the *model, view,* and *controller.* Together, these three components are called the model-view-controller (MVC) triad. Any subview within a window can have an MVC triad that is different from its superview or other subviews. Some views are noninteractive, meaning they never have a need for acquiring control. For consistency with the MVC concept, these views have a controller that is an instance of class **NoController.**

The functions of the three components of the MVC triad and their properties are first described in Section 9.6.1. In Section 9.6.2, summaries are given for the abstract superclasses **View** and **Controller.** Finally, three examples are given that illustrate the MVC concept. The first example (in Section 9.6.3) uses an existing MVC triad in the Smalltalk system that is relatively simple. The second example (in Section 9.6.4) creates a new (and even simpler) MVC triad. A detailed discussion of what actually happens when this MVC application is invoked is given in Section 9.6.5. The third example illustrates the use of a valuable tool for investigating the properties of any MVC triad. Opening an inspector on a MVC triad is discussed in Section 9.6.6.

9.6.1   Interaction of model, view, and controller

The three components of the MVC triad have the following functionality and properties:

- *model*—an object that represents the data to be displayed. The model can be an instance of any appropriate class that represents the data most efficiently. For simplicity and elimination of extensive new protocol for all classes that can serve as models, the protocol of the model has no internal reference to its view or controller. Since the model contains information relative to the amount of data to be displayed in a view, it is often desirable to add a method for computing a bounding box to the model protocol.

- *view*—an object that is the visual display of the data represented by the model. Protocol in the view subclass determines how the data are to be displayed. Keeping the MVC triad together as a family with consistent information is the primary responsibility of the view. Private data within the view protocol are used to connect the view with its model and controller. A view consists of a top view and zero or more subviews. In many cases the top view is an instance of **StandardSystemView.** This has the advantage of providing the standard blue button menu options for collapsing, framing, moving, etc., for the new view. There are a number of key methods in **View** that need to be redefined in a new subclass of **View.** These include displayView, defaultWindow, and defaultControllerClass.

- *controller*—an object that provides the protocol for user interaction with the view and its model. Protocol in the controller subclass provides menus and action messages for the view and its model. Private data within the controller protocol are used to connect the controller with its model and view. The controller maintains an interface with the controller manager for coordination with other active controllers. In most cases control is acquired through positioning of the cursor in combination with pressing or clicking the mouse buttons. Therefore, most controller classes are subclasses of **MouseMenuController,** which is a direct subclass of the superclass of all controllers, **Controller** (see Figure 9.1). Key methods in **Controller** that need redefinition in most subclasses include initialize-YellowButtonMenu, isControlActive, controlInitialize, and controlTerminate.

The basic sequence of events for the operation of MVC triads is given below. The steps outlined here are general in nature. More detailed explanations for the exact steps required to invoke an MVC application are given in Section 9.6.5.

1. New MVC applications are invoked with instance creation methods in the view class of the application. Sending one of these methods to the view class causes creation of the view, display of the model, and passage of control to the controller for the application. There are key methods in the view and controller class hierarchy that are part of this process. A more detailed discussion of these key methods is given in Section 9.6.5 for the histogram MVC example presented in Section 9.6.4.

2. When a new MVC triad is created, its controller is added to a list of scheduled controllers. This list is an instance variable, scheduledControllers, in class **ControlManager.** The global variable **ScheduledControllers** is the single instance of **ControlManager.** Protocol in **ControlManager** provides capability for accessing, scheduling, and modifying any controller in the list of scheduled controllers. This is accomplished by sending appropriate messages to **ScheduledControllers**

3. **ScheduledControllers,** the global instance of **ControlManager,** constantly monitors the position of the cursor and the state of the mouse buttons. When the cursor is moved within a view and a button is clicked, **ScheduledControllers** gives control to the controller for that view. The controller for the view is established as the value of another instance variable, activeController, in the control manager.

4. When a controller becomes the active controller, it receives the following sequence of messages from the startup message to activeController.

```
self controlInitialize.
self controlLoop.
self controlTerminate.
```

The active controller retains control and stays in the controlLoop until it relinquishes control. Of course, the user can move the cursor to another view and click a mouse button to terminate and change the active controller. Control can also be terminated by pressing certain special keys on the keyboard. The details of the controlLoop message are

```
controlLoop
        self isControlActive whileTrue: [
                Processor yield. self controlActivity].
```

The message controlActivity has method details that define specifically what the controller does. It is redefined for specific controller subclasses to reflect the actions that are possible when that controller is active. An example of the details of controlActivity is given for the System Transcript window in MVC Example 9A later in this section. The object **Processor** is the only instance of class **ProcessorScheduler.** It coordinates the use of the physical processor by all processes requiring service. The message yield sent to **Processor** gives other processes at the same priority a chance to run.

Without the support for polymorphic redefinition of the message selectors controlInitialize, isControlActive, controlActivity, and controlTerminate, the protocol for the controller classes would be many times more difficult to understand. The method controlLoop, is typically not redefined by subclasses.

5. When a new controller becomes active, it initiates a control sequence that varies with the kind of controller. Details of the control sequence are contained in the methods controlInitialize, isControlActive, controlActivity, and controlTerminate for each controller subclass. It typically polls the sensor for user input and prompts the view to update itself and the model. The active controller can pass control back to the control manager, back to the controller from which it gained control, or to a new MVC controller based on a user-selected menu option.

6. The message display sent to a view causes the following sequence of messages to be sent.

```
self displayBorder.
self displayView.
self displaySubViews.
self noSelectionSelected.
```

This message, display, is sent by any action that requires updating of the view, including the *restore display* option on the main system menu. The view and all its subviews are redisplayed with updated model information, by displaying the border first, followed by the top view and its subviews. The last message shows no selection in the updated view (i.e., text that was reverse videoed is not).

9.6.2   Protocol summaries for **View** and **Controller**

View is an abstract superclass of all views. It defines protocol for use by instances of its subclasses. This class is one of the largest in the Smalltalk system, with over a hundred methods. A detailed description of the protocol for class **View** is given below.

Protocol Summary for Class View

Definition—The hierarchy for class **View** is **Object—View.** Class **View** has 14 instance variables, model, controller, superView, subViews, transformation, viewport, window, displayTransformation, insetDisplayBox, borderWidth, borderColor, insideColor, boundingBox, and selectionSelected. It has no class variables or pool dictionaries. It has 2 class methods in 1 category and 114 instance methods in 26 categories.

Private data—Class **View** has 14 instance variables.

model—an instance of any class that represents data to be presented graphically in a view on the screen.

controller—an instance of one of the **Controller** subclasses, an instance of a special class called **NoControllerAllowed,** or nil. The controller manages interaction between the user and a view.

superView—an instance of one of the **View** subclasses, or nil. The superview is the dominant view within a complex view.

subViews—an instance of **OrderedCollection** that contains a collection of instances of one of the **View** subclasses. These subviews are part of the current **View** instance.

transformation—an instance of **WindowingTransformation** that provides scaling and translation of objects from a source view to a destination view. This instance variable describes how objects are to be scaled or translated for display in the current view.

viewport—an instance of **Rectangle** that defines the viewing port of the super view, or nil.

window—an instance of **Rectangle** in view coordinates, or nil.

displayTransformation—an instance of **WindowingTransformation,** or nil.

insetDisplayBox—an instance of **Rectangle** in display screen coordinates, or nil.

borderWidth—an instance of **Rectangle** in display screen units, or zero (meaning no border). This parameter specifies a border for the view.

borderColor—an instance of **Form** that defines the color of the border rectangle.

insideColor—an instance of **Form** that specifies the inside color for the view, or nil (meaning transparent).

boundingBox—an instance of **Rectangle** in view coordinates, or nil.

selectionSelected—an instance of **Boolean.** A value of true means the corresponding **windowForm** (for a **StandardSystemView**) was saved with the selection.

Instance methods—Class **View** has 114 instance methods in 26 categories. A summary is given below of the categories and methods.

initialize-release—two methods (**initialize, release**) that initialize the view and release the view and its subviews from its model's list of dependents, respectively. The method **initialize** sets the instance variable **subViews** to an empty ordered collection, **transformation** to scale of 1.0 and translation of 0.0, **borderWidth** to zero, and **borderColor** to black. Both methods are inherited from **Object** and redefined.

testing—one method (**containsPoint:**) that is new protocol and answers true if the parameter point is within the view's display box.

model access—two methods (**model, model:**) that answer or set the view's model. Both are new protocol.

superView access—four methods (**isTopView, resetSubViews, superView, topView**) for testing if a particular view is a top view, for accessing the superview or topview of a view, and for setting the collection of subviews to an empty collection. All four methods are new protocol.

subView access—four methods (**firstSubView, lastSubView, subViewContaining, subviews**) for returning the first, last, or all subviews of the receiver or for returning the first subview that contains a specified point. All methods are new protocol.

controller access—five methods (**controller, controller:, defaultController, defaultControllerClass, model: controller:**) for accessing and setting the controller for the receiver view. One method, model: controller:, also sets the model for the view. All five methods are new protocol.

basic control sequence—one method (**subViewWantingControl**) that answers the first subview in the ordered collection of subviews that wants control. The subviews are queried in a reverse order, from lowest level to highest. This method is new protocol.

window access—four methods (**defaultWindow, insetWindow, window, window:**) for accessing the instance variable window and its features, as well as setting its value. All methods are new protocol.

viewport access—one method (**viewport**) that returns a copy of the instance's viewport. This method is new protocol.

display box access—four methods (**boundingBox, computeBoundingBox, displayBox, insetDisplayBox**) for accessing information about the display rectangular region represented by the view. All methods are new protocol in this hierarchical chain.

lock access—four methods (**isLocked, isUnlocked, lock, unlock**) that answer the status of the view and change the status. A view is unlocked if its instance variables displayTransformation and insetDisplayBox are both nil. These methods are new protocol.

subView inserting—twelve methods (**addSubView:, addSubView: above, addSubView: align: with:, addSubView: below:, addSubView: ifCyclic:, addSubView: in: borderWidth:, addSubView: toLeftOf:, addSubView: toRightOf:, addSubView: viewport:, addSubView: window: viewport:, insertSubView: above:, insertSubView: before: ifCyclic:**) for adding subviews to a view. All 12 are new protocol.

subView removing—five methods (**releaseSubView:, releaseSubViews, removeFromSuperView, removeSubView:, removeSubViews**) for removing and releasing a specified subview or all subviews. These methods are new protocol.

displaying—ten methods (**display, display:, displayAfterMove:, displayBorder, displaySubViews, displaySubViews:, displayView, displayView:, inspect, restore:**) for displaying a view and its subviews or inspecting the view's MVC triad. The method inspect is inherited from **Object** and redefined. The other nine methods are new protocol.

selection access—five methods (**isSelectionSelected, noSelectionSelected, saveSelection, selectionIsSelected, setSelection:**) for setting or accessing the instance variable selectionSelected and for saving a selection. All methods are new protocol.

deEmphasizing—nine methods (**deEmphasize, deEmphasize: andClip:, deEmphasizeSubViews, deEmphasizeSubViews: andClip:, deEmphasizeView, deEmphasizeView: andClip:, emphasize, emphasizeSubViews, emphasizeView**) for changing the emphasis of a view. This action is used to indicate whether a view is active or not. All methods are new protocol.

display transformation—three methods (**displayTransform:, displayTransformation, inverseDisplayTransform:**) for transforming between display coordinates and the receiver's coordinates. All are new protocol.

transforming—eight methods (**align: with:, scale: translation:, scaleBy:, transform:, transformation, transformation:, translateBy:, window: viewport:**) for transforming (scaling, translating, coordinate system) of the view. All these methods are new protocol.

bordering—seven methods (**borderColor, borderColor:, borderWidth, borderWidth:, borderWidthLeft: right: top: bottom:, insideColor, insideColor:**) for accessing or setting values for the border width, border color, and inside color of the view. All methods are new protocol.

scrolling—two methods (**repaintScrollBar, scrollBy:**) for scrolling by a specified amount in the x- or y-directions and for resetting the scroll bar of the view. Both are new protocol.

clearing—four methods (**clear, clear:, clearInside, clearInside:**), all new protocol, for repainting the view or its inside display box, using default or specified colors.

indicating—three methods (**flash, highlight, highlightAndClip:**) for either flashing the view or inverse videoing its inset display box. All three are new protocol.

updating—two methods (**update, update:**) that are normally implemented by the receiver's model specifying an action to be taken when there is a change in the view. These methods are new protocol.

user interface—two methods (**emphasizedDisplayForm, emphasizedDisplayForm:**) that return either false or the receiver. These are new do-nothing messages. No existing methods in the system send these messages.

private—nine methods (**computeDisplayTransformation, computeInsetDisplayBox, getController, getViewport, getWindow, isCyclic:, setTransformation:, setWindow:, superView:**) used by other methods in class **View.**

text style—one method (**textStyle:**) that sets the text style for all the subviews of the view. This method is new protocol.

Class methods—Class **View** has two class methods in one category. A summary is given below of the categories and the methods.

instance creation—two methods (**identityTransformation, new**) that are used to create instances of class **View.** The method **new** is inherited from **Behavior** and redefined. The other method is new protocol.

Controller is an abstract superclass of all controllers. Its protocol summary follows.

Protocol Summary for Class **Controller**

Definition—The hierarchy for class **Controller** is **Object—Controller.** Class **Controller** has three instance variables, model, view, and sensor. It has no class variables or pool dictionaries. It has 1 class method in one category and 18 instance methods in seven categories.

Private data—Class **Controller** has three instance variables.

model—any object that represents the model for this particular MVC triad. The value of model is established by protocol in the **View** subclass for this MVC triad.

view—an instance of one of the **View** subclasses, representing the view for this controller. The value of view is established by protocol from the appropriate view subclass of an MVC triad.

sensor—an instance of **InputSensor** whose value is initialized to the default (global variable sensor).

Instance methods—Class **Controller** has 18 instance methods in seven categories. A summary is given below of the categories and methods.

initialize-release—two methods (**initialize, release**) that set the default value for the private data sensor and break the cycle between a controller and its view. Both are inherited from **Object** and redefined.

model access—two methods (**model, model:**) for answering or setting the model for this controller. Both are new protocol.

view access—two methods (**view, view:**) for answering or setting the view for this controller. Both are new protocol.

sensor access—two methods (**sensor, sensor:**) for answering or setting the sensor for this controller. Both are new protocol.

basic control sequence—four methods (**controlInitialize, controlLoop, controlTerminate, startup**) that give control to the receiver, maintain a control loop, and give control back to the sender of the message startup when finished. All three methods are new protocol.

control defaults—four methods (**controlActivity, controlToNextLevel, isControlActive, isControlWanted**) that handle the passing of control to other controllers. All four are new protocol.

cursor—two methods (**centerCursorInView, viewHasCursor**) that center the cursor in the view of the receiver or answer true if the cursor is within that view. Both are new protocol.

Class methods—Class **Controller** has one class method in one category, as summarized below.

instance creation—One method (**new**) is inherited from **Behavior** and redefined.

9.6.3   Example of an existing MVC triad in the Smalltalk image

This example illustrates the protocol of a relatively simple MVC triad that is part of the Smalltalk system. It illustrates the MVC triad for the System Transcript window, which is an instance of class **TextCollector.** It is relatively simple because it has only one subview. Its top view is an instance of **StandardSystemView,** whose controller is an instance of **StandardSystemController.** As a collector of text, it has a yellow-button menu that includes the standard text editing options (cut, paste, copy, and so forth). Since its top view is a standard system view, it has the standard blue-button menu options shared by all standard system views. The controllers for this window must be able to intercept and handle the menus for the yellow and blue buttons.

MVC Example 9A

The three components of this MVC triad are described below:

Model—Defined by protocol in class **TextCollector.** The model is the global variable **Transcript,** an instance of **TextCollector.** The hierarchy chain for **TextCollector** is **Object—StringHolder—TextCollector.** Basically a text collector is a model for holding structured string infomation (the role of a string holder) with the ability to add contents using stream protocol. It is simply a collector of text.

View—Defined by protocol in class **TextCollectorView.** The view for this example is an instance of **TextCollectorView.** The hierarchy chain is **Object—View—StringHolderView—TextCollectorView.** Thus the view for the Transcript window inherits all the protocol from **View** (recall it has over 100 methods) and from **StringHolderView.** It is the responsibility of the text collector view to display information contained in the text collector and to maintain communication between the model and controller. The top view for this example is an instance of **StandardSystemView.**

Controller—Defined by protocol in class **TextCollectorController.** The controller for this example is an instance of **TextCollectorController.** The hierarchy chain for this class is **Object—Controller—MouseMenuController—Scroll-**

Controller — ParagraphEditor — StringHolderController — TextCollector Controller. Class **TextCollectorController** has only four instance methods, so it appears to be very simple. It inherits most of its active protocol from its superclasses. For example, the yellow-button menu and messages are inherited from class **StringHolderController,** and the blue-button menu and messages are provided in class **StandardSystemController** (the controller for the top view of the Transcript window).

The message controlActivity for the Transcript window is inherited by its controller from a superclass, **ParagraphEditor.** Details of the method represented by this message are given below. This method gives the details of acceptable activity while the **TextCollectorController** is active.

ParagraphEditor methodsFor 'control defaults'
controlActivity
             self scrollBarContainsCursor
                      ifTrue: [self scroll]
                      ifFalse: [self processKeyboard.
                               self processMouseButtons]

The control activities consist of three possible options, *scrolling, processing the keyboard inputs,* or *processing the mouse buttons when pressed or clicked.* The text collector controller stays in this loop until it is no longer the active controller. It typically gives up control temporarily when the yellow-button menu options *do it* or *print it* are selected. It gives up control on a more permanent basis when the user selects a different window on the screen.

If, for example, the user presses the yellow button, then processMouse-Buttons first determines that the yellow button was pressed and prompts the view to display the yellow-button menu on the screen. Once the user has selected a menu option, that option is executed. Depending on the details of the option, the view is prompted to update itself and the model. Listing 9.17 gives details of the method update: in class **TextCollectorView.** It shows the three updating actions required for the Transcript window. All three instruct the controller to take appropriate actions. The controller updates the model and causes the view to re-display itself with updated model information. Yes, it is somewhat of a circle.

Figure 9.17 shows additional details about the Transcript MVC triad using a tool that is explained in more detail in MVC Example 9C in Section 9.6.6. For each component, details are shown of the private data (of the class and all its superclasses). The view shown defaults to the top view (for the Transcript window, the top view is a standard system view) and its controller (a standard system controller). The instance variable subViews list all the subviews for the view. Note in the figure that the Transcript window has only one subview, an instance

Listing 9.17
Details of
TextCollectorView
Method update:

TextCollectorView methodsFor: 'updating'

```
update: aParameter
    self topView isCollapsed ifTrue: [model appendEntry].
    (self controller isKindOf: TextCollectorController)
        ifTrue:
            [aParameter = = #appendEntry
                ifTrue: [↑controller appendEntry].
            aParameter = = #update
                ifTrue: [↑controller changeText: model contents asText].
            aParameter = = #refresh
                ifTrue:  [↑controller viewToTop]]
```

Figure 9.17
Inspecting the
MVC Triad—
Inspector on a
System Transcript
Window

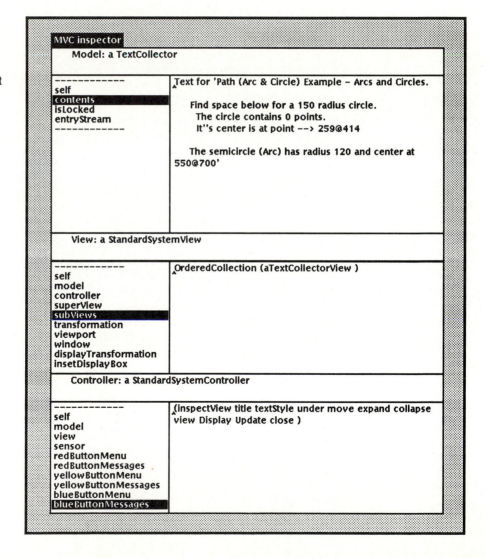

of **TextCollectorView.** The controller description has no way of accessing the subview controller.

MVC Example 9A has sought to provide an overview of the workings of one of the system MVC triads. It is rather intricately interwoven with many of the system subclasses. The next example is a new MVC triad that is made as simple as possible to show what functions each component of the MVC triad is to perform.

9.6.4   A new and simple MVC triad example

The following example illustrates protocol for a new and simple MVC triad for displaying a histogram, with various display options as menu selections in the display window. A new class, **Histogram,** is added as a subclass of **Dictionary.** (Recall that an instance of **Dictionary** was used to generate a histogram of occurrences of letters in a text file in Chapter 7.) Most of the details of the model are the inherited protocol for any object of class **Dictionary.** Two more new classes, **HistogramView** and **HistogramController,** are added to represent the view and controller for this example. Details of all three new classes are given in Listings 9.18, 9.19, and 9.20. Figure 9.18 shows results of using the histogram MVC triad to display a histogram.

Listing 9.18
Protocol
Description for
Class **Histogram**

```
Dictionary variableSubclass: #Histogram
    instanceVariableNames: ''
    classVariableNames: ''
    poolDictionaries: ''
    category: 'Histogram-MVCExample'
```

Histogram comment: ''

Histogram methodsFor: 'measurement'

boundingBox
    "Compute the minimum rectangle that will hold the histogram.
        Assumes barWidth = 2 and barSpacing = 1."
    ↑Rectangle origin: 0@0 extent: (self size * (2 + 1) @ self maxValue)

maxValue
    "Answer the maximum value in the histogram."
    | max |
    max ← 0.
    self associationsDo: [:assoc | max ← max max: assoc value].
    ↑max

Listing 9.19
Protocol
Description
for Class
HistogramView

View subclass: #HistogramView
instanceVariableNames: 'barWidth barSpacing '
classVariableNames: ''
poolDictionaries: ''
category: 'Histogram-MVCExample'

HistogramView comment: 'I display histograms as bar charts. The bar width is specifiable or defaults to DefaultBar. Default spacing between bars is 10 pixels. Labeling can be added as menu option. Display size can be rescaled as user option.

Default bar size is a Quadrangle of width 10 pixels, inside color veryLightGray, and a 1-pixel black border, height = 1. Must scale to get actual bar for display'

HistogramView methodsFor: 'window access'

defaultWindow
"Answer the minimum bounding rectangle for the histogram display."
| rect |
rect ← model boundingBox.
rect ← Rectangle
origin: rect origin
extent: rect extent * ((barWidth + barSpacing / 3) @ 1).
↑ rect expandBy: 50

HistogramView methodsFor: 'controller access'

defaultControllerClass

^HistogramController

HistogramView methodsFor: 'displaying'

addLabels
"Add key/values as labels on the histogram, using scale factors."
| maxValue ticPos ticForm origin |
origin ← (self displayTransform: self window bottomLeft) rounded.
ticForm ← (Form new extent: 10@3) black.
maxValue ← model maxValue.
ticPos ← origin + (75@-50) - (15@maxValue).
ticForm
displayOn: Display
at: ticPos - (0@1). "Center the tics on the vertical axis."
'1.0' displayOn: Display at: ticPos - (30@7).
'Maximum value is ', maxValue printString
displayOn: Display
at: ticPos - (30@35).

```
    1 to: 2 do: [ :i |
        ticPos ← ticPos + (0@(0.5 * maxValue)).
        ticForm displayOn: Display at: ticPos - (0@1).
        (1.0 - (0.5*i)) printString
            displayOn: Display
            at: ticPos - (30@7)].
        model associationsDo: [ : assoc |
        (String with: assoc key)
            displayOn: Display
            at: origin + (75@-40) + ((assoc key asciiValue - 97)
                * (barWidth + barSpacing) @0)]
```

displayView
```
    "Display a filled rectangle for each key in the histogram."
    | height origin |
    origin ← (self displayTransform: self window bottomLeft) rounded.
    model associationsDo: [ :assoc |
        height ← assoc value rounded.
        (Quadrangle region: (0@0 extent: barWidth@height)
            borderWidth: ((barWidth*0.1) max: 1)
            borderColor: Form black
            insideColor: Form veryLightGray)
            displayOn: Display
            at: origin + (75@-50) + ((assoc key asciiValue - 97)
                * (barWidth + barSpacing) @ (0-height))].
```

HistogramView methodsFor: 'private'

setBarParams
```
    barWidth ← 15.
    barSpacing ← 5
```

HistogramView class
    instanceVariableNames: "

HistogramView class comment: "

HistogramView class methodsFor: 'examples'

example1
```
    "This example creates a view on a histogram."
    | sourceFile key histogram |
    "Open file for read only and build histogram as a Dictionary of Associations."
    sourceFile ← FileStream oldFileNamed: '/safe/fileIn/project1.st'.
    histogram ← Histogram new: 26.
    1 to: 26 do: [ :i |
        histogram add: (Association key: (i + 96) asCharacter value: 0)].
```

Listing 9.19
(continued)

```
[sourceFile atEnd] whileFalse:[
    (key ← sourceFile next) isLetter ifTrue: [
        histogram at: (key ← key asLowercase) put: (histogram at: key) + 1] ].
HistogramView openOn: histogram

"  HistogramView example1  "
```

HistogramView class methodsFor: 'instance creation'

```
openOn: aHistogram
    "Create and schedule a view of aHistogram."
    | topView histogramView |
    histogramView ← self new
        setBarParams;
        model: aHistogram;
        borderWidth: 2;
        insideColor: Form white.
    topView ← (StandardSystemView
        model: aHistogram
        label: 'Histogram Plot'
        minimumSize:  histogramView defaultWindow extent)
        addSubView: histogramView.
    topView controller open
```

Listing 9.20
Protocol
Description
for Class
**Histogram-
Controller**

```
MouseMenuController subclass: #HistogramController
    instanceVariableNames: ''
    classVariableNames: 'HistogramYellowButtonMenu HistogramYellowButtonMessages '
    poolDictionaries: ''
    category: 'Histogram-MVCExample'
```

HistogramController comment: ''

HistogramController methodsFor: 'menu messages'

```
addLabels
    "Add labels to the histogram"
    view addLabels

toPrinter
    "Send the histogram to the printer, scaled so one screen fills a page."
    Cursor execute showWhile: [
        (Form fromDisplay: (view topView displayBox expandBy: 30))
            outputToPrinterHor: 150
            offset: 150@130]
```

HistogramController methodsFor: 'control defaults'

isControlActive
↑ super isControlActive & sensor blueButtonPressed not

HistogramController methodsFor: 'private'

initializeYellowButtonMenu
self yellowButtonMenu: HistogramYellowButtonMenu
yellowButtonMessages: HistogramYellowButtonMessages.

HistogramController methodsFor: 'initialize'

initialize
super initialize.
self initializeYellowButtonMenu

HistogramController class
instanceVariableNames: ''

HistogramController class comment: ''

HistogramController class methodsFor: 'class initialization'

initialize
"Initialize the menu for the mouse yellow button."
HistogramYellowButtonMenu ←
PopUpMenu
labels: 'add labels\to printer' withCRs
lines: #(1).
HistogramYellowButtonMessages ← #(addLabels toPrinter)

"HistogramController initialize"

Figure 9.18
MVC Histogram
Example

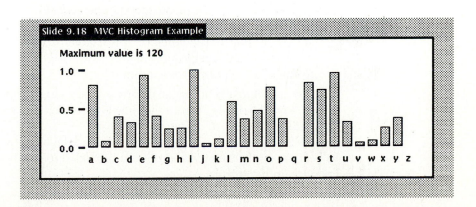

MVC Example 9B

A summary of the protocol and its functionality are given below for the model, view, and controller of a simple MVC triad for displaying a histogram.

Model—Two new instance methods are added. The first, **boundingBox**, computes and returns the minimum-size rectangle that will hold a display of the histogram. The size is based on an assumed mimimal display pattern using bars of width 2 and spacing between bars of width 1 pixel. These values can be scaled by the view protocol that does the actual display. The second method, **maxValue**, simply returns the maximum value in the histogram.

View—The class **HistogramView** is a subclass of **View.** Some of the methods included in this new class are required and expected to be there. If they are not, then defaults are assigned that do not correctly represent the histogram view. For example, the methods **defaultWindow**, **defaultControllerClass**, and **displayView** are required. They define the default minimum window size for the view, the default controller for the view, and the details for displaying a histogram, respectively. These messages are sent by controller and view superclasses, and they are expected to be redefined in every view subclass.

Other protocol in the view class includes messages for displaying labels on the histogram (**addLabels**), setting new values for the bar width and spacing (**setBarParams**), creating an instance of **HistogramView** (**openOn:**), and an example (**example1**) that uses this MVC triad. Note that the top view is a standard system view. Thus it can be framed, moved, retitled, closed, and modified using other standard blue-button menu actions.

Controller—The controller is a subclass of **MouseMenuController,** since the histogram MVC triad is to provide user interaction. Two yellow-button menu options (*add labels, to printer*) are included for additional processing of the MVC triad. The controller subclass must redefine any options or functions that are different from those inherited from its superclass. Specifically, new protocol is added (class method **initialize**, instance methods **initialize**, **initializeYellowButtonMenu**, **isControlActive**) to make the new yellow-button menu effective and to define when the controller is to be active.

Two other methods (**addLabels**, **toPrinter**) define actions to be taken for the two yellow-button menu options. The **addLabels** option passes responsibility to the view for displaying labels. The **toPrinter** option does not involve any display functions; therefore, it is handled completely by the controller method. Its only interaction with the view is to retrieve the rectangular box from the screen that is to be printed.

The title bar of the histogram display is modified using the blue-button menu option *title*. The display box for the view is expanded by a border of 30 pixels in the method **toPrinter**, to include the title bar.

Other functions can be added to this example; however, the goal has been to keep it simple. New capabilities can be added to this basic MVC triad as an exercise for the reader.

9.6.5   Invoking MVC applications—what really happens

With the aid of MVC Example 9B it is possible to provide a more detailed discussion of the sequence of events that take place when an MVC application is activated. Details of selected methods are presented below that describe the sequence of events for the histogram MVC example.

Look for a moment at the details of class method **example1** in class **HistogramView.** The temporary variable **histogram** is established as a dictionary of associations that contains the actual histogram key/value pairs. Most of the method details are involved with this operation. The last executable expression in the method,

HistogramView openOn: histogram

invokes the MVC triad. The message **openOn:** is an instance creation message sent to class **HistogramView.**

Method **openOn:** first creates an instance of **HistogramView** with the expression **histogramView ← self new.** This newly created instance is next sent four instance messages to set bar parameters, establish a model, set the width of its display border, and set its inside color to white.

The second action by method **openOn:** is to define a top view as a standard system view. This is accomplished with the expression

topView ← (StandardSystemView
        model: aHistogram
        label: 'Histogram Plot'
        minimumSize: histogramView defaultWindow extent)

Next **histogramView** is added as a subview of this newly created top view. At this point a standard system view has been defined with a subview that is an instance of **HistogramView.** The model is established as the parameter aHistogram.

The third and final action by method **openOn:** is to pass control to the controller for the top view. Since the top view is a standard system controller, details of message **open** are found in class **StandardSystemController.** The method for **open** is shown in Listing 9.21.

The first expression in method **open** invokes the **controlTerminate** message of the currently active controller. This allows that controller to perform any cleanup or save operations it deems necessary before relinquishing control. The second expression sets the instance variable **activeController** in class **Control-**

Listing 9.21
Protocol for
Method open
in Class
**StandardSystem-
Controller**

StandardSystemController methodsFor: 'scheduling'

open
    "Terminate the currently active controller and open a window for the receiver of this
        message. "
    ScheduledControllers activeController controlTerminate.
    ScheduledControllers noActiveController.
    self realOpen.

Listing 9.22
Protocol for
Method realOpen
in Class
**StandardSystem-
Controller**

StandardSystemController methodsFor: 'scheduling'

realOpen
"Create an area on the screen in which the receiver's scheduled controller can be
    displayed. Make it the active controller."
view resize.
status ← #open.
ScheduledControllers scheduleActive: self

Listing 9.23
Protocol for
Method
scheduleActive:
in Class
ControlManager

ControlManager methodsFor: 'scheduling'

scheduleActive: aController
"Make aController be scheduled as the active controller. Presumably the active
    scheduling process asked to schedule this controller and that a new process
    associated this controller takes control. So this is the last act of the active scheduling
    process."
Cursor normal show.
self scheduleActiveNoTerminate: aController.
Processor terminateActive

Manager to nil (**ScheduledControllers** is the only instance of class **Control-
Manager**). The last expression in open actually opens the new controller (thus it
is called realOpen).

Details of method realOpen in class **StandardSystemController** are shown in
Listing 9.22. The expression view resize sends the message getFrame, which
prompts the user to define a rectangle for displaying the view. It computes defaults for minimum size and needed transformations for display in the user-
selected window. Instance variable status is set to #open. The last expression,
ScheduledControllers scheduleActive: self, invokes the message scheduleActive: in
class **ControlManager.** Details of this method are given in Listing 9.23.

The method scheduleActive: first sets the cursor to normal and then sends
itself (**ScheduledControllers**) the message scheduleActiveNoTerminate: with the
current controller as a parameter. Note that the current controller has not yet
been made the active controller. That is accomplished in messages sent by
method scheduleActiveNoTerminate:. The last expression in method schedule-
Active: (Listing 9.23) is not executed until the current controller relinquishes
control.

Listing 9.24 gives details of the **ControlManager** method scheduleActiveNo-
Terminate:. The expression self schedulePassive: aController establishes the current controller as the first one in an ordered collection of controllers. It is still
not activated. The second expression, self scheduled: aController from: Processor
activeProcess, actually passes control from the currently active process (the result of Processor activeProcess) to the current controller. Details of how this is
done are given in the method scheduled: from: in Listing 9.25.

The method scheduled: from: in class **ControlManager** first checks to see if the active control process is the same as the active controller. If it is, the active controller is allowed to terminate gracefully with **activeController controlTermi-nate**. The message **self activeController: aController** is the last step in the long chain to make the current controller active. Details of method **activeController:** are shown in Listing 9.26.

The first expression in Listing 9.26 assigns the current controller to be the active controller. Method **promote:** guarantees that the current controller is the first scheduled controller in the ordered collection. The next expression is the most important in the entire control sequence. It first sends the message **startup** to the active controller. That controller then remains in control until its conditions

Listing 9.24
Protocol for
Method
scheduleActive-
NoTerminate:
in Class
ControlManager

ControlManager methodsFor: 'scheduling'

scheduleActiveNoTerminate: aController
  "Make aController be the active controller. Presumably the process that requested the
    new active controller wants to keep control to do more activities before the new
    controller can take control. Therefore, do not terminate the currently
active process."
    self schedulePassive: aController.
    self scheduled: aController
      from: Processor activeProcess

Listing 9.25
Protocol for
Method scheduled:
from: in Class
ControlManager

ControlManager methodsFor: 'private'

scheduled: aController **from:** aProcess
    activeControllerProcess = = aProcess
      ifTrue:
        [activeController ~ ~ nil
            ifTrue: [activeController controlTerminate].
        aController centerCursorInView.
        self activeController: aController]
      ifFalse:
        [aController view display]

Listing 9.26
Protocol for
Method
activeController:
in Class
ControlManager

ControlManager methodsFor: 'accessing'

activeController: aController
  "Set aController to be the currently active controller. Give the user control in it."
    activeController ← aController.
    self promote: activeController.
    activeControllerProcess ←
        [activeController startUp.
        self searchForActiveController] newProcess.
    activeControllerProcess priority: Processor userSchedulingPriority.
    activeControllerProcess resume

Listing 9.27
Protocol for
Method startup in
Class **Controller**

Controller methodsFor: 'basic control sequence'

startUp
  "Give control to the receiver. The default control sequence is to initialize (see
      Controller | controlInitialize), to loop (see Controller | controlLoop), and then to
      terminate (see Controller | controlTerminate). After this sequence, control is returned
      to the sender of Control | startUp. The receiver's control sequence is used to
      coordinate the interaction of its view and model. In general, this consists of polling
      the sensor for user input, testing the input with respect to the current display of the
      view, and updating the model to reflect intended changes."
  self controlInitialize.
  self controlLoop.
  self controlTerminate

for relinquishing control are met. Details of **startup** are given in Listing 9.27 for class **Controller.**

Details of the method **controlInitialize** include messages for displaying the view. Then the control loop is entered, and the view remains active until the criteria for **isControlActive** fail for the current controller. After a controller relinquishes control, the method **activeController:** in Listing 9.26 searches for the controller requesting control.

The purpose of this walkthrough is to clarify the sequence of operations that take place whenever a new MVC application is invoked. These are the same steps that are involved every time a different window on the display screen is selected to have control.

9.6.6   An MVC triad inspector

The following example illustrates the use of a tool called the MVC inspector for accessing information about any MVC triad. This tool is added to the blue-button menu options of any selected standard system view as part of the anonymous file-in protocol that is provided with the Tektronix system. It sends the message **inspect** to the top view (**aStandardSystemView**) of the selected window. The message **inspect** is part of the protocol of class **View.**

An inspector is opened on the MVC triad of the selected view. Separate subviews provide inspection of the model, view, and controller. The private data of each of these three components can be accessed by this inspector.

MVC Example 9C

Listing 9.28 gives details of the file that installs the MVC inspector as a blue-button menu option for all standard system views. Figure 9.19 shows an inspector opened on a browser window. The private data (instance variables) are shown for each component class represented. The view and controller are restricted to be instances of **StandardSystemView** and **StandardSystemController** or their subclasses. **BrowserView** is a subclass of **StandardSystemView.**

The subviews shown in Figure 9.19 identify the various subviews of a browser window. The four subviews for selecting category, class, method category, and message are all instances of **SelectionInListView.** Each must display a list of items from which the user can select one.

This chapter has presented protocol summaries for several classes important to graphics operation in Smalltalk and examples of the use of some graphics

Listing 9.28
Details of *file-In*
File for Adding
MVC Inspection to
Blue Button Menu

"Filing in this file places an inspect item on the blue button menu of every system view. Using this menu item causes a special kind of inspector to be brought up which shows the internal state of the view and its associated controller. This code is from the Xerox May 85 Smalltalk Newsletter and is excellent for exploring MVC coding examples."!

!*StandardSystemController class methodsFor:* 'class initialization'!

initialize
 "StandardSystemController initialize"
 ScheduledBlueButtonMenu ← PopUpMenu labels:
'inspect
title
style
under
move
frame
collapse
repaint
close' lines: #(3 8).
 ScheduledBlueButtonMessages
  ← #(inspectView title textStyle under move expand collapse viewDisplayUpdate close)

"StandardSystemController initialize.
StandardSystemController allInstancesDo: [:c | c initializeBlueButtonMenu]"! !

!*StandardSystemController methodsFor:* 'menu messages'!

inspectView
 "Provide an action for inspecting my view"
 self view inspect! !
StandardSystemController initialize!
StandardSystemController allInstancesDo: [:controller |
 controller initializeBlueButtonMenu].

Figure 9.19
Inspecting the
MVC Triad—
Inspector on a
Browser Window

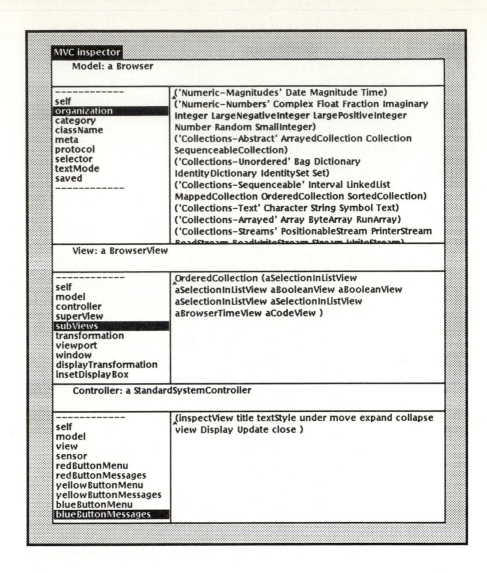

protocol. It has by no means included a complete demonstration of the existing graphics protocol. Additional protocol is demonstrated in the examples presented in Chapters 10 and 11.

Exercises

9.1   Explain in your own words why classes **Point** and **Rectangle** are considered to be primitive graphics classes.

9.2   Class **BitBlt** represents an object that is actually an operation (an action). Reasons are given in the text for why this action is represented by a class instead of methods in the display object classes. Give all the reasons, pro and con, for a separate class.

9.3   Develop an example program that tests all the arithmetic protocol for points. Based on their support for coercion, verify all possible arithmetic combinations of points with various kinds of numbers.

9.4   There are 32 accessing methods in class **Rectangle.** Using techniques and criteria given in the text, identify which of these are key methods.

9.5   Develop an example program that tests all the instance creation methods defined for rectangles.

9.6   **BitBlt** Example 9A shows the 16 combination rules for black patterns in the source and destination forms. Change the pattern in the source form to gray and then run the example. Comment on interpretations of the merged patterns.

9.7   Develop a comparative list of new, inherited, and redefined protocol for the **DisplayObject** class and all its subclasses. Pay particular attention to like categories of messages. Comment on the significance of the existing hierarchy. Should any of the classes be arranged differently?

9.8   Develop an example that illustrates the editing protocol of class **Form.**

9.9   Implement the protocol in classes **Form** and **DisplayScreen** that supports graphic output to your printer. Details of the methods will need to be modified for each different printer. Test your implementation.

9.10 Develop an example that allows the user to define a new cursor shape using a form editor.

9.11 A number of techniques have been presented for displaying mathematical curves such as the sin x / x curve. Compare various **Path** methods and the **Pen** method for smoothness of the curve versus time required to plot the curve. Do a parametric analysis of any selectable parameter (such as number of points).

9.12 For your system identify all the methods in the **View** class that interact with the model. This provides a summary of the ways in which a model and its view interact. (Hint: Use protocol in **SystemDictionary** to find all accesses to model in class **View**).

9.13 Repeat Exercise 9.12 for the methods in class **Controller** that access the model.

9.14 Repeat Exercise 9.12 for all accesses in **View** of the controller and all accesses in **Controller** of the view.

10

Improved Problem Solutions Using the Full Power of Object-Oriented Programming

This chapter describes in more detail the concept of object-oriented problem solving. It uses previous examples in the text to illustrate how the object-oriented methodology has already been applied. Most of these examples are very short in length and designed to illustrate protocol in various Smalltalk classes. Consistency with the object-oriented approach is emphasized instead of efficiency.

This chapter further illustrates the object-oriented concept by introducing a new example problem solution. The new example is a specific problem solution of small to medium size that builds on existing protocol in the Smalltalk image. It is a discrete event simulation of a bank serving customers. Simulations are natural applications for the object-oriented methodology. The number of tellers is specifiable as are average service times for each teller and the average inter-arrival time for customers. Rationale for where to attach the new protocol in the image is given, along with a discussion of the private and shared data and class and instance methods supporting each class.

10.1   Being True to the Object-Oriented Paradigm

The object-oriented paradigm, as characterized in Chapter 1, has several features that can be used as guidelines for developing object-oriented software systems. First, and most importantly, the problem is characterized in terms of the objects that are part of it. The major objects in many cases are distinct enough that they are described by new classes. Minor objects that refine the definitions of the major objects are typically described as private or shared data for the major objects. They are typically instances of existing classes.

The second most important step is to define the message protocol for accomplishing actions with the major objects. Refinement and addition of new messages are usually required as development of a problem solution, using the messages, progresses. Messages are defined using a top-down or bottom-up approach. The final cadre of messages will include both global and localized actions. Global messages are those that initiate a sequence of messages to solve a major subproblem. An example of global messages

solutionObject initialize; getInputs; runProgram; outputResults.

The major object for this example problem is **solutionObject**. It is sent four global messages (**initialize, getInputs, runProgram,** and **outputResults**) that initiate sequences of less-global messages. The four global messages represent typical major operations in solving many computer problems. The details of the global messages are continually refined, until a hierarchy of complete messages is developed. Grouping of messages at a given hierarchical level can be accomplished partially by using message categories in Smalltalk.

In the refinement of messages from global to localized, the software developer uses judicious encapsulation. Repeated segments of code are avoided by implementing the code as a lower-level new message. Excessive use of iterative loops is not consistent with good object-oriented programming. Iteration is best accomplished using low-level messages for enumeration that are part of the image. If necessary, new messages for enumerating can be added in any class. This characteristic of object-oriented programming is, in the authors' view, less important and more difficult to follow than the others just described.

Many of the examples presented in previous chapters are not necessarily examples of good object-oriented programming. Their major goal was to show in one place how to exercise protocol in selected classes. For convenient display of results, the Transcript window was often used. These were the overriding considerations in the development of the class protocol examples. A more object-oriented approach to the examples produces multiple new messages supporting the actions taken. This creation of supporting messages is done for some of the examples. The **Rectangle** examples in Chapter 9 use a new message, **showRect: aPoint,** for displaying rectangles at a specified point on the display screen.

A newcomer to Smalltalk has difficulty following the sequence of messages that are part of apparently simple methods. In many cases these message sequences are interwoven in a complex way with messages in many classes. Tools in the System Browser help the user follow the path of these messages. It is still confusing until the user gains more familiarity with the image and its large list of classes and messages.

Problem solutions in Smalltalk add new capability to the image. Although it is possible to develop executable Smalltalk code in a separate file for solving a specific problem, it is more desirable to include the components of the solution as new classes, instances, and methods. This was illustrated for the **sieve** described in an earlier chapter. It was first implemented as a separate code file. Later it was added as a new message in class **Integer.** Execution of code in a separate file is more awkward than execution of example messages in a class.

Adding incremental capability to an existing base of workable software (the image) is an example of incremental problem solving. This concept is well supported by Smalltalk. If a problem has a solution that is an incremental change from existing capability, then its solution is more quickly achieved. Smalltalk supports the development of new problem solutions in much the same way that human beings acquire new knowledge. We always build on existing knowledge. Chapter 11 discusses further the concept of incremental problem solving and uses the concept to develop new problem solutions.

The approach in this book has been to build slowly from familiar concepts to a more object-oriented implementation of problem solutions. The larger example described in the remainder of this chapter has a solution that is object-oriented.

10.2   A New Example in Object-Oriented Problem Solving—Statement of the Problem

This section defines a new problem of small to medium size that is to be solved using Smalltalk object-oriented methodology and incremental problem solving techniques. The problem is a bank simulation. The overall problem is defined and discussed, along with potential new classes that support a solution to the problem.

A bank needs information to determine the number of tellers it should have to meet desired goals on average service time and the amount of time tellers are free. An optimum solution minimizes teller free time, minimizes the number of tellers required, and minimizes the wait time for customers. Simulations based on models for random events, such as customer arrival time and time required to service a customer, provide useful information for achieving optimum staffing.

The arrival and service of customers in a bank are separate Poisson processes. The time between arrivals of customers (interarrival time) and the time required to service a customer (teller service time) can be modeled as exponentially distributed random variables. The simulation program is to generate customer arrival and teller service times (for each teller). An event is defined as the next occurrence of either: (1) a customer arrives or (2) a customer has been served and leaves.

The sequence of events described above continues until the bank closes. This requires that the real time be maintained and updated for each event. Customers arriving at the bank enter a waiting line for service. The first customer in the line goes to the next available teller. If the line is empty a new customer goes directly to a teller, if one is available. If more than one teller is available, the customer picks one at random. Other options include the use of separate lines for each server. If this option is chosen, logic must be introduced for a customer choosing a line (probably the shortest line). The first example implementation uses a single waiting line.

Specifiable inputs include: (1) average time between customer arrivals (average interarrival time), (2) number of tellers, (3) average service time (for each teller), and (4) number of hours bank is open.

Statistics computed for the simulation include: (1) number of hours bank open (from input), (2) total number of customers served, (3) average interarrival time of customers (from input), (4) maximum number of customers in waiting line during entire simulation, (5) average number of customers in waiting line (averaged over total time), and (6) average wait time in the line. For each teller the following statistics are computed: (1) server number, (2) average service time (from input), (3) number of customers served, and (4) percent of time spent serving customers.

Potential classes that can be part of the solution are the following: (1) a class representing the customers, (2) a class representing the tellers, (3) a class representing the simulation time, and (4) a class representing the random interarrival times and customer service times for each teller (e.g., exponentially distributed random numbers).

10.3 Defining the Objects and Methods in the Problem Solution—Using Existing Capabilities and Defining New Protocol

This section presents a detailed discussion of the objects, actions, private data, shared data, and approach to solving the problem. Actual classes are identified and their place in the image hierarchy is specified. All private and shared data are identified.

One of the first objects identified as being part of a discrete event simulation over a specified time is the actual simulation (real) time. This object has sequential values that represent times of events. Events are a new customer arrival or completed service of a customer. At any event in the simulation, this time object represents the real time. Because of its importance, a new class representing this object may be desirable. It logically should be a subclass of **Time** so it has access to the available protocol in the image for time objects.

A second object that is part of the simulation is a customer. For this simple problem, customer features are of no interest except for their arrival time. Thus the customer object can be represented simply as an arrival time (actually an interarrival time, the time that has elapsed since the last customer arrival). This object can be given a name that is a time. However, it is far more meaningful to define a customer as an object and let the interarrival time be part of its private data. This latter approach is more consistent with object-oriented programming.

Since the only requirement of customers is to return a new interarrival time, class **Customer** is a special class that can be installed as a subclass of **Object.** An alternative is to install **Customer** as a subclass of **Random.** The interarrival times are computed from an instance of **Random.** Installing **Customer** as a subclass of **Object** keeps open the possibility of adding other non–time-related features as a maintenance item, while maintaining a consistent hierarchical position in the image.

A third object is the waiting line that contains customers. Since the courtesy rule of first-come-first-served is followed by customers, the best representation of the waiting line is a queue data structure. Class **OrderedCollection** in the Smalltalk image has protocol for representing queues. Thus it is logical that the waiting line be an instance of **OrderedCollection.**

The waiting line is a special case of a queue. For example, it is required that statistics such as maximum size and average size be computed. Further, this queue contains only customers (interarrival times). To maintain more under-standable encapsulation, a new class, **CustomerQueue,** is defined that has pri-vate data to represent the actual queue of customers. Statistics are computed on this private data to obtain average and maximum size. Because of its depen-dence on class **Customer,** a logical place to install **CustomerQueue** is as a sub-class of **Customer.**

A fourth object is a teller. A teller is characterized by an average service time, an identifying number (since there are multiple tellers), and performance statis-tics such as number of customers served or percent service time. In addition a teller has a status parameter whose value determines if the teller is busy or not. A new class, **Server,** can be installed as a subclass of **Object,** to represent an indi-vidual server.

A fifth object is an array of tellers. Each element in the array is an instance of **Server.** Since this object has size that varies with user input (the user is prompted to enter the number of tellers for a simulation), it is best implemented as an object in the simulation main driver program.

Normally a main driver program is implemented as a class method under the category *examples* for one of the major classes in a software system. For the bank simulation, none of the above newly defined or existing classes provides the logical home for such an example method. The details of a simulation are still complex, even with the support of the above classes and objects.

A simulation requires the following minimal operations: (1) prompt the user for input parameters (hours bank open, number of servers, average service time for each server, average interarrival time for customers), (2) run the actual simulation getting next events and updating all statistics until the bank closes and all customers are served, and (3) compute final statistics and display the re-sults. Each of these operations is relatively complex and requires several differ-ent methods if the object-oriented paradigm is to be followed.

To provide a convenient encapsulation and to follow the object-oriented paradigm, a new class called **BankSimulation** is defined as a subclass of **Object.** Its purpose is to serve as a main driver for the bank simulation. Its private data and methods use the other classes to actually run a simulation.

All classes that are new to the bank simulation problem are grouped under the class category **BankSimulation.** Their hierarchy is shown in Figure 10.1. Only the classes in category **BankSimulation** are shown in boldface in the figure. A protocol summary is given below for each of the classes to define the private

**Figure 10.1
BankSimulation**
Hierarchy of
Classes

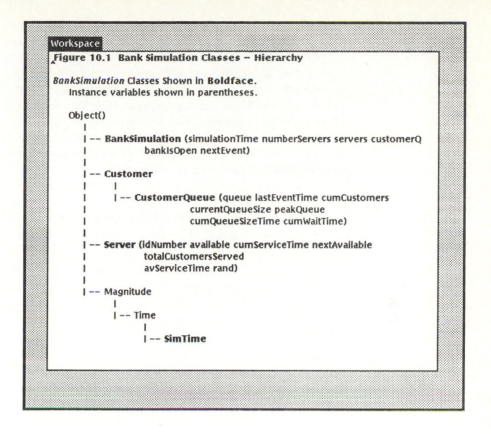

```
Workspace
 Figure 10.1  Bank Simulation Classes – Hierarchy

BankSimulation Classes Shown in Boldface.
   Instance variables shown in parentheses.

Object()
   |
   | -- BankSimulation (simulationTime numberServers servers customerQ
   |              bankIsOpen nextEvent)
   |
   | -- Customer
   |      |
   |      | -- CustomerQueue (queue lastEventTime cumCustomers
   |                     currentQueueSize peakQueue
   |                     cumQueueSizeTime cumWaitTime)
   |
   | -- Server (idNumber available cumServiceTime nextAvailable
   |            totalCustomersServed
   |            avServiceTime rand)
   |
   | -- Magnitude
   |      |
   |      | -- Time
   |             |
   |             | -- SimTime
```

data and categories of messages. Section 10.4 gives a complete listing of the protocol for all the bank simulation classes.

BankSimulation is the main driver class for running the bank simulation. Its instances are actual simulation runs. It includes a class method for executing the bank simulation program and methods for the major functional tasks of prompting for user input, determining the next event, computing statistics, and displaying results.

Protocol Summary for Class **BankSimulation**

Definition—The hierarchy for class **BankSimulation** is **Object—BankSimulation.** Class **BankSimulation** has six instance variables, simulationTime, numberServers, servers, customerQ, bankIsOpen, and nextEvent. It has no class variables or pool dictionaries. It has 2 class methods in one category and 15 instance methods in three categories.

Private data—Class **BankSimulation** has six instance variables.
   simulationTime—an instance of **Number** that is the total simulation time in

minutes. The user is prompted to enter a value in hours. This is converted to minutes since the basic time unit for the simulation is minutes.

numberServers—an instance of **Integer** that is the number of tellers for the simulation. The user is prompted to enter this value.

servers—an instance of **Array** that is an array of servers. The size of the array is determined by user input. The array contains numberServers instances of **Server.**

customerQ—an instance of **CustomerQueue** that is the active queue of customers. This private data is initialized to be an empty ordered collection.

bankIsOpen—an instance of **Boolean** that shows true if the bank is still open.

nextEvent—an instance of **Association** whose key value is zero if the next event is a customer arrival and anInteger if the next event is that server anInteger becomes free. In all cases the value of the association is the next event time.

Instance methods—Class **BankSimulation** has 15 instance methods in three categories. A summary is given below of the categories and methods.

initialize—one method (**init**) that prompts the user for inputs and establishes values for private data.

run methods—eleven methods (aServerStillBusy, bankIsOpen, customerArrived, customersWaiting, getNextEvent:, nextEventIsCustomerArrival, nextEventIsService, processNextEvent, run, serverAvail, serviceCompleted) that control the sequence of events for running the bank simulation. Specifically, the following methods and functionality are given:

aServerStillBusy—returns a Boolean true if any server is still busy.

bankIsOpen—returns a Boolean true if the next event time is less than or equal to the simulation time (total time bank is open).

customerArrived—This message is sent if the next event is a customer arrival. Serve the customer if a server is available or add the customer to the queue.

customersWaiting—Return true if the customer queue is not empty.

getNextEvent: open—Set the value of the association **nextEvent**. The key is tied to a customer (0) or a server number, and the value is the event time. If **open** is false, then the next event can only be a service (no new customer arrivals).

nextEventIsCustomerArrival—Return true if the key of **nextEvent** is zero.

nextEventIsService—Return true if the key of **nextEvent** is not zero. Next event is a service.

processNextEvent—Either serve a customer or accept a new customer arrival dependent on the key and value of **nextEvent**.

run—Execute the bank simulation program. Contains loops for processing the next event until the bank is closed and then clearing the customer line after the bank is closed.

serverAvail—Answer a random choice from among available servers. Answer zero if no server is available.

serviceCompleted—Either serve a customer if there is one or set the server free (available).

Statistics—four methods (customerStats, hours, stats, tellerStats) for computing and displaying statistics for a simulation run. Details for each method are given below:

customerStats—Computes statistics for the customer queue maximum size, average size, and customer average wait time, and displays results in the Transcript window.

hours—Shows the number of hours the bank is open in the Transcript window.

stats—overall statistics control method. It first calls hours, customerStats, then tellerStats.

tellerStats—Computes and displays in the Transcript window statistics for each teller.

Class methods—Class **BankSimulation** has two class methods in one category. A summary is given below of the category and the methods.

example—two methods (**example, title**) that run a bank simulation example and display a title in the Transcript window, respectively.

SimTime has only one purpose, the maintenance of the overall real time of the simulation. As such it has only one class variable, which is the real time. It is a class variable so no instances of **SimTime** need be created to track this time. There are no instances of **SimTime** and no instance methods. It has class methods for initializing, setting, and returning the value of the class variable CurrentTime. The following is a summary of the protocol for class **SimTime.**

Protocol Summary for Class SimTime

Definition—The hierarchy for class **SimTime** is **Object—Magnitude—Time—SimTime.** Class **SimTime** has no instance variables or pool dictionaries. It has one class variable, CurrentTime. It has three class methods in one category. It has no instance methods.

Shared data—Class **SimTime** has one class variable.

CurrentTime, an instance of **Number,** which is the current simulation time. It is initialized to have value zero.

Instance methods—Class **SimTime** has no instance methods.

Class methods—Class **SimTime** has three class methods in one category. A summary is given below of the categories and the methods.

accessing—Three methods (**init, setTime:, getTime**) that initialize CurrentTime to zero, set its value, or return its value, respectively.

Class **Customer** has the purpose of establishing a random number generator and an average interarrival time. Instances of **Customer** are interarrival times based on this average. It has three class variables that represent the random number generator, the average interarrival time, and the value of the interarrival time for an instance of **Customer.**

The definition of the actual interarrival time as a class variable instead of an instance variable is unusual. It is justified from the viewpoint that the actual interarrival time can be accessed by a message to the class **Customer.** This makes the protocol for generating new customer arrivals simpler. Although instances of **Customer** are actually created, they are never accessed after their return of the next interarrival time. If other features of a customer are needed for later processing, then additional protocol is necessary.

A detailed summary of the protocol for class **Customer** is given below.

Protocol Summary for Class Customer

Definition—The hierarchy for class **Customer** is **Object—Customer.** Class **Customer** has no instance variables or pool dictionaries. It has three class variables ArrivalTime, AverageIAT, and RandomTime. It has four class methods in one category and one instance method in one category.
>   **ArrivalTime**—This time is an instance of **Number** that is the actual arrival time (in simulation time reference) for a customer. The current simulation time is updated by the current customers interarrival time (an exponentially distributed random value with average = AverageIAT).
>   **AverageIAT**—The average interarrival time for all customers generated as instances of **Customer.** This parameter is set from a user-input value.
>   **RandomTime**—an instance of **Random,** that is the uniform random number generator. It generates numbers uniformly distributed between 0 and 1, exclusive.

Pool data—Class **Customer** has no pool dictionaries.

Instance methods—Class **Customer** has one instance method in one category, as summarized below.
>   *accessing*—one method (**newValue**) that returns the sum of the current simulation time and the next exponentially distributed customer interarrival time.

Class methods—Class **Customer** has four class methods in three categories. A summary is given below of the categories and methods.
>   *accessing*—two methods (**avgIAT, current**) that return the value of the class variables AverageIAT and ArrivalTime, respectively.
>   *instance creation*—one method (**next**) that creates an instance of **Customer** and returns the next arrival time in simulation time reference.
>   *initialize*—one method (**init**) that initializes the random number generator and sets the value of AverageIAT, based on a user-prompted input.

Class **CustomerQueue** provides functionality for maintaining a queue of customers with random arrival and departure times. Arrival times are based on instances of superclass **Customer.** Departures are determined externally by class **Server** for the bank simulation. A detailed summary of the protocol for class **CustomerQueue** follows.

Protocol Summary for Class CustomerQueue

Definition—The hierarchy for class **CustomerQueue** is **Object—Customer—CustomerQueue.** Class **CustomerQueue** has seven instance variables, queue, lastEventTime, cumCustomers, currentQueueSize, peakQueue, cumQueue-SizeTime, and cumWaitTime. It has no class variables or pool dictionaries. It has one class method in one category and nine instance methods in three categories.

Private data—Class **CustomerQueue** has seven instance variables.
  queue—an instance of **OrderedCollection** that is the actual queue of arrival times for customers.
  lastEventTime—an instance of **SimTime** that is the time of the last event (arrival or removal of a customer) for the queue.
  cumCustomers—cumulative integer count of the number of customers who entered the queue.
  currentQueueSize—the integer number of customers currently in the queue.
  peakQueue—the integer maximum number of customers in the queue.
  cumQueueSizeTime—cumulative product of queue size and time it is that size over the simulation run.
  cumWaitTime—cumulative wait time before being served for all customers who entered the queue.

Instance methods—Class **CustomerQueue** has nine instance methods in three categories. A summary is given below of the categories and methods.
  accessing—two methods (**insert, remove**) that insert or remove a customer and update all statistical parameters.
  initialize—one method (**init**) that initializes a new instance of **CustomerQueue** to have an empty **OrderedCollection** for private data queue and initializes all statistical parameters to zero.
  statistics—six methods (**averageQueueSize, averageQueueWaitTime, maximumQueueSize, size, totalCustomers, totalWaitTime**) that compute and return values for overall statistics for the queue. The method **size** returns the current size of the queue in number of customers.

Class methods—Class **CustomerQueue** has one instance method in one category, as summarized below.
  instance creation—one method (**new**) that creates an instance of **CustomerQueue** and initializes all instance variables. This method is polymorphically redefined from **Behavior.**

Class **Server** represents servers of customers in a customer queue. It tracks availability of a server and establishes service times as a random time. An instance of **Server** is created for each teller in a bank simulation program. A protocol summary for class **Server** follows.

Protocol Summary for Class Server

Definition—The hierarchy for class **Server** is **Object—Server.** Class **Server** has seven instance variables, idNumber, available, cumServiceTime, nextAvailable, totalCustomersServed, avServiceTime, and rand. It has no pool dictionaries. It has one class variable, **Large**. It has 1 class method in one category and 13 instance methods in three categories.

Private data—Class **Server** has seven instance variables.

idNumber—an integer that identifies each server. This value is established at instance creation time. It is the responsibility of the user to establish unique i.d. numbers for each server.

available—an instance of **Boolean** that has value true when a server is not busy.

cumServiceTime—total time the server is busy.

nextAvailable—the time at which a server is next available (based on the time for serving a customer). The time for serving a customer is an exponentially distributed random variable based on the value of **avServiceTime**.

totalCustomersServed—the total number of customers served by this server.

avServiceTime—the average time for servicing a customer by this server. This value is established by user input at instance creation time.

rand—an instance of **Random** that is established at instance creation time. It provides the uniformly distributed random numbers from which a new service time is computed.

Shared data—Class **Server** has one class variable.

Large—an instance of **LargePositiveInteger,** initialized to have value **999999**. This is a value assigned to the next available service time for a server that indicates the server is available. It is the value assigned to **nextAvailable**, the time to service a customer, for an available server. This guarantees the server will not show up as the next event as having completed a service.

Instance methods—Class **Server** has 13 instance methods in three categories. A summary is given below of the categories and methods.

initialize—one method (**initialize: time:**) that initializes the private data for a new instance of **Server.**

service—one method (**serveCust**) that completes service of a customer (whenever a customer service completion is the next event) and updates statistics for the server.

statistics—eleven methods (addToServiceTime:, addToTotalServed, fraction-OfTimeService, getTotalServed, busy, getAvServiceTime, getNextAvailable, id, setNextAvailable:, setServerBusy, setServerFree) that control the status of a server and update or access statistical information about the server. Details for each method follow.

addToServiceTime: aTime—Update the instance variable, cumServiceTime, by adding **aTime** to it.

addToTotalServed—Increment the instance variable totalCustomersServed by one.

fractionOfTimeService—Answer the ratio of cumServiceTime to current simulation time.

getTotalServed—Answer the value of the instance variable totalCustomers-Served.

busy—Answer the negation of the instance variable available.

getAvServiceTime—Answer the value of the instance variable avServiceTime.

getNextAvailable—Answer the value of the instance variable nextAvailable.

id—Answer the value of the instance variable idNumber.

setNextAvailable: aTime—Set the value of the instance variable nextAvailable to aTime.

setServerBusy—Set the value of the instance variable available to false.

setServerFree—Set the instance variable available to true and the instance variable nextAvailable to Large.

Class methods—Class **Server** has one class method in one category, as summarized below.

instance creation—One method (**init:**) that creates an instance of **Server,** with a user-specified idNumber. It prompts the user for an average service time also.

10.4   A First Solution to the Problem

This section defines the methods for a first implementation of the problem solution that is relatively simple. It uses the Transcript window to display a textual summary of the simulation run. Input is accepted from **FillInTheBlank** prompters. The bank has a specifiable number of tellers but has only one serving line. No checks are made for bad input, so the results can vary widely based on user input for average service times for the tellers and average interarrival time for customers. Listings 10.1 through 10.5 give complete protocol for the bank simulation software. An example is given as the **BankSimulation** class method **example**.

Listing 10.1
Protocol
Description
for Class
BankSimulation

Object subclass: #BankSimulation
    instanceVariableNames: 'simulationTime numberServers servers customerQ
        banklsOpen nextEvent '
    classVariableNames: ''
    poolDictionaries: ''
    category: 'BankSimulation'

BankSimulation comment: 'This class is established as a superclass of all classes used in the
    bank simulation for convenience of organization. It includes methods for establishing
    input parameters and running the simulation. Version 2 is more object-oriented in its
    approach than Version 1.

        simulationTime -- real time in minutes to run the simulation
        numberServers -- the number of bank tellers serving customers
        servers -- an array of numberServers bank tellers
        customerQ -- an instance of class CustomerQueue representing the customers
        banklsOpen -- a boolean that answers true if currentTime is less than simulationTime
        nextEvent -- an Association identifying next event as customer arrival (key = 0) or
            service (key = serverNo) with value given as the time of the next event.'

BankSimulation methodsFor: 'statistics'

customerStats
```
    Transcript cr;
        show: ' Total customers: ',(customerQ totalCustomers printString),
            ' with average IAT of: ',(Customer avgIAT) printString, ' minutes'; crtab.
    Transcript
        show: ' Max line: ',(customerQ maximumQueueSize printString),
            '. Avg line: ',((customerQ averageQueueSize)truncated printString),
            ' Avg wait: ',(customerQ averageQueueWaitTime printString),' minutes'.
```

hours
```
    Transcript cr; cr;
        show: ' Bank open for: ',((simulationTime /60.0)printString),' hours'.
```

stats
```
    "Compute and display in Transcript the statistics for a simulation run"
    self hours; customerStats; tellerStats
```

tellerStats
```
    Transcript cr; cr;
        show: ' Server    AvgServTime    NoCustServed    PercentServTime'.
    1 to: numberServers do: [ :serverNo |
        Transcript cr; show: '      ',serverNo printString, '           ',
            (servers at: serverNo) getAvServiceTime printString, '                ',
            (servers at: serverNo) getTotalServed printString, '              ',
            (((servers at: serverNo) fractionOfTimeService *100.0) truncated min: 100)
            printString]
```

BankSimulation methodsFor: 'run methods'

aServerStillBusy
"Answer true if any server is still busy"
1 to: numberServers do: [:i | (servers at: i) busy ifTrue: [↑true]].
↑false

bankIsOpen
↑bankIsOpen ← nextEvent value < = simulationTime

customerArrived
"Next event is a customer arrival;
    serve customer if server available or add cutomer to queue"
| nextServerNo |
(self customersWaiting not and: [((nextServerNo ← self serverAvail) = 0) not])
    ifTrue: ["Customer goes directly to server"
        customerQ insert; remove. "Keeps stats updated"
        (servers at: nextServerNo) serveCust]
    ifFalse: [customerQ insert "Add customer to Q"]

customersWaiting
"Return true if customer queue not empty"
↑customerQ size > 0

getNextEvent: open
"Set nextEvent to an association with key tied to customer
    or server number and value = time.
    If not open then only a server is possible"
| temp |
open
    ifTrue: [nextEvent ← Association new
        key: 0
        value: (Customer new value)]
    ifFalse: [nextEvent ← Association new
        key: 0
        value: 999999].
1 to: numberServers do: [:index |
    (temp ← (servers at: index) getNextAvailable) < nextEvent value
        ifTrue: [nextEvent key: index value: temp "Find min event time"]]

nextEventIsCustomerArrival
↑nextEvent key = 0

nextEventIsService
↑ (nextEvent key = 0) not

processNextEvent
"Process either a service or a customer arrival"
SimTime setTime: nextEvent value.
self nextEventIsService ifTrue: [self serviceCompleted].
self nextEventIsCustomerArrival ifTrue: [self customerArrived]

Listing 10.1
(continued)

```
run
    "Execute the bank simulation program"
    [self bankIsOpen] whileTrue: [
        self getNextEvent: true; processNextEvent].
    "Bank is now closed"
    [self customersWaiting or: [ self aServerStillBusy]] whileTrue: [
        self getNextEvent: false; processNextEvent]


serverAvail
    "Answer random choice server number from available servers. Answer 0 if none available"
    | choice size |
    choice ← servers select: [ :aServer | aServer busy not]. "New collection, available servers"
    (( size ← choice size) = 0)
        ifTrue: [↑0]
        ifFalse: [ ↑(choice at: ((size * (Random new next)) truncated + 1)) id]
            "Pick random index in choice, return the id number of the server at that index"


serviceCompleted
    "Customer service completed. Accept next customer, if there is one, or set server free."
    self customersWaiting
        ifTrue: [ "Take a customer from Q and service"
            customerQ remove.
            (servers at: nextEvent key) serveCust]
        ifFalse: ["No customers to serve; set the server free"
            (servers at: nextEvent key) setServerFree]



BankSimulation methodsFor: 'initialize'


init
    "prompt user for inputs and establish constants for the simulation"
    bankIsOpen ← true.
    nextEvent ← Association key: 0 value: 0.
    simulationTime ← (FillInTheBlank
        request: 'Enter number of hours bank open:  ') asNumber *60.
    numberServers ← (FillInTheBlank
        request: 'Enter number of tellers:  ') asNumber.
    servers ← (Array new: numberServers). "Create array of servers, install avg service times."
    1 to: numberServers do: [ :serverNo |
        servers at: serverNo put: (Server init: serverNo)].
    Customer init.
    customerQ ← CustomerQueue new
```

BankSimulation class
    instanceVariableNames: ''

BankSimulation class comment: ''

BankSimulation class methodsFor: 'example'

example
    "To run the bank simulation program select and execute the following expression
        BankSimulation example
    "
    self title.
    self new init; run; stats

title
    Transcript clear; refresh;
        show: 'Bank Simulation Program - L. J. Pinson Version 2, May 31, 1987'

Listing 10.2
Protocol
Description for
Class **SimTime**

Time subclass: #SimTime
    instanceVariableNames: ''
    classVariableNames: 'CurrentTime '
    poolDictionaries: ''
    category: 'BankSimulation'

SimTime comment: 'Includes methods for setting and getting CurrentTime. There are no
    instances of SimTime.'

SimTime class
    instanceVariableNames: ''

SimTime class comment: ''

SimTime class methodsFor: 'accessing'

getTime
    ↑CurrentTime

setTime: aSimTime
    CurrentTime ← aSimTime

SimTime class methodsFor: 'initialize'

init
    self setTime: 0

Listing 10.3
Protocol
Description for
Class **Customer**

Object subclass: #Customer
    instanceVariableNames: ''
    classVariableNames: 'ArrivalTime AverageIAT RandomTime '
    poolDictionaries: ''
    category: 'BankSimulation'

Customer comment: 'This is the superclass of CustomerQueue. Its purpose is to establish a
    random number generator and an average value for arrival time. Subsequent instance
    generation produces an arrival time based on that average with an exponential
    distribution. Instance of Customer are interarrival times.

        AverageIAT -- the average interarrival time, input from user programs
        ArrivalTime -- the value of an instance of Customer; a time relative to simulation start
        time
        RandomTime -- a random number generator'

Customer methodsFor: 'accessing'

value
    "Answer the current simtime + the next exponentially distributed random number as
    customer ArrivalTime"
    ↑ArrivalTime ← (SimTime getTime - (AverageIAT * (RandomTime next) ln))

Customer class
    instanceVariableNames: ''

Customer class comment: ''

Customer class methodsFor: 'accessing'

avgIAT
    ↑AverageIAT

current
    ↑ArrivalTime

Customer class methodsFor: 'instance creation'

new
    "Create an instance of Customer."
    ↑self basicNew

Customer class methodsFor: 'class initialization'

init
    "Set statistical average and start random number generator for all customers"
    RandomTime ← Random new.
    AverageIAT ← (FillInTheBlank
        request: 'Enter average customer arrival time(minutes): ') asNumber

Listing 10.4

Protocol
Description
for Class
CustomerQueue

Customer subclass: #CustomerQueue
    instanceVariableNames: 'queue lastEventTime cumCustomers currentQueueSize
    peakQueue cumQueueSizeTime cumWaitTime '
classVariableNames: ''
poolDictionaries: ''
category: 'BankSimulation'

CustomerQueue comment: 'This class provides functionality for maintaining a queue of
    customers with random arrival and departure times. Arrival times are based on instances
    of superclass Customer. Departures are determined externally by class Server for the
    bank simulation. Instance variables are:

        queue -- the actual queue of customers as an OrderedCollection of arrival times
        lastEventTime -- the time of the last event (insertion or removal) for the queue
        cumCustomers -- cumulative count of number of customers that entered the queue
        currentQueueSize -- number of customers in queue at current time
        peakQueue -- maximum number of customers in queue over a simulation run
        cumQueueSizeTime -- cumulative queue size - time product over a simulation run
        cumWaitTime -- cumulative wait time for all customers that entered the queue before
            being served'

CustomerQueue methodsFor: 'accessing'

insert
```
| arrivalTime |
arrivalTime ← SimTime getTime.
queue addLast: arrivalTime.
cumCustomers ← cumCustomers + 1.
cumQueueSizeTime _ cumQueueSizeTime + (currentQueueSize *
    (arrivalTime - lastEventTime)).
currentQueueSize ← currentQueueSize + 1.
(currentQueueSize > peakQueue) ifTrue: [ peakQueue ← currentQueueSize].
lastEventTime ← arrivalTime
```

remove
```
"Remove first time in the queue. Update statistics."
| currentTime |
cumWaitTime ← cumWaitTime + (currentTime ← SimTime getTime)
    - (queue removeFirst).
cumQueueSizeTime ← cumQueueSizeTime + (currentQueueSize
    * (currentTime - lastEventTime)).
currentQueueSize ← currentQueueSize - 1.
lastEventTime ← currentTime
```

CustomerQueue methodsFor: 'initialize'

init
```
queue ← OrderedCollection new. "Establish a queue using ordered collection."
lastEventTime ← 0.
cumCustomers ← 0.
currentQueueSize ← 0.
ArrivalTime ← SimTime init. "Set Customer ArrivalTime and SimTime CurrentTime to 0"
```

Listing 10.4
(continued)

```
peakQueue ← 0.
cumQueueSizeTime ← 0.
cumWaitTime ← 0.
```

CustomerQueue methodsFor: 'statistics'

averageQueueSize
    ↑cumQueueSizeTime/(SimTime getTime)

averageQueueWaitTime
    ↑cumWaitTime/cumCustomers

maximumQueueSize
    ↑peakQueue

size
    ↑currentQueueSize

totalCustomers
    ↑cumCustomers

totalWaitTime
    ↑cumWaitTime

CustomerQueue class
    instanceVariableNames: ''

CustomerQueue class comment: ''

CustomerQueue class methodsFor: 'instance creation'

new
    "Create an instance of me. Establish initial values."
    ↑self basicNew init

Listing 10.5
Protocol
Description for
Class **Server**

Object subclass: #Server
    instanceVariableNames: 'idNumber available cumServiceTime nextAvailable
        totalCustomersServed avServiceTime rand '
    classVariableNames: 'Large '
    poolDictionaries: ''
    category: 'BankSimulation'

Server comment: 'This class represents servers of customers in a CustomerQueue. It tracks
    availability of a server and statistics for the server. An instance of Server must be created
    for each server in the application program.

        avServiceTime -- average time for serving a customer established at instance
            creation time

idNumber -- an integer that identifies each server established at instance creation
    time
available -- a boolean true if server is not busy
cumServiceTime -- cumulative time the server is busy
nextAvailable -- time to serve a customer (based on exponentially distributed time
    with avServiceTime). Set to Large if server is not busy.
totalCustomersServed -- cumulative number of customers served by this server
rand -- a random number generator established at increation time
Large -- a constant 999999 indicating non-busy status for a server'

Server methodsFor: 'initialize'

initialize: aNumber **time:** aTime
    "Establish a new instance with id number aNumber and average service time aTime"
    idNumber ← aNumber.
    avServiceTime ← aTime.
    cumServiceTime ← 0.
    totalCustomersServed ← 0.
    nextAvailable ← Large.
    available ← true.
    rand ← Random new.

Server methodsFor: 'service'

serveCust
    | r |
    self setNextAvailable: (SimTime getTime - (r ← (avServiceTime * (rand next) ln))).
    self addToServiceTime: (0-r); addToTotalServed; setServerBusy

Server methodsFor: 'statistics'

addToServiceTime: aTime
    cumServiceTime ← cumServiceTime + aTime

addToTotalServed
    totalCustomersServed ← totalCustomersServed + 1

fractionOfTimeService
    ↑cumServiceTime asFloat/(SimTime getTime)

getTotalServed
    ↑totalCustomersServed

Server methodsFor: 'status'

busy
    ↑available not

Listing 10.5
(continued)

```
getAvServiceTime
    ↑avServiceTime

getNextAvailable
    ↑nextAvailable

id
    ↑idNumber

setNextAvailable: aTime
    nextAvailable ← aTime

setServerBusy
    available ← false

setServerFree
    available ← true.
    nextAvailable ← Large


Server class
    instanceVariableNames: ''

Server class comment: ''


Server class methodsFor: 'instance creation'

init: aNumber
    "Establish an instance of server with id number aNumber and user specified average
        service time"
    Large ← 999999.
    ↑ self basicNew
        initialize: aNumber
        time: (FillInTheBlank
            request: 'Enter average service time(minutes) for server ',
                aNumber printString, ':  ') asNumber
```

Figures 10.2 through 10.5 show examples resulting from running the bank simulation program. Figure 10.2 is an example run with three tellers and the bank open only two hours. Its purpose is to get a feeling for how busy the tellers are for an average customer arrival of 0.4 minutes. As can be seen in Figure 10.2, the tellers are busy approximately 100 percent of the time and the average time in the waiting line is long, about 30 minutes. Figure 10.3 represents an eight-hour day with customers arriving about one per minute on the average. Three servers with average service times of one, two, and three minutes are used. The servers are busy about half the time, and customers have a very short average wait time. The results of Run 3 are shown in Figure 10.4. It is the same as Run 2

Figure 10.2
BankSimulation
example—Run 1:
Three Tellers—
Two Hours

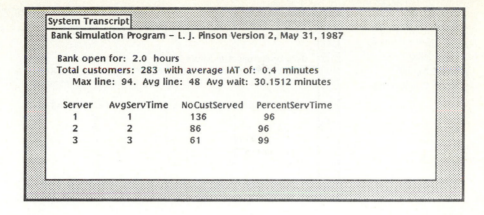

```
System Transcript
Bank Simulation Program – L. J. Pinson Version 2, May 31, 1987

Bank open for:  2.0  hours
Total customers: 283  with average IAT of:  0.4  minutes
    Max line:  94.  Avg line:  48  Avg wait:  30.1512 minutes

    Server    AvgServTime    NoCustServed    PercentServTime
    1         1              136             96
    2         2              86              96
    3         3              61              99
```

Figure 10.3
BankSimulation
example—Run 2:
Three Tellers—
Eight Hours

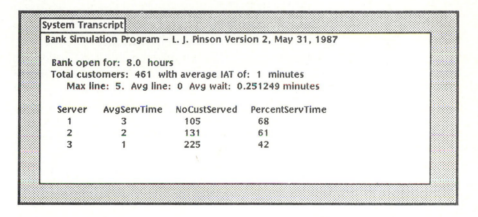

```
System Transcript
Bank Simulation Program – L. J. Pinson Version 2, May 31, 1987

Bank open for:  8.0  hours
Total customers:  461  with average IAT of:  1  minutes
    Max line:  5.  Avg line:  0  Avg wait:  0.251249 minutes

    Server    AvgServTime    NoCustServed    PercentServTime
    1         3              105             68
    2         2              131             61
    3         1              225             42
```

Figure 10.4
BankSimulation
example—Run 3:
Three Tellers—
Eight Hours—More
Customers

```
System Transcript
Bank Simulation Program – L. J. Pinson Version 2, May 31, 1987

Bank open for:  8.0  hours
Total customers:  1195  with average IAT of:  0.4  minutes
    Max line:  318.  Avg line:  156  Avg wait:  86.3245 minutes

    Server    AvgServTime    NoCustServed    PercentServTime
    1         2              319             99
    2         1              650             98
    3         3              226             99
```

**Figure 10.5
BankSimulation**
example—Run 4:
Five Tellers—
Eight Hours—
More Customers

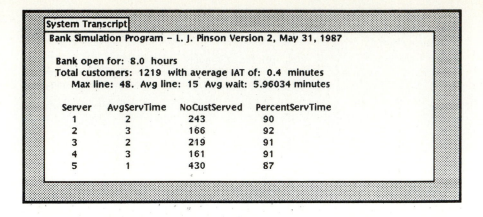

```
System Transcript
Bank Simulation Program – L. J. Pinson Version 2, May 31, 1987

Bank open for: 8.0 hours
Total customers: 1219 with average IAT of: 0.4 minutes
   Max line: 48. Avg line: 15 Avg wait: 5.96034 minutes

Server    AvgServTime    NoCustServed    PercentServTime
1         2              243             90
2         3              166             92
3         2              219             91
4         3              161             91
5         1              430             87
```

except that the bank has increased its number of customers by approximately two and one half times. In this example, the tellers are overloaded and customers must wait over an hour on the average.

The situation in Run 3 is unacceptable—customers will change banks if they must wait over an hour for service. The bank can project the effect of adding more tellers. This result is shown as Run 4 in Figure 10.5. Two new tellers are added with average service times of two and three minutes, respectively. The result is an average wait time for customers of less than six minutes. Additionally, all servers are busy most of the time. This is an almost ideal situation from the viewpoint of the bank's management.

In Chapter 11, incremental capability is added to the bank simulation problem solution as well as other example problems.

Exercises

10.1 Reasons are given in this chapter for defining a class called **BankSimulation** to serve as a main control class for all the other bank simulation classes. Can you think of any reasons why this choice is not good? Compare reasons for and against the chosen hierarchy. Develop an alternative hierarchical arrangement of the classes that are part of this example.

10.2 Develop a list of new, inherited, and redefined protocol for the classes in the bank simulation. Use this information to discuss the merits of the chosen class hierarchy.

10.3 Install and test the bank simulation software in your Smalltalk system.

10.4 Define specific measurable criteria for determining when a bank is performing well. Suggestions include a weighted average of the customer wait times, number of customers served in a given time period, and idle time for servers.

10.5 Perform experimental runs of the bank simulation software to determine which of the following two cases provides better banking performance. Case 1: All servers have the same average service time. Case 2: All servers have different average service times but the average (of the average service times) across all servers is the same as in Case 2.

11

Incremental Problem Solving—
Adding Capabilities to the Smalltalk Image

This chapter illustrates incremental problem solving by adding, in two stages, incremental capability to the bank simulation problem introduced in Chapter 10. In addition to adding new capability to the solution, some modifications are made that make the solution more object-oriented. Modification is also made to the binary tree classes introduced in Chapter 4.

Additional discussion is first given on the rationale for incremental problem solving. The concept is further clarified and a methodology used by the authors is described. This methodology is applied to the examples as indicated.

The first example modifies the bank simulation problem so that each server has a separate line of customers to serve. A second example adds animation to the original bank simulation problem. A third example adds an MVC triad to the binary tree class for graphically displaying and interacting with binary trees.

11.1   Incremental Problem Solving—
Definition and Examples

The concept of incremental problem solving is further defined and clarified and illustrated by using previous examples in the text. It is emphasized how these previous solutions were actually incremental solutions that build on existing capabilities in the Smalltalk image. Most of the previous examples dealt with protocol illustrations. In some cases new classes and/or methods were added to the Smalltalk image.

The addition of printer support is a good example of incremental problem solving. It builds on existing capabilities. This kind of problem solving is supported in many languages by providing separate libraries, which are typically understood from a study of separate documentation provided for each library. To use the capability of any library requires inclusion of its source code or linking of specific object modules. In Smalltalk, any part of the image is available to the user at all times. This includes the ability to browse the source code and to use the protocol by sending appropriate messages.

Printer support required the addition of a new class called **PrinterStream** as a subclass of **WriteStream.** In addition, new instance methods were added to classes **String, Form,** and **DisplayScreen.** Protocol in the superclasses of **Printer-Stream, DisplayScreen, Form, WriteStream,** and **String** is available to support printer control and output of both text and graphics. Protocol in classes **File-Stream** and **TekSystemCall** (a hardware interface class) is also important to the new printer protocol. Without the support of existing classes and methods in the Smalltalk image, the addition of printer support is a far more difficult and time-consuming project.

The Smalltalk approach is not as efficient in terms of memory utilization and speed of computation. The image is quite large (over a megabyte and continually growing), and interpreters are slow compared to compiled code for execution. The major advantage to the Smalltalk approach is the efficiency of the use of human resources. The edit-compile-link-execute cycle of other languages is replaced with a simple edit-execute cycle. Execution may even be halted and resumed when bugs are encountered and repaired. Smalltalk provides an excellent set of tools and an approach that makes incremental problem solving fast and easy.

Other previous examples of incremental problem solving include the addition of new number classes in Chapter 6. Addition of classes for handling both imaginary and complex numbers required the addition of two new classes, **Imaginary** and **Complex.** In addition modifications were made to existing methods in classes **Float, Fraction, Number,** and **Scanner** to support the new classes. Inheritance of existing protocol from the superclasses **Number, Magnitude,** and **Object** made the task of adding these new classes relatively simple.

The process of attaching new classes to a selected point in the image hierarchy makes incremental problem solving easier. Without the support for inheritance and polymorphism, incremental problem solving has much larger increments and results in more redundancy. One of the key factors in the practice of incremental problem solving using Smalltalk is knowing where to attach new protocol to the existing hierarchy. There are often several choices for where to add the new classes. How does one make the best choice?

The most important information for assisting the user in deciding where to attach new classes is an understanding of what is already in the hierarchy. With that understanding, users can then apply their own set of rules and logic for where new classes belong. As more new classes are added, there will come a time when reorganization of the hierarchy structure may be desirable. We sometimes reorganize our filing cabinets, so this should come as no surprise. Fortunately, Smalltalk provides tools that make reorganization a faster and safer process.

Existing classes in Smalltalk provide the protocol for inspecting, browsing, finding all senders, finding all implementors, finding all dependents, and even obtaining explanations for any message or object in the complete Smalltalk image. No other language or environment provides this capability. With these tools, reorganization is not only possible; it is not too painful. Smalltalk also provides protocol for cleaning up its own act (removing all nonreferenced objects, compressing changes, compressing sources, and so forth) and for cloning specified portions of itself.

Examples in the following sections are incremental problem solutions. They build on previously developed solutions to provide enhanced capability.

11.2   Enhancing the Capability of an Existing Problem Solution

This section adds multi-line queueing to the bank simulation problem. An enhanced bank simulation problem solution is required that is consistent with the following rules.

1.   The user specifies the total time for the bank to be open in hours.

2.   The user specifies a number of servers and average service times for each. Actual service time is an exponentially distributed random variable. Each server has a separate customer waiting line.

3.   The user specifies an average interarrival time for customers. The actual interarrival time is an exponentially distributed random variable.

4.   Statistics are to be kept and reported on the customers and the servers. In addition to statistics reported for the single-line bank simulation problem, maximum size, average size, and average wait time are to be reported for each serving line.

5.   Customers arriving at the bank enter the shortest line or the line with the lowest number (an arbitrary choice).

6.   Tellers always serve customers from their own waiting line first. If a teller becomes available and has an empty customer waiting line, then the teller takes a customer from the longest of the other non-empty lines. A server is set free only when no customers are waiting in any line.

Much of the functionality for solving this problem already exists in the classes supporting the single-line bank simulation problem. For example, customers have not changed. They still enter the bank based on the same kind of statistical arrival time. Their arrival time is still the only significant feature for customers. Customers still wait in a line. The only difference is that there are multiple lines. It is expected that the classes **Customer** and **CustomerQueue** can be used as is for the multi-line problem.

Servers still perform the same functions as for the single-line simulation. They serve a customer and keep track of their own statistical performance. The line or lines from which customers arrive is not determined by the server. It is expected that the class **Server** can be used as is.

The logic and protocol for directing customers to a waiting line and to a server are in class **BankSimulation.** The protocol needs to be modified for the multi-line case.

The most logical way to add multi-line capability to the bank simulation problem is to add a subclass to **BankSimulation.** This is valid if much of the protocol in **BankSimulation** is usable by the new subclass without modification. The major differences between the single-line and multi-line problems can be summarized easily as follows:

1. Instead of the single serving line, customerQ, an array of customer queues is required, one for each server. The solution is to define a new instance variable, waitingLines, that is an array of instances of **CustomerQueue. CustomerQueue** has protocol for maintaining statistics on each line.

2. The initialization method must establish the array of customer queues and attach them uniquely to the servers.

3. A new feature (not required) is added that reports the number of customers in line at the close of day as unHappyCustomers, a new instance variable. Except for this reporting of the number of unhappy customers, the method run (as defined in **BankSimulation**) need not be changed.

4. The arrival of customers is different because a customer now must choose a line to enter. The method customerArrived must be redefined to properly insert the customer into the appropriate queue. The logic is that the customer enters the shortest line, as described above.

5. The removal of customers from a queue for servicing is different. An available server always accepts a customer from his or her own line if it is not empty. If it is empty, then a customer from the longest line is accepted. The method serviceCompleted must be redefined to properly remove customers from the queues.

6. Items 4 and 5 indicate a need for determining the longest and shortest waiting line for correct handling of customer arrivals and customer servicing. Two new methods, getLongLine and getShortLine, are required new protocol.

7. To determine if customers are waiting requires checking all waiting lines. The method customersWaiting must be redefined. The same argument holds for determination of the total number of customers served. Method totalCustomers is added as new protocol to answer the total number of customers served across all waiting lines.

8. Reporting of customer statistics is done for each line. The method customerStats must be redefined.

The following is a complete summary of the protocol available to a new subclass of **BankSimulation,** called **MultiLineBankSimulation.** The summary identifies inherited, polymorphically redefined, and new protocol for this subclass. The other existing bank simulation classes (**SimTime, Customer, CustomerQueue, Server**) are used by **MultiLineBankSimulation** without modification.

Inherited, Redefined, and New Protocol in Class MultiLineBankSimulation

Inherited protocol—Inherited from **BankSimulation** and used without modification.

> *Private data*—Five instance variables (**simulationTime, numberServers, servers, bankIsOpen, nextEvent**) are inherited and used. One instance variable (**customerQ**) is inherited but not used. It is not appropriate for the multi-line case.

> *Instance methods*—Nine methods (**hours, tellerStats, aServerStillBusy, bankIsOpen, getNextEvent:, nextEventIsCustomerArrival, nextEventIsService, processNextEvent, serverAvail**) are inherited and used.

Inherited and redefined protocol—Inherited from **BankSimulation** and polymorphically redefined.

> *Instance methods*—Seven methods (**initialize, customerArrived, customersWaiting, run, serviceCompleted, customerStats, stats**) are inherited and redefined.

> *Class methods*—Two methods (**example, title**) are inherited and redefined to reflect minor changes.

New protocol—Defined specifically to support multi-line bank simulations.

> *Private data*—One new instance variable (**waitingLines**) is required. It represents an array of customer waiting lines. Another instance variable (**unHappyCustomers**) is not required but is added as a new feature. It could have been added to the superclass **BankSimulation;** indeed, that is the more logical place for it, since this information is useful for the single-line simulation as well. The reader may wish to do this.

> *Instance methods*—Four methods (**getLongLine, getShortLine, totalCustomers, unHappyCustomers**) are added as new protocol.

The only change in the image hierarchy from this incremental enhancement is that class **MultiLineBankSimulation** has been added as a subclass of **BankSimulation**. Listing 11.1 gives a complete protocol description for class **MultiLineBankSimulation**.

Listing 11.1
Protocol
Description
for Class
**MultiLineBank-
Simulation**

BankSimulation subclass: #MultiLineBankSimulation
    instanceVariableNames: 'waitingLines unHappyCustomers '
    classVariableNames: ''
    poolDictionaries: ''
    category: 'BankSimulation'

MultiLineBankSimulation comment: 'This class is a subclass of BankSimulation that add multi-waiting lines. Each server has a separate waiting line and takes customers from his own line. If a server is available and has an empty waiting line, the server takes a customer from the longest line. Polymorphically redefined protocol is given for handling multiple waiting lines. New instance variables are:

waitingLines - an array of instances of CustomerQueue. Each queue is   bound to a
server id number.
unHappyCustomers - the number of customers in line at the close of day for the
bank.'

MultiLineBankSimulation methodsFor: 'initialize'

init
"prompt user for inputs and establish constants for the simulation"
bankIsOpen ← true.
unHappyCustomers ← 0.
nextEvent ← Association key: 0 value: 0.
simulationTime ← (FillInTheBlank
    request: 'Enter number of hours bank open: ') asNumber * 60.
numberServers ← (FillInTheBlank
    request: 'Enter number of tellers: ') asNumber.
servers ← (Array new: numberServers).
    "Create an array of servers and install average service times."
waitingLines ← (Array new: numberServers).
    "Create and initialize a waiting line for each teller."
1 to: numberServers do: [:serverNo |
    servers
        at: serverNo
        put: (Server init: serverNo).
    waitingLines
        at: serverNo
        put: CustomerQueue new].
Customer init

MultiLineBankSimulation methodsFor: 'run methods'

customerArrived
"Next event is a customer arrival; serve customer if server available or add cutomer to
    queue of shortest line."
| nextServerNo shortLine |
shortLine ← self getShortLine.   "an integer index tied to server."
(self customersWaiting not and: [((nextServerNo ← self serverAvail) = 0) not])
    ifTrue: ["Customer goes directly to server"
        (waitingLines at: nextServerNo)
            insert; remove. "Keeps stats updated"
        (servers at: nextServerNo) serveCust]
    ifFalse: ["Add customer to shortest line"
        (waitingLines at: shortLine) insert]

customersWaiting
"Return true if any customer queue not empty"
1 to: numberServers do: [:server |
    (waitingLines at: server) size > 0 ifTrue: [↑true]].
↑false

Listing 11.1
(continued)

getLongLine
```
"Answer the index of the longest queue in waitingLines"
| temp |
temp ← 1.        "Initialize to line 1."
1 to: numberServers do: [ :serverNo |
    (waitingLines at: serverNo) size > (waitingLines at: temp) size
        ifTrue: [ temp ← serverNo]].
↑temp
```

getShortLine
```
"Answer the index of the shortest queue in waitingLines"
| temp |
temp ← 1.        "Initialize to line 1."
1 to: numberServers do: [ :serverNo |
    (waitingLines at: serverNo) size < (waitingLines at: temp) size
        ifTrue: [ temp ← serverNo]].
↑temp
```

run
```
"Execute the bank simulation program"
[self bankIsOpen] whileTrue: [self
    getNextEvent: true;
    processNextEvent].
"Bank is now closed"
unHappyCustomers ← self unHappyCustomers.
[self customersWaiting or: [ self aServerStillBusy]] whileTrue: [self
    getNextEvent: false;
    processNextEvent]
```

serviceCompleted
```
"Next event is completed service.
    Get next customer if there is one, else set server free."
| nextServer |
nextServer ← servers at: nextEvent key.
self customersWaiting
    ifTrue: [ "Take a customer from own line and service.
            If own line is empty choose customer from longest line."
        (waitingLines at: nextServer id) size > 0
            ifTrue: [ (waitingLines at: nextServer id) remove ]
                "Remove customer from server line."
            ifFalse:[ (waitingLines at: self getLongLine) remove ].
                "Remove customer from longest line."
        nextServer serveCust]
    ifFalse: ["No customers to serve; set the server free"
        nextServer setServerFree]
```

MultiLineBankSimulation methodsFor: 'statistics'

customerStats

```
Transcript crtab;
    show: 'Total customers served:  ',
        (self totalCustomers printString),', with average IAT of:  ',
        (Customer avgIAT) printString, '  minutes'.
```

```
Transcript cr; cr;
    show: ' Statistics for each waiting line'; cr;
    show: ' Server   MaxQueueSize   AvgQueueSize   AvgWaitTime'; cr
1 to: numberServers do: [ :serverNo |
    Transcript
        show: '     ', serverNo printString , '            ',
            (waitingLines at: serverNo) maximumQueueSize printString,'                 ',
            (waitingLines at: serverNo) averageQueueSize truncated printString,
            '          ',
            (waitingLines at: serverNo) averageQueueWaitTime printString,
            '  minutes']
```

stats
```
"Compute and display in Transcript the statistics for a simulation run"
self hours; customerStats; tellerStats.
Transcript cr; cr;
    show: ' Customers in line at close of day:  ',
        unHappyCustomers printString.
```

totalCustomers
```
"Answer total customers served in all lines."
| total |
total ← 0.
1 to: numberServers do: [ :server |
    total ← total + (servers at: server) getTotalServed ].
↑total
```

unHappyCustomers
```
"Answer total customers waiting in all lines at end of banking hours."
| total |
total ← 0.
1 to: numberServers do: [ :serverNo |
    total ← total + (waitingLines at: serverNo) size ].
↑total
```

MultiLineBankSimulation class
    instanceVariableNames: ''

MultiLineBankSimulation class comment: ''

MultiLineBankSimulation class methodsFor: 'example'

example
```
"To run the bank simulation program select and execute the following expression
        MultiLineBankSimulation example                    "
self title.
self new init; run; stats
```

title
```
Transcript clear; refresh;
    show: 'Bank Simulation Program - L. J. Pinson Version 3, August 8, 1987'; crtab;
    show: 'This version uses  a separate waiting line for each teller.'; crtab;
    show: 'When an available teller''s waiting line is empty, '; crtab;
    show: 'a customer is taken from the longest line.'; cr; cr
```

Figure 11.1
MultiLineBank-
Simulation—
Run 2: Three
Tellers—Eight
Hours

```
System Transcript

Bank Simulation Program – L. J. Pinson Version 3, August 8, 1987
    This version uses  a separate waiting line for each teller.
    When an available teller's waiting line is empty,
    a customer is taken from the longest line.



Bank open for:  8.0  hours
    Total customers served: 521, with average IAT of:  1  minutes

Statistics for each waiting line
    Server      MaxQueueSize      AvgQueueSize      AvgWaitTime
       1             4                 0             0.290001   minutes
       2             3                 0             0.450863   minutes
       3             3                 0             0.379649   minutes

    Server      AvgServTime       NoCustServed      PercentServTime
       1             1                262               56
       2             2                143               66
       3             3                116               72

Customers in line at close of day:  1
```

Figure 11.2
MultiLineBank-
Simulation—
Run 2: Three
Tellers—Eight
Hours—More
Customers

```
System Transcript

Bank Simulation Program – L. J. Pinson Version 3, August 8, 1987
    This version uses  a separate waiting line for each teller.
    When an available teller's waiting line is empty,
    a customer is taken from the longest line.



Bank open for:  8.0  hours
    Total customers served: 1157, with average IAT of:  0.4  minutes

Statistics for each waiting line
    Server      MaxQueueSize      AvgQueueSize      AvgWaitTime
       1            119                53             102.698   minutes
       2            119                48             60.1052   minutes
       3            118                58             148.969   minutes

    Server      AvgServTime       NoCustServed      PercentServTime
       1             2                340               99
       2             1                613               99
       3             3                204               99

Customers in line at close of day:  354
```

**Figure 11.3
MultiLineBank-
Simulation—**
Run 3: Five
Tellers—Eight
Hours

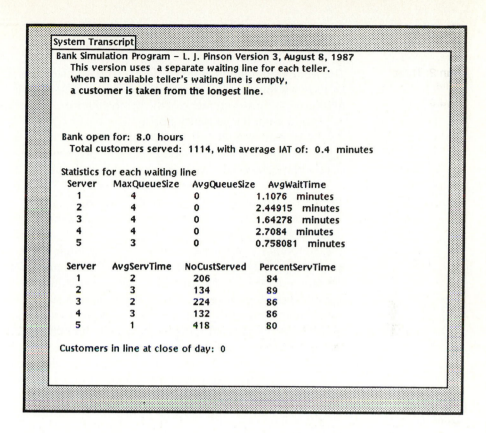

```
System Transcript
Bank Simulation Program – L. J. Pinson Version 3, August 8, 1987
    This version uses  a separate waiting line for each teller.
    When an available teller's waiting line is empty,
    a customer is taken from the longest line.


Bank open for: 8.0  hours
    Total customers served: 1114, with average IAT of: 0.4  minutes

Statistics for each waiting line
    Server    MaxQueueSize    AvgQueueSize    AvgWaitTime
      1            4               0           1.1076    minutes
      2            4               0           2.44915   minutes
      3            4               0           1.64278   minutes
      4            4               0           2.7084    minutes
      5            3               0           0.758081  minutes

    Server    AvgServTime    NoCustServed    PercentServTime
      1            2              206             84
      2            3              134             89
      3            2              224             86
      4            3              132             86
      5            1              418             80

Customers in line at close of day:  0
```

It is of interest to compare the relative performance of the bank simulations for single and multiple waiting lines with all other conditions held constant. Three cases were presented in Figures 10.3, 10.4, and 10.5 (Runs 2, 3, and 4) for the single serving line. These three cases are repeated for multiple serving lines. It is not our purpose to discuss the statistical significance of these simulations. Rather, they illustrate that the results are in the expected range. There are no flags that indicate an error in the software.

Figure 11.1 shows the results of Run 2, with three tellers whose average service times are three, two, and one minutes, respectively. The average customer interarrival time is one minute, and the bank is open for eight hours. Compare this result with that of Figure 10.2.

Figure 11.2 shows the results of Run 3, with a two-and-one-half times increase in customer arrivals. Compare this result with that of Figure 10.3. There are many unhappy customers.

Figure 11.3 shows the results of Run 4, with five tellers (two more added). Compare this result with that of Figure 10.4.

11.3   Graphics Enhancement of the Bank Simulation

This section adds graphics display to the bank simulation problem for the single customer waiting line. The multi-line bank simulation is not supported by this modification. However, much of the protocol for the single-line graphics can be used for a multi-line graphics display. The major differences are in definitions for the display of waiting lines. Additionally, instances of a class for animation using multiple waiting lines should inherit protocol from both the animation class and the multi-line class already established. Either a reorganization of the class hierarchy is required or multiple inheritance is required. Multiple inheritance is defined to be a part of Smalltalk. Actual support for multiple inheritance is provided in some implementations of Smalltalk but not others.

A new class, **AnimatedBankSim,** is added as a subclass of **BankSimulation** that supports the animated version of a single-line bank simulation. For this modification, the existing support classes (**Customer, CustomerQueue,** and **Server**) require additional protocol. The approach used is to add subclasses to each of these three classes with new protocol to support the animation. This keeps the three classes clean and allows the new subclasses to inherit needed protocol from them. Three new subclasses (**AnimatedCustomer, Animated-CustomerQueue,** and **AnimatedServer**) are added to the class hierarchy. Class **SimTime** is still used without modification by the animated bank simulation.

A description of the logic for the animation is first presented. Then a protocol summary is given for the new classes that identifies inherited, redefined, and new protocol. Complete listings of the new classes are given next. Finally, several figures show the result of the animated bank simulation at selected key points in the simulation.

11.3.1   Logic for the animation

The logic for the animated bank simulation is identical in part to the logic for the single-line simulation represented by class **BankSimulation.** It has additional logic that deals with how the objects are to be displayed on the screen. This additional logic is best presented by describing a typical display.

Figure 11.4 shows a typical bank display. It is a snapshot taken during the execution of a simulation. Action was frozen and the image dumped to a printer by pressing a function key. Multiple presses send multiple copies to the printer. After the printout is obtained, the simulation automatically resumes. This makes it easy to dump visual displays of the simulation at any point of interest. Example images described later are obtained in this way.

The bank structure is a bordered rectangular area with an inner partition where customers wait. Tellers are positioned behind counters along the east wall of the bank. Their spacing and positions are centered vertically (with a maximum of 10 tellers). The size of the bank is fixed. An entry door is posi-

Figure 11.4
AnimatedBank-
Sim—Bank Layout

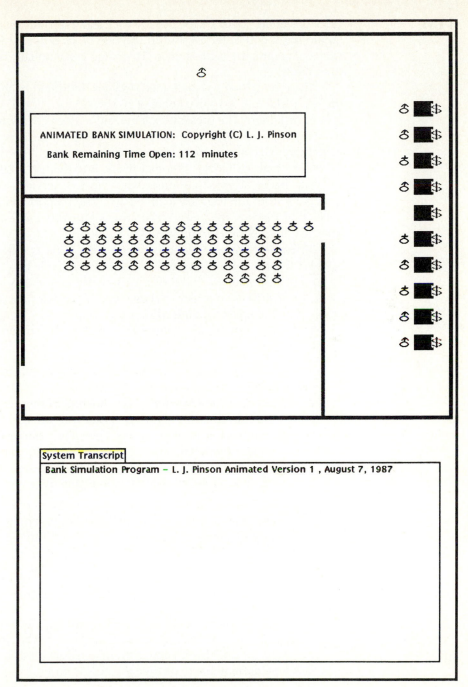

tioned near the south end of the west wall, and a separate exit door is positioned at the north end of the west wall. The title block is for information display on remaining time the bank is open. This value is continually updated throughout the simulation.

The waiting line has the folded structure indicated by the customers in Figure 11.4. The line has a maximum of 10 rows (5 are shown) with a total capacity of 142 customers. The present implementation does not test for a full line before moving a new arriving customer to the end of the line; however, the line is updated immediately to reflect the correct line content. The only difference is in whether a male or female customer image is to be displayed.

The figure shows a customer who was just serviced by teller number 5 (counting from the top) leaving the bank. The partition and counters are gray (they look black in the figure). The images for male and female customers and for the tellers (**$** sign) are indicated in the figure.

When the simulation time is reached, the bank is closed. The entry door closes (becomes part of the black border), and the title block indicates the bank is closed. Customers in the line at closing are continually served until all are gone. Once the last customer has been served, the exit door is closed and a large happy face is displayed in the customer waiting area.

The major new responsibilities for handling the animated version consists of three events.

1. Initialization methods must create and display the initial bank image including the walls, doors, partitions, counters, and tellers. This is the responsibility of class **AnimatedBankSim.** Class **AnimatedTeller** must provide support for creating images of tellers. Initialization of the customer class must include creation of male and female images. This responsibility is handled by class **AnimatedCustomer.** Initialization of the queue of customers must add the creation of a queue of images. This is the responsibility of the initialization methods in class **AnimatedCustomerQueue.**

2. Arrival of customers must now cause the movement of a customer image to the waiting line and/or to a teller if the line is empty. Method **customerArrived** in **BankSimulation** is the only method affected. It must be redefined in **AnimatedBankSim** to add the graphic animation. The queue of customer images must be updated, as well as the queue of arrival times.

3. Completion of the servicing of a customer must now cause the customer image to be moved to the exit door. The queue of customer images and the queue of customer arrival times are both updated. The next customer in the waiting line is moved to the available teller for servicing. Method **serviceCompleted** in **BankSimulation** is the affected method. It must be redefined in **AnimatedBankSim** to provide the new features.

These three events require redefinition of only a few key methods that deal with initialization, customer arrivals, and service completions. In addition, several new methods for supporting the actual graphic displays are needed. The approach is to (1) identify required new private or shared data, (2) install the subclasses, (3) identify and redefine those inherited methods that need to be changed, and (4) identify and add new protocol required to support the redefined methods.

A summary of the actual classes added follows. It is the result of applying the described approach. Total maintenance time was approximately 12 hours to provide this incremental capability. Much of this time was spent learning new things about the graphics classes.

11.3.2   Protocol summary (inherited, redefined, and new)

The new hierarchy of classes supporting the animated bank simulation is given in Figure 11.5. The animation classes are given in boldface. Four new subclasses (**AnimatedBankSim, AnimatedCustomer, AnimatedCustomerQueue,** and **AnimatedServer**) are required that provide incremental capability to their super-

Figure 11.5
Animated Bank
Simulation
Classes—
Hierarchy

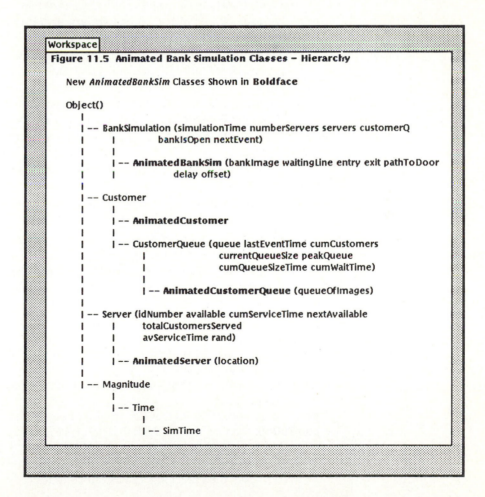

```
Workspace
Figure 11.5  Animated Bank Simulation Classes – Hierarchy

New AnimatedBankSim Classes Shown in Boldface

Object()
 |
 | -- BankSimulation (simulationTime numberServers servers customerQ
 |     |              bankIsOpen nextEvent)
 |     |
 |     | -- AnimatedBankSim (bankImage waitingLine entry exit pathToDoor
 |     |              delay offset)
 |     |
 | -- Customer
 |     |
 |     | -- AnimatedCustomer
 |     |
 |     | -- CustomerQueue (queue lastEventTime cumCustomers
 |     |     |              currentQueueSize peakQueue
 |     |     |              cumQueueSizeTime cumWaitTime)
 |     |     |
 |     |     | -- AnimatedCustomerQueue (queueOfImages)
 |
 | -- Server (idNumber available cumServiceTime nextAvailable
 |     |              totalCustomersServed
 |     |              avServiceTime rand)
 |     |
 |     | -- AnimatedServer (location)
 |
 | -- Magnitude
 |     |
 |     | -- Time
 |           |
 |           | -- SimTime
```

classes. Each of these new classes is summarized below in terms of inherited, redefined, and new protocol.

Class **AnimatedBankSim** has major responsibility for generating instructions for the insertion and removal of customers from both the image queue and the arrival time queue. Actual insertion and deletion are implemented by classes **CustomerQueue** and **AnimatedCustomerQueue.** Further, this class has responsibility for generating and updating the actual display image. A detailed summary of its inherited, redefined, and new protocol follows.

Inherited, Redefined, and New Protocol for Class AnimatedBankSim

Inherited protocol—Inherited from **BankSimulation** and used without modification.

    Private data—All six instance variables (**simulationTime, numberServers, servers, bankIsOpen, nextEvent, customerQ**) are inherited and used.

    Instance methods—Twelve methods (**hours, tellerStats, stats, customerStats, aServerStillBusy, bankIsOpen, getNextEvent:, nextEventIsCustomerArrival, nextEventIsService, processNextEvent, customersWaiting, serverAvail**) are inherited and used. One method (**init**) is inherited but not used. Initialization is accomplished with a new method (**init:**).

    Class methods—One method (**example**) is inherited but not used. Examples of **AnimatedBankSim** are executed using a new method (**example: at:**).

Inherited and redefined protocol—Inherited from **BankSimulation** and polymorphically redefined.

    Instance methods—Three methods (**customerArrived, run, serviceCompleted**) are inherited and redefined.

    Class methods—One method (**title**) is inherited and redefined to reflect minor changes.

New protocol—Defined specifically to support animated single-line bank simulations.

    Private data—Seven new instance variables (bankImage, waitingLine, entry, exit, pathToDoor, delay, offset) are required. Their descriptions are as follows.

    bankImage—an instance of **Form** that is the structure of the bank (walls, doors, and partitions).

    waitingLine—an instance of **Path** that defines where customers are to stand in the graphic display.

    entry—an instance of **Point** that defines the upper-left edge of the bank entrance.

    exit—an instance of **Point** that defines the upper-left edge of the bank exit.

    pathToDoor—an instance of **Path** that defines the path customers follow to exit the bank.

    delay—an **Integer** that is a user-specified delay in milliseconds. This value slows down the movement of customers if desired.

offset—an instance of **Point** that lets the user specify an offset for displaying the bank image on the screen. All other displayed objects are adjusted to this offset.

Class Variables—One new class variable (**HappyFace**) is added just for fun. It is an instance of **Form** and is shaped like a happy face. The user must create this image using a form editor and install it as **HappyFace** by executing AnimatedBankSim initialize.

Instance Methods—Eleven methods (init:, addFeatures, addTellers, createBankImage, createBankStructure, defineExitPath, defineWaitingLine, setDelay:, customerAt: moveTo:, updateTimeDisplay:, updateWaitingLine) are added as new protocol. Their functionality is described below.

init: aPoint—Prompt the user for all specifiable inputs and initiate creation of the bank image. Parameter aPoint is assigned to instance variable offset.

addFeatures—Add title and a block for displaying time remaining for the bank to be open. Adjust for offset and display on the bank image.

addTellers—Compute the location of tellers to be centered in the teller service area (based on the number of tellers) and display the teller images and images for service counters. This method also sets values for one of the private data values for each teller, its location.

createBankImage—This method creates a level of abstraction that sends all the other messages that are part of creating a complete bank image. It also defines the instance variables entry and exit.

createBankStructure—Create the walls, doors, and partitions and display with adjustment for the specified offset point.

defineExitPath—Define a path that is the collection of points a customer follows to exit the bank. Set this path to be the value of the instance variable pathToDoor.

defineWaitingLine—Define a path that is the collection of points at which customers wait in line. Set this path to be the value of the instance variable waitingLine.

setDelay: anInteger—Set the value of instance variable delay to anInteger.

customerAt: aLocation **moveTo:** aPoint—This method moves a customer image at point aLocation to point aPoint smoothly without flashing and while restoring the background.

updateTimeDisplay: status—This method displays either the remaining time the bank is to be open (for status = #open) or the message that the bank is closed (for status = #closed).

updateWaitingLine—When the line changes (a customer arrives or is served), this method redisplays the existing line of customers, advancing the line if a customer has left.

Class methods—One method (**example: at:**) initiates an example run of the animated bank simulation with user-specified delay and offset as parameters.

Inherited, Redefined, and New Protocol for Class **AnimatedCustomer**

Inherited protocol—Inherited from **Customer** and used without modification.

Class variables—Three class variables (**ArrivalTime, AverageIAT, Random-Time**) are inherited and used.

Instance methods—One instance method (**value**) is inherited and used.

Class methods—Four methods (**init, new, avgIAT, current**) are inherited and used.

New protocol—Defined specifically to support animated customers.

Class variables—Three new class variables (**BlankCustomer, MaleCustomer, FemaleCustomer**) are added to this class. They are instances of **Form.** All are 16-by-16 pixels and contain bitmaps that represent a blank background, a male customer, or a female customer.

Instance methods—One method (**image**) that answers a MaleCustomer or FemaleCustomer at random. The probability for either is one-half. The image for a customer and its arrival time are independent processes.

Class methods—Two methods (**initialize, blank**) that define the class variables MaleCustomer, FemaleCustomer and BlankCustomer and return a BlankCustomer image respectively.

Inherited, Redefined, and New Protocol for Class **AnimatedCustomerQueue**

The primary purpose of this class is to maintain a queue of customer images.

Inherited protocol—Inherited from **CustomerQueue** and used without modification.

Private data—Seven instance variables (**queue, lastEventTime, cumCustomers, currentQueueSize, peakQueueSize, cumQueueSizeTime, cumWaitTime**) are inherited and used.

Instance methods—Six methods (**averageQueueSize, averageQueueWaitTime, maximumQueueSize, size, totalCustomers, totalWaitTime**) are inherited and used. They are all methods for maintaining statistics on the queue.

Class methods—One method (**new**) is inherited and used.

Inherited and redefined protocol—Inherited from **CustomerQueue** and polymorphically redefined.

Instance methods—Three methods (**init, insert, remove**) are inherited and redefined. All three send a call to their inherited superclass message of the same name and add protocol for initializing, inserting into, and removing from the queue of customer images.

New protocol—Defined specifically to support graphic display of a queue of animated customers.

Private data—One new instance variable (**queueOfImages**) is required. It is an ordered collection of customer images.

Instance methods—Two methods (last, displayQueue:) are added as new protocol. Their functionality is defined below.

last—Returns the last image in the queue of images.

displayQueue: aBlock—This method executes **aBlock** for each image in the queue of images. It supports the display of the images as part of the animated bank simulation.

Inherited, Redefined, and New Protocol for Class AnimatedServer

The primary purpose of this class is to define an image for tellers and to maintain a location reference for displaying that image on the screen.

Inherited protocol—Inherited from **Server** and used without modification.

Private data—Seven instance variables (**idNumber, available, cumService-Time, nextAvailable, totalCustomersServed, avServiceTime, rand**) are inherited and used.

Class variables—One class variable (**Large**) is inherited and used.

Instance methods—Thirteen instance methods (**busy, getAvServiceTime, getNextAvailable, id, setNextAvailable:, setServerBusy, setServerFree, addToServiceTime:, addToTotalServed, fractionOfTimeService, getTotalServed, serveCust, initialize: time:**) are inherited and used.

Class methods—One method (**init:**) is inherited and used.

Inherited and redefined protocol—None of the protocol inherited from **Server** is redefined.

New protocol—Defined specifically to support graphic display of servers.

Private data—One new instance variable (**location**) is added as an instance of **Point.** It is the location on the screen at which an instance of **AnimatedServer** is displayed. This provides a constant record of this important location in the animated version of the bank simulation.

Class variables—One new class variable (**TellerImage**) is added to represent the image of a teller. It is a 16-by-16 **Form** whose bitmap represents a teller.

Instance methods—Two new instance methods (**location, location:**) are added as new protocol. They return and set the value, respectively, for instance variable location.

Class methods—Two new class methods (**initialize, image**) are added as new protocol. They define and answer the TellerImage, respectively.

11.3.3   Listings of new classes

Complete protocol listings for the new animation classes supporting the bank simulation are given in the following listings. Listing 11.2 gives complete protocol for the class **AnimatedBankSim,** Listing 11.3 gives protocol for **Animated-Customer,** Listing 11.4 for **AnimatedCustomerQueue,** and Listing 11.5 gives complete protocol for the class **AnimatedServer.**

Listing 11.2
Protocol
Description
for Class
AnimatedBankSim

BankSimulation subclass: #AnimatedBankSim
        instanceVariableNames: 'bankImage waitingLine entry exit pathToDoor delay offset '
        classVariableNames: 'HappyFace '
        poolDictionaries: ''
        category: 'BankSimulation'

AnimatedBankSim comment: 'This class provides an animated version of the bank simulation program. Because of display limitations the number of tellers is limited to a maximum of ten. The following new class and instance variables are added:

    HappyFace -- a very large Form.
    bankImage -- a Form that is the graphic image of the bank.
    waitingLine -- an instance of Path representing the center of the 'roped-off' waiting line.
    entry -- a Point thast defines the edge of the entrance door.
    exit -- a Point that defines the edge of the exit door.
    pathToDoor -- an instance of Path that defines the path taken by customers to exit after being served.
    delay -- an Integer in milliseconds that delays the graphics display.
    offset -- a Point that is the offset from 0@0 to display the bank image.'

AnimatedBankSim methodsFor: 'run methods'

customerArrived
    "Next event is a customer arrival; serve customer if server available or add customer to queue"
        | nextServerNo customerImage endOfLine canServeNow |
        canServeNow ←
                (self customersWaiting not and:
                        [((nextServerNo ← self serverAvail) = 0) not]).
        customerQ insert.
        endOfLine ← waitingLine at: customerQ size.
        customerImage ← customerQ last.
        customerImage
                displayOn: Display
                at: offset + entry + (30@30). "Inside the door"
        self
                customerAt: offset + entry + (30@30)
                moveTo: endOfLine.

```
            self updateWaitingLine.
            canServeNow
                    ifTrue: [ "Customer goes directly to server"
                            self
                                    customerAt: endOfLine
                                    moveTo:  (servers at: nextServerNo) location.
                            customerQ remove.
                            self updateWaitingLine.
                            (servers at: nextServerNo) serveCust]


customerAt: aLocation moveTo: aPoint
            "Move the receiver customer image from aLocation to aPoint"
            | imageToMove increment rect index point |
            rect ← Rectangle
                        origin: aLocation - (8@8)
                        extent: 16@16.
            imageToMove ← Form fromDisplay: rect.
            (Form extent: 16@16) white
                        displayOn: Display
                        at: rect origin rule: Form over. "erase the image"
            aPoint = = exit
                        ifTrue: [ index ← 0.
                                imageToMove
                                            follow: [ (Delay forMilliseconds: delay) wait.
                                                        pathToDoor at: (index ← index + 1)]
                                            while: [index < pathToDoor size].  ]
                        ifFalse: [  increment ← aPoint - aLocation // 16.
                                index ← 0.
                                imageToMove
                                            follow: [(Delay forMilliseconds: delay) wait.
                                                    (index ← index + 1) < 16
                                                            ifTrue:     [point ← aLocation +
(index * increment)]
                                                            ifFalse:    [point ← aPoint] ]
                                            while: [point ~ = aPoint] .
                                imageToMove
                                            offset: -8@-8;
                                            displayOn: Display
                                            at: aPoint
                                            rule: Form over].


run
            "Execute the bank simulation program"
            [self bankIsOpen] whileTrue: [
                    self
                            getNextEvent: true;
                            processNextEvent;
                            updateTimeDisplay: #open].
            "Bank is now closed. Shut the entry door."
            self
                    updateTimeDisplay: #closed.
```

Listing 11.2
(continued)

```
                            (Form extent: 6@60) black
                                    displayOn: Display
                                    at: offset + entry
                                    rule: Form over.
                            [self customersWaiting or: [self aServerStillBusy]]
                                    whileTrue: [self
                                            getNextEvent: false;
                                            processNextEvent].
                            "Shut the exit door and display happy face."
                            (Form extent: 6@60) black
                                    displayOn: Display
                                    at: offset + exit
                                    rule: Form over.
                            HappyFace displayAt: offset + (80@275)
```

serviceCompleted
```
                    "Customer service completed. Accept next customer if there is one, or set server
free."
                    | nextServer |
                    nextServer ← servers at: nextEvent key.
                    self
                            customerAt: nextServer location
                            moveTo: exit.
                    self customersWaiting
                            ifTrue: [ "Take a customer from Q and service"
                                    customerQ remove.
                                    nextServer serveCust.
                                    self
                                            customerAt: waitingLine firstPoint
                                            moveTo: nextServer location;
                                            updateWaitingLine]
                            ifFalse: ["No customers to serve; set the server free"
                                    nextServer setServerFree]
```

updateTimeDisplay: status
```
                    "Update time display with time remaining if open or closed if closed."
                    | timeRemaining |
                    timeRemaining ← (simulationTime - SimTime getTime) truncated.
                    self bankIsOpen
                            ifTrue: ['Bank Remaining Time Open: ', timeRemaining printString, '
minutes      '
                                                            displayAt: offset + (40@180)]
                            ifFalse: [ 'Bank is closed'                              '
                                                            displayAt: offset + (40@180)]
```

updateWaitingLine
```
                    "Line has changed; redisplay it."
                    | index |
                    index ← 1.
```

```
customerQ size = 0 ifFalse: [
        customerQ displayQueue: [ :image |
                image
                                displayOn: Display
                                at: (waitingLine at: index)
                                rule: Form over.
                        index ← index + 1]].
index < waitingLine size ifTrue: [
        index to: waitingLine size do: [ :i |
                AnimatedCustomer blank
                displayOn: Display
                at: (waitingLine at: i)
                rule: Form over]]
```

AnimatedBankSim methodsFor: 'initialize'

addFeatures
```
        "Add title and time left for bank to be open to display."
        (Form extent: 430@100) white;
                borderWidth: 2;
                displayAt: offset + (15@125).
        'ANIMATED BANK SIMULATION:  Copyright (C) L. J. Pinson'
                displayAt: offset + (30@150).
        'Bank Remaining Time Open: '
                displayAt: offset + (40@180)
```

addTellers
```
        "Compute teller locations and display with counters."
        | counter y1 |
        y1 ← 600 - (40 * (numberServers - 1)) // 2.
        counter ← (Form extent: 30@24)
                offset: -15@-12;
                gray;
                borderWidth: 1.
        1 to: numberServers do: [ : i |  "set locations and display tellers"
                (servers at: i)
                        location: offset + (600@(i-1*40+y1)).
                counter
                        displayOn: Display
                        at: (servers at: i) location + (30@0)
                        rule: Form over.
                (AnimatedServer image)
                        displayOn: Display
                        at: (servers at: i) location + (50@0)
                        rule: Form over]
```

createBankImage
```
        "Create the image of tellers and bank details"
        entry ← 0@515.
        exit ← 0@30.
```

Listing 11.2
(continued)

```
self
        createBankStructure;
        addTellers;
        defineWaitingLine;
        defineExitPath;
        addFeatures.
```

createBankStructure
```
"Create the walls, doors and partitions and display at offset point."
        | cage rect |
bankImage ← (Form extent: 675@600) white;
        borderWidth: 6.
bankImage
        displayOn: Display
        at: offset
        rule: Form over.
rect ← Rectangle origin: 0@0 extent: 475@350.
cage ← Form extent: rect extent.
cage white;
        border: rect
        width: 6
        mask: Form gray.
cage
        displayOn: Display
        at: offset + (0@250)
        rule: 7.
(Form extent: 6@60) white
        displayOn: Display
        at: entry + offset
        rule: Form over.
(Form extent: 6@60) white
        displayOn: Display
        at: exit + offset
        rule: Form over.
(Form extent: 6@50) white
        displayOn: Display
        at: offset + (469@275)
        rule: Form over.
```

defineExitPath
```
"Define the exit path taking into account the offset. Go out the door."
| y1 deltaY |
y1 ← 600 - (40 * (numberServers - 1)) // 2.
deltaY ← y1 - 55 // 10.
pathToDoor ← Path new.
        1 to:  11 do: [ :i | pathToDoor
                add: offset + (550@(y1 - (i - 1 * deltaY)))].
        1 to: 21 do: [ :i | pathToDoor
                add: offset + (550 - (i * 25) @ 55)].
```

defineWaitingLine
```
"Define the path that is the waiting line taking into account the value of offset."
waitingLine ← Path new.
1 to: 16 do: [ :line | waitingLine
        add: 375 - (line - 1 * 25)@0].
```

```
            2 to: 10 do: [ :pos | 1 to: 14 do: [ :line |
                    pos odd
                            ifTrue: [waitingLine
                                    add: 325 - (line - 1 * 25)@(pos - 1 * 20) ]
                            ifFalse:[waitingLine
                                    add: line - 1 * 25@(pos - 1 * 20) ]]].
            waitingLine ← waitingLine translateBy: offset + (75@300).
```

init: aPoint
```
        "prompt user for inputs and create the bank image at offset aPoint.
                Different from super class because must limit number of servers."
        offset ← aPoint.
        bankIsOpen ← true.
        nextEvent ← Association key: 0 value: 0.
        simulationTime ← (FillInTheBlank
                request: 'Enter number of hours bank open:  ') asNumber *60.
        numberServers ← (FillInTheBlank
                request: 'Enter number of tellers (max = 10):  ') asNumber.
        numberServers ← 10 min: numberServers.
        servers ← (Array new: numberServers).
                "Create server array and install average service times."
        1 to: numberServers do: [ :serverNo |
                servers
                        at: serverNo
                        put: (AnimatedServer init: serverNo)].
        AnimatedCustomer init.
        customerQ ← AnimatedCustomerQueue new.
        self createBankImage
```

setDelay: anInteger
```
        "Set delay for graphics to anInteger milliseconds."
        delay ← anInteger
```


AnimatedBankSim class
        instanceVariableNames: ''

AnimatedBankSim class comment: ''

AnimatedBankSim class methodsFor: 'example'

example: milliseconds at: aPoint
```
    " To run the animated simulation select and execute the following expression
        milliseconds is delay for graphics; good value is 50 to watch show.


                                AnimatedBankSim example: 0 at: 7@20  "
        self title.
        Form
                slideBorder: (Rectangle origin: 0@0 extent: 690@1024)
                width: 4.
        self new
                setDelay: milliseconds;
                init: aPoint;
                run;
                stats
```

Listing 11.2
(continued)

title

Transcript clear; refresh;
show: 'Bank Simulation Program - L. J. Pinson Animated Version 1 ,
August 7, 1987'

AnimatedBankSim class methodsFor: 'class initialization'

initialize

"Set form for HappyFace. Must first generate it somewhere else."
HappyFace ← Form fromUser

Listing 11.3
Protocol
Description
for Class
AnimatedCustomer

Customer subclass: #AnimatedCustomer
instanceVariableNames: ''
classVariableNames: 'BlankCustomer FemaleCustomer MaleCustomer '
poolDictionaries: ''
category: 'BankSimulation'

AnimatedCustomer comment: This class generates images for the animated line. The image
and the arrival time are independent of each other. New Instance variables are:

BlankCustomer -- a Form like the background for representing no customer.
FemaleCustomer -- a Form representing the graphic image of a female customer.
MaleCustomer -- a Form representing the graphic image of a male customer.

AnimatedCustomer methodsFor: 'accessing'

image

"Answer a random male or female form for the customer image."
RandomTime next < 0.5
ifTrue: [↑MaleCustomer]
ifFalse:[↑FemaleCustomer]

AnimatedCustomer class
instanceVariableNames: ''

AnimatedCustomer class comment: ''

AnimatedCustomer class methodsFor: 'inquiries'

blank

↑BlankCustomer

AnimatedCustomer class methodsFor: 'class initialization'

initialize
    "Initialize super class and establish class variables."
    MaleCustomer ← Form extent: 16@16
        fromArray: #(
                2r0000000011000000
                2r0000001111110000
                2r0000011011011000
                2r0000110011001100
                2r0001100110000110
                2r0000000110000000
                2r0000000110000000
                2r0000111111100000
                2r0011100000111000
                2r0110000000001100
                2r1100000000000110
                2r1100000000000110
                2r0110000000001100
                2r0011100000111000
                2r0000111111100000
                2r0000000000000000)
        offset: -8@-8.
    FemaleCustomer ← Form extent: 16@16
        fromArray: #(
        2r0000000011000000
        2r0000000011000000
        2r0000000011000000
        2r0000111111111100
        2r0001111111111000
        2r0000000110000000
        2r0000000110000000
        2r0000111111100000
        2r0011100000111000
        2r0110000000001100
        2r1100000000000110
        2r1100000000000110
        2r0110000000001100
        2r0011100000111000
        2r0000111111100000
        2r0000000000000000)
        offset: -8@-8.
    BlankCustomer ← (Form extent: 16@16)
        white;
        offset: -8@-8.

"AnimatedCustomer initialize"

Listing 11.4
Protocol
Description
for Class
**Animated-
CustomerQueue**

CustomerQueue subclass: #AnimatedCustomerQueue
    instanceVariableNames: 'queueOfImages '
    classVariableNames: ''
    poolDictionaries: ''
    category: 'BankSimulation'

AnimatedCustomerQueue comment: 'I inherit protocol from CustomerQueue. In addition I maintain a queue of images that are obtained from instances of AnimatedCustomer (forms). I add the following new instance variable.

        queueOfImages -- an instance of OrderedCollection containing 16 x 16 forms for male & female customers.'

AnimatedCustomerQueue methodsFor: 'display'

displayQueue: aBlock
    "Execute aBlock for each image in queueOfImages."
    queueOfImages do: aBlock

AnimatedCustomerQueue methodsFor: 'accessing'

insert
    "Insert an image in queueOfImages and a time in queue."
    | nextImage |
    nextImage ← AnimatedCustomer new image. "Get a male or female image."
    super insert.
    queueOfImages addLast: nextImage

last
    "Answer the last image in the line."
    ↑queueOfImages last

remove
    "Update stats for the queue, remove first customer (time) in queue, and remove and answer the image at front of queueOfImages."
    super remove.
    ↑queueOfImages removeFirst

AnimatedCustomerQueue methodsFor: 'initialize'

init
    super init.
    queueOfImages ← OrderedCollection new.

Listing 11.5
Protocol
Description
for Class
AnimatedServer

Server subclass: #AnimatedServer
    instanceVariableNames: 'location '
    classVariableNames: 'TellerImage '
    poolDictionaries: ''
    category: 'BankSimulation'

AnimatedServer comment: 'I inherit most of my protocol from my superclass, Server. I add an image for tellers and a location where I am displayed in the bank. I add the following new data objects.

        TellerImage -- a 16 x 16 form that is the teller image.
        location -- an instance of Point where I am to be displayed.'

AnimatedServer methodsFor: 'accessing'

location
    "Answer location of image."
    ↑location

location: aPoint
    "Set a point in front of server for customers to stand."
    location ← aPoint

AnimatedServer class
    instanceVariableNames: ''

AnimatedServer class comment: ''

AnimatedServer class methodsFor: 'class initialization'

initialize
    "Set the form for the animated teller."
    TellerImage ← Form extent: 16@16
        fromArray: #(
                2r0000000110000000
                2r0000000110000000
                2r0000011111100000
                2r0001110110111000
                2r0011000110001100
                2r0011000110001100
                2r0011000110000000
                2r0001110110000000
                2r0000011111100000
                2r0000000110111000
                2r0000000110001100
                2r0011000110001100
                2r0011000110001100
                2r0001110110111000
                2r0000011111100000
                2r0000000110000000)
        offset: -8@-8

Listing 11.5
(continued)

"AnimatedServer initialize"

AnimatedServ   class methodsFor: 'image retrieval'

image
        ↑TellerImage

11.3.4   Example results

The following figures illustrate some of the key features of the animated bank simulation software. Figure 11.6 shows the status early in the day and with no waiting time. There are servers idle, and a new customer is approaching the service area.

Figure 11.7 illustrates the situation at the close of business when there are still customers in line to be served. The entry door is closed, and customers are being cleared from the waiting line. Teller number 7 is just receiving a new customer to serve.

Figure 11.8 shows the final result after all customers have left the bank from the example in Figure 11.7. Both doors are closed, and the large happy face is displayed. Statistical summaries are presented in the Transcript window for the run. For this run the bank was open only one hour.

11.4   Adding an MVC Triad to the Binary Tree Classes

This section adds new subclasses to the binary tree classes for supporting graphic display and interaction with binary trees. In addition to providing a display of the tree structure, menu options are included for inserting a new node, removing an existing node, and for producing a hardcopy printout of the tree display. A model-view-controller triad is developed to support the graphic display and interaction with binary trees. The three components are described below.

- **model**—Class **Tree** is the model for binary trees. Its supporting classes, **TreeNode** and its subclasses, are also important to the MVC triad. The model may be an instance of the **Tree** subclass **ExpressionTree,** as well.

- **view**—A new class, **TreeView,** is defined as a subclass of **View.** It provides protocol for displaying the binary tree.

- **controller**—A new class, **TreeController,** is defined as a subclass of **Mouse-MenuController.** Its purpose is to provide user interaction with the tree view.

Both the new classes **TreeView** and **TreeController** are included in the class category *Trees—Ordered.* This maintains a consistent grouping of all the tree

**Figure 11.6
AnimatedBank-
Sim**—Early in the
Day—Servers Idle

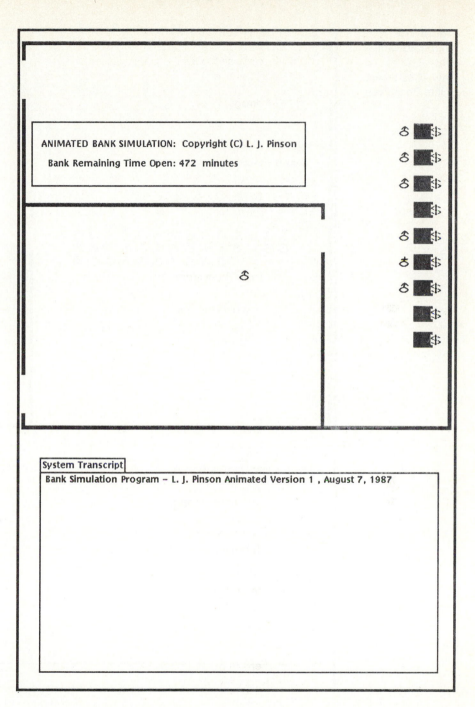

Figure 11.7 AnimatedBank-Sim—End of Day—Customers Still to Be Served

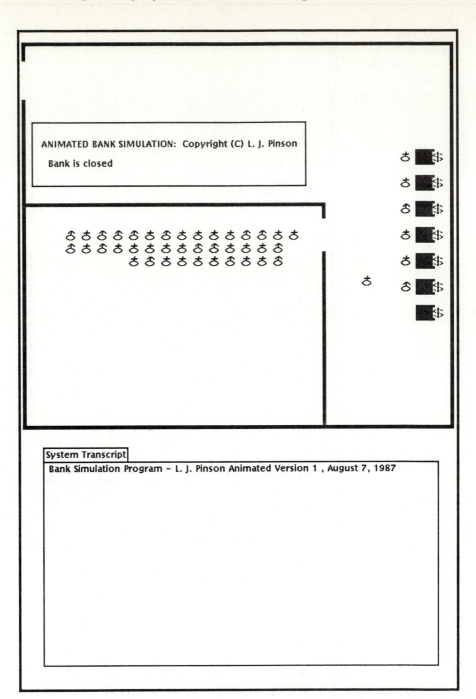

**Figure 11.8
AnimatedBank-
Sim**—End of
Day—All
Customers Cleared

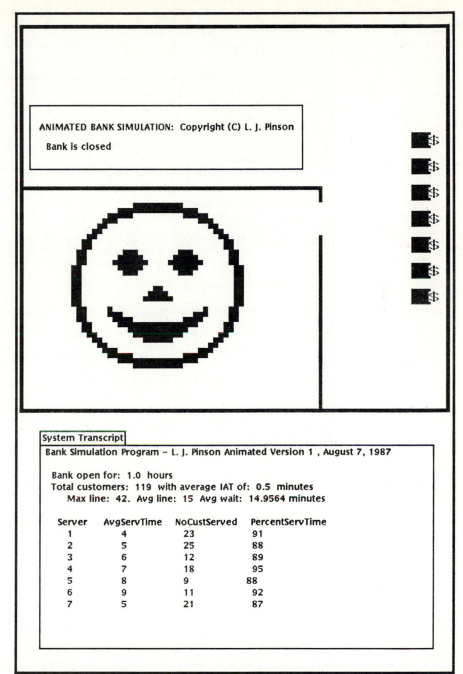

ANIMATED BANK SIMULATION: Copyright (C) L. J. Pinson

Bank is closed

System Transcript

Bank Simulation Program – L. J. Pinson Animated Version 1 , August 7, 1987

Bank open for: 1.0 hours
Total customers: 119 with average IAT of: 0.5 minutes
   Max line: 42. Avg line: 15 Avg wait: 14.9564 minutes

Server	AvgServTime	NoCustServed	PercentServTime
1	4	23	91
2	5	25	88
3	6	12	89
4	7	18	95
5	8	9	88
6	9	11	92
7	5	21	87

Figure 11.9
Hierarchy for
Binary Tree MVC
Support

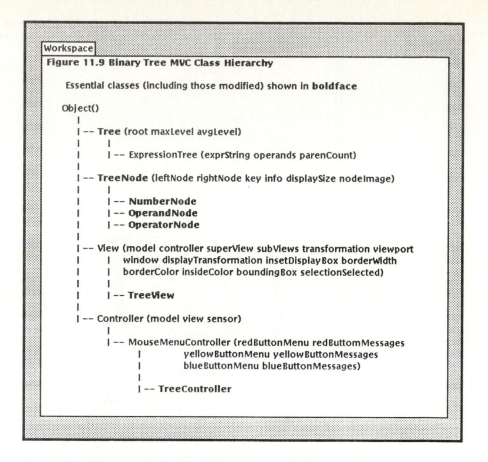

```
Workspace
Figure 11.9 Binary Tree MVC Class Hierarchy

Essential classes (including those modified) shown in boldface

Object()
   |
   | -- Tree (root maxLevel avgLevel)
   |      |
   |      | -- ExpressionTree (exprString operands parenCount)
   |
   | -- TreeNode (leftNode rightNode key info displaySize nodeImage)
   |      |
   |      | -- NumberNode
   |      | -- OperandNode
   |      | -- OperatorNode
   |
   | -- View (model controller superView subViews transformation viewport
   |      |     window displayTransformation insetDisplayBox borderWidth
   |      |     borderColor insideColor boundingBox selectionSelected)
   |      |
   |      | -- TreeView
   |
   | -- Controller (model view sensor)
          |
          | -- MouseMenuController (redButtonMenu redButtomMessages
          |            yellowButtonMenu yellowButtonMessages
          |            blueButtonMenu blueButtonMessages)
          |
          | -- TreeController
```

classes. Much of the required protocol for views and controllers is explained in Chapter 9. This knowledge is applied here to define the new classes **TreeView** and **TreeController.** In fact, most of the protocol for these new classes is developed by cut-and-paste operations on methods with the same message selectors in classes **HistogramView** and **HistogramController.** In addition, these two classes inherit most of their protocol from their superclasses.

Figure 11.9 gives an updated hierarchy chart for the tree classes. The new classes supporting graphics are shown in boldface.

Because of the recursive methods used for traversing binary trees (for display or access) that are included in class **TreeNode,** much of the display protocol for **TreeView** depends on messages to tree nodes. In the implementation described below, new methods are added to **TreeNode** to support the graphic display of the tree. This choice violates the principle stated in Chapter 9 that a model does not know how to display itself. Because of the doubly recursive techniques already available in **TreeNode,** the choice is justified for this example.

Details follow for new protocol in the model classes **Tree, TreeNode,** and subclasses of **TreeNode.** Complete protocol summaries are given for classes

TreeView and **TreeController.** Then examples are given of the actual use of the tree MVC triad. Finally, complete listings are given for the view and controller classes. This is consistent with the goal of providing a complete understanding of the incremental solution.

11.4.1   Details of new protocol in the model classes

- **Tree** method **computeBoundingBox**—This method supports protocol in **TreeView** (defaultWindow) for setting the minimum rectangle required to display an instance of **Tree.** It sends the message setNodeDisplayParams to its root node.

- **TreeNode** methods **setNodeDisplayParams** and **setNodeDisplay-Params:**—These two methods recursively compute the required display rectangle for each node in the tree. A new instance variable in **TreeNode,** displaySize, is an instance of **Point** that is the extent of the required display rectangle for each node. The value of this instance variable is established for each node by these two methods. The minimal spacing is computed unless the value of a new class variable, **Delta,** is set to a point value other than 0@0. Setting Delta to a non-zero value causes the nodes to be separated further when displayed.

  The value of Delta is set by a new class method, setDelta: aPoint, in class **TreeNode.** Its value is set by the message setNodeParams: aPoint in **TreeView.** The current implementation sets Delta to 30@30.

  The method setNodeDisplayParams: also sets the value of a new instance variable, nodeImage, for each node. This instance variable is an instance of **Form** that is the image for a given node. These images consist of rectangles with the key value displayed inside. The actual details of a node's image are a subclass responsibility for each kind of node.

- Methods **setNodeImage** and **nodeImage** in classes **TreeNode, NumberNode, OperatorNode,** and **OperandNode**—Method setNodeImage computes the minimum size rectangle required to display contents representative of each kind of node. It is implemented as subclassResponsibility in **TreeNode.** In **NumberNode** the key value (a number) is displayed in a rectangle. In **OperandNode** a string key value is displayed. In **Operator-Node** the key value and info fields are both displayed. The info field in an **OperatorNode** denotes relative precedence of the operator key. Method nodeImage is implemented only in class **TreeNode.** It answers the node image for all subclasses.

- Methods **displaySize** and **displaySize:** aPoint—These methods are implemented in class **TreeNode** to answer and set the value of displaySize, respectively.

- **TreeNode** method **showImageAt:** aPoint **as:** direction—This is a doubly recursive method for displaying the nodes in the tree. This message is sent by the **TreeView** method displayView. Parameter direction is one of the symbols (#left #right #center) to denote that the next node is a left off-spring, right offspring, or the root node, respectively. This knowledge is required for proper computation of offsets for the display point. Parameter **aPoint** carries the most recent display point into the next recursive level.

Listing 11.6 gives complete details of the new model methods for MVC support of the binary tree classes.

Listing 11.6
New Model
Methods
Supporting
the Binary Tree
MVC Triad

Tree methodsFor: 'printing and display'

computeBoundingBox
    "Answer the minimum rectangle for displaying the tree."
    ↑Rectangle origin: 0@0 extent: root setNodeDisplayParams

TreeNode class methodsFor: 'accessing'

setDelta: aPoint
    "Set the spacing between node images for display."
    Delta ← aPoint

TreeNode methodsFor: 'accessing'

nodeImage
    "Answer the rectangle that is the node display image."
    ↑nodeImage

displaySize
    "Answer the minimum size to display the node and its subtrees."
    ↑displaySize

TreeNode methodsFor: 'printing and display'

setNodeDisplayParams
    "Answer the extent of the minimum display rectangle for the root."
    ↑self setNodeDisplayParams: self

setNodeDisplayParams: aNode
    "Set the nodeImage and answer the extent of the minimum display rectangle."
    | lSize rSize |
    aNode isNil ifTrue: [^0@0].
    aNode setNodeImage.
    aNode isLeaf ifTrue: [aNode displaySize: aNode nodeImage extent].
    lSize ← self setNodeDisplayParams: aNode left.
    rSize ← self setNodeDisplayParams: aNode right.
    aNode displaySize: lSize x + rSize x + (Delta x max: aNode nodeImage extent x)
            @ (aNode nodeImage extent y + (lSize y max: rSize y)).
    ↑aNode displaySize

showImageAt: aPoint **as:** direction
    "Display the nodeImage at aPoint.
     Direction is left or right from parent node."
    | dx dy location line |
    line ← Line new form: (Form dotOfSize: 2).
    dx ← nodeImage extent x // 2 max: Delta x // 2.
    dy ← nodeImage extent y // 2 max: Delta y // 2.
    direction = #left
       ifTrue: [location ← aPoint + (0-dx@dy).
          self right isNil ifFalse: [
             location ← location - (self right displaySize x @ 0)]].
    direction = #right ifTrue: [
       location ← aPoint + (dx@dy).
       self left isNil ifFalse: [
          location ← location + (self left displaySize x @ 0)]].
    direction = #center ifTrue: [
       location ← aPoint + (dx@0).
       self left isNil ifFalse: [
          location ← location + (self left displaySize x @ 0)]].
    direction = #center ifFalse: [
       line beginPoint: aPoint.
       line endPoint: location.
       line displayOn: Display].
    nodeImage displayOn: Display at: location.
    leftNode isNil ifFalse: [
       self left showImageAt: location + (0-dx@dy) as: #left].
    rightNode isNil ifFalse: [
       self right showImageAt: location + (dx@dy) as: #right].

TreeNode methodsFor: 'private'

setNodeImage
    "Set the rectangular image for the node, subclass responsibility."
    ↑self subclassResponsibility

displaySize: aPoint
    "Set the extent of the display size for a node and its subtrees."
    displaySize ← aPoint

NumberNode methodsFor: 'private'

setNodeImage
    | width height form |
    width ← self key printString size * 10.
    height ← 14.
    form ← Form extent: (width + 10)@(height + 11).
    form white; borderWidth: 2.
    self key printString
       displayOn: form
       at: form boundingBox center - (width//2@(height-7)).
    nodeImage ← form offset: (0@0 - (form boundingBox center))

Listing 11.6
(continued)

OperandNode methodsFor: 'private'

setNodeImage
```
    | width height form |
    width ← self key size * 9.
    height ← 14.
    form ← Form extent: (width + 14)@(height + 11).
    form white; borderWidth: 2.
    self key
        displayOn: form
        at: form boundingBox center - (width//2@(height-7)).
    nodeImage ← form offset: (0@0 - (form boundingBox center))
```

OperatorNode methodsFor: 'private'

setNodeImage
```
    | width height form aKey |
    aKey ← String with: self key.
    width ← aKey size * 10.
    height ← 28.
    form ← Form extent: (width + 10)@(height + 11).
    form white; borderWidth: 2.
    aKey
        displayOn: form
        at: form boundingBox center - (width//2@16).
    self info printString
        displayOn: form
        at: form boundingBox center - (width//2@0).
    nodeImage ← form offset: (0@0 - (form boundingBox center))
```

Protocol Summary for Class TreeView

Definition—The hierarchy for class **TreeView** is: **Object—View—TreeView.** Class **TreeView** has no instance variables, class variables, or pool dictionaries. It has one class method in one category and five instance methods in five categories.

Instance methods—Class **TreeView** has five instance methods in five categories. A summary is given below of the categories and methods.
   controller access—one method (**defaultControllerClass**) that sets the default controller class to **TreeController.**
   window access—one method (**defaultWindow**) that sets the default window size.
   displaying—one method (**displayView**) that sends appropriate messages to the model for displaying the nodes in the tree.

updating—one method (**update**) that resets the minimum display size whenever the model changes. This message is sent by menu messages in **TreeController** that insert or delete nodes from a tree.

private—one method (**setNodeParams:**) that establishes the value of the **TreeNode** class variable Delta to be a specified point.

Class methods—Class **TreeView** has one class method in one category, as summarized below.

instance creation—one method (**openOn:**) that creates an instance of **TreeView** on a binary tree.

Protocol Summary for Class TreeController

Definition—The hierarchy for class **TreeController** is **Object—Controller—MouseMenuController—TreeController.** Class **TreeController** has no instance variables, class variables, or pool dictionaries. It has one class method in one category and six instance methods in four categories.

Instance methods—Class **TreeController** has six instance methods in four categories. A summary is given below of the categories and methods.

initialize—one method (**initialize**) that sends the message initialize to its superclass and sends the private message initializeYellowButtonMenu.

menu messages—three methods (**deleteNode, insertNode, toPrinter**) that correspond to the three yellow-button menu options.

control defaults—one method (**isControlActive**) that establishes conditions for maintaining control.

private—one method (**initializeYellowButtonMenu**) for activating the yellow-button menu items and action messages.

Class methods—Class **TreeController** has one class method in one category, as summarized below.

class initialization—one method (**initialize**) that establishes the yellow-button menu options and action messages.

11.4.2   Listings of new classes

Complete protocol listings for the new binary tree classes supporting graphics display and interaction are given in the following listings. Listing 11.7 gives complete protocol for class **TreeView.** Listing 11.8 gives complete protocol for class **TreeController.**

Listing 11.7
Protocol
Description for
Class **TreeView**

```
View subclass: #TreeView
    instanceVariableNames: ''
    classVariableNames: ''
    poolDictionaries: ''
    category: 'Trees-Ordered'
```

TreeView comment: 'I display binary trees on the screen.'

TreeView methodsFor: 'private'

setNodeParams: aPoint
```
    "Establish spacing between node images."
        TreeNode setDelta: aPoint.
```


TreeView methodsFor: 'displaying'

displayView
```
    "Display a  box with a key for each node in the tree."
    model root
        showImageAt: (self displayTransform: self window origin) + (50@50)
        as: #center.
```


TreeView methodsFor: 'controller access'

defaultControllerClass
```
        ↑TreeController
```


TreeView methodsFor: 'window access'

defaultWindow
```
    "Answer the minimum bounding rectangle for the tree display."
    ↑model computeBoundingBox expandBy: 50
```


TreeView methodsFor: 'updating'

update
```
    "The model has changed, update the view."
    self topView minimumSize: self defaultWindow extent
```

TreeView class
   instanceVariableNames: ''

TreeView class comment: ''

TreeView class methodsFor: 'examples'

example1
   "This example creates a view on a binary tree with 20 random integers in it."
   | tree rand |
   tree ← Tree new.
   rand ← Random new.
   1 to: 15 do: [:i |
       tree insert: (NumberNode new: (rand next * 1000) truncated)].
   TreeView openOn: tree

   " TreeView example1 "

example2
   "This example creates a view on Tree example2a."
   TreeView openOn: Tree example2a

   " TreeView example2 "

example3
   "This example creates a view on an expression tree."
   | tree |
   tree ← ExpressionTree new getExpression; buildTree.
   TreeView openOn: tree

   " TreeView example3 "

TreeView class methodsFor: 'instance creation'

openOn: aTree
   "Create and schedule a view of a binary tree."
   | topView treeView |
   treeView ← self new
       setNodeParams: 30@30;
       model: aTree;
       borderWidth: 2;
       insideColor: Form white.
   topView ← (StandardSystemView
       model: aTree
       label: 'Binary Tree'
       minimumSize: treeView defaultWindow extent)
       addSubView: treeView.
   topView controller open

Listing 11.8
Protocol
Description
for Class
TreeController

MouseMenuController subclass: #TreeController
    instanceVariableNames: ''
    classVariableNames: 'TreeYellowButtonMenu TreeYellowButtonMessages '
    poolDictionaries: ''
    category: 'Trees-Ordered'

TreeController comment: I accept menu options 'insert and delete' for views of binary trees.

TreeController methodsFor: 'menu messages'

deleteNode
    "Prompt user for a new key value and delete from tree. Update display."
    | aKey rootKey |
    model class = ExpressionTree ifTrue: [
       ↑Transcript cr;
          show: 'Deletion from expression trees not allowed'].
    rootKey ← model root key.
    aKey ← FillInTheBlank
       request: 'Enter key to delete (',
         ((rootKey isKindOf: Number)
            ifTrue: ['number only']
            ifFalse:['string only']), ')'
       initialAnswer: ''.
    (rootKey isKindOf: Number)
       ifTrue: [aKey ← aKey asNumber].
    model delete: aKey.
    view clearInside; update; displayView

insertNode
    "Prompt user for a new key value and insert in tree. Update display."
    | aKey rootKey |
    model class = ExpressionTree
       ifTrue: [↑Transcript cr;
          show: 'Cannot insert into expression tree.'].
    rootKey ← model root key.
    aKey ← FillInTheBlank
       request: 'Enter key to insert (',
         ((rootKey isKindOf: Number)
            ifTrue: ['number only']
            ifFalse:['string only']), ')'
       initialAnswer: ''.
    (rootKey isKindOf: Number)
       ifTrue: [aKey ← aKey asNumber.
         model insert: (NumberNode new: aKey)]
       ifFalse: [model insert: (OperandNode new: aKey)].
    view clearInside; update; displayView

toPrinter
>"Send the histogram to the printer, scaled so one screen fills a page."
>Cursor execute showWhile: [
>>(Form fromDisplay: (view topView displayBox expandBy: 30))
>>outputToPrinterHor: 150 offset: 150@130]

TreeController methodsFor: 'control defaults'

isControlActive
>↑super isControlActive & sensor blueButtonPressed not

TreeController methodsFor: 'private'

initializeYellowButtonMenu
>self yellowButtonMenu: TreeYellowButtonMenu
>>yellowButtonMessages: TreeYellowButtonMessages.

TreeController methodsFor: 'initialize'

initialize
>super initialize.
>self initializeYellowButtonMenu

TreeController class
>**InstanceVariableNames:** ''

TreeController class comment: ''

TreeController class methodsFor: 'class initialization'

initialize
>"Initialize the menu for the mouse yellow button."
>TreeYellowButtonMenu ←   PopUpMenu
>>labels: 'insert node\delete node\to printer' withCRs
>>lines: #(1 2).
>TreeYellowButtonMessages ←
>>insertNode deleteNode toPrinter)
>
>"TreeController initialize"

**Figure 11.10
TreeView**
example1—MVC
Display of Binary
Tree with 20
Random Integers

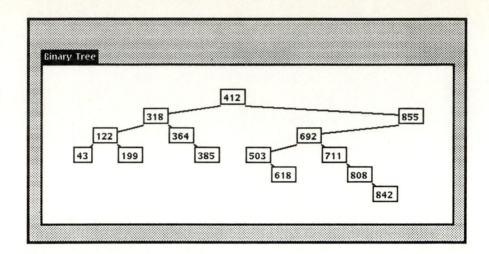

11.4.3   Example results

Tree MVC Example 11A

The following figures show results of using the binary tree MVC triad. Each menu option is exercised. The first example is for a binary tree with number nodes. It is initiated by executing **TreeView example1**. A tree with 20 random integers is generated and displayed. Results are indicated in Figure 11.10. The logic for the display is illustrated in this figure. The left subtree of a node is always completely to the left of the node, and the right subtree is displayed completely to the right of the node. Also note that the displayed node has size adjusted to the length of the number.

Tree MVC Example 11B

A second example is presented by executing **TreeView example2**. It starts with a tree generated by the **Tree** class method **example2a** whose details are given in Listing 11.9. Figure 11.11 shows the initial display of this tree with five number nodes in it. Several modifications are made to the tree using the *insert* and *delete* options from the yellow-button menu. After the changes are made, the binary tree window has its title modified. It is then dumped to the printer using the yellow-button menu option *to printer*. Prior to dumping the image to the printer, the display background is set to white.

The result is shown in Figure 11.12 The insertions and deletions are accomplished in the following order: (**del 12000; ins 48, 500, 190, 800, 10, 1000, 60; del 500; ins 80, 300**). As the size of the tree display exceeds the window, one only

Tree class methodsFor: 'examples'

example2a

"Generate a binary tree with 10 integer keys. Display keys inorder and postorder in
Transcript. Delete odd integers and redisplay."

" Tree example2a "

```
| tree |
Transcript clear; refresh;
    show: 'Insertion of integers (1..10) into a binary tree.'.
tree ← Tree new.
tree insert: (NumberNode new: 50 ) .
tree insert: (NumberNode new: 45).
tree insert: (NumberNode new: 95).
tree insert: (NumberNode new: 75).
tree insert: (NumberNode new: 12000).
↑tree
```

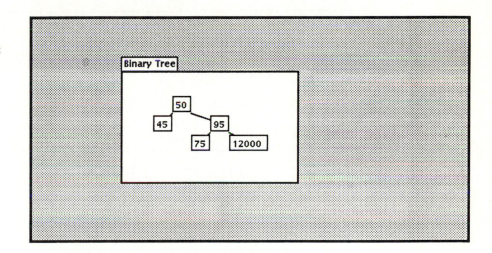

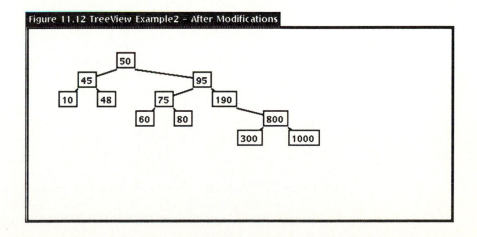

**Figure 11.13
TreeView**
example3—MVC
Display of an
Expression Tree

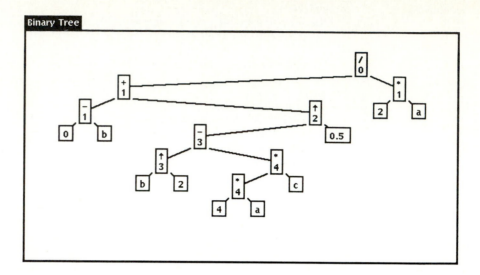

needs to reframe the window (using the blue-button menu) to adjust the minimum size.

Tree MVC Example 11C

This example generates a view of an expression tree. The expression entered is that given in Figure 4.4 in Chapter 4. It is the quadratic equation solution. Figure 11.13 shows the resulting expression tree display. For expression trees the *insert* and *delete* menu options do nothing but display an error message in the Transcript window.

These examples are not complete in terms of the functionality that may be desirable for binary and expression trees. For example, an interesting exercise is to add a menu option for expression trees that lets the user evaluate the expression. This is relatively easy and is left as an exercise for the reader.

Exercises

11.1 Figure 11.5 shows the complete hierarchy for the bank simulation classes. Based on the knowledge of all these classes and special cases (i.e., single-line, multi-line, and animated) analyze the hierarchical structure and decide if a different class hierarchy is possible. Evaluate it in comparison to the existing hierarchy for number of required methods, compactness, and consistency with object-oriented programming.

11.2 Implement the software for all three examples in this chapter on your Smalltalk system. Discuss any difficulties and their solutions. (The code is kept as generic as possible to minimize any system-specific problems).

11.3 Modify the binary tree example so that an existing node in a tree can be deleted by simply moving the mouse cursor to that node and clicking the mouse left button. Why should the mouse middle or right buttons not be used for this purpose?

11.4 Modify the animated bank simulation program to provide animation of either the single- or multi-line simulations.

11.5 Modify the binary tree MVC example so that the window is automatically redrawn whenever a node is inserted or deleted.

11.6 Repeat Exercise 11.5 for the histogram MVC example developed in Chapter 9.

11.7 Add an *evaluate* menu option to the binary expression tree MVC example. Add all details necessary for evaluation of the expression in the expression tree. To what menu should this option be attached, and why?

11.8 Add new capability to the binary expression tree class in the form of a finite-state machine for verifying the validity of an algebraic expression. The current version checks only for matching parentheses. Define appropriate classes and methods for adding this incremental capability to expression trees. What impact does this have on the other binary tree classes? What impact does it have on the MVC triad for binary trees?

APPENDIX

1

Smalltalk Syntax

This appendix provides a brief summary of the Smalltalk syntax.

A1.1   Concepts and Reserved Words

A1.1.1   Object, class, instance, message, method— the five fundamental concepts

Understanding Smalltalk requires understanding the five concepts: object, message, class, instance, and method. They are defined in a circular fashion in terms of each other. Once they are understood, the remainder of the task for understanding Smalltalk is to become totally familiar with the image.

Object
In Smalltalk, everything is an object. This is true for data structures, physical devices, concepts, files, executable program segments, source code segments, and elements of the supporting environment such as compilers and debuggers. One needs to think in terms of objects and the actions to be performed on or by those objects.

Class
A class is an object that defines properties for specific kinds of objects. Classes have names that indicate the kinds of objects they represent. Objects represented by a class are called instances of the class. Classes are arranged in a hierarchy with subclasses representing more specific kinds of objects than their superclasses. Subclasses inherit properties from their superclasses. Part of the protocol description for a class provides a way to create new instances of the class. All the actions to which an object responds are defined in its class description.

Instance

An instance is an object of a specific class. Its properties are defined by the protocol description for the class of which it is an instance. The actions to which an instance responds are defined in its class protocol.

Message

A message is an action identifier that is sent to an object. It instructs the object to perform some action. An object will respond to the message only if it is included in the protocol description of the class of which the object is an instance. All messages to which instances of a class can respond must be defined in the protocol description of the class or its superclasses. Messages are inherited by a class from its superclasses.

Method

Methods are the implementation details of messages. The protocol description of a class includes method details for each message to which instances of the class can respond. The method defines exactly how the object responds to a message. Methods usually send messages to other objects.

A1.1.2   Reserved words

There are only five reserved words in Smalltalk. These are the pseudovariables **nil**, **true**, **false**, **self**, and **super**. Pseudovariables are used like variables except their values cannot be reassigned. The first three are constants. The last two have value dependent on the context in which they are used.

nil

The reserved word **nil** is a constant-valued object used to represent uninitialized objects. When new objects are created without initialization, they are assigned the value **nil**.

true

The reserved word **true** is a constant-valued object representing Boolean truth.

false

The reserved word **false** is a constant-valued object representing Boolean nontruth.

self

The reserved word **self** is a pseudovariable object used in methods to refer to the receiver of the message for which the method gives details. The value of **self** is always the object that received the message. Messages sent to **self** in the method details must be defined in the protocol of the class of the receiver.

super

The reserved word **super** is a pseudovariable object used in methods to refer to the receiver of the message for which the method gives details. The value of **super** is always the object that received the message. The only difference between **self** and **super** is that messages to **super** are first sought in the class description of the superclass of the class of the receiver. This provides a mechanism for superceding the same message in the class of the receiver.

A1.1.3   Virtual image, virtual machine, primitives

The virtual image is the software representing all the classes and objects that are part of the system. It contains compiled versions of all methods and provides access to the source code for all the compiled methods.

The virtual machine is the hardware, the interpreter and other machine microcode that provide functionality for using the virtual image.

Primitives are low-level methods, implemented in assembly language, that help bridge the gap between the image and the machine. They are optimized for efficiency and are the method details for selected key messages in the image. Some implementations of Smalltalk provide support for user-generated primitives.

A more detailed discussion of the virtual machine and of the standard primitives is given in Part Four of Goldberg and Robson.

A1.2   Literals

Smalltalk provides support for literals as instances of five classes: **Character, Number, String, Symbol,** and **Array.** This includes each subclass of **Number** (**Integer, Float, Fraction**).

A1.2.1   Character

A character literal is any ASCII character preceded by a $ sign (e.g., $A $5 $= $$ $" $' $q $| $} $] $($%).

A1.2.2   Number

Numbers begin with a digit (0..9) or a minus sign. Floating point numbers are identified by inclusion of a decimal point and/or an exponent. The exponent consists of the character *e* followed by a signed integer (with or without a minus sign). Rational fractions are identified by ordinary division of two integers (using the / operator). The radix of a number can be specified by preceding a number with xxr where xx is the radix. The default radix is 10. Examples of numbers follow.

456	an **Integer**
−34	a negative **Integer**
2r111	binary representation for **Integer** 7
2.56	a **Float**
−4.1	a negative **Float**
1.0e−20	a **Float**
−3.5e10	a negative **Float**
16rFF.C	a hexadecimal **Float**
5/7	a **Fraction**
6/3	a **Fraction** that becomes an **Integer** 2
.25	an error (cannot begin with decimal point)
1.	an error (cannot end with decimal point)
1.0e.5	an error (exponent must be an **Integer**)

New protocol added in Chapter 6 of this book provides literal support for instances of **Imaginary** and **Complex.** Examples are given below for these two classes.

j6	an **Imaginary** (**Integer**)
j22.9	an **Imaginary** (**Float**)
j3/8	an **Imaginary** (**Fraction**)
j8r177	an **Imaginary** (radix 8 **Integer**)
−j1.5e−8	a negative **Imaginary** (**Float**)
j−1	a **Complex** (−1 + j1)
22.6+j8r22	a **Complex**
j(3)	error (support not provided)

A1.2.3   String

A string is any sequence of characters enclosed between single quotes. Single quotes can be embedded in the string if they are doubled. Examples are given below.

‘This is a string.’
‘It’’s another string example.’
‘Strings may contain $ &) | @ any special symbol.’

A1.2.4   **Symbol**

A symbol is an identifier, binary selector, or keyword selector preceded by a pound sign, #. All symbols are unique. Thus any new symbol defined must have a unique sequence of characters, or else it is not a new symbol. Examples of symbols follow.

#aSymbol	an identifier
#*	a binary selector
#at:put:	a keyword selector
#2Times	error (identifiers must begin with a letter)

A1.2.5   **Array**

An array is a data structure whose elements can be any valid object. Literal arrays are arrays of literals. Arrays are delimited by the special symbols #(and). Elements of an array can be arrays. An example of an array is

#($d 22.4 2r1101 symbol ('string' symbol2 (2 13.5)))

Arrays and symbols within an array drop the preceding # sign.

A1.3   Delimiters and Special Symbols

A tabular listing of all special symbols and their meanings is given below. Normal symbols for arithmetic operations and comparison are not given; they are defined in the **Object** and **Number** classes and are typically the same as those used in most languages. In Smalltalk they can be redefined. The following symbols (except for the comma) cannot be redefined.

"	double quote (comment delimiters)
'	single quote (string delimiters)
$	dollar sign (precedes character literals)
#	pound sign (precedes symbols and arrays)
#( )	array delimiters
.	period (statement separator)
,	comma (concatenation operator)
;	semicolon (separator for multiple messages to an object)
:	colon (terminator for some keyword messages and precedes a block parameter)
|	vertical bar (temporary variable delimiter and separator for block parameter)
:=	colon-equal (assignment in some versions of Smalltalk)
←	left arrow (assignment in standard Smalltalk-80)
↑	up arrow (precedes object whose value is to be returned from a method)
( )	parentheses (specify higher precedence inside)
[ ]	square brackets (block delimiters or precedence control)
{ }	curly brackets (control precedence)

A1.4   Variables and Identifiers

A1.4.1   Identifiers and readability

No special symbols or separators are allowed as part of identifiers. The method for making multiword identifiers more readable concerns their case. Although not required, the convention for case of characters in identifiers is followed by all Smalltalk implementations. Following this convention makes Smalltalk code more readable. All multiword identifiers use uppercase for the first character of all words after the first word. If the identifier is a parameter, temporary variable, or instance variable, the first character of the first word is lowercase. If the identifier is a class variable, class name, or global variable, the first character of the first word is uppercase.

A1.4.2   Variables—instance, class, temporary, global, pool, parameters

Instance Variables (Private)
Instance variables are private to instances of a class. Their values are unique to each instance, yet all instances of a class will have the same set of instance variables. Instance variables are accessible only by the instance methods of a class and its subclasses.

Class Variables (Shared)
Class variables are shared by all instances of a class and its subclasses. They have the same values for all instances. Class variables are accessible by the class methods and the instance methods of a class and its subclasses.

Temporary Variables (Private)
Temporary variables have scope that is limited to the method or Smalltalk program in which they are defined. They cannot be accessed outside their scope. They exist only while the program or method is activated.

Global Variables (Shared)
Global variables are accessible by any method in the Smalltalk system. A dictionary of global variables and their values is kept as the system dictionary, **Smalltalk.** All the class names are global variables. **Smalltalk** is also a global variable that is defined in **Smalltalk.**

Pool Variables (Shared)

Pool variables are shared by classes that specifically include them in their protocol definition. They are global to those classes only.

Parameters (Private)

Parameters are objects defined in the method details for message selectors. They are private to the method and cannot be accessed outside the method.

A1.5   Messages

There are three kinds of messages in Smalltalk: unary, binary, and keyword. Keyword messages have almost unlimited variety. Each is defined below with examples.

A1.5.1   Unary

Unary messages are defined by single identifiers. For example,

tree class	message class answers the class of tree
0.3 sin	message sin answers the sin of 0.3
Array new	message new creates a new instance of **Array**
pen up	message up sets the status of pen to up

A1.5.2   Binary

Binary messages are defined by an identifier with exactly one parameter. The parameter follows the identifier. For example,

x ∗ y	message ∗ is sent to x with parameter y
2 @ 3	message @ is sent to 2 with parameter 3
6 // 5	message // is sent to 6 with parameter 5

A1.5.3   Keyword

Keyword messages consist of any number of identifier/parameter pairs. Each identifier (selector) is terminated by a colon to distinguish it from the parameter. The message consists of all the keywords. The keywords are distributed with parameters interspersed for increased readability. For example,

array at: 2 put: 'string'
25 max: 50
image displayOn: Display at: aPoint rule: 7

The first example sends the message **at: put:** to object **array** with parameters **2** and '**string**'. It inserts '**string**' into position **2** of **array**. The second example sends the message **max:** to object **25** with parameter **50**. It answers the maximum of the receiver (**25**) and the parameter (**50**). The third example sends the message **displayOn: at: rule:** to object **image** with parameters **Display**, **aPoint**, and **7**. It displays **image** on the **Display** at location **aPoint** using combination rule **7**.

The user can define messages in any of the three categories.

A1.6   Expressions, Precedence, and Deferred Execution

Expressions consist of objects and messages. The result of sending a message to an object is always an object. An expression that does not have a message (i.e., an object only) always returns the object if it is evaluated. The object occurs first in an expression, followed by one or more messages.

Multiple messages to one object are separated by semicolons. The order of precedence is left to right, with the leftmost message being evaluated first. Left-to-right precedence is overridden by the relative precedence of the three kinds of messages. Unary messages have highest precedence, followed by binary messages, with keyword messages last. Left-to-right precedence can be overridden by the insertion of parentheses. Expressions inside parentheses have highest precedence.

Expressions in blocks are not executed until the message **value** is sent to the block. For example, the following block is defined and later evaluated.

```
| aBlock |
aBlock ← ['This is a string' displayAt: 500@500].
Display white.
aBlock value.
```

The block is created with an expression for displaying a string on the display screen at a specified location. The display screen is cleared (set to white). Then the string is actually displayed on the screen at location (500, 500). Blocks may also have parameters. The protocol for blocks with parameters is demonstrated in the chapters.

The following expression creates a form that is a white rectangle of size 100-by-50 pixels with a black border of 2 pixels and displays it on the display screen with the upper left corner at location (200, 200). It overwrites what is already on the display beneath it.

```
((Form extent: 100 @ 50) white borderWidth: 2)
displayOn: Display
at: 200 @ 200
rule: Form over
```

The sequence of messages follows the pattern determined by relative precedence, as given below.

1. The object **100** is sent the message @ with parameter **50**. The result is an object (a new instance of **Point**) with x-coordinate = 100 and y-coordinate = 50.

2. The object **Form** (a class name) is sent the message **extent:** with parameter **aPoint** (the result of Step 1). The result of this message is a new instance of **Form** with rectangular size specified by **aPoint** (100 pixels wide by 50 pixels high).

3. The object that is the new form created in Step 2 is sent the unary message **white**. The result is the same form created in Step 2 with its bitmap set to white (all zeros).

4. The form that results from Step 3 is sent the keyword message **borderWidth:** with parameter **2**. The result is the same form with a two-pixel wide black border added to its bitmap.

5. The form resulting from Step 4 is sent the keyword message **displayOn: at: rule:** with parameters **Display**, **200 @ 200**, and **Form over**. Execution is deferred because two of the parameter objects are expressions with higher precedence than this message. They must first be evaluated.

6. The first message left to right is a binary message. The message @ is sent to object **200** with parameter **200**. The result is a new instance of **Point** with coordinates x = 200 and y = 200. This object is now the parameter for the message selector **at:** in Step 5.

7. The next expression sends the unary message **over** to the class name object **Form**. The result is an integer that represents the combination rule for overwriting. This object is now the parameter for the message selector **rule:** in Step 5.

8. Finally the expression in Step 5 is executed. It displays the rectangle on the display as described above. In addition to performing the actual display, this expression returns an object that is the form itself.

Summary Protocol of the Smalltalk Image

This appendix gives protocol for providing a printout of the Smalltalk-80 image. Two examples of protocol summary printouts are given. The image is the Tektronix Version 2.2.0c image with all modifications developed in this book.

First, the added methods that produce the protocol printout for the Smalltalk virtual image are presented. Existing classes and methods provide the framework for these new methods. Specifically, from the System Browser there are messages sent that provide the ability to access any part of the Smalltalk image. The message printHierarchy is sent to a class name to display the hierarchy of that class in the browser text subview. Using this method and methods for setting the emphasis of characters, several new methods are added to class **Behavior** for printing out the image hierarchy.

The hierarchy option in the browser lists all super- and subclasses of the selected class name with appropriate indentation. It also lists all instance variables for each class. As a first example for printing the complete image hierarchy, a new method, toPrinterHierarchyNamesOnly, is developed in class **Behavior.** Details of the method are given in Listing A2.1. It prints only the class names with indentation.

Listing A2.1
Details of
Behavior Method
toPrinterHierarchy-
NamesOnly

Behavior methodsFor: 'printing'

toPrinterHierarchyNamesOnly
   "Send the emphasized hierarchy of the receiver to the printer"

   | fileStream |

   Transcript refresh; cr; cr;
      show: 'Sending to printer, hierarchy for class: ', self name.
   fileStream ← Disk file: (self name, 'Hierarchy.prn') asFileName.
   fileStream emphasis: 3. "italic"
   Smalltalk timeStamp: fileStream.
   fileStream cr; cr.
   fileStream nextPutAll: self printEmphasizedHierarchyNamesOnly.
   fileStream close.
   (self name, 'Hierarchy.prn') asFileName printFile: 20.
   fileStream remove.

The method toPrinterHierarchyNamesOnly sends the message printEmpha-sizedHierarchyNamesOnly, which is developed from an existing method, print-Hierarchy, in class **Behavior.** Details of printEmphasizedHierarchyNamesOnly are given in Listing A2.2.

Listing A2.2
Details of
Behavior Method
printEmphasized-
Hierarchy-
NamesOnly

Behavior methodsFor: 'printing'

printEmphasizedHierarchyNamesOnly
   "Answer a description containing the names and instance variable names of all of the
      subclasses and superclasses of the receiver. Add boldface emphasis to the class
      names"

      | aStream index supers |
   index ← 0.
   aStream ← WriteStream on: (String new: 16).
   self allDynamicSuperclasses reverseDo: [:aClass |
      aStream crtab: index.
      index ← index + 1.
      aStream emphasis: 2.
      aStream nextPutAll: aClass name.
      supers ← aClass superclasses.
      supers size > 1 ifTrue:[
         aStream nextPutAll: ' [also a '.
         (supers copyFrom: 2 to: supers size) do: [:s |
            aStream space; emphasis: 2; nextPutAll: s name].
         aStream nextPut: $]]].
   aStream cr.
   self
      printEmphasizedNameOfSubclassesOn: aStream
      callingSuperclass: self dynamicSuperclass
      level: index.
   ↑aStream contents

The method printEmphasizedHierarchyNamesOnly sends the message print-EmphasizedNameOfSubclassesOn: callingSuperclass: level:. It is also developed from an existing class in class **Behavior.** Details of this modified method are given in Listing A2.3.

Listing A2.3
Details of
Behavior Method
printEmphasized-
NamesOf-
SubclassesOn:
callingSuperclass:
level:

Behavior methodsFor: 'private'

printEmphasizedNameOfSubclassesOn: aStream **callingSuperclass:** whichSuper
   level: level

   "As part of the algorithm for printing a description of the receiver, print the subclass on
      the file stream, aStream, indenting level times."

      | subs supers |
   aStream crtab: level.

Listing A2.3
(continued)

```
aStream emphasis: 2.
aStream nextPutAll: self name.
supers ← self superclasses.
supers size > 1 ifTrue: [
    aStream nextPutAll: ' [also a'.
    (supers copyWithout: whichSuper) do: [:s |
        aStream space; emphasis: 2; nextPutAll: s name].
    aStream nextPut: $] ].
subs ← self subclasses.
self = = Class ifTrue: [
    aStream crtab: level + 1;
        nextPutAll: '... all the Metaclasses ...'.
    subs ← subs reject: [:sub | sub isMeta]].
"Print subclasses in alphabetical order"
(subs asSortedCollection: [:x :y | x name < y name]) do: [:sub |
    sub
        printEmphasizedNameOfSubclassesOn: aStream
        callingSuperclass: self level: level + 1]
```

An example method is added as class method **example1** to class **Behavior.** Its details are given in Listing A2.4. The example sends the message **toPrinterHierarchyNamesOnly** to **Object.** The result is a complete hierarchy list (names only) of the entire Smalltalk image. The result is shown in Listing A2.5.

Listing A2.4
Details of
Behavior
example1

Behavior class methodsFor: 'examples'

example1
    "Example of hierarchy printout of a class.
        This example prints the entire image hierarchy."

    Object toPrinterHierarchyNamesOnly

    " Behavior example1 "

Listing A2.5
Complete Image
Hierarchy
(names only)

```
Object
    BankSimulation
        AnimatedBankSim
        MultiLineBankSimulation
    Behavior
        ClassDescription
            Class
                ... all the Metaclasses ...
            Metaclass
                MetaclassForMultipleInheritance
    Benchmark
    BinaryChoice
```

BitBlt
   CharacterScanner
      CharacterBlockScanner
      CompositionScanner
      DisplayScanner
   Pen
Boolean
   False
   True
Browser
   Debugger
   MethodListBrowser
Change
   ClassRelatedChange
      ClassChange
         ClassDefinitionChange
         ClassOtherChange
            ClassCommentChange
         ClassReorganizationChange
      MethodChange
         MethodDefinitionChange
         MethodOtherChange
   OtherChange
ChangeSet
Checker
ClassCategoryReader
ClassOrganizer
   SystemOrganizer
Collection
   Bag
   MappedCollection
   SequenceableCollection
      ArrayedCollection
         Array
            LiteralArray
         ByteArray
            BytecodeArray
         RunArray
         String
            Symbol
         Text
         WordArray
            DisplayBitmap
      Interval
         TextLineInterval
      LinkedList
         Semaphore
      OrderedCollection
         Signal
         SortedCollection
         WireList

Listing A2.5
(continued)

```
Set
    Dictionary
        Histogram
        IdentityDictionary
            MethodDictionary
        LiteralDictionary
        StrikeFontManager
        SystemDictionary
        TextStyleManager
    IdentitySet
CompiledMethod
    TimedCompiledMethod
Compiler
ComplexSignal
Controller
    BinaryChoiceController
    FormMenuController
    MouseMenuController
        BitEditor
        ClockController
        FinancialHistoryController
        FormEditor
        HistogramController
        ScreenController
        ScrollController
            ListController
                LockedListController
                    ChangeListController
                SelectionInListController
            ParagraphEditor
                StringHolderController
                    ChangeController
                    FillInTheBlankController
                        CRFillInTheBlankController
                    ProjectController
                    TextCollectorController
                    WorkspaceController
                TextController
                    CodeController
                        AlwaysAcceptCodeController
                        OnlyWhenSelectedCodeController
        StandardSystemController
            NotifierController
        TreeController
        WireListController
    MovieController
    NoController
    SwitchController
        IndicatorOnSwitchController
        LockedSwitchController
ControlManager
```

Customer
>**AnimatedCustomer**
>**CustomerQueue**
>>**AnimatedCustomerQueue**

Delay
DisplayObject
>**DisplayMedium**
>>**Form**
>>>**Cursor**
>>>**DisplayScreen**
>>**DisplayText**
>>>**Paragraph**
>>>**TextList**
>**EvaluationNode**
>**InfiniteForm**
>**OpaqueForm**
>**Path**
>>**Arc**
>>>**Circle**
>>**Curve**
>>**Line**
>>**LinearFit**
>>**Spline**
>**PositionNode**
>>**MovingNode**
>>>**BounceInBoxNode**
>**SequenceNode**
>**SuperpositionNode**
>**WindowNode**

DrunkenCockroach
Explainer
FileModel
>**FileList**

FinancialHistory
FormButtonCache
HanoiProgs
>**HanoiDisk**
>>**HanoiDiskRules**
>**TowerOfHanoi**
>>**AnimatedTowerOfHanoi**
>>>**TowerByRules**

InputSensor
InputState
Inspector
>**ContextInspector**
>**DictionaryInspector**

InstructionStream
>**ContextPart**
>>**BlockContext**
>>**MethodContext**
>**Decompiler**
>**InstructionPrinter**

Listing A2.5
(continued)

KeyboardEvent
Link
    Process
Magnitude
    Character
    Date
    LookupKey
        Association
    MessageTally
    Number
        Complex
        Float
        Fraction
        Imaginary
        Integer
            LargeNegativeInteger
            LargePositiveInteger
            SmallInteger
  Time
    SimTime
Message
MethodDescription
MusicFormatter
  MorseCode
ParseNode
    AssignmentNode
    BlockNode
    CascadeNode
    DecompilerConstructor
    Encoder
    LeafNode
        LiteralNode
        SelectorNode
        VariableNode
    MessageNode
    MethodNode
    ReturnNode
ParseStack
Pipe
Point
PopUpMenu
    ActionMenu
    IconPopUpMenu
ProcessHandle
ProcessorScheduler
ProjectBrowser
ProtocolBrowser
Rectangle
    CharacterBlock
    Quadrangle
RemoteString

Scanner
   ChangeScanner
   Parser
Server
   AnimatedServer
SharedQueue
ShellInterface
StatusPrompter
Stream
   PositionableStream
      ReadStream
      WriteStream
         PrinterStream
         ReadWriteStream
            ExternalStream
               FileStream
                  FileDirectory
               PipeStream
                  PipeReadStream
                  PipeWriteStream
   Random
StrikeFont
StringHolder
   ChangeList
   FillInTheBlank
   Project
   TextCollector
   Workspace
StructOutputTable
Subtask
Switch
   Button
   OneOnSwitch
SyntaxError
SystemTracer
TekFileStatus
TekSystemCall
TextStyle
Tile
Tree
   ExpressionTree
TreeNode
   NumberNode
   OperandNode
   OperatorNode
UndefinedObject
Variables2
   Variables3
View
   BarChartView
   BinaryChoiceView

Listing A2.5
(continued)

BrowserTimeView
DisplayTextView
FinancialHistoryView
FormMenuView
FormView
    FormHolderView
HistogramView
ListView
    ChangeListView
    SelectionInListView
MovieView
SignalView
StandardSystemView
    BrowserView
    ClockView
    InspectorView
    NotifierView
StringHolderView
    FillInTheBlankView
    ProjectView
    TextCollectorView
    WorkspaceView
SwitchView
    BooleanView
TextView
    CodeView
        OnlyWhenSelectedCodeView
TreeView
WireListView
WindowingTransformation

Another version that prints the indented class names and the instance variables in parentheses is presented below in Listings A2.6, A2.7, A2.8, A2.9, and A2.10. It represents an incremental modification to the case in which names only are printed. Both examples depend on existing protocol for supporting printer output (class **PrinterStream** and **String** methods printFile: and outputToPrinter).

Listing A2.6
Details of
Behavior Method
toPrinterHierarchy

Behavior methodsFor: 'printing'

toPrinterHierarchy
    "Send the emphasized hierarchy of the receiver to the printer"

    | fileStream |

    Transcript refresh; cr; cr;
        show: 'Sending to printer, hierarchy for class: ', self name.
    fileStream ← Disk file: (self name, 'Hierarchy.prn') asFileName.
    fileStream emphasis: 3. "italic"

```
Smalltalk timeStamp: fileStream.
fileStream cr; cr.
fileStream nextPutAll: self printEmphasizedHierarchy.
fileStream close.
(self name, 'Hierarchy.prn') asFileName printFile: 20.
fileStream remove.
```

Listing A2.7
Details of
Behavior Method
printEmphasized-
Hierarchy

Behavior methodsFor: 'printing'

printEmphasizedHierarchy
    "Answer a description containing the names and instance variable names of all of the
        subclasses and superclasses of the receiver. Add boldface emphasis to the class
        names"

```
    | aStream index supers |
index ← 0.
aStream ← WriteStream on: (String new: 16).
self allDynamicSuperclasses reverseDo: [ :aClass |
    aStream crtab: index.
    index ← index + 1.
    aStream emphasis: 2.
    aStream nextPutAll: aClass name.
    aStream space; emphasis: 1.
    aStream print: aClass instVarNames.
    supers ← aClass superclasses.
    supers size > 1 ifTrue: [
        aStream nextPutAll: ' [also a '.
        (supers copyFrom: 2 to: supers size) do: [:s |
            aStream space; emphasis: 2;
                nextPutAll: s name; space;
                    emphasis: 1; print: s allInstVarNames].
        aStream nextPut: $] ]].
aStream cr.
self
    printEmphasizedSubclassesOn: aStream
    callingSuperclass: self dynamicSuperclass
    level: index.
↑aStream  contents
```

Listing A2.8
Details of
Behavior Method
printEmphasized-
SubclassesOn:
callingSuperclass:
level:

Behavior methodsFor: 'private'

printEmphasizedSubclassesOn: aStream **callingSuperclass:** whichSuper **level:** level
    "As part of the algorithm for printing a description of the receiver, print the subclass on
        the file stream, aStream, indenting level times."

```
    | subs supers |
aStream crtab: level.
aStream emphasis: 2.
aStream nextPutAll: self name.
```

Listing A2.8
(continued)

```
aStream emphasis: 1.
aStream space; print: self instVarNames.
supers ← self superclasses.
supers size > 1 ifTrue: [
    aStream nextPutAll: ' [also a'.
    (supers copyWithout: whichSuper) do: [:s |
        aStream space; emphasis: 2;
            nextPutAll: s name; space;
            emphasis: 1;
            print: s allInstVarNames asArray].
    aStream nextPut: $] ].
subs ← self subclasses.
self = = Class ifTrue: [
    aStream crtab: level + 1;
        nextPutAll: '... all the Metaclasses ...'.
    subs ← subs reject: [:sub | sub isMeta]].
"Print subclasses in alphabetical order"
(subs asSortedCollection: [:x :y | x name < y name]) do: [:sub |
    sub
        printEmphasizedSubclassesOn: aStream
        callingSuperclass: self
        level: level + 1]
```

Listing A2.9
Details of
Behavior
example2

Behavior class methodsFor: 'examples'

example2
```
    "Example of hierarchy printout of a class.
        This example prints the entire image hierarchy."

    Object toPrinterHierarchy

    " Behavior example2 "
```

Listing A2.10
Complete Image
Hierarchy (names
and instance
variables)

```
Object ()
    BankSimulation ('simulationTime' 'numberServers' 'servers' 'customerQ' 'bankIsOpen'
        'nextEvent' )
        AnimatedBankSim ('bankImage' 'waitingLine' 'entry' 'exit' 'pathToDoor' 'delay'
            'offset' )
        MultiLineBankSimulation ('waitingLines' 'unHappyCustomers' )
    Behavior ('superclass' 'methodDict' 'format' 'subclasses' )
        ClassDescription ('instanceVariables' 'organization' )
            Class ('name' 'classPool' 'sharedPools' )
                ... all the Metaclasses ...
                Metaclass ('thisClass' )
                    MetaclassForMultipleInheritance ('otherSuperclasses' )
    Benchmark ('dummy' 'verboseTranscript' 'reporting' 'reportStream' 'fromList' )
    BinaryChoice ('trueAction' 'falseAction' 'actionTaken' )
```

BitBlt ('destForm' 'sourceForm' 'halftoneForm' 'combinationRule' 'destX' 'destY' 'width'
    'height' 'sourceX' 'sourceY' 'clipX' 'clipY' 'clipWidth' 'clipHeight')
    CharacterScanner ('lastIndex' 'xTable' 'stopConditions' 'text' 'textStyle' 'leftMargin'
        'rightMargin' 'font' 'line' 'runStopIndex' 'spaceCount' 'spaceWidth'
        'outputMedium')
        CharacterBlockScanner ('characterPoint' 'characterIndex' 'lastCharacter'
            'lastCharacterExtent' 'lastSpaceOrTabExtent' 'nextLeftMargin')
        CompositionScanner ('spaceX' 'spaceIndex')
        DisplayScanner ('lineY' 'runX')
    Pen ('frame' 'location' 'direction' 'penDown')
Boolean ()
    False ()
    True ()
Browser ('organization' 'category' 'className' 'meta' 'protocol' 'selector' 'textMode'
    'saved')
    Debugger ('context' 'receiverInspector' 'contextInspector' 'shortStack' 'sourceMap'
        'sourceCode' 'processHandle')
    MethodListBrowser ('methodList' 'methodName')
Change ('file' 'position')
    ClassRelatedChange ('className')
        ClassChange ()
            ClassDefinitionChange ('superclassName' 'classType' 'otherParameters')
            ClassOtherChange ('type')
                ClassCommentChange ()
            ClassReorganizationChange ('reorganization')
        MethodChange ('selector' 'category')
            MethodDefinitionChange ()
            MethodOtherChange ('type')
    OtherChange ('text')
ChangeSet ('classChanges' 'methodChanges' 'classRemoves' 'reorganizeSystem'
    'specialDoIts')
Checker ()
ClassCategoryReader ('class' 'category')
ClassOrganizer ('globalComment' 'categoryArray' 'categoryStops' 'elementArray')
    SystemOrganizer ()
Collection ()
    Bag ('contents')
    MappedCollection ('domain' 'map')
    SequenceableCollection ()
        ArrayedCollection ()
            Array ()
                LiteralArray ()
            ByteArray ()
                BytecodeArray ()
            RunArray ('runs' 'values')
            String ()
                Symbol ()
            Text ('string' 'runs')
            WordArray ()
                DisplayBitmap ()
        Interval ('start' 'stop' 'step')
            TextLineInterval ('internalSpaces' 'paddingWidth')

Listing A2.10
(continued)

```
                          LinkedList ('firstLink' 'lastLink' )
                              Semaphore ('excessSignals' )
                          OrderedCollection ('firstIndex' 'lastIndex' )
                              Signal ()
                              SortedCollection ('sortBlock' )
                              WireList ()
                   Set ('tally' )
                       Dictionary ()
                           Histogram ()
                           IdentityDictionary ('valueArray' )
                               MethodDictionary ('keyArray' )
                           LiteralDictionary ()
                           StrikeFontManager ()
                           SystemDictionary ()
                           TextStyleManager ()
                       IdentitySet ()
           CompiledMethod ('header' 'literals' 'instructions' 'sourceCode' )
               TimedCompiledMethod ('timeOfCreation' )
           Compiler ('sourceStream' 'requestor' 'class' 'context' )
           ComplexSignal ('real' 'imaginary' )
           Controller ('model' 'view' 'sensor' )
               BinaryChoiceController ()
               FormMenuController ()
               MouseMenuController ('redButtonMenu' 'redButtonMessages' 'yellowButtonMenu'
                   'yellowButtonMessages' 'blueButtonMenu' 'blueButtonMessages' )
                   BitEditor ('scale' 'squareForm' 'color' )
                   ClockController ('clockProcess' )
                   FinancialHistoryController ()
                   FormEditor ('form' 'tool' 'grid' 'togglegrid' 'mode' 'previousTool' 'color'
                       'unNormalizedColor' 'xgridOn' 'ygridOn' 'toolMenu' 'underToolMenu' )
                   HistogramController ()
                   ScreenController ()
                   ScrollController ('scrollBar' 'marker' 'savedArea' )
                       ListController ()
                           LockedListController ()
                               ChangeListController ()
                           SelectionInListController ()
                       ParagraphEditor ('paragraph' 'startBlock' 'stopBlock' 'beginTypeInBlock'
                           'emphasisHere' 'initialText' 'selectionShowing' 'currentFont'
                           'echoLocation' 'echoForm' )
                       StringHolderController ('isLockingOn' )
                           ChangeController ()
                           FillInTheBlankController ()
                               CRFillInTheBlankController ()
                           ProjectController ()
                           TextCollectorController ()
                           WorkspaceController ()
                       TextController ()
                           CodeController ()
                               AlwaysAcceptCodeController ()
                               OnlyWhenSelectedCodeController ()
```

            StandardSystemController ('status')
                NotifierController ()
          TreeController ()
          WireListController ()
      MovieController ()
      NoController ()
      SwitchController ('selector' 'arguments' 'cursor')
          IndicatorOnSwitchController ()
          LockedSwitchController ()
ControlManager ('scheduledControllers' 'activeController' 'activeControllerProcess'
   'screenController')
Customer ()
      AnimatedCustomer ()
      CustomerQueue ('queue' 'lastEventTime' 'cumCustomers' 'currentQueueSize'
          'peakQueue' 'cumQueueSizeTime' 'cumWaitTime')
          AnimatedCustomerQueue ('queueOfImages')
Delay ('delayDuration' 'resumptionTime' 'delaySemaphore' 'delayInProgress')
DisplayObject ()
      DisplayMedium ()
          Form ('bits' 'width' 'height' 'offset')
              Cursor ()
              DisplayScreen ()
          DisplayText ('text' 'textStyle' 'offset' 'form')
             Paragraph ('clippingRectangle' 'compositionRectangle' 'destinationForm' 'rule'
                'mask' 'marginTabsLevel' 'firstIndent' 'restIndent' 'rightIndent' 'lines'
                'lastLine' 'outputMedium')
              TextList ('list')
          EvaluationNode ('evalBlock' 'boundingBox')
          InfiniteForm ('patternForm')
          OpaqueForm ('figure' 'shape')
          Path ('form' 'collectionOfPoints')
              Arc ('quadrant' 'radius' 'center')
                Circle ()
              Curve ()
              Line ()
              LinearFit ()
              Spline ('derivatives')
          PositionNode ('contents' 'location')
              MovingNode ('velocity')
                BounceInBoxNode ()
          SequenceNode ('subNodes' 'position')
          SuperpositionNode ('subNodes')
          WindowNode ('window' 'contents')
DrunkenCockroach ('currentTile' 'tilesVisited')
Explainer ('class' 'selector' 'instance' 'context' 'methodText')
FileModel ('fileName')
    FileList ('list' 'myPattern' 'isReading' 'fileMenu')
FinancialHistory ('cashOnHand' 'incomes' 'expenditures')
FormButtonCache ('offset' 'form' 'value' 'initialState')
HanoiProgs ()
    HanoiDisk ('name' 'width' 'pole' 'rectangle' 'image')
        HanoiDiskRules ('previousPole')

Listing A2.10
(continued)

        TowerOfHanoi ('stacks' 'timeToRun' 'steps' 'smoothMoves')
           AnimatedTowerOfHanoi ('howMany' 'mockDisks')
               TowerByRules ('oldDisk' 'currentDisk' 'destinationDisk')
InputSensor ('keyboardMap')
InputState ('x' 'y' 'bitState' 'lshiftState' 'rshiftState' 'ctrlState' 'lockState' 'metaState'
    'keyboardQueue' 'deltaTime' 'baseTime' 'timeProtect')
Inspector ('object' 'field')
    ContextInspector ('tempNames')
    DictionaryInspector ('ok')
InstructionStream ('sender' 'pc')
    ContextPart ('stackp')
        BlockContext ('nargs' 'startpc' 'home')
        MethodContext ('method' 'receiverMap' 'receiver')
    Decompiler ('constructor' 'method' 'instVars' 'tempVars' 'constTable' 'stack'
        'statements' 'lastPc' 'exit' 'lastJumpPc' 'lastReturnPc' 'limit' 'hasValue')
    InstructionPrinter ('stream' 'oldPC')
KeyboardEvent ('keyCharacter' 'metaState')
Link ('nextLink')
    Process ('suspendedContext' 'priority' 'myList')
Magnitude ()
    Character ('value')
    Date ('day' 'year')
    LookupKey ('key')
        Association ('value')
    MessageTally ('class' 'method' 'tally' 'receivers')
    Number ()
        Complex ('real' 'imaginary' 'modulus' 'angle')
        Float ()
        Fraction ('numerator' 'denominator')
        Imaginary ('magnitude')
        Integer ()
            LargeNegativeInteger ()
            LargePositiveInteger ()
            SmallInteger ()
    Time ('hours' 'minutes' 'seconds')
        SimTime ()
Message ('selector' 'args')
MethodDescription ('status' 'whichClass' 'selector')
MusicFormatter ('bytes')
    MorseCode ('letterSpace')
ParseNode ('comment')
    AssignmentNode ('variable' 'value')
    BlockNode ('arguments' 'statements' 'returns' 'nArgsNode' 'size' 'remoteCopyNode'
        'sourceRange' 'endPC')
    CascadeNode ('receiver' 'messages')
    DecompilerConstructor ('method' 'instVars' 'nArgs' 'literalValues' 'tempVars')
    Encoder ('scopeTable' 'nTemps' 'supered' 'requestor' 'class' 'literalStream'
        'selectorSet' 'litIndSet' 'litSet' 'sourceRanges' 'lastTempPos')
    LeafNode ('key' 'code')
        LiteralNode ()
        SelectorNode ()
        VariableNode ('name' 'isArg')

MessageNode ('receiver' 'selector' 'precedence' 'special' 'arguments' 'sizes' 'pc')
MethodNode ('selectorOrFalse' 'precedence' 'arguments' 'block' 'literals' 'primitive'
 'encoder' 'temporaries')
ReturnNode ('expr' 'pc')
ParseStack ('position' 'length')
Pipe ('readFdn' 'writeFdn' 'fileDescriptor')
Point ('x' 'y')
PopUpMenu ('labelString' 'textStyle' 'lineArray' 'frame' 'form' 'marker' 'selection')
ActionMenu ('selectors')
IconPopUpMenu ('markerTabs')
ProcessHandle ('process' 'controller' 'interrupted' 'resumeContext' 'proceedValue')
ProcessorScheduler ('quiescentProcessLists' 'activeProcess')
ProjectBrowser ('projects' 'currentProject')
ProtocolBrowser ('list' 'classDictionary' 'selectedClass' 'selectedSelector')
Rectangle ('origin' 'corner')
CharacterBlock ('stringIndex' 'character')
Quadrangle ('borderWidth' 'borderColor' 'insideColor')
RemoteString ('sourceFileNumber' 'filePositionHi' 'filePositionLo')
Scanner ('source' 'mark' 'hereChar' 'aheadChar' 'token' 'tokenType' 'currentComment'
 'buffer' 'typeTable' 'jScan' 'parenCount')
ChangeScanner ('file' 'chunkString')
Parser ('here' 'hereType' 'hereMark' 'prevToken' 'prevMark' 'encoder' 'requestor'
 'parseNode' 'failBlock' 'lastTempMark' 'correctionDelta')
Server ('idNumber' 'available' 'cumServiceTime' 'nextAvailable' 'totalCustomersServed'
 'avServiceTime' 'rand')
AnimatedServer ('location')
SharedQueue ('contentsArray' 'readPosition' 'writePosition' 'accessProtect' 'readSynch')
ShellInterface ('result' 'resultView' 'command' 'executeView' 'commandListView'
 'executableText' 'shellTask' 'shellIn' 'shellOut')
StatusPrompter ('a' 'l' 's' 'x' 'result')
Stream ()
PositionableStream ('collection' 'position' 'readLimit')
ReadStream ()
WriteStream ('writeLimit')
PrinterStream ('fileDescriptor' 'currentFont')
ReadWriteStream ()
ExternalStream ()
FileStream ('name' 'directory' 'mode' 'fileDescriptor' 'filePosition'
 'fileMode')
FileDirectory ()
PipeStream ('fileDescriptor' 'mode')
PipeReadStream ('foundEnd')
PipeWriteStream ()
Random ('seed')
StrikeFont ('xTable' 'glyphs' 'name' 'stopConditions' 'type' 'minAscii' 'maxAscii'
 'maxWidth' 'strikeLength' 'ascent' 'descent' 'xOffset' 'raster' 'subscript' 'superscript'
 'emphasis' 'ascentForStdAsciiChars' 'descentForStdAsciiChars')
StringHolder ('contents' 'isLocked')
ChangeList ('listName' 'changes' 'selectionIndex' 'list' 'filter' 'removed' 'filterList'
 'filterKey' 'changeDict' 'doItDict' 'checkSystem' 'fieldList')
FillInTheBlank ('actionBlock' 'actionTaken')

Listing A2.10
(continued)

Project ('projectWindows' 'projectChangeSet' 'projectTranscript' 'projectHolder' 'title')

TextCollector ('entryStream')

Workspace ('localVariableDictionary')

StructOutputTable ('globalDict' 'mapArray' 'idCount')

Subtask ('taskId' 'status' 'program' 'args' 'environment' 'initBlock' 'accessProtect' 'termStatus' 'priority' 'waitSemaphore' 'terminateBlock')

Switch ('on' 'onAction' 'offAction')

Button ()

OneOnSwitch ('connection')

SyntaxError ('class' 'badText' 'processHandle')

SystemTracer ('hashTable' 'hashTblSize' 'file' 'writeDict' 'specialObjects' 'initialProcess' 'gradeFiles' 'largeObjFile' 'largeObjCount' 'writtenObjCount' 'knownObjectsCount')

TekFileStatus ()

TekSystemCall ('operationType' 'operation' 'D0In' 'D0Out' 'D1In' 'D1Out' 'D2In' 'A0In' 'A0Out' 'errno')

TextStyle ('fontArray' 'lineGrid' 'baseline' 'alignment' 'firstIndent' 'restIndent' 'rightIndent' 'tabsArray' 'marginTabsArray' 'outputMedium' 'lineGridForLists' 'baselineForLists' 'lineGridForMenus' 'baselineForMenus')

Tile ('location' 'floorArea')

Tree ('root' 'maxLevel' 'avgLevel')

ExpressionTree ('exprString' 'operands' 'parenCount')

TreeNode ('leftNode' 'rightNode' 'key' 'info' 'displaySize' 'nodeImage')

NumberNode ()

OperandNode ()

OperatorNode ()

UndefinedObject ()

Variables2 ('instVarLevel2')

Variables3 ('instVarLevel3')

View ('model' 'controller' 'superView' 'subViews' 'transformation' 'viewport' 'window' 'displayTransformation' 'insetDisplayBox' 'borderWidth' 'borderColor' 'insideColor' 'boundingBox' 'selectionSelected')

BarChartView ()

BinaryChoiceView ()

BrowserTimeView ()

DisplayTextView ('rule' 'mask' 'editParagraph' 'centered' 'textStyle')

FinancialHistoryView ()

FormMenuView ()

FormView ('rule' 'mask')

FormHolderView ('displayedForm')

HistogramView ('barWidth' 'barSpacing')

ListView ('list' 'selection' 'topDelimiter' 'bottomDelimiter' 'lineSpacing' 'isEmpty' 'textStyle')

ChangeListView ()

SelectionInListView ('itemList' 'printItems' 'oneItem' 'partMsg' 'initialSelectionMsg' 'changeMsg' 'listMsg' 'menuMsg')

MovieView ()

SignalView ()

StandardSystemView ('labelFrame' 'labelText' 'isLabelComplemented' 'savedSubViews' 'minimumSize' 'maximumSize' 'windowForm' 'windowFormFlag' 'textStyle')

BrowserView ()
ClockView ('cacheForm' 'cacheBox' 'myProject' 'date')
InspectorView ()
NotifierView ('contents')
StringHolderView ('displayContents' 'textStyle')
FillInTheBlankView ()
ProjectView ()
TextCollectorView ()
WorkspaceView ()
SwitchView ('complemented' 'label' 'selector' 'keyCharacter' 'highlightForm' 'arguments' 'textStyle')
BooleanView ()
TextView ('partMsg' 'acceptMsg' 'menuMsg' 'textStyle')
CodeView ('initialSelection')
OnlyWhenSelectedCodeView ('selectionMsg')
TreeView ()
WireListView ()
WindowingTransformation ('scale' 'translation')

3

Descriptive Protocol Summaries
for Selected Classes

This appendix provides additional descriptive protocol summaries for selected classes in the Smalltalk image. Descriptive summaries are given in various chapters for classes that are key to understanding the material in that chapter. The summaries in this appendix are supplemental and are organized by the chapter in which each is discussed.

A3.1   Chapter 1

None.

A3.2   Chapter 2

None.

A3.3   Chapter 3

Protocol Description Summary for Class **BlockContext**

Definition—The hierarchy for class **BlockContext** is **Object—Instruction-Stream—ContextPart—BlockContext.** It has three instance variables, nargs, startpc, and home. It has no class variables or class methods. It has 27 instance methods in nine categories. In addition, **BlockContext** has interited protocol from its three superclasses.

Private data—Class **BlockContext** has three instance variables.

> **nargs**—an instance of **Integer** representing the number of block arguments.
>
> **startpc**—an instance of **Integer** that points to the beginning of a block of code. It is essentially an initial program counter for the block.
>
> **home**—an instance of **MethodContext** whose **CompiledMethod** contains the block represented by an instance of **BlockContext.**

Instance methods—There are 27 instance methods in nine categories. The categories and corresponding number of methods are:

> *initialize-release*—one method for initializing all private data for a block context.
>
> *accessing*—five methods for accessing private data in the block context.
>
> *temporaries*—two methods for accessing or changing indexed variables in the home context.
>
> *evaluating*—five methods for evaluating a block context with zero, one, two, three, or more arguments.
>
> *controlling*—four methods representing while loops (e.g., **whileFalse:**).
>
> *scheduling*—four methods related to control of multiprocesses.
>
> *instruction decoding*—two methods relating to stack manipulation for instruction decoding.
>
> *printing*—one method, **printOn:.**
>
> *private*—three methods for handling program counter initialization and error conditions.

Class methods—Class **BlockContext** has no class methods.

A3.4   Chapter 4

None.

A3.5   Chapter 5

Protocol Summary for Class BinaryChoice

Definition—The hierarchy for class **BinaryChoice** is **Object—BinaryChoice.** It has three instance variables, trueAction, falseAction, and actionTaken. It has no class variables or pool dictionaries. It has six class methods in two categories and seven instance methods in three categories. **BinaryChoice** also inherits protocol from its superclasses (both classes and metaclasses).

Private data—Class **BinaryChoice** has three instance variables.

trueAction—an instance of **BlockContext,** representing a sequence of expressions to execute if the positive choice is made.

falseAction—an instance of **BlockContext,** representing the sequence of expressions to execute if a negative choice is made.

actionTaken—an instance of **Boolean,** which is true or false depending on whether one of the actions has been taken.

Instance methods—There are seven instance methods in three categories. They are all used internally by instances of class **BinaryChoice.** They are sent by class methods. The categories and corresponding number of methods are:

initialize-release—three methods that each set the value for one of the three instance variables.

menu messages—two methods, **selectTrue** and **selectFalse,** that execute the appropriate expression block dependent on user response to the binary prompt.

accessing—two methods for determining the status, **active** or **actionTaken,** for an instance of a binary choice prompter.

Class methods—There are six methods in two categories. These messages are the interface to this class for users. The categories and corresponding methods are:

instance creation—five methods for creating instances of **BinaryChoice.** Differences in the five methods relate to where the prompter view is displayed, whether it accepts only a true alternative or false alternative or both. One method simply returns a true or false; it does not evaluate a block of expressions.

examples—one method, **example,** that illustrates one of the five instance creation methods.

Protocol Summary for Class FillInTheBlank

Definition—The hierarchy for class **FillInTheBlank** is **Object—StringHolder— FillInTheBlank.** It has two instance variables, actionBlock and actionTaken. It has no class variables or pool dictionaries. It has nine class methods in two categories and five instance methods in three categories.

Private data—Class **FillInTheBlank** has two instance variables.

actionBlock—an instance of **BlockContext,** representing a sequence of expressions to execute with the user response as a parameter.

actionTaken—an instance of **Boolean** that is true or false depending on whether the action block has been executed at least once.

Instance methods—There are five instance methods in three categories. They are all used internally by instances of class **FillInTheBlank.** They are sent by class methods. The categories and corresponding number of methods are:

initialize-release—One method, **initialize,** sets the value for the instance variable actionTaken to false. It also initializes inherited instance variables from the superclass **StringHolder.**

menu messages—one method, **selectAction,** that executes the action block dependent on user response to the binary prompt.

accessing—three methods for establishing values for the two instance variables.

Class methods—There are nine methods in two categories. These messages are the interface to this class for users. The categories and corresponding methods are:

instance creation—six methods for creating instances of **FillInTheBlank.** Differences in the six methods relate to where the prompter view is displayed, whether it requires a response or not, and if the initial block argument is specified. One method simply returns the user response, with no action taken.

examples—three example methods that illustrate three instance creation methods.

Protocol Summary for Class FileStream

Class **FileStream,** in conjunction with class **FileDirectory,** provides protocol for file manipulation.

Definition—The hierarchy for class **FileStream** is **Object—Stream—Positionable-Stream—WriteStream—ReadWriteStream—ExternalStream—FileStream.** It has six instance variables, name, directory, mode, fileDescriptor, filePosition, and fileMode. It has three class variables, BufferSize, OpenFileStreams, and SystemCall. It has no pool dictionaries. It has 12 class methods in 3 categories and 67 instance methods in 16 categories. In addition, **FileStream** inherits protocol from all its superclasses.

Private data—Class **FileStream,** has six instance variables.

name—an instance of **String,** identifying the file within a directory.

directory—an instance of **FileDirectory** containing the file. If the directory is unknown, this instance variable has a value of nil.

mode—an instance of **Symbol,** representing the mode of the file (e.g., #ReadOnly, #WriteOnly, #ReadWrite).

fileDescriptor—an instance of **SmallInteger,** representing a code assigned by the operating system to the **FileStream.** This instance variable is assigned a value by a message sent to class **TekSystemCall,** (or the appropriate class representing the operating system).

filePosition—an instance of **Integer,** representing the position within a file.

fileMode—an instance of **Symbol,** indicating the current permission for the fileDescriptor of the file.

Shared data—Class **FileStream** has three class variables.

BufferSize—an instance of **Integer** that is the size in bytes of the file buffer. Default value is 1024.

OpenFileStreams—an instance of **OrderedCollection.** Each time a new file is opened, it is added to this collection.

SystemCall—Set equal to the class name **TekSystemCall.**

Instance methods—There are 67 instance methods in 16 categories. The categories and corresponding number of methods are:

accessing—nine methods for adding characters or collections of characters to the **FileStream** and accessing the next byte, the entire contents, or the size of the file.

testing—One method, **atEnd,** returns a Boolean true if the position in the file is at the end; else false.

positioning—five methods for determining the current position and setting a new position within a file.

nonhomogeneous positioning—two methods for skipping or padding to a boundary. The boundary is determined by a specified size in bytes.

printing—one method, **printOn:,** that returns a descriptive string defining the file.

editing—one method, **edit,** for opening a view on the file. Contents of the file are displayed in the view.

copying—one method, **copy,** that returns a copy of the receiver file with a different file descriptor.

file accessing—seven methods for accessing the file name, path, description, directory, and for removing or renaming the file.

file testing—eight methods for determining the status of the file. Status includes such features as its existence, its mode (read, write, etc.), whether it's open, and its filetype (text, binary, etc.).

file modes—six methods for setting the mode of the file.

file status—four methods, including the method **close,** for disassociating the file descriptor from its file name.

file in-out—three methods for filing in a file or creating a file with a description of the system changes.

alto file compatibility—two methods, both of which return **self.**

private descriptor modes—seven methods called by other methods in this class for actually creating files with a specified mode or releasing a file descriptor.

private—nine methods used by other methods in this class for performing specified file operations.

converting—one method, **asFileDirectory,** that treats the full name of the current file as a directory.

Class methods—There are 12 class methods in three categories.

class initialization—one method, **initialize,** that initializes the three class variables.

instance creation—nine methods for creating new instances of **FileStream.** Different methods are used for creation of instances on old or new files with various modes.

external references—two methods for releasing external references to the receiver and closing all instances.

Protocol Summary for Class **InputSensor**

Definition—The hierarchy for class **InputSensor** is **Object—InputSensor.** It has one instance variable, keyboardMap. It has three class variables, Current-Cursor, CurrentInputState, and DefaultKeyboardMap. It has no pool dictionaries. It has 5 class methods in three categories and 30 instance methods in four categories.

Private data—Class **InputSensor** has one instance variable.

keyboardMap—an instance of **String** containing 5 * 256 characters. These characters represent the keyboard map for five different states of the *shift, control,* and *caps lock* keys. The keyboard can be remapped by the user.

Shared data—Class **InputSensor** has three class variables.

CurrentCursor—an instance of **Cursor** that is a 16-by-16 pixel pattern representing the cursor.

CurrentInputState—an instance of **InputState,** representing the attached hardware.

DefaultKeyboardMap—the default mapping of the keyboard. The private data variable keyboardMap is initialized to be equal to this default.

Instance methods—There are 30 instance methods in four categories. The categories and corresponding number of methods are:

keyboard—eight methods for detecting a keyboard event and flushing or reading the keyboard buffer.

mouse—ten methods for detecting various combinations of button presses from the mouse and for returning the coordinates of the mouse position.

current cursor—four methods for returning or setting the current cursor shape and position.

private—eight methods supporting the other methods in this class. They deal with changing and updating the values of the instance variable keyboardMap and the class variables CurrentCursor and CurrentInputState.

Class methods—There are five class methods in three categories.

class initialization—two methods. Method **initialize** establishes the values for the class variable DefaultKeyboardMap. Method **install** creates and installs the value for the class variable CurrentInputState.

instance creation—one method, **new,** that creates and initializes a new instance of **InputSensor.**

constants—two methods, **default** and **initSensor,** that return and create the global variable **Sensor** as an instance of **InputSensor.**

A3.6   Chapter 6

Protocol Summary for Class Time

Instances of class **Time** represent times.

Definition—The hierarchy for class **Time** is **Object—Magnitude—Time.** Class **Time** has three instance variables, hours, minutes, and seconds. It has no class variables or pool dictionaries. It has 14 class methods in three categories and 14 instance methods in six categories.

Private data—Class **Time** has three instance variables.

> **hours**—an instance of **Integer,** representing the number of hours in the instance of time.

> **minutes**—an instance of **Integer,** representing the number of minutes in the instance of time.

> **seconds**—an instance of **Integer,** representing the number of seconds in the instance of time.

Instance methods—Class **Time** has 14 instance methods in six categories. The categories and number of methods are:

> *comparing*—four methods (**<, =, hash, hashMappedBy:**) with the same selectors as those inherited from superclass **Magnitude. Time** polymorphically redefines one method and defines three other subclassResponsibility methods for comparison given in superclass **Magnitude.**

> *accessing*—three methods (**hours, minutes, seconds**) that return one of the three instance variable values, respectively.

> *arithmetic*—two methods, one (**addTime:**) for adding time and one (**subtractTime:**) for subtracting time.

> *printing*—two methods (**printOn:, storeOn:**) that provide protocol for printing and storing instances of time on a stream.

> *converting*—one method (**asSeconds**) that converts the receiver time to seconds.

> *private*—two methods (**hours:, hours: minutes: seconds:**) that assign the appropriate instance variables to have values represented by the parameters in these messages.

Class methods—Class **Time** has 14 class methods in three categories. The categories and number of messages are:

> *instance creation*—four methods (**fromFileSystemSeconds:, fromSeconds, now, readFrom:**) for creating instances of class **Time.**

> *general inquiries*—six methods (**abbreviatedDateAndTimeNow, dateAndTimeNow, millisecondClockValue, millisecondsToRun:, timeWords, totalSeconds**) that answer specific times and formats. Included are messages that return the current date and time, time in milliseconds, and time since Jan. 1, 1901. Also included is the message millisecondsToRun:, which accepts a block as its parameter and times execution of the block in milliseconds.

private—four methods (**currentTime:, from:, millisecondClockInto:, secondClockInto:**) used by other class methods in the *general inquiries* and *instance creation* categories.

Protocol Summary for Class **Imaginary**

Class **Imaginary** represents imaginary numbers. Instances of this class are represented as numbers preceded by the symbol j.

Definition—The hierarchy for class **Imaginary** is **Object—Magnitude—Number—Imaginary**. It has one instance variable, **magnitude**. It has no class variables or pool dictionaries. It has 1 class method in one category and 15 instance methods in seven categories.

Private data—Class **Imaginary** has one instance variable.

magnitude—a number representing the magnitude of the imaginary number.

Instance methods—Class **Imaginary** has 15 instance methods in seven categories. The categories and number of methods are:

arithmetic—four methods (**+, *, −, /**) representing the four basic arithmetic operations, add, multiply, subtract, and divide. These are polymorphically redefined from class **Number.**

accessing—one method (**magnitude**) that returns the value of the instance variable **magnitude**. This is new protocol.

coercing—two methods (**coerce:, generality**), one that defines the generality of imaginary numbers and one that defines coercion of an imaginary number to be imaginary (both these methods are redefined from **Number**).

converting—two methods (**asImaginary, asComplex**) for converting to imaginary or complex numbers (new protocol).

comparing—four methods (**<, =, hash, hashMappedBy:**) that are polymorphically redefined from **Magnitude.**

printing—one method (**printOn:**) that defines how imaginary numbers are to be appended to a stream. This method is inherited from **Object** and redefined.

private—one method (**setMagnitude:**) that is used to establish the magnitude of an imaginary number. This method is used by instance creation methods (new protocol).

Class methods—Class **Imaginary** has one class method in one category as described below.

instance creation—One class method (**new:**) that creates a new instance of **Imaginary** with the parameter set as the magnitude. This method is inherited from **Behavior** and redefined.

Protocol Summary for Class **Complex**

Class **Complex** represents complex numbers. Instances of this class are represented in both rectangular form as a real and imaginary part or in complex form as a magnitude and an angle.

Definition—The hierarchy for class **Complex** is **Object—Magnitude—Number—Complex.** It has four instance variables, real, imaginary, modulus, and angle. It has no class variables or pool dictionaries. It has 2 class methods in one category and 21 instance methods in seven categories.

Private data—Class **Complex** has four instance variables.

real—a number representing the real part of the complex number in rectangular form.

imaginary—a number representing the imaginary part of a complex number in rectangular form.

modulus—a number representing the modulus of a complex number in polar form.

angle—a number representing the angle of a complex number in polar form.

Instance methods—Class **Complex** has 21 instance methods in seven categories. The categories and number of methods are:

arithmetic—four methods (**+, *, −, /**) representing the four basic arithmetic operations, add, multiply, subtract, and divide.

accessing—four methods (**real, imaginary, modulus, angle**) that return the values of the four instance variables real, imaginary, modulus, and angle, respectively.

coercing—two methods (**coerce:, generality**), one (generality) that defines the generality of complex numbers and one (coerce:) that defines coercion of a complex number to be complex.

converting—two methods (**asComplex, asImaginary**) for converting to complex or imaginary numbers. Conversion of complex numbers to imaginary numbers is valid only if the real part of the complex number is zero.

comparing—four methods (**<, =, hash, hashMappedBy:**) that are polymorphically redefined.

printing—three methods (**printOn:, printPolar, printPolar:**). One method (printOn:) defines how complex numbers are to be appended to a stream (default is rectangular form). Two methods define ways for printing complex numbers in polar form as a string or on a stream.

private—two methods (**setModulus: setAngle:, setReal: setImaginary:**) that are used to establish the rectangular and polar instance variables of a complex number. These methods are used by instance creation methods.

Class methods—Class **Complex** has two class methods in one category as described below.

instance creation—two class methods (**modulus: angle:, real: imaginary:**) that create a new instance of **Complex** based on specified rectangular instance variables or polar instance variables.

A3.7   Chapter 7

Protocol Summary for Class Bag

Definition—The hierarchy for class **Bag** is **Object—Collection—Bag.** Class **Bag** has one instance variable, **contents.** It has no class variables or pool dictionaries. It has 1 class method in one category and 12 instance methods in six categories.

Private data—Class **Bag** has one instance variable.

> **contents**—an instance of **Dictionary** that contains the contents (the objects) of the bag. An object is stored once, and a tally is kept of the occurrences of each unique object.

Instance methods—Class **Bag** has 12 instance methods in six categories. A summary follows of the categories and methods.

> *accessing*—five methods (**at:, at:put:, size, sortedCounts, sortedElements**). Method **size** is polymorphically redefined from its version in **Collection.** Methods **at:** and **at: put:** are redefined to block their use since bags have no indices or keys. These methods are inherited from **Object.**

> *testing*—two methods (**includes:, occurrencesOf:**) that test presence of an element and number of occurrences of an element in the bag, respectively. These methods are inherited from **Collection** and redefined.

> *removing*—one method (**remove: ifAbsent:**) for removal with an alternative if the element is absent. This method is inherited from **Collection** and redefined.

> *adding*—two methods (**add:, addWithOccurrences:**) for adding one or multiple copies of an element to the bag. The message **add:** is polymorphically redefined from **Collection.**

> *enumerating*—One method (**do:**) is implemented as subclassResponsibility in **Collection.** It is therefore defined in **Bag** in a way suitable for enumerating the elements of a bag. The other six inherited enumeration methods, upon close examination, all depend on the key method, **do:**.

> *private*—one method (**setDictionary**) that creates a new **Dictionary** instance for private data, **contents.** This method is used for creation of a new instance of **Bag.**

Class methods—Class **Bag** has one class method in one category, as summarized below.

instance creation—one method (**new**) that is a polymorphic redefinition of the same method inherited from class **Behavior.** In addition, new bags can be created using the instance creation methods inherited from **Collection** (the four different with messages).

Protocol Summary for Class Set

Of the 22 instance methods and 4 class methods defined in **Set,** 11 instance methods and all 4 class methods are polymorphic redefinitions of inherited methods. Aside from the 9 private methods, only 2 new methods are defined in class **Set.** The key instance methods in class **Set** are add:, remove: ifAbsent:, and do:. The methods new and new: are redefined to include initialization of the instance variable tally.

Definition—The hierarchy for class **Set** is **Object—Collection—Set.** Class **Set** has one instance variable, tally. It has no class variables or pool dictionaries. It has 4 class methods in three categories and 22 instance methods in eight categories.

Private data—Class **Set** has one instance variable.

tally—an instance of **Integer** that is the number of elements in a set.

Instance methods—Class **Set** has 22 instance methods in eight categories. A summary of the categories and methods follows.

accessing—three methods (**at:, at: put:, size**) of which two (at:, at: put:) are redefined from class **Object** to block their use. Sets are not indexed. The other method (**size**) is inherited from **Collection** and redefined.

testing—Two methods (**includes:, occurrencesOf:**) are inherited from **Collection** and redefined. The method occurrencesOf: returns either a one or a zero.

removing—One method (**remove: ifAbsent:**) is inherited from **Collection** and redefined.

adding—two methods (**add:, grow**) for adding elements to a set. Method add: is inherited from **Collection** and redefined. Method grow is new protocol.

enumerating—Two methods (**collect:, do:**) are inherited from **Collection** and redefined.

printing—one method (**storeDefinitionOn: auxTable:**) inherited from **Object** and redefined.

copying—two methods (**deepCopy, structureCopyWithDict:**), both of which are inherited from **Object** and redefined.

private—nine methods (**atNewIndex: put:, find: ifAbsent:, findElementOrNil, fixCollisionsFrom, fullCheck, noCheckAdd:, rehash, setTally, swap: with:**) that are used by other methods in the protocol for class **Set.**

Class methods—Class **Set** has four class methods in three categories, as summarized below.

instance creation—two methods (**new, new:**) that are inherited from **Behavior** and redefined.

constants—one method (**maxSize**) inherited from **Collection** and redefined.

private—One method (**readDefinitionFrom: map:**) is inherited from **Object** and redefined.

Protocol Summary for Class Dictionary

Definition—The hierarchy for class **Dictionary** is **Object—Collection—Set—Dictionary.** Class **Dictionary** has no instance variables, class variables, or pool dictionaries. It has no new class methods. It has 38 instance methods in 12 categories.

Instance methods—Class **Dictionary** has 38 instance methods in 12 categories. A summary of the categories and methods follows.

accessing—ten methods (**associationAt:, associationAt: ifAbsent:, associations, at:, at: ifAbsent:, at: put:, keyAtValue:, keyAtValue: ifAbsent:, keys, values**). Of these 10 methods, 2 (at:, at: put:) are inherited from **Set** and redefined. The other 8 are new protocol.

testing—two methods (**includes:, occurrencesOf:**) that are inherited from **Set** and redefined.

removing—two methods (**remove:, remove: ifAbsent:**), inherited respectively from **Collection** and **Set,** are redefined to block their use by instances of **Dictionary.** Removal of an element from a dictionary involves removing an association. This must be done by accessing the key in the association. New protocol for correct removal of elements in a dictionary is added in the category *dictionary removing,* below.

adding—three methods (**add:, grow, declare: from:**), of which two (add:, grow) are inherited from **Set** and redefined.

enumerating—three methods (**collect:, do:, select:**), of which two (collect:, do:) are inherited from **Set** and redefined. The method select: is inherited from **Collection** and redefined.

printing—three methods (**printOn:, storeOn:, storeDefinitionOn: auxTable:**). The first two are inherited from **Collection** and redefined, and the last is inherited from **Set** and redefined.

converting—One method (**asSortedCollection**) is inherited from **Collection** and redefined. Sorting of dictionaries is based on the key in each element.

dictionary testing—two methods (**includesAssociation:, includesKey:**) for determining if a dictionary contains a key or an association, respectively.

dictionary removing—four methods (**removeAssociation:, removeAssociation: ifAbsent:, removeKey:, removeKey: ifAbsent:**) that provide protocol for removing elements from a dictionary based on finding their key value or a specified association.

dictionary enumerating—two methods (**keysDo:, associationsDo:**) that iterate over the keys or the associations, respectively.

user interface—one method (**inspect**) that creates an inspector for viewing the contents of a dictionary.

private—five methods (**errorKeyNotFound, errorValueNotFound, findKey: ifAbsent:, findKeyOrNil:, rehash**) that are used by other methods in the protocol for class **Collection.**

Class methods—Class **Dictionary** has no class methods.

Protocol Summary for Class **SequenceableCollection**

SequenceableCollection is an abstract superclass of the collection classes that have a well-defined order associated with their elements. It does not have instances; rather, its subclasses will have instances that inherit protocol defined in **SequenceableCollection.**

Definition—The hierarchy for class **SequenceableCollection** is **Object—Collection—SequenceableCollection.** Class **SequenceableCollection** has no instance variables, class variables, or pool dictionaries. It has no class methods. It has 35 instance methods in eight categories.

Instance methods—Class **SequenceableCollection** has 35 instance methods in eight categories. A summary of the categories and methods follows.

accessing—eleven methods (**atAll: put:, atAllPut:, first, indexOf:, indexOf: ifAbsent:, indexOfSubCollection: startingAt:, indexOfSubCollection: startingAt: ifAbsent:, last, replaceFrom: to: with:, replaceFrom: to: with: startingAt:, size**) for accessing the elements of a **Sequenceable-Collection.** One method (**size**) is inherited from **Collection** and redefined. The other methods are new protocol.

removing—One method (**remove: ifAbsent:**) is polymorphically redefined to block its usage by a **SequenceableCollection.**

adding—one method (**grow**) for making the instance larger by a specified size called growSize. The size is essentially doubled until doubling is not possible. Then it is incremented by an amount that brings its total size up to DefaultMaximumSize (as defined by the class variable in **Collection**).

enumerating—eight methods (**collect:, do:, findFirst:, findLast:, reverse, reverseDo:, select:, with:do:**) Of these, three (**do:, collect:, select:**) are inherited from **Collection** and redefined (**do:** is implemented as subclassResponsibility in **Collection**). The other five methods are new protocol defined in **SequenceableCollection.**

converting—Two methods (**asArray, mappedBy:**) are new protocol for converting to an array or a mapped collection.

private—two methods (**errorOutOfBounds, swap: with:**) that are used by other methods in the protocol for class **SequenceableCollection.**

copying—seven methods (**,** **,** **replaceFrom: to:, copyReplaceAll: with:, copyReplaceFrom: to: with:, copyWith:, copyWithout:, shallowCopy**) for making copies of instances of **SequenceableCollection** by concatenation (the comma message selector), or by copying selected portions of the receiver, or by using conditional copying.

comparing—Three methods (**=, hash, hashMappedBy:**) are inherited from **Object** and redefined.

Class methods—Class **SequenceableCollection** has no class methods.

Protocol Summary for Class **ArrayedCollection**

ArrayedCollection is an abstract superclass of all the collection classes that have a fixed-range integer, external key. It does not have instances; rather, its subclasses will have instances that inherit protocol defined in **ArrayedCollection.** Since the methods for instance creation for most of the subclasses of **Arrayed-Collection** are identical, the instance creation protocol is defined in **Arrayed-Collection** instead of its subclasses. This discussion illustrates a long chain of abstract classes supporting the subclasses that actually represent objects that can be created. That is, the chain of classes given by **Object—Collection—Sequence-ableCollection—ArrayedCollection** is an abstract chain defining protocol for use by the subclasses of **ArrayedCollection.**

Definition—The hierarchy for class **ArrayedCollection** is **Object—Collection—SequenceableCollection—ArrayedCollection.** Class **ArrayedCollection** has no instance variables, class variables, or pool dictionaries. It has seven class methods in two categories and five instance methods in four categories. Most of the protocol of its subclasses is inherited.

Instance methods—Class **ArrayedCollection** has five instance methods in four categories. A summary is given below of the categories and methods.

accessing—one method (**size**) that returns the number of elements in the receiver collection. This method is inherited from **Sequenceable-Collection** and redefined using a primitive call, which provides more efficiency.

adding—One method (**add:**) is inherited from **Collection** and redefined to block its use. All instances of subclasses of **ArrayedCollection** have a fixed number of elements. Therefore elements cannot be added.

printing—One method (**storeOn:**) is inherited from **Collection** and redefined for arrayed collections.

private—Two methods (**defaultElement, storeElementsFrom: to: on:**) are new protocol that are used by other methods in the protocol for class **ArrayedCollection.**

Class methods—Class **ArrayedCollection** has seven class methods in two categories, as summarized below.

instance creation—Six methods (**new, new: withAll:, with:, with: with:, with: with: with:, with: with: with: with:**) for creating instances of the subclasses of **ArrayedCollection.** Of these, **new** is inherited from **Behavior** and redefined. The four methods using **with:** are inherited from **Collection** and redefined. One method (**new: withAll:**) is new protocol.

constants—One method (**maxSize**) is inherited from **Collection** and redefined.

Protocol Summary for Class OrderedCollection

Instances of **OrderedCollection** have order that is determined by the sequence in which objects are added or removed. They are accessible by keys that are external indices. Instances of this class are used to implement stacks, queues, deques, or ordered linked lists.

Definition—The hierarchy for class **OrderedCollection** is **Object—Collection—SequenceableCollection—OrderedCollection.** Class **OrderedCollection** has two instance variables, firstIndex and lastIndex. It has no class variables or pool dictionaries. It has 3 class methods in two categories and 40 instance methods in six categories.

Private data—Class **OrderedCollection** has two instance variables.

firstIndex—an instance of **Integer** representing the index position of the first element in the **OrderedCollection.**

lastIndex—an instance of **Integer** representing the index of the last element in the **OrderedCollection.**

Instance methods—Class **OrderedCollection** has 40 instance methods in six categories. A summary of the categories and methods follows.

accessing—seven methods (**after:, at:, at: put:, before:, first, last, size**) for accessing elements in an ordered collection. Of these, two (**at:, at: put:**) are inherited from **Object** and redefined, three (**first, last, size**) are inherited from **SequenceableCollection** and redefined, and two (**after:, before:**) are new protocol.

removing—four methods. One (**remove: ifAbsent:**) is inherited from **SequenceableCollection** and redefined. The other three methods (**removeAllSuchThat:, removeFirst, removeLast**) are new protocol for removing elements based on the result of a block, removing the first element, or removing the last element.

adding—nine methods (**add:, addAfter:, addBefore:, addAll:, addAllFirst:, addAllLast:, addFirst, addLast:, grow**). Two methods (**add:, addAll:**) are inherited from **Collection** and redefined. One method (**grow**) is inherited from **SequenceableCollection** and redefined. The other six methods are new protocol that deal with special ways to add elements to an instance of **OrderedCollection.**

enumerating—Five methods (**collect:, do:, reverse, reverseDo:, select:**) are all polymorphically redefined from class **SequenceableCollection.**

copying—five methods. One (**copyEmpty**) is new protocol, and four (**copyFrom: to:, copyReplaceFrom: to: with:, copyWith:, copyWithout:**) are inherited from **SequenceableCollection** and redefined.

private—ten methods (**errorFirstObject, errorLastObject, errorNoSuchElement, errorNotFound, find:, insert: before:, makeRoomAtFirst, makeRoomAtLast, removeIndex, setIndices**) that are used by other methods in the protocol for class **OrderedCollection.** One of these (errorNotFound) is polymorphically redefined from class **Collection.**

Class methods—Class **OrderedCollection** has three class methods in two categories, as summarized below.

instance creation—two methods (**new, new:**) that are inherited from class **Behavior** and redefined.

constants—one method (**maxSize**) that is inherited from **Collection** and redefined.

Protocol Summary for Class MappedCollection

MappedCollection represents an access mechanism to an existing collection. Mapping can determine a reordering or partial listing of the collection. The key elements of an instance of **MappedCollection** are its domain and map. The domain has key/value pairs that map the elements from an existing collection into a mapped collection. The domain is the existing collection.

Definition—The hierarchy for class **MappedCollection** is **Object—Collection—MappedCollection.** Class **MappedCollection** has two instance variables, map and domain. It has no class variables or pool dictionaries. It has 2 class methods in one category and 12 instance methods in six categories.

Private data—Class **MappedCollection** has two instance variables.

map—an instance of **Dictionary** or a subclass of **SequenceableCollection** that gives a one-to-one correspondence between the keys of the mapped collection and keys in the existing collection. This mapping determines the value for any key in the mapped collection as the value of the mapped key in the existing collection.

domain—an instance of **Dictionary** or a subclass of **SequenceableCollection,** representing the existing collection from which the mapped collection is generated.

Instance methods—Class **MappedCollection** has 12 instance methods in six categories. A summary of the categories and methods follows.

accessing—four methods (**at:, at: put:, contents, size**), of which two (at:, at: put:) are inherited from **Object** and redefined, and one (size) is inherited from **Collection** and redefined. The other method (contents) is new protocol that returns the values of the elements from the **domain** that are mapped by the **map**.

adding—One method (**add:**) is inherited from **Collection** and redefined to block its usage. Elements cannot be added to a mapped collection.

enumerating—Three methods (**collect:, do:, select:**) are inherited from **Collection** and redefined.

printing—One method (**storeOn:**) is inherited from **Object** and redefined.

copying—One method (**copy**) is inherited from **Object** and redefined.

private—two methods (**setCollection: map:, species**) that set the values for the two instance variables and answer the specific class of the **domain** respectively.

Class methods—Class **MappedCollection** has two class methods in one category, as summarized below:

instance creation—two methods (**collection: map:, new**). The first method is used to create an instance of **MappedCollection** from a user-specified domain collection and map. The second method (**new**) is inherited from **Behavior** and blocked. Instances of **MappedCollection** cannot be created using **new**.

A3.8   Chapter 8

Protocol Summary for Class Stream

Stream is an abstract superclass of all the stream classes. It does not have instances; rather, its subclasses will have instances that inherit protocol defined in **Stream. Stream** defines protocol that is common to all streams. In some cases a subclass will redefine an inherited method or block its use.

Definition—The hierarchy for class **Stream** is **Object—Stream.** Class **Stream** has no instance variables, class variables, or pool dictionaries. It has 1 class method in one category amd 10 instance methods in three categories.

Instance methods—Class **Stream** has 10 instance methods in three categories. A summary of the categories and methods follows.

accessing—eight methods (**contents, next, next:, next: put:, nextMatchFor:, nextPut:, nextPutAll:, nextPutAll: startingAt: to:**) that return or change the contents of a stream. These methods are all new protocol; some are redefined by subclasses. Three of the methods (**next, nextPut:, contents**) are key methods in the inheritance hierarchy, since they are implemented as **subclassResponsibility** in **Stream.** These three methods can be blocked at any subclass level and effectively block most of the other five *accessing* methods that appear to be inherited and usable.

testing—one method (**atEnd**) that answers whether the position is at the end of the stream. This method is implemented as subclassResponsibility.

enumerating—one method (**do:**) for enumerating across the elements of a stream. It evaluates the parameter block for all elements in the stream from the current position to the end of the stream. It is the responsibility of the user to establish the position in the stream.

Class methods—Class **Stream** has one class method in one category, as summarized below.

instance creation—One method (**new**) that is inherited from class **Behavior** and redefined to block its use. New instances of the stream subclasses are created with the messages on: and with:.

Protocol Summary for Class **Random**

Instances of **Random** are streams whose initial element value is determined from a clock-driven seed. Subsequent values are derived from the previous value using algorithms for producing the desired uniform distribution of numbers. The protocol for instances of **Random** is limited and requires polymorphic blocking of certain inherited protocol messages.

Definition—The hierarchy for class **Random** is **Object—Stream—Random.** Class **Random** has one instance variable, **seed.** It has no class variables or pool dictionaries. It has one class method in one category and five instance methods in three categories.

Private data—Class **Random** has one instance variable.

seed—an instance of **Integer,** limited to 16-bit accuracy. This is required by the algorithm for generating the elements of a **Random** stream.

Instance methods—Class **Random** has five instance methods in three categories. A summary is given below of the categories and methods.

accessing—three methods (**contents, next, nextPut:**), two of which (contents, nextPut:) are polymorphically blocked from use. They are inherited from **Stream.** The other message (next) is an implementation of the random number generation algorithm. It is inherited from **Stream** (where it is defined as subclassResponsibility).

testing—One method (**atEnd**) is inherited from **Stream** and redefined to always return false. A stream of random numbers has no end so long as the next message is sent. Thus the user generates exactly as many random numbers as desired, without pre-specifying how many.

private—one method (**setSeed**) that is used during instance creation to set a new initial seed value.

Class methods—Class **Random** has one class method in one category as summarized below.

instance creation—one method (**new**) that is inherited from class **Stream** and redefined. Recall that this message was blocked in class **Stream.** It is the preferred way to create an instance of **Random.**

Protocol Summary for Class ReadStream

ReadStream is a class whose instances are set for reading only. The protocol for writing to these instances is blocked.

Definition—The hierarchy for class **ReadStream** is **Object—Stream—PositionableStream—ReadStream.** Class **ReadStream** has no instance variables, class variables, or pool dictionaries. It has one class method in one category and three instance methods in two categories.

Instance methods—Class **ReadStream** has three instance methods in two categories, which are summarized below.
   accessing—two methods (**next, nextPut:**), of which the first is inherited (as subclassResponsibility) from **Stream** and the second is inherited from **Stream** and blocked. Read streams cannot write.
   private—One method (**on: from: to:**) that is used for creating an instance by the instance creation method of the same selector. This method takes into account the fact that the stream cannot have its position fall outside the range of elements in the collection.

Class methods—Class **ReadStream** has one class method in one category, as summarized below.
   instance creation—One method (**on: from: to:**) is inherited from **PositionableStream** and redefined.

Protocol Summary for Class WriteStream

Instances of **WriteStream** have write only status. The size of their collections can grow as needed to accommodate new elements written onto the stream.

Definition—The hierarchy for class **WriteStream** is **Object—Stream—PositionableStream—WriteStream.** Class **WriteStream** has one instance variable, writeLimit. It has no class variables or pool dictionaries. It has 3 class methods in one category and 21 instance methods in six categories.

Private data—Class **WriteStream** has one instance variable.
   writeLimit—an instance of **Integer** that is initialized to equal the number of elements in the collection over which an instance of **WriteStream** is streaming. Its value is increased whenever additional elements are written onto the collection.

Instance methods—Class **WriteStream** has 21 instance methods in six categories. A summary is given below of the categories and methods.

accessing—four methods (**contents, next, nextPut:, size**), all of which are inherited and redefined. One method (contents) is inherited from **PositionableStream.** Two methods (next, nextPut:) are inherited from **Stream.** Method next was implemented as subclassResponsibility in **Stream.** Its definition in **WriteStream** is to block its use, since write streams cannot access using next. The other method (size) is inherited from **Object.**

positioning—Two methods (**position:, reset**) are inherited from **PositionableStream** and redefined.

character writing—eight methods (**cr, crtab, crtab:, emphasis, emphasis:, ff, space, tab**) for appending special characters to the stream. Most of these are self-explanatory or easily understood from their method details. All are new protocol.

printing—two methods (**print:, store:**) for printing or storing the object parameter on the stream instance. These messages implement the counterpart of the messages printOn: and storeOn: in other classes that reverse the role of parameter and receiver. Both are new protocol.

file in-out—one method (**nextChunkPut:**) that appends its parameter string to the stream and adds terminators ($!) where appropriate. Chunks are the format used for creating files that can be filed in (i.e, added to a Smalltalk image). This method is new protocol.

private—four methods (**on:, on: from: to:, pastEndPut:, with:**), of which two (on:, on: from: to:) are inherited from **PositionableStream** and redefined. The other two are new protocol. These methods are used by other methods in the protocol for class **WriteStream.**

Class methods—Class **WriteStream** has three class methods in one category. A summary is given below of the category and the methods.

instance creation—three methods (**on: from: to:, with:, with: from: to:**) that are used to create instances of **WriteStream.** The first (on: from: to:) is inherited from **PositionableStream** and redefined. The other two are new protocol.

Protocol Summary for Class **ReadWriteStream**

Instances of **ReadWriteStream** can be thought of as write streams modified to permit reading as well.

Definition—The hierarchy for class **ReadWriteStream** is **Object—Stream—PositionableStream—WriteStream—ReadWriteStream.** Class **ReadWriteStream** has no instance variables, class variables, or pool dictionaries. It has no class methods. It has eight instance methods in three categories.

Instance methods—Class **ReadWriteStream** has eight instance methods in three categories. A summary of the categories and methods follows.

accessing—two methods (**contents, next**) that are inherited from **Write-**

Stream and redefined. These two methods were blocked in **WriteStream** to disallow reading. They are redefined to be active for **ReadWrite-Stream.**

file status—one method (**close**) that sets the stream status to be closed. At this level it does nothing, but is used in **FileStream** to set the file status to closed.

file in-out—five methods (**fileIn, fileOutChanges, fileOutChangesFor:, printOutChanges, timeStamp**) that support the filing in/out in chunk format of a specified file, all system changes, changes for a specified class, or the current time stamp. The message printOutChanges appends all changes to the receiver stream in a format that has standard emphasis added and no terminators ($!). It produces a more easy-to-read copy of the changes. All five are new protocol.

Class methods—Class **ReadWriteStream** has no class methods.

Protocol Summary for Class ExternalStream

Definition—The hierarchy for class **ExternalStream** is **Object—Stream—PositionableStream—WriteStream—ReadWriteStream—ExternalStream.** Class **ExternalStream** has no instance variables, class variables, or pool dictionaries. It has 1 class method in one category and 19 instance methods in five categories.

Instance methods—Class **ExternalStream** has 19 instance methods in five categories. A summary of the categories and methods follows.

accessing—one method (**next:**) that returns a specified number of next elements of the collection of this stream. This method is inherited from **PositionableStream** and redefined.

nonhomogeneous positioning—seven methods (**padTo:, padTo: put:, padToNextWord, padToNextWordPut:, skipWords:, wordPosition, wordPosition:**) for positioning the stream position reference using various criteria. All seven methods are new protocol.

nonhomogeneous accessing—nine methods (**nextBytes: into:, nextNumber:, nextNumber: put:, nextSignedInteger, nextString, nextStringPut:, nextWord, nextWordPut:, nextWords: into:**) for reading and writing elements in a nonhomogeneous way in the receiver stream. All nine methods are new protocol and unique to this class.

positioning—one method (**resetContents**) that is new protocol and resets both the position and readLimit for the collection of the stream.

private—one method (**bulkRead: into:**) that is new protocol defined as subclassResponsibility. Its intent is to read large amounts of data into a buffer. Currently the only subclass that implements this method is **FileStream.**

Class methods—Class **ExternalStream** has one class method in one category, as summarized below.

instance creation—One method (**new**) is inherited from **Stream** as a blocked message. Here it is redefined to be a valid instance creation message for instances of **ExternalStream.**

Protocol Summary for Class FileDirectory

Definition—The hierarchy* for class **FileDirectory** is **Object—Stream—PositionableStream—WriteStream—ReadWriteStream—ExternalStream—FileStream—FileDirectory.** Class **FileDirectory** has no instance variables, class variables, or pool dictionaries. It has 5 class methods in one category and 30 instance methods in nine categories.

Instance methods—Class **FileDirectory** has 30 instance methods in nine categories. A summary of the categories and methods follows.

> *accessing*—five methods (**completePathname, contents, directoryName, fullName, versionNumbers**) that return strings describing the directory name, its path, and list of files. One method (**contents**) is inherited from **ReadWriteStream** and redefined. One method (**fullName**) is inherited from **FileStream** and redefined. The other three methods are new protocol. Method **versionNumbers** returns false, indicating that version numbers are not supported for file directories.

> *testing*—three methods (**includesKey:, isEmpty, statusOf:**), one of which (**isEmpty**) is inherited from **PositionableStream** and redefined. The other two are new protocol that check for the existence of and the status of a file name in the directory.

> *adding*—One method (**addKey:**) is new protocol that adds a new file name to the directory or notifies an error if the file name already exists.

> *removing*—One method (**removeKey:**) is new protocol that removes a file name or answers an error if it does not exist.

> *enumerating*—three methods (**do:, filesMatching:, namesDo:**), of which one (**do:**) is inherited from **Stream** and redefined. The other two are new protocol that find matching patterns in file names or evaluate a block for all file names in the directory.

> *file accessing*—eleven methods (**checkName: fixErrors:, directoryNamed:, file:, fileClass, isLegalFileName:, isLegalOldFileName:, newDirectory:, newFile:, oldFile:, oldWriteOnlyFile:, rename: newName:**) for accessing files in the directory. All 11 are new protocol.

> *file copying*—two methods (**append: to:, copy: to:**) for appending one file to another or copying the contents of one file to another. Both are new protocol.

> *alto file compatibility*—one method (**findKey:**) that is new protocol.

---

*The current version of Smalltalk from ParcPlace Systems has **FileDirectory** as a subclass of **Object.**

private—three methods (**beginWriting, directoryFromName: setFileName:, initFileName:**), of which one (beginWriting) is inherited from **FileStream** and redefined to block its use. The other two are new protocol used by other methods in **FileDirectory.**

Class methods—Class **FileDirectory** has five class methods in one category. A summary is given below of the category and the methods.

instance creation—five methods (**currentDirectory, directory: directoryName:, directoryFromName: setFileName:, directoryNamed:, fileNamed:**) for creation of instances of **FileDirectory.** One method (fileNamed:) is inherited from **FileStream** and redefined to block its use. Directories are not created from a file name.

A3.9   Chapter 9

Protocol Summary for Class Point

Definition—The hierarchy for class **Point** is **Object—Point.** Class **Point** has two instance variables, **x**, and **y**. It has no class variables or pool dictionaries. It has 1 class method in 1 category and 45 instance methods in 12 categories.

Private data—Class **Point** has two instance variables.

x—an instance of **Number** (preferably an integer) that is the x-coordinate of the point.

y—an instance of **Number** (preferably an integer) that is the y-coordinate of the point.

Instance methods—Class **Point** has 45 instance methods in 12 categories. A summary of the categories and methods follows.

accessing—four methods (**x, x:, y, y:**) that return and set the values for instance variables **x** and **y**, respectively.

comparing—nine methods (**<, <=, =, >, >=, hash, hashMappedBy:, max:, min:**) for equality and inequality comparison as well as other comparisons. Three methods (=, hash, hashMappedBy:) are inherited from **Object** and redefined. The other six are new protocol for this hierarchy chain. Equality for two points is satisfied if their private data, **x** and **y**, match.

arithmetic—seven methods (***, +, −, /, //, abs, negated**) that define arithmetic operations for points. All seven are new protocol.

truncation and round off—two methods (**rounded, truncateTo:**), both of which are new protocol. A rounded point is one whose private data are rounded to the nearest integer.

polar coordinates—three methods (**complexProduct:, r, theta**) that compute the complex product of two points, its radius, and its angle in polar coordinates. These methods are useful for the display of points using a polar coordinate reference system.

point functions—eight methods (**dist:, dotProduct:, grid:, normal, point-NearestLine: to:, transpose, truncatedGrid:, unitVector**) that are defined specifically for operating on instances of class **Point.** In each case the result of sending the message to a point is another point with characteristics determined by the particular message. All eight are new protocol.

converting—three methods (**asPoint, corner:, extent:**). The first returns the receiver point. The second two are messages for defining new instances of class **Rectangle.** The receiver in both cases is interpreted as the **origin** (upper left corner) point of the rectangle. These methods are new protocol.

coercing—two methods (**coerce:, generality**) that define the special coercing of a two-dimensional object and set its generality at 90. Since arithmetic operations are defined for points and their private data consist of numbers, they are implemented to support the generality of numbers concept described in Chapter 6. Although it has not been added, protocol to coerce a point to a complex number (with the x-coordinate as the real part and the y-coordinate as the imaginary part) could be useful for certain problem applications. New protocol can be added to class **Complex** for converting complex numbers to points. This would be useful for the display of complex numbers on a two-dimensional graph.

transforming—two methods (**scaleBy:, translateBy:**) for scaling and translating a point. The parameter in each case is also an instance of **Point.** This allows independent scaling or translation for the x- and y-directions.

copying—two methods (**deepCopy, shallowCopy**) that are both inherited from **Object** and redefined for improved performance.

printing—two methods (**printOn:, storeOn:**) that are inherited from **Object** and redefined specific to points.

private—one method (**setX: setY:**) that is used to set the private data of new instances of **Point.**

Class methods—Class **Point** has one class method in one category, as summarized below.

instance creation—One method (**x: y:**) that is used to create instances of **Point.**

Protocol Summary for Class Rectangle

Definition—The hierarchy for class **Rectangle** is **Object—Rectangle.** Class **Rectangle** has two instance variables, **origin** and **corner.** It has no class variables or pool dictionaries. It has 8 class methods in one category and 57 instance methods in eight categories.

Private data—Class **Rectangle** has two instance variables.

origin—an instance of **Point** that is the upper left corner of the rectangle.

corner—an instance of **Point** that is the lower right corner of the rectangle.

Instance methods—Class **Rectangle** has 57 instance methods in eight categories. A summary of the categories and methods follows.

accessing—thirty-two methods (**area, bottom, bottom:, bottomCenter, bottomLeft, bottomRight, bottomRight:, center, center:, corner, corner:, extent, extent:, height, height:, left, left:, leftCenter, origin, origin:, origin: corner:, origin: extent:, right, right:, rightCenter:, top, top:, topCenter, topLeft, topLeft:, topRight, width, width:**) that return specific points or features of a rectangle or allow those features to be set to new values. As is common in Smalltalk protocol, messages without a colon terminator return information, and messages that use the same identifier with a colon terminator set new values for specified parameters. The intent of many of the 32 messages is apparent from the selector name. All these messages represent new protocol.

comparing—three methods (**=, hash, hashMappedBy:**) that are inherited from **Object** and redefined. Equality for two rectangles is satisfied if their private data, **origin** and **corner**, match.

rectangle functions—eight methods (**amountToTranslateWithin:, areasDiffering:, areasOutside:, expandBy:, insetBy:, insetOriginBy: cornerBy:, intersect:, merge:**) that are specific to rectangles. In most cases the result is also a rectangle. These methods are new protocol.

testing—three methods (**contains:, containsPoint:, intersects:**) that test if the receiver rectangle contains or is equal to another rectangle, contains a specified point, or intersects another rectangle. All three methods are new protocol.

truncation and round off—one method (**rounded**) that rounds the private data (**origin, corner**) to have integer values for **x** and **y** coordinates. This method does not produce a rectangle with round corners, as the message selector might imply.

transformation—six methods (**align: with:, moveBy:, moveTo:, negated, scaleBy:, translateBy:**) for translating and scaling the receiver rectangle to produce a different rectangle. The **negated** method causes a reflection about the origin. The resulting rectangle will have negative coordinates. All these methods are new protocol.

copying—one method (**copy**) inherited from **Object** and redefined to be a deep copy.

printing—two methods (**printOn:, storeOn:**) inherited from **Object** and redefined.

Class methods—Class **Rectangle** has eight class methods in one category, as summarized below.

instance creation—eight methods (**fromUser, fromUser:, fromUserAspectRatio, left: right: top: bottom:, origin: corner:, origin: extent:, origin-**

FromUser:, originFromUser: grid:) that are used to create instances of **Rectangle.**

Protocol Summary for Class DisplayBitmap

Definition—The hierarchy for class **DisplayBitmap** is **Object—Collection—SequenceableCollection—ArrayedCollection—WordArray—DisplayBitmap.** Class **DisplayBitmap** has no named instance variables, class variables, or pool dictionaries. As a **variableWordSubclass**, its private data consists of indexable words (16-bit quantities). It has three class methods in two categories and nine instance methods in two categories.

Private data—Class **DisplayBitmap** has no named instance variables. Its private data consists of indexable words (16-bit quantities).

Instance methods—Class **DisplayBitmap** has nine instance methods in two categories. A summary is given below of the categories and methods.

 accessing—five methods (**address, at:, at: put:, raster, size**), of which one (**size**) is inherited from **SequenceableCollection** and redefined. Two (**at:, at: put:**) are inherited from **Object** and redefined. The other two are new protocol. Messages **at:** and **at: put:** access the actual display words in the bitmap. Messages **address, raster,** and **size** return information about the starting memory location, number of words per row, and total number of words, respectively, of the display bitmap.

 private—four methods (**longAt:, memoryAt:, memoryAt: put:, memoryLongAt: put:**) that are used by the *accessing* methods. Of these, one (**longAt:**) uses a call to **super** to access the **size, address,** and **raster** parameters for a bitmap. The other three access quantities in the display bitmap itself.

Class methods—Class **DisplayBitmap** has three class methods in two categories, as summarized below.

 instance creation—two methods (**basicNew:, new:**) that are inherited from **Behavior** and redefined using a different primitive method. There is only one other class in the Smalltalk system that redefines **basicNew:**.

 constants—one method (**maxSize**) that answers the value of the **Collection** class variable DefaultMaximumSize.

Protocol Summary for Class BitBlt

Definition—The hierarchy for class **BitBlt** is **Object—BitBlt.** Class **BitBlt** has 14 instance variables, destForm, sourceForm, halftoneForm, combinationRule, destX, destY, width, height, sourceX, sourceY, clipX, clipY, clipWidth, clipHeight.

It has no class variables or pool dictionaries. It has 3 class methods in two categories and 27 instance methods in four categories.

Private data—Class **BitBlt** has 14 instance variables.

destForm—an instance of **Form** that is the destination object for the copy operation of a bit-block transfer.

sourceForm—an instance of **Form** that is the source object from which the copy operation is performed.

halftoneForm—a 16-by-16 pixel instance of **Form** that is repeatedly combined with each subarea of the source form prior to the copy operation. The bits actually copied into the destination form are the result of ANDing the halftone form and the source form.

combinationRule—an instance of **Integer** between 0 and 15 that is the code for one of the 16 possible combination rules for black and white pixels. Definitions for the combination rules are given in Goldberg and Robson on page 361.

destX—an instance of **Integer** that is the x-coordinate of the origin of a rectangle in the destination form into which the copy operation is to be performed.

destY—an instance of **Integer** that is the y-coordinate of the origin of a rectangle in the destination form into which the copy operation is to be performed.

width—an instance of **Integer** that is the x-direction extent of the rectangle in the destination form into which the copy operation is to be performed. It is also the x-direction extent of the rectangle in the source form from which the copying is to be performed.

height—an instance of **Integer** that is the y-direction extent of the rectangle in the destination form into which the copy operation is to be performed. It is also the y-direction extent of the rectangle in the source form from which the copying is to be performed.

sourceX—an instance of **Integer** that is the x-coordinate of the origin of the rectangle in the source form from which the copying is to be performed.

sourceY—an instance of **Integer** that is the y-coordinate of the origin of the rectangle in the source form from which the copying is to be performed.

clipX—an instance of **Integer** that is the x-coordinate of the origin of the clipping rectangle in the destination form.

clipY—an instance of **Integer** that is the y-coordinate of the origin of the clipping rectangle in the destination form.

clipWidth—an instance of **Integer** that is the x-direction extent of the clipping rectangle in the destination form.

clipHeight—an instance of **Integer** that is the y-direction extent of the clipping rectangle in the destination form.

Instance methods—Class **BitBlt** has 27 instance methods in four categories. A summary of the categories and methods follows.

accessing—twenty methods (**clipHeight:, clipRect, clipRect:, clipWidth:, clipX, clipY, combinationRule:, destForm:, destOrigin:, destRect:,**

destX:, destY:, height:, mask:, sourceForm:, sourceOrigin:, source-Rect:, sourceX:, sourceY:, width:) that set values for the instance variables of **BitBlt.** One method (clipRect) returns the parameters defining the clipping rectangle. All these methods are new protocol.

copying—one method (**copyBits**) that performs the actual bit-block transfer. It requires that an instance of **BitBlt** first be established and that the appropriate parameters be established using other protocol in this class.

line drawing—two methods (**drawFrom: to:, drawLoopX: Y:**) for drawing lines. The first method uses the second to determine when a move in the minor direction is required. The second method is based on an algorithm for drawing lines between two points on a rectangular grid. Both methods are new protocol.

private—four methods (**copyBitsAgain, paintBits, paintDrawLoopX: Y:, setDestForm: sourceForm: halftoneForm: combinationRule: destOrigin: sourceOrigin: extent: clipRect:**) that support the creation of instances, line drawing, and the copy operation.

Class methods—Class **BitBlt** has three class methods in two categories, as summarized below.

instance creation—two methods (**destForm: sourceForm: halftoneForm: combinationRule: destOrigin: sourceOrigin: extent: clipRect:, toReverse:**) that are used to create instances of **BitBlt.**

private—one method (**exampleAt: rule: mask:**) that is used by examples of **BitBlt** for demonstrating the combination rules.

Protocol Summary for Class Pen

Definition—The hierarchy for class **Pen** is **Object—BitBlt—Pen.** Class **Pen** has four instance variables, frame, location, direction, and penDown. It has no class variables or pool dictionaries. It has 1 class method in one category and 25 instance methods in five categories.

Private data—Class **Pen** has four instance variables.

frame—an instance of **Rectangle** that defines the rectangular region within which the pen can draw.

location—an instance of **Point** that is the current location of the pen.

direction—an instance of **Integer** that defines the direction in which the pen is pointing. Direction is measured in degrees clockwise from the positive x-direction (i.e., right is 0, up is 270).

penDown—an instance of **Boolean** that defines whether the pen is down (true) or not. A pen cannot draw unless it is down.

Instance methods—Class **Pen** has 25 instance methods in five categories. A summary of the categories and methods follows.

initialize-release—one method (**defaultNib:**) that sets the nib (tip of the pen and also the **sourceForm** for **BitBlt**) to a specified diameter dot. The dot is an instance of **Form.** New instances of **Pen** are initialized to have a nib diameter of one pixel. This method is new protocol.

accessing—six methods (**direction, frame, frame:, location, sourceForm:, width:**) that return the direction, frame, or location of the pen and set a new frame or source form. Method width:, is inherited from **BitBlt** and redefined to block its use. Method sourceForm: is inherited from **BitBlt** and redefined. The other four methods are new protocol.

coloring—three methods (**black, color:, white**) that set the pen's mask to black or white. The method, color: does nothing in a monochrome system. All three are new protocol.

moving—nine methods (**down, fillIn:, go:, goto:, home, north, place:, turn:, up**) for changing the pen position to up or down, for changing the pen direction, and for moving the pen's position.

geometric designs—six methods (**dragon:, filberts: side:, hilbert: side:, hilberts:, mandala: diameter:, spiral: angle:**) that demonstrate the drawing of geometric patterns with instances of class **Pen.**

Class methods—Class **Pen** has one class method in one category, as summarized below.

instance creation—One method (**new**) creates an instance and initializes its destination form to be the **Display,** its frame to be the entire display screen, and its default nib to be a black dot of diameter one pixel. The new pen is centered on the screen, pointing north (up) and is down (ready for writing).

Protocol Summary for Class DisplayObject

DisplayObject is an abstract superclass of all the display object classes. It does not have instances; rather, its subclasses will have instances that inherit protocol defined in **DisplayObject.** There are five major subclasses under **DisplayObject.** They are **DisplayMedium, DisplayText, InfiniteForm, OpaqueForm,** and **Path. DisplayObject** defines protocol that is common to all display objects. In some cases a subclass will redefine an inherited method or block its use.

Definition—The hierarchy for class **DisplayObject** is **Object—DisplayObject.** Class **DisplayObject** has no instance variables, class variables, or pool dictionaries. It has no class methods. It has 27 instance methods in six categories.

Instance methods—Class **DisplayObject** has 27 instance methods in six categories. A summary of the categories and methods follows.

accessing—six methods (**extent, height, offset, offset:, relativeRectangle, width**) that return information about the display object's bounding box, a rectangle. Of these, one method (offset) is implemented as subclass-Responsibility. All six are new protocol.

truncation and round off—one method (**rounded**) that converts the receiver bounding box to an integer representation. This method is new protocol.

transforming—three methods (**align: with:, scaleBy:, translateBy:**) for moving or scaling the display object. All three methods are new protocol in this hierarchy chain.

display box access—two methods (**boundingBox, computeBoundingBox**) that return the display object's rectangular region for information content. The first method calls the second, which is implemented as subclassResponsibility. Both are new protocol.

displaying-generic—ten methods (**displayOn:, displayOn: at:, displayOn: at: clippingBox:, displayOn: at: clippingBox: rule:, displayOn: at: rule:, displayOn: transformation: clippingBox:, displayOn: transformation: clippingBox: align: with:, displayOn: transformation: clippingBox: align: with: rule: mask:, displayOn: transformation: clippingBox: fixedPoint:, displayOn: transformation: clippingBox: rule: mask:**) for displaying objects. Of the 10, one method (displayOn: at: clippingBox: rule: mask:) is called by the remaining 9, and it is implemented as subclassResponsibility. All are new protocol.

displaying-Display—five methods (**backgroundAt:, display, displayAt:, follow: while:, moveTo: restoring:**) that provide ways to display a display object on the display screen (represented by the global variable **Display**). The background already on the display screen is preserved if desired.

Class methods—Class **DisplayObject** has no class methods.

Protocol Summary for Class **Form**

Definition—The hierarchy for class **Form** is **Object—DisplayObject—DisplayMedium—Form.** Class **Form** has four instance variables, bits, width, height, and offset. It has no pool dictionaries. It has one class variable, OneBitForm. It has 26 class methods in 4 categories and 49 instance methods in 15 categories.

Private data—Class **Form** has four instance variables.

bits—an instance of **WordArray** that is the bitmap for the form.

width—an instance of **Integer** that is the width in pixels of the rectangular form.

height—an instance of **Integer** that is the height in pixels of the rectangular form.

offset—an instance of **Point** that gives the offset for displaying the form. If a form is to be displayed at **aPoint**, the offset is first added to **aPoint** and then displayed. This provides an easy mechanism for displaying the form centered about a point.

Shared data—Class **Form** has one class variable.

OneBitForm—an instance of **Form** that is one-by-one bit in size and whose bitmap contains only zeros.

Instance methods—Class **Form** has 49 instance methods in 15 categories. A summary of the categories and methods follows.

initialize-release—one method (**fromDisplay:**) that sets the bitmap for an instance of **Form** from a user-specified rectangle on the display screen.

accessing—six methods (**extent:, extent: offset:, extent: offset: bits:, offset, offset:, size**) for setting values for the private data of **Form** and returning the size in bits of its bitmap. Two methods (offset, offset:) are inherited from **DisplayObject** and redefined. The method size is inherited from **Object** and redefined.

copying—One method (**deepCopy**) is inherited from **Object** and redefined.

displaying—four methods (**copyBits: from: at: clippingBox: rule: mask:, displayOn: at: clippingBox: rule: mask:, displayOn: transformation: clippingBox: align: with: rule: mask:, drawLine: from: to: clippingBox: rule: mask:**). The first and last are inherited from **DisplayMedium** and redefined. The middle two are inherited from **DisplayObject** and redefined.

display box access—one method (**computeBoundingBox**) inherited from **DisplayObject,** where it is implemented as subclassResponsibility.

displaying-Display—two methods (**follow: while:, moveTo: restoring:**) that are inherited from **DisplayObject** and redefined.

pattern—four methods (**bits, bits:, valueAt:, valueAt: put:**) for returning or setting the receiver's bitmap and for returning or setting a single bit at a specified location in the bitmap. All four are new protocol.

bordering—two methods (**borderWidth:, borderWidth: mask:**) for painting a black border of specified pixel width around a form. The second method allows specification of a mask color other than black. Both methods are new protocol.

coloring—One method (**fill: rule: mask:**) is inherited from **DisplayMedium** (where it was subclassResponsibility) and redefined. This is the key method for coloring the rectangular region of a form.

image manipulation—eleven methods (**convexShapeFill:, copy: from: in: rule:, magnifyBy:, nextLifeGeneration, reflect:, rotate2:, rotateBy:, shapeFill: interiorPoint:, shrinkBy:, spread: from: by: spacing: direction:, wrapAround:**) for manipulating the size or orientation of a form's bitmap and other image characteristics. All are new protocol.

printing—six methods (**outputToPrinterHor: offset:, outputToPrinterVert: offset:, scanLineStringAt:, showBits:, storeOn:, storeOn: base:**) that either store or print a form and display its bit pattern as ones and zeros. All are new protocol except for storeOn:, which is inherited from **Object** and redefined.

file in-out—one method (**writeOn:**) that is new protocol and saves the form on a specified file in a format that allows reconstruction of the form.

editing—five methods (**bitEdit, bitEditAt:, bitEditAt: scale:, edit, editAt:**) for creating instances of either the **BitEditor** or the **FormEditor** classes. These classes provide protocol for editing forms on a micro or macro scale.

private—three methods (**isAllWhite, setExtent: fromArray: setOffset:, setExtent: fromCompactArray: setOffset:**) used by other methods in class **Form.** All are new protocol.

scheduling—one method (**openAs:**) for opening a view on the receiver with the parameter of this message as its label. This is new protocol.

Class methods—Class **Form** has 26 class methods in four categories, as summarized below.

class initialization—two methods (**initialize, initializeMasks**) that set values for the class variable **OneBitForm** and establish the forms representing the various masks (e.g., white, gray, lightGray,) respectively. Both methods are new protocol.

instance creation—ten methods (**dotOfSize:, extent:, extent: fromArray: offset:, extent: fromCompactArray: offset:, fromDisplay:, fromUser, fromUser:, readFormFile:, readFrom:, stringScanLineOfWidth:**) for creating new instances of **Form.** Instances can be created by user specification from a rectangle on the display screen, by reading a form file, from an array, or as a circular dot. All methods are new protocol except for read-From:, which is inherited from **Object** and redefined.

mode constants—six methods (**and, erase, over, paint, reverse, under**) that give names to six of the combination rule codes used by **BitBlt.** All are new protocol.

mask constants—eight methods (**background, background:, black, darkGray, gray, lightGray, veryLightGray, white**) for returning or setting the background mask and for answering the form that represent various "colors." All are new protocol.

Protocol Summary for Class Cursor

Instances of class **Cursor** are 16-by-16 forms whose bit patterns represent the various cursor shapes used by the Smalltalk system. There are 13 standard cursor shapes that are the class variables of **Cursor.** The user can easily define new cursor shapes if desired.

Definition—The hierarchy for class **Cursor** is **Object—DisplayObject—DisplayMedium—Form—Cursor.** Class **Cursor** has no instance variables or pool dictionaries. It has 14 class variables, BlankCursor, CornerCursor, CrossHairCursor, CurrentCursor, DownCursor, MarkerCursor, NormalCursor, OriginCursor, ReadCursor, SquareCursor, UpCursor, WaitCursor, WriteCursor, and XeqCursor. It has 19 class methods in four categories and 8 instance methods in three categories.

Shared data—Class **Cursor** has 14 class variables. Each represents a specific system cursor shape in Smalltalk, except that **CurrentCursor** is the current cursor shape.

BlankCursor—an instance of **Cursor** that has a blank bitmap.

CornerCursor—an instance of **Cursor** that has the shape of a lower right corner of a rectangle.

CrossHairCursor—an instance of **Cursor** that has the shape of a crosshair.

CurrentCursor—an instance of **Cursor** that is the current cursor shape. It is typically one of the other cursor shapes defined as class variables in **Cursor.**

DownCursor—an instance of **Cursor** that has the shape of a downward-pointing half arrow.

MarkerCursor—an instance of **Cursor** that has the shape of a boldface right-pointing arrow.

NormalCursor—an instance of **Cursor** that is a northwest-pointing arrow. This is the normal cursor shape.

OriginCursor—an instance of **Cursor** that has the shape of the upper left corner of a rectangle.

ReadCursor—an instance of **Cursor** that has the shape of a pair of glasses.

SquareCursor—an instance of **Cursor** that has the shape of a small square.

UpCursor—an instance of **Cursor** that has the shape of an upward-pointing half arrow.

WaitCursor—an instance of **Cursor** that has the shape of an hourglass.

WriteCursor—an instance of **Cursor** that has the shape of a pencil.

XeqCursor—an instance of **Cursor** that has the shape of the normal cursor with a star positioned in its upper right corner.

Instance methods—Class **Cursor** has eight instance methods in three categories. A summary is given below of the categories and methods.

printing—one method (**printOn:**) that is inherited from **Object** and redefined.

displaying—six methods (**beCursor, centerCursorInViewport, show, showGridded:, showGridded: while:, showWhile:**) that are new protocol for displaying instances of **Cursor.**

updating—one method (**changed:**) that is inherited from **Object** and redefined. Its purpose is to notify all dependents of **Cursor** that the cursor has changed.

Class methods—Class **Cursor** has 19 class methods in four categories, as summarized below.

class initialization—one method (**initialize**) that creates instances of **Cursor** (the class variables except **CurrentCursor**) representing the 13 standard cursor shapes.

instance creation—two methods (**extent: fromArray: offset:, new**) that are used to create instances of **Cursor.** The method **new** is inherited from **Behavior** and redefined to create a cursor with zeroed bitmap. The method extent: fromArray: offset: is inherited from **Form** and redefined to restrict the size to 16 by 16.

current cursor—three methods (**currentCursor, currentCursor:, cursor-Link:**) that return or set the current cursor and cause the cursor to track or not track the pointing device. All three methods are new protocol.

constants—thirteen methods (**blank, corner, crossHair, down, execute, marker, normal, origin, read, square, up, wait, write**) that return the instance of cursor represented by each of the 13 standard cursor shapes. All are new protocol.

Protocol Summary for Class **DisplayScreen**

Class **DisplayScreen** has one instance, the global variable **Display.** It is a subclass of **Form** that provides protocol for interacting directly with the display screen.

Definition—The hierarchy for class **DisplayScreen** is **Object—DisplayObject—DisplayMedium—Form—DisplayScreen.** Class **DisplayScreen** has no instance variables, class variables, or pool dictionaries. It has 4 class methods in two categories and 30 instance methods in six categories.

Instance methods—Class **DisplayScreen** has 30 instance methods in six categories. A summary is given below of the categories and methods.

displaying—two methods (**beDisplay, flash:**) that set the receiver to be the current display and cause the display to flash (reverse video twice), respectively. Both are new protocol.

printing—four methods (**outputToPrinterHor, outputToPrinterHor:, outputToPrinterVert, outputToPrinterVert:**) that send the display screen bitmap to a printer. They provide portrait (vertical) or landscape (horizontal) orientation and options on specifying resolution or using the default resolution for the printer. All four are new protocol added to support class **PrinterStream.**

file in-out—two methods (**hardcopy, writeOn:**) that send the display bitmap to a file and save the display image with parameters to a file, respectively. Method **writeOn:** is inherited from **Form** and redefined. The other method is new protocol.

copying—one method (**deepCopy**) inherited from **Form** and redefined to block its use. There is only one instance of this class, and it is the display screen.

display functions—nineteen methods (**capsLockOn, disableCursorPanning, disableJoydiskPanning, disableScreenSaver, enableCursorPanning, enableJoydiskPanning, enableScreenSaver, getDisplayReport, getViewportLocation, makeDisplayBlank, makeDisplayVisible, setDisplayStateFrom:, setInverseVideo, setMouseBounds:, setMouseBoundsUpper: lowerCorner:, setNormalVideo, setViewportLocation:, viewport, viewportCenter**) for interacting with the display screen. The panning methods are used for a small display screen. *Caution:* Sending the message **makeDisplayBlank** causes all display to the screen to go blank. It is not recommended except in an executable sequence of code that eventually sends the message makeDisplayVisible. Otherwise, the only way out may be to reboot the system.

private—two methods (**resetFrom: extent:, resetFrom: extent: offset:**) that are sent by class methods of **DisplayScreen.** Both are new protocol.

Class methods—Class **DisplayScreen** has four class methods in two categories, as summarized below.

current display—three methods (**currentDisplay:, displayExtent:, display-Height:**) for modifying the width, height, and/or bitmap of the current display screen image. All three are new protocol.

display box access—one method (**boundingBox**) that is inherited from **DisplayObject** and redefined. It returns the rectangle that bounds the display.

Protocol Summary for Class DisplayText

Definition—The hierarchy for class **DisplayText** is **Object—DisplayObject—DisplayText.** Class **DisplayText** has four instance variables, text, textStyle, offset, and form. It has one pool dictionary, **TextConstants.** It has no class variables. It has 3 class methods in one category and 17 instance methods in five categories.

Private data—Class **DisplayText** has four instance variables.

text—an instance of **Text** that is the text string to be displayed.

textStyle—an instance of **TextStyle** that defines all the pertinent features for the font of the display text.

offset—an instance of **Point** that defines an offset from a display point for the actual display of the text.

form—an instance of **Form** used to cache the display text. It is set to nil in most cases. A value is assigned to this instance variable by sending the message form to the class name **DisplayText.**

Pool data—Class **DisplayText** has one pool dictionary.

TextConstants—an instance of **Dictionary** that defines defaults for keyboard control sequences, character features, and emphasis.

Instance methods—Class **DisplayText** has 17 instance methods in five categories. A summary is given below of the categories and methods.

accessing—ten methods (**form, lineGrid, numberOfLines, offset, offset:, string, text, text:, textStyle, textStyle:**) that return or set new values for instance variables and return other features of the display text. Two methods (offset, offset:) are inherited from **DisplayObject** and redefined. The other eight methods are new protocol.

displaying—two methods (**displayOn: at: clippingBox: rule: mask:, displayOn: transformation: clippingBox: align: with: rule: mask:**), both of which are inherited from **DisplayObject** and redefined.

display box access—two methods (**boundingBox, computeBoundingBox**), both of which are inherited from **DisplayObject** and redefined.

converting—one method (**asParagraph**) that converts the display text to an instance of **Paragraph.** This method is new protocol.

private—two methods (**composeForm, setText: textStyle: offset:**) that are used by instance creation methods in **DisplayText.**

Class methods—Class **DisplayText** has three class methods in one category, as summarized below.

instance creation—three methods (**text:, text: textStyle:, text: textStyle: offset:**) for creating new instances of **DisplayText** with various combinations of style and offset. These methods are new protocol.

Protocol Summary for Class **Path**

Path is an abstract superclass of its subclasses that represent specific kinds of paths. Paths are typically defined by an equation. As an abstract class, **Path** has no instances. It defines protocol shared by instances of its subclasses.

Definition—The hierarchy for class **Path** is **Object—DisplayObject—Path.** Class **Path** has two instance variables, form and collectionOfPoints. It has no class variables or pool dictionaries. It has 2 class methods in one category and 27 instance methods in nine categories.

Private data—Class **Path** has two instance variables.

form—an instance of **Form** that is the display object to be displayed at each point in the path. This instance variable defaults to a one-pixel black dot unless defined differently by a creation method.

collectionOfPoints—an instance of **OrderedCollection** that contains points representing the path. As an ordered collection, points in the path have the order of their insertion. Addition of a new point always occurs at the end of the collection. However, accessing protocol provides the mechanism for changing any point in the collection.

Instance methods—Class **Path** has 27 instance methods in nine categories. A summary of the categories and methods follows.

accessing—fourteen methods (**at, at: put:, first, firstPoint, firstPoint:, form, form:, last, offset, secondPoint, secondPoint:, size, thirdPoint, thirdPoint:**) that return selected points in the path and access or set the values of private data. Of these, three (at:, at: put:, size:) are inherited from **Object** and redefined. One method (offset) is inherited from **DisplayObject** and redefined to block its use. The remaining 10 methods are new protocol.

testing—One method (isEmpty) is new protocol that tests to see if the private data collectionOfPoints are empty.

displaying—two methods (**displayOn: at: clippingBox: rule: mask:, dis-**

playOn: transformation: clippingBox: align: with: rule: mask:), both of which are inherited from **DisplayObject** and redefined.

display box access—One method (**computeBoundingBox**), implemented as subclassResponsibility in **DisplayObject,** is inherited and redefined.

transforming—Two methods (**scaleBy:, translateBy:**) are inherited from **DisplayObject** and redefined for paths.

adding—one method (**add:**) that is new protocol for adding a point to the collection of points defining the path.

removing—one method (**removeAllSuchThat:**) that is new protocol for removing all points in the collection of points for which a block evaluates to true.

enumerating—two methods (**collect:, select:**) that are new protocol. They implement the same functionality for the private data collectionOfPoints as they do for instances of the collection classes.

private—three methods (**initializeCollectionOfPoints, initializeCollectionOfPoints:, collectionOfPoints**) that return or initialize the private data collectionOfPoints. All three methods are new protocol.

Class methods—Class **Path** has two class methods in one category, as summarized below.

instance creation—two methods (**new, new:**) that are used to create instances of **Path.** Both methods are inherited from **Behavior** and redefined.

A3.10   Chapter 10

None.

A3.11   Chapter 11

None.

References

Budd, Timothy A. 1987. *A Little Smalltalk*. Reading, Mass.: Addison-Wesley.

Cox, Brad. 1986. *Object-Oriented Programming: An Evolutionary Approach*. Reading, Mass.: Addison-Wesley.

Digitalk, Inc. 1986. *Smalltalk/V: Tutorial and Programming Handbook*. Los Angeles: Digitalk.

Goldberg, Adele. 1984. *Smalltalk-80: The Interactive Programming Environment*. Reading, Mass.: Addison-Wesley.

Goldberg, Adele, and David Robson. 1983. *Smalltalk-80: The Language and Its Implementation*. Reading, Mass.: Addison-Wesley.

Goldberg, Adele, and David Robson. *Smalltalk-80: The Language*. Reading, Mass.: Addison-Wesley. A revision of previous reference.

Hewlett-Packard. 1987 *Laserjet Series II Technical Reference Manual,* Part Number 33440-90905. Palo Alto, Calif.: Hewlett-Packard.

Kaehler, Ted, and Dave Patterson. 1986. *A Taste of Smalltalk*. New York: Norton.

Krasner, Glenn. 1983. *Smalltalk-80: Bits of History, Words of Advice*. Reading, Mass.: Addison-Wesley.

Stroustrup, Bjarne. 1986. *The C++ Programming Language*. Reading, Mass.: Addison-Wesley.

Wiener, Richard S., and Lewis J. Pinson. 1988. *An Introduction to Object-Oriented Programming and C++*. Reading, Mass.: Addison-Wesley.

Index